GEORGETOWN UNIVERSITY ROUND TABLE ON LANGUAGES AND LINGUISTICS 1991

Linguistics and language pedagogy:
The state of the art

James E. Alatis, *Editor*

Georgetown University Press, Washington, D.C.

Bibliographic notice

The title of the series includes the year of a Round Table and omits both the monograph number and the meeting number, thus: *Georgetown University Round Table on Languages and Linguistics 1991*, with the regular abbreviation *GURT '91*. Full bibliographic references should show the form:

Byrnes, Heidi. 1991. In search of a sense of place: The state of the art in language teaching methodology. In: Georgetown University Round Table on Languages and Linguistics 1991. Washington, D.C.: Georgetown University Press.

Copyright © 1991 by Georgetown University Press
All rights reserved
Printed in the United States of America

Library of Congress Catalog Number: 58-31607
ISBN 0-87840-126-1
ISSN 0186-7207

Contents

James E. Alatis, *Dean, Georgetown University School of Languages and Linguistics, and Chair, Georgetown University Round Table on Languages and Linguistics 1991*
Welcoming remarks 1

Rita Esquivel, *Director, Office of Bilingual Education and Minority Languages Affairs, U.S. Department of Education*
Some words of greeting 5

James E. Alatis, *Dean, Georgetown University School of Languages and Linguistics*
H. G. Widdowson: An introduction 9

Peter D. Strevens, 1922–1989 / IN MEMORIAM 10

H.G. Widdowson, *University of London*
The description and prescription of language 11

Donald Freeman, *School for International Training*
'Mistaken constructs': Re-examining the nature and assumptions of language teacher education 25

Mary McGroarty, *Northern Arizona University*
What can peers provide? 40

Craig Chaudron, *University of Hawai'i at Manoa*
What counts as formal language instruction? Problems in observation and analysis of classroom teaching 56

Vicki Galloway, *Georgia Institute of Technology*
Reflective teachers 65

Jack C. Richards, *City Polytechnic of Hong Kong*
Content knowledge and instructional practice in second language teacher education 76

Edward M. Anthony and Lionel Menasche, *University of Pittsburgh*
Teaching vocabulary: The current word 100

Gail L. Robinson, *San Diego State University*
Second culture acquisition 114

Sandra Silberstein, *University of Washington*
Dangerous liaisons: Pitfalls in second language reading research   123

Sandra C. Browne, *Language Consultant*
A pedagogy of corporate-level ESP training for international
scientists and engineers   131

Joan Morley, *University of Michigan*
Perspectives on English for academic purposes   143

Patricia L. Carrell, *University of Akron*
Strategic reading   167

Dorothy M. Chun, *University of Texas at Austin*
The state of the art in teaching pronunciation   179

Elizabeth Joiner, *University of South Carolina*
Teaching listening: Ends and means   194

Pamela Kaleugher Levac, *Georgetown University*
Teaching language communicatively: An examination of the
presentation of phonology to first-year students   215

Marianne Celce-Murcia, *University of California at Los Angeles*
Language and communication: A time for equilibrium and
integration   223

Ann Raimes, *Hunter College, City University of New York*
Instructional balance: From theories to practices in the teaching
of writing   238

Nadine O'Connor DiVito, *Georgetown University*
Looking at and towards the future in French textbooks   250

Diane Larsen-Freeman, *School for International Training*
Consensus and divergence on the content, role, and process of
teaching grammar   260

L. Kathy Heilenman, *University of Iowa*
Writing in foreign language classrooms: Process and reality   273

Robert C. Kleinsasser, *Memphis State University*
Sandra Savignon, *University of Illinois at Urbana*
Linguistics, language pedagogy, and teachers' technical cultures   289

Anita L. Wenden, *York College, City University of New York*
Metacognitive strategies in L2 writing:
A case for task knowledge   302

Sally Sieloff Magnan, *University of Wisconsin-Madison*
Social attitudes: The key to directing the evolution of grammar
teaching   323

Earl W. Stevick, *Independent researcher*
Ann, Bert, Carla, Derek, and Oakley's Thesis   335

June K. Phillips, *Tennessee Foreign Language Institute*
An analysis of text in video newscasts:
A tool for schemata building in listeners   343

Heidi Byrnes, *Georgetown University*
In search of a sense of place: The state of the art in language
teaching methodology   355

Kenneth Chastain, *University of Virginia*
Second-language learning: Engaging, simulating, and converting   368

Linda Schinke-Llano, *Millikin University*
The shifting sands of bilingual education   379

Janet Swaffar, *University of Texas at Austin*
Normative language and language use: The separate implications
for instructional practices and materials   386

Genelle G. Morain, *University of Georgia*
X-raying the international funnybone: A study exploring
differences in the perception of humor across cultures   397

Stephen D. Krashen, *University of Southern California*
The Input Hypothesis: An update   409

Rebecca M. Valette, *Boston College*
Whither accuracy? The state of the art in foreign language
testing at the secondary level   432

Marguerite Ann Snow, *California State University, Los Angeles*
Content-based instruction: A method with many faces   461

JoAnn Crandall, *Center for Applied Linguistics*
Literacy, language, and multiculturalism   471

Maria Tarasevitch, *Moscow State Linguistic University*
Soviet phraseology: Problems in the analysis and teaching of
idioms   484

John M. Sinclair, *University of Birmingham*
Shared knowledge   489

Hanna Komorowska, *University of Warsaw*
Second language teaching in Poland prior to the reform of 1990   501

Elli Doukanari, *Georgetown University*
Greek diglossia to Greek dimorphia:
A new dilemma for linguists and teachers   509

Leo van Lier, *Monterey Institute of International Studies*
Language awareness: The common ground between linguist
and language teacher   528

Suzanne Flynn, *Massachusetts Institute of Technology*
The relevance of linguistic theory to language pedagogy:
Debunking the myths   547

Jan Svartvik, *Lund University, Sweden*
What can real spoken data teach teachers of English?   555

Flor Aarts, *Katholieke Universiteit Nijmegen, The Netherlands*
Lexicography and syntax: The state of the art in learner's
dictionaries   567

Dennis R. Preston, *Eastern Michigan University*
Language teaching and learning: Folk linguistics perspectives   583

Maria Ibba, *Università Cattolica del Sacro Cuore, Rome*
Metaphors we are healed by: On the use of metaphors in
medical language   603

Acknowledgments and Permissions

The following publishers have generously given permission to use facsimiles of the term "declare" as published in their copyrighted works. As reproduced in this volume in the paper entitled "Lexicography and syntax: The state of the art in learner's dictionaries" by Flor Aarts, these facsimiles are the following:

From OALD. Oxford Advanced Learner's Dictionary of Current English. Copyright 1989. 4th edition. A. P. Cowie, editor. Oxford: Oxford University Press.

From Collins COBUILD English Language Dictionary. Copyright 1987. J. Sinclair, editor. London and Glasgow: Collins.

From LDOCE. Longman Dictionary of Contemporary English. Copyright 1987. 2nd edition. D. Summers, editor. Essex: Longman.

The following publisher has generously given special permission to reproduce six copyrighted cartoons from *The New Yorker* Magazine, Inc. They are one cartoon each by Eric Teitelbaum, Charles Barsotti, Arnie Levin, P. Steiner, J. B. Handelsman, and Eldon Dedini © copyright 1990. These are reproduced in this volume in the paper by Genelle C. Morain entitled "X-raying the international funnybone: A study exploring differences in the perception of humor across cultures."

Welcoming remarks

James E. Alatis
Dean, Georgetown University School of Languages and Linguistics
Chair, Georgetown University Round Table on Languages and Linguistics
1991

Good evening, ladies and gentlemen. My name is James E. Alatis and I am Dean of the School of Languages and Linguistics at Georgetown University. It is my great honor to welcome you to the campus and the Georgetown University Round Table, *GURT 1991*, for short. For me, the Round Table is one of this University's most important contributions to our field. For in this forum, we have the opportunity to assemble students, researchers, faculty members, and other professionals to discuss research and review the most important trends in the discipline. We are fortunate to have with us at this conference the most distinguished authorities on our conference theme: *Linguistics and language pedagogy: The state of the art.* This Round Table represents a forty-two year unbroken tradition of excellence, and based on the speakers and topics included in our program, I can say without a moment's hesitation, that this year's conference will surely be among the most important and exciting. A key to the success of the Round Table is, I believe, its very manageable size. We are fortunate that we are able to attract scholars who would be prized plenary speakers at any language or linguistics conference in the world and yet, our conference is small enough that our participants are not overwhelmed by the sheer crush of people and the scale of the facilities. We are delighted that you are here and encourage you to be an active participant in our proceedings.

Through a combination of tradition and necessity, *GURT* was held during Georgetown's spring break. We clung to the tradition partly because it was a tradition—we are fond of tradition around here—and partly because it made long-term scheduling for the Round Table so much easier. Such scheduling was also a necessity until very recently because we needed more classroom and auditorium space than was available while classes are in session. The opening of the Leavey Center and its conference center eliminated the need for classroom space. The clear advantage is that more of our students and faculty are on campus and able to participate in the conference and rub elbows with the stars, or at least that portion of the constellation not already on Georgetown's faculty.

Two years ago, the *GURT* conference opened under a thick coat of ice; the following year, we sweltered under record temperatures. This year, perhaps protected by the confluence of Easter, Passover, Greek Orthodox Holy Week, and Ramadan, it seems we shall be meeting under more temperate circumstances. We frequently call upon the GURT organizers to make the impossible happen, but even I was impressed to learn that they arranged to have the cherry blossoms in full bloom for you. This, ladies and gentlemen, is a full service conference.

Before I get any further into my remarks, I would like to express my gratitude to the many people who have done such a fine job organizing the conference. The pastor of my church cautions against ever thanking people by name to avoid omitting others. This is sage advice, but on this occasion, it is advice I cannot follow. I would be remiss if I did not acknowledge the tremendous debt owed Carol Kreidler who has coordinated GURT for three years now. Her scholarly judgment, devotion to her field, and administrative wizardry have given us the continuity which had hitherto not been one of *GURT's* most prominent features. Indeed, I had almost begun to take her wonderful work for granted, but this year, I had a potent reminder that we must never take anything—or anyone—for granted. On New Year's Day, Carol suffered a stroke. Thank goodness, Carol is well on her way to a complete recovery and, even while recuperating in the hospital, was fully involved in keeping conference planning on an even keel. Carol is here this evening and I would like to offer her these roses as a modest token of our gratitude, and on behalf of everyone here, offer our best wishes for your continued recovery. Thank you, Carol.

I take a small share of the credit for the remarkable progress Carol has made because I am confident her fear that I would begin meddling into the organization of *GURT* provided tremendous incentive to get her back on the job. However, this was an unnecessary concern because Carol has been supported throughout the planning process by three of our superb graduate students. Carolyn Straehle, Rebecca Freeman, and Yuchen Fan have done a wonderful job, and, together with Carol Kreidler, are responsible for everything right about the conference. Again, on behalf of everyone at GURT, I would like to thank you all most sincerely.

Of course, even these three stalwarts would not be able to put on a conference of the complexity of the Round Table without a small army of helpers. Offered nothing more than the occasional doughnut or slice of Domino's pizza, a highly-credentialed army of graduate students formed an assembly line and put together all those packets and have staffed the registration areas. So, to all of you, and I know who you are and you know who you are, our sincerest thanks.

Before I turn to our speakers, I would like to congratulate the organizers and participants in the pre-sessions of the Round Table which took place today. A quick review of the conference program demonstrates that these pre-sessions bring us a level of both diversity and specialization which the Round Table itself cannot approach. We are happy to provide a forum for these sessions and hope we shall be able to continue to do so in the future.

You will see from your program that I am now about to introduce Rita Esquivel, Director of the Office of Bilingual Education and Minority Languages Affairs of the U.S. Department of Education. It is not only an honor, but also a great pleasure for me to welcome this impressive colleague with the intimidating title, because she is not only a highly-placed government official, she is, more importantly, one of us.

Rita Esquivel was appointed Director of OBEMLA, as her office is called, in May 1989 by President Bush. Serving first under Secretary Cavazos and now under Secretary Alexander, she has worked tirelessly to ensure that all language-minority residents of this country have an equal opportunity to pursue their own version of the American dream. To recall a phrase used by my friend, G. Richard Tucker, at another *GURT* 10 years ago, Rita Esquivel has been working with us toward a language-competent society. That is, I believe, an achievable dream and one shared by this School, by the Center for Applied Linguistics and, I am sure, by everyone here this evening.

Rita grew up in San Antonio, Texas. She received her Bachelor's and Master's degrees in education from Our Lady of the Lake University in San Antonio. For ten years, she taught in the Edgewood and San Antonio elementary schools. Taking Howard Greeley's advice, she went west, where for another ten years, she taught elementary school classes and Spanish to junior high school students, served as a counselor, and taught English as a second language to adults at the college level. In 1973, Rita crossed the Maginot line to administration, holding positions of increasing importance and responsibility in the Santa Monica-Malibu Unified School District. She has been an elementary school principal, coordinator of community relations, supervisor of state and federal projects and assistant superintendent of schools.

Ms. Esquivel has been a persuasive and effective advocate in the Bush administration for Bilingual Education. In an era of tight budgets, she has secured increased funding from the Congress for fellowships and other teacher-enhancement programs. She is a much-sought-after speaker throughout the United States and we are pleased to have her with us tonight. Ladies and gentlemen, please welcome Rita Esquivel, Director of the Office of Bilingual Education and Minority Languages Affairs.

Some words of greeting

Rita Esquivel
Office of Bilingual Education and Minority Languages Affairs
U.S. Department of Education

It is a great pleasure for me to share a few words with this distinguished assembly. And it is a special pleasure, on this occasion, to convey to the *Georgetown University Round Table on Languages and Linguistics 1991* the greetings of Lamar Alexander, who took office on March 18 as Secretary of Education. The U.S. Department of Education appreciates and strongly encourages the kind of work that you are doing because it provides the theoretical foundations for the labors of policy makers and teachers. I cannot underline too strongly how significant is the enterprise which will engage you these next few days. The ideas you will hear, the hypotheses you will debate, the questions you will frame are fraught with implications for more than one area of contemporary life.

Language instruction, the teaching of verbal and written communication, and, above all, the skilled linking of one language with another—and, therefore, one worldview with another—have become critical social concerns. They are the subject of public discourse (and, inevitably, of ideological warfare). But the issues are far too important to be left to ideologues. Certainly, learned practitioners, many of whom are speaking at this conference, can use debate as a tool to increase our knowledge of the language-learning process and to explore new, inventive ways of teaching language. But outside this hall the reality of linguistic diversity presses hard against the classroom teacher, the vocational educator, the employer.

If the scholarly work of an assembly such as this was ever peripheral to the major processes of society, it is no longer so. In an era in which the migration of peoples is a constant, the scholarly study of language and of language acquisition has import far beyond communities of academics and foreign-language teachers. Last year, when officials of the U.S. Department of Education met with counterparts in European countries, they discovered a high level of interest in the American experience of bilingual education. Large groups of immigrants are crossing national borders to work; their children are appearing in the schools. And immediately the transmission of information and the development of learning patterns in a population that does not know the language of instruction become focal points. Last year, also, as senior education officers from the United States and Mexico explored possible avenues for collaboration, we learned that the questions of language and second-language acquisition confront Mexico on a massive scale. The growing presence of indigenous peoples in Mexican schools and the enactment of free trade agreements between the two countries are now posing strong challenges related to the learning of language and, at bottom, to the function of language as *a*—if not *the*—major vehicle in social and cultural transactions of every sort.

Over the past few months data from our own 1990 Census are confirming the impressions our experience has already left: that the last ten year have brought a dramatic influx of immigrants *in every region of the country*. The Asian population has tripled; the Hispanic population has grown by fifty percent. (That sounds like two groups; you know they include many more.) Though less numerous, other immigrant groups have also multiplied. At the beginning of the current school year, for example, every elementary school in Cambridge, Massachusetts, enrolled at least one Russian-speaking child. The state of Virginia counts ninety-five different languages in its student population. A single middle school in a nearby Maryland suburb copes with children who speak twenty languages. The Title VII projects funded and supervised by the Office of Bilingual Education and Minority Languages Affairs serve students of 148 languages. We, the people, are, in fact, multilingual and multicultural.

All non-English-speaking persons in this country—be they university graduates or unschooled laborers—know that a mastery of English is the true passport into this society. It enables one to consult a doctor or discuss a child's progress with the teacher or follow an employer's directions. More important still, it is the key to participation in community action and political discourse and corporate decision making. At the same time, the worlds of diplomacy and commerce, of scientific research and ecumenical dialogue, of pharmaceutical experiment and ecological activism are realizing vividly that the capacity for high-level thinking, speaking, and interacting in more than one language is now indispensable. (Some people, of course, have been saying that for decades. The difference is that today many more *know* it—at times because of irremediable mistakes.) Samuel Betances puts the case boldly: 'Anyone who says he can get along in the United States without speaking English is a fool. And anyone who thinks that he can move into the twenty-first century speaking only English is a fool, too.'

I mentioned that 148 languages are represented in current Title VII programs. Among them are Arabic and Arapaho, Cambodian and Choctaw, Farsi and Hmong, Polish and Punjabi, Russian and Tagalog,

Urdu and Vietnamese, and many more. As we work with people all over the land, we find ourselves puzzling over questions like: 'What really happens in the language-acquisition process?', 'What is the relation between language structures and conceptual structures, between language and worldview?', 'How do human beings link the languages they already know with those they seek to learn?' Those questions are not purely speculative. Their answers unlock insights about the *how to's* of curriculum design and teaching methodology. I don't need to tell you that our current knowledge does not begin to answer these questions. Meanwhile our children—and the hundreds of thousands of adults who seek incorporation as responsible citizens—can't wait. So I thank you for the work you have already done, I cheer your work, and I urge you to pursue it zealously. May these few days be a step in the continuing process.

H. G. Widdowson: An introduction

James E. Alatis
Dean, Georgetown University School of Languages and Linguistics

Now, as a reward for listening to me so patiently, relieved only briefly by Ms. Esquivel's gracious remarks, I shall turn the podium over to Professor H.G. Widdowson who will deliver our opening address. Given our conference theme, I can think of no more appropriate speaker.

Professor Widdowson received his A.B. from King's College at Cambridge. His Ph.D. in Linguistics, which was awarded in 1973, is from the University of Edinburgh. His professional career has included terms with the British Council in Sri Lanka and Pakistan. He has held teaching appointments in Indonesia and Scotland, and, since 1977, he has been Professor of Education at the University of London.

Perhaps his university's most 'frequent flyer', he has lectured and offered seminars in, at last count, thirty-eight countries. One begins to understand why he is in such demand after a brief review of Professor Widdowson's scholarly achievements. He is respected as both an editor and author for his scholarly judgment, masterful command of the field, and sophisticated yet accessible style of writing. For me to detail his contributions would be so time-consuming as to preclude his address. Therefore, I shall just scratch the surface.

He is applied linguistics advisor for Oxford University Press, the founding editor of *Applied Linguistics*, coeditor of the Cambridge University Press *Annual Review of Applied Linguistics*, and coeditor for applied linguistics and contributor to *The Oxford International Encyclopedia of Linguistics*. He has published six books through Oxford University Press and has been translated into Japanese, French, and Italian. His numerous articles have appeared in the most prestigious refereed journals in the world. Most important of all, he spoke at *GURT* last year to rave reviews, and I am disinclined to tamper with success. This evening, Professor Widdowson will speak to us on 'The description and prescription of language'. Ladies and gentlemen, please join me in welcoming our distinguished speaker to the podium.

PDS / *In Memoriam*

*What can we say? We fumble words and fail
For what we feel to find the turn of phrase.
Sadness eludes our rhetoric and stays.
Our verbal gesturing is to no avail.*

*The usual expressions are so trite:
We mourn his passing and we share the grief.
This ritual idiom brings no relief,
It is outside, like noises in the night.*

*Echoes that sound out silences, that's all,
The empty space of past no words can fill.
He will write us no more letters now; he will
Never again be there to take our call.*

*Now in his absence we all feel alone.
And in his death we recognize our own.*

H.G.W.

The description and prescription of language

H. G. Widdowson
University of London

When linguists talk about the principles of their enquiry, what they have to say not uncommonly resonates with a high moral tone. They say, for example, that they consider all linguistic systems as equal and treat them all, languages and dialects alike, with the same even-handed detachment. They say, too, that they are concerned with the description and not the prescription of language. They tell it how it is, they give you the facts, and indulge in no value judgements. But is it possible to be so aloof from reality? All languages may be equal in linguistic principle, but as we all know well enough some are (to invoke George Orwell) more equal than others in social practice. And these egalitarian principles do not seem to be applied very generally to different theories or descriptions of language. Although there is no discrimination against languages, there is very definitely discrimination against ideas about language. Tolerance is much less in evidence here. Linguists have no hesitation in saying that certain ideas held by the uninformed commoner or language teacher are ill-conceived, inadequate, or hopelessly wrong, and they will rubbish the theories of colleagues with relish in prescribing their own. So value judgements **are** made. Linguists do not deal with objective fact. They do not tell it how it is, but how, from their particular point of view, it seems to be. And this point of view is sustained by eliminating all others, so that the diversity of experience is reduced in the interests of intellectual security.

The principles of equality and objectivity are comfortable illusions. Descriptions of language are not more or less correct but more or less influential, and therefore prescripive in effect. They tell us less about truth than about power, about the privilege and prestige accorded to acknowledged authority. Reality is cast in the image of the beholder, and it is the image of the most influential beholders which prevails. All of this is the expression of the relativist and pluralist position on the nature of knowledge whose most prominent advocate is Paul Feyerabend (e.g. Feyerabend 1987). It finds expression too in other areas of enquiry, in the archaeology and sociology of knowledge, in the writing of Michel Foucault and Paulo Freire. There is a growing ground-swell of thought which questions the validity of aloof detachment and the claims of access to objective fact. This effectively re-interprets the term social science. It is not that sociology, linguistics, and so on can emulate the principles and practices of the physical sciences in some quasi positivist fashion, but that all science, even the most apparently objective, is a socio-cultural construct. It is not that social science is a science; it is that all science is social science. 'The new philosophy puts all in doubt.' We cannot any longer be sure of our facts. It is not a very comfortable position to be in.

And some people, of course, do not accept the position anyway. This, for example, is what John Sinclair has to say:

> We are teaching English in ignorance of a vast amount of basic fact. This is not our fault, but it should not inhibit the absorption of new material (Sinclair 1985:252).

The basic fact that John Sinclair is referring to is that which emerges from the computer analysis of text. This is descriptive fact about English usage, the new material now documented in the COBUILD dictionary and grammar (COBUILD 1987, 1990). And the assumption is that such basic descriptive fact, about which teachers were previously ignorant, can now serve as the basis for pedagogic prescriptions. For the first time, teachers are in a position to help their learners with **real** English. The position is comfortable. It is based on the certainties of fact and reality: basic fact and real English. Teachers can follow the injunction of Mr Gradgrind: 'Teach these boys and girls nothing but Facts. Facts alone are wanted in life.' And descriptive facts about language alone are wanted in language teaching. Teach these boys and girls nothing but the facts of real English. But is it quite so straightforward? What kind of fact is it that comes out of the computer analysis of a corpus of text? And how basic is it from the pedagogic point of view? Can it be so confidently, so positively projected into direct prescriptions for learning?

Corpus linguistics, of which the COBUILD work is an impressive example, provides for the description of what Chomsky calls 'Externalized language' or 'E- language', that is to say the description of performance, the actualized instances of attested behaviour (Chomsky 1986, 1988). This he distinguishes from the study of 'Internalized language' or 'I-language', that is to say, the enquiry into competence as abstract knowledge, linguistic cognition. Here, whether or not a particular expression is actually attested is irrelevant to the model of description since its purpose is to account not only for sentences which happen, incidentally, to have occurred, but also those that never have, and perhaps never will. It is, so to speak, a model of absences for which presences provide only partial and unreliable evidence. In E- language descriptions, presences are the only evidence there is, and knowledge is equivalent to a generalization from behaviour. It is not that performance is an actualization of competence, but that competence is an abstraction from performance. The only facts about what people know are those which can be directly inferred from what they have done.

But we are talking here about Chomsky's notion of competence. What of the broader definition of that concept? What of communicative competence? Let me remind you that Hymes has proposed that this can be defined in reference to four aspects of knowledge that a 'normal member of a community' can bring to bear in deciding whether and to what degree something, a linguistic expression for example, is formally 'possible', 'feasible', 'appropriate', or actually 'performed' (Hymes 1972:281-2).

It is clear that I-language study ('I-linguistics') is concerned with the first two of these aspects, the possible and the feasible. 'E-linguistics', on the other hand is concerned with the other two, with the actualized occurrence of language in contexts of communication. One E-linguistic line, discourse analysis (broadly conceived) takes up the matter of appropriateness and deals with the pragmatic use of language in the transaction of social business, the interaction of social relations, the negotiation of indexical meaning of different kinds: reference, force, and effect. Another E-linguistic line focuses on performance frequency, the extent to which linguistic forms actually occur. This is corpus linguistics of the COBUILD kind, which we might in contrast call text rather than discourse analysis.

The crucial question that arises is how these different aspects of language knowledge are to be accounted for in linguistic descriptions. Chomsky's view is that you go for the possible. Sinclair's view is that you go for the performed. Grammarians like Randolph Quirk and his colleagues would line up with Chomsky in this respect since their work (as exemplified by Quirk et al. 1972, 1985, etc.) is essentially descriptive of what they know of English as representative users, and what they know, as grammarians, of other descriptions of English, checked out against information about actual occurrence but not determined by it. Theirs is not data driven description. By the account of one of the team, Sidney Greenbaum, the corpus was used as a stimulus to enquiry and a source of supplementary evidence. As Greenbaum puts it:

> The major function of the corpus is . . . to supply examples that represent language beyond that corpus . . . (Greenbaum 1988:83).

Beyond the corpus, let us note. In the grammar of Greenbaum, Quirk and colleagues, primacy is given to the possible, and not to the performed. But they do seek correspondence with occurrence and work to some notion of normality. Unlike Chomsky, therefore, they conflate the possible with the feasible. We will not find in their descriptions any unfeasible expressions of the *This is the malt the rat the cat the dog chased killed ate* variety. The competence they account for has the implication of performance.

The work of Sinclair and his colleagues, on the other hand, conflates the possible with the performed. It is not that the description is derived from the grammarian's knowledge and then checked against the data as a secondary source. The data represent the primary source. Sinclair has argued that the evidence which emerges from computer analyses does not 'merely give us a better documented description of the language' but indicates inadequacies in the categories of description themselves, that is to say, the categories of what is possible in the language. He says:

> The categories and methods we use to describe English are not appropriate to the new material. We shall need to overhaul our descriptive systems (Sinclair 1985:252).

The clear implication here is that linguistic description should be confined to an account of what is actualized as behaviour. You do not represent language beyond the corpus: the language is represented by the corpus. What is not attested in the data is not English; not real English at any rate. In reference to the Hymes' scheme, what is not performed is just not possible. And linguists and language teachers alike have in their ignorance been guilty of descriptive sins of both omission and commission: failing to present real patterns of common occurrence, and presenting patterns of language which are unreal because they occur very rarely, if at all.

There is no doubt that computerized text analysis does reveal a vast amount of quantitative information, fact indeed, about the frequency of linguistic tokens, the recurrence and co-occurrence of words. It provides a detailed profile of what people do with the language. It is a fascinating revelation and its importance should not be minimized. But what does it tell us of what people know? If it is the case that what is not performed is not possible in Hymes's terms, then what is not part of the corpus is not part of competence. This, of course, is directly contrary to the Chomsky view. It is contrary also to the principles of description followed by Quirk and his associates. Here is Greenbaum again:

> We cannot expect that a corpus, however large, will always display an adequate number of examples. . . . We cannot know that our sampling is sufficiently large or sufficiently representative to be confident that the absence or rarity of a feature is significant (Greenbaum 1988:83-84).

Significant of what? Significant, presumably, of what users know as distinct from what they do.

All this raises the question of what it is that a linguistic description is actually meant to describe, of what its facts are facts about, and whether these facts are the most relevant to prescriptions for language learning. The distinction between I-language and E-language descriptions refers to what aspects of language are to be described. But it carries implications also about the perspective of enquiry, the relationship between the describer and the data. The description of internalized language requires a first person perspective. You really have no choice if you are seeking to prise knowledge out from the recesses of the mind: knowledge which is not realized as behavioural evidence available to the observer, human or electronic. In the tradition of generative linguistics, this has involved linguists acting as their own informants. The assumption has been that they can draw introspectively on their own competence as representative members of the speech community whose language they are describing. The difficulty is, of course, that as linguists they are also members of another community, the community of linguists with all its disciplinary sub-culture of different and incompatible attitudes and values and this disqualifies them as representative informants. Thus we are sometimes presented with the rather unedifying spectacle of linguists trying to pull themselves up by their own bootstraps, citing sentences which are representative only of their own idiosyncratic limitations. There is a corrective to such eccentric behaviour. We can (as Greenbaum again points out) elicit judgements from members of the speech community whose integrity has not been tainted by linguistics. This too has its methodological difficulties, of course, since elicitation involves, in some degree at least, the externalization of language which you are trying to avoid: the setting up of conditions for elicitation will tend, not surprisingly, to condition informant response. You can narrow down these conditions, and constrain response, but then you run the risk of getting your own judgements played back to you. Confirmation is never difficult to find if you look for it where you put it yourself in the first place.

The description of E-language text such as is carried out by corpus linguistics of the COBUILD kind does not have to contend with this problem of probing for knowledge, quite simply because it is only concerned with its realizations as behaviour. It adopts a third person perspective and only describes what can be observed. It may thereby reveal, as Sinclair claims, the need for new categories of description, but these cannot be 'member' categories, categories, that is to say, of the members of the speech community itself which account for their intuitions about the language. You could of course argue along traditional behaviourist lines and say that such intuitions will be made manifest in what people do and so we do not have to needlessly hypothesize any separate existence. What is real is only what is actual. This, of course, is the argument that Chomsky attacked with such vehemence in his review of Skinner. It is anathema to I-linguistics, as he sees it. This is no wonder, for, if true, his own enquiry would be pointless.

But the argument is not very welcome in E-linguistics either: the E-linguistics, that is, of the discourse analysis kind that deals with appropriacy of use, Hymes's third aspect of communicative competence. In this area of description, there has been an increasing recognition of the importance of participant rather than observer perspectives, even to the point of denying validity to any description of language which is not member oriented. Ethnography has in many places become synonymous with ethnomethodology. Descriptions aim to be from the inside looking out, not from the outside looking in. There is no privileged status for observers. For they only see what their own preconceptions dispose them to see, and so simply confirm their own prejudices, which carry weight only by virtue of their prestige. In this respect, discourse analysts tend more and more towards the relativism that I referred to at the beginning of this paper. They too are imbued with the epistemological spirit of the times. To the extent that they favour a direct confrontation with actual data, they make common cause with the text analysis of corpus linguistics. But to the extent that they define that data in terms of participant experience and recognise that there are psycho-sociological goings on in members' minds behind behavioural appearances, they line up with Chomsky. For them, as for Chomsky, the actual language is evidence for realities beyond it. The kind of realities are, of course, different. But they are alike in that they are not accessible to third person observation but only to first person awareness. Though one approach is concerned with E-language as experienced by members other than the analyst, and the other with I-language as intuited by the analyst as member, it is in both cases description which is inside out, so to speak, rather than outside in.

The question arises as to whether (and to what degree) an approach to description can capture member knowledge of language from the inside out without depending on the unrepresentative and unreliable intuitions of the analyst. I mentioned earlier the difficulties of elicitation, and these should not be discounted. Nevertheless, elicitation is just about the only way of getting at what people know if you do not trust the evidence of naturally occurring behaviour alone. And it does provide us with interesting evidence that the way people know their language does not neatly match up either with the analyst's description or with the evidence of actual occurrence. I should make it clear that I am referring here to what we might call 'conceptual' elicitation, that which seeks to probe directly into member categories of knowledge, rather than elicitation of a 'contextual' kind, which requires subjects to give instances of what language they would normally use in a given context. We would expect the data from contextual elicitation, to correspond relatively closely to the findings of frequency emerging out of corpus analysis. We would suppose that what people indicate they **would** say in a given context is not likely to be greatly different from what they actually **do** say in such contexts. It would be disturbing for the claims of corpus linguistics, if there were disparities between subject response in contextual elicitation and computer concordance. Contextual elicitation ought to spring no surprises for corpus linguists. All the same, there **are** surprises. The correspondence between what people claim they **would** say, and what they actually **do** say cannot be taken on trust. And with conceptual elicitation it turns out that there are very clear disparities, not only with respect to the way the linguistic analyst describes language, but also with respect to actual patterns of language use as revealed by computer processing of text.

Consider the kind of conceptual elicitation carried out by Eleanor Rosch (Rosch 1975, Aitchison 1987:ch 5). Her work is well known, but let me remind you of it and bring it within the context of the present discussion. She devised a questionnaire to elicit from subjects the word which sprang most immediately to mind as an example of a particular category. These categories were, in the terms of lexical semantics, hyperonyms or superordinate terms, and the subjects were asked to identify a particular hyponymous word as having some marked mental prominence for them. Lexical analysis in terms of sense relations treats all such words as equal co-hyponyms. It turns out that as cognitive representations, however, some hyponyms are more equal than others. With remarkable consistency, subjects homed in on one hyponym as in some sense representative of the category. This Rosch refers to as the prototype word. Thus the prototypical hyponym for *bird* was *robin* for *vegetable* was *pea* and so on.

There is an obvious explanation for such findings. When prompted by the word *vegetable* the word *pea* comes more readily to mind, rather than, say, *asparagus* or *mangelwurzel* quite simply because it is a word of more common occurrence. If this were so, then the prototype would appear in the frequency profile of words in computer print-outs, and there would be no need to go to all this trouble to identify it by elicitation. If this were so. But it seems that it is not so. The obvious explanation appears to be wrong. For prototypical prominence in the mind does not accord with frequency of actual occurrence. The word *cauliflower*, for example, has a higher prototype score than the word *potato* and in the clothing category *bathing-suit* is more prominent than *shoe*. I do not have any evidence immediately to hand, but I would imagine that these cognitive representations would not correspond with the relative frequency of these words. The mental lexicon seems to have an identity which eludes the abstractions of structural semantics on the one hand

and the actuality of text analysis on the other. There is competence of a kind here that does not directly declare itself. Prototypical prominence can be considered as one criterion for the identification of what has been called nuclear or core vocabulary (Stubbs 1986, Carter 1987), and this I will come back to presently. But is this cognitive phenomenon confined to lexis? What of syntax? Can we also talk about prototype sentences as well as words? Synonymous with *nucleus* and *core* is the word *kernel* and that word, for anyone acquainted with linguistics, has its own reverberant associations: *the kernel sentence*. This figured prominently in the early days of generative grammar as a central concept in the model of description, and then disappeared. Chomsky despatched it summarily in 1965, but he seemed to do so with some regret. This is what he says:

> The notion 'kernel sentence' has, I think, an important intuitive significance, but since kernel sentences play no distinctive role in generation or interpretation of sentences, I shall say nothing more about them here (Chomsky 1965:18).

And nothing more is said about them elsewhere either as far as I know. But this begs a tantalizing question. If these kernel sentences have such an important intuitive significance, then why is their importance not reflected in grammatical description? If they do not have any distinctive role in the grammar, then what role do they have? The answer is, I think, that they have a role in the mind, an intuitive role indeed. They are prototype sentences which elude description in much the same way as prototype words do. They cannot be accounted for in analytic models of syntactic structure (on Chomsky's own admission) any more than prototype words can be accounted for in analytic models of lexical structure. And they certainly do not figure as high frequency units in text: a brief glance at a computer print-out would reveal that they are actually of uncommon occurrence. Where they do figure is in descriptive grammars, and their presence there can be said to be justified by their intuitive significance, their psychological reality, as prototypes. They may not be authentic as units of behaviour, but they can be said to have their own authenticity as units of knowledge.

And they figure very prominently too, of course, in pedagogic **prescriptions** of language. They are the stock-in-trade of language teaching. Teachers may have been labouring under a descriptive delusion, in ignorance of certain basic facts about actual usage, but they seem to have been reasonably well informed as far as the intuitive significance of the kernel sentence is concerned and its prescriptive relevance for the process of learning, whatever the authenticity of its status as actual use.

It should be noted, too, that the notion of the lexical prototype has also in some respects been anticipated in work on the pedagogic prescription of language. I refer here to the concept of disponibilité, or availability of words. This was proposed thirty-five years ago in the pioneer research which led to the specification of the core or nuclear language to be included in *Le Français Fondemental* (Gougenheim et al. 1956). The research involved the analysis of actually occurring data and this revealed certain frequencies, in the same way as does modern corpus analysis, although necessarily without the finesse that modern technology can now provide. But it was recognized that there was something real to be accounted for which was not actual in the data. French people had a knowledge of words which they did not necessarily act upon in their behaviour: words which the researchers themselves felt, intuitively, they ought to include in spite of their poor showing in performance. To quote from the description of the research that appears in *The Linguistic Sciences and Language Teaching* by Halliday, McIntosh and Strevens:

> There remained the problem of words absent from the list which were nevertheless intuitively felt to be necessary. Two of the names of days of the week, for example, *mercredi* and *vendredi*, failed to appear in the texts, yet that could hardly justify their omission from a basic teaching vocabulary. The biggest single group of words that seemed to the researchers to be inadequately represented in the lists was the category of abstract nouns. French people obviously knew a great many words of this kind and therefore had them available for use, but it seemed that they might not use any particular noun very frequently (Halliday et al. 1964:194).

The researchers therefore carried out an exercise in conceptual elicitation, not dissimilar to that of Eleanor Rosch that I referred to earlier. They identified a number of categories: clothing, furniture, animals, occupations and so on, and elicited responses by questionnaire from thousands of school children all over France as to which common everyday nouns they thought it would be most useful to know in respect to such topics. To quote Halliday and his colleagues again:

> Under the heading of 'furniture', for example, *table* was universally given, but *vitrine* was rather rare. The quality of being mentioned by a high proportion of those answering the questionnaire for a given topic was termed *disponibilité*, which might be translated as 'availability'; thus the word *table* is more *disponible* as a word relating to furniture than is *vitrine* (Halliday et al. 1964:195).

The parallels with the Rosch research are obvious. Just as the word *table* is more readily available in the French mind than the word *vitrine* so, for the English-speaking informants, *pea* and *robin* come more readily to mind than *asparagus* and *ostrich*. In both cases we have cognitive representations which emerge from elicitation but which may not show up in the frequency profiles of actual occurrence. But there is a difference.

The research of Rosch reveals something of the language users' mental lexicon. The prototype is a descriptive category of member competence which lurks in the mind beyond immediate awareness. The French research did not elicit user response in the same way. It asked its subjects to make a conscious judgement about words which it would be most useful to know. So availability or disponibilité is a 'prescriptive' criterion and not a 'descriptive' category. Words which are identified as disponible are prescribed for learning because they are useful; not because they are frequently used, but because they appear to be readily available in the minds of users. We are concerned here not primarily with what language users know but with what language learners *need* to know.

Language teaching cannot simply be based on descriptive facts, whether these are facts of attested frequency of usage which emerge from text analysis or facts of pyschological reality in the minds of users such as conceptual elicitation might reveal. These are 'factors' to be considered, of course, but not facts to be uncritically incorporated into prescriptions. Their relevance is not self-evident. It has to be established by reference to pedagogic criteria. This is because, obviously enough, our business in language teaching is not with the members of language user communities but with the members of language learner communities. They too develop cognitive representations of lexis and grammar, prototype words and sentences which they may or may not make manifest in actual performance, and which constitute the interim competence of their interlanguage. To the extent that second language acquisition research has indicated the nature of such representations, it too provides us with factors to consider. But again, factors to consider, not facts to conform to. For even if we were confident that we knew what the mental grammars and lexicons of learners (some learners at least) were like, pedagogy would not, as a matter of fact, be bound by them. They would provide a point of reference, but only *one* point of reference. There are others to be taken note of as well in plotting a course of instruction. To be effective, such a course might well lead the learners in directions very different from those they would be naturally disposed to follow. One might argue, indeed, that if it did not, there would hardly be any point in plotting a course in the first place.

Language prescriptions for the inducement of learning cannot be based on a database. They cannot be modelled on the description of externalized language, the frequency profiles of text analysis. Such analysis provides us with facts, hitherto unknown, or ignored, but they do not of themselves carry any guarantee of pedagogic relevance. The pioneers of corpus analysis, though their techniques were crude, unaided by technology, showed a subtlety of perception in this regard not always evident in their successors. Prescription cannot be modelled on the description of internalized language either, on cognitive representations, or mental prototypes, whether elicited from the minds of the language user or language learner community. The user prototype shows us where learners have eventually to arrive, and the learner prototype where they would go if left to their own devices. The purpose of pedagogy is to point them in the right direction. And this purpose does require the specification of prototypes of a kind, but the kind must be such as to activate the process of learning. A prototype, according to the *Oxford Advanced Learners Dictionary*, is a model, a preliminary version, and is used, according to the *COBUILD Dictionary*, as a basis for later improved models. Exactly so: pedagogic prescription specifies a succession of prototypes, preliminary versions of the language, each a basis for later improved models. In this way, learners are guided through the stages of induced interlanguage by a process of gradual approximation to the norms of the language user community. For learners the language is not real or authentic until they have learned to realize and authenticate it.

This process of authentication through interim versions of the language has to be guided by reference to other factors as well as those of frequency and range of actual use, as was recognized by the pedagogic pioneers in text analysis that I referred to earlier (see Palmer 1922/64, Mackay 1965). Such factors have to do with usefulness rather than use. Thus words and structures might be identified as 'pedagogically' core or nuclear, and preferred as a prototype at a particular learning stage because of their coverage or their generative value, because they are catalysts which activate the learning process, whatever their status might be in respect to their actual occurrence in contexts of use.

It might be objected that this means that things have to be first learned and then unlearned. The answer to this is that all learning proceeds by unlearning, by recurrent revisions of previous knowledge. This assumption informs the language pedagogy, underwritten by SLA research, which acknowledges learner error as evidence of learning at different phases of interlanguage. How this is consistent with an insistence on authenticity is far from clear. There seems, on the contrary, a contradiction here which needs to be resolved. But teachers of other subjects, too, accept the need to deal with approximations. They, too, accept the need to be economical with the truth in the interests of effective pedagogy. Teachers of science, for example, would not claim to be presenting concepts in the early stages of instruction which would carry an unchanged validity right through to advanced levels of study. If they did, they would simply baffle and alienate their students and learning would never get off the ground. So they deal initially with simplifications, and these are recurrently complexified, with reduced and interim versions which are gradually modified so as to conform more closely to the authenticity of established thought and practice. I see no reason why language teaching should not proceed by reference to the same basic pedagogic principles of catalysis and approximation.

This does not, to be sure, deny the relevance of the facts revealed by the corpus description of usage, or the elicitation of user knowledge. They do indeed reveal facts, particularly about collocation and the formulaic associations of syntax and lexis, which are not otherwise accessible. But they represent the goal towards which the learners have to be directed, and these facts will need to be incorporated into pedagogic prototypes at appropriate stages. It would be as much a mistake to uncritically dismiss these facts as it would be to uncritically accept them. The point is that their relevance and appropriacy to the learning process are matters of empirical pedagogic enquiry. What form such an enquiry might take I have indicated elsewhere (Widdowson 1990). But that is a different story which there is no time here and now for me to tell.

In an article about Interlanguage some years ago, Bialystok and Sharwood Smith liken language knowledge to a library:

> The language user's mental library may be said to contain a number of books as part of its stable repertoire (i.e. information in long-term storage). These books are not treated as totally unrelated units, but are arranged together in some system; this is what distinguishes a library collection from an indiscriminate pile of books (Bialystok and Sharwood Smith 1985:105).

They then go on to point out that we need to distinguish between knowing the content of the books and knowing how they are classified, and the procedures to be employed in getting effective access to them: knowledge of language on the one hand, ability for use on the other (Widdowson 1989). It is a nice analogy and one which I can use to draw my own conclusions. Language knowledge is organized as a library by some sort of classification system. You cannot infer the system by finding out how many books are borrowed. And a description of which books are taken out does not tell you about the contents of the library. It provides information, of course, about how the library is used and this may be a matter of considerable relevance, but we would not normally conclude that the books that remain on the shelves are not part of the real library at all. But what of classification? Librarians, like linguists, have developed complex systems of their own which are not self-evident to the lay person, and not determined by the nature of books as such, nor, for that matter, by the behaviour of borrowers. It might be argued that these systems are an imposition and that any classification should conform to some natural book acquisition and innate cataloguing device, and that what we should do is simply present people with piles of books and let them sort them out for themselves.

The point I would make is that the sorting system they came up with might not be the most helpful to them in organizing content or making it readily accessible. They might be disposed to classify according to size, or publisher, or colour of cover. On the other hand, the Dewey classification system, well suited no doubt to the Bodleian or the Library of Congress, would be too complex and cumbersome for their modest collection. Learners need some guidance in finding an effective system for cataloguing what they have got and dealing with new accessions, whether we are talking of books or linguistic knowledge.

Analogies can, of course, always be pushed to the point of absurdity. But it is not, I think, misleading to conceive of language learning as the gradual extension of knowledge comparable to the accumulation of books. There is the similar need to devise and revise systems of classification as a continuous process to accommodate new accessions and to ensure access in the way which appears empirically by classroom experience to be the most effective for learning. And this devising and revising is a matter of pedagogic prescription which directs learners through interim systems or models of knowledge, preliminary versions which are the basis for improvement: the prescription, in short of a succession of prototypes, from precedent to precedent, gradually approximating to the norms of competence and performance of user communities.

To alter the analogy, descriptions of language, whether of I-language or E- language, tell us a good deal about the destinations that language learners are travelling towards. But they do not provide any directions as to how they are to get there. Only prescriptions can do that: not prescriptions which are absolute whatever the circumstances, but relative in that they are relevant to the requirements of effective language learning in different teaching/learning situations. The prescription of language for such contexts of instruction can, and should, be informed by the description of language in contexts of use, but not be determined by it. And the cognitive representations, the prototypes, as interim interlanguage versions which activate learning are not the same as those which figure as established features of knowledge in the minds of language users. For prescription has its own conditions of adequacy to meet, and it is the business of language pedagogy, and nobody else's business, to propose what these conditions might be.

References

Aitchison, J. 1987. Words in the mind: An introduction to the mental lexicon. Oxford: Blackwell
Bilaystok, E. and M. Sharwood Smith. 1985. Interlanguage is not a state of mind: An evaluation of the construct for second-language acquisition. Applied Linguistics Vol 6 No 2. 101-117.
Carter, R. 1987. Vocabulary. Applied Linguistic Perspectives. London: Allen and Unwin.
Chomsky, N. 1965. Aspects of the theory of syntax. Cambridge, Mass.: MIT Press.
Chomsky, N. 1986. Knowledge of language: Its nature, origin and use. New York: Praeger.
Chomsky, N. 1988. Language and problems of knowledge. Cambridge, Mass.: MIT Press.
COBUILD. 1987. English language dictionary. London: Collins.
COBUILD. 1990. English grammar. London: Collins.
Feyerabend, P. 1987. Farewell to reason. London: Verso.
Gougenheim, G., R. Michea, P. Rivenc, and A. Sauvageot. 1956. L'Elaboration du français é lé mentaire. Paris: Didier.
Greenbaum, S. 1988. Good English and the grammarian. London: Longman.
Halliday, M. A. K., A. McIntosh, and P. Strevens. 1964. The linguistic sciences and language teaching. London: Longman.
Hymes, D. 1972. On communicative competence. In: J. Pride, and J. Holmes, eds. Sociolinguistics. Harmondsworth: Penguin Books.
Mackay, R. F. 1965. Language teaching analysis. London: Longman.
Palmer, H. R. 1922. The principles of language study. London: Harrap. Reprinted London: Oxford University Press 1964.
Quirk, R., S. Greenbaum, G. Leech, and J. Svartvik. 1972. A grammar of contemporary English. London: Longman.
Quirk, R., S. Greenbaum, G. Leech, and J. Svartvik. 1985. A comprehensive grammar of the English language. London: Longman.
Rosch, E. 1975. Cognitive representations of semantic categories. In: Journal of Experimental Psychology: General. 104: 192-233.
Sinclair, J. M. 1985. Selected issues. In: Quirk, R. and H. G. Widdowson, eds. English in the world. Cambridge: Cambridge University Press.
Stubbs, M. J. 1986. Educational linguistics. Oxford: Blackwell.
Widdowson, H. G. 1989. Knowledge of language and ability for use. Applied Linguistics. Vol. 10 No 2:
Widdowson, H. G. 1990. Aspects of language teaching. Oxford: Oxford University Press.

'Mistaken Constructs':
re-examining the nature and assumptions of language teacher education

Donald Freeman*
School for International Training

Introduction: 'A way of not seeing'. This paper concerns what seems to be a contradiction: that to see and value some aspects of a situation or phenomenon, you have to overlook others. Jean Renoir, the French director who pioneered in black-and-white films, talked about this contradiction when he said that what fell outside of the camera's view was as important as what was included in the shot. In a sense, he said, one defined and implied the other.

In this paper, I want to examine the issue of what is framed through the lens of accepted ideas in language teaching. I will argue that as a field we have been concentrating—for whatever reasons—on the wrong things in the education of language teachers. We have accepted theories and constructs from the allied disciplines of applied linguistics, second language acquisition, and language pedagogy, at the expense of building an independent, classroom-based understanding of language teaching and learning. It is not that such borrowing is wrong, or that the particulars of what has been borrowed are mistaken, but that the use of constructs from these allied fields has obscured some crucial elements in language teaching. In mapping out the terrain of language teaching using borrowed constructs, issues which do not fit within those constructs have been missed or overlooked.

The process is actually quite natural. Kenneth Burke, the philosopher, made the point in different words when he remarked that 'a way of seeing is also a way of not seeing' (1935:70). Thirty years later, historian of education, David Tyack took Burke's comment as a point of departure in an essay comparing various 'ways of seeing' the issue of compulsory education. Tyack (1976:355-356) observed that:

---

* In developing my ideas for this paper, I benefited from discussions at Carleton University with Devon Woods, Dick Allright, and Jean Handscombe, and at Harvard Graduate School of Education with Courtney Cazden and members of the seminar on language in education.

Socialization within the academic disciplines focuses on inquiry: economists explain events in economic terms, sociologists in sociological ways, psychologists by their own theories. Splintering even occurs within fields: Freudians and behaviorists, for example, see the world through quite different lenses.

Burke and Tyack, in very distinct types of endeavors, make the argument which frames this paper: that attending to a situation or phenomenon requires that some aspects are rendered as significant or meaningful, while the others, simply by virtue of not being attended to, are in effect not seen.

I will take this contradiction as a point of departure for analyzing three central aspects of what is seen—and therefore not seen—in the field of foreign and second language teaching. In the concern for what should take place to classrooms—as content, methodology, and processes of language acquisition—we fail to look at lessons for what they are: sets of social and discoursal relationships. We also often do not see that teachers' understandings are a central and given part of the relationship between teaching and learning (see Prabhu 1991). To ground the discussion here, I will begin with a brief description of part of a language lesson, excerpted from field notes of a research project I am doing.

Rainey's French II class: The imparfait and the passé composé.
As the first period class bell sounds, the kids straggle in. The group of seventh and eighth graders is a 'French II - Honors' class, which means they have actually been studying the language for three years and seem fairly comfortable with using it in their own fractured, English- derived way. Their teacher, Rainey, is in her fifth year teaching; she is a highly energetic woman with a contagious sense of humor.

While the kids are settling in, Rainey asks one boy how he slept.
Rainey: *Tu t'es bien dormi hier soir?* 'Did you sleep well last night?'
The boy: *Oui... oh, no, I mean, non. Je n'ai pas dormi parce que mon chien...* 'Yes..., no. I didn't sleep because my dog'
Another student: *Ce n'est pas son chien, c'est le chien de Mr. Worder.* 'It isn't his dog, it's Mr Worder's dog.'
The boy: *Non, c'est mon chien... Je sais. Je l'ai ecouté...* 'No, it is my dog. I know; I listened to it.'
... *entendu* 'heard', Rainey adds absent-mindedly. (She glances down at her lesson plan and then back at the class.)
Rainey: *Bon, allez, on commence...* 'OK let's start'

Rainey hands out a worksheet containing sentences which have blanks with the verb indicated in parentheses. The instructions read, 'Fill in the blanks with either the *imparfait* or the *passé composé* '. The students work dutifully on the sheet. As they finish, they stare out the window at the rain, or put their heads down on their books.

Rainey calls them back together: *OK. Qui a la premiè re phrase? Dis-la moi et je vais l'écrire au tableau* . . . 'OK. Who has the first sentence? Tell me and I'll put it up on the board.'

After some cajoling, a boy volunteers. He reads from his sheet: <u>*Nous prenions le petit dé jeuner quand nos copains*</u> . . . (pauses) . . . *sont entrés*. Rainey writes the sentence as he says it.
Rainey: *Bon* . . . *'sont entré s' avec 's'. Pourquoi avec 's'?* 'Good, came in *(sont entrés)* with an 's'. Why with an 's'?'
The boy: *Parce que, 'nos copains'*. . . *pluriel.* 'Because, it's 'our friends' . . . plural.

(Observation notes: 10/25/90)

Rainey's lesson is interesting in a number of ways. While it is typical of many foreign language lessons, it also offers an unintended juxtaposition which provides a means of entry into the issues I want to examine in this paper. In the first part, two students are talking about what happened the previous night with the dog; in the second, they are completing a worksheet which uses the same verb forms.

It may be tempting simply to fault Rainey for not recognizing the parallel: the opportunity implicit in the first part to do what she has planned explicitly in the second. Some might criticize her understanding of the content: that she seems stuck on grammar and doesn't realize that she can accomplish the same ends communicatively. Or some might fault her understanding of methodology: that she is depending on written worksheets in place of interactive activities which would aim for communicative rather than linguistic competence. Still another criticism might be that she is overly committed to what she has planned for the lesson and so misses the opportunity which she has created in a natural and unplanned exchange with her students.

These critiques are not particularly useful for three reasons. First, they each depend on and so reenforce the status quo: <u>seeing the lesson in terms of accepted constructs of content, methodology, and teaching.</u> Second, the critiques reduce the lesson to one instance of less-than-optimal teaching, rather than accepting it as it takes places in order to understand the complexities which it presents. And thirdly, they ignore the fact that lessons of this type are more common than not in classrooms (see Applebee 1981). I would argue therefore that it is more productive to take the lesson, to try to understand on its own terms, to play Elbow's 'believing game' (1973) with it.

If we step away from the perspective of remediation and critique, some interesting questions emerge. Why does Rainey seem to feel the first part of the lesson is not teaching, while the second one is? What is it about the second part which makes her see the content as legitimate and more important than the first? What in Rainey's experience—as a student in classrooms and in teacher education—may have led her to this view of her practice? With this orientation in mind, I would like to critically examine three assumptions which guide our given and accepted view of language teaching. These assumptions, which I will refer to as constructs, provide the basis for seeing language teaching, and lessons such as Rainey's, in particular and accepted ways. The first has to do with the construct of content in lessons; the second with methodology; and the third with the act of teaching itself.

These constructs can obscure others ways of seeing Rainey's lesson, and language teaching more generally. For alternatives, I will turn to the literature of educational research, particularly in the domains of teacher thinking and expertise research.[1] In doing so, I would emphasize that I am not necessarily proposing that we substitute these alternative ways of seeing for the constructs on which we now depend. Instead, I use them as a means to examine what we are assuming about linguistics and language pedagogy, in the interests of developing—to borrow anthropologist Clifford Geertz's term (1973)—a 'thicker description' of classroom language teaching.

Construct #1: Content. We generally assume—and encourage teachers to think—that there is something distinct and separable in lessons which we refer to as the content. Defining what we call the content of language lessons is generally within the purview of applied linguistics. However to seeing language as content depends on isolating it from the flow of contextual interactions which make up the classroom. The objectification and abstraction of language which makes this way of seeing possible has its roots in the Structural Linguistics of de Saussure and the Prague school (Butt 1990, Doe 1988). The British literary critic Raymond Williams argues that until the structuralists, language was largely seen as what he terms a 'constitutive activity.' With the advent of structural analyses, Williams writes (1977:32), 'Language . . . became a tool or an instrument or a medium taken up by individuals to communicate, as distinct from the faculty which made (those individuals) . . . not only able to relate and communicate, but . . . possess the active practice of language.'

Williams' observations about the divorce of language as an 'active process' from language as a system offer another way of seeing content

---

1 Research in teacher cognition generally dates from the deliberations of two panels in 1975- 1977, the (U.S.) National Institute of Education Report on 'Teaching as clinical problem-solving' (1975) and the parallel although unrelated report of the Working Group on Classroom Decision-making of the (U.K.) Social Science Research Council (Sutcliffe 1977). The best known summaries of such research are Shavelson and Stern (1981) and Clark and Peterson (1986); see also Freeman (1990a).

in language lessons. When it is an 'active process' and a 'constitutive human faculty,' language becomes embedded in the interpersonal and interactional context of the lesson. It cannot be the abstract 'tool, instrument, medium' or set of competences on which applied linguistics depends. To conceive of language as 'constitutive activity' implies that the content in lessons be redefined. It is not abstract knowledge but something which is contextual and interactive.

Researchers in teacher cognition have followed a similar line in proposing that the knowledge which teachers use in preparing and conducting their lessons is actually distinct from the disciplinary facts and knowledge on which those lessons are based. Shulman (1984), a leading proponent of this view, draws on a distinction originally made by Schwab between 'substantive' and 'syntactic' knowledge structures. 'Substantive' structures are defined as 'those systems that define and constitute facts and meanings of the domain;' 'syntactic' ones, in contrast, 'are the procedures of inquiry for determining the warrant of assertions offered' (Shulman 1984:199). Using this orientation towards content, Shulman can make the important and worthwhile distinction between knowing the subject matter, which is 'substantive' knowledge, and knowing how to teach it to others, which is 'syntactic'. He offers contrast between the literary critic, who must know how to recognize 'good' poetry, and the literature teacher, who must know that and, in addition, how to get her students to recognize and understand its 'goodness'.

Teachers often depend more on their 'substantive' knowledge of what they are teaching than on their 'syntactic' knowledge of how to make that information accessible to learners. In the French lesson, Rainey leans heavily on her substantive knowledge of the imparfait and the passé composé and seems not to have developed the syntactic knowledge of how to have the students develop that language. This may be because in her training as a teacher and in the educational materials from which she constructs her lessons, the subject matter has been conceived and presented as an abstract system of language. She has not been introduced to French as a 'constitutive activity,' but rather as a 'tool' for communication.

Shulman (1987, 1986b) has proposed another way to see content, as 'pedagogical content knowledge.'[2] Pedagogical content knowledge bridges the dichotomy between 'substantive' and 'syntactic' knowledge. Shulman defines it as 'the ways of representing and formulating the subject that make it comprehensible to others.' To develop such knowledge, teachers must know:

---

2 For a recent discussion of pedagogical content knowledge in various subject matters, see the *Journal of Teacher Education,* 41 (3), May-June 1990.

the aspects of content most germaine to its teachability. . . . (This) includes an understanding of what makes topics easy or difficult: the conceptions and preconceptions which students of different ages and backgrounds bring with them to the learning (Shulman 1986b:9).

In this definition, pedagogical content knowledge in the field of language teaching cannot be constructed out of concepts from applied linguistics and second language acquisition, each of which possesses a set of substantive knowledge structures in its own right. To develop pedagogical content knowledge, teachers like Rainey need to think of French in a new way, as the 'constitutive activity' which brings a particular class of students together. They need to avoid the mistaken construct that there is content in a lesson which is separable from how it is presented and who is learning it.

There is some research to suggest that teachers are naturally inclined to think about lessons in this way. They conceive of such pedagogical content knowledge primarily in terms of phrasings of classroom activity. However this conception does not fit with the construct of content as abstract, objectified subject matter which they encounter in their teacher education. In that environment, they are asked to break down such knowledge into content and delivery, or methodology. This distinction is not because language teaching and learning actually operate in this manner, but because it is how we know how to present teaching knowledge to teachers-in-training. Rainey may somewhere have been introduced to the idea that chatting with students is not itself a 'pedagogical' activity, while doing a work sheet is. So she sees the worksheet as the lesson, while chatting is not. This is not simply a problem in methodology however, it centers on how teachers learn what is worth doing in classrooms.

Construct #2: Methodology. How do teachers gain pedagogical content knowledge? This question is at the heart of the second construct. Instruction in methodology occupies a central place in our thinking of how teachers learn to teach; we operate from an assumption that it is efficient and productive to teach teachers isolated forms of pedagogy— commonly called methods, activities, or techniques—which they can then apply in their practice. But training in methodology contradicts teachers' assertions that they learn how to teach by doing it (Richards and Hino 1983). Teachers contend that classroom practice is virtually the only way to understand what one has to do as a teacher.

Their contention is borne out in findings from a five-year study of the influences of teacher education on classroom teaching in English and mathematics conducted by the (U.S.) National Center for Research on Teacher Education (NCRTE). These researchers write 'Teachers acquire seemingly indelible imprints of teaching from their own experiences as

students and these imprints are tremendously difficult to shake.'
(Kennedy 1990:7) The 'indelible imprints' seem to develop through a
process of emulation, or 'apprenticeship of observation' (Lortie 1975).
As the NCRTE study explains, the mathematics of such influence are
quite simple:

> By the time we receive our bachelor's degree, we have observed
> teachers and participated in their work for up to 3,060 days. In con-
> trast, teacher preparation programs usually require (about) 75 days
> of classroom experience. What could possibly happen during these
> 75 days to significantly alter the practices learned during the preced-
> ing 3,060 days? (Kennedy 1990:4).

It therefore stands to reason that Rainey is to some degree replicat-
ing the teaching which she received, not only in language classes but in
other subjects as well. The influences of her training on the lesson were
most likely far less than those of her own experience. The fact is that
teacher education is, in the larger scheme of teachers' understandings, a
far weaker intervention than we suppose it to be. Teachers see their
lessons more in terms of what can be done, given the circumstances,
than in terms of what they should do. A high school Spanish teacher in a
longitudinal study which I am doing expresses the sentiment quite
clearly (Freeman 1991):

> I don't even think in terms of methodology now. . . . Just whatever is
> available to me at that time (in the lesson) that's going to work. I
> might take two or three different things. . . . I add, borrow, and steal
> from every place as long as it works (CB: I: 11/14/90).

To say that teachers learn from their 'apprenticeship of observation'
as students does not entirely explain what they do in the classroom. Certainly the methodology encountered, or assimilated, through formal
teacher education plays an important part in their ways of doing things in
the classroom. However methodology *per se* becomes a mistaken construct when it is assumed to be the way in which teachers learn to teach.
This view tends to distract us from seeing that as adults, teachers do not
come to their professional preparation *tabula rasa*; indeed they bring a
tremendous amount of background knowledge and schema which influence—if not shape—their thinking and development.

There is a parallel in the research classroom discourse. Cazden
(1988) has suggested that the teacher-inquiry student-response teacher-
evaluation sequence which is the norm in most classrooms, may function
as a discoursal and interactional 'default option.' In other words, it may
be the form of exchange which teachers and students tend to fall back on

in the absence of other intentional ways of organizing their talk and activity. It would make sense that this IRE structure embodies in classroom discourse what become memories of teaching and furnishes teachers' tacit knowledge of how to conduct lessons. It would further make sense that attempts to encourage teachers to present language communicatively run head on into the powerful default potential of this IRE norm. So perhaps Rainey feels that she is teaching when she operates within the standard IRE structure of the worksheet, while she does not in the freer conversational exchange which precedes it.

In place of the construct of methodology, we need to consider the teacher's existing and developing understandings of teaching. In teacher education, it will be more productive, and ultimately more effective, to realize that teachers-in-training are transforming what they already know about teaching rather than to think of them as learning new methods or ways of behaving in the classroom. Several in our field have called attention to the existence of such pre-existing understandings in teachers, referring to them as the teacher's 'sense of coherence' (Brumfit 1983), 'beliefs, assumptions and knowledge' (Woods 1989), 'belief structures' (Johnson 1990), or 'sense of plausibility' (Prabhu 1990); I have called these understandings the teacher's 'conception of practice' (Freeman 1991). The issue is not the pluralism of labels, but the recognition of the phenomenon itself. It focuses us on what teachers know; not on what they need to learn.

Construct #3: The act of teaching as arranging lessons. The first two mistaken constructs have to do with what to teach and how to teach it. Rather than conceiving of the content in lessons as an abstract, objectified body of linguistic material, I have suggested it be seen as 'pedagogical content knowledge,' a composite which integrates subject matter with its means of presentation to particular students. And rather than thinking of methodology as a matter of teachers adopting specific techniques or activities, or the attendant beliefs or theoretically-derived rationales, it may make sense to see teachers' knowledge more comprehensively, as conceptions of practice which integrate and extend the understandings built up through the 'apprenticeship of observation.' In light of these alternatives, the third assertion will come as no surprise. I think it is mistaken to think of the act of teaching as put together out of independent or even distinct choices or decisions about what to teach and how to teach it.

This construct for assembling the act of teaching out of content and methodology is problematic in two ways. It is does not adequately account for the classroom as a context or for the teacher as a developing person. In the field of language education generally, there has certainly been a great deal of concern over context, however it is generally expressed in socio-cultural or socio-political terms (Cazden 1988, Doe

1988). I am suggesting a different, perhaps more ordinary, sense of context as the landscape of personalities and interactions in the classroom. Lessons, as temporally-defined episodes of teaching and learning, bring together groups of people in particular places to accomplish their own, at times divergent, ends; this is at once their strength and often their downfall (Prabhu 1991, Allwright 1989). It thus makes a certain amount of sense that research on beginning teachers is virtually unanimous in citing the achievement of effective functioning of the classroom through management and discipline as their primary concern (Doyle 1983, 1977; Bullough 1989).

The issue of managing classrooms is central to teaching. Rainey observes about her teaching: 'Having students work together has been very powerful too, although it also presents a management problem that relates back to keeping students accountable.' (Document: 2/23/91) Like Rainey, most teachers quickly learn that establishing routines allows them to control and create order in interaction. As Doyle (1977:51), a principal researcher in this area, has argued: 'Learning to teach involves learning the 'texture of the classroom' and a set of behaviors congruent with the demands of that setting.' Knowing how to organize classrooms is the teacher's central concern.

> (Our) analysis suggests that, from the teacher's perspective, learning is an epiphenomenon in classrooms, something that accompanies classroom events and is effected by them, but that has little immediate or direct role in the daily processes of classroom life (Carter and Doyle 1987:157).

The NCRTE findings offer a similar picture:

> (T)eachers tend to avoid thought-provoking work and activities and to stick to predictable routines . . . because students are easier to manage and student outcomes easier to control when tasks are routine (Kennedy 1990:4).

If these findings seem unencouraging, it may be because we have been unwilling to conceive of teaching in terms of the strengths and weaknesses of classrooms as contexts. The perspective on teaching as managing interaction suggested here must be embedded within the broader domain of teachers' work lives and schools as places where they carry out those lives. Classrooms are not isolated environments, nor does what goes on in them necessarily reflect in a causal manner the decisions, priorities, or commitments of the wider setting, as curriculum planners might have us believe. So increased attention is being paid to the structure of teaching as work (Apple and Jungck 1990, Lightfoot

1985, Apple 1985) and to schools as environments which enable or detract from teachers' ability to perform their jobs effectively (Rosenholtz 1989, Kleinsasser 1990).

It is equally important to realize that the teacher's relation to context is hardly a fixed or unchanging one, however. Teachers are people; their understandings and priorities grow and develop over time. Research on teacher expertise confirms and extends this observation. It suggests that over the first five years in the classroom, teachers' thinking can develop from a prescriptive, rule-oriented orientation towards what goes on in the classroom to an embedded, contextual clustering of responses and judgments (Berliner 1988, 1986; Freeman 1990b). Thus their pedagogical content knowledge can grow more complex, as they learn to account for an increasing number of dimensions and variables within the classroom situation. Other researchers who examine teacher socialization from a developmental perspective (Oja 1990, Oja and Smulyan 1989) emphasize the evolution of teachers' abilities as a function of their intellectual development. What is common to both types of the research is the commitment to understanding teachers as individuals who change and develop over time.

Taken together, the contextual view of classrooms and the developmental view of teachers' work lives presents a way of looking at the act of teaching which is far more intricate than the current view that teachers simply combine content and methodology to produce lessons. Considering issues of place, in the classroom as a context, and time, in the teacher's intellectual development, presents a dynamic view of the act of teaching. It is less a matter of arranging lessons than one of negotiating among demands; the negotiation both reflects and depends on the teacher's understanding of the context and her own abilities. Thus when Rainey moves from the open social interaction of chatting in the first part of her lesson to the managed interaction of the worksheet in the second, the change can seem quite complex from this perspective. It may reflect her socialized expectation of what an organized lesson should look like, as well as her level of expertise in enacting that expectation.

Summary and proposals. I have argued against three mistaken constructs which are prevalent in our thinking about language teaching. In pursuit of a 'thicker description' of what goes on in classrooms, I have drawn alternative constructs from educational research suggesting that:

> First, pedagogical content knowledge offers a different and potentially useful perspective on what teachers know in order to teach.
> Second, the idea of a conception of practice can replace the construct of methodology as discrete behaviors which teachers learn to carry out. This idea of methodology is misleading since it overlooks

the fund of experience and tacit knowledge about teaching which the teachers already have by virtue of their lives as students.

And third, we compound the first two mistakes when we see lessons as put together out of decisions about what to teach and how to teach it. This focus distracts us from the role of classrooms as contexts which must be organized by teachers. We also lose the perspective that teachers possess levels of individual proficiency at such organization which changes over time.

These three alternatives have a common root: they all center on the teacher. To base our thinking on the content, as defined by applied linguistics, or the methodology, as defined by various theorists and proponents, is one way of seeing language teaching. However, these constructs overlook the crucial point of the teacher's role. The recent work from educational research which I have cited shares a common paradigm which is generally referred to as 'cognitive' (Kagan 1988) to distinguish it from the 'process-product' view of teaching as an activity which is measurable by its outcomes (Shulman 1986a). I believe we can borrow quite profitably from this different orientation in order to reconceptualize the terrain of language teaching. To do so will shift our way of seeing; it may help to illuminate complexities which we have not attended to in the past.

In closing I want to outline the characteristics which these alternative constructs from the cognitive paradigm bring to understanding classroom language teaching. While the alternatives themselves are useful, the contrasts which they provoke are more important. How is our understanding enhanced by contrasting the constructs with these alternatives? What do they contribute to a 'thicker description' of language teaching?

Contingent knowledge. First, the alternatives allow for an understanding which is more contingent and less absolute than those which are currently in use. Our present mistaken constructs reenforce a compartmentalized view of teaching which does not encourage a focus on the interaction of elements. The alternatives are far more contingent; they emphasize the network of influences and connections which create what happens in the classroom. Pedagogical content knowledge connects what is taught to how it is taught and to who is learning it; a conception of practice connects the teacher's past experience and 'apprenticeship of observation' to her present perceptions and actions.

Developmental knowledge. Second, the alternatives promote the idea that language teaching is developmental and not static. If learning to teach must occur in real time, then we ought to question why almost all teacher education programs are predicated on the idea of 'front-loading.'

Teachers are exposed to most or all of what they will need to know early in their careers and then are expected somehow to make this knowledge serve their teaching over time.³ The assumption of such 'front-loading' can really only appear reasonable as long as we conceive of content and methodology as fixed entities, and conversely we do not focus on the characteristics of teachers as learners and on the intricate environments in which they work.

Constructed knowledge. If we begin to think of what teachers know as contingent, rather than absolute, and developmental, rather than static or atemporal, it makes sense that such knowledge has to be constructed by the individual. The constructs of content and methodology encourage us to think of teaching knowledge as transmitted and received; the alternatives make that view untenable. Seeing what is taught as pedagogical content knowledge and how it is taught as based on a conception of practice illuminates the highly personal nature of what teachers know. To say that teachers' knowledge depends on who they are as individuals means that it will be idiosyncratic, but it will also have common features. Such a view of teachers' knowledge has clear implications for teacher education; principally that we must no longer think of it as a matter of transmitting information but rather as a process of constructing understandings.

Conclusion. Taken together, these three characteristics of what teachers know—that it is contingent, developmental, and constructed—offer a different way of seeing language teaching. The business of seeing as not-seeing is a common phenomenon, hardly confined to our field. Through this paper, I hope to have raised the issue of what is taken for granted in the common constructs in the field of language teaching. Offering alternatives, drawn from the other domains of educational research, is hardly a panacea; it may, however, jar our collective assumptions and thinking. It is also an appeal to become more flexible and accommodating as we try to better understand language teaching and language teacher education. The fact that shared assumptions about the nature of content, methodology, and the act of teaching have become reified as accepted constructs should not force us to accept them as the truth. As the historian Tyack points out, our truths are in large measure a function of our disciplinary backgrounds.

But they are truths nonetheless. So the issue is how to combine and thus make them more complex; it is not one of asserting certain truths and rejecting others. As Tyack (1976:388) concludes his essay:

---

3 Stern (1983) referred to this common form of teacher education as an 'input-output' model.

The different kinds of interpretation do call our attention to different actors, motives, and evidence and in this sense one could say that the historian interested in the phenomenon . . . might simply add together the various sets of observation. . . . There are problems with simple additive eclecticism however. To argue that one should not mix interpretations promiscuously does not mean that it is unwise to mix confront alternative conceptualizations or to attempt to integrate them into a more complex understanding.

In thinking about Rainey's lesson from this perspective, we are led to a different set of questions about it and through them to a more emic view of her. There is quite simply a whole lot that we do not have direct access to in a lesson or in teaching, more generally, aspects which reflect features of the teacher's 'mental life' (Walberg 1977) in practice. However it is a mistake to ignore these aspects because we are unable to see them through our current constructs.

References

Allwright, D. 1989. Interaction in the language classroom: Social problems and pedagogic possibilities. Paper presented at Les É tats Gé né raux des Langues, Paris.
Apple, M. 1985. Education and power. New York: Routledge.
Apple, M. and S. Jungck. 1990. 'You don't have to be a teacher to teach this unit:' Teaching, technology and gender in the classroom. American Educational Research Journal, 27, (2). 227-254.
Applebee, A. 1981. Writing in secondary schools: English and the content areas. Research Report #21. Urbana, IL: National Council of Teachers of English.
Berliner, D. 1988. The development of expertise in pedagogy. Washington, DC: American Association of Colleges for Teacher Education.
Berliner, D. 1986. In search of the expert pedagogue. Educational Researcher, 15, (7). 5-13.
Brumfit, C. 1983. Creating coherence in ELT teacher training. In R.R. Jordan (ed). Case Studies in ELT. London: Collins.
Bullough, R. Jr. 1989. First-year teacher: A case study. New York: Teachers College Press.
Burke, K. 1935. Permanence and change. New York: New Republic.
Butt, D. 1990. Talking and thinking: The patterns of behavior. Oxford: Oxford University Press.
Carter K. and W. Doyle. 1987. Teachers' knowledge structures and comprehension processes. In: J. Calderhead (ed). Exploring teachers' thinking. London: Cassell Publications. 147-160.
Cazden, C. 1988. Classroom discourse: The language of teaching and learning. Portsmouth NH: Heineman.
Clark, C. and P. Peterson. 1986. Teachers' thought processes. In: M. Wittrock (ed). Handbook of research on teaching (3rd ed.) New York: Macmillan Publishing. 255-297.

Cummings, A. 1989. Student teachers' conceptions of curriculum: Towards an understanding of language teacher development. TESL Canada/Revue TESL du Canada, 7, (1). 33-51.

Doe, J. 1988. Speak into the mirror: A story of linguistic anthropology. Washington, DC: University Press of America.

Doyle, W. 1983. Academic Work. Review of Educational Research, 53. (2). 159-199.

Doyle, W. 1977. Learning the classroom environment: An ecological analysis. Journal of Teacher Education, 28, (6). 51-55.

Elbow, P. 1973. Writing without teachers. New York: Oxford University Press.

Freeman, D. (in press). Collaboration: Constructing shared understandings in a second language classroom. In: D. Nunan (ed). Collaborative language learning and teaching. Cambridge: Cambridge University Press.

Freeman, D. 1991. 'The same things done differently.' Doctoral dissertation: Harvard Graduate School of Education.

Freeman, D. 1990a. Teachers' knowledge: The grammar of experience. Plenary presentation: TESOL Mid-Summer Meeting, East Lansing, MI.

Freeman, D. 1990b. 'Thoughtful work': Reconceptualizing the research literature on teacher thinking. Qualifying Paper: Harvard Graduate School of Education.

Geertz, C. 1973. The interpretation of cultures. New York: Basic Books.

Johnson, K. 1990. The theoretical orientations of ESOL teachers: The relationship between beliefs and practices. Unpublished manuscript.

Journal of Teacher Education. 1990. Theme: Pedagogical content knowledge. Journal of Teacher Education, 41, (3).

Kagan, D. 1988. Teaching as clinical problem-solving: A critical examination of the analogy and its implications. Review of Educational Research, 58, (4), 482-505.

Kennedy, M. 1990. Policy issues in teacher education. East Lansing, MI: National Center for Research on Teacher Education.

Kleinsasser, R. 1990. Foreign language teaching: A tale of two technical cultures. Doctoral dissertation: University of Illinois at Urbana.

Lightfoot, S. L. 1985. The lives of teachers. In: Shulman, L. and G. Sykes (eds). Handbook of teaching and policy. New York: Longman. 241-261.

Lortie. D. 1975. Schoolteacher: A sociological study. Chicago: University of Chicago Press.

National Institute of Education (NIE). 1975. Teaching as clinical problem-solving. Report of Panel #6; National Conference on Studies in Teaching. Washington, DC: National Institute of Education.

Oja, S. 1990. Developmental theories and the professional development of teachers. Paper presented at the American Educational Research Association Annual Meeting, Boston, MA.

Oja, S. and L. Smulyan. 1989. Collaborative action research: A developmental process. London: Falmer Press.

Prabhu, N.S. 1991. The dynamics of the language lesson. Invited address; TESOL Convention, New York, NY.

Prabhu, N.S. 1990. There is no best method: Why? TESOL Quarterly, 24, (2): 161-176.

Richards. J. and N. Hino. 1983. Training ESOL teachers: The need for needs assessment. In: J. Alatis, H. Stern, and P. Strevens (eds). Applied linguistics and the preparation of language teachers: Towards a rationale. Washington, DC: Georgetown University Press. 312-327.

Rosenholtz, S. 1989. Teachers' workplace: The social organization of schools. New York: Longman.
Shavelson, R. and P. Stern. 1981. Research on teachers' pedagogical thoughts, judgments, decisions, and behaviors. Review of Educational Reseach, 51. (4) 455-498.
Shulman, L. 1987. Knowledge-base and teaching: Foundations of the new reform. Harvard Educational Review, 57, (1): 1-22.
Shulman, L. 1986a. Paradigms and research programs in the study of teaching. In: M. Wittrock ed. Handbook of Research on Teaching (3rd ed.). New York: Macmillan. 3-36.
Shulman, L. 1986b. Those who understand: Knowledge growth in teaching. Educational Researcher, 15, (2): 4-14.
Shulman, L. 1984. The practical and the eclectic: A deliberation on teaching and educational research curriculum inquiry, 14, (2): 183-200.
Stern, H. 1983. Language teacher education. In: J. Alatis, H. Stern, and P. Strevens eds. Applied linguistics and the preparation of language teachers: Towards a rationale. Washington, DC: Georgetown University Press. 342-362.
Sutcliffe, J. 1977. Introduction to the 'Volume on classroom decision-making. Cambridge (UK) Journal of Education, 7, (1): 2-3.
Tyack, D. 1976. Ways of seeing: An essay on the history of compulsory schooling. Harvard Educational Review, 46, (3): 355-389.
Walberg, H. 1977. Decision and perception: New constructs for research on teaching effects. Cambridge (UK) Journal of Education, 7 (1): 12-20.
Williams, R. 1977. Marxism and literature. Oxford: Oxford University Press.
Wilson, S., L. Shulman, and A. Richert. 1987. '150 different ways' of knowing: Representations of knowledge in teaching. In: J. Calderhead (ed). Exploring teachers' thinking. London: Cassell Publications. 104-124.
Woods, D. 1989. What studying ESL teachers' decisions in context tells us. Unpublished manuscript.

What can peers provide?

Mary McGroarty
Northern Arizona University

Virtually all current second language teaching theory, if it falls into any of the so-called communicative camps, provides for group work in the language classroom. The possible advantages of group work have been discussed for some time (e.g. Long et al. 1976, Long and Porter 1985, Gaies 1985). Here I want to review some of those advantages, supplementing the discussion with data from learner discourse in second language classes; note some of the unanswered questions that accompany group work; and then suggest some tentative guidelines for teachers who wish to incorporate techniques of group work into their own classwork.

First, the matter of definition. In considering the possibilities of peer interaction for instruction, it is essential to ask who are the 'peers' and what are the 'groups' of interest. The answer varies for foreign and second-language settings, and for discussions of L2 learning versus cooperative learning in content-area classrooms. It is worthwhile to acknowledge this variation explicitly since the matter of peer skill profiles affects the applicability of group work. In most of the L2 literature, 'peers' have been defined as, in effect, students of the same level of proficiency in the L2 who are otherwise more or less equivalent in educational background, first language literacy, and educational setting. Thus discussions of group work have focused, naturally, on how such students make use of interaction with others to develop L2 skills. In the cooperative learning literature (e.g. Kagan 1986, Slavin 1983), a peer is a student of the same age or grade level. In the peer tutoring literature (e.g. Sapiens 1982), a peer is a person of similar background, but perhaps two or three years ahead of the students being tutored.

Before being able to answer the question of 'What can peers provide?' we must establish who the available peers are. The answer will be different in each of the three configurations I have noted. Peers of the same level in a second language can provide input useful for comprehension practice, communicative exchange, and some feedback for clarification; peers of the same grade level who are more fluent or native speakers of a second language can provide a wider range of the second language for comprehension practice, exchange, and clarification, if tasks are structured appropriately. While most of my discussion here will address the situation of peers as students of the same L2 level in a second language classroom, I will also allude to some of the work done on peer learning in cooperative learning settings in bilingual programs because of the usefulness of that model for content-area teachers; because content-based L2 instruction is a vital aspect of current L2 methodology, it is important to see what kind of methodological bridges can be built between language and content teaching. Use of peer interaction in appropriately structured learning tasks is certainly one of those, and one which reflects as well broader currents in cognitive psychology which emphasize the contribution that social interaction makes to cognitive as well as linguistic development (Moll 1989).

The term 'group work' in the L2 classroom can also refer generally to any kind of activity where students are placed into pairs or groups of any size smaller than that of the whole class. Thus the term includes several different arrangements, each with its own possibilities and constraints for the amount and kind of language to be produced. In some cooperative learning models, notably but not only those developed and investigated by Kagan (1989, 1986) and Slavin (1983), group work is further structured by use of explicit roles which can be assigned according to expertise in parts of a task to be completed, or social and interactional responsibilities for managing parts of a task (e.g. materials organizer; clarifier of instruction; encourager, etc.). The structures or social roles used to guide the activity are an integral part of the way teachers influence group interaction; certain roles often have characteristic language patterns that students are taught and expected to use, a feature akin to choice of linguistic functions in many approaches to communicative language teaching (Coelho 1988). In models of native language instruction that fall under the broad umbrella of the label 'collaborative learning' (e.g. Bayer 1990), the use of small groups constituted randomly is seen to be an essential tool in promoting free use of expressive language; there is explicit disavowal of using designated roles to shape interaction. Group work in an L2 classroom may or may not be comparable to other models of cooperative or collaborative learning depending on how it is structured, a topic I will discuss presently.

Now to the matter of what peers in second language classes can provide each other. The five linguistic advantages related to group work are (a) more opportunity to produce output, which then acts as input for learning; production of (b) more redundant language, which can encourage skills in fluency and comprehension; production of language which is (c) appropriate in level of linguistic accuracy; (d) appropriate in the shape of linguistic units; and (e) more varied in discourse patterns.

None of these is a novel observation, but all deserve careful review. That use of group work affords more students more opportunity to produce language than they have in teacher-fronted settings has long been evident. In traditional teacher-centered classrooms, whether we consider those serving native speakers or second language learners, students have little opportunity to express themselves to either teachers or peers (Goodlad 1984, Dunkin and Biddle 1973). The structure of traditional teacher-centered classrooms gives only one person at a time the chance to speak, and, for over twenty-five years, most observational research has indicated that the speaker is the teacher 60 to 70% of the time (Bellack 1966, Chaudron 1988). Thus, any classroom activity which gives students more opportunity to speak will improve potential communicative skills (Bejarano 1987, Long and Porter 1985).

However, the lecture-style or 'lock step' (Long et al. 1976) classroom is not the only culprit in depriving L2 students of the chance to communicate: in open-plan or completely individualized elementary, middle, or high school classrooms, students may be left to their own devices to carry out their work or complete worksheets in relative isolation (Wong Fillmore 1989, 1982), thus depriving them of the chance to hear or produce very much of the second language. Classrooms following a predominately 'open plan' or individualized model of content instruction thus also unwittingly restrict access to spoken models of the second language if students don't know it well before they begin. The kind of interaction most suitable for second language teaching does not happen automatically in such classrooms; it must be integrated into instructional planning from the start if it is to occur regularly enough to assist L2 learners (Enright and McCloskey 1988).

Some examples will make the claim of more opportunity to produce the L2 more concrete. These and many following come from a thesis done in a university level Dutch class for English speakers; the researcher, Jeanine Deen, wished to see what the differences between teacher-centered and a jigsaw-type cooperative activity were in amount of talk even in the rather small (13 students) Dutch L2 class. She used two measures, number of turns taken and T-units in each language, as indicators of quantity. In the teacher-centered setting, students produced 220 turns at talk, while the teacher took 201; in the cooperative activity, students took 2,005 turns, nearly ten times as many as they had taken in the teacher-centered condition, and the teacher took 142, a difference that was statistically significant (Deen 1987: 36). Data from the utterances produced as well as the turn taking behavior provided further confirmation of the hypothesis that students would produce more of the second language in the cooperative learning activity, as Table 1 shows.

In this class, then, there was no doubt that the group-based activity led to production of more of the second language. Indeed, it led to

Table 1. Frequencies of L2 / L1 T-units in teacher-centered vs. cooperative learning Dutch L2 class (Deen 1987:43)

	Teacher-centered		Cooperative learning	
	Students	Teachers	Students	Teachers
Dutch (L2)	176	583	1,127	196
Mixed	7	7	160	37
English (L1)	33	20	793	5
Total:	116	610	2,080	238

greater production of all types of language (L2, L1, and mixed utterances), but the far greater number of L2 T-units shows that students, even in a class that was, by some standards, small as a whole, produced much more of the second language when the small group tasks required them to do so.

The second advantage, redundancy of language, has special benefits for L2 learners at earlier stages of proficiency. Commentators have long noted the sometimes deadly simplicity of L2 classroom talk and, for that matter, L2 materials (Long and Sato 1983). In classrooms where all students are L2 learners, a teacher's "going by the book" can result in extreme boredom for all, particularly if the teacher is a not a fluent speaker of the L2 who must rely on verbatim repetition of the L2 text or grammatical discussions in L1 to keep the class moving. (Fortunately, evidence indicates that nonnative teachers who have achieved good proficiency in an L2 are capable of adjusting their language to the students' instructional level. See Milk 1990.)

In classes which combine native speakers with students of limited English proficiency, LEP students typically receive less teacher and peer communication, and communication at a lower linguistic and cognitive level (Schinke-Llano 1983). By breaking the class into groups or pairs, teachers can allow students to create messages for each other that may, in the case of L2 learners, be more redundant than statements in a text; ESL learners mixed in with native speakers will also be able to hear more redundant language.

The process of asking and answering questions and working out tasks with various degrees of uncertainty provides a natural context for greater redundancy in communication as students exchange information and requests. This redundancy, again contextualized within tasks relevant to the curriculum, supports growth of comprehension. Experimental evidence from adult learners of English shows that greater redundancy, achieved either through deliberate repetition and re-insertion of topics in discourse (Chaudron 1983) or by the natural repetition of words and phrases in conversation (Pica, Young, and Doughty 1987), improves comprehension. An important caveat: the repetition and redundancy of L2 group work is grounded in task demands and natural communicative requirements. It is thus different from the rote repetition that can characterize audio-lingual drills, if such are handled inexpertly. Because it is based on interactional needs, the repetition and rephrasing in group work retains communicative relevance. Indeed, because of the requirement that each response be appropriately contingent to its predecessor, there is no chance for students to parrot responses.

Let us see what this means in actual interaction. Here are three students from the Dutch L2 class puzzling out the nature of the cartoon story that one of them must retell for the small group:

Example 1. Students beginning cartoon retelling task, Dutch L2 class (from Deen 1987: 145).

Student language:	Translation:
Mia: *Het gaat over//*	'It's about (it = the story)'
James: *Het gaat?*	'It goes?'
Mia: *Gaat over*	'Is about'
It, the story is about	
James: *Oh.*	
Mia: *Het gaat over de kat.*	'It's about the cat.'
James: *De de kat?*	'The the cat?'
Mia: *De kat.*	'The cat.'
James: *K-A-T?*	[Spells in English]
Bea: *Ja.*	'Yes.'
Mia: *K-A-T.*	

Here students have not only repeated one of the key lexical items, *cat* (which is, after all, a cognate) three times and spelled it twice to insure comprehension; one of the more proficient students also repeated the sentence structure *Het gaat over* three times, and, in doing so, provided an indirect correction through modeling for the student who was confused about its meaning as he tried to figure out the meaning of the story being recounted.

Even when classes are not aimed principally at developing oral proficiency and thus do not emphasize speaking activity, group work in writing can also provide redundancy that supports comprehension. I observed one such example during my own effort to learn some Navajo in a beginning level class composed of seventeen students, twelve of Navajo background and five who were not. Assigned to write sentences with various adverbs, among them *a do'* 'also', I wrote a sentence with an initially misplaced form which was corrected by my partner, who had a better sense of Navajo word order:

Example 2. Students writing sample sentences, Navajo L2 class.

Student language:
Mary (writing): **Tom Kin ánígóó a do' deeyá* . 'Tom to Flagstaff also is going.'
Mary (speaking): *Is this right?*
Linda: *No, a do' goes here.*
Linda (gestures to her own paper and writes): *Tom a do' Kin ánígóó deeyá* . 'Tom is also going to Flagstaff.'
Mary (copies): *Tom a do' Kin ánígóó deeyá.* 'Tom is also going to Flagstaff.'

In this example, even though students do not do a great deal of speaking, they have repeated the correct form through nonverbal interaction and writing. Besides simply offering an example of the correct placement of the adverb, though, the students have generated repetition of the entire sentence which includes elements such as the postposition -*góó* and the sentence-final verb, both of which pose problems for English speakers. Thus the redundancy even in this interaction, directed not at oral proficiency but at writing, helped to model a critical feature of the L2 for the less proficient learner.

The input students provide for each other is also at an appropriate level of accuracy. Let us be clear about what this means. Learner production is not flawless, either in structure or semantic features, but it does, in general, conform to the communicative demands of being adequately informative and clear insofar as learners' proficiency allows. This, indeed, is a key to understanding its possible relevance to the L2 classroom, especially in the post structuralist language teaching world of the 1990s. Where errors were once viewed as anathema, we now see them as part of the learning process. Though there is still, and ought to be, lively debate regarding the balance between insistence on accuracy versus insistence on fluency in the L2 classroom (see, for example, Celce-Murcia's plenary paper here), all but the most hidebound pedagogues would now admit that some error types are not just inevitable but developmentally appropriate in the course of L2 learning, and that some errors—notably over-generalization of target language forms—indicate real progress in acquisition of L2 patterns.

The principal pedagogical issue for group work, as for all communicative techniques and, for that matter, cooperative or collaborative techniques for native speakers, is that we do not yet know at what point, if any, overt intervention in the form of correction or counterexample can be expected to nudge performance further toward the L2 standard form. That is, we know that group work provides communicative practice, but we do not yet know how much, if at all, it provides for the shaping of performance in the direction of target language norms in pronunciation, grammar, or lexical choice (Ellis 1990:114-116). This is the methodological correlate of what Gass has called the negative evidence problem in L2 acquisition (Gass 1989).

A recurring worry in L2 classrooms is that, left to talk with teach other, students will make so many errors that they will acquire an imperfect version of the L2. Indeed, the lack of more proficient interlocutors is one of the factors that led Swain to point out the need for 'comprehensible output' in French immersion classrooms (Swain 1985). The question of fine tuning of grammatical competence broadly defined (taken here to include all the dimensions noted by Canale and Swain 1980: phonological, morphological, and syntactic) remains an open one, as I will argue in the next section. Nevertheless, available evidence seems rather robust to date in showing that, during group work, students make either the same relative number of errors as they do in teacher-centered interaction (Pica and Doughty 1985a) or, in fact, may make a far lower proportion (if sometimes higher absolute number) of errors in group work because of the their much greater opportunity to produce language. In the beginning level Dutch class described previously, Deen (1987) found that the proportion of errors in cooperative student work was far lower than that in teacher-led interaction, primarily because students had such abundant practice opportunities that they used much more language overall (Deen 1987:55). Furthermore, the language they used was pragmatically accurate, though much of it structurally simple as would be expected for a beginning level class. While I do not propose here that group work in an L2 classroom can substitute, especially as students become more proficient, for interaction with more fluent speakers, either native speakers or more advanced learners, it is nonetheless clear that, in itself, use of group or pair work can provide not only more practice but practice at a level of accuracy appropriate to the learners, in part because the small group interaction, with its greater opportunity for student participation and negotiation, provides more opportunity for learners to correct themselves and each other.

Sometimes students may correct one another overtly, as in Example 2 where my partner told me directly that my sentence was deviant and also supplied the correct form. Much more common than direct correction in group work (as in conversation), though, is the indirect correction that takes place through modeling of the correct form. A particularly nice example comes from the university Dutch class, in which the successive rounds of recounting and reporting show us one student, Melvyn, who makes two attempts to produce the correct ordinal form and finally does so on the third attempt:

Example 3. Student self-correction at three different times in group work (Deen 1987:45,46).

Student language:
Jean: *Zij is de tweeëntwintigste van de klas.* 'She's the twenty-second in the class.'
Melvyn: *Ja, dat is x.* 'Yes, that is x.'
Jean: *Zij is stom.* 'She is dumb.'
Martin: *Ja.* 'Yes.'
Melvyn: **De tweeëntwintig.* 'The twenty-two.'
... [Later in discussion]:
Melvyn: **Tweeëntwintig van de klas.* 'Twenty-two in the class.'
Martin: *Yeah, tweeëntwintigste.* 'Yeah, twenty-second.'
... [Later in Melvyn's report]:
Melvyn: *Eh, zij is de tweeëntwintigste van, van haar klas.* 'Eh, she is the twenty-second in, in her class.'

We do not know, of course, whether production of the correct form is entirely fortuitous, nor do we know how stable a part of Melvyn's vocabulary it is. We can nonetheless see that through group work he has had a chance to try out an incorrect hypothesis, receive indirect correction from a classmate, and later produce the appropriate form; group work has here provided the scaffolding (Moll 1989, Hawkins 1987) needed to help him express information that is accurate not only semantically but in appropriate linguistic form.

Production of language in appropriate units, the fourth advantage I note for group work, is apparent in all three of the examples set out above. In group work, as in conversation, students do not always produce complete sentences; they offer one- or two-word responses, ask brief questions, or offer short confirmations, as well as creating sentences. Learners prompt each other more often than native speakers do (Porter 1983). These shorter pieces of language, termed 'satellite units' by Bygate (1988), help learners maintain the flow of interaction. Thus, as in conversation, learner production matches demands of communicative relevance while not always being structurally explicit. Again, such practice assists in developing fluency and pragmatic skills (though it may well be distressing for language instructors trained with The Complete Sentence as the optimal goal) and is thus appropriate for at least some activities in communicatively oriented classrooms.

The final advantage I wish to emphasize is the chance for learners to produce a greater range of discourse functions, notably questions, in group work. In the Dutch L2 class, students asked 93% (469 out of a total of 503) of the questions in the cooperative learning condition; in the teacher-centered condition, the teacher asked 86% (217 out of 251) (Deen 1987:38), a significant difference. Not only the higher percentage but the much higher number of questions bear comment: in the small group setting, students had many more opportunities to ask questions than they had even in a small teacher-centered class, where the teacher's authority role can discourage question asking.

The type as well as the number of questions is pedagogically important. Group work related to task accomplishment, if the task is chosen well, leads to production of referential questions, questions in which the person asking does not know the answer and truly needs the information. In contrast, display questions (*Is this a pencil? Is this book red?*, etc.), often a prominent feature of teachers' classroom language, request learners to produce information already known to the questioner, thus rendering their communicative value nil. Besides being grounded in genuine communicative need, as questions related to task accomplishment typically are (Christison 1988), referential questions typically produce more complex responses (Brock 1986, Long et al. 1984) and can stimulate requests for clarification, elaboration, and other meaning-based expansions (Pica 1987). Group work using appropriate tasks can thus promote use of referential questions which should in turn enhance the level of discussion. Additionally, where roles such as praiser, encourager, or manager are used in the set-up of group tasks, the language that goes with each role (e.g. *Good job!, You figured that out, Try again, I think we can do this, It's her turn next, Put the scissors away,*) may help to expand the learner's L2 repertoire, particularly when students are beginners who are building up their store of second language forms to use for different functions. Some foreign language research suggests that roles help to equalize opportunities for interaction, particularly for learners in the early stages of L2 acquisition (Açiköz 1991).

Now to the unanswered questions. Given that, through group work, peers can promote more language production, greater redundancy, practice at appropriate levels of accuracy, production of conversationally appropriate units and a greater range of discourse functions, why should we not use it even more than we do? The answer is that, while group work can provide these benefits, it is no panacea for all the difficulties related to L2 instruction, nor does it provide similar benefits to all students in all circumstances. A number of questions remain.

Chief among them is the nature of the tasks used to generate pair or group discussion. Two sets of dimensions are particularly relevant here, one related to language and one to content. As investigations of both ESL (e.g. Pica and Doughty 1985b, 1988; Duff 1986) and foreign language classrooms (Kinginger and Savignon 1991) have shown, the nature of the tasks used plays a critical role in shaping the possibilities for interaction. Not all small-group tasks afford equal opportunity for conversational participation and modification, even when pairs are used: if tasks are directed at language form, requiring production or translation of particular units, they will elicit more comments and correction on formal linguistic properties, while tasks requiring more personal opinion or information exchange will generate more language overall in a more conversational format (Kinginger and Savignon 1991:102). Furthermore, even within the domain of tasks broadly defined as 'communicative,' there are important differences in the kind of language elicited from learners: on comparing two tasks, one a 'find the difference' and one a 'twenty questions' activity, Bygate (1991) found that the former elicited significantly longer average turns and a greater number of clause units but significantly fewer single phrase, phrase-only, and interrogative utterances. Thus the possibilities for the five possible benefits I have noted must be explored within the constraints of specific task formats. The relative utility of different tasks may well differ for students of differing proficiency levels: beginners may have to struggle to generate enough language to propose elaborate solutions to ambiguous situations, while high intermediate or advanced L2 students may chafe at having to supply short word or phrase answers when they are capable of proposing and defending solutions to a problem.

In practice, this means there is no single best task type for teachers interested in communicative classwork. Even the choice between one- and two-way tasks (with the former essentially requiring one partner to listen to new information provided by the other, and the latter requiring two or more members of the interaction to provide information) must be made according to instructional goal and proficiency level. A pilot study of one- versus two-way tasks (Ju 1989) concluded that learners, particularly learners at lower proficiency levels, had more opportunity for extended practice in listening to and producing extended discourse in the new language in a one-way condition. The researcher speculated that this would be useful for them in building confidence in their ability to understand the new language even if such tasks did not provide for the more rapid exchange of information observable when both parties to an interaction had to contribute. As Long (1989) has suggested, there are different optimal task types for learners of different proficiency levels. It may be that beginners may benefit from combinations of pair and small-group tasks different from those that can develop the proficiency of more advanced students. For L2 learners and teachers, then, the most effective use of group work must be defined according to both level of learner proficiency and linguistic demands of the task itself in terms of the presence of information exchange, the demands made on interlocutor comprehension, the kind of discourse required to complete the task, and the kind of follow-up activity, if any, included (Eyring 1989, Danielson and Porter 1991).

The questions related to the negotiation of content in small group work are, perhaps, more critical outside of the L2 classroom in content-area settings, where the heterogeneity at issue includes not only student language background but differing levels of academic experience and background in the subject taught, be it social studies, mathematics, or science. Investigators have noted that most L2 research on group work uses brief tasks unrelated to previous class work (Rulon and McCreary 1986). In an L2 class, where the main purpose of group or pair work is functional use of the L2, the factor of amount of new information or cognitive load of a particular task is not often a major consideration. Indeed, many of the tasks used to investigate group work (retelling cartoon stories, negotiating who should survive on a desert island after a plane crash, giving a partner instructions to produce a simple line drawing of different objects) have no particular relevance to other academic domains except insofar as they provide students the chance to develop L2 proficiency.

However, when the issue of developing proficiency in an L2 is added to that of developing an academic knowledge base in a particular subject, the matter of appropriate task selection takes on another dimension. If teachers are interested in using small group work to teach science or social studies as well as develop L2 proficiency in students who are not native speakers, another set of judgments regarding cognitive as well as linguistic demands of the task comes into play (Kagan and McGroarty, in preparation; Cohen 1986). Teachers must then balance demands for complexity of linguistic form and pace of turn-taking with those of the density of new information involved to allow for an optimal balance of language practice and content learning. In the content area classroom, group work needs to include opportunities for negotiation and clarification of content area issues and feedback on accuracy of information as well as clarification, overt or covert, of language forms and functions. Thus instructional decisions regarding the appropriate constitution of groups, the rubric used for assigning roles (if any are used), and the nature of tasks themselves may well differ from those made for second language classrooms.

Moreover, the role of the native language in group work in content area classrooms is likely to differ from its function in the L2 classroom: use of the L1 is often controlled or restricted in the L2 setting, where the purpose is to develop L2 skill, while use of the native language may well have a wider scope in the content area classroom, and appropriately so, particularly when students have some academic background or previous schooling in the first language relevant to the subject they are studying

(McGroarty 1989). Here only systematic documentation of effective practices in each setting will begin to provide some guidance for teachers interested in exploring the usefulness of peer work in their own classrooms.

Beyond the matters of linguistic and cognitive goals of instruction are additional social and cultural considerations that affect the usefulness of peer work in L2 in content area classrooms. Evidence indicates some gender-related differences in group participation in both L2 (Pica et al. 1989, Duff 1986) and L1 classrooms (Webb and Kenderski 1985), though gender-related differentials have not been observed in every L2 setting (Açiköz 1991). Hence, teachers who work with students of both genders in the same classroom need to insure that the tasks and settings they use provide for equal participation. Furthermore, cultural preferences for various kinds of group structures may play a role in designing appropriate learning tasks in L2 and content-area classrooms. Research on small group learning in elementary classrooms serving students of different ethnic backgrounds has indicated that optimal group size for native Hawaiian children was larger than that preferred by Navajo students of the same age, who worked best when placed in groups of two of three children of the same gender (Tharp and Gallimore 1989: 182-185). Use of peer work in the L2 classroom (or in any classroom, for that matter) must be tested out within the same set of cultural constraints that shape all educational behavior in whatever setting is of interest.

What guidelines, then, can direct teacher decisions in the selection of small group activities in L2 classes? Most obviously, teachers can be confident that the use of small group or pair activity can indeed promote fluency, give practice in turn-taking, provide for language practice at an appropriate level of redundancy and accuracy, encourage a wider range of discourse functions, and, depending on whether a one- or two-way task is used, provide relatively more practice in listening to and producing language, as in a one-way task, or in appropriate and more frequent conversational turn-taking, as in two-way tasks. Teachers must also be aware that learner proficiency level is a crucial selection factor: tasks involving an 'opinion gap' rather than provision of more narrowly defined information may be beyond the linguistic resources of students below the low intermediate level (Danielson and Porter 1991). For content-area classrooms, considerations of effective use of peer work must include some determination of the cognitive as well as linguistic demands of small group or pair tasks. Such considerations will affect the formation of groups, the instructions given to students, the emphasis on second language use during the activity, and the nature of follow-up activities used.

In summary, peers can provide each other with much valuable input and practice during the course of second language learning. The relative value of peer work in any given classroom, though, will depend on both the instructional goals of the particular classroom and the availability of alternative means of realizing those goals outside the classroom. This means that peer work may well have different optimal configurations in foreign language, second language, and content area classrooms. The challenge for L2 researchers and teachers alike is now to document the outcomes of peer work in different settings, noting the relative efficacy of different group sizes and different tasks, and to examine whether and how the use of peer work affects level of L2 and, where appropriate, subject area mastery over time. With greater breadth of descriptive information across settings and, if possible, longitudinal data from learners whose curriculum has systematically included group work, we will be better able to generate a more adequate model of what peers in L2 learning can and cannot provide.

References

Açiköz, Kamile. 1991. Cooperative, competitive, and traditional techniques and foreign language achievement. Paper presented at 25th TESOL Convention, New York City, March.

Bayer, Ann Shea. 1990. Collaborative-apprenticeship learning: Language and thinking across the curriculum, K-12. Mountain View, Calif.: Mayfield Publishing.

Bejarano, Yael. 1987. A cooperative small-group methodology in the language classroom TESOL Quarterly. 21. 483-504.

Brock, Cynthia. 1986. The effects of referential questions on ESL classroom discourse. TESOL Quarterly. 20. 47-59.

Bygate, Martin. 1991. Strategies in oral communication: Towards a typology of tasks. Paper presented at 25th TESOL Convention, New York City, March.

Bygate, Martin. 1988. Units of oral expression and language learning in small group interaction. Applied Linguistics. 9.59-82.

Canale, Michael, and Merrill Swain. 1980. Theoretical bases of communicative approaches to second language teaching and testing. Applied Linguistics. 1. 1-47.

Chaudron, Craig. 1988. Second language classrooms. Cambridge: Cambridge University Press.

Chaudron, Craig. 1983. Simplification of input: Topic restatements and their effects on L2 learners' recognition and recall. TESOL Quarterly. 17. 437-458.

Christison, Mary Ann. 1988. Research on cooperative learning in the ESL classroom. Paper presented at TESOL Summer Meeting, Flagstaff, Ariz.

Coelho, Elizabeth. 1988. Cooperative group learning in the language classroom. Workshop presented at 22nd TESOL Convention, Chicago, Ill. March.

Cohen, Elizabeth G. 1986. Designing groupwork: Strategies for the heterogeneous classroom. New York: Teachers College Press.

Danielson, Dorothy, and Patricia Porter. 1991. Addressing some criticisms of group work. Demonstration presented at 25th TESOL Convention, New York City. March.

Deen, Jeanine Y. 1987. An analysis of classroom interaction in a cooperative learning and teacher-centered setting. M.A. in T.E.S.L. thesis, University of California, Los Angeles.

Duff, Patricia A. 1986. Another look at interlanguage talk: Taking task to task. In: Talking to learn. ed. by R. R. Day. 147-181. Rowley, Mass.: Newbury House.
Dunkin, Michael J., and Bruce J. Biddle. 1974. The study of teaching. New York: Holt, Rinehart, and Winston.
Ellis, Rod. 1990. Instructed second language acquisition. Oxford, England: Basil Blackwell.
Enright, D. Scott, and Mary Lou McCloskey. 1988. Integrating English. Reading, Mass.: Addison-Wesley.
Eyring, Janet L. 1989. Teacher experiences and student responses in ESL project work instruction: A case study. Ph.D. dissertation, University of California, Los Angeles.
Gaies, Stephen J. 1985. Peer involvement in language learning. Orlando, Fl.: Harcourt Brace Jovanovich.
Gass, Susan M. 1989. Language universals and second-language acquisition. Language Learning. 39. 497-534.
Goodlad, John I. 1984. A place called school. New York: McGraw-Hill.
Hawkins, Barbara. 1988. Scaffolded classroom interaction in a minority language setting. Ph.D. dissertation. University of California, Los Angeles.
Ju, Kyoung Sook. 1989. One- and two-way tasks in second language learning. Term paper for English 658 (Second Language Acquisition), Northern Arizona University.
Kagan, Spencer. 1989. The structural approach to cooperative learning. Educational Leadership. 47. 4:12-15. Los Angeles, CA: Evaluation Dissemination, and Assessment Center, California State University.
Kagan, Spencer. 1986. Cooperative learning and sociocultural factors in schooling. In: Beyond language: Social and cultural factors in schooling language minority students, 231-298.
Kagan, Spencer, and Mary McGroarty. In preparation. Principles of cooperative learning and language acquisition for language and content gains. In: Cooperative learning for ESL students [tentative title]. Englewood Cliffs, N.J.: Prentice Hall Regents/Center for Applied Linguistics.
Kinginger, Celeste S., and Sandra J. Savignon. 1991. Four conversations: Task variation and classroom learner discourse. In: Languages in school and society: Policy and pedagogy, ed. by Mary McGroarty and Christian Faltis, 85-106. Berlin: Mouton de Gruyter.
Long, Michael H. 1989. Task, group, and task-group interaction. University of Hawai'i Working Papers in ESL, Vol. 8 (2):1-26.
Long, Michael H., and Patricia A. Porter. 1985. Group work, interlanguage talk, and second language acquisition. TESOL Quarterly. 19. 207-228.
Long, Michael H., L. Adams, M. McClean, and F. Castanos. 1976. Doing things with words—verbal interaction in lockstep and small group classroom situations. In: On TESOL '76, ed. by Ruth Crymes and John Fanselow. 137-153. Washington, D.C.: TESOL.
Long, Michael H., Cynthia Brock, Graham Crookes, G. Deicke, L. Potter, and S. Zhang. 1984. The effect of teachers' questioning patterns and wait-time on pupil participation in public high school classes in Hawai'i for students of limited English proficiency. Technical report 1. Honolulu: Center for Second Language Classroom Research, University of Hawai'i at Manoa.

McGroarty, Mary. 1989. The benefits of cooperative learning arrangements in second language instruction. NABE Journal. 13. 127-143.
Milk, Rober D. 1990. Can foreigners do 'foreigner talk'? A study of the linguistic input provided by non-native teachers of EFL. Texas Papers in Foreign Language Education. 1,4:274-288
Moll, Luis. 1989. Teaching second language students: A Vygotskyan perspective. In: Richness in writing: Empowering ESL students, ed. by Donna M. Johnson and Duane H. Roen, 55- 69. White Plains, N.Y.: Longman.
Pica, Teresa. 1987. Second language acquisition, social interaction, and the classroom. Applied Linguistics. 8. 3-21.
Pica, Teresa, and Catherine Doughty. 1988. Variations in classroom interaction as a function of participation pattern and task. In: Second language discourse, ed. by Jonathan Fine, 41- 55. Norwood, N.J.: Ablex.
Pica, Teresa, and Catherine Doughty. 1985a. Input and interaction in the communicative language classroom: A comparison of teacher-fronted and group activities. In: Input in second language acquisition, ed. by Susan M. Gass and Carolyn G. Madden, 115-132. Rowley, Mass.: Newbury House.
Pica, Teresa, and Catherine Doughty. 1985b. The role of group work in classroom second language acquisition. Studies in second language acquisition. 7. 233-248.
Pica, Teresa, Richard Young, and Catherine Doughty. 1987. The impact of interaction on comprehension. TESOL Quarterly. 21. 737-758.
Pica, Teresa, Lloyd Holliday, Nora Lewis, and L. Morgenthaler. 1989. Comprehensible output as an outcome of linguistic demands on the learner. Studies in Second Language Acquisition. 11. 63-90.
Porter, Patricia A. 1983. Variations in the conversations of adult learners of English as a function of the proficiency level of the participants. Ph.D. dissertation, Stanford University.
Rulon, Kathryn A., and Jan McCreary. 1986. Negotiation of content: Teacher-fronted and small-group interaction. In: Talking to learn, ed. by Richard R. Day, 182-199. Rowley, Mass.: Newbury House.
Sapiens, Alexander. 1982. Instructional language strategies in bilingual Chicano peer tutoring and their effect on cognitive and affective learning outcomes. Ph.D. dissertation, Stanford University.
Schinke-Llano, Linda A. 1983. Foreigner talk in content classrooms. In: Classroom oriented research in second language acquisition, ed. by Herbert W. Seliger and Michael H. Long, 146-165. Rowley, Mass.: Newbury House.
Slavin, Robert. 1983. Cooperative learning. New York: Longman.
Swain, Merrill. 1985. Communicative competence: Some roles of comprehensible output in its development. In: Input in second language acquisition, ed. by Susan M. Gass and Carolyn G. Madden, 235-253. Rowley, Mass.: Newbury House.
Tharp, Roland, and Ronald Gallimore. 1989. Rousing minds to life. Cambridge: Cambridge University Press.
Webb, Noreen M., and Cathy M. Kenderski. 1985. Gender differences in small-group inter action and achievement in high- and low-achieving classes. In: Gender differences in classroom interaction, ed. by Louise Cherry Wilkinson and C.B. Marrett. Orlando, Fla.: Harcourt Brace Jovanovich.

Wong Fillmore, Lily. 1989. Teachability and second language acquisition. In: The teachability of language, ed. by Mabel L. Rice and Richard L. Schiefelbusch, 311-332. Baltimore: Paul H. Brookes.

Wong Fillmore, Lily. 1982. Instructional language as linguistic input. In: Communicating in the classroom, ed. by Louise Cherry Wilkinson, 283-296. New York: Academic Press.

What Counts as Formal Language Instruction? Problems in Observation and Analysis of Classroom Teaching

Craig Chaudron*
University of Hawai'i at Manoa

I would like to sketch out here some of the important questions that I believe face the researcher, teacher trainer, teacher in training, or curriculum evaluator in documenting and understanding the nature of formal language teaching. As the pendulum of methodological trends swings away from an entirely naturalistic, 'communicative' focus in language teaching toward one in which some attention is paid to learners' formal accuracy and the provision and exercising of certain target forms, we have seen a gradual increase in classroom-based observational and experimental research on formal aspects of L2 instruction.

While the scale of some studies on formal language instruction is impressive (such as the Canadian research at OISE, seen in Harley et al. 1990, and in Montreal at McGill and Concordia University, described below), not to mention showing great ingenuity of design and precision in linguistic focus, and while I believe in the value of some degree of formal focus in instruction, I must call attention to the need for researchers to provide sufficient evidence for their eventual claims as to the nature and effects of instruction. The history of research on L2 instruction, going back to the "methods comparison" research of the 1960's, is littered with studies that have failed in one way or another to document the actual language teaching events in the programs or methods they were comparing. I have discussed several such problems in recent work (Chaudron 1988, 1991), so that I will not attempt here to remind you of the past research.

Current arguments for formal language instruction. Nor can I take much space here to recapitulate the arguments for the role of formal

---

* I would like to acknowledge the contribution of Beverly Edge, supported by a 1988-1989 Research Corporation of the University of Hawai'i graduate research grant ot the Department of ESL, in the accumulation of materials for and development of some ideas in this paper.

language instruction in the L2 curriculum. These have been thoroughly laid out, for example, in work by Long (1983, 1985, 1988) and Larsen-Freeman & Long (1991), by the 'consciousness-raising' literature (Rutherford 1987, Rutherford & Sharwood-Smith 1983, 1988), by Pienemann and his colleagues in Australia (1984, 1989, Pienemann & Johnston 1987), and by several of the Canadian teams I just referred to (Lightbown 1991, Lightbown & Spada 1987, 1990, White, Spada, Lightbown & Ranta, in press). Briefly put, the argument is that formal instruction stands to promote a more rapid advancement through natural sequences of target language (TL) development, as well as a likely higher degree of ultimate attainment in the TL. Also, as Schmidt (1990) has recently argued convincingly, the source of such effectiveness may be that formal instruction provides focal opportunities for learners to "notice the gap" between their developing grammars or lexis and target forms, in other words, it promotes their conscious awareness. A student in the Ph.D. in SLA program at Hawai'i, Aki Shimura, has recently conducted an experiment showing that only a learner who *noticed* the English rule for reflexive use, which is anomalous for Japanese learners, acquired it on a measure of grammatical judgment. Other research on metacognitive skill acquisition, such as that of learner planning (O'Malley, et al 1985, O'Malley & Chamot 1990, Crookes 1989) also demonstrates the potential advantages for target-like attainment of learners' *control* over their own output. And in a recent review (Chaudron & Russell 1990) we found several studies showing significant correlations between learners' formal knowledge or representations of the TL, and their performance (e.g. Grigg 1986, Hulstijn & Hulstijn 1984, Jeffries 1985).

I take it as axiomatic that these general arguments need, nevertheless, to be further demonstrated and proven by means of classroom-based observation and experimentation. Fortunately, a number of researchers, including some of the aforementioned, have been following this agenda in recent years. Yet this direction of research is fraught with problems. My purpose in the following is to call attention to the need for greater rigor in the conduct of such research, and in particular, to the need for explicit documentation of the teaching-learning process as learners acquire L2 skills and knowledge.

Evaluation criteria in observation. I will state first three criteria which I believe must be applied to observational data on formal instruction in order to be sure of their adequacy, and then I will outline what sorts of evidence can be presented in research that would be judged by these criteria. The criteria are 1) accuracy in target structure description, 2) match of structure with learner stage of development, and 3) frequency of behavior. I point out these criteria only because they are so often implicit in the conduct of research, yet I think each must be considered in a full assessment of the extent of formal instruction observed. I also will insist, as I have in the past (Chaudron 1988, Chaudron, Crookes & Long 1988) on the overarching need in such research for *reliability* assessment of observations. This should go without saying, yet surprisingly few classroom researchers ever bother to report *that* they assessed interobserver reliability, much less *what* it was.

The first criterion that must be evaluated in observation is whether or not the teacher's, the syllabus's, or the learner's own performance, characterization, or description of the formal structures involved are *accurate*. It should be obvious that if a teacher's language or explanation is in fact an incorrect version of the TL, any assessment of the formal nature of the resulting acquisition risks being distorted. We see many such potential dangers in the literature, most explicitly shown in Kasper's (1982) study of teaching-induced errors. The second criterion, a critical one for all the experimental research on stage development in instruction, is that instruction needs to be *oriented to the learner's particular stage of development* (as demonstrated, e.g. in Pienemann's work on German as a second language word order instruction, 1984). Failure to observe this criterion is probably one source of Ellis' (1984) lack of finding of an advantage for instruction to learners in question formation. A final criterion for adequacy of observational data is needed, which has proven to be one of the fundamental pitfalls of comparative research, namely, the documentation of the relevant *frequencies* of teacher and learner behaviors *in all conditions under investigation*. Thus, the uniqueness of an instructional treatment can fail to be established, as was the case in a large-scale study on group instruction in ESL in Israel (Bejarano 1988), and it would appear as well, in Harley's (1989) important experiment in French immersion classes.

Types of behavior / evidence for observation. The following is a selected listing of types of behavior or evidence in teaching that can be used to document the fact or nature of formal instruction. I will argue that each researcher should attempt to demonstrate as fully as possible the nature of formal instruction, offering evidence in the form of several of these types, in order to avoid the later discovery that the true source of learners' development, if any, is obscured or remains uninterpretable. I am listing these types in what I view to be a cline of decreasing accessibility to the researchers' observation, as determined by the time and effort that is likely needed to observe and evaluate them. It should be obvious, however, that for several reasons, the more difficult to access may be the more important to observe.

(1) Syllabus content or materials. In numerous cases, researchers have provided the materials used to elicit or promote formal language use, as in Harley's (1989) detailed description of materials for the teaching of the French passé composé versus imparfait distinction, or Eckman, et al.'s (1989) complete set of instructional sentences for teaching certain English relative clause types, or White et al.'s (in press) recent materials and exercises for teaching French learners to understand question formation in ESL. Whatever the specific application of such materials (in these cases, primarily experimental), it is useful for comparison across studies to assess language teaching materials with respect to a *scale* of formal focus, such as that proposed recently by Loschky & Bley-Vroman (1990). According to increasing constraints on output, they suggest that some language teaching tasks would *naturally* generate target forms, while in others, the forms would have *utility* for the attainment of task goals, and in still others, the accurate use of the forms would be *essential* to the completion of the task. Although in the actual performance on the White, et al. or Eckman, et al. experiments, we would assume that learner output of target forms was most constrained, i.e. *essential* to the task, it would help our understanding of the operation of such tasks to have documented when the forms were indeed produced by the learners, and when they might not have been.

(2) Explicit instruction and rule formulation. In early research on L2 instruction, *implicit* versus *explicit* rule presentation was contrasted in a number of studies (see, e.g. Levin 1972). This is clearly a level of teacher behavior that deserves to be documented in research studies, for as Færch (1986) has shown, teachers will vary considerably in the precision and formality of their rule formulations. I would not argue that a complete, formalized rule should always be presented in either materials or classroom teacher talk, yet it is probably helpful that some abstraction of forms, whether learner-generated or teacher-formulated rule of thumb, be part of the classroom focus at some point. We see this evidenced, for instance, in Shaffer's (1989) study of French and Spanish contrasting forms. In many studies, however, we lack the evidence of how much and in what form rules were explicitly stated by either the teachers or learners.

(3) Teacher focus and reference. Short of being fully explicit in rule formulation, classroom-based evidence is needed to at least document the fact of the teacher's focus on form or reference to specific target structures. I believe that this is probably the most common source of observations of formal focus in global observation systems such as the COLT system used by the OISE research teams (Allen, et al. 1983, Fröhlich, et al. 1985, Spada 1987). Lightbown & Spada (1990) have recently attempted to show that an overall greater teacher focus on form is the probable source of one ESL teacher's success in promoting her students' advanced use of English target forms such as the *there is/there* *are* construction. Lightbown & Spada do have to call upon more detailed analysis of transcripts and the teacher's comments, however, to show that in fact, the teacher was specifically treating these forms. Otherwise, research employing correlational methods alone to associate focus on form with learner progress cannot establish a direct explanatory link between the two.

(4) Teacher correction; (5) Teacher formal explanation; (6) Teacher follow-up with learner practice / transfer. For the previous reason, I look for research to document an explicit use of teacher correcting, provision of formal explanations, and encouraging further follow-up by learners, as a source of direct evidence of formal language teaching. Those who are familiar with a model for corrective feedback I proposed some years ago (Chaudron 1977) will not be surprised to read this lament of the inadequate documentation of teacher correcting behavior in most classroom research, or even in many of the experiments cited here. In White, Spada, Lightbown, & Ranta (in press), study on instruction in ESL question formation, the argument is made for the need for *negative* evidence to the learner. We have been aware of such a need in instruction for quite some time (e.g. Schachter 1984), yet I believe that precisely in such experimental studies, it is incumbent on the researcher(s) to document that not only were *instances* of target forms provided that constitute negative evidence for learners' hypotheses, but teachers' *feedback* to learners' misuse was explicitly negative. And further, whether other treatment was or was not provided. For instance, the recent 'Garden Path' research on French language instruction by Tomasello & Herron (1988, 1989) attempts to demonstrate the effectiveness of error correction at an appropriately timed moment, namely after the learners have generated a false overgeneralization of target rules. If we temporarily take at face value the findings of these latter two studies, we should be quite encouraged. Yet one who is familiar with the procedures and events of typical classrooms would appreciate having a more complete record of what transpired. Was *one* instance of correction all that was necessary? Did the learners follow up with questions or practice? What sort of corrective treatment did the teacher use each time? Just 'No!'?

It is difficult to categorize or classify the many different variations of teacher feedback, and the model for analysis I proposed almost 15 years ago probably needs refinement for specific situations, but I would urge than any further research on teacher formal focus and provision of negative input adopt a bit more careful application of such a model.

(7) Learner inquiry; (8) Learner overt application; (9) Learner covert application. None of the previous sorts of evidence are meant to place the burden of proof for formal focus on the teacher and curriculum, however, for in the end, if learners' processing of the target language is not activated in any formal way, I think we are merely talking about behavioral reinforcement. As I suggested earlier, there is good reason to believe that L2 learners' own representations of the target language rules and forms play an important role in their development and ultimate performance. These last, learner-oriented types of behavior or evidence for formal instruction, which are perhaps the most difficult to observe, must be examined carefully by researchers conducting instructional or classroom-oriented experiments and observations. This may entail the additional use of elicitation instruments to assess learners' metalinguistic judgments, and their own rule formulations, recall and think-aloud protocols, and the like (see Færch & Kasper 1988). Audio or video tapes and transcripts of learning events will only rarely afford us that glimpse into the more active learner's mind, inquiring about the difference between forms A and B. I recognize the enormity of the researcher's task who wants to find out what learners were actively doing in the process of some controlled experiment, but techniques can be devised to explore such questions, and until they are employed in research on formal instruction, we will not truly have an idea of its nature and effectiveness.

Conclusion. I hope I have not been misunderstood. The bulk of research on formal instruction to date is carefully conducted and challenging to the researcher, and I am certain that as we proceed with refinements, more careful observation and experimentation, we will come to greater insights and direct, effective applications to language teaching. The advent of communicative, task-based language teaching materials (Long 1985, Candlin & Murphy 1987, Nunan 1989), if it incorporates built-in focus on accuracy for the achievement of the tasks (cf. Long 1988b) is not a step backwards into more traditional grammar-translation exercises, yet we must pursue classroom-based research to determine how such materials are assimilated by learners in the course of instruction.

References

J. P. B. Allen, M. Fröhlich & N. Spada. 1984. The communicative orientation of language teaching: An observation scheme. In J. Handscombe, R. A. Orem & B. P. Taylor, (Eds.), *On TESOL '83: The Question of Control*, pp. 231252. Washington, D. C.: TESOL.

Y. Bejarano. 1987. A cooperative small-group methodology in the language classroom. *TESOL Quarterly*, 21, 483504.

C. N. Candlin & D. F. Murphy, (Eds.). 1987. *Language Learning Tasks*. Englewood Cliffs, NJ: Prentice-Hall.

C. Chaudron. 1977. A descriptive model of discourse in the corrective treatment of learners' errors. *Language Learning* 27 (1), 29-46.

C. Chaudron. 1988. *Second Language Classrooms: Research on Teaching and Learning.* Cambridge: Cambridge University Press.

C. Chaudron. 1991. Validation in second language classroom research: The role of observation. In R. Phillipson, E. Kellerman, L. Selinker, M. Sharwood Smith & M. Swain, (Eds.), *Foreign/Second Language Pedagogy: A Commemorative Volume for Claus Færch,* pp. 187-196. Philadelphia: Multilingual Matters.

C. Chaudron, G. Crookes & M. H. Long. 1988. *Reliability and Validity in Second Language Classroom Research.* Technical Report No. 8, Center for Second Language Classroom Research, Social Science Research Institute, University of Hawaii, Honolulu.

C. Chaudron & G. Russell. 1990. The validity of elicited imitation as a measure of second language competence. Expanded version of paper presented at the Ninth World Congress of Applied Linguistics, Thessaloniki-Halkidiki, Greece.

G. Crookes. 1989. Planning and interlanguage variation. *Studies in Second Language Acquisition,* 11 (4), 367383.

F. R. Eckman, L. Bell & D. Nelson. 1988. On the generalization of relative clause instruction in the acquisition of English as a second language. *Applied Linguistics,* 9 (1), 120.

R. Ellis. 1984. Can syntax be taught? A study of the effects of formal instruction on the acquisition of *Wh-* questions by children. *Applied Linguistics* 5, 138155.

C. Færch. 1986. Rules of thumb and other teacher-formulated rules in the foreign language classroom. In G. Kasper (Ed.), *Language, Teaching, and Communication in the Foreign Language Classroom,* pp. 125-143. Aarhus, Denmark: Aarhus University Press.

C. Færch & G. Kasper, (Eds.). 1987. *Introspection in Second Language Research.* Philadelphia: Multilingual Matters.

M. Fröhlich, N. Spada & P. Allen. 1985. Differences in the communicative orientation of L2 classrooms. *TESOL Quarterly,* 19, 2757.

T. Grigg. 1986. The effects of task, time, and rule knowledge on grammar performance for three English structures. *Working Papers,* 5 (1), 161212, Department of ESL, University of Hawai'i.

B. Harley. 1989. Functional grammar in French immersion: A classroom experiment. *Applied Linguistics,* 10 (3), 331359.

B. Harley, P. Allen, J. Cummins & M. Swain, (Eds.). 1990. *The Development of Second Language Proficiency.* Cambridge: Cambridge University Press.

J. H. Hulstijn & W. Hulstijn. 1984. Grammatical errors as a function of processing constraints and explicit knowledge. *Language Learning,* 34 (1), 2343.

S. Jeffries. 1985. English grammar terminology as an obstacle to second language learning. *The Modern Language Journal,* 69 (4), 385390.

G. Kasper. 1982. Teaching-induced aspects of interlanguage discourse. *Studies in Second Language Acquisition,* 4, 99113.

D. Larsen-Freeman & M. H. Long. 1991. *An Introduction to Second Language Acquisition Research.* London: Longman.

L. Levin. 1972. *Comparative Studies in Foreign Language Teaching.* Stockholm: Almqvist and Wiksell.

P. M. Lightbown. 1991. What have we here? Some observations on the influence of instruction on L2 learning. In R. Phillipson, E. Kellerman, L. Selinker, M. Sharwood Smith & M. Swain, (Eds.), *Foreign/Second Language Pedagogy: A Commemorative Volume for Claus Færch*, pp. 197212. Philadelphia: Multilingual Matters.

P. M. Lightbown & N. Spada. 1987. Learning English in intensive programs in Quebec schools: 198687. Manuscript, Concordia University.

P. M. Lightbown & N. Spada. 1990. Focus-on-form and corrective feedback in communicative language teaching: Effects on second language learning. *Studies in Second Language Acquisition*, 12 (4), 429448.

M. H. Long. 1983. Does second language instruction make a difference? A review of research. *TESOL Quarterly* 17, 359382.

M. H. Long. 1985. A role for instruction in second language acquisition: Task-based language teaching. In K. Hyltenstam & M. Pienemann, (Eds.), *Modelling and Assessing Second Language Development*, pp. 7799. San Diego: College-Hill Press.

M. H. Long. 1988a. Instructed interlanguage development. In L. Beebe (Ed.), *Issues in Second Language Acquisition: Multiple Perspectives*, pp. 115141. New York: Newbury House.

M. H. Long. 1988b. Focus on form: A design feature in language teaching methodology. Paper presented at the NFLC/European Cultural Foundation Conference on Empirical Research on Second Language Learning in Institutional Settings, Bellagio, Italy.

L. Loschky & R. Bley-Vroman. 1990. Creating structure-based communication tasks for second language development. *University of Hawai'i Working Papers in ESL*, 9 (1), 161212.

D. Nunan. 1989. *Designing Tasks for the Communicative Classroom*. Cambridge: Cambridge University Press.

J. M. O'Malley, A. U. Chamot, G. Stewner-Manzanares, R. P. Russo, & L. Kupper. 1985. Learning strategy applications with students of English as a second language. *TESOL Quarterly* 19, 285296.

J. M. O'Malley & A. U. Chamot. 1990. *Learning Strategies in Second Language Acquisition*. New York: Cambridge University Press.

M. Pienemann. 1984. Psychological constraints on the teachability of languages. *Studies in Second Language Acquisition*, 6, 186214.

M. Pienemann. 1989. Is language teachable? Psycholinguistic experiments and hypotheses. *Applied Linguistics*, 10 (1), 5279.

M. Pienemann & M. Johnston. 1987. Factors influencing the development of language proficiency. In D. Nunan (Ed.), *Applying Second Language Acquisition Research*, pp. 45141. Adelaide: National Curriculum Resource Centre, AMEP.

W. Rutherford. 1987. *Second Language Grammar: Learning and Teaching*. London: Longman.

W. Rutherford & M. Sharwood-Smith. 1983. Consciousness raising and universal grammar. *Applied Linguistics*, 6 (3), 274282.

W. Rutherford & M. Sharwood-Smith, (Eds.). 1988. *Grammar and Second Language Teaching: A Book of Readings*. New York: Newbury House.

J. Schachter. 1984. A universal input condition. In W. E. Rutherford (Ed.), *Language Universals and Second Language Acquisition*, pp. 167183. Philadelphia: John Benjamins.

R. W. Schmidt. 1990. The role of consciousness in second language learning. *Applied Linguistics*, 11 (2), 129158.

C. Shaffer. 1989. A comparison of inductive and deductive approaches to teaching foreign languages. *The Modern Language Journal*, 73 (4), 395403.

N. M. Spada. 1987. Relationships between instructional differences and learning outcomes: A process-product study of communicative language teaching. *Applied Linguistics*, 8 (2), 136161.

M. Tomasello & C. Herron. 1988. Down the Garden Path: Inducing and correcting overgeneralization errors in the foreign language classroom. *Applied Psycholinguistics*, 9 (3), 237246.

M. Tomasello & C. Herron. 1989. Feedback for language transfer errors: The Garden Path technique. *Studies in Second Language Acquisition*, 11 (4), 385395.

L. White, N. M. Spada, P. M. Lightbown, & L. Ranta. In press. Input enhancement and L2 question formation. *Applied Linguistics*.

Reflective teachers

Vicki Galloway
Georgia Institute of Technology

Elliott Eisner (1988) observes that ballet dancers, who practice their art to perfection, have mirrors to see for themselves how they are doing. And of teachers and teachers of teachers he asks: 'Where are our mirrors?'

Indeed, the past decade in teacher education has produced a virtual circus world of images and reflections. Society's mirrors have been aimed at every part of the educational colossus, its wrinkles, its scars, its bruises. Some mirrors have been aimed at capturing impressions of the expanse of the system; others, mere chips of glass, have turned blemishes into deformities. It may be that we have too many mirrors—so many that we are blinded by the reflections, confused by the reversals, duplications, distortions.

For each of the hundreds of investor/participant groups in the U.S. educational system, there is a slightly different angle of vision, resulting in a slightly different prescription for the improvement of the image. It is commonly accepted that education is, and has been, in crisis. But why? According to the deans of colleges of education who formed the Holmes group, the culprit is time—there is simply not enough time in the traditional baccalaureate program to equip teachers with the knowledge and skills needed for the complex and intellectually challenging profession of teaching. According to the group of professionals in education and other fields who formed the Carnegie Forum (1986), the culprits are lack of national standards and lack of realistic professional working climates. A few tenacious individuals insist the problem lies in the lack of traditional curricula and disciplined classrooms for learning. The 80s have produced a grand flurry of panel and commission reports focusing on such issues as national certification standards, post baccalaureate teacher education programs, candidate competency testing, career ladder programs, alternative licensing, program accreditation standards, and so on.

This activity has not been limited to generic teacher education concerns. Professional membership organizations have assumed a proactive stance in proclaiming the type of preparation deemed necessary or desirable for entrance into the professions of Science teacher, Math teacher,

Foreign language teacher. The American Associations of Teachers of French (AATF) and Teachers of Spanish and Portuguese (AATSP) have issued standards for levels of advancement in terms of teacher and teacher candidate skills and knowledge. The American Council on the Teaching of Foreign Languages (ACTFL 1988) has developed guidelines for program development in the pedagogical and specialization areas of foreign language teacher education.

The 80s are marked by administrative and organizational images of teachers, and administrative and organizational efforts to take charge, to exercise better control of aspects deemed significant in the development of teachers—better control of time, better control of program quality, better control of teacher candidate experiences, better control of our own expectations. Our decade of conference room discussion and deliberation has given us blueprints to facilitate some much needed renovations in the structure of our educational house. Perhaps our greatest efforts now can be directed toward exploring what it is like to live there, to understanding what goes on in the bedrooms of education—the very personal worlds of classrooms. Perhaps in the 90s we will adjust our mirrors so that they reflect not the blurred vision of teachers as a group, but a more distinct image of the teacher as an individual. Efforts to exercise control *over* teacher quality may well be futile if they are not informed by clear notions of control needs *in* teachers themselves.

Control is a prominent and powerful notion in this culture. The society that produced and maintains this complex educational system is a society that promotes independence, rewards initiative, values responsibility, cherishes ownership, rejects absolute authority, and encourages involvement, self motivation, and decision-making. Control of oneself is a virtue; control by others is anathema. Feeling 'in control' requires being comfortable 'on the edge', for the same society that values options also abhors incorrect selection.

Individual notions of control are at the very core of actions. Some of us exercise control through predictability, sameness, routine procedures. Some of us achieve a sense of control through avoidance of risk. And for some, control is a limited commodity—the more one person has, the less is available for others. The issue of teacher perceptions of and needs for control has become more and more complicated during the past twenty years, with the emergence of communicative goals and approaches to teaching, and with expanding understandings of learners and foreign language learning. The notion of control in traditional classrooms was absolute and obvious: students, seated at their desks relied on the teacher at the front of the class to indicate to them their precise moment of recitation, the precise content and form of their recitation, the precise error in their recitation. The questions of control had *yes/no* answers and dealt with such topics as discipline, order, textbook coverage, adherence to methodological training, and award of grades. We've torn down these classrooms, at least in our current approaches to educating teachers, but in stuffing teachers with new and better knowledge and skills, have we attended sufficiently to their accompanying control needs? Have we devoted effort to helping prospective and veteran teachers alike pull from themselves new definitions and satisfying realizations of control? Have we attended to the more subtle, yet more powerful, internal control systems of individuals, to helping teachers shift notions of control from the observable act to the swift pulling of strings that goes on behind the curtain—the careful and purposeful design of a firm structure that allows freedom of movement and of exploration. Control is a powerful need and one that teachers rightly need to feel in order to perform well in the complex environment in which they work. Yet, if no attention is given to this need, it will surface regardless—often, unfortunately, in defiance or in adjustment of the knowledge gained in teacher preparation programs. We have seen this happen repeatedly: knowledge of learner differences has led to labeling and tracking for ease of administration of instruction—for ease of control; learner based methods have been reduced to unquestioned instructional rules for ease of control; concepts such as cooperative learning are reduced to simple movement of desks for pair and group manipulative practice—for ease of control.

Researchers note that what is missing from the knowledge base of teaching are the voices of teachers themselves—the questions teachers ask, the interpretive frames teachers use to understand and improve their classrooms (Cochran-Smith and Lytle 1990:2). Teachers in classrooms today are experiencing a very real control conflict. Here are some of their voices:

    1. 'In regards to correction of errors, I have been *trained* to correct just about everything, although the trend nowadays is to get away from the very nitty-gritty and to simply concentrate on "is the message being communicated?" That's something I really need to work on because I have been trained to go after every little detail.'

    2. 'I'm trying to talk less and listen more and get the students to take more control of the classroom . . . I do a lot of pair work but I don't know if it's working because I can't get around to every pair during a class period.'

    3. 'Over the last few years I would say that I am far less structured, less afraid of loosening the reins on students as far as getting up and moving around my room, or speaking out, or getting off track.'

Striking in these teachers' assessments of their instruction and directions of change is the predominance of visible, mechanical, surface-level description of controllables—the focus on particulars of their own behavior, which are motivated by a somewhat reductionist view (for ease of control) of current pedagogical theory. One hears in these comments a desire to say the right thing, to do what is considered to be right by others. But this desire is accompanied by fear, tentativeness, lack of conviction. None of these teachers revealed to us their own belief systems, and, as Combs (1988:39) notes:

> No matter how promising a strategy for reform, if it is not incorporated into teachers' belief systems, it will be unlikely to affect behavior in the desired directions.

Jarvis and Taylor (1990) suggest that teacher education of tomorrow is going to be more individualized, better contextualized, more analytical, intensely *reflective,* and further that to achieve these aims, video—not of staged demonstrations, but of actual classrooms—will be our most powerful and perfect instrument. Video will afford us context specificity—the opportunity to anchor pedagogical learnings in rich educational contexts. Video may provide us with the complex data that are truly worthy of reflection. The video camera gives us peripheral vision, long looks rather than glances, the close-ups and wide angles that the human eye is not capable of capturing and holding. Video provides the opportunity to seize and explore the complexity of a single moment from the many moments that adhere to form situations. But as another mirror, it can only provide images. What we 'see' in these images are interpretations, constructed from our own schemata, constrained by what we are prepared to see, what our experience, imagination, and belief systems allow us to see. If the video camera is to serve us as a mirror in the education of teachers, we must begin with some insights from teachers themselves: What does the teacher see and select to see and what meanings are attached to these images?

The high school teachers whose comments appear above opened their classrooms to three days of filming as part of an ACTFL project funded by the Department of Education during the two year period from 1988 to 1990. The aim of this project was to create a staff development video program based on real life classrooms and real life teaching for the purpose of developing teachers' skills in context-embedded observation, analysis, and application of pedagogical knowledge through a process of individual teacher reflection (See ACTFL, 1991; Galloway, 1991). A crucial step prior to developing the materials to accompany the video and activate the reflection process was that of gathering information in response to the questions above: What does the teacher see and select to see and what meanings are assigned to these observations? We needed teachers to inform and guide us in reflecting on the process of reflection.

To this aim, small groups of high school and college foreign language teachers were shown selected segments that comprise the video and were simply asked to record their observations and offer commentary. No viewing framework was provided other than that of general pedagogical topics—segments were grouped for observational focus on the following aspects of teacher task control: use of time, use of group, learner accountability, and task transition. The results were the following predominant categories of observations:

(1) Teachers focused on teacher personalities: enthusiasm and energy vs. dullness, monotony and repetition.

(2) Teachers focused on teacher acts: movement and position, correction, delivery of instructions and follow up, individual assistance, intervention, innovative quality of techniques.

(3) Teachers focused on teacher language use: fluency, accuracy, pronunciation.

(4) Teachers focused on student language use: speaking opportunities, manipulative vs. communicative language use, distribution of practice.

(5) Teachers focused on logistical issues: seating arrangements, student movement, class size, small group formation.

(6) Teachers focused on student performance: attentiveness, cooperativeness, preparation, discipline.

(7) Teachers focused on general pedagogical approach or use of particular method (TPR, natural approach, direct method, grammar translation, etc.).

(8) Teachers evaluated teachers or offered alternative techniques without identifying problems in observed techniques.

(9) Teachers empathized with teachers: they were quick to praise, reluctant to criticize.

Threaded throughout these comments was a single theme: observation of the particulars, the acts, the discrete behaviors of other teachers. While a few teachers made occasional insightful probes into such notions as task purpose and expectations, and learner strategy use, these comments were more the exception than the rule. The picture afforded by these comments was one of a teacher observational system comprised of clusters of surface-level specifics. In assessing the effectivness of these classrooms, teacher observers displayed familiarity with foreign language pedagogical concepts which they applied with frequency. However, it was evident that observation was to remain at this level of *familiarity*. There was little thoughtful stretching. There was little true reflection.

John Dewey (1933), father of many of our finest ideas in education, first defined reflection as behavior which involves active, persistent, and careful consideration of beliefs in terms of both source and consequence. The opposite of reflection, then, is mindless adherence to unexamined practices or principles (Cochran-Smith and Lytle 1991:37). The growing body of literature on critical reflective thinking emphasizes the creativity and intellectual challenge of this pursuit that 'celebrates the organic above the artificial' (Wellington 1991:4). Reflection goes beyond analysis, beyond decision making, certainly beyond mere recall and playback to the formation of deep connections. Beause reflection is not easy, because it takes time, it is a luxury not frequently enjoyed by busy people, and teachers and teachers of teachers are busy people.

Researchers cite the following factors, other than time, that appear to be necessary conditions for reflective thought: volition, purpose, guidance and control, structure and formality (Killion and Todnem 1991). Reflection takes teachers beyond the actions they perform automatically and with confidence to live at the limits of their knowledge and competence (Scarda-malia 1988). The very deliberate act of stretching beyond one's comfort zone requires guidance, initially from experts, but ultimately from within. Tracy Kidder in her best seller, *Among Schoolchildren*, gives us a rather unsettling picture of teachers isolated (Kidder 1990:51):

> Like everyone else, teachers learn through experience, but they learn without much guidance. One problem . . . is that experience, especially the kind that is both repetitious and disappointing, can easily harden into narrow pedagogical theories. Most schools have a teacher with a theory built on grudges.

Reflection requires focus. As Combs (1988:39) states: 'If I don't know what is important, then everything becomes important.' In developing a program that fosters reflection in teachers, then, a necessary motivation would be to direct teachers' attention away from the particulars of discrete acts and automatic answers—away from collections and into connections of knowledge. Strong and others (Strong et al. 1990:26) remind that 'The devil's in the details . . . Sources of conflict are in the specifics. If you want to find common ground, find the big ideas.' The teachers who viewed our video of the classroom offered commentary on teachers. But perhaps the biggest ideas lay not in observable acts of teachers. For the big ideas, we needed to turn to learners.

The learner as a focus of reflection on the teaching-learning process truly carries us out of our comfort zone to the edge of our competence. We are accustomed to studying learners through the teacher's world, but far less accustomed to exploring teaching through the learner's world. To reflect on this world, we have to cross the major barriers of training—of long held assumptions and rigid control systems. Teachers are accustomed to discussions with other teachers, but reflective thought is highly personal and may well require the support and formality of a reflective act. To help the teachers who were using the classroom video move into the learner's world, we chose to have them write, creatively— not as teachers, but as students. Writing is a truly personal activity, well suited to truly personal thought. Writing allows self dialogue, expression of that inner speech that guides our thinking. The writing tasks of our teacher-observers were of different types, but always emanated from a student perspective—interior monologues that focused on the moment, to stream of consciousness thoughts that produced elliptical notes throughout the segment. Some particularly insightful thinking resulted from a notewriting task. As the video played, teachers were to assume the identity of a particular student and indulge themselves in the unlawful act of writing a note to a friend during class time. However, since there is more to a student's life than those moments in the foreign language classroom, their notes were not only to focus on the classroom of the moment, but to incorporate the real world. Teachers' notes reflected the entire gamut of emotions: worries about tests and relationships, anger about a morning locker incident, humor, boredom, excitement, guilt, and fear. After this exercise, teachers were asked to describe what had taken place in the classroom during the segment. Some found they had involved themselves so much in the student's imaginings, that they could not remember the specific details of what went on in the class. They had performed their roles well. The problem was obviously not in the teachers' ability to empathize with a student. The problem was in using this empathic understanding and connecting it to pedagogy.

To use this perspective to reflect on and inform pedagogy, a framework was required. This framework needed to be one, again, based on a big idea, a familiar idea. We returned to the notion of control and needs for control—this time, not through the eyes of teachers, but through the minds of learners. The teachers listened as the students in the video commented on their classes. What they heard are the types of student comments that can only be described as typical. In fact, as teachers, we have all heard them so frequently that perhaps we ceased paying much attention to them long ago. But if these comments are typical and timeless, surely they must reflect some truths. As teachers listened to the comments, they were asked to interpret them in terms of learner control needs (See Table 1).

What the teachers came up with afforded a new basis for observing and reflecting on what takes place in the classroom (See Table 2). The teachers were now equipped to return to the video with a different perspective and stretch their thought from a new edge of competence. If these were the control needs of learners, then such teacher issues as whether or not to stand at the front of the class paled in significance. In

Table 1. Student comments.

---

1. 'We learned . . . more commands, you know. What did I learn? I learned, oh gosh, well, it was kind of new but I'm catching on to it . . . I really didn't learn much.'
2. 'The thing I don't like about the class is that I get bored sometimes cause I know, like, mostly, a lot of things, but I just try to concentrate and do the best I can.'
3. 'She asks you questions, she goes around the room, you know, makes it not just a class where you come in and sit down, do your work and then leave, you know. She makes it part of your life.'
4. 'There's one thing I don't like about this class, is when he starts getting in a bad mood or he won't really yell, but he'll say stuff that you don't understand, but you're supposed to understand and then he'll like, wait for the answer. And you're like "I didn't understand it. You said it too fast".'
5. 'Sometimes it's hard for me to pay attention to what other people are saying because if you don't know what they're talking about in the first place, it's hard to catch on. Even if we know what we're looking for, it's hard to understand.'
6. 'When I was performing in front of the class I felt scared, cause everyone was watching me. I would have felt embarrassed if I would have messed up or anything like that. It scared me. I would like to perform in a small group. It's better because when you make a mistake, they don't laugh.'
7. 'To speak is easier than to listen. To listen is . . . I can't really catch all the words. When I speak I know what I'm saying. I'm really involved in it when I'm talking to the teacher and the other students.'
8. 'I didn't talk that much today. I mean, she usually chooses on me more. I wish I could've talked more 'cause I like speaking Spanish. I don't do it exactly like, you know, really good or anything as if I've been speaking it for a while but, you know, I try and I do pretty good.'
9. 'When we were going over the homework that was boring. You're just reading the same stuff that you did last night so, that was sort of boring.
10. The way she keeps doing everything, like . . . I'm learning a lot quicker. I'm catching on, like a lot. The way like she keeps reviewing and doing different things. It helps me a lot.'
11. 'Push me more, I guess. I don't know. Make me try more . . . I can't say make me, but tell me to try more and if I don't, then discipline, I guess. It's not discipline, it's just that I don't try. It's . . . I don't know how she can make me try harder, except tell me, and that usually doesn't work.'

---

fact, it was not what the teacher did, but the hows, whats, whens, and whys of what the teacher planned for learners to do—the task—that was the appropriate focus. A debate that had previously raged over a teacher correction incident they had observed shifted out of the right-wrong realm of teacher behaviors into more productive discussion as to how to reconstruct the task itself in order to diminish high error potential. With this new perspective, teachers applied their pedagogical proficiency with acumen and, indeed, brilliance.

Eisner's (Eisner 1991:14) comments about student discovery is equally appropriate to teachers: 'What really counts in schools is teaching children that the exploration of ideas is sometimes difficult, often exciting, and occasionally fun.' The preparation for the journey into

Table 2. Learner control needs.

---

1. **Self monitoring.** Opportunities to experience personal growth through awareness of what one is learning to do and how it fits in with established goals.
2. **Cognitive involvement.** The need for tasks that stimulate and energize purposeful thought and action.
3. **Authenticity.** Tasks and contexts that have direct applicability to the real world and that are perceived by learners as usable and useful. Tasks that make sense.
4. **Ownership.** The need for personal involvement, for equality, and for shared responsibility in learning. The need to develop a sense of partnership with the teacher in the pursuit of common learning goals.
5. **Clear expectations.** The need to understand task demands and maintain a sense of the expectations of others.
6. **Sense of community.** The need to feel connected to others in ways that have important consequences; the need for opportunities to interact with others as partners.
7. **Dignity.** The need to feel important, confident, and capable.
8. **Flexibility.** The need to work and learn in accord with one's own style, pace, and modality preferences.
9. **Communication.** The need to make and be responsible for one's own decisions in self expression. The need to create.
10. **Sense of accomplishment.** The opportunity to exercise personal responsibility, to self-assess and to reward.
11. **Variety.** A rejection of sameness in task or task repetition for display purposes.
12. **Integration of learning.** The need for tasks that constantly re-enter and recombine previous knowledge in light of new knowledge or insights, heightened awareness.
13. **Psychological investment.** The need for suppport in learning to recognize and assume personal responsibility for one's own development.

---

reflection were at least as important as the journey itself. As so-called experts, we certainly could have handed teachers literature on student needs, but the process of discovering these through the learners themselves proved to be much more powerful.

Personal and individual realization of the needs of learners may well provide the organic data that will help us direct our efforts more often, more deeply, at the edge of competence. What seems to be true of real reflective thinking is that it leads to formation of connections that enable deeper connections. And it is these deeper connections that subsequently form the base of more connections, and so on, in a fulfilling and enduring growth process.

These teachers went through a process of shifting attention from the teacher, to that which links the teacher and learner in the teaching-learning process: The task. As Marzano (Marzano et al. 1990) reminds us: 'The effective classroom climate is practically invisible. It is crafted by the artful teacher in subtle but intentional ways.'

Perhaps tomorrow's teacher education will focus on helping teachers enjoy both the comfort and challenge in real, lasting control—the kind that comes from developing control in the learner. But if this is our aim as teacher educators, we will need to be less convinced of the power of our answers and more devoted to the search for questions. As teacher developers, we must be willing to live at our own edge of competence as well. There, we will find our mirrors; and there we will find such excitement and challenge that the motivation to share the process of discovery will be overpowering. There is a crisis in education; there always will be a crisis in education in this society. And we may be thankful for this crisis—it keeps all of us—administrators, teachers, teachers of teachers—on the edge of our competence, where real learning and reflection can take place.

References

American Council on the Teaching of Foreign Languages (ACTFL). 1991. Changing Perspectives (Video program). Yonkers, NY: ACTFL

American Council on the Teaching of Foreign Languages (ACTFL). 'ACTFL provisional program guidelines for foreign language teacher education.' Foreign Language Annals 21: 71-82.

Carnegie Forum on Education and the Economy. 1986. A Nation Prepared: Teachers for the Twenty-First Century. New York: Carnegie Forum.

Cochran-Smith, M., and S.L. Lytle. 1990. 'Research on teaching and teacher research: The issues that divide.' Educational Researcher. 19(2): 2-11. As cited in: Georgea Mohlman Sparks-Langer and Amy Berstein Colton. 1991. 'Synthesis of research on teachers' reflective thinking.' Educational Leadership. 48(6):37-44.

Combs, Arthur W. 1988. 'New assumptions for educational reform.' Educational Leadership. 45(2):38-41.

Dewey, John. 1933. How we think: A restatement of the relation of reflective thinking to the educative process. Lexington, MA: D. C. Heath.

Eisner, Elliot W. 1991. 'What really counts in schools.' Educational Leadership. 48(5): 10-17.

Eisner, Elliot W. 1988. 'The ecology of school improvement.' Educational Leadership. 45(5):24-29.

Galloway, Vicki. 1991. Changing Perspectives. Yonkers, NY: ACTFL.

Jarvis, Gilbert A., and Sheryl V. Taylor. 1990. 'Reforming foreign and second language teacher education.' In: New Perspectives and New Directions in Foreign Language Education, ed. by Diane Birckbichler, 159-182. Lincolnwood, IL: National Textbook Company.

Kidder, Tracy. 1990. Among Schoolchildren. New York: Avon.

Killion, Joellen P., and Guy R. Todnem. 1991. 'A process for personal theory building.' Educational Leadership. 48(6):4-17.

Marzano, Robert J., Debra J. Pickering, and Ronald S. Brandt. 1990. 'Integrating instructional programs through dimensions of learning.' Educational Leadership. 47(5):17-23.

Scardamalia, Marlene. 1988. 'Cognition research drives development of collaborative, intentional, computer-linked learning.' The Holmes Group Forum. 3(1): 5-7.

Sparks-Langer, Georgea Mohlman, and Amy Berstein Colton. 1991. 'Synthesis of research on teachers' reflective thinking.' Educational Leadership . 48(6): 37-43.

Strong, Richard W., Harvey F. Silver, J. Robert Hanson, Robert J.Marzano, Pat Wolfe, Tom Dewing, and Wende Brock. 1991. 'Thoughtful education: Staff development for the 1990s.' Educational Leadership. 47(5): 25-29.

Wellington, Bud. 1991. 'The promise of reflective practice.' Educational Leadership. 48(6): 4-5.

Content knowledge and instructional practice in second language teacher education

Jack C. Richards
City Polytechnic of Hong Kong

This paper seeks to examine approaches to Second Language Teacher Education (SLTE) by considering two issues: content knowledge, and instructional practice. The status of both these domains within the field of SLTE will first be examined, and then implications for the design of SLTE progams will be considered. While the training and preparation of second language teachers is a well established activity within the field of language teaching, with a wide variety of courses, degree programs, and professional diplomas and certificates being offered worldwide, the recognition of second language teacher education as an emerging generic *field*, is relatively new. This paper considers the extent to which SLTE has developed a coherent theoretical foundation and evolved a specific body of educational practices.

In planning SLTE programs, the basic decisions which have to be considered are the same as those involved in planning any kind of instructional program—namely, what do we teach, and how do we teach it? Decisions of the first kind have to do with what can be termed 'pedagogical content knowledge', and the latter with 'instructional practice'. For example, a decision that prospective language teachers should study something about cross cultural communication is part of the domain of Pedagogical Content Knowledge. A decision that they should acquire this information by attending a workshop in which they take part in simulation-activities designed to raise issues concerning cultural differences in communicative styles, is a question of Instructional Practice. Issues raised in making decisions in both of these domains form the focus for the rest of this paper.

1 Pedagogical content knowledge. In the present context, Pedagogical Content Knowledge is defined as the core set of theories, concepts, and practices regarding second language learning and teaching which form the content of Second Language Teacher Education. Marks (1990, 9) defines Pedagogical Content Knowledge as:

a class of knowledge that is central to the teacher's work and that would not typically be held by nonteaching subject-matter experts or by teachers who know little of that subject matter.

In order to determine the Pedagogical Content Knowledge of the field of SLTE, it is necessary to identify the sources of this knowledge. At least four sources are available in SLTE: expert opinion, task analysis, teacher-perceived needs, and current practice or 'tradition'. Expert opinion refers to the views of subject matter specialists and other experts as to what it is that prospective second language teachers need to know. Task analysis refers to deriving pedagogical content knowledge from an analysis of the situations in which teachers work, the tasks they typically perform on the job, and the kinds of skills they need for performing those tasks. Teacher-perceived needs refers to teachers' expressions of need for professional development. Current practice refers to what SLTE programs currently offer to teachers in training. These four sources can provide guidance in setting up new programs and in evaluating how well the profession is meeting its aims.

1.1 Expert knowledge. A long accepted practice in determining curriculum content is to ask experts what they think the clients need to know. In a field such as SLTE which draws on a number of source disciplines, it is not always clear who the relevant experts are. This has not always been the case. Forty years ago, linguists regarded themselves as experts in second language teaching and had a considerable influence on both the content and process of second language teacher training programs (Richards and Rodgers 1986). Few would expect linguists to have a major input to the design of SLTE programs today, but there is no consensus as to what the most appropriate expertise is. It could come from such fields as General Education, Instructional Design, Curriculum Development, Teacher Education, Second Language Acquisition, or Applied Linguistics, depending on one's persuasion.

Views of language teaching specialists as to what constitutes the core body of theory, concepts, skills, and practices in the field are most readily seen in what they write about the field. Comparison of the content of introductory textbooks in the field reveals a reasonable base of current expert opinion.

(1) Rivers'(1981) *Teaching foreign language skills*, for example, covers the following thirteen areas:

1   Objectives of Language Teaching
2   Language Teaching Methods
3   Theories of Language and Language Learning
4   Structured Practice

5 Teaching Sounds
  6 Listening Comprehension
  7 The Speaking Skill: Learning the Fundamentals
  8 The Speaking Skill: Expressing Personal Meaning
  9 The Reading Skill
 10 The Writing Skill
 11 Cultural Understanding
 12 Testing: Principles and Techniques
 13 Technology and Language Learning Centers

(2) Omaggio's *Teaching language in context* (1986), another comprehensive introduction to language teaching, covers the following:

  1 First Principles
  2 Methodology in Transition
  3 The Role of Context in Comprehension and Learning
  4 A Proficiency-Oriented Approach to Listening and Reading
  5 Developing Oral Proficiency
  6 Becoming Proficient in Writing
  7 The Accuracy Issue
  8 Classroom Testing
  9 Teaching for Cultural Understanding
 10 Planning Instruction for the Proficiency-Oriented Classroom

(3) A book representing the British approach in TESOL, Abbott and Wingard's *The teaching of English as an international language* (1981) treats these topics:

  1 Approaches to English Teaching
  2 Pronunciation—perception and production
  3 Comprehension and listening
  4 Comprehension and reading
  5 Oral fluency
  6 Writing
  7 Assessment
  8 Error analysis
  9 Remedial work
 10 Planning your teaching
 11 The teacher and the class
 12 Putting things in perspective

(4) Another British text, Harmer's *The practice of English language teaching* (1983), includes:

1 Why do people learn languages
2 What a native speaker knows
3 What a language student should learn
4 Language learning and language teaching
5 Teaching the productive skills
6 Introducing new language
7 Practice
8 Communicative activities
9 Receptive skills
10 Class management
11 Planning

These books share some common themes. They reflect a skills-oriented approach, rather than one which attributes a primary role to the teaching of grammar or literature. They include consideration of such issues as theories of language, second language learning, and learner errors. They do not advocate a specific method of teaching (such as the Audiolingual Method or The Natural Approach.) They differ in the extent to which they deal with cultural issues, classroom management, and assessment.

(5) How did an earlier generation of experts define the core content of the field? Brooks' *Language and language learning* (1960)—a classic in the days of Audiolingualism—includes chapters on the following issues:

1 Theory of Language
2 Language and Talk
3 Mother Tongue and Second Language
4 Language Learning
5 Language Teaching
6 Language and Culture
7 Language and Literature
8 Objectives of the Language Course
9 Continuity for the Learner
10 Methods and Materials
11 The Language Laboratory
12 Tests and Measurements
13 Building a Profession

(6) Bright and McGregor's *Teaching English as a second language* (1970), another influential book in the seventies which represents the British approach to TEFL at that time, has chapters on the following topics:

1 Generalisations
2 Vocabulary
3 Reading
4 Writing
5 Speech
6 Drama
7 Poetry
8 Grammar

In comparing an earlier generation of books with more recent texts, we see that most of the issues identified by Brooks thirty years ago are still considered central to the field. More recent books, however, acknowledge the last twenty years of research and theorizing in such areas as second language acquisition, language comprehension, language transfer, and interlanguage. Likewise, the 'skills plus grammar and literature' focus seen in books such as Bright and McGregor have now been supplemented by treatment of syllabus design and testing and a more sophisticated linguistic base, drawing from disciplines such as sociolinguistics and psycholinguistics. However, both recent and earlier texts typically present a view of language content which consists of subject matter knowledge (i.e. language and language related matters) and skills (i.e. presenting new materials, practice techniques, and classroom management).

1.2 Task analysis. Another source for determining the content of SLTE programs is through identifying the kinds of things that teachers do on the job, and deriving components for a teacher education program from the information obtained. As Connell (1985:69) states, 'Teachers are workers, teaching is work, and the school is a workplace'.

In order to identify priorities to be addressed in a teacher education program, Smith (cited in Fanselow and Light 1977:5) suggests it is necessary to:

(a) analyze the job of teaching into the tasks that must be performed,
(b) specify the abilities required for the performance of these tasks,
(c) describe the skills or techniques through which the abilities are expressed,
(d) work out training situations and exercises for the development of each skill.

Information on the task base of teaching was obtained from a survey of expatriate TESOL teachers in Japan (Richards and Hino 1983).

Respondents (N=116) indicated that the ten tasks they most frequently had to undertake were:

1. teach speaking
2. teach listening
3. prepare materials
4. use audiovisual aids
5. design curriculum/syllabuses
6. prepare tests
7. teach writing
8. teach reading
9. interpret test scores
10. do administrative work

The same subjects indicated that the methods they most frequently employed in the classroom were

1. Combination of Methods
2. Direct Method
3. Notional/Functional
4. Audiolingual
5. Total Physical Response

In a recent study of Hong Kong English teachers, (Richards et al. 1990) a number of dimensions of teachers' work were identified in a questionnaire study. In response to a question on the kinds of teaching activities and techniques teachers employed, the ten most frequently cited activities were (N=137):

1. doing reading/writing exercises in the textbook
2. written grammar exercises
3. composition
4. pair/group work
5. reading aloud
6. dictation
7. oral grammar exercises
8. pronunciation drills
9. role-play
10. games

The differences between the teaching practices of teachers in the Japanese and Hong Kong study reflect the conversational focus of many English language programs in Japan, and the exam-based teaching seen in many Hong Kong schools. The teaching approaches and methods the Hong Kong teachers identified as those used most frequently were:

1   grammar-based approach: studying the structures of the language
2   a functional approach: using language for communicative purposes
3   a situational approach: learning language used in particular contexts
4   a reading approach: learning language through reading
5   an eclectic approach geared to meeting the requirements of the examinations

As with most areas of SLTE, information on the tasks that teachers actually carry out as part of their professional life is generally unreported, though information on the roles and practices of teachers in particular programs is available (e.g. Shaw and Dowsett 1986, Nunan 1987).

Attempts to derive educational goals and content from analysis of the tasks that teachers perform in their work has been identified with a 'reconstructionist' approach to educational planning, i.e. one which emphasizes the importance of planning, efficiency and rationality and which stresses the practical aspects of education. In second language teaching this approach emphasizes the promotion of practical skills, makes use of objectives, and advocates a systematic approach to needs analysis, program development, and syllabus design (Clark 1987). It is typically identified with a 'training' approach to teacher education; that is, one which sees the teacher as a skilled craftsperson or technician, who is concerned 'primarily with the successful accomplishment of ends decided by others' (Zeichner and Liston 1987:27).

1.3 Teacher-perceived needs. In the case of inservice-program design, teachers can also be consulted directly about the kind of professional development and training they think they need. In the Japanese study cited above (Richards and Hino 1984), when asked what issues they would like to study more about if they were to pursue a Master's degree in TESOL, experienced expatriate English teachers in Japan without graduate TESOL qualifications indicated preferences for the following topics/areas (N=75):

1   teaching of listening
2   teaching of speaking
3   second language acquisition
4   materials writing, selection, and adaptation
5   curriculum and syllabus design

6   use of audiovisual aids
7   psycholinguistics
8   sociolinguistics
9   teaching of writing
10 teaching of reading

This prioritizing of needs reflects the kinds of work which expatriate English teachers in Japan are typically engaged in, i.e. teaching, speaking, and listening skills in conversation programs. Using teachers as a source of information about program content raises the tricky question of 'Do teachers really know what they need to know?' The difference between what teachers think they need to know and what experts think teachers need to know is often striking. Many teachers disavow any interest in the theoretical issues which occupy an important place in graduate TESOL programs. For example, comments such as the following were typical in the Japan study just cited:

> I would not be interested in any theoretical courses. I am only interested in things that could be used tomorrow.
> I would have little interest in theory and research per se.

Compare these views with an expert's opinion of what teachers' need:

> The professional teacher of English as a Second Language needs pedagogical training to be a teacher, and academic training in English language and linguistics to be a professional in our field. But of the two, there is a certain priority for English language and linguistics, for a decision on the nature of language and on the psycholinguistic mechanisms of language acquisition will determine to a large extent our decision on the principles and methods of teaching (Diller, cited in Richards and Hino 1984).

1.4 Current practice. Another source for the content of SLTE programs is information about what is typically offered in current programs. What kinds of courses and learning experiences are typically provided in second language teacher education programs around the world? Information of this kind is available from various sources, including directories of programs as well as surveys of aspects of different programs (e.g. Richards and Crookes 1988). In the Japanese survey, teachers with MA TESOL degrees were asked to indicate the subjects they studied as part of their graduate training. The data was collected in 1982 and the average number of years since graduation was 7 (N= 41). The following courses had been taken:

Rank Subject/Area of Studies		Percent Who Took Course Work in Area
1	phonology/phonetics	97%
2	transformational grammar	95
3	structural linguistics	92
4	second language acquisition	88
5	first language acquisition	85
6	contrastive analysis	84
7	teaching of speaking	79
8	teaching of writing	79
9	teaching of listening	76
10	teaching of reading	76
11	sociolinguistics	75
12	method analysis	73
13	psycholinguistics	73
14	practice teaching	72
15	traditional grammar	70
16	error analysis	68
17	semantics	66
18	materials writing, selection, and adaptation	63
19	language testing	63
20	history of language teaching	58
21	curriculum/syllabus design	58
22	use of audiovisual aids	57
23	pedagogical grammar	56
24	varieties of English	52
25	classroom management	47
26	discourse analysis	46
27	statistics and research	46
28	bilingual education	45

It can be seen that 'theory' courses predominated in the graduate courses taken by most of these teachers. A useful source of information about the content of graduate TESOL programs is the *Directory of Professional Preparation Programs in TESOL in the United States 1989-1991* (Kornblum 1989). The directory lists all graduate programs available in the U.S., and also contains information about the required courses in such programs.

The content of the courses listed varies widely, since U.S. programs are directed at different kinds of students: the focus may be research oriented, oriented towards teaching skills, or directed towards the requirements of state school systems. Thus the required courses in the program offered at California State University, Domingues Hills, are:

Phonology   Contrastive analysis
Morphology   Linguistic theory
Syntax   Teaching methods (2 courses)
Psycholinguistics   English literature

By contrast the program offered at Eastern Michigan University has the following required courses:

Observation and analyses of ESL programs
Theoretical foundations of second language pedagogy
A pedagogical grammar and phonology of ESL
Methods of TESOL (Reading, Writing, Grammar)
ESL materials: review, adaptation and development (Reading, Writing, Grammar)
Methods of TESOL (Listening, Speaking, Pronunciation)
ESL materials: review, adaptation, development (Listening, Speaking, Pronunciation)
Foreign language testing and evaluation
TESOL practicum
TESOL seminar

An examination of the course requirements in a sample of 50 MA TESOL programs listed in the TESOL directory reveals the following required courses:

Type of required course in MA TESOL programs	Number of programs which require each course
TESOL methods and materials	47
English grammar/syntax	36
linguistics	36
practice teaching	33
phonology	32
second language acquisition	29
syllabus/curriculum design	24
testing	24
research in TESOL	16
language and culture	12
teaching reading	11
contrastive/error analysis	11
sociolinguistics	11
bilingual education	10
teaching writing	10
history of English	7
psycholinguistics	5

Discussion. Pedagogical content knowledge in SLTE programs typically consists of courses selected from two main areas: subject matter knowledge (language theory, English grammar, phonology, second language learning, etc.) and teaching skills (methodology, classroom management, presentation, and practice techniques, etc.).

Traditionally, language-based courses have been given a major emphasis, and this is partly a reflection of the history of the TESOL profession. In a survey of MA TESOL programs in 1977, Acheson (1977:33) noted:

> The lack of concern with such *educational* matters as competency and performance in the classroom is partly explicable by the fact that only about ten of America's 50 TESOL departments appeared to be affiliated to schools, departments, or colleges of education. The remaining 40 were attached to departments of linguistics, English, foreign languages, speech, or other adminstrative units in the academic institutions. Furthermore in many cases, it is surmised that the preparation of teacher educators in the TESOL teacher preparation programs has been exclusively in linguistics, rather than in education and/or the *teaching* of ESOL.

The current *Directory of Professional Programs in TESOL in the United States* (TESOL 1989) gives a somewhat similar picture of where MA TESOL programs are currently located:

Home department	Number of programs
English	46
Education/Curriculum	41
Linguistics	25
Foreign languages	10
ESL/TESOL	6
Other	19

Some 28% of programs are now located in departments of education, compared with the 20% found in Acheson's survey. As to what the core disciplines underlying SLTE are, the lack of consensus is seen in the widely different components of programs as well as in the fact that they are located in such a spectrum of different university departments. This supports Freeman's (1989:27) observation:

> Language teacher education has become increasingly fragmented and unfocused. Based on a kaleidoscope of elements from many different disciplines, efforts to educate individuals as language teachers often lack a coherent, commonly accepted foundation. In its place,

teacher educators and teacher education programs substitute their own individual rationales, based on pedagogical assumptions or research, or function in a vacuum, assuming—yet never articulating—the bases from which they work.

This kind of problem is not unfamilar in other areas of teacher education. Students preparing to enter the general teaching profession, for example, are generally required to take courses in 'the psychology of education', but increasingly both student teachers and educators have begin to ask why such a subject should be required, what such a field is supposed to include, what relevance it has to classroom practice, and how it should be taught (cf. the entry on *Teacher Training* in Harre and Lamb 1986).

Freeman (1989) argues that SLTE is confused about its pedagogical content base because the profession has failed to appreciate the distinction between language teaching and the areas of inquiry on which it is based (linguistics, applied linguistics, methodology, SLA, etc.). He points out that applied linguistics and methodology should not be confused with teaching itself, and 'should not be the primary subject matter of language teacher education' (1989:29). In a paper with a similar focus, Richards (1987:205) noted that 'there has been little systematic study of second language teaching processes that could provide a theoretical basis for deriving practices in second language teacher education'. It was argued that pedagogical content knowledge in SLTE should be derived from a theory of teaching; that is, a statement of the general principles that account for effective teaching, including a specification of the key variables in language teaching and how they are interrelated. This would focus on examining the concepts and thinking processes that guide the effective second language teacher. Freeman (1989:31) sees this as a focus on language teaching as 'a decision-making process based on four constituents: knowledge, skills, attitude, and awareness'. Such a reorientation of the content of SLTE programmes would entail a reexamination of the teaching approaches used in such programs. It is to this dimension of SLTE that we now turn.

2 Instructional practice in SLTE. How is the content of SLTE programs typically taught and what instructional options are available? Unfortunately, there is no data avilable on this issue, though observation of and participation in a number of such programs suggests that most often 'information transmission' is the major mode of instruction. The assumption is that by providing teachers with information about language, language learning, and methodology, teachers themselves will be able to apply such information to their own classroom practices. There is a considerable irony here. For years, language teaching specialists have argued 'teach them the language, not *about* the language'. But in SLTE programs, the focus is often on giving information, rather than on exploring the process of teaching itself.

If an attempt is made to link theory with practice, it is generally through the practicum or teaching practice experience. In a survey of the practicum course in US graduate programs (Richards and Crookes 1988) it was found that the second most frequently cited objective for the practicum was 'to apply instruction from theory courses'. Often however, this application is left entirely to chance, and the practicum is run as a self-contained and independent component of the student teacher's teacher education program.

What alternatives are available if we are interested in developing second language teacher education programs which move beyond subject matter knowledge and teaching techniques and which focus in a substantial way on the process of teaching itself? A starting point is the development of goals which acknowledge teaching and the study of language teaching as the fundamental content of the field of second language teacher education. The following are examples of goals which identify the teaching process itself as the subject matter of SLTE.

- to develop a high level of competence in language teaching and its related activities,
- to develop a personal theory of teaching and a reflective approach to one's own teaching,
- to become aware of the contexts of teaching (settings, participants, curriculum, materials) and the effects of these on teaching and learning,
- to recognize the theories and beliefs underlying one's own teaching practices,
- to understand the roles of teachers and learners in the classroom and the different levels of interaction they take part in,
- to develop awareness of different options available in language teaching and the consequences of selecting different options,
- to acquire skills needed for classroom based inquiry,
- to recognize the kinds of decision-making teaching involves and to utilize decision-making effectively in one's own teaching,
- to be able to analyze and evaluate one's own teaching practice,
- to be able to redirect goals and strategies in teaching,
- to know how to initiate change in one's own classroom and how to monitor the effects of such changes.

In developing teacher education programs, activities are then needed which enable these kinds of goals to be realized. While lectures, seminars, and discussions will continue to provide one mode of input to program implementation, more experientially based approaches are needed to address the kinds of goals identified above. Activities of this kind include the following:

(1) Observing teaching in different settings
   a. Observation of experienced teachers
   b. Peer observation
   c. Study of video protocols of lessons

(2) Experiencing teaching in different settings
   a. Microteaching
   b. Practice teaching
   c. Team teaching
   d. Internships

(3) Investigating teaching and learning
   a. Case studies
   b. Investigative projects
   c. Analysis of lesson protocols

(4) Reflecting critically on teaching/learning experiences
   a. Diaries
   b. Language learning experiences
   c. Reflective teaching
   d. Self-monitoring

(5) Focusing on critical events in teaching
   a. Problem-solving
   b. Role plays and simulations

(6) Carrying out project-work
   a. Action research
   b. Curriculum and materials projects

Let us now consider how some of these activities can be used used in preservice and inservice programs in teacher education. Examples are drawn largely from programs currently being taught or developed at the City Polytechnic of Hong Kong, an in-service degree for teachers of English and a pre-service BA (Hons) degree in TESL.

2.1 Observing teaching in different settings. Observation of teaching is a standard component of most teacher education programs. In both pre- and in-service courses it can serve to help develop concepts that can be used to describe and analyze the nature of classroom events. In pre-service programs, observation (both of live teachers and of videotaped lessons) can be used to help teachers develop a terminology to describe and discuss teaching, and to provide data with which to examine central concepts in their own teaching. In our work with in-service teachers, teachers are first taught techniques of ethnographic observation in order to disassociate observation from the notion of evaluation, to develop the ability to focus on the objective description of classroom events, and to develop a language to describe classroom processes. In the pre-service program, observation has a related focus. Since the participants in this program have no teaching experience, observations of different kinds of ESL classes are intended to orient student teachers to the nature of the second language classroom, its organization, practices, and norms, and to enable student teachers to develop an awareness of the kinds and levels of interaction that happen in language classrooms.

2.2 Experiencing teaching in different settings. In our pre-service degree we are exploring a number of alternatives to depending solely on the teaching practicum as a source for practical experience of teaching. One avenue we are exploring involves a re-examination of micro-teaching.

Microteaching is traditionally associated with a training-based view of teaching. This view is built on on the assumption that teaching can be broken down into individual skills that can be isolated and practiced individually, such as drilling, correcting errors, and presenting new vocabulary or grammar. While this skills-based view of teaching has been criticized as offering a limited view of teaching, microteaching activities can be used to provide different kinds of teaching experiences, which can then be used as a basis for reflection and analysis.

> The emphasis is placed not on mastering a specific isolated skill, for example, but on identifying and reacting to the total teaching act. The task given to the students is accordingly more holistic and the expectations from the feedback sessions are both broader and less precise (Kornblueth and Schoenberg 1990:17).

Cruickshank et al. (1981) have developed an approach which has the following features:

(1) Student teachers are divided into small groups of four to six.
(2) Each are given an identical lesson to teach and have a few days to prepare for teaching to the small group.
(3) Content is not drawn from their academic subject (i.e. future English teachers might present a geography lesson: this is intended to encourage focus on the process of teaching rather than on the content).

(4) Lessons are taught within a 15 minute time frame.
(5) A reflection process follows, within each group and then with the class as a whole.

Modifications of this approach are used in the pre-service program.

2.3 Investigating teaching and learning. A primary goal in inservice programs is to provide teachers with ways of looking at their own classrooms from a different perspective. Activities which promote self-inquiry and critical thinking are central for continued professional growth, and are designed to help teachers move from a level where their classroom actions are guided by routine to a level where their practices are guided by reflection and critical thinking.

One course in the in-service program, for example, focuses on exploring classroom processes. Each week one aspect of classroom life is examined. Topics covered include structuring, learner roles and strategies, teacher roles, teacher decision-making, tasks, grouping, teacher-student interaction, and classroom language. Initially in seminar sessions, video protocols of actual lessons are used to identify different dimensions of classroom behaviour. Each week the teachers audiotape one of their own lessons and then write a reflective response to it, focusing on the topic under discussion that week. An assignment during a week in which the topic of teacher decision-making was being discussed consists of the following activity:

A. **Planning decisions.** As you plan a lesson for the coming week, make notes of the planning decisions you made:
   (1) What alternatives did you consider?
   (2) How did your belief system influence your decisions?
   (3) What final decisions did you make? Why?

B. **Interactive decisions.** Audio-record the lesson you planned. Later that day, review the lesson by listening to the recording and comparing the actual lesson to your plan. Write a commentary on your lesson focusing on the interactive decisions that you made during the lesson:
   (1) What happened during the lesson that you did not plan for?
   (2) What kinds of interactive decisions did you make? Why?
   (3) On reflection, do you think an alternative decision would have been better? Why?

Investigation of different aspects of language teaching, language learning, and language use, is a strand running through many of the courses in both the pre-service and in-service programs. In a course on pedagogic grammar, for example, as part of a unit on aspect and tense in

English, students might build up a data base of native-speaker usage (based on occurences in newspapers or other sources) as well as of learner usage (based on a written corpus either collected by teachers themselves or provided by the course instructor). This is then used to test out particular theories of tense and aspect or of second language acquisition. Or in a course on second language acquisition, teachers might administer a language attitude questionnaire to their students, to compare published findings on language attitudes with data from their own students. With students in pre-service programs, small scale investigative projects help develop an awareness of the significance of issues they study in their theory courses, as well as give them a familiarity with collecting and analyzing different kinds of language data. This is also true at the in-service level, but here such activities help teachers develop a research orientation to their own classrooms and to appreciate their potential roles as classroom researchers.

2.4 Reflecting critically on teaching/learning experiences. Activities which involve critical reflection focus on conscious recall and examination of experiences as a basis for evaluation and decision making and as a source for planning and action. Reflection is seen as a process which can facilitate both learning and understanding, and plays a central role in several recent models of teacher development. Zeichner and Liston (1986:4) suggest that a teacher education program which seeks to develop a reflective view of teaching seeks to develop student teachers who:

> are willing and able to reflect on the origins and consequences of their actions, as well as the material and ideological constraints and encouragements embedded in the classroom, school, and societal contexts in which they live. These goals are directed towards enabling teachers to develop pedagogical habits and skills necessary for self-directed growth and towards preparing them, individually and collectively to participate as full partners in their making of educational policies.

2.4.1 The three-part process. Many different approaches are available to engage teachers and student teachers in critical reflection. Central to any approach however is a three-part process which involves:

(1) The event itself. The starting point is an actual teaching or learning episode, such as a lesson in a foreign language (for pre-service students, where a goal might be the study of language learning strategies) or a lesson taught by a student teacher or a practicing teacher. While the focus of critical reflection is usually the student's own learning or teaching, reflection can also be stimulated by observation of another person's teaching, hence both peer observation and team teaching can also be employed.

(2) Recollection of the event. The next stage is to produce an account of what happened, without adding explanation or evaluation. This might be through the written description of an event, through the use of a video or audio recording, or through the use of checklists or other procedures.

(3) Review and response to the event. The student or teacher now returns to the event and reviews and questions it. The goal here is to process the event at a deeper level.

2.4.2 Procedures. Procedures used in programs at City Polytechnic of Hong Kong include:

(1) Autobiographies. Groups of up to 10 students meet regularly with the teacher. Throughout the course each person creates a written account of experiences and observations in teaching. These are read aloud and discussed during the weekly sessions.

(2) Reaction sheets. Reaction sheets are shorts responses written after particular learning activities have been completed. The students are encouraged to 'stand back from what they had been doing and think about what it meant for their own learning and what it entailed for their work as teachers of others' (Powell 1985:46). In a teaching practicum, for example, students work in pairs with a co-operating teacher, and take turns teaching lessons. One serves as observer while the other teaches, and both complete a reflection sheet after each lesson. They then compare their responses in a follow-up session.

(3) Journals. Journals or diaries are another experience which can help develop a reflective orientation towards teaching. With the journal experience, the student or teacher regularly enters information about lessons he or she taught (or learning activities of other kinds), and regularly reviews these, with the help of classmates (if journals are shared with peers) or the teacher. Journal writing experiences provide a record of significant learning experiences, help the participants understand their own self-development process, and foster a creative interaction between the student and other classmates or the instructor.

2.5 Focusing on critical events in teaching. An important dimension of teaching is interactive decision-making, that is, the ability to analyze a classroom problem, determine what range of options is available, and decide on the best course of action. Decision-making for some educationists is the most crucial dimension of the teacher's work. In teacher education, decision-making can be approached in a number of different ways, including through the use of problem solving and role play.

Pennington (1990:145) gives examples of problem-solving activities which involve a sequence of activities beginning with individual or small group discussion of a problem and then moving to whole-class discussion. For example:

Student case:
You are a teacher in a a large second language program whose administration includes a director of courses or department chair, several student advisors, and a clerical assistant. In speaking informally with you, a student from your class suddenly states that she is very much dissatisfied with her situation in the United States, so much so that she wishes to return immediately to her home country.

Questions:
1. What is the immediate problem?
2. What might be the direct and indirect causes of the immediate problem?
3. What other potential or actual problems do you see?
4. What else do you need to know (e.g. about the student or about the situation relating to the problem)?
5. How do you obtain the information that you need?
6. What should you say or do (a) when meeting with the student and (b) after meeting with the student?
7. What other people (if any) need to become involved?
8. What are some of the things to watch out for or to be particularly sensitive to?

Pennington points out that such an activity can easily lead to a discussion of such things as:

(1) the difficulty of determining the source of student problems
(2) the appropriate role of the teacher
(3) the extent to which teachers should become involved in students' personal problems.

Role play is another useful activity which can help develop an awareness of the kinds of beliefs and values implicit in teaching and how these can lead to different kinds of decisions and classroom actions.

Pennington (1990) illustrates how role play activities can be used in conjunction with video viewing to explore different perspectives on the same classroom event. In the example she gives, student teachers or teachers in-service first view a short video segment of a class several times, completing viewing tasks from three different perspectives. On first viewing, an objective viewpoint is taken, and details about the lesson are recorded. On second viewing, the viewpoint of someone who has a positive view of the teacher/lesson is taken, and positive behaviours are noted. On the third viewing, a negative viewpoint is taken and negative aspects of the lesson are noted. The following role play activity is then enacted:

> **As a follow-up to the video** that you just observed, two or more role plays will take place. You will take the role of either the person just observed or the teacher's new supervisor. Both positive and negative roles are provided so that you may try out different combinations of these. Assume that you are having a conference soon after the observation has taken place, as part of the normal teaching evaluation process. The aim of the meeting is to review performance in the class observed and to reach agreement on two potential areas for professional growth/improvement and to develop concrete action steps that both parties can agree on to accomplish the goals.
>
> **Teacher: Positive role:**
> You have basic confidence in yourself and your teaching, yet you realize that there is always room for growth and improvement. In the conference, your primary objective is to establish a good working relationship with your new supervisor. Secondarily, you would like to get some constructive advice about your classes from the supervisor, whom you know to have considerable experience and expertise in language teaching.
>
> **Teacher: Negative role:**
> You lack basic confidence in yourself and your teaching, and you are not comfortable accepting feedback on your teaching unless it is 100% positive. Because of negative experiences with a previous supervisor, you feel threatened by this conference. Your primary objective is to convince your new supervisor that you are doing a good job and that no one needs to worry about you. Secondarily, you want to establish the fact that you have job security and do not have to listen to any advice.
>
> **Supervisor: Positive role:**
> You are a confident and supportive person, with positive attitudes about teachers and teaching. You strongly believe that a 'carrot'

rather than a 'stick' is more effective in changing behavior. Your primary objective is to establish a good working relationship with the teacher. Secondarily, you would like to discuss areas of common ground based on your observation of the teacher's class.

Supervisor: Negative role:
You lack confidence in your abilities as both teacher and supervisor. As a consequence, you tend to take a defensive, condescending stance toward those you supervise. Your primary objective is to establish that you are an experienced expert, and know how the teacher can improve teaching performance. Secondarily, you want to establish that you have control over the teacher's job (Pennington 1990:149).

Goals:	Action steps:
(To: 1, 2, 3, . . .)	(By: 1, 2, 3, . . .)

2.6 Carrying out project work. The use of classroom-based or school-based project work is another strategy available in in-service programs, and often provides a valuable link between campus-based program input and the contexts in which teachers work or in which student teachers do practice teaching or internships. Action research is a central activity in our in-service program, and takes its name from two processes that are central to action research: a data-gathering component (the research element), and a focus on bringing about change (the action component). Many of the courses in the in-service program include an obligatory action-research project. These projects involve a four-part sequence of activities:

(1) **Identify a problem.** Through observation of their own classrooms, teachers identify some aspect of their teaching that they would like to change. For example, a teacher may decide that the class is too teacher dominated, that students are not having many opportunities to speak, and that he or she would consequently like to increase the amount of student participation in lessons.

(2) **Develop a strategy for change.** The next step, developed in consultation with peers or with the instructor, is to work out an action plan that will address the problem. For example, the teacher may decide to change the classroom seating arrangement, or keep a record of how often students initiate talk during lessons. The teacher might use a simple coding instrument for this purpose.

(3) **Implement the strategy.** The teacher decides to put his or her plan into operation for a fixed period of time, say, two weeks. During this time he or she monitors students' classroom participation, by audiotaping lessons and by inviting a colleague into the class to complete an observation form which records how often students participated in the lesson and for what purpose.

(4) **Evaluate the results.** The teacher decides if the action plan has brought about the intended changes in style of teaching, and reflects on the goals, procedures, and outcomes of the project.

Conclusions. In a recent summary of trends in second language teacher education, Richards and Nunan (1990:xii) suggest that for SLTE to move forward there should be:

- a movement away from a 'training' perspective to an 'education' perspective and recognition that effective teaching involves higher-level cognitive processes, which cannot be taught directly,
- the need for teachers and student teachers to adopt a research orientation to their own classrooms and to their own teaching,
- less emphasis on prescriptions and top-down directives and more emphasis on an inquiry-based and discovery-oriented approach to learning (bottom-up),
- a focus on devising experiences that require the student teacher to generate theories and hypotheses and to reflect critically on teaching
- less dependence on linguistics and language theory as a source discipline for second language teacher education, and more of an attempt to integrate sound, educationally based approaches,
- use of procedures that involve teachers in gathering and analyzing data about teaching.

In order for this to happen, this survey has suggested that practitioners of SLTE need to reach consensus as to what the fundamental nature of the field is and how its pedagogical content knowledge should be defined. In many situations, SLTE still reflects the history of its development as a branch of applied linguistics. A consistent approach or philosophy of second language teacher education has not yet emerged to serve as a basis for sound instructional practice. If the movement away from language-based approaches to more teaching-based ones gains momentum in the future however, both pedagogical content knowledge and accompanying instructional practices will need to be evaluated to ensure that teaching assumes a more prominent role within the field of second language teacher education.

References

Acheson, P. 1977. English for speakers of other languages: A survey of teacher preparation programs in American and British colleges and universities. In: Bilingual, ESOL, and foreign language teacher preparation: Models, practices, issues. Edited by John F.Fanselow and Richard L. Light. Washington, D.C.: TESOL.
Abbott, G and P. Wingard. 1981. The teaching of English as an international language. Glasgow: William Collins.
Bright, J.A and G.P. McGregor. 1970. Teaching English as a second language. London: Longman.
Brookes, Nelson. 1960. Language and language learning: Theory and practice. New York: Harcourt, Brace and World.
Clark, John L. 1987. Curriculum renewal in school foreign language learning. Oxford: Oxford University Press.
Connell, R.W. 1985. Teachers' work. Sydney: George Allen and Unwin.
Cruikshank, D.T., J. Holton, D. Fay, J. Williams, B. Myers, and J. Hough. 1981. Reflective teaching. Bloomington, Ind.: Phi Delta Kappa.
Kornblum, Helen. 1989. Directory of professional preparation programs in TESOL in the United States: 1989-1991. Alexandria, Va.: TESOL.
Fanselow, John F., and Richard L. Light, eds. 1977. Bilingual, ESOL, and foreign language teacher preparation: Models, practices, issues. Washington, D.C.: TESOL.
Freeman, Donald. 1989. Teacher training, development, and decision making: A model of teaching and related strategies for teacher education. TESOL Quarterly. 23,1. 27-46.
Harmer, J. 1983. The practice of English language teaching. London: Longman.
Harre, Rom, and Roger Lamb, eds. 1986. The dictionary of developmental and educational psychology. Cambridge, Mass: MIT Press.
Kornblueth, I., and S. Schoenberg. 1990. Though the looking glass: Reflexive methods in teacher training. TESOL Newsletter XXIV, 5: 17-18.
Marks, R. 1990. Pedagogical content knowledge: From a mathematical case to a modifed conception. Journal of Teacher Education. May-June 1990:3-12.
Nunan, D. 1987. The teacher as curriculum developer. Adelaide: National Curriculum Resource Centre.
Omaggio, A. C. 1986. Teaching language in context. Boston: Heinle and Heinle.
Pennington, Martha. 1990. A professional development focus for the language teaching practicum. In: Jack C. Richards and David Nunan, eds. Second language teacher education. New York: Cambridge University Press. 132-152.
Powell, J. P. 1985. Autobiographical learning. In: David Boud, Rosemary Keogh, and David Walker, eds. Reflection: Turning experience into learning. London: Kogan Page.
Richards, Jack C., and N. Hino. 1983. Training ESOL teachers: The need for needs assessment. Georgetown University Roundtable on Languages and Linguistics 1983. Edited by James E. Alatis, H. H. Stern, and Peter Strevens. Washington, D.C.: Georgetown University Press. 312-326.
Richards, Jack C., and Ted Rodgers. 1986. Approaches and methods in language teaching. New York: Cambridge University Press.

Richards, Jack C. 1987. The dilemma of teacher education in TESOL. TESOL Quarterly. 21. 209-226.
Richards, Jack C., and Graham Crookes. 1988. The practicum in TESOL. TESOL Quarterly. 22. 1:9-26.
Richards, Jack C., Peter Tung, and Peggy Ng. 1990. The culture of the language teacher. In: W. M. Rivers. 1981. Teaching foreign-language skills. Chicago: University of Chicago Press.
Shaw, J.M., and G. W. Dowsett. 1986. The evaluation process in the adult migrant education program. Adelaide: National Curriculum Resource Centre.
Zeichner, K., and D. Liston. 1987. Teaching student teachers to reflect. Harvard Educational Review. 57.1: 23-48.

Teaching vocabulary: The current word

Edward M. Anthony and Lionel Menasche
University of Pittsburgh

Introduction. Some weeks ago William Safire, the *New York Times* columnist, put better than we could the feelings we had when we first faced up to the problem of preparing a state of the art paper on vocabulary teaching. Mr. Safire pointed this out: Because a Constitutional provision requires a 'state of the Union' report, (and we quote him directly):

> ... every January, governors intone their 'State of the State', mayors their 'State of the City', and executives everywhere their 'state-of-the-whatever'.

Among Mr. Safire's less majestic 'whatevers' might be included 'state of the art' papers on vocabulary teaching. What follows is our assessment—partial (in two different senses) and incomplete; hopefully, however, it may be helpful in a small way.

We also hope in this, our response to Dean Alatis's generous invitation to contribute to the Georgetown University Round Table, that we can escape Safire's concluding assessment of the delivery of 'states of the whatever', addresses, which was:

> As a result, the state of the audience is bored to the point of stupefaction.

But there remains one other aspect. It does not take long for preparers of papers of this sort to realize that an art like teaching vocabulary does not hold still willingly for an examination, and that what we say today may have been true late yesterday but is unlikely to continue to be true tomorrow.

And here a quotation from another non-language teacher is apropos of the 'state of the art'. T.S. Eliot, when interviewed by *Time* magazine more than 35 years ago said about William Shakespeare:

> About anyone so great as Shakespeare, it is probable that we can never be right, and if we can never be right, it is better that we should from time to time change our way of being wrong.

We say the same about the smaller subject of vocabulary teaching, which can never be done in a fully satisfactory manner, but which can profitably change its way of being wrong from time to time. With that, let us turn to examine our subject.

First of all, we will present a set of guidelines or touchstones which we believe ought to be reflected in vocabulary teaching, the training of teachers in how to teach words and their meanings, and, of course, in those portions of foreign language texts devoted to vocabulary.

The criteria are intended to reflect certain basic characteristics of the lexicon of a language—or at least the English language. In brief, we will state our assumptions about what vocabulary is like and discuss a few of its salient characteristics which in our judgment are crucial to consider in developing and carrying out an effective program of teaching the vocabulary of a foreign language. Our effort here is, to echo Eliot, just 'our way of being wrong'.

1 Rationale. Discussions of vocabulary center on the meanings of words, of course. We have no desire to be sucked into the vortex of an attempt to define minutely just what a word is. We are well-advised to leave that for consideration in a different arena.

For us it is enough to accept as a starting point *Webster's Ninth New Collegiate Dictionary*. It provides one satisfactorily imprecise definition of 'vocabulary': a 'stock of words employed by a language, group, individual, or work or in a field of knowledge.'

2 The givens. We begin by citing two starting points to our approach.

First, our presentation will not be a measured recitation of all texts recently published accompanied by a brief inventory of their contents. We have found it necessary and practical within the constraints of this assignment to try to be selective and representative rather than comprehensive in our report of what is going on.

We have excluded, for instance, texts espousing what we call the 'sadistic swimming-teacher approach': Just throw your students off the dock—they'll learn to swim! We believe that if you throw the student of a foreign language off the linguistic dock into a sea of words, a certain number will drown, some will dog-paddle awkwardly and inaccurately through the lexicon, others will tend to come up only slightly damp or even dry. A few perhaps survive, but the percentage is probably low—at least in formal education situations.

Second, we admit that we will tend willy-nilly to be evaluative. In this paper we will thus first state and explain our own criteria for judging vocabulary pedagogy, and then we will briefly consider some theoretical positions and areas of current interest, some recent teacher-training materials, and some recent ESL student textbooks. We will conclude by summarizing the state of the art in relation to our evaluative criteria.

3 The criteria.

3.1 The contextual criterion. Texts ought to recognize that words cluster together and refer to events which also cluster together within a culture, and derive much of their meaning from the various contextual dimensions in which they appear: lexical, grammatical, or non-linguistic/cultural, for example.

The lexical context tells us that the word *pitch*, used at one time with the term *soprano* and at others with the words *roof*, or *southpaw*, shifts meanings as its lexical context changes.

In the grammar context, *mother* as a noun usually signifies a biological relationship and is ordinarily gender-restricted, except in some direct address situations, but as a verb is not. *Father*, on the other hand, remains stubbornly gender-bound, whether noun or verb. A cat—even a tomcat—may *mother* a guinea pig, but would find it difficult to father one.

And, in a nonlinguistic flower-garden context, the word *bulb* might refer to a tulip, but in a dark basement it could be described in watts.

A text, we think, is more effective if it presents its words in consistent contexts whether linguistic or non-linguistic; illustrations (pictures) are an example of the latter, but consistency is important: the illustration must match the text. A well-remembered text used the phrase *patch of clouds* and accompanied it with a picture of a *patch* on a small boy's trousers.

Our first criterion for judgment thus insists that good texts present words in context, and potential teachers must be aware of this, for a word combines a form with meanings—sometimes a large number of meanings.

3.2 The method criterion. Our second touchstone is methodological and consists in how this *yes/no*-question can be answered: Have the texts for teachers or students considered the instructional environments in which the lessons are intended to be presented? Some of the components of the learning environment are: EFL and/or ESL situations; the extent of the teachers' education; the age and aims of the students; the goals of the socio-politico-educational milieu; and of course the cultural background of the student body, including the problems peculiar to a particular cultural/linguistic group. A reader from some years back entited *Six Physicists* assumed not only a society in which the tasks of a physicist are understood but also a phonological system that can deal with all those fricatives in all those environments. (In Bangkok, where one of us first came in contact with the book, students and some teachers talked of [sɪk fɪt sa sɪt] in class.)

3.3 The word-type criterion. A third evaluative subject concerns the attention paid to the various ways in which words can be divided up into groups. We feel somewhat diffident about this criterion because it is open-ended, and our divisions are only one way in which to divide the lexicon, but as general check-points perhaps they have some value. Again, we may phrase the evaluative procedure in the form of *yes/no*-questions, as follows:

Are the writers of the text aware of the distinctions between frequency and usefulness of contexts and items? Medical terminology is useful but less frequent than the terminology of foods, for example. *Ten-forty* may be less frequent than *twenty to eleven* but may be more useful because more regular.

The latter example can also be used to illustrate the need to direct another question to the authors of texts: Have they considered the distinctions between vocabulary production and vocabulary recognition? The student of English might be taught to understand when someone says (or writes, for that matter) *twenty to eleven*; but at least in the beginning stages that student might be restricted to producing only members of the pattern that *ten-forty* represents.

On occasion the evaluator might want to ask whether the text writer or teacher trainer is aware of and has considered the sometime vagueness of the borders between grammar and vocabulary. Sometimes the distinction seems to be related to a continuum of versatility, one end of which is represented by words like *the*, *then*, or *should*, and leans toward the grammatical; the other end is exemplified by *zygapophysis* and *zyzzogeton* and tilts toward the lexical.

3.4 The sociolinguistic criterion. Does the work under examination recognize vocabulary distinctions related to who is interacting with whom and under what circumstances? At the very least, does the text aim at a level of communication that is sociolinguistically sufficiently broad to allow satisfactory multilevel communication enabling the native speaker-listener to concentrate on the message rather than the form?

3.5 The inter-intralanguage criterion. This criterion deals with the place of translation in teaching vocabulary, and is a familiar one. Opinions differ, but word-for-word translation has long been considered a weak classroom technique. Here the evaluator watches for excesses.

Let us keep in mind the statistics that some of us here today learned at the feet of Charles C. Fries: If the most frequent 500 words in English have 14,070 meanings, how odd it would be if the most frequent 500 words in another language had the same 14,070 meanings.

3.6 The qualitative criterion. A last grab-bag of criteria is here lumped together, some subjective. And they can be approached in the answers to these questions:

Are the materials integrated?
Do they show imagination?
Is there any evidence of innovation?

And last of all, and crucially important:

Is there evidence of an effort to provide overt opportunities or at least directions to lead students toward the practice of what has been presented?

4 Theoretical positions and areas of current interest. Traditionally, the possible approaches to vocabulary teaching, which have appeared in various forms in different theories and materials, often overlapping, have been the following six:

(1) Teach the *words of a written text*. This is still current and may be considered the prime mode of pedagogy for students who are able to read at an intermediate or higher level.

(2) Teach the *words of an invented situation*. This is still current in all specially designed materials based on scenarios, which can take the form of pictures or spoken descriptions or written descriptions.

(3) Teach *lists of words that are not related* to each other in any way. This is not current and probably never has been a way of achieving real success in vocabulary pedagogy, although some students like to enter words and definitions in notebooks.

(4) Teach *lists of related words*. This is quite common. Such lists are usually connected with situational topics or chapter themes in textbooks and are often derived from invented or real scenarios in text or pictorial form.

(5) Teach *words only as they arise from a need to express meanings in real situations*. This is current and popular since it is a concomitant of the communicative approaches to language teaching and of the trend towards greater authenticity of source materials.

(6) Teach a *core list of words systematically—a lexical syllabus—and then vocabulary for special purposes*. This approach has been given attention in the past based on word frequency counts. It still attracts followers, but, other than in dictionaries, there are very few sets of systematically developed materials covering several thousand words.

These six approaches, and aspects of them, are taken up in much current work on lexical acquisition, which exhibits a wide range of interests and foci, some of which we briefly mention here by way of background. The wide range of current work may be exemplified by Hudson (1989) on the one hand and Cowie (1990) on the other. Hudson is concerned with the development of a formal lexical acquisition model that will account for how meanings are acquired. Cowie (1990:196) reviews current trends in EFL lexicography, pointing out that '. . . English monolingual dictionaries designed for foreign learners have increased astonishingly in number, variety, and authority' during the past decade. Other areas of current interest to theorists, as noted by Gass (1988) include knowledge of the lexicon (what is entailed in knowing a word); connections between elements within the lexicon and between the lexicon and other components of language; lexical simplification; the influence of the native language; lexical prototypes; and vocabulary in context. Some of these issues, and others, are discussed in Carter's 1988 state of the art article in *Language Teaching*. As a final example, we may note that a further area attracting recent interest is the methodology involved in assessing the size of an individual's vocabulary; Goulden, Nation, and Read (1990:356) explore this issue and come to the interesting conclusion that 'the average educated native speaker has a vocabulary of around 17,000 words and has acquired them at the average rate of about two to three words per day'—a finding that supports what would previously have been regarded as a conservative estimate.

5 Teacher training texts/articles. In the 1970s, it was often noted that vocabulary was a neglected area in language teaching, as in Richards (1976) and Judd (1978). Judd also noted that vocabulary instruction was usually indirect, i.e. not taught in itself, but was a peripheral part of an activity with some other focal point, most often a reading activity and less often of listening, speaking, or writing. In Paulston and Bruder's teacher training text (1976), for instance, vocabulary is discussed only in the chapter on reading. Indirectness in teaching words is still the norm, but the call for much greater attention to vocabulary pedagogy has in part been answered. It is not now as neglected an area as it used to be although, as Carter (1988:14) rightly points out, 'there is still a long way to go . . . before the the sophistication reached at other linguistic levels is achieved.'

In the area of teacher training, the last fifteen years or so have seen a dramatic increase in the number of texts devoted wholly to lexical analysis and pedagogy. About fifteen years ago, one could have noted that the special advice was in articles or single chapters or parts of single chapters in books (e.g. Paulston and Bruder 1976, Nilsen 1976, Chastain 1976). Now we have several excellent texts which are devoted entirely to teaching vocabulary, most of them published within the last five years. They include Taylor (1990), Nation (1990), Carter and McCarthy (1988), Gairns and Redman (1986), Allen (1983).

The trend is, first, a reflection of the way in which teacher training materials in general have become increasingly specialized over the last decade; more and more frequently—almost in a geometric progression—we are seeing specialized texts for different skill areas and for different aspects of skill areas, techniques, and methods. Such increasing specialization is likely to continue. In the next decade we may well see whole books dealing with topics as comparatively narrow as, for example, the pegagogical uses of word-counts, or teaching vocabulary for speaking, or teaching vocabulary for composition, or teaching vocabulary through context clues exercises.

Second, the trend is also a reflection of the greatly increased emphasis on authentic communicativeness in learner interactions in the classroom, even at beginning and intermediate levels. This emphasis leads to an increased focus on content words as the components of language that most readily convey basic semantic content. In its most basic form, some degree of meaning can be conveyed by 'stringing' lexical items without regard to structural rules (while the reverse is not possible—grammatical rules alone, slots without fillers, convey no useful semantic content).

Third, there has been increasing research in and theoretical analysis of lexis and lexical acquisition. For many decades, debate moved back and forth in relation to the role of grammar in various methods, but vocabulary, especially in terms of content words, was not given any serious consideration as an integral component of methodology. However, it was and continues to be given special attention in word counts (as in West's General Service List 1953) and in lexicographical developments in English as a foreign language. The lexicography has yielded several dictionaries designed specifically for learners of English (e.g. the *Longman dictionary of contemporary English* 1978).

In the teacher-training texts that are part of this trend towards increasing specialization, major foci include: vocabulary size and the concept of a core vocabulary; what it means to know a word; vocabulary in relation to the four skills; learner strategies (such as mnemonics and guessing words from context); morphological analysis; cognates; and lexis and discourse (Nation 1990, Carter 1987, Cohen 1990).

Those who advise teachers and students 'how to', may be exemplified by Taylor (1990), Morgan and Rinvolucri (1986), and Berwald (1986). Taylor's book and Morgan and Rinvolucri's are typical of the trend towards providing teachers with resource material which they can dip into for ideas and exercises. Taylor presents a series of chapters which together reflect a sequence of stages that vocabulary learners are to be put through. The spirit of her procedure is captured in the title of

Chapter 2: 'The communicative teaching of vocabulary', which focuses on the presentation of new items. Subsequently, she discusses the immediate follow-up to the initial presentation, exercises for consolidation, and vocabulary in discourse. Morgan and Rinvolucri provide a rich mix of activities divided by 'styles of activity' as follows: pre-text, text, pictures and mime, word sets, personal reactions to words, dictionary use, and lists.

Berwald attempts to divert teachers from a reliance on the vocabulary of textbooks. He provides a comprehensive review of how to make use of mass media to teach French culture and vocabulary using authentic materials. His media sources cover a wide range, including newspaper headlines and stories, comic strips, advertisements, TV guides, maps, mail order catalogues, and tourist guides. He advises teachers to prepare a vocabulary sheet to accompany the text and suggests a traditional way of indicating the meanings of selected words: provide simple definitions and give examples in sentence contexts.

Methods texts for teachers also include the type that gives a general overview of all skills, some of which we will now consider.

Richard-Amato, in *Making it happen* (1988) follows methodological principles of the 'Natural Approach' and aims to encourage acquisition, rather than learning. Accordingly, there is little emphasis on form, whether grammatical or lexical, and much on interactional communication in a low-anxiety atmosphere. Indeed, her book does not even list 'vocabulary' or 'words' or 'lexis' in the index. There is, however, some reference to word acquisition at various places in the text, especially in discussing the earlier stages of language acquisition.

Very different from Richard-Amato is the basic methods text by Bowen, Madsen, and Hilferty (1985). Their approach is skills-based, and it presents vocabulary in two sections—one for oral language and one for written language. The distinction is artificial, but the authors justify it by stating that the lexis of oral language is more often informal and that the oral language situation gives different kinds of opportunities for identifying and learning new terms and for feedback from interlocutors. Bowen, Madsen, and Hilferty offer no single methodology in their collection of techniques and procedures for language teaching, preferring a pragmatic eclecticism (1985:69). Their formulation for vocabulary learning might be called 'mainstream current word', a communicative strategy: 'Probably the best way to build a strong vocabulary is through extensive participation as a respondent in real communication situations. This means talking to lots of people in English—or at least doing a lot of listening. . . . It also means doing a lot of reading to enlarge one's vocabulary in the written language' (Bowen, Madsen, and Hilferty 1985:324).

Different from both Richard-Amato and Bowen et al. and exemplifying a more recent emphasis on the strategies that students use in language learning, is the recent book by Rebecca Oxford, *Language learning strategies: What every teacher should know* (1990). Oxford divides strategies into direct (memory, cognitive, and compensation) and indirect (social, affective, and metacognitive) and applies these to all four skills. The book does not isolate grammar or vocabulary for separate treatment in terms of strategies, but indicates how they can be woven into all communicative exercises—abundant examples of which are provided.

6 The treatment of vocabulary in some recent ESL textbooks. The overwhelming trend in textbooks continues to be to present new words in relation to the the development of the four skills, especially the receptive skills. Extensive courses with an exclusive focus on vocabulary, covering several thousand words, are rare.

6.1 Vocabulary-only, multi-volume series. Within the domain of textbooks that focus primarily on vocabulary development, there is little available. We are aware of only two major attempts to provide a careful introduction to several thousand words, both being multi-volume series. They are the Barnard series (early 1970s) and the Rogerson et al. series (late 1980s). (For convenience, the name of the first author only, out of nine, is used in referring to the 'Rogerson' series). These two series exemplify changes and consistencies in pedagogical strategies during the period from the early 1970s to the late 1980s.

Similarities between the two series are that they both assume a certain number of words as known (Barnard: 1,000, Rogerson 600); both focus each unit on a specific topic; and, at the beginning of each unit, both present word lists in a format which indicates parts of speech.

Regarding differences between the series, we note the following: Barnard aims to teach 2,000 new words, while Rogerson covers 3,000. Each unit in Rogerson is graded in its exercises: '. . . there is a three-tiered system of exercises sequenced to take the student from easy, open-book, fairly controlled exercises through more difficult, less controlled exercises to a final phase with communicative exercises' (Rogerson 1988:xiv). There is no such gradation in Barnard. Another difference is that Barnard is intended as a self-study series for students who plan to attend English-medium universities or professional programs. Rogerson is more general in intent. Barnard's pedagogical strategy is to provide lengthy definitions and discussions of each word and follow this up with dictation activities, reading passages, and a vocabulary test. In the explanations, exercises, and tests, there is extreme reliance on a fill-in-the-letters technique of providing the first and last letter (or letters) of words being studied. This technique is not used at all in Rogerson. Finally, the feature that most distinguishes Rogerson from Barnard is this: in

Barnard, only the definitions contain known vocabulary (previously taught or assumed), whereas in the Rogerson series *all* definitions, examples, and exercises and reading passages in Volumes 1 to 6 contain *only* vocabulary which has been previously taught in the series. This remarkable feature does mean that there is no material from naturally occurring sources, but the gain is that all input is controlled—all input is comprehensible for students working sequentially through the volumes. This clearly reflects a fundamental tenet of the Natural Approach even though the authors make no explicit linkage to the approach in their introduction.

6.2 Textbooks for specific skills. It is a well-established tradition in language teaching that learning new words can be part of developing any of the skills, and, as mentioned earlier, systematic vocabulary development is often linked to the teaching of reading. A reading textbook of the most common variety—which includes reading passages and attached exercises—will almost invariably include some vocabulary work. Sometimes this has a dual function, to increase knowledge of vocabulary found in the passages, and also, when the word study precedes the reading, to develop schemata that will improve text comprehension. An example, published this year for low intermediate students, is Krahnke's *Reading together: A reading/activities text for students of English as a second language*. Each chapter includes an introductory vocabulary exercise which aims 'to get the students to begin to find word meanings' (from other students or from dictionaries) 'and be able to state them using their own resources', and also 'to begin to develop a sense of topic or schema' about the subject dealt with in the various readings (Krahnke, *Teacher's manual* 1991:8). Almost all the readings are followed by vocabulary exercises based on words in the readings. Typically, the exercises get students to connect words and definitions, though in different formats (multiple choice or matching words and definitions).

As in most reading textbooks, there are exercises that force students to use context clues to guess word meaning. Such exercises are the meeting ground of lexical acquisition and reading strategy development. Here, they are presented once early in each chapter in the form of a cloze passage. Krahnke states that the point of the exercise is 'to develop the students' ability to use discourse information of all kinds (grammatical, semantic, informational, morphological) to guess what words might fit into a blank'. The author emphasizes that the exercise must be done in the form of interactional groupwork—'The discussion among the students is where much of the learning takes place.' Increasing 'lexical resources needed for the topic' is considered to be a 'secondary objective' of the exercise (Krahnke, *Teacher's manual*, 10-11).

A recent intermediate listening text for ESL, *Face the issues* (Numrich 1990) also places vocabulary exercises before the text. The intention is simply and rather vaguely stated: 'to prepare the students for vocabulary and expressions used in the listening section' (Numrich 1990:v). The exercise types are (1) a blend of context clues, based on a reading passage or written sentences, and definition matching to support and check on the guessing from context, and (2) selecting the non-synonymous word from a group of three, the other two of which are synonyms of the selected word from the text.

Numrich includes very few vocabulary exercises after listeners have heard the text. They are sometimes the focus of an exercise section called 'Looking at language' and include such lexical items as puns, idioms, and verbs commonly associated with cooking.

An example of a writing text for intermediate to advanced ESL students is *Thinking to write: A composing-process approach to writing*, by Watkins-Goffman and Berkowitz. In line with virtually all writing texts, this gives little systematic attention to vocabulary study. Occasionally, in the prewriting phase, student writers are asked to consider words that will make their writing more specific or more interesting. Transition words (referred to as 'linkers' in this text) are given some attention in the revising phase of some units, e.g. for comparing and contrasting. In the introduction to the text, students are advised to keep a notebook of new words which they have looked up in a glossary, dictionary, or thesaurus and to write a sentence for each as an aid to remembering them. An innovative and useful lexical feature in this text is its glossary, printed as an appendix, of almost 200 difficult or less common or key words. These words appear in various places in the text—in reading selections, explanations, or exercises—and are printed in boldface so that the student will realise that they are glossed in the appendix and will have the choice of continuing to read without interruption or pausing to turn to the glossary.

A recent pair of speaking texts for high-beginning to low-intermediate students is *Interactions I: A speaking activities book* and *Interactions II: A speaking activities book*, by Keller and Thrush. Both are organized in thematic chapters and strongly emphasize what might be called the current orthodoxy of the ESL classroom: task-oriented and problem-solving activities conducted as far as possible in pairs and groups. In these texts, vocabulary is not presented for its own sake, although a fairly good vocabulary is necessary to do the activities. While the authors assume that the students will have most of the requisite lexical knowledge, topic-related words and expressions are frequently provided as part of the description of the task or activity. However, they are rarely defined.

7.0 Conclusion. We summarize the state of the art in relation to our six evaluative criteria, as outlined at the beginning of this paper, in this way:

7.1 The contextual criterion. Contextualization of new words is central in current pedagogy and textbooks. Dealing with new words in real contexts is considered the prime mode of acquisition for most learners who advance beyond the beginning stages of language learning.

7.2 The method criterion. Methodological issues related to environments in which vocabulary teaching occurs are generally implicit in the materials used; e.g. students' lexical goals are reflected in English for special purposes texts. Sometimes the strategy is explicit (as in the Rogerson series using only previously learned words in presenting new ones).

7.3 The word-type criterion. New words are not generally divided into groups and taught as members of the groups in current pedagogy. Frequency and usefulness, for instance, are not taken into account in any tightly controlled way in most materials. Grammatical and content word distinctions are not used as ways of organizing the lexical material. The production and recognition distinction does, however, appear as an organizing principle in Volume 7 of the Rogerson series.

7.4 The sociolinguistic criterion. The sociolinguistic variable is one which is apparent mainly in dictionary indications of formality and informality. Stylistic lexical variation based on interlocutor and situation is not very evident in pedagogy, except insofar as the overwhelming drive is to teach some standard, educated variety. In ESL situations, the less formal vocabulary is learned 'on the street', not in the classroom.

7.5 The inter-intralanguage criterion. Translation is not a major feature of the current work in pedagogy. It is regarded as having some real value at the beginning levels, especially for concrete and specific terms. Its value lies in opening a way into the new language to establish some basic communicative ability. But this value dramatically and progressively decreases as the learner moves into intermediate and advanced levels.

7.6 The qualitative criterion. In this regard, we note that there is increasing innovation in teaching vocabulary—the pool of techniques and procedures is being enriched by activities resource books for teachers, innovative lexicographic developments (e.g. the Collins COBUILD project), the use of authentic texts; imaginative and well-planned vocabulary series, and increasingly various and stimulating opportunities for communicative practice.

Finally, we would note that in the preface to his *A history of English language teachingy*, Howat (1984:xiv) remarks that 'progress in the teaching of languages, as in many practical arts, is neither a function solely of theoretical principle, however persuasive, nor of an unthinking reaction to the demands of the immediate market, but of the alchemy which, whether by accident or by design, unites them to a common purpose.' It is this alchemy that we have tried to reflect in our review of the current work in vocabulary pedagogy; theoretical principle being represented by texts aimed at training teachers, and practical needs by student textbooks.

References

Allen, Virginia F. 1983. Techniques in teaching vocabulary. New York: Oxford.
Barnard, H. 1971, 1972, 1975. Advanced English vocabulary: Workbooks 1-4. Rowley, Mass.: Newbury House.
Berwald, Jean-Pierre. 1986. Au courant: Teaching French vocabulary and culture using the mass media. Washington, D.C.: Center for Applied Linguistics.
Bowen, J. Donald, Harold Madsen, and Ann Hilferty. 1985. TESOL techniques and procedures. Rowley, Mass.: Newbury House.
Carter, Ronald. 1987. Vocabulary: Applied linguistics perspectives. London: Allen and Unwin.
Carter, Ronald. 1987. Vocabulary and second/foreign language teaching. Language Teaching, January 1987. 3-16.
Carter, Ronald and Michael McCarthy. 1988. Vocabulary and language teaching. London: Longman.
Chastain, Kenneth. 1976. Developing second-language skills: Theory to practice. 2nd ed. Chicago: McNally.
Cohen, Andrew. 1990. Language learning: Insights for learners, teachers and researchers. New York: Newbury House.
Cowie, A. P. 1989. Pedagogical descriptions of language: Lexis. Annual Review of Applied Linguistics 10. 196-209.
Eliot, T. S. 1956. Time, January 30.
Fries, Charles C. 1945. Teaching and learning English as a foreign language. Ann Arbor: University of Michigan Press.
Gairns, Ruth and Stuart Redman. 1986. Working with words. Cambridge: Cambridge University Press.
Gass, Susan M. 1988. Second language vocabulary acquisition. Annual Review of Applied Linguistics 9. 92-106.
Goulden, Robin, Paul Nation, and John Read. 1990. How large can a receptive vocabulary be? Applied Linguistics 11. 341-363.
Howatt, A. P. R. 1984. A history of English language teaching. Oxford: Oxford University Press.
Hudson, Wesley. 1989. Semantic theory and L2 lexical development. In: Linguistic perspectives on SLA. Edited by Susan M. Gass and Jacquelyn Schachter. Cambridge: Cambridge University Press.

Judd, Elliot L. 1978. Vocabulary teaching and TESOL: A need for reevaluation of existing assumptions. TESOL Quarterly 12. 71-76.
Keller, Deborah P. and Emily A. Thrush. 1987. Interactions I: A speaking activities book. New York: Random House.
Keller, Deborah P. and Emily A. Thrush. 1987. Interactions II: A speaking activities book. New York: Random House.
Krahnke, Karl. 1991. Reading together: A reading/activities text for students of English as a second language. New York: St. Martin's Press.
Morgan, John and Mario Rinvolucri. 1986. Vocabulary. Oxford: Oxford University Press.
Nation, I.S.P. 1990. Teaching and learning vocabulary. New York: Newbury House.
Nilsen, Don L. F. 1976. Contrastive semantic vocabulary instruction. TESOL Quarterly 8. 347-362.
Numrich, Carol. 1990. Face the issues: Intermediate listening and critical thinking skills. New York: Longman.
Oxford, Rebecca. 1990. Language learning strategies: What every teacher should know. New York: Newbury House.
Paulston, Christina B. and Mary N. Bruder. 1976. Teaching English as a second language: Techniques and procedures. Cambridge, Mass.: Winthrop.
Richard-Amato, Patricia A. 1988. Making it happen. New York: Longman.
Richards, Jack C. 1976 The role of vocabulary teaching. TESOL Quarterly 10. 77-89.
Rogerson, Holly, Betsy Davis, Gary Esarey, Suzanne T. Hershelman, Carol Jasnow, Carol Moltz, Linda M. Schmandt, Dorolyn A. Smith, and Courtenay M. Snellings. 1988, 1989, 1990. Words for students of English, Volumes 1-7. Ann Arbor: University of Michigan Press.
Safire, William. 1991. Perspectives. Pittsburgh Post-Gazette, January 7.
Sinclair, J. M., ed. 1987. Collins COBUILD English language dictionary. London: Collins.
Summers, D., ed. 1978, 1987. LDOCE Longman dictionary of contemporary English. 2d ed. London: Longman.
Taylor, Linda. 1990. Teaching and learning vocabulary. New York: Prentice Hall.
Watkins-Goffman, Linda and Diana G. Berkowitz. 1990. Thinking to write: A composing-process approach to writing. New York: Maxwell Macmillan.
West, M. P. 1953. A general service list of English words. London: Longman.

Second culture acquisition

Gail L. Robinson
San Diego State University

Introduction. I think we would all probably agree that language learning and culture learning are the business of language educators. Even for those who have chosen not to address culture explicitly most of us have claimed that language learning will open the door to another culture. . . . In fact, we've justified language requirements on that basis. Over the past decade, our concern has been opening the door to another culture 'to promote more positive interaction.' 'Interaction' has been viewed as the key to language learning (Rivers 1987). However, an analysis of language curricula, recent textbooks, and attitudinal research shows that little is happening in the university classroom that can really open that cultural door, at least during those first two years that encompass most language requirements. This phenomenon is something that over a decade ago I called the 'magic-carpetride-to-another-culture syndrome' (Robinson 1978).

As far back as 1973, the St. Lambert experiment showed that children can become functionally bilingual without intervening on attitudes toward speakers of the language. (It was reported that the experimental (French immersion) students held attitudes as 'equally positive' as the monolingual English students (Tucker and d'Anglejan 1973). And how positive were these attitudes? According to measures of ethnocentrism, both groups held quite negative attitudes toward the French! More importantly, the experimental program had no effect on attitudes, even though the children achieved functional bilingualism! A study currently being conducted by Nocon at our National Foreign Language Resource Center, San Diego State University, almost two decades later, has come up with the disillusioning find that—again—language study during the required years does not affect student attitudes toward the target culture or speakers of the language. In fact, this study of approximately 500 students of 1st and 3rd semester Spanish shows a clear hostility to the requirement itself (Nocon 1991).

While there has been little if any research which shows that language proficiency leads to a positive attitude toward the culture, we do have evidence of the reverse—that is, that a positive attitude toward the culture, or 'integrative orientation', does facilitate language acquisition. So achieving our cultural goals **will** help fulfill our language ends.

Today I would like to suggest that the reason we are still not achieving our cultural goals is because we simply have not looked at what it is that is acquired in the name of culture learning, how culture is acquired and modified, and by what processes.

We often speak of first language acquisition and its application to second language acquisition and learning. However, rarely do we speak of **first culture acquisition** and its application to **second culture acquisition** and learning. If we are serious about our cultural goals, we have to take a serious look at what anthropology and psychology have to offer the second language teacher and learner. In other words, we will need to do more than add 'cultural notes' to our textbooks. First, I would like to talk about traditional views of culture as **knowledge** and contrast this with a symbolic view of culture as **synthesis**.

Traditional views of culture as knowledge. Like linguists and language methodologists, anthropologists have different theories about what culture is and what the subject of study should be. The goal of 'culture acquisition' is actually new, if not radical, for anthropologists as well as language educators. For example, even the Princeton anthropologist Clifford Geertz suggested that the principal task of interpretive anthropology is not to acquire culture but to gain knowledge **about** the culture, much like the grammarian whose goal is to **describe** language with metalanguage rather than to emphasize language proficiency **itself**. For example, Geertz wrote:

> The essential vocation of interpretive anthropology is not to answer our deepest questions, but to make available to us answers that others, guarding other sheep in other valleys, have given, and thus to include them in the consultative record of what man has said (Geertz 1973).

Our tradition of teaching culture has focused to date on such knowledge about how **others** live **their** lives. However, for the purpose of changing our feelings and perceptions about people from different cultures—opening that door to promote more positive interaction—we are talking about a degree of culture acquisition. For culture acquisition we need to go beyond such **knowledge** to how culture itself is **created** and **transmitted**.

A symbolic view of culture: the color purple. Symbolic anthropology seems to offer the most valuable insights in this arena. To the symbolic anthropologist, culture is neither static nor objective and therefore can not be 'objectively described'. Cultural meaning to the symbolic anthropologist is dynamic and subjective. To quote Dolgin et al.:

> Meaning is the product, not only of the association of 'raw' experience with an already-defined 'code' name, but of the integration of successive past and present . . . experiences into a coherent whole, a life- world, which each individual creates and also internalizes . . . and projects onto his or her interactions with others (Dolgin et al. 1977).

This dynamic notion theoretically dwells on the **interdependence between the meaning within the learner and the cultural experience**. For language learners who already have an established culture, second cultural acquisition implies the development of **cultural versatility**. What we want to strive for is what I call 'the color purple' (quite distinct from Spielberg's movie!). For example, let us imagine that the learner's current meaning, based on past experience, is 'blue'; and the new second cultural objective is 'red'. According to symbolic anthropology, proof of acquiring the second cultural objective would be the color 'purple'.

The idea behind the 'color purple' is that it represents a synthesis between the learner, his or her own culture, and the new cultural objective to be acquired. Let me give an example of a 'purple' response. While studying English as a Second Language at the Center for Language and Crosscultural Skills in San Francisco, one particular unit of work focused on a cultural theme: understanding the American Dream. In one activity students studied this part of a speech by Martin Luther King:

> I have a dream:
> I have a dream, that one day
> this nation will rise up
> and live out the true meaning of its creed.
> I have a dream . . .
> that all men are created equal.

After hearing, studying, analyzing, and repeating the speech, students were asked to write and present their own speeches, using the style of King, but conveying their own dreams. One female Japanese student responded:

> I have a dream, that one day
> all women can get a job
> with the same wages and the
> same conditions as men—
> I have a dream, that one day

the good facilities will be built where people
take good care of children
and children won't feel so lonely (M. Takagi).

Another female student, who had previously suffered from a life threatening kidney illness responded:

I have a dream, that in this world
there will be no hopeless, cureless diseases . . .
I have a dream
that people won't be afraid of death . . .
and someday I yearn
my own fear will also be conquered (N. Matsuo).

I would like to contrast this notion of culture acquisition as synthesis with what goes on in many language programs, regardless of their designation as 'natural approach', 'communicative approach', 'community language learning', 'content-based instruction', etc. In many instances, there are no cultural objectives at all—no 'red'. In an attempt to make language learning 'meaningful', we are sometimes concerned with a focus on 'blue': relating language to current student interests to the exclusion of new cultural information.

Within literature programs the reverse seems to prevail: we analyze the way **they** live: we ask for red responses, not purple. Subjectivity is often viewed as a dirty word. In contrast, psychological theories of perception suggest that all perception is, to a degree, subjective.

Psychological theories of perception

Subjectivity of perception. The notion that we can learn about others **exclusively** by knowing ourselves, by producing blue in response to instruction, is as naive as the notion that we can learn about others **exclusively** by studying about them—by imitating red.

How many of you have heard the cliché, 'let's see it from their perspective?' I have conducted a series of perceptual experiments which suggests that the latter is simply not possible. In the experiment, the audience is divided into two groups. Each group sees six different slides, alternatively closing and opening their eyes. With eyes open, all participants from both groups view the last slide together. However, the overwhelming majority of each group consistently interpret the same slide quite differently, say one side sees a fish, one side sees a child. The experiment clearly illustrates that our learners are not a cultural *tabula rasa* upon which they can paint an objective 'red'. If they do, red is likely the result of 'imitation' rather than 'internalization'. The new object of learning must be processed through their own cultural experience for the 'culturally broadening experience' that we have long talked about to take place. The essence of the culturally broadening experience is the literal perceptual expansion to become perceptually or culturally versatile, e.g. able to see both the fish **and** the child. (By 'perception' I am referring to cognition, affect, and **all** the sensory modes.)

The clear implication for culture acquisition in the second language classroom is to structure tasks and assignments so as to elicit the 'color purple'—elicit a synthesis between the learner, the learner's home culture, and the target cultural objective. That is the road to **cultural versatility**, which includes perceptual versatility—being able to see the rat and the man.

Cue salience and perceptual errors. The next point I want to take from the psychology of person perception refers to the target cultural objective itself: the object of perception or what instructors choose to bring student attention **to**. How many of us begin discussions about the target culture with ideas, institutions, or behaviors that are **different**? . . . how many of those 'cultural notes' refer to things which are different? According to the psychology of person perception, this is quite normal. We tend to perceive things which are different more readily than things which are similar to ourselves. Things which stand out are called 'salient cues'. The only problem with this normal tendency is that it is the basis for stereotyping and negative attitudes toward people of other cultures, wherever differences are perceived. Let me explain. In the normal process of person perception, what is different stands out and is more readily perceived. To make matters worse, there is also an automatic tendency toward perceptual errors: that is, we misjudge the frequency of salient cues. For example, if only ten people in the exhibition hall were wearing long gowns, someone may comment, 'why is **everyone** wearing a long gown?' In another example, some years ago in Sydney I conducted a study in which I asked all seventh grade children in one school their general impressions of people from different countries. The school was in an area inhabited by many Italian immigrants. Anglo-Australian students frequently commented, 'They're always abrupt', 'they're always shouting', 'they're always wearing black'. (Actually, only a **few** women dressed in black came to pick up their children from school daily, but not only were they more noticed than those dressed like the mainstream, but their frequency of occurrence was also grossly misjudged. ('Does anyone notice a basis for stereotyping here?')

Tendency for perceptual consistency. Another sad but true feature of person perception is that we base our first impressions of others—say of a new culture—on very limited information, but once these impressions are formed they are very difficult to change because of our tendency for perceptual consistency. And if these first impressions include the initial perception of differences, we're in for trouble. For example, in the Sydney study I just mentioned I asked students, 'Have you ever met or spoken with someone from another country? If so, what were your impressions and why?' It is interesting to contrast these **specific** impressions of people they had met with the **general** impressions mentioned earlier.

First, students made three times as many negative comments about foreign people in general as they did about those they had met. Second, even a positive experience with and impression of a **specific** person did not alter the same student's general **negative** impression or frame of reference in many cases This points to the importance of establishing positive first impressions and an **initial** focus on similarity so that a positive frame of reference may be formed.

If the normal process of perception **automatically** provides an obstacle or interference to second culture acquisition, then we must **deliberately** devise methods to intervene, just as we deliberately treat areas of linguistic interference, especially with adult second language learners. However, the **treatment** for what I shall call **cultural interference** due to mismatching perceptual cues is quite different from **linguistic interference**. To counter the normal perceptual bias which accounts for much cultural interference, three strategies are useful:

(1) Actively look for similarities as an initial point of departure. While looking for similarities may sound trivial, it is a critical point of departure in order to counter the perceptual bias of exaggerating differences. The latter differences result in negative first impressions, which lead to false stereotypes. (While living abroad I have frequently caught myself taking pictures of the folkloric and exotic, people with painted faces or colorful costumes, rather than of the typical. How many of you are guilty of the same? However, this is **only the beginning**—an important point of departure, because **we must deal with the differences which are causing the obstruction.**

(2) Empathy/Similarity through analogy: A search for the similarity beneath the difference. A productive approach to understanding the differences is through **analogy**. In other words, ask students to look at the difference and through analogy find something that is similar to themselves or their cultures. For example, if one is presenting the different forms of housing in Spanish speaking countries, or the role of family unit, and how they differ from our own, it is also important to focus on how they are similar, e.g. how they serve similar functions. I am **not** suggesting singing a joint chorus of 'It's a small world after all'. Indeed, the differences are very real, even if greatly exaggerated. What I **am** suggesting is a **deliberate search** for the similarity beneath the difference—what I call **'similarity through analogy'**. When confronting false stereotypes, the same strategy is useful, particularly when empathy is stimulated. For example, during one discussion of cultural differences in a language program, students perceived speakers of the language to be 'defensive'. For homework students were assigned to complete the following, referring to themselves: 'I felt defensive when . . .', 'I felt angry when . . .' In developing social studies courses, Bruner and associates found that the stimulation of emotion was a useful means of decreasing prejudice of children towards the Eskimos.

By concentrating on the information-giving aspects of films on the Eskimos, prejudice increased, but by encouraging children to try to understand the feelings, they decreased the danger of prejudice.

(3) Use of ethnography. A third useful technique for helping students to counter automatic perceptual biases and develop positive perceptions of others is by doing an ethnographic-type interview. Very simply stated, an ethnographic interview is an interview in which the interviewer tries to elicit the feelings and experiences of the interviewee. It's unlike a typical news reporter interview in that the questions are not pre-planned, and they are deliberately open. After beginning with a general question, 'How does it feel to . . .', each subsequent question builds directly upon what the interviewee has said. An ethnographic interview is more akin to the psychological counselling interview than say, to a news reporter's questions. After the interviewee responds, the ethnographic interviewer continually probes, 'What do you mean?' The goal is to find out the natural categories of meaning within the interviewee rather than through pre-conceived questions of the interviewer. An ethnographic interview typically takes place over a minimum of several days. The process of conducting the interviews is valuable as a direct means of breaking down cultural barriers for at least five reasons:

(1) the commitment of time on the part of both the ethnographer and informant(s);
(2) the depth of discussion or observations related to a particular topic;
(3) the need for creative listening;
(4) the self-awareness of one's own communication style and one's own culture; and

(5) the role of being a participant as well as an observer, and thereby sharing part of the target cultural experience (Robinson 1988:81).

At the National Foreign Language Resource Center, San Diego State University, we are currently evaluating the effects of ethnography on student attitudes towards Spanish speakers. The study is being conducted with third semester students of Spanish.

In summary, we have seen that perceptual errors or biases play a large part in inhibiting cultural acquisition and we have seen a few strategies for creating deliberate positive perceptions of the second culture instead of automatic negative ones. I have elaborated other strategies to counter such psychological biases elsewhere (Robinson 1988).

However, many cultural differences are **not** the results of skewed perceptions, but of accurately perceived differences, such as communication style differences. Communication style differences in the areas of paralinguistics, body language, and pragmatics are gaining credibility as important areas of study for the culturally-oriented language classroom. While these type of differences and associated negative attitudes are more easily remedied than those derived from psychology biases, the remedy also lies in acquiring part of the second culture, in developing cultural versatility—in developing new skills—rather than in acquiring knowledge 'about' the differences. I have reported strategies for developing cultural diverse speech styles in Rivers 1987, Chapter 11.

Conclusion. In conclusion, if our goal is to open the door to other cultures in order to promote positive interaction, it seems time to revamp our language curricula to include second culture acquisition. We will need to replace traditional views of culture as knowledge with views of culture acquisition as the development of cultural versatility. The way students respond to cultural objectives will be different. A symbolic view of culture suggests that students will then be seeing 'the color purple' in response to instruction.

We will need to use new, special strategies to counter normal cognitive errors which cause learners to focus on exaggerated differences. Examples of new strategies include deliberately searching for similarities, developing empathy through analogy, and using ethnographic techniques.

In closing, it may be time to abandon old cliché s such as, 'Let's see it through their eyes'. It is time to realize that opening the door to another culture for the purpose of promoting positive interaction means developing cultural versatility: acquiring the skills and perceptions of the second culture, to the extent possible. Thank you.

Selected References

Dolgin, J., D. Kemnitzer, and D. Schneider, eds. 1977. Symbolic anthropology. New York: Columbia University Press.
Geertz, Clifford. 1973. Interpretation of culture. New York: Basic Books.
Nocon, Honorine D. 1991. Attitudes and motivation of beginning students of Spanish at a border university. San Diego State University.
Robinson, Gail L. 1988. Crosscultural understanding: Processes and approaches for FL, ESL, and bilingual educators. New York: Prentice Hall International.
Robinson, Gail L. 1987. Culturally diverse speech styles. In: Wilga Rivers, ed. Interactive language teaching. New York: Cambridge University Press.
Robinson, Gail L. 1981. Issues in second language and crosscultural education. Boston: Heinle & Heinle.
Robinson, Gail L. 1978. The magic-carpet ride to another culture syndrome: An international perspective. Foreign Language Annals. New York. April.
Tucker, G. R., and A. d'Anglejan. 1973. Cognitive and attitudinal consequences of bilingual schooling: The St. Lambert project through grade five. Journal of Educational Psychology. 65 (2):141-159.

Dangerous liaisons:
Pitfalls in second language reading research

Sandra Silberstein*
University of Washington

Disclaiming the detached perspective of the critical outsider, this paper explores issues in second language reading research from the perspective of the uncomfortable, committed participant. The discussion examines current techniques for gauging reading comprehension, noting the pitfalls and promise of each. Using Japanese language research as an example, we find that the issues raised become more interesting and vexing in the context of comparative research across languages.

How does one evaluate reading, particularly across languages? In a research context, time limitations and demands for comparability often lead by default to reading assessment procedures that parallel general approaches to the testing of reading. Perhaps the most widely used format in language testing is the multiple-choice. Its advantages are obvious and explain the ubiquity of such tests. Students (and researchers) worldwide are accustomed to them; they are easy to score (they have near perfect reliability with a single nonnative scorer); and it is sometimes claimed that cleverly constructed distractors can show where a reader went astray. So-called main idea distractors, for example, can be written to reflect readings that are too narrow, too broad, or incorrect.

What are the disadvantages? The most obvious are the questionable assumptions on which the multiple-choice format rests: that reading is an isolated skill which can be assessed using individual items, and that it is possible to know what these items test. This weakness arguably obtains for short-answer tests as well. Reviewing the literature and his own research, Alderson (1990) tentatively concludes that judges disagree when asked what particular reading items test; moreover, there appears to be a lack of relationship between what an item is claimed to be testing and its difficulty and discrimination.

---

* My thanks to J. Charles Alderson, Clifford Hill, and Kate Parry for allowing me to cite forthcoming work; to Hiskao Kikuchi and John Treat for consulting on Japanese language issues; and to colleagues Anne Doyle, Juan Guerra, David Moore, and Kathryn Shanley for comments on an earlier draft.

A final difficulty lies with the format itself. Notwithstanding 'the limits of authenticity in language testing' (Spolsky, 1985; see also Hughes and Porter, 1985), one cannot help but notice that multiple-choice items present post facto tasks seldom resembling anything that a real reader might do with a real text. (We do not typically finish reading a passage to discover that we have developed questions for which there are always four plausible responses.) For cross-linguistic research, the problems multiply.

These problems most recently confronted me in research designed to compare reading and writing interactions in first and second language (Carson et al. 1990a, 1990b). Our goal was to develop comparable reading and writing tasks across several languages. In this context, the limitations of the multiple-choice format seemed insuperable. If one wants to create comparable tasks in several languages, who will create the questions for these passages? Who will translate them? Few researchers possess native-speaker intuitions in more than two languages. Moreover, the very existence of comparative rhetorics suggests that multiple-choice tasks may not be comparable across languages.

Examining what might be regarded as the other end of a spectrum, recalls present another means of gauging reading comprehension. In a typical variant of this format, students are asked to recall what they have read. An advantage is that, in some sense, students define the reading task, recounting what they have gained from a text. However, it is possible to exaggerate claims of authenticity for the recall format. The uncontextualized test setting does not provide current and prior contexts in which to read; it is difficult to develop realistic reading goals in a contrived test setting. We assume that readers in authentic contexts recall what is interesting and important to them as social beings. The typical research setting, particularly when testing large numbers of readers across languages, presents no social or intellectual context. Consider the authenticity of reading goals typically demanded in recalls: 'Remember all you can about this text and tell us about it without reference to the passage.'

When working across languages, recalls present additional problems: Who will administer the recalls in diverse settings? Who will translate the responses? Who will score them? What would be the reliability of this format across, and even within, languages? Again, the problems seem insurmountable.

Finally, the cloze format appears both promising and vexing. In its requirement that students reconstruct gapped texts, the cloze procedure has the advantage that it intervenes in the reading process, testing during, not after, the fact. In contrast to the multiple-choice format, cloze passages are relatively easy to construct (in some languages), and seem comparable. Their scoring presents far fewer challenges to reliability than that of recalls.

The literature on cloze testing remains inconclusive. Some researchers counsel caution. Alderson (1979) claims that changing the deletion rate or the scoring procedure, or using a different text may result in a substantially different test. Klein-Braley (1983) provides additional evidence to suggest that all cloze tests are not parallel. Johnson (1982:64) agrees with Alderson (1979) that the cloze procedure tests rather 'low order' or 'core' elements of language (e.g., grammar and vocabulary) rather than 'higher order' skills such as reading comprehension. Most recently, Grabe and Vigueiredo (1991) wonder whether, in its demand for language production, the second language cloze test may go beyond reading to test overall language proficiency.

There are, however, alternative voices. A recent defense of cloze testing, for example, is presented by Jon Jonz (1990). His paper, winner of the 1991 Newbury House Distinguished Research Award, reports a more promising study, arguing that the fixed-rate cloze procedure has a high rate of sensitivity to intersentential ties and lexical selections and that the kinds of language knowledge required to complete cloze tests are virtually the same from one test to the next. For her population, Bensoussan (1984) found that cloze and multiple-choice formats yielded similar results. Similarly, Pike (1979:77) found the cloze procedure 'performed very satisfactorily' in estimating performance on a reading comprehension multiple-choice criterion measure. In the context of Grabe and Vigueiredo's (1991) observations, researchers may want to restrict cloze to students above a threshold of language proficiency; nonetheless, as a response to the deficiencies of other reading comprehension measures, the cloze procedure remains intriguing.

However, application of the cloze procedure across languages presents substantial challenges. For the reading-writing interaction studies (Carson et al. 1990a, 1990b), I was charged with generating and interpreting the Japanese language data. To guarantee comparability with other language tests, we sought a random, that is, fixed-rate deletion pattern. It proves a straight-forward task to delete every seventh word in languages where linguistic and orthographic words correspond. However, the Japanese orthographic system marks clausal (and sometimes phrasal) but not lexical boundaries; that is, there is no tradition of word boundaries in orthographic convention. This issue is typically ignored in the literature. In a cross-linguistic study of cloze in English, Swedish, and Japanese, for example, Grundin et al. (1978:51) state only that 'cloze tests were prepared according to established principles'.

One approach to constructing a Japanese cloze passage is to count and delete what might be termed semantically loaded morphemes. This often produces a unit suspiciously similar to an English word. The level of judgment involved in identifying semantic units can suggest a procedure reminiscent of a rational-deletion test. I have found only one alternative, suggested by an expert in Japanese language instruction (J. Treat, personal communication). He notes that romanized Japanese language texts adopt a common convention: Nominals, verbals, and particles are grouped together. What would be, for example, a four-word string in English (*would have been going*) is coded as a single linguistic unit. For purposes of consistency, we settled on this scheme for counting and deleting Japanese 'words'.

Although I was worried that students would be unable to reconstruct texts containing such long and substantial gaps, Japanese subjects consistently scored highest on the cloze tests (Carson et al. 1990b). Scoring exact responses only, the mean percent correct was 62% for Japanese, compared with 21% correct for Chinese speakers, and 58% for Spanish speakers. Using an acceptable scoring procedure, those figures jumped to 92% for the Japanese, 64% for the Chinese, and 71% for the Spanish speakers. These results are consistent with those of Grundin et al.: Among Japanese-, Swedish-, and English-speaking students, the Japanese students earned higher overall cloze scores. The remarkable linguistic agreement of Japanese speakers is the topic of another discussion; it suffices to say that cross-linguistic research presents many unexpected challenges and findings.

Any review of the cloze procedure highlights the need for more research. Joan Carson and I have undertaken a study designed to compare the effects of cloze and other assessment procedures on the rank ordering of Japanese and Chinese readers. We are asking students in Japan and the People's Republic of China to complete both a cloze passage and a standardized college entrance exam. It may be that 'good' reading is in some sense a language- or culture-specific notion.

The 'reading' portions of entrance exams provide representations of cultural perspectives on reading. There are some surprises in these local definitions. For example, some standard components of Japanese entrance exams which we have omitted are passages designed to test reading of non-vernacular historical forms of Japanese, the approximate equivalent of middle English, but used up until modern times. We have, however, retained questions on Japanese etymology, although these would not be included in a typical English language reading test. Entailed in our research design is the assumption that reading in all its aspects may not be culturally universal and that research on reading assessment instruments must accommodate cultural differences in the very definition of reading.

Such accommodation, however, may not solve the more fundamental issues suggested by this survey of test formats. Most contemporary approaches to testing remain perilously poor approximations of actual reading. An unexamined adoption of test formats to reading research may indeed prove a 'dangerous liaison'.

In an intriguing manuscript, *The Test at the Gate*, Clifford Hill and Kate Parry note the lack of correspondence between current models of the reading process and the types of testing formats examined here. They note the following, often unacknowledged, assumptions that underlie the construction of most reading tests, assumptions that reflect what they term an *autonomous* model of reading (following Street 1984):

(1) Each passage should be presented as an isolated and self-sufficient unit. There are no indications 'apart from the "linguistic cues"' (p. 9) to identify the kind of text presented.
(2) Tests and test takers are thought to be autonomous: Resultant test scores 'are taken as a reflection of individual abilities, unmediated by parents or teachers, home or school' (p.13).
(3) Reading is considered an autonomous skill. As Hill and Parry note, 'other qualities, such as the background knowledge that individuals have, their ability to use it in obtaining new information from text, or their capacity for remembering and using this new information are all considered irrelevant.' (p. 15).
(4) Test makers generally try to construct items 'that cannot be answered without reference to the text, even by someone who knows about the subject matter' (p. 15). Remarkably, in this model, a physicist should have little advantage confronting a test passage on physics.

Further evidence of the autonomy assumptions underlying much current testing practice is the fact that test results are assumed to be representative of an individual's ability to read diverse texts. Hill and Parry summarize: The autonomous model of literacy 'treats reading as an autonomous skill that is independent of other factors and transferable across all kinds of texts' (p.16).

In critiquing these assumptions, Hill and Parry propose what they term a *pragmatic* (highly contextualized) model of literacy, shifting attention from the physical to the 'essentially social character of text' (p. 18). They join those who argue against textual autonomy, noting that text often depends for its interpretation on oral mediation and that such interpretation is far from invariant. Moreover, 'writers do not simply refer to the world they are writing about, they associate themselves with particular communities of language users' (p. 19).

For Hill and Parry, all written discourse 'takes the form of an exchange' (p. 24) between reader and writer: 'the presumed social identity of the writer is crucial in determining how a reader responds to a text;

and so, of course, is the social identity that readers construct for themselves' (p. 24). Hill and Parry develop a model of reading as a reciprocal exchange in which readers also construct themselves as writers. 'In constructing the author's identity. . . readers must view the text in a social context, as embodying some kind of social purpose' (p. 28), for example, to inform rather than to persuade.

Note how widely this social, contextual model of reading diverges from a testing model in which the reading of autonomous passages is assumed to represent the complete repertoire of autonomous readers. Hill and Parry's work challenges us to seek assessment procedures consistent with a pragmatic model of literacy. Responses to this challenge remain elusive.

It would be seductive to close this discussion in the form of a challenge. I could note that, in keeping with contemporary models of the reading process, readers will have constructed an identity and point of view for me. Readers should now be able to imagine the sorts of solutions I might find plausible. This paper, thus ended, is a test.

However tempting this witty evasion, further exploration is in order. Min-imally, the foregoing discussion should provide questions that can define a research agenda:

(1) Is there a difference between research on the reading process (how individuals read texts and tests) and research designed to gauge whether one has read successfully? Qualitative research may be necessary to further explore the reading process. Can qualitative insights usefully inform the development of large-scale, cross-linguistic assessment measures that are both practical and economical?
(2) To what extent does the dynamic nature of contemporary research on reading and testing recommend the use of multiple formats for reading assessment? Researchers might use multiple testing instru-ments and/or multiple formats within a single test.
(3) To what extent can/should test formats be made authentic?
(4) Is reading both a universal cognitive process and a social, locally defined practice? If both, can we capture the contextualized, social nature of reading in a test setting?

There have been some interesting attempts to define reading test formats in terms of the issues raised here. Swaffer et al. (1991:154) argue for formats that are reader- rather than text-based, diagnosing 'not only test-based products, but reader-based processing'. As such, their discussion focusses on assessment tools that interrogate students' abilities to draw meaning from texts as individual readers in a social context. Arens et al. argue for tests that reveal how readers 'connect text meaning' (p. 171). In their scheme, reading tests should:

(1) Assess student schemata as a factor in test selection;
(2) include items that reveal a grasp of intersentential links;
(3) enable students to demonstrate their view of textual organization;
(4) if feasible, allow some reader conceptualization of text meaning in the native language;
(5) ascertain the reasoning behind a student's conclusions;
(6) enable students to demonstrate a grasp of the text's cultural and authorial characteristics (pp. 154-156).

A full discussion of specific test formats is presented in Arens et al. (1990). Additionally relevant for our purposes is their suggestion that test formats should provide 'flexibiity in acknowledging individual interpretations' (p. 159).

Appealing as is the Arens et al. discussion, we are again reminded by Alderson's research (1990, in press) that appealing models of the reading/ testing process do not guarantee that we know what individual items actually test. Ultimately, a serviceable testing taxonomy must be grounded in empirically determined function rather in than functional asssumptions. Alderson (in press) offers an intriquing route to assess our tests. He suggests qualitative research using two different forms of test-taker self-observation: introspective ('concurrent', 'think aloud' [p. 4] formats) and retrospective (based on interviews) and aptly characterizes of our research needs:

> What a reading test tests is not simply what its constructors say it tests, nor what a set of judges considers it to test. It must surely and crucially relate to what happens inside a test-taker's head when he or she responds to an item. Finding out that information, and discovering how generalizable the results are, is a neglected but important research endeavour.

The most optimistic assumptions concerning our understanding of the assessment process will likely not be supported as testing research matures. In the current context, special caution will be required of many in second language reading research.

Selected References

Alderson, J. C. 1979. The cloze procedure and proficiency of English as a foreign language. TESOL Quarterly. 13:219-226.

Alderson, J.C. 1990. Testing reading comprehension skills, part one. Reading in a foreign language. 6:425-438.

Alderson, J.C. In press. Testing reading comprehension skills, part two: Test-taker's accounts. Reading in a foreign language. 7.

Alderson, J.C., and Y. Lukmani. 1989. Cognition and reading: Cognitive levels as embodied in test questions. Reading in a foreign language. 5:253-270.

Bensoussan, M. 1984. A comparison of cloze and multiple-choice reading comprehension tests of English as a foreign language. Language Testing. 1:101-104.

Carson, J.E., P. L. Carrell, S. Silberstein, B. Kroll, and, P. A. Kuehn. 1990a. Reading-writing relationships in first and second language. TESOL Quarterly. 24:245-266.

Carson, J.G., P. L. Carrell, S. Silberstein, B. Kroll, and P. A. Kuehn. 1990b. The transfer of literacy skills across and within languages. Paper presented at the 24th Annual TESOL Convention, San Francisco, Calif.

Grabe, W., and M. B. Vigueiredo. 1991. Learning to read in Portuguese: An introspective case study. Paper presented at the 25th Annual TESOL Convention, New York.

Grundin, H.U., Br. L. Courtney, J. Langer, R. Pehrsson, H. A. Robinson, and T. Sakamoto. 1978. Cloze procedure and comprehension: An exploratory study across three languages. 48-60. In: D. Feitelson, ed., Cross-cultural perspectives on reading and reading research. Newark, Del.: International Reading Association.

Hill, C., and K. Parry. 1990. The test at the gate: International perspectives on literacy assessment. Manuscript submitted for publication.

Hughes, A., and D. Porter, eds. 1985. Authenticity in language testing [Special issue]. Language Testing, 2.

Johnson, R. K. 1982. Questioning some assumptions about cloze testing. In: J.B. Heaton, ed. Language testing. 59-72. Modern English Publications.

Jonz, J. 1990. Another turn in the conversation: What does cloze measure? TESOL Quarterly. 24:61-83.

Klein-Braley, C. 1983. A cloze is a cloze is a question. In: J.W. Oller, Jr. ed., Issues in language testing research. 218-228. Rowley, Mass.: Newbury House.

Pike, L. W. 1979. An evaluation of alternative item formats for testing English as a foreign language Report No. TOEFL-RR-2. Princeton, N. J.: Educational Testing Service. ERIC Document Reproduction Service No. ED 206 627.

Spolsky, B. 1985. The limits of authenticity in language testing. Language Testing, 2, 31-40.

Street, B. V. 1984. Literacy in theory and practice. New York: Cambridge University Press.

Swaffer, J.K., K. M. Arens, and H. Byrnes. 1991. Reading for meaning: An integrated approach to language learning. Englewood Cliffs, N. J.: Prentice Hall.

A pedagogy of corporate-level ESP training for international scientists and engineers

Sandra C. Browne*
Language Consultant

Overview. The teaching of English as a second language to research scientists and engineers in international corporations requires a task-based pedagogy which takes into account the high intellectual skills and strong learning abilities of the clientele. The paper discusses the role of the language consultant, outlines a pedagogy for language instruction, and suggests topics and materials for English for Special Purposes in the corporate setting.

In the past ten years some U.S. corporations, particularly those with research and development staffs, have instituted in-house English language programs for their international employees. While good progress has been and is being made in the development of such programs, it is clear that more U.S. corporations will need to institute their own English language training programs in order to remain competitive.

One of the most fundamental challenges of corporate-level language work is convincing upper management that significant benefits will accrue to the company through improving international employees' communicative competence in English.

In the corporate world of the United States, two negative factors contribute to a general lack of attention to the language problems of international employees who communicate poorly in English: (1) accom-modation to the international speaker's accent and language use on the part of supervisors and department heads, which in turn contributes to (2) the employee's lack of motivation to improve his or her English communication skills.

From the point of view of the language expert, the linguistic problems encountered are serious deterrents to effective communication which merit attention. In the corporate arena, however, language training

---

* My thanks to Joan Morley and Fred Lupke for their comments and suggestions regarding the content of this paper and to Richmond Browne for his editing. The opinions and suggestions put forth are, of course, my own.

is not high on the list of priorities. The relationship between the ability to communicate well in English and better transfer of technological information, improved product design, and more successful marketing is not immediately obvious to many company directors.

However, once language training has been agreed upon, management expectations for improvement are often very high. The language consultant must, therefore, demonstrate efficiency, clarity of purpose, and a logical approach to the language training process from the outset.

Applied linguistics in the service of pedagogy is a useful motto here. It means that the teaching of English as a Second Language to professional scientists and engineers requires analytical skills, based upon linguistic principles, in combination with a focused approach to the art of teaching.

The pedagogy described in this paper is based on an English for Specific Purposes (ESP) approach and is based on a two-pronged needs analysis: the corporate career-specific language requirements and the person-specific speech communication needs of the individual.

The language consultant: 'teacher' or 'trainer?' In the corporate milieu, part of the job of the language consultant is to convince management that the expertise being provided requires a rather sophisticated linguistic background. At this level of English language instruction what constitutes *teaching English* is more appropriately termed *language training* or *coaching*.

It is important to the profession that consultants in English for Specific Purposes (ESP) who work in American corporate environments clarify this specialized use of terminology to their clientele. *Language teaching* implies no prior knowledge on the part of the student or client and is often termed *remedial* in business settings. *Language training* implies the augmenting of given knowledge and fits better with the international client's own view of his English language proficiency.

Labels aside, the point I hope to have made here is that the pedagogy required to improve the English language performance of international speakers of English in the corporate world should be based upon careful analysis of task-based language function in the workplace.

Pedagogy in the corporate world. In designing an ESP pedagogy for the corporate world, the language consultant must consider the results the company expects the training to achieve. Both written and oral English skills are of major concern—with oral skills often primary.

Most of the information used for corporate decision making is, both initially and finally, oral. The process of decision making moves from group discussion of how a problem is to be investigated, through the research and development stages, to a formal written report, followed by an oral presentation to management of the process and the results.

The consultant/trainer therefore needs to build a program which will address both the English language performance skills the corporation requires and the current English language skills deficits of the research scientists and engineers who work for the corporation.

In designing a program for this situation, the consultant should consider two factors: (1) what level of language proficiency is sufficient for a given corporate position, and (2) what rhetorical skills are necessary to satisfactory job performance.

The first factor, level of language proficiency for a given corporate level, concerns the language needs of the client in the work environment. Not all researchers or engineers have to worry about interviews with the press or teleconferencing, for example, but some do.

The second factor, rhetorical skills, includes formal oral presentations and written reports, informal speech at group meetings, informal in-house memoranda, calls for papers and/or abstracts for professional conferences, professional review of colleagues' scientific papers, monthly summary reports to managers, and press interviews and teleconferences.

English for academic purposes and English for special purposes. Unlike academia, where the focus is on educating the student—a pedagogical approach which centers around new vs. old information—in the corporate world, the factors discussed above require a task-based pedagogy based upon the needs of the corporation.

Further, if the program is an in-house program, the consultant is sponsored by the corporation, not the client. Thus the training must focus on those language skills necessary for better communication within the company.

Designing a task-based pedagogy which meets the functional criteria of management, the employees, and the consultant is not a task to be undertaken by the faint of heart. The challenge involves more than a thorough knowledge of English grammar, as many academics turned 'consultant' have discovered. As Robert Kaplan recently said, 'what you have to be really good at is framing a problem and demonstrating problem-solving skills'[1]

The international English-speaking research scientists and engineers who choose to participate in English language training at this level of

---

[1] This is one of Robert Kaplan's seven axioms 'On the fine art of consultin', delivered as part of the 'Colloquium on consulting in ESL', TESOL, 1990, San Francisco. Other panel consultants were William Action, Sandra Browne, Ann Cessaris, and Adrian Pilbeam.

their careers expect a pedagogy designed to improve their language performance in specific ways. They view the language consultant as a trainer who will teach them those English language skills which will be readily perceived by their immediate supervisors as improved performance skills and will lead to better job evaluations and greater career success.

The pedagogical approach chosen should, then, be responsive to such basic issues as the status of the consultant vis-à-vis both management and the prospective client.

Requirements of the language pedagogy. In the corporate world of the United States, language training is largely, and falsely, viewed as remedial. Therefore, the pedagogy chosen must be able to satisfy the following requirements: (1) documented improvement in English language skills, (2) client satisfaction with the program, (3) management and client approval of the consultant's expertise, and (4) cost/benefit factors.

(1) Documented improvement. Management needs to be shown examples of problem-solving approaches that are effective and efficient. For oral skills, 'before' and 'after' videos work well. For written skills, documentation of im-proved writing skills over time is helpful.

(2) Client satisfaction. International clients become impatient if the trainer is unclear in purpose or if the materials are poorly chosen. In general, clients' language goals are quite specific, though often stated in a somewhat negative way. For example, many clients believe the myth that pronunciation cannot be changed after the age of nine or that they are too old to learn how to change the mechanics of sentence structure in English. They want to be shown that they are not wasting their time.

The language consultant must be able to be successful in demonstrating to the client that the pedagogical approach in use is appropriate to the task at hand.

(3) Consultant expertise. To management, the relation between the professional linguistic insights of the language consultant and improved communication in the workplace is often hard to discern. Thus the consultant must work to sustain a good reputation. This means that references, outside publications, and especially evaluations from clients are important.

(4) Cost benefit. U.S. corporations are discovering that it is very expensive to hire a Ph.D. engineer who speaks English as a second language only to find that the person does not have the language skills necessary to advancement within the corporation.

The cost vs. benefit issue must be posed, in this setting, as one of long-term value to the corporation. Management needs to be assured that their investment in English language training will ultimately save the corporation both time and money.

Program design which takes into account these four requirements will enable clients, management and the consultant to justify continued support for a successful language training program.

Designing task-based programs. Because the major audience for this paper is concerned with pedagogy in the field of applied linguistics in academia, it might be useful to point out some important differences between designing task-based programs in English for academic purposes and designing them for corporate use.

In corporate language training, one can operate in a less restricted atmosphere than at a college or university because of the following factors:

1. The pedagogical design can be flexible in time frame and the number of clients.
2. Program content can be individually designed to suit the language needs of the client.
3. Evaluation depends upon performance in the real world rather than upon academic success.

In the corporate world, these differences can be marketed as advantages for everyone. Program design, in particular, can be tailored to the needs of the individual client.

Individual task-based tutorials. Language skills even as disparate as pronunciation and the linguistic editing of written material are often better suited to individual tutoring than to a classroom or seminar approach.

The conduct of the tutorial can and should reflect a pedagogical style which is comfortable for both the tutor and the client. In the sample procedure which follows, the English language training is designed to mimic that of professional coaching in music or sports. The focus is to build upon the existing skills and knowledge of the client.

In a one-to-one tutorial session it is useful to have a researcher or engineer bring in material in progress. Here is a seven-step sample procedure for a one hour tutorial:

1. Client brings in draft of written material.
2. Tutor makes a photocopy of the material.

3. Client reads the material into a tape recorder.
4. Tutor listens and notes prosodic, grammatical, and rhetorical problems, marking them on the photocopy.
5. Joint aural review of the tape follows, using the tutor's marked copy for reference.
6. Summary of the most important linguistic points; demonstration of prosodic features (pronunciation, rhythm, intonation); explication of grammatical problems (article usage, verb tenses, prepositions, etc.); discussion of appropriate rhetorical style for the material
7. Assignment of follow-up material based upon the client's immediate needs.

A similar procedure can be used for rehearsals of oral presentations, videotaping the client and ajusting the critique to matters of oral rhetoric and visual presentation skills.

A caution is in order with regard to videotaping. Since much of the material in a corporate research environment is restricted or confidential, it is important that the consultant assure management and the client of the confidentiality of this procedure. If the corporation is large enough, the consultant can voluntarily become a 'dedicated consultant,' i.e. one who does not contract out work with other firms. If this is not the case, some form of consent agreement should be initiated by the consultant.

Language consultant expertise and linguistic training. Ideally, the education needed to provide the consultant with the necessary background to create a task-based pedagogy in the corporate world is one which includes solid training in articulatory and acoustic phonetics and in the phonology of the English language, some familiarity with the sound systems of the major languages of the world, a good understanding of the morphology and grammar of the English language, knowledge of rhetorical styles (both oral and written), some background in theories of adult second language acquisition and teaching methodologies, and several years of language teaching experience.

The ability to speak other languages well also contributes positively to the consultant's image as a professional. Few businessmen know the distinction between an linguist and a polyglot. To them, a linguist is someone who speaks a lot of languages, not someone who analyzes the structure(s) and function(s) of language(s).

From the corporate point of view, the language consultant should be able to provide international clients with the best materials and advice available in order that they achieve improved English language performance in those areas important to professional development. In a research situation, this includes improving the ability to represent the corporation at outside conferences and professional meetings.

To provide clients with the range of language training needed also requires a somewhat special set of materials and equipment. For the individual tutorials, dual track audio tape recorders, video equipment, and a computerized speech training system are recommended.

Because the computerized speech training system I use is not widely known among applied linguists, a brief technical description follows.

The Video Voice Speech Training System. Video Voice is a combination of specialized hardware and computer software which uses a patented speech analyzer to sample voice frequency data and input it to a computer.[2]

Using low-pass filter chips, the analyzer produces four voltage signals which are proportional to the following speech characteristics: (1) pitch (20-480 HZ), (2) intensity, (3) Formant 1 (20-750 HZ), and (4) Formant 2 (750-2,800 HZ).

The output can be displayed in a variety of ways on a color monitor.

What is special about this speech analyzer system is that the software includes a template for American English Vowel sounds which allows the tutor and the client to model vowel sounds. To work on /iy/ and /I/, for example, a menu might have high frequency vocabulary items taken from the client's professional work, a set of minimal pairs constructed by the language consultant, or a mix of items. This template is not available on any of the other speech analyzers currently on the market.

Using a speech analyser to improve spoken English. A speech analyzer system is especially useful in identifying overlapping vowel articulations. For example, Mandarin Chinese speakers often have difficulty with the words *man* and *men*, substituting their own centralized and somewhat raised vowel (See Maddieson 1986:346). The ability to see what they say helps clients to accurately target these and other American English vowel sounds.

Most speech analyzers plot pitch across time to provide live visual feedback on rhythm and speech rate. This type of display is also useful for work on American English consonant clusters and linking across word boundaries. Used together with Morley's and Dauer's prosodic materials, rapid improvement in connected speech can be made (See Morley 1979, 1991; Dauer, forthcoming)

---

[2] Video Voice Speech Training System is marketed by Micro Video, P.O. Box 7357, Ann Arbor MI 48107.

For example, visual feedback can be used to show a Farsi speaker how to eliminate a neutral vowel before English words beginning with /s/. The tutor can ask the client to model his speech and then demonstrate how to link the final consonant or vowel of the preceding syllable to the /s/. This changes a phrase like *in-situ* estudies and *Raman* espectroscopy to *in-situ studies* and *Raman spectroscopy*.

The speech analyzer amplitude display plots intensity data over time and is appropriate for problems involving syllable stress. For example, one Gujarati speaker was having trouble with polysyllabic English words which had second syllable accent like *constituent, alternative,* and *miraculous*. After ten trials per tutorial session over a period of a few weeks, the speaker was able to produce an appropriate English syllable accent for these words and others of the same pattern.

A speech analyzer pitch display is useful for intonation practice with *Wh-* and *Yes-No*-questions, tag questions, and general practice in widening a speaker's pitch range. For instance, Hindi speakers often use a pitch rise at the end of every phrase group, producing a lilting, somewhat sing-song effect which can interfere with the listener's attempts to parse what is being said. Again, visualization of what is being produced, together with oral training, can be productive.

Speech therapists have used this type of equipment for some time in dealing with pathological speech problems. Applied linguists should consider adapting this technology for language training.

English language training in the corporate world. In the American corporate world, language training does not come first. Most large companies do, however, have a professional in-house staff made up of technical writers, graphic artists, photographers, and video specialists who write, design, and produce newsletters and reports of various types.

Within some corporations, the technical writing instructor teaches a course on how to write in the company style. These classes are generally taught from the point of view of English as a first language and thus gram-matical and rhetorical problems stemming from a non-native English language background are necessarily given minimal attention.

Since most technical writers are not trained in ESL or linguistics, it is therefore not surprising that their writing classes are oriented to the problems of Americans whose first (and most often only) language is English.

However, as John Swales has recently noted, with the increasing number of Ph.D. engineers who speak English as a second language now working for U.S. corporations, the problems of writing and speaking in English have come to require advanced English language training within an ESP framework (See Swales 1991:75).

It is in the interest of international employees and management for the language consultant to point out that a trained linguist can help the company's international employees improve their written English skills through examination of each client's rhetorical skills.

ESP grammar workshops. Having described a tutorial procedure for integrating English speaking and writing skills, I would like to outline a pedagogy for workshop/seminars on a few specific problem areas of English, some of which I have outlined elsewhere (Browne 1987).

ESL professionals know well that there are certain grammatical areas of the English language which pose problems for nearly all speakers of English as a second language.

The list of items varies, depending upon the level of English skills already acquired. At an advanced level, however, the list usually includes the use of the English article system, the meaning and function of modals and conditionals, and two-part verbs, idioms and prepositions.

Finding this to be true of the international professionals I work with, I have designed three workshops to address these topics.

The format for each of the workshops is the same:

1. One and one-half hour workshops once a week for a period of 8 weeks (12 contact hours),
2. A reference grammar and course pack materials,
3. A seminar style room set-up with video camera and VCR, overhead projector and audio tape recorder for taping client presentations
4. Limited class size (10 to 12 participants).

Participants in the workshop are assigned a specific time slot in which they are asked to present and discuss in class samples from their own writing of the grammatical issue(s) under discussion.

This format is not particularly new. It has been around in the liberal arts areas of academia for some time, but it is not common in the sciences and engineering.

What the clients find interesting about the format is that it provides them with an excellent opportunity to investigate differences in varying language structures vis-à-vis the structures of English.

For example, a Romanian participant may enlighten the group by stating that the preposition *cu* meaning 'with' in Romanian is not used in verb plus particle expressions. That is, the preposition cannot be attached to a verb and acquire a new meaning. In Romanian, it seems, a man cannot be *bored* with his wife (although he can be *bored* about her, using the Romanian *de*).[3]

A Hindi or a Chinese participant may have differing reactions to this linguistic fact. The Hindi may be amused; the Chinese puzzled. This

---

3 My thanks to Abraham Horowitz for this example.

may be due to the fact that Hindi has prepositions in the Indo-European sense and Mandarin does not, or it may also be the result of an awakening to the fact that languages are organic entities with different lexicons and structures.

The point is that the linguistic facts of both English and the first language are important to the pedagogical necessity to explicate problems in second language acquisition. As Schacter and Celce-Murcia (1990:281-82) have suggested, a combination of contrastive analysis and error analysis may constitute a useful approach.

Occasionally, one participant in a workshop may offer an explanation of a fact about American English to another participant which, while less elegant and linguistically informed than the instructor's own, makes the point succinctly. The existence of language differences is demonstrated prima facie by these interactions and language interference needs only the gentlest mention.

From a pedagogical point of view, the most difficult part of designing workshops on English grammar and use is limiting the scope of the problems addressed.

In dealing with the English article system, Huckin and Olsen (1983) provide a good starting point. Their two chapters on articles are designed for scientists and engineers who speak English as a second language. Huckin's flow chart, in particular, serves as a useful introduction to an explication of the function of the English article system in technical writing.

For work on modals and conditionals, Azar's recent textbook (Azar 1989) provides clear and concise charts of sequence of tenses and implied meaning. The charts can be used as a base for a series of in-class oral exercises using situations common to the participants' professional lives.

Additional material culled from Leech 1987, Frank 1972, Bander 1983, and Celce-Murcia and Larsen-Freeman 1983 helps to present a useful view of how communication in English is subtly modified through tense and aspect.

Prepositions and idioms present a serious challenge to any applied linguist. Because of their morphological history, prepositions are often presented in partitioned lists (cf. Frank 1972 and Bander 1983).

Quirk, Greenbaum, Leech and Svartvik (1976) usefully define the base meanings of spatial prepositions, which are often used in technical descrip-tions. Prepositions of instrument and cause are also relatively easy to disambiguate in English. The real problem lies in the use of prepositions as particles attached to verbs, nouns, and adjectives.

The question of form and function is a particularly difficult one for those who have been taught English grammar as a set of parts of speech. Such clients often use a 'labeling response' to parsing prepositional phrases or idioms. No matter how an item functions in the phrase, it is viewed as belonging to a fixed grammatical category.

It is important to train international clients to view language as functional, i.e. that the role the item plays in the phrase is more important than the dictionary label.

To address this issue, one can begin with the base meaning of prepositions in technical writing and then move to the function of prepositions in two-part verbs, nouns, and idioms.

I have assessed my success rate in trying to prove to international scientific professionals that prepositions can function both as true prepositions with diectic meaning and as particles with little independent meaning. The success rate is variable and modest. However, for the client who gets this distinction straight a significant linguistic insight has been achieved, i.e. that in language, form and function are not always synonymous.

An important part of this training is to include social contexts in which prepositions and idioms are used in the workplace. Non-English speaking employees of international corporations are often confused and intimidated when slang and swear words are used casually in American English speech.

A classic support text for slang and swearing is Elizabeth Claire's *Dangerous English* (Claire 1986). In my workshops, selected portions of this text have become home rule guides for what the young children of the participants are and are not permitted to say. In most cases, though, learning how to respond to slang and swearing is more of an issue than learning how to use it.

A pedagogy which can successfully present the types of English language training outlined above must be carefully tailored to meet the needs of the clients. It must also be linguistically valid.

As an applied linguist working on-site in a large corporation, it is my job to provide the training outlined here and to be responsive to the changing language training needs of the research scientists and engineers who are my clients. This is a substantial pedagogical responsibility.

The language consultant's role is to provide the best explication of the linguistic facts and appropriate materials for resolving an applied linguistic problem. If the client's ability to use English more accurately and effectively to perform his professional duties is the result, then the pedagogy has been a success.

Summary. The focus of the English language training (ESP) described in this paper is to outline a pedagogy to improve research scientists' and engineers' use of American English in the international corporate world.

A model pedagogy for advanced English language training of this clientele is outlined, together with some consideration of the factors which motivate advanced English language training in this setting. Sample tutorials and workshops are described, together with hardware and software equipment, textbooks and reference materials. The content is intended to suggest ways in which a language consultant might address the issues involved.

References

Azar, Betty Schrampfer. 1989. Understanding and using English grammar. 2nd ed. Englewood Cliffs, N.J.: Prentice-Hall.
Bander, Robert G. 1983. American English rhetoric. 3rd ed. New York: Holt, Rinehart and Winston.
Browne, Sandra C., and Thomas N. Huckin. 1987. Pronunciation tutorials for nonnative technical professionals: A program description. In: Current perspectives on pronunciation: Practices anchored in theory. ed. by Joan Morley. Washington, DC: TESOL Publications.
Celce-Murcia, Marianne and Diane Larsen-Freeman. 1983. The grammar book: An ESL/EFL teacher's course. Rowley, Mass.: Newbury House.
Claire, Elizabeth. 1986. A foreign student's guide to dangerous English! Rochelle Park: Eardley Publications.
Dauer, R. M. (forthcoming). A practical guide to speaking American English, Englewood Cliffs, N.J.: Prentice-Hall.
Frank, Marcella. 1972. Modern English: A practical reference guide. Englewood Cliffs, N.J.: Prentice Hall.
Huckin, Thomas N., and Leslie A. Olsen. 1983. English for science and technology: A handbook for nonnative speakers. New York: McGraw Hill.
Kaplan, Robert B. 1990. Colloquium on consulting in ESL. San Francisco: TESOL '90.
Leech, Geoffrey N. 1987. Meaning and the English verb. 2nd ed. London: Longman.
Maddieson, Ian. 1986. Patterns of sounds. Cambridge Studies in Speech Science and Communication. Cambridge: Cambridge University Press.
Morley, Joan. 1979. Improving Spoken English. Ann Arbor: University of Michigan Press.
Morley, Joan. 1991. Improving spoken English: Consonants in context. Ann Arbor: University of Michigan Press.
Quirk, Randolph and Sidney Greenbaum, Geoffrey Leech and Jan Svartvik. 1976. A Grammar of contemporary English. 6th impression. London: Longman.
Schacter, Jacquelyn and Marianne Celce-Murcia. 1990. Some reservations concerning error analysis in second language learning. In: Contrastive analysis, error analysis, and related aspects, ed. by Betty Wallace Robinett and Jacquelyn Schacter, 272-284. Ann Arbor: University of Michigan Press.
Swales, John M. 1991. International graduate students in Anglophone research worlds. In: Rackham Reports, School of Graduate Studies, ed. by Homer C. Rose, Jr., 72-83. Ann Arbor: The University of Michigan.

Perspectives on English for academic purposes

Joan Morley
University of Michigan

1 Introductory comments. The term English for Academic Purposes (EAP) has come to be used today in the field of second language teaching as a rubric broad enough to encompass a variety of kinds of instruction. Because of this diversity, in any discussion of a particular program, it is necessary at the outset to set out some of the parameters and some of the perspectives from which the 'rubric' is approached. This, then, is the purpose of this introductory commentary.

The specialized EAP program discussed in this paper is a university program currently under development at the University of Michigan English Language Institute (ELI), an academic unit in the College of Literature, Science, and the Arts, and an independent credit-granting program since 1986. It is a program for non-native speakers of English (NNSs) in which the primary focus is on English for (Advanced) Academic Purposes (EAP), but with specialized attention to English for (Career-) Specific Purposes (ESP) as well.

Although for the most part the single term 'EAP' is used throughout the paper, the intended reference is to the dual EAP/ESP nature of the work. Our advanced students' special needs call for this EAP/ESP mix as many of them have the following 'mixed' status:

(a) enrolled graduate students pursuing master's and/or doctoral degrees,
(b) teaching assistants and /or research assistants,
(c) (and some are) practicing professionals already engaged in preparing field-specific publications and presentations.

Some of the NNS 'students' are, in fact, on leave from academic, government, or business positions in their home countries, a not unusual situation in many American graduate schools. In addition to regularly enrolled students, courtesy participation in the program's specialized courses, speaking clinic, and writing laboratory is extended to international post-doctoral students, visiting scholars, and regular faculty members, as scheduling permits.

Around ninety percent of the 650-700 course enrollments during the academic year are students at the graduate level, with the majority engaged in doctoral studies across the university's colleges and professional schools. Since the beginning, the ELI's program has focused on ways to identify and meet the needs of this particular segment of the higher education population by designing specialized courses and evaluation procedures and by undertaking relevant research relating to issues of language use, language learning processes, and effective instructional modes.

As pedagogical, assessment, and research agenda have been formulated for this special clientele, one outstanding fact has emerged: Many of these students are students who may be able to 'survive' linguistically, but who are 'at risk' as far as any chance for real 'success' is concerned in the sophisticated uses of language required for participation in the academic community. That is, they are students upon whom greater and greater second language demands are made, but for whom only minimal language attention has been provided in many American universities until relatively recently. The serious need is for specialized courses in English for academic purposes (EAP) to complement (or replace) existing general purpose English classes (often in the format of pre-matriculation intensive programs) and existing university courses (such as composition and public speaking courses intended for native speakers (NSs)).

Looking at peer institutions across the United States it becomes clear that this is a growing problem, especially in large research universities. At the same time, it is well-documented that there is an ever-increasing ascendancy of English as the world's international language of scholarship and research (Swales 1989, 1991). English is today the dominant language in science and technology, medicine and health care fields, commerce, business and industry, and much more. It should come as no shock to find that three-quarters of the world's information stored in computer banks is in English.

It will soon be the case, if indeed it is not already largely true, that the student graduating from an English-speaking university with a master's or doctoral degree who does not have a sophisticated field-specific command of English may not be fully prepared to meet the challenges of his or her profession in tomorrow's world. In point of fact, English language expertise is becoming a priority academic/professional requirement whether inter-national higher education graduates choose to return to their home countries or whether they choose to stay in the United States—and more and more students are doing just that today, moving into American university teaching and research positions and into business and industry (Huckin and Olsen 1984; Browne, in this volume). It is no longer 'enough' to equip international graduate students with general

English skills with which to survive when the need is for a high level of academic and career-specific facility with English, one that will enable them to succeed, both during their campus careers and beyond.

Another dimension in which the international graduate student may well be at risk is one that involves a *critical thinking/critical language* interface. Consider this: the average graduate student probably never will pass through any more time-compressed more critical period of intense intellectual growth in his or her lifetime. Some non-native speakers may not be able to take full advantage of this once-in-a-life-time opportunity to develop their potential—both intellectually, and linguistically in English as a medium of scholarly communication in their chosen field—unless they have sound instructional guidance in developing the breadth and depth and 'richness' of their English language use at the same time that significant conceptual development is taking place. Their chance to grow linguistically as well as intellectually is an imperative, not only in specific degree-related course work and research projects, but also in formal and informal opportunities to speak and to write in their field in English.

It is not difficult to identify international graduate students who are at risk, ones who may never be able to realize their potential to become fully participating members of the academic and professional community of their choice. And more the rule than the exception, these students do not have to be told that their language is not equal to their needs; certainly after a semester in graduate school most begin to become aware of their limitations.

In the following story insightful second language concerns are expressed by a cross-section of international graduate students.

2 Students reflect: 'On being a minority speaker of the language of the majority'. As is the case on campuses across the United States, on the third Monday in January, the University of Michigan celebrates Diversity Day as a part of a two-week commemoration that honors the life and the work of Dr. Martin Luther King. This is also a time when the University reaffirms its commitment to fostering an atmosphere of mutual respect and appreciation for all members of the University community. Each department, each unit, within the University is responsible for presenting a special program, not only for its own constituency, but for the wider academic community as well.

For Diversity Day 1991, the Program in Linguistics and the English Language Institute sponsored an open forum discussion in which panel members addressed the topic 'On Being a Minority Speaker of the Language of the Majority'. Two sub-panels approached the topic from quite different points of view. One was from the perspectives of non-native speakers of the language of the majority; one was from the perspectives of second dialect speakers, specifically, speakers of 'New Yorican' (i.e. New York Puerto Rican) and speakers of Black English.

For the NNS portion of the presentation several graduate students who were (or had been) enrolled in one or more of the EAP courses offered by the English Language Institute were invited to participate. Each represented well the special nature of our clientele.

The NNS panelists were: Antonio, a Fulbright visiting scholar and pro-fessor of Economics in Mexico City (at UM for a year and a half doing research on industrial productivity in Mexico and South Korea); Yong from Korea, a Ph. D. candidate in Political Science and International Relations (at UM for two and a half years doing research in Russian and Eastern European Studies, with an already well-established publications record); Hiro, from Japan, first year M.A. student planning to follow through to the Ph. D. program in Applied Economics; Yi Jen, from Taiwan, enrolled in a Ph. D. program in Social Work; Sergei, from Bulgaria, a doctoral student in Nuclear Engineering; Mei, from Beijing, a third-year doctoral student in Microbiology.

The topic, 'On Being a Minority Speaker of the Language of the Majority', proved to be a very provocative one; in fact, 'it hit a nerve'. The following concerns were expressed at a 'dress rehearsal' and expanded upon during the formal panel presentation and question period.

Antonio's immediate reaction to the topic was this: 'I can't control the context.' As we discussed this very insightful observation with Antonio, he appeared to mean that he didn't have the linguistic skills to 'take the floor' quickly and smoothly and politely during a professional discussion with several native speaker colleagues, and he couldn't shift the topic deftly in order to situate what he wanted to say within a context that was satisfactory to him. He felt he always had to try to find a way to bond to whatever context existed, instead of being able to create his own. As he expressed it, he felt he always had to 'run after' the conversation, 'catch it', hold it, and then try to turn it to his own advantage, a skill that native speakers use so adroitly that they usually are unaware of it.

One of Yong's concerns was also about academic conversations with colleagues in his department. He said, 'I seem to be misunderstood, and I say things that must sound angry; but I don't mean to be angry; I don't know how to control my language so that I can express my views without people walking away.'

Yi Jen opened her comments with this: 'I can't write what I want to mean and have it come out right—and I don't want my professor rewriting my reports and my articles; I want to be able to write them myself; I have to publish in English, even right now.'

From Hiro came: 'People don't seem to take my views seriously— and I'm a little bit hurt inside, and sometimes I'm a little bit angry and I don't know how to express my views so that they'll take me seriously.'

Sergei said, 'My big problem in discussion is really two problems: to keep going with the ideas I want to express and to find the language I need.' It turns out that what he seemed to mean was his difficulty in juggling both the ongoing planning and structuring of language with its central focus on the intellectual content, and at the same time the struggle to find appropriate words, grammatical phrase structuring, effective use of stress and intonation.

Mei expressed her lack of confidence in 'public' speaking: 'I can talk all right with the professor and the other students before the seminar begins, but then during the actual class, I get so nervous and my heart beats so fast that I'm even afraid to raise my hand.'

Initially it may have seemed to the audience, to any casual listener, that these speakers were so skilled in using English as a second language (in this generalist setting) that they were beyond—some of them far beyond—any need for English language instruction of any kind. But the very linguistic and communicative concerns they expressed soon dispelled any notion that they were not prime candidates for continued, and, in fact, specialized attention to the development of sophisticated language uses within the demanding intelle-tual situation in which they find themselves immersed.

These revealing Diversity Day introspections about language limitation and its affective and intellectual dimensions are only 'local' anecdotes. But nationwide there is growing evidence, especially at large research universities, that more and more demands are being made on students in graduate studies for sophisticated writing skills and sophisticated oral communication skills. For example, the graduate student newsletter of the University of Michigan Rackham School of Graduate Studies solicits and publishes in each issue a listing of graduate student publications and presentations. They note: 'We want to publish the major honors and prizes you attain, as well as your professional presentations and publications.' (*Rackham Graduate Student Newsletter*, University of Michigan, Ann Arbor: Winter, 1991).

In addition, most departments and other academic units also routinely publish lists of the scholarly activities of their graduate students. Competition for establishing a publications and presentations record is a fact of life, not only after graduation but before, a competition that clearly disadvantages those international students whose language skills have limitations.

Moreover, there is every indication that graduate students are going to continue to meet these kinds of performance standards, and more. Swales (1991) has provided convincing evidence that more and more expectations are being placed on the English proficiency of international doctoral students and that these expectations are trending upward rapidly. There is increasing departmental emphasis on monitoring writing and speaking skills at the Ph.D. qualifying and 'prelim' stages. Many departments are increasingly concerned about the language performance of their International Teaching Assistants (ITAs), especially ITA testing (which is now mandatory at UM for prospective ITAs in the literary college and the college of engineering) and ELI instructional follow-up when a prospective ITA has performed poorly on the test. In addition, Swales reports that there is a trend, particularly in science departments and engineering departments, to build publications and presentations right into the degree structure.

Finally, reflecting once more on Diversity Day, both panelists and audience members had a good experience. The panelists were quite perceptive and candid in sharing their linguistic experiences, and audience members were responsive participants in the discussion. Both groups were 'winners'—and there is a strong sense in which the English Language Institute also was a 'winner'. Why? Because, with solid University of Michigan administrative support, the ELI has undertaken a new mission and undergone a radical revision of program over the past five years and has been putting into place an increasingly comprehensive program of special EAP courses and evaluative procedures. The primary focus of the program is on meeting the needs of NNS graduate students like Antonio and Yong, and many more students with even more severe language limitations. In addition, special attention is also given to undergraduate NNSs who need language development.

Once again, as noted in the introduction, the goal is not English for survival, (although we provide it for some students as a first step); rather, the goal is guiding students in the development of academic and professional English for success. The intent is to provide instructional opportunities that will enable students to develop the kinds of sophisticated writing and speaking skills they will need in order to become successful, fully participating members of the academic community, on campus and beyond into their careers. In paraphrasing Widdowson (1978), for many of these students, to assume that they will 'pick up' these communication skills on their own may be too optimistic a view to take.

It should be clear at this point that the purpose of this EAP program is language development, not language remediation.

3 The new Michigan program: Transition and early developments. In Chapter 1, 'The Origins of ESP', (*English for Specific Purposes*, 1987), Hutchinson and Waters observe that, 'As with most developments in human activity, ESP was not a planned and coherent movement, but rather a phenomenon that grew out of a number of converging trends.' Certainly, as our program took shape, developments were not entirely 'coherent' in the beginning as we struggled to make the transition from an intensive English program (IEP) to a specialized EAP program.

3.1 Programs compared

3.1.1 General differences.
The IEP and EAP clientele differ considerably; their needs differ considerably. The intensive program focused primarily on 'future' applicability; the EAP courses emphasize 'here and now' applicabilty with a strong sense of immediacy, indeed urgency. The intensive classes were not credit courses; the EAP courses grant one or two undergraduate or graduate credits. The fact that the EAP courses offer credit marks them as having academic credibility in the mainstream university system and attests to the seriousness of the scholarly endeavor in the eyes of the University. They can be looked upon as on a par with advanced-level foreign language courses. High standards and rigorous criteria for accomplishment can be established and maintained as students take EAP courses concurrently with their other academic courses.

3.1.2 Student population.
For the most part the intensive program was structured for non-matriculated, relatively young, pre-university students. In general their maturity, needs, and interests were quite different from those of the relatively advanced, more mature University of Michigan students now enrolled in EAP courses. As a large midwest research university located away from large immigrant growth areas, UM has a very limited number of undergraduate international students, only 13.8% of the total international population of over 2,300 according to statistics published by the UM International Center in September 1990. This accounts for the fact that the majority of the students currently enrolled in the EAP courses, around ninety percent, are graduate students, and, in fact, most are on doctoral degree programs. In the main, then, they are farther up the academic ladder and more focused, with a whole host of different needs and interests.

3.1.3 Curriculum.
As new EAP courses were designed, little of the IEP course content was found appropriate for the new clientele. Ultimately most of the old curriculum was abandoned, although some of the lower level EAP courses continued to focus on general language skills. At intermediate levels, however, attention shifted to the development of specific language skills that can be generalized to apply in academic contexts to a wide variety of university disciplines. Some work was arranged into two-course sequences of increasing difficulty and opportunities for specialization, such as two levels of academic writing, two levels of language and communication, and two levels of academic listening, among others. At advanced levels, courses were designed to focus more

narrowly in order to place emphasis on writing and speaking styles of those types of academic discourse which are also areas of professional career communication. These include: writing research papers for publication, giving conference reports on research in progress, participating in discussions in a variety of settings, interviewing and counseling clients, teaching university courses, and more.

3.1.4 A new mission. Historically, after offering parallel IEP and EAP programs for about three years, in April 1987, the English Language Institute of the University of Michigan closed the door on the old intensive program (a door that had opened in June 1941, as the first of its kind in the world). The present university-wide mission of the ELI is to provide a variety of courses in English for Academic Purposes for nonnative speakers enrolled at the University of Michigan and to carry out relevant research.

3.2 EAP program start-up: Testing and referrals.

3.2.1 Testing. In making the transition from IEP to main stream university service, there was an immediate need to develop a systematic way to identify international students 'at risk' because of limitations in their linguistic and communicative skills. The Academic English Evaluation (AEE) was developed by the ELI Testing Division to re-evaluate incoming NNSs. At the present time most newly admitted international students, both graduate and undergraduate, are required to take this advanced level EAP test. In fact, the Testing Division is now considering the development of a screening instrument targeted specifically for graduate students.

It has been surprising to find that seventy-five percent of all students who take the AEE appear to have insufficient language skills to handle the rigorous language demands of advanced university work. Data gathered by the Testing Division over the past two years show this to be the case in spite of the fact that all students admitted to Michigan must have a score of at least 560 on the TOEFL or the equivalent on the MELAB. These findings suggest, pre-admission proficiency scores notwithstanding, that there is a significant number of students entering the university who have language limitations. Some are relatively minor, to be sure, but a number have severe limitations, which place them 'at risk' at the survival level, let alone at the success level. On the basis of the test scores on the AEE and an oral interview, students are counseled to enroll in sequences of courses to meet their needs. Courses can be required or optional as indicated by the student's performance levels.

The Testing Division also has developed a special Oral Interview Test for testing prospective international teaching assistants (ITAs). (See section 5.1 in this paper for a detailed discussion.)

3.2.2 Departmental referrals. It has been an important part of our development to establish strong departmental relationships in order to encourage faculty members and student advisors to refer 'at-risk' students for EAP language courses, clinical services, and testing, including ITA testing. One significant liaison with departments has resulted from the practice of having a professor from the prospective ITA's department as a member of the the three-person testing team administering ITA evaluations. Inasmuch as over 400 ITA tests are administered each year by the English Language Institute, significant numbers of faculty members from departments across the campus are now involved in close 'hands on' observation of the work of the ELI.

3.2.3 Self-referrals. Another referral 'source', and one not to be overlooked, is self-referral, and especially the 'satisfied customer' route. That is, the student who returns for course after course and encourages friends to enroll. The value of establishing a reputation with students for serious study and demanding credit courses that satisfy student needs (a reputation spread through the international student 'grapevine') cannot be underestimated and is a powerful incentive for us to strive for quality control in our teaching.

3.3 Course development. The major responsibility of the new program has been the development of a comprehensive curriculum of effective EAP courses. The goal has been to design courses that provide a sequence of linguistic and communicative language development activities, with well-defined tasks that are relevant and applicable to the students' present campus academic needs and beyond. (See section 5.2 of this paper for a detailed discussion.)

3.4 Research. In support of its new mission in the University, the ELI is currently engaged in research and development across a number of key growth areas. These include English for Specific Purposes instruction and particularly task-based instruction, applied discourse analysis, language assessment, applications of audio and video technology with special emphasis on self-access programming, and adult second language acquisition. This aspect of the program has been strongly encouraged by the literary college and the English Language Institute itself, with financial support both for professorial faculty who have joint appointments in ELI and in the Program in Linguistics, and for ELI professional instructional and testing faculty. Support has included released time for research and development projects, in-service guest faculty workshops and demonstrations, and resources for professional conference participation.

3.4.1 A focus on discourse and genre. Today it is essential that a comprehensive EAP program of instruction and research concern itself with discourse patterns beyond the sentence, both forms and functions. Areas of discourse focus must include: studying how sentences are combined to produce meaning; analyzing organizational patterns in written and spoken texts; identifying linguistic markers with which these patterns are signalled; comparing the systematic differences in the way information is conveyed in written versus oral communication.

In observing language use in academic contexts, one has only to do a casual sampling of class lectures, seminar presentations or faculty meetings across the campus, or to read departmental memoranda, laboratory reports, or research articles in a range of scholarly journals to discover that language is 'different' and used 'differently' across disciplines. John Myhill, who teaches Introduction to Discourse Analysis in the UM Program in Linguistics, characterizes this difference as follows: 'Part of being a member of a professional community (e.g. doctors) is learning the 'genre' of official interaction in that community, the linguistic forms used which mark someone as a member of that community.'

Swales in an extensive treatment of genre analysis (1990) defines a genre as comprising a class of communicative events, the members of which share some set of communicative purposes. He notes that, 'These purposes are recognized by the expert members of the parent discourse community, and thereby constitute the rationale for the genre. This rationale shapes the schematic structure of the discourse and influences and constrains choice of content and style.'

Native speakers are in a language-privileged position to be able to recognize these (often very subtle) differences that when mastered, will mark them as informed 'insiders' in the organization and presentation of information in the field-specific genre. NNSs are not in such a fortunate situation. Again, in Widdowson's words, to assume that NNS students will pick up these communication skills on their own may be too optimistic a view to take.

3.4.2 A focus on diversity. There is no escaping the fact that EAP students will come from a range of fields across the university. This brings with it the immediate need to turn attention to what language looks like and sounds like when it is used in specific communicative events designed to accomplish particular communicative purposes in the students' fields.

In the area of spoken discourse, for example, in the graduate EAP oral communication seminar, *Speaking in Research Contexts*, some of the discipline-specific academic genre in which students have been working include the following: juried oral presentations required by design courses in the graduate program in the School of Architecture and Urban Planning (where over 25% percent of the student population is non-native speakers; see Briggs 1987); oral qualifying examinations required for admission to candidacy in the College of Engineering's Department of Mechanical Engineering (over 50 percent of the enrollment, NNSs); oral case presentations of patient dental work required by the School of Dentistry (over 10 percent, NNSs); oral data collection interviews in conjunction with graduate course work in the School of Public Health (over 16 percent NNSs); conference paper presentations in the U.S., Canada, Mexico, the UK and various locations in Europe and Asia, in a range of disciplines (geology, art history, applied economics, Spanish historical linguistics, Russian literature, microbiology, civil engineering, psychology, aerospace science, industrial and operations engineering and more).

3.4.3 A focus on language analysis. How can we cope with the problem of studying such diversity, and often in a limited 'need-to-know-now' time frame? How can we identify similarities and differences across disciplines? As a 'here-and-now' working protocol, class 'case study' assignments and consultation with departmental faculty on campus are valuable sources of information; in the larger picture, more formal research needs to be pursued.

A productive way for students to gather and share oral language infor-mation is by means of a 'case-study' project in which carefully specified observation assignments are carried out by all students in the EAP class. For example, as a new oral communication seminar begins each semester, with students from a variety of fields, language 'discovery' activities can be set to develop language awareness. Such tasks can be aimed at helping students to analyze different oral language events in their own departments (e.g. class seminars, case reporting, departmental forums, research in progress reports) and to report back to the seminar. A series of observation tasks can focus on the nature and structuring of language organization and presentation, forms and conventions, functions and formats. The benefits for students are language awareness, sharpening observation skills, and developing language analysis strategies. The benefits for the instructor are the entries in a log of field-specific discourse information. Johns (1988) has done experimental work in this area, observing that, '. . . we can make additional use of students in formulating curriculum, by teaching them to be ethnographers, to stand back from the lecture or laboratory situation and examine the language and socio-linguistic rules.'

A second useful way to gather information about different fields is, of course, to talk with faculty members in different departments, discussing oral and written assignments, studying written texts, and wherever possible, videotaping oral presentations (e.g. seminar presentations, lectures, laboratory sessions, professor-student individual office hour conferences).

3.5 A summary of program goals. Three overall program goals may be summarized as follows:

(a) To provide a coherent program of specialized course work in English for academic/professional purposes so that students can develop competence in sophisticated language skills.
(b) To help students develop confidence in their abilities as speakers, listeners, readers, and writers of English as a second language. In the NNS classroom context students often feel less pressured and less intimidated by 'linguistic competition', something they often experience in NS groups.
(c) To foster a special sense of 'community' within the EAP classroom. As Swales (1991) has observed, it is important to capitalize on the social value of bringing together groups of often quite isolated individuals from all over the campus to share educational and linguistic experiences. In addition, the cross-cultural understanding that can develop among students brought together in the EAP con-text can contribute to a reduction of the following problem voiced by Dean John D'Arms, UM Rackham School of Graduate Studies (1988): 'In a university of our size and scale . . . where the concentration of foreign graduate students is often heavily field-specific, nationality cliques (like racial cliques) form, breeding resentment and social cleavage rather than collegiality.' Through participation in multi-lingual, multi-cultural groups students in the EAP classes can develop mutual understanding and mutual respect, and some form lasting intercultural friendships.

Once again, the primary purpose of the English Language Institute program is to provide special purpose developmental English instruction.

4 EAP/ESP in the larger context: World affairs, linguistics, and learning. In the introductory chapter of *The Origins of ESP* (1987), Hutchinson and Waters propose three factors as common to the emergence of all ESP programs. Their first factor is called 'the demands of a Brave New World', a reference to the influence of world events on language use. Their second factor is called 'a revolution in linguistics', and the reference here is to the influence of emerging new ideas in the study of language, specifically, a shift away from a focus only on the formal features of language usage to an examination of language use in real communication (in Widdowson's terms, 1978). Their third factor is called 'focus on the learner', a reference to the developments in educational psychology that emphasize the central importance of learners and their attitudes toward learning (in Rodgers' terms, 1969). In the following section these three factors will be examined in the context of developments in the United States in general and at the University of Michigan in particular.

4.1 World affairs and international students in the United States.

4.1.1 Global influences and trends in the United States. Hutchinson and Waters note that following World War II, there was an unprecedented demand for an 'international' language as the result of the expansions in scientific, technical, and economic activity. For a variety of well-known reasons, this international role fell to English.

Strevens (1988), in discussing the development of ESP, observed that, 'Another main contribution to the development of ESP has come from the enormous spread of English.' He went on to note that estimates of the numbers of people in the world who use English for some purpose or other varies between 750 million and 1.5 billion, but that only 300 million of them are native speakers. In contrast, before 1940 the total number (both NSs and NNSs) was perhaps half a million. This means that the number of English speakers has tripled in the last fifty years with substantial increases in the ranks of NNSs.

In the United States over the past fifty years there has been an enormous increase in the numbers of international students in institutions of higher education. Enrollments rose from 8,000 in 1943 (the first year the Institute for International Education (IIE) compiled figures), to a post World War II figure of 26,000 in 1950, and a record high of over 387,000 for the academic year 1989-1990, a fifteen-fold increase from 1950 to 1990. The rate of increase slowed appreciably during the late 1970s, but picked up again in the mid 1980s. While it appears that previous estimates of a million international students by the turn of the century may not materialize, the continued acceleration of upward trending is still predicted.

Over these years predominant countries of origin have changed continuously, reflecting the influences of both national and international developments. During the 1980s more students came from Asia (up from 30% to 54%) and fewer from the Middle East and other oil-dependent areas (down from 25-30% to 10%). Today the leading countries of origin are China, Taiwan, Japan, India, Korea, and after Canada, Malaysia, Hong Kong, and Indonesia.

An examination of the changes in countries of origin reveals that more and more students today are coming from prosperous regions of the world and fewer from poorer regions. This is an important factor when we consider what graduate students will do when they graduate; that is, what they are likely to do career-wise, when they leave their U.S. universities. While the majority will return to their home countries, often to important roles in academia, government, business, and industry, increasing numbers will remain in the United States. Swales (1991) calls our attention to a recent report that the United States has passed legislation raising the immigration quota for skilled foreign professionals from 55,000 to 140,000 a year (1991). Leave or stay, post-university job responsibilities impact on the kinds of professional career-specific language skills these graduates will need, and trends today are toward a demand for increasingly sophisticated and complex English language skills in both written and oral domains. (See Huckin and Olsen, 1984; see Browne, this volume.)

As the English language skills of NNS recipients of advanced degrees become corporate and higher education employer concerns, increasingly the existence of inadequate language preparation for such positions may come to reflect badly on the graduating institution of higher education. Although a university can, indeed, claim that it is not 'responsible' for language skills, on the other hand it may become harder for a university to justify allowing a student to graduate with a prestigious doctoral or master's degree, after 3 to 7 years of graduate study, with (often severe) limitations in language facility. And of course the negative impact on the individual NNS and his or her career development is yet another issue, a moral issue.

4.1.2 Trends and developments at Michigan. At the University of Michigan international enrollments grew from two students in 1847, (one from Mexico and one from Wales) to 600 in 1941, and figures of 2,300 to 2,500 over the last three to four years, with a sizeable 30% increase in the 1970s. Today NNSs make up over 6 1/2% of the total enrollment of 36,000 students on the Ann Arbor campus but they comprise over 15% of the total graduate school enrollment of nearly 13,200 students.

While on many campuses in the United States international undergraduates outnumber graduates three to two, it is quite the reverse at Michigan and other major research universities. In fact at Michigan the figures are over 86% enrolled in graduate and professional schools, but less than 14% in undergraduate schools. And of special interest, over 400 NNSs of this graduate population serve as Graduate Student Teaching Assistants (GSTAs) on campus, about 22% of the total GSTA population.

In 1989-1990 the number of countries represented at Michigan was 98, with more than 100 students from 6 of these countries: Taiwan, Korea, China, India, Canada, and Japan. As for the fields of study, the highest percentages of NNSs at Michigan were in: Engineering, over 44% with 15 of its 28 depart-ments over 40%; Architecture and Urban

Planning, over 25%; Literature, Science and the Arts, over 19%; Art, over 18%; School of Public Health, over 16%; Business Administration, nearly 15%.

4.1.3 Admissions policies. Now it is time to look at the following question posed by Dean John D'Arms, UM Graduate School, (*The University Record*, May 22, 1988) and some of his observations on the important topic of admissions: 'What are the forces driving universities in the United States to admit international students in such large numbers?' The main reason, says D'Arms, is pragmatic; that is, many doctoral programs, especially in the technical fields, have seen a tremendous decline in the number of qualified domestic applicants beginning in the mid seventies. In fact, since 1975 the total number of Ph.D. degrees awarded annually by American universities has declined from 33,500 to roughly 30,000, but over the same period of time, the number of those degrees earned by international students has increased steadily from 1,000 to more than 3,000 annually.

'It seems clear', says D'Arms, 'that shortages in domestic student supply, rather than truly enlightened attitudes toward international education, have been driving a good deal of our behavior in graduate admissions.'

And why have domestic enrollments declined? For some clear domestic economic reasons: one is insufficient financial aid for U.S. students (while many international students receive help from their home governments); another is the lure of lucrative jobs in business and industry that engineering and hard science majors can get when they have completed a bachelor's degree. In fact, it has been pointed out, again by D'Arms (1988), that '. . . certain so-called problems of international educational exchange—such as the very high proportion of foreign students in some engineering, mathematics, and other graduate programs, and the notorious problem of the unintelligible foreign teaching assistant—are not really 'international problems' at all. Instead, they are not very good international solutions to very substantial domestic manpower and resource problems . . .'

4.1.4 The 'ITA problem'. The so-called 'ITA problem' has become a serious concern, especially in universities that employ large numbers of teaching assistants to serve as faculty for undergraduate teaching. The higher the number of international students at the doctoral level, of course, the higher the number of international TAs, for they are drawn from that academic level; thus Michigan has a significant numbers of ITAs. In fall, 1990, out of nearly 1,800 TAs, 409, (close to 22%) were non-native speakers.

Increasingly over the past several years ITAs' command of English—or lack of it—has become a growing concern on many campuses across the United States and it also has become a source of political pressures and English language policy decision at the state government level. In the last three or four years a substantial number of state legislatures have intruded into higher education decision-making by passing legislation forcing universities to test English language skills of ITAs, and in some cases, all NNS faculty members, much to the consternation of university governance. Specifically, twelve states have either passed legislation or adopted state-wide policies to assess ITA oral English proficiency and legislation has been introduced in many more states.

In Michigan, in 1986, both the State House and the State Senate took up the ITA issue vis-à-vis state supported institutions of higher education. Although legislation was introduced, no final action was taken. James Duderstadt (now University of Michigan president) viewed such legislation as 'undermining the autonomy of an institution to determine its own faculty' (*Michigan Daily*, May 9, 1986) and State Senator Lana Pollack called such action unconstitutional because it would dictate to colleges how to run their affairs (*Ann Arbor News*, January 29, 1988).

As a result of mounting concerns since 1986, the University of Michigan and other state institutions that employ large numbers of ITAs have moved ahead briskly to put ITA testing and training into place. In our situation, the literary college which employs large numbers of ITAs (272 out of 1,222 in the autumn of 1990) turned to the English Language Institute to take responsibility for developing ITA testing and for establishing special language courses. (For information on ITA developments at Michigan, see Ard 1987, Ard and Swales 1986, Axelson and Madden 1990, Briggs and Hofer 1990, and Rounds 1987.)

The (then) dean of the College of Literature, Science, and the Arts, Peter Steiner, felt strongly that the ELI should be addressing the needs of the enrolled NNS students on campus, including the ITAs, rather than the needs of non-Michigan students in the intensive course, and expressed those views to ELI Director, John Swales, as follows: 'I don't see why the ELI spends all its time on courses for strangers when we have so many of our own students who need help.' Indeed, the English Language Institute welcomed the opportunity to shift its emphasis away from the externally-based IEP program to an internally-based EAP program, one situated within the mainstream affairs of the university.

Certainly the language needs of the ITAs were a major concern for ELI as faculty attention turned to testing and teaching issues. But just as important for us was the opportunity to open up a whole range of EAP course work, not only for international students in their role as teachers, but for international students in their roles as students and researchers in the demanding university milieu.

The pressure on the university to deal with the ITA problem was a catalyst that allowed us to undertake the development of a comprehensive EAP program, and now that the total program is in place, it has proved its worth and is recognized today as an essential program in the life of the university. (See section 5 in this paper for more information.)

4.2 A 'Revolution in linguistics' and a 'Focus on the learner'. In the following discussion the attention turns from the 'demands of a Brave New World' to the second and third features identified by Hutchinson and Waters as instrumental in shaping the development of ESP programs, that is a 'revolution in linguistics' and a 'focus on the learner'.

During the past fifty years, as perspectives on language learning and language teaching have changed significantly, the ELI's teaching, testing, and research have reflected those changes. Roughly the first half of the ELI's 50 years followed the approach stance associated with 'The Oral Approach' developed by Charles C. Fries and staff members in the 1940s and 1950s. (See Morley et al. 1984, for a historical review.) In the late 1960s and 1970s this gave way to a pragmatic skills-based orientation. Through the 1980s instructional methods/materials have followed a communicative language teaching approach stance more and more, including incorporation of task-based methodology and genre-based materials in many parts of the EAP curriculum.

Some of the significant developments in theoretical models—learning models, linguistics models, instructional models—that inform much of the state-of-the-art work in the field today, and our work as well, may be summarized as follows (Morley 1991):

> . . . from a language learning perspective of 'outside-in', to one of 'inside-out', in a changed concept of language acquisition that views the learner as the active primemover in the learning process (Corder 1967) and an emerging paradigm shift in which learners are seen as active creators, not as passive recipients in a process which is cognitively driven, not behaviorally conditioned; focus is on the learner and individual learning styles and strategies (Oxford 1990, O'Malley and Chamot 1989, Wenden and Rubin 1987)

> . . . from a focus on language as simply a formal system, to a focus on language as both a formal system and a functional system that exists to satisfy the communicative needs of its users (Halliday 1970, 1973, 1978)

> . . . from linguistic preoccupation with sentence-level grammar to widening interest in semantics, pragmatics, discourse, and speech act theory (Austin 1962, Searle 1970).

... from an instructional focus on linguistic form and correct usage, to one on function and communicatively appropriate use (Widdowson 1978, 1983)

... from an orientation of linguistic competence, to one of communicative competence (Hymes, 1972), and a specific competence model which brings together a number of viewpoints in one linguistically-oriented and pedagogically-useful framework: grammatical competence, sociolinguistic competence, discourse competence, and strategic competence (Canale and Swain 1980)

5 A summary of current program developments.

5.1 Testing developments. One of the tests developed by the ELI Testing Division for the new program is the Academic English Evaluation (AEE). This is an advanced level EAP test which is administered to most new University of Michigan international students, both graduates and undergraduates, even though all admitted students must have achieved a preadmission score of 560 or higher on the TOEFL or an equivalent score on the MELAB. ELI works closely with both graduate and undergraduate admissions officers in this regard.

The opportunity to assess the language skills of potentially 'at risk' students coming on campus has been one of the most important areas of change in ELI mission. Through the AEE we are able to focus on an analysis of the language strengths and weaknesses of incoming students in order to determine course recommendations for those 'at risk'. The AEE test includes measures of writing, editing of written text, listening, grammar, vocabulary, reading, and an oral interview to access speaking and pronunciation intelligibility level.

A second important test developed over the last several years is the ITA Oral Interview Test for evaluating the language skills of prospective international teaching assistants. Students must perform at appropriate levels before they are given permission to teach. The College of Literature, Science, and the Arts (since 1982) and the College of Engineering (since 1988) have required international students whose native language is not English to have their competence in classroom English evaluated prior to appointments as teaching assistants.

The ITA test is a highly specialized individual oral test which has four parts: an interactive interview with a team of three evaluators, a lesson presentation with questions from the 'audience' of evaluators, an interactive office hour task, and responses to video-taped student questions. Evaluators include three persons: a member of the ELI testing staff, a member of the ELI teaching faculty, and a professor from the ITA's department. We have been extremely fortunate to have the cooperation of departmental faculty members as evaluators. They provide good insights, valid judgments of the prospective TA's knowledge of the subject matter and effectiveness of the presentation, and moral support.

5.2 Curriculum developments. The goal over the last several years has been to develop a curriculum in both written and oral communication for academic and career-specific purposes at increasing levels of sophistication. There are now 34 EAP courses in place. Most courses give one hour of credit, although a few carry two or three hours of credit. Usually sixteen to twenty courses are taught each semester but we may offer as many as twenty-eight sections in a given term. Enrollments average 425 in the fall semester and around 250 in the winter semester. ELI courses are taken concurrently with other academic courses, although many doctoral students have finished their course work and are working on their research. The comprehensive EAP curriculum includes different kinds of courses designed to meet a variety of academic needs:

(a) Integrated academic skills. As a special program for non-native speakers who have conditional-only admission to the University—that is, students who do not have sufficient language proficiency to enroll in more than one or two academic/content courses—ELI offers a sequence of two semi-intensive integrated academic courses. These courses, each for three hours credit, focus on improving academic language skills across the disciplines and include reading and vocabulary building, lecture comprehension and note taking, writing, and discussion.

(b) Intermediate and Advanced Level EAP courses. Twenty-one academic English courses are offered, eleven in written communication and ten in oral communication. A number of these courses are arranged in two-course sequences of increasing difficulty.

Intermediate level courses focus on the sub-genre level, working with the development of language skills that are generalizable to specific fields across the university. These courses deal with writing and grammar in academic contexts, lecture comprehension, interactive listening and communication, academic speaking, and interviewing, among many other offerings.

Special advanced courses are designed to guide students in developing facility with the field-specific genre required for successful written and oral language performance. Included are three graduate-level writing courses (critical reading and writing, research papers and thesis writing, and dissertation prospectus and dissertation writing), and two graduate-credit courses in oral communication (discussion and oral argumentation, and speaking in research contexts).

(c) **International Teaching Assistant (ITA) courses.** These courses are restricted to non-native graduate students who currently hold, or are being considered for, teaching assistantships at the University. The most comprehensive ITA work is provided through three-week intensive summer workshop courses, *Teaching in the U.S.: Pedagogy, Culture and Language,* a requirement for all new ITAs in the literary college. These collaborative workshop-courses are jointly sponsored by the UM Center for Research on Learning and Teaching (CRLT) and the English Language Institute. The CRLT offers follow-up class observation and consultation services throughout the academic year and the ELI offers five additional courses during the fall and winter semesters. ELI courses deal with topics such as introduction to ITA work, ITA presenting skills, ITA interacting skills, ITA interactions with undergraduates, and an ITA seminar and practicum.

(d) **Special topics in English for Specific Purposes (ESP).** The ELI designs special courses for individual departments, schools, or colleges upon request. At the present time two business courses are offered: *MBA Writing for Non-native Speakers* (1 or 2 credits) and *Oral Communication in Business for Non-native Speakers* (1 or 2 credits).

(e) **Spring semester general purpose academic skills courses.** During the Spring semester the ELI does not offer the regular course selection but provides three general academic skills courses.

(f) **Special language services.** In addition to the 34 courses, the ELI operates a Speaking Clinic and a Writing Laboratory. These are one-on-one-tutorial facilities for NNSs who have taken or are taking ELI courses in the relevant areas or are deemed not to need regular classroom instruction.

(g) **Advanced intensive summer programs.** Two special six-and-a-half-week intensive summer programs complete ELI programming. One summer program is English for Academic Purposes. The other is English for Business and Management Studies.

5.3 Current directions in research and development. Research and development interests of English Language Institute faculty members cut across a range of topics relating to language learning and teaching. Each faculty member is involved in one or more of the following areas:

(a) **Testing and evaluation research areas.** ITA testing; testing listening skills; test/retest variations; the development of codes and descriptions for scoring compositions; the effects of task and topic assignment on writing test performance; pronunciation and intelligibility profiles; oral and communicative feedback and assessment.

(b) **ITA research interests.** Accommodation in NS/NNS interactions, especially between ITAs and their undergraduate students; analysis of the structure of office hour interactions; discourse and performance of ITAs; ITA training.

(c) **Discourse interests.** A discourse-based grammar of research English; the rhetoric of economics; conference abstracts, with a focus on process, product, and reception; lecture listening and rhetorical markers; analysis of genre-specific oral discourse; business English; the effect of rhetorical consciousness-raising on performance.

(d) **Instructional research and materials development interest areas.** Communication tasks and language performance, with applications to course design and materials development; self-access self-study instructional modules; methods and materials for teaching advanced grammar; milieu specific pronunciation teaching.

(e) **Second language acquisition interests.** SLA interaction data, especially communicative effectiveness and interaction; teaching input and variant interlanguage forms in different contexts, especially across discourse domains.

6 Concluding comments. The language deficits of 'at risk' NNS students in higher education have long been recognized in the university community. How many dissertations over the years have been ghost-written or undergone massive editing by members of doctoral committees (D'Arms 1988)? How many students have had the 'double standard' applied? That is, how often do professors assert that students' English is quite adequate to be an RA or a TA and to finish a degree, but not good enough to hire for an academic position or to have as a preferred colleague for an external consultant partnership (Olsen, in Swales 1991).

We continue to accept international students into our universities in unprecedented numbers. And there are questions to be asked and answered.

In Graduate School Dean D'Arms (1988) words: 'Academic substance and academic style come together when we consider the familiar and often discussed subject of 'communication skills'. My question is this: ought we not be conceptualizing what we mean by these 'skills' in more sophisticated, and less egocentric, ways?'

D'Arms (1988) has also observed that many of these students will play roles in their own societies, not just as professionals, but as policy-makers and in management. He notes further that those roles will require communication skills that extend far beyond the ability to speak and write clearly in English, and that the University has the responsibility to help foreign students attain a strong command of the language and use it to gain confidence and power in their academic careers.

In preparing this paper and reviewing developments at Michigan over the past several years and the English Language Institute's part in them, there is a clear pattern of concrete measures that have been put into place and definitive steps taken on behalf of NNS students. University of Michigan President James Duderstadt is firmly committed to internationalization of the university and fostering diversity on its campus. ELI's work makes a solid contribution to these developments at the University of Michigan.

Appendix. EAP courses** and special program for international students (English Language Institute, The University of Michigan).

110	Integrated Academic Skills.	112	Integrated Academic Skills.

Written communication:
300 Writing & grammar in academic contexts.
310 Reading and vocabulary.
312 Grammar I.
313 Academic grammar II.
320 Academic writing I.
321 Academic writing II.
322 Term paper writing.
410 (GR/UG*)(1) Critical reading & writing.
520 (GR*)(2) Research papers & thesis writing.
600 (GR*)(2) Dissertation prospectus & dissertation writing.

Special spring courses:
342 Oral academic skills.
343 Written academic skills.
344 Pronunciation skills.

ITA courses:
380 Introduction to ITA work.
381 ITA Presenting skills.
383 ITA Interacting skills.
392 ITA Interactions with undergraduates.
584 (GR*)(1) ITA seminar & practicum.
993 (GR*)(1) College teaching in the U.S.: Pedagogy, culture, & language.

Oral communication:
330 Language & communication I.
331 Language & communication II.
332 Lecture comprehension.
333 Interactive-listening & communication.
334 Academic speaking.
336 Pronunciation I.
337 Pronunciation II.
338 Voice and articulation.
392 Interviewing.
434 (GR/UG*)(1) Discussion & oral argumentation.
601 (GR*)(2) Speaking in research contexts.

Business courses:
393 MBA writing for non-native speakers.
394 Oral communication in business for non-native speakers.

Tutorial services:
Speaking clinic.
Writing laboratory.

Advanced intensive summer programs:
English for business & management studies (6 1/2 weeks).
English for academic purposes (6 1/2 weeks)

* GR - Graduate credit; UG - Undergraduate credit.
** These one-credit and two-credit courses are open to graduate and undergraduate students who are enrolled at the University of Michigan.

References

Ard, J. 1987. The foreign TA problem from an acquisition-theoretic point of view. English for Specific Purposes. 6.2:133-144.
Ard, J. and J. M. Swales. 1986. English for international teaching assistants: What ESL institutions can offer. TESOL Quarterly 20.2:21-22.
Austin, J. L. 1962. How to do things with words. Oxford: Clarendon Press.
Axelson, E. and C. Madden. 1990. Video-based materials for communicative ITA training. Issues and Developments in English and Applied Linguistics. 5:1-12.
Briggs, S. 1987. When course success varies from discourse success. English for Specific Purposes. 6.2:153-156.
Briggs, S., and B. Hofer. 1990. Undergraduate perceptions of ITA effectiveness. In: J. Nyquist, R. Abbott, D. Wulff, and J. Sprague, eds. Preparing the professoriate of tomorrow's teachers: Selected readings on ITA training. Dubuque, Iowa: Kendall/Hunt.
Briggs, S., S. Hyon, P. Aldridge, and J. Swales. 1990. The international teaching assistant: An annotated critical bibliography. Ann Arbor: The English Language Institute of the University of Michigan.
Browne, S. C. 1991 A pedagogy of corporate-level ESP training for international scientists and engineers. In: Georgetown University Round Table on Languages and Linguistics 1991. Washington D. C.: Georgetown University Press.
Canale, M., and M. Swain. 1980. Theoretical bases of communicative approaches to second language teaching and testing. Applied Linguistics. 1.1:1-47.
Corder, S.P. 1967. The significance of learners' errors. International Review of Applied Linguistics 5.161-170.
D'Arms, J. 1988. Foreign students, international studies, and the internationalization of the university. Rackham Reports 1987-1988 Issue 1-19.
Halliday, M. A. K. 1970. Language structure and language function. In: J. Lyons, ed. New horizons in linguistics. Baltimore, Md.: Penguin. 140-165.
Halliday, M. A. K. 1973. Exploration in the functions of language. London: Edward Arnold.
Halliday, M. A. K. 1978. Language as social semiotic. London: Edward Arnold.
Huckin, T. and L. Olsen. 1984. The need for professionally oriented ESL instruction in the United States. TESOL Quarterly 18.2: 273-294.
Hutchinson, T. and A. Waters. 1987. English for specific purposes: A learning-centered approach. Cambridge: Cambridge University Press.
Hymes, D. 1972. On communicative competence. In: Pride and Holmes, ed. 1972.
Johns, A. 1988. ESP and the future: Less innocence abroad. In: M. L. Tickoo, ed. ESP: State of the Art. Singapore: SEAMEO Regional Language Centre. 21-26.
Morley, J. 1991. Current directions in second language teaching. In: W. Grabe and R. Kaplan, ed. Introduction to applied linguistics. Reading, Mass.: Addison Wesley. 79-105.
Morley, J., B. W. Robinett, L. Selinker, and D. Woods. 1984. ESL theory and the Fries legacy. The Language Teacher: JALT Journal. 6.2:171-208.
O'Malley, J. M., and A. Chamot. 1989. Learning strategies in second language acquisition. New York: Cambridge University Press.
Oxford, R. 1990. Language learning strategies. New York: Newbury House.
Rodgers, S. 1969. Freedom to learn. Merrill.

Rounds, P. 1987. Characterizing successful classroom discourse for NNS teaching assistant training. TESOL Quarterly. 21.4:643-671.
Searle, J. 1970. Speech acts. Cambridge, Mass.: Cambridge University Press.
Strevens, P. 1988. ESP after twenty years: A reappraisal. In: M. L. Tickoo, ed. ESP: State of the art. Singapore: SEAMEO Regional Language Centre. 1-13.
Swales, J. 1989. English as international language of research. In: J.Morley, ed. American lectures: New listening materials. Fudan PRC: University of Fudan Press. 68-73.
Swales, J. 1990. Genre analyis. Cambridge: Cambridge University Press.
Swales, J. 1991 International graduate students in anglophone research worlds. Rackham Reports 1990-1991 Issue 72-88.
Wenden, A., and J. Rubin. 1987. Learner strategies in language learning. Englewood Cliffs, N.J.: Prentice-Hall Regents.
Widdowson, H. G. 1978. Teaching language as communication. Oxford: Oxford University Press.
Widdowson, H. G. 1983. Language purpose and language use. Oxford: Oxford University Press.

Strategic reading

Patricia L. Carrell
University of Akron

In the past several years, both first and second language reading research has begun to focus on reading strategies. Reading strategies are of interest for what they reveal about the ways readers manage interactions with written text and also for how strategies are related to reading comprehension. The term 'strategies' is used deliberately, rather than the more traditional term 'skills', because the term 'strategies' refers to actions that readers select and control to achieve desired goals or objectives (Johnston and Byrd 1983; Paris et al. 1983; van Dijk and Kintsch 1983). The term 'strategies' emphasizes the reader's active participation and actual way of doing something, or the reader's performance, whereas the term 'skills' may suggest the reader's competence or only passive abilities which are not necessarily activated. 'Strategies' may be relatively conscious and non-automatic, or relatively subconscious and automatic.

Strategies run the gamut from such traditionally recognized reading skills as skimming and scanning, to rereading, contextual guessing or skipping unknown words, tolerating ambiguity, making predictions, confirming or disconfirming inferences, and using cognates to comprehend, to more recently recognized strategies such as activating background knowledge (Zvetina 1987) and recognizing text structure (Block 1986; Carrell, in press).

In exploratory, descriptive investigations with small numbers of individual learners using think-aloud techniques, studies by both Hosenfeld and Block have identified apparent relations between certain types of reading strategies and successful or unsuccessful foreign or second language reading. In Hosenfeld's (1977) study of high school students in this country reading French, German, or Spanish, but thinking-aloud in English, her example of a 'successful' French reader: (1) kept the meaning of the passage in mind during reading, (2) read in what she termed 'broad phrases', (3) skipped words viewed as unimportant to total phrase meaning, and (4) had a positive self-concept as a reader. By contrast, Hosenfeld's unsuccessful French reader: (1) lost the meaning of sentences as soon as they were decoded, (2) read in short phrases, (3) seldom skipped words as unimportant and viewed words as equal in terms of their contribution to total phrase meaning, and (4) had a negative self-concept as a reader.

Block (1986), in a study of generally nonproficient readers—specifically entering university freshmen, both native and nonnative English speakers, enrolled in remedial reading courses in the U.S.—found that four characteristics seem to differentiate the more successful from the less successful of these nonproficient readers: (1) integration, (2) recognition of aspects of text structure, (3) use of general knowledge, personal experiences, and associations, and (4) response in extensive versus reflexive modes. In the reflexive mode, readers relate affectively and personally, directing their attention away from the text and toward themselves, and focusing on their own thoughts and feelings rather than on the information in the text; in the extensive mode, readers attempt to deal with the message conveyed by the author, focus on understanding the author's ideas, and do not relate the text to themselves affectively or personally. Among the nonproficient readers Block investigated, one subgroup, which she labeled 'integrators', integrated information, were generally aware of text structure, responded in an extensive mode, and monitored their understanding consistently and effectively. They also made greater progress in developing their reading skills and demonstrated greater success after one semester in college. The other subgroup, which Block labeled 'nonintegrators', failed to integrate, tended not to recognize text structure, and seemed to rely much more on personal experiences, responding in a reflexive mode. They also made less progress in developing their reading skills and demonstrated less success after one semester in college.

Several additional studies have similarly shown relationships between various reading strategies and successful or unsuccessful second language reading (Hauptman 1979; Devine 1984; Knight et al. 1985; Sarig 1987).

Yet, the picture is much more complex than suggested by these early studies. Unfortunately, the relationships between strategies and comprehension are not simple and straightforward; use of certain reading strategies does not always lead to successful reading comprehension, while use of other strategies does not always result in unsuccessful reading comprehension. Research results reported by Anderson (1990) show that there are no simple correlations or one-to-one relationships between particular strategies and successful or unsuccessful reading comprehension. His research, with native Spanish-speaking university level intensive ESL students reading in English as their second language and self-reporting their strategy use, suggests much individual variation in successful or unsuccessful use of the very same reading strategies. Rather than a single set of processing strategies that significantly contributed to successful reading comprehension, the same kinds of strategies were used by both high and low comprehending readers. However, those readers reporting the use of a higher number of different strategies tended to score higher on the comprehension measures. Anderson concludes from his data that successful second language reading comprehension is 'not simply a matter of knowing what strategy to use, but the reader must also know how to use it successfully and [to] orchestrate its use with other strategies. It is not sufficient to know about strategies, but a reader must also be able to apply them strategically' (Anderson 1990:19).

Another study, by Pritchard (1990), has shown that cultural content schemata interact with reading processing strategies to affect comprehension. Pritchard had sixty 11th grade readers—30 each from the U.S. and the Pacific island nation of Palau—reading culturally familiar and unfamiliar passages in their native language. From verbal report data provided by the students as they read each passage, Pritchard compiled a taxonomy of 22 processing strategies and organized it into five categories: (1) developing awareness, (2) accepting ambiguity, (3) establishing intrasentential ties, (4) establishing intersentential ties, and (5) using background knowledge. Pritchard found that students used strategies in categories (1) and (3) significantly more often for culturally unfamiliar than for the familiar passage, and strategies in categories (4) and (5) significantly more often for the culturally familiar than for the unfamiliar passage. From students' retellings, Pritchard confirmed the earlier findings of Steffensen et al. (1979) that students recalled significantly more idea units and produced more elaborations as well as fewer distortions for the culturally familiar than for the unfamiliar passage. Pritchard concludes that cultural schemata influence readers' processing strategies and the level of comprehension they achieve.

Thus, the picture is complex and the details are still emerging. Much more research is needed to show precisely which reading strategies in which combinations are positively related to successful reading for which groups of readers and in which reading situations. Nonetheless the research to date clearly shows the important role that processing strategies play in reading comprehension.

Metacognitive awareness or perceptions of reading strategies. Much of the early research on reading strategies, as typified by Hosenfeld and Block, was focused upon strategy use—i.e. post hoc identification of strategies used by readers in the process of reading, usually via think-aloud techniques—and did not investigate readers' awareness of strategies; that is, their metacognitive awareness. Although Block did identify three apparently metacognitive strategies in her study—one which she called 'commenting on behavior or process', a second she called 'monitoring comprehension', and a third 'correcting behavior'—none of these is mentioned in her results to relate to reading proficiency. Further, Anderson's results point to the need to understand not only reading strategies, but strategic use of reading strategies in second language reading.

First language reading researchers, most notably Brown and her collaborators (e.g., Baker and Brown 1984) have investigated several different aspects of the relationship between metacognitive ability (literally cognition about cognition) and effective reading.

Two dimensions of metacognitive ability have been recognized (Flavell 1978): (1) knowledge of cognition, and (2) regulation of cognition. The first, knowledge of cognition, includes the reader's knowledge about his or her own cognitive resources and the compatibility between the reader and the reading situation. If a reader is aware of what is needed to perform efficiently, then it is possible to take steps to meet the demands of a reading situation more effectively. If, however, the reader is not aware of his or her own limitations as a reader or of the complexity of the task at hand, then the reader can hardly be expected to take preventative actions to anticipate or recover from problems.

Related to this first aspect of metacognition is the reader's conceptualization of the reading process: how the reader conceptualizes what s/he is doing in reading. Devine in 1984 investigated second language readers' conceptualizations about their reading in a second language by analyzing transcripts of reading interviews for evidence of beginning ESL readers' theoretical orien-tations toward reading in their second language. 'Depending on the language units they considered important to effective reading,' Devine classified subjects as 'sound-, word-, or meaning-oriented...' (Devine 1984:97). Devine found that meaning-centered readers demonstrated good to excellent comprehension on a retelling task from an oral reading, while sound-centered readers were judged to have either poor or very poor comprehension (Devine 1984:104).

Devine's result is reminiscent of first language reading research which has generally shown that younger and less proficient readers tend to focus on or conceptualize reading as a decoding process rather than as a meaning-getting process (Myers and Paris 1978, Canney and Winograd 1979, Garner and Kraus 1981-82, Paris and Myers 1981, Gambrell and Heathington 1981).

In a recent study of foreign language reading, Barnett (1988) investigated the relationships among reading comprehension, strategy use, and perceived strategy use or strategy awareness. She found that all three were significantly correlated for cognitively mature university-level readers of French as a foreign language. She concluded:

> ... students who effectively consider and remember context as they read [i.e. strategy use] understand more of what they read than

students who employ this strategy less or less well. Moreover, students who think they use those strategies considered most productive [i.e. perceived strategy use or strategy awareness] actually do read through context better and understand more than do those who do not think they use such strategies (Barnett 1988:156).

In a 1989 study, Carrell investigated relationships between readers' meta-cognitive awareness or judgments about various types of reading strategies and their reading ability in both their first and second language. Subjects were adult, college-level readers of English and Spanish as both first and foreign or second languages. Results showed that for reading in the first language, either English or Spanish, perceptions or judgments about 'local' reading strategies (e.g. focusing on grammatical structures, sound-letter correspondences, word-meaning, and text details) tended to be negatively correlated with reading performance. For example, for the Spanish L1 group, if subjects tended to disagree with statements such as 'When reading silently in Spanish, the things I do to read effectively are to focus on "mentally sounding out parts of words," "the grammatical structures," "understanding the meaning of each word," and "the details of the content" '—all local reading strategies—they tended to be better readers of Spanish as the native language. Furthermore, if they tended to disagree that sound-letter information or grammatical structure made reading in their L1 difficult, then they also tended to read significantly better. In other words, to put it in a positive way, if subjects tended to agree that what might be characterized as 'local', bottom-up, decoding types of reading strategies were not particularly effective, but also did not cause them particular difficulty, then reading performance in the L1 tended to be better. The English L1 group showed these same tendencies with regard to subjects' perceptions about 'local' reading strategies. Obviously, one would expect this correlation for proficient L1 readers who have the requisite language decoding skills to process texts automatically for effective reading comprehension.

For reading in the second or foreign language, some differences emerged between the L2 groups. For the Spanish-as-a-foreign-language group (American students studying university-level Spanish), at rather low proficiency levels of Spanish, and reading in Spanish as a foreign rather than a second language, perceptions about some of the 'local' reading strategies were positively correlated with reading performance. For the ESL group (native speakers of Spanish studying ESL at an American university), at relatively higher proficiency levels of English than the other group was at Spanish, and reading in English as a second rather than a foreign language, perceptions about 'global' reading strategies (such as, use of background knowledge, focus on text gist, and textual organization) were positively correlated with reading performance.

That article concludes that the ESL group, of more advanced proficiency levels, tended to be more 'global' or top-down in their perceptions of effective reading strategies. The Spanish-as-a-foreign-language group, at lower proficiency levels, tended to be more 'local' or bottom-up in their perceptions of effective reading strategies. Because of their lower proficiency level in the foreign language, they may have been more dependent on bottom-up decoding skills; they may have needed and may have been aware of their need to 'hold in their bottoms' as Eskey (1988) has argued. That is, we may be seeing metacognitive reflexes of the language 'short circuit' in the sense of Clarke (1980).

In a more recent study, Carrell (1991) reports relationships between ESL students' awareness of text structure, measured in two different ways, and reading comprehension as measured by reading recalls. Subjects who demonstrated awareness of text structure by using the structure of the reading passages to organize written recalls showed superior recall as measured both quantitatively and qualitatively. Other studies of ESL readers' metacognitive awareness or perceptions of their processing strategies on reading achievement have been reported in Waxman and Padron (1987) and Padron and Waxman (1988).

Metacognitive strategy training. Traditionally, reading instruction has involved either direct instruction on decoding skills or informal teaching of comprehension. Those who advocate major emphasis decoding mechanisms in reading tend also toward direct, explicit, deductive instructional approaches, while those who emphasize attention to reading for meaning tend toward learner-directed, informal, inductive instructional approaches. Yet, as Resnick (1979) has argued, there is no reason, in principle, why one cannot have direct instruction in comprehension, or for that matter—although perhaps more difficult to imagine—informal instruction in decoding. This part of the paper is concerned with relatively direct, explicit instruction in comprehension-fostering reading strategies.

The definition of metacognition given above referred to two aspects of metacognition: (1) knowledge of cognition, and (2) regulation of cognition. This part of the paper is, therefore, concerned with the second aspect—regulation of cognition—the control readers have of their own actions while reading for different purposes. Successful readers monitor their reading, 'plan strategies, adjust effort appropriately, and evaluate the success of their ongoing efforts to understand' (Brown et al. 1986:49).

Metacognitive control, in which readers consciously direct the reasoning process, is a particularly important aspect of strategic reading. When readers are conscious of the reasoning involved, they can access and apply that reasoning to similar reading in future situations. However, current approaches to comprehension instruction, especially in second language reading pedagogy, do not always provide students with sufficient explicit information to enable them to assume metacognitive control (Duffy, Roehler, and Herrmann 1988).

Several first language researchers have advocated metacognitive training, especially metacomprehension training in reading, with the goal of teaching individuals how to adjust their cognitive activity in order to promote more effective comprehension (Gavelek and Raphael 1985; Brown et al. 1981; Baker and Brown 1984). In fact, in first language reading research, direct instruction of reading comprehension strategies via teacher explanation (e.g. Brown et al. 1981; Brown 1981; Brown and Palincsar 1982; Cook and Mayer 1983; Brown et al. 1984) has been shown to 'yield consistently positive results' (Winograd and Hare 1988: 121). For second language reading, prior to the requisite research being done, we had only Casanave's (1988) assumption that such instruction would be beneficial:

> In accordance with Baker and Brown (1984), I am assuming that in class-room settings, inefficient readers who enhance their awareness of the nature of reading and of their own reading strategies will ultimately be better readers than those who do not. Such awareness lies at the foundation of effective instruction in comprehension monitoring (Casanave 1988:285).

While relatively little metacognitive strategy training research has yet been conducted in second language reading, three relevant studies may be cited (Padron 1985, Sarig and Folman 1987, Carrell et al. 1989).

Carrell et al. (1989) undertook a study of metacognitive strategy training for second language reading that specifically focused on explicit training in two reading strategies: semantic mapping and the experience-text-relationship method. Both of these reading strategies have in common the activation of prior background knowledge, the reading of texts against the activated background knowledge, and, finally, the relating of information gained from the reading to the prior background knowledge. Semantic mapping attempts to organize the information in the form of a visual learning adjunct called a 'map'; experience-text-relationship method does not include the organization or mapping step. With adult, high-intermediate level, intensive ESL students of varied native language backgrounds, we provided training in either semantic mapping or the experience-text-relationship method. Each group of students also received training in metacognitive awareness and regulation of these strategies, i.e. explicit information on what the strategy consisted of, why the strategy was considered to be effective and what it was designed to accomplish, when to use the strategy, and, conversely, when not to, and how to evaluate their own success in the use of the strategy. A control group, which received no specialized strategy or awareness training, was also run.

Results showed that metacognitive strategy training in semantic mapping and in the experience-text-relationship method were both effective in enhancing second language reading when compared with the control group. Results also showed that on some measures while training in each strategy enhanced second language reading, on other measures there were differences between them. In other words, it seemed to make a difference how second language reading ability was assessed. Finally, results showed that there were significant interactions between students' learning styles and the effectiveness of training the two different strategies. Students' individual learning styles played a role in the effectiveness of training each strategy; students with different learning styles benefitted differentially from each strategy training.

The results of this study suggested that second language reading pedagogy, especially for adult students in academic ESL programs, should benefit from the inclusion of explicit, comprehension-fostering metacognitive strategy training, and, furthermore, that the types of such training should be varied to accommodate individual students' differing learning styles.

Brown et al. (1981:20) see the principal aim of instruction in metacognitive awareness and regulation as getting the students to understand the interactive nature of reading, and the active role played by the reader:

> What we are advocating is an avoidance of blind training techniques and a serious attempt at informed, self-control training, that is, to provide novice learners with the information necessary for them to design effective plans of their own. The essential aim of training is to make the trainee more aware of the active nature of learning and the importance of employing problem-solving, trouble-shooting routines to enhance understanding. If learners can be made aware of (1) basic strategies for reading and remembering, (2) simple rules of text construction, (3) differing demands of a variety of tests to which their information may be put, and (4) the importance of activating any background knowledge which they may have, they cannot help but become more effective learners. Such self-awareness is a prerequisite for self-regulation, the ability to orchestrate, monitor, and check one's own cognitive activities.

The results in Carrell et al. (1989) suggest that effective second language reading pedagogy must include not only training and practice in the use of task-specific strategies (i.e. strategy training), instruction in orchestrating, overseeing, and monitoring these strategies (i.e. self-regulation training), but, more importantly, information about the significance and outcome of these strategies and the range of their utility (i.e. awareness training). Too often students in second language reading programs, who receive instruction only in the skills or strategies, fail to use them intelligently and on their own volition in other reading situations because they do not appreciate the reasons why such strategies are useful nor do they understand where and when to use them. Adding instruction in awareness and regulation, or knowledge about a strategy's evaluation, rationale, and utility should greatly increase the positive outcomes of instruction.

This approach is, in effect, training for lateral transfer in the sense of Gagne (1967), i.e. explicitly instructing students about what the strategy is, why it should be learned, where, when, and how to use a strategy in a variety of appropriate domains, and how to evaluate their use of the strategy (Winograd and Hare 1988). Such instruction would go far beyond much of what passes for second language reading pedagogy today, which is often limited to repeated but relatively unguided and uninformed exposure to a task, and materials saturated with directives but short on explanations. Such instruction should enable us to produce readers who are 'strategic strategy users'.

Research on reading strategies has not only demonstrated that reading strategies are important to second language reading—perhaps not a very startling result by itself—but further that readers' metacognitive awareness of strategies is also related in important ways to successful and unsuccessful second language reading, and, finally, and perhaps least obviously, that explicit, overt training of both reading strategies and of awareness and regulation of strategies can contribute significantly to successful second or foreign language reading pedagogy.

References

Anderson, Neil J. 1990. Individual differences in strategy use in second language reading and testing. Unpublished paper presented at the conference on Research Perspectives in Adult Language Learning and Acquisition, Ohio State University, Columbus, October 1990.
Baker, Linda and Ann L. Brown. 1984. Metacognitive skills and reading. Handbook of reading research, ed. by P. David Pearson, 353-94. New York: Longman.
Barnett, Marva A. 1988. Reading through context: How real and perceived strategy use affects L2 comprehension. Modern Language Journal 72.150-62.
Block, Ellen. 1986. The comprehension strategies of second language readers. TESOL Quarterly 20.463-94.

Brown, Ann L. 1981. Metacognition: The development of selective attention strategies for learning from texts. Directions in reading: Research and instruction, ed. by Michael L. Kamil, 21-43. Washington, D.C.: National Reading Conference.
Brown, Ann L., Bonnie B. Armbruster, and Linda Baker. 1986. The role of metacognition in reading and studying. Reading comprehension: From research to practice, ed. by Judith Orasanu, 49-75. Hillsdale, N.J.: Erlbaum.
Brown, Ann L., Joseph C. Campione, and Jeanne D. Day. 1981. Learning to learn: On training students to learn from texts. Educational Researcher 10.14-21.
Brown, Ann L., and Annemarie Sullivan Palincsar. 1982. Inducing strategic learning from texts by means of informed, self-control training. Topics in Learning and Learning Disabilities 2.1-17.
Brown, Ann L., Annemarie Sullivan Palincsar, and Bonnie B. Armbruster. 1984. Instructing comprehension-fostering activities in interactive learning situations. Learning and comprehension of text, ed. by Heinz Mandl, Nancy L. Stein and Tom Trabasso, 255-86. Hillsdale, NJ: Erlbaum.
Canney, George, and Peter Winograd. 1979. Schemata for reading and reading comprehension performance. (Technical Report No. 120). Urbana, Ill.: University of Illinois, Center for the Study of Reading.
Carrell, Patricia L. 1989. Metacognitive awareness and second language reading. Modern Language Journal 73.121-34.
Carrell, Patricia L. [in press]. Awareness of text structure: Effects on recall. Language Learning.
Carrell, Patricia L., Becky G. Pharis, and Joseph C. Liberto. 1989. Metacognitive strategy training for ESL reading. TESOL Quarterly 23.647-78.
Casanave, Christine Pearson. 1988. Comprehension monitoring in ESL reading: A neglected essential. TESOL Quarterly 22.283-302.
Clarke, Mark A. 1980. The short circuit hypothesis of ESL reading—or when language competence interferes with reading performance. Modern Language Journal 64.203-9.
Cook, Linda K., and Richard E. Mayer. 1983. Reading strategies training for meaningful learning from prose. Cognitive strategy research: Educational applications, ed. by Michael Pressley and Joel R. Levin, 87-131. New York: Springer-Verlag.
Devine, Joanne. 1984. ESL readers' internalized models of the reading process. On TESOL '83, ed. by Jean Handscombe, Richard Orem, and Barry P. Taylor, 95-108. Washington, D.C.: TESOL.
Dijk, Teun A. van, and Walter Kintsch. 1983. Strategies of discourse comprehension. New York: Academic Press.
Duffy, Gerald G., Laura R. Roehler, and Beth Ann Herrmann. 1988. Modeling mental processes helps poor readers become strategic readers. The Reading Teacher 41.762-7.
Eskey, David E. 1988. Holding in the bottom: An interactive approach to the language problems of second language readers. In: Interactive approaches to second language reading, ed. by Patricia L. Carrell, Joanne Devine, and David E. Eskey, 93-100. Cambridge: Cambridge University Press.
Flavell, John H. 1978. Metacognitive development. In: Structural/process theories of complex human behavior, ed. by Joseph M. Scandura and Charles J. Brainerd, 217-45. Alphen a.d. Rijn, Netherlands: Sijthoff and Noordhoff.

Gagne, Robert A. 1967. Learning and individual differences. Columbus, Ohio: Merrill.
Gambrell, Linda B., and Betty S. Heathington. 1981. Adult disabled readers' metacognitive awareness about reading tasks and strategies. Journal of Reading Behavior 13.215-22.
Garner, Ruth, and Katherine Kraus. 1981-82. Good and poor comprehender differences in knowing and regulating reading behaviors. Educational Research Quarterly 6.5-12.
Gavelek, James R., and Taffy E. Raphael. 1985. Metacognition, instruction, and the role of questioning activities. In: Metacognition, cognition, and human performance: Instructional practices, ed. by D. L. Forrest-Pressley, G. E. MacKinnon, and T. Gary Waller, 103-36. Orlando, Fla.: Academic Press.
Hauptman, Philip C. 1979. A comparison of first and second language reading strategies among English-speaking university students. Interlanguage Studies Bulletin 4.173-201.
Hosenfeld, Carol. 1977. A preliminary investigation of the reading strategies of successful and nonsuccessful second language learners. System 5.110-23.
Johnston, Peter, and Margie Byrd. 1983. Basal readers and the improvement of reading comprehension. Searches for meaning in reading/language processing and instruction, ed. by Jerome A. Niles and Larry A. Harris, 140-7. Rochester, NY: National Reading Conference.
Knight, Stephanie L., Yolanda N. Padron, and Hersholt C. Waxman. 1985. The cognitive reading strategies of ESL students. TESOL Quarterly 19.789-92.
Myers, Meyer, II, and Scott G. Paris. 1978. Children's metacognitive knowledge about reading. Journal of Educational Psychology 70.680-90.
Padron, Yolanda N. 1985. Utilizing cognitive reading strategies to improve English reading comprehension of Spanish-speaking bilingual students. Unpublished doctoral dissertation, University of Houston.
Padron, Yolanda N., and Hersholt C. Waxman. 1988. The effect of ESL students' perceptions of their cognitive strategies on reading achievement. TESOL Quarterly 22.146-50.
Paris, Scott G., Marjorie Y. Lipson, and Karen K. Wixson. 1983. Becoming a strategic reader. Contemporary Educational Psychology 8.293-316.
Paris, Scott G., and Meyer Myers II. 1981. Comprehension monitoring, memory, and study strategies of good and poor readers. Journal of Reading Behavior 13.5-22.
Pritchard, Robert. 1990. The effects of cultural schemata on reading processing strategies. Reading Research Quarterly 25.273-95.
Resnick, Lauren B. 1979. Theories and prescriptions for early reading instruction. Theory and practice of early reading, Vol. 2, ed. by Lauren B. Resnick and Phyllis A. Weaver, 321-38. Hillsdale, N.J.: Erlbaum.
Sarig, Gissi. 1987. High-level reading in the first and in the foreign language: Some comparative process data. In: Research in reading in English as a second language, ed. by Joanne Devine, Patricia L. Carrell, and David E. Eskey, 105-20. Washington, D.C.: TESOL.
Sarig, Gissi, and Shoshana Folman. 1987. Metacognitive awareness and theoretical knowledge in coherence production. Unpublished paper presented at the Communication and Cognition International Congress, Ghent, Belgium.

Steffensen, Margaret S., Chitra Joag-Dev, and Richard C. Anderson. 1979. A cross-cultural perspective on reading comprehension. Reading Research Quarterly 15.

Waxman, Hersholt C., and Yolanda N. Padron. 1987. The effect of students' perceptions of cognitive strategies on reading achievement. Unpublished paper presented at the annual meeting of the Southwest Educational Research Association, Dallas.

Winograd, Peter, and Victoria Chou Hare. 1988. Direct instruction of reading comprehension strategies: The nature of teacher explanation. In: Learning and study strategies: Issues in assessment, instruction, and evaluation, ed. by Claire E. Weinstein, Ernest T. Goetz, and Patricia A. Alexander, 121-39. San Diego: Academic Press.

Zvetina, Marina. 1987. From research to pedagogy: What do L2 reading studies suggest? Foreign Language Annals 20.233-8.

The state of the art in teaching pronunciation

Dorothy M. Chun
University of Texas at Austin

Introduction. In the last several decades, two general responses to teaching pronunciation were prevalent: the first was to teach articulatory phonetics in an essentially structuralist fashion, i.e. to isolate the sounds to be learned, contrast them with the L1 sounds, and provide exercises for practicing them; and the second, a fairly common response from the 1960s to the early 1980s, was simply to avoid or ignore it.[1] However, pronunciation teaching seems to be undergoing a revival. Based on the research and the handbooks from the second half of the 1980s, two main trends emerge: first, the more recent focus on oral communication has sparked interest in the teaching of pronunciation units larger than the word, particularly stress and intonation of phrases and sentences, and second, computer technology is being increasingly used as an additional source for improving pronunciation, not only of individual sounds but also of tones in tonal languages and intonation in non-tonal languages.

This paper will show how intonation is slowly regaining recognition as an integral part of foreign language competence and proficiency, i.e. there has been a marked shift in focus from individual sounds or phonemes to sentence intonation, suprasegmentals, and other features of the larger context of utterances. As one way to implement this shift in emphasis, we turn to computer software that provides help not only with vowels and consonants but with intonational contours as well, and we also examine the research on the effectiveness of visual feedback for improving pronunciation and intonation.

1 The research agenda for the last decade. Leather (1983) suggests two reasons why pronunciation is ignored, i.e. why pronunciation is often thought to be a dispensable component of second- or foreign-language learning. First, the shift in pedagogical concern from linguistic form to communicative function has focused on 'getting the message across' rather than on 'getting the sounds correct.' Second, theoretical linguistics has not provided helpful input for teaching applications: the

---

1 Cf. Yule (1990:107) and Morley (1987:preface).

phonemic approach of structuralist linguistics has not proven to be enormously successful, and generative linguistics has offered little in the practical realm.

To correct this deficiency, Leather suggests seven research areas, only one of which does not have some relevance to either intonation or computer technology. Only the fifth area, 'Constraints on pronunciation mastery,' is not tied in some way to the teaching of intonation or the use of computers. These constraints include: age; personal variations in aptitude, motivation, and attitude; individual rather than developmental differences, e.g. patterns of hemispheric specialization in the brain; psychological variables like 'empathy,' and 'intuition,' 'self-esteem,' 'flexibility of ego boundaries,' e.g. studies with alcohol and tranquilizing drugs.[2]

All of the other six research areas deal directly or indirectly with intonation or computer technology. Leather's first research question is 'What are our pronunciation goals?' We must decide whether we are striving, e.g. for 'near-native accents,' for 'comfortably intelligible' pronunciation, or for 'socially acceptable' pronunciation. This last option is what takes us beyond the segmentals (consonants and vowels) to the suprasegmentals (stress and intonation). For learners to communicate in a socially acceptable way, they need to know, for example, how to ask questions politely and how to interrupt, more than how to pronounce certain sounds perfectly. While the ACTFL Guidelines do not address pronunciation at great length, the emphasis seems to be equally divided among straight *linguistic* competence as well as *sociolinguistic, discourse,* and *strategic* competence.[3]

Leathers' second research area focuses precisely on this 'reversal of emphasis from segmentals to prosodic patterns.' Previously, the teaching and learning of segmentals was primary, while intonation was considered a 'luxury.' However, if students are to develop all four types of language competence, then learning to express nuances of meaning beyond the face value of individual words or phrases and being able to argue or keep the floor can no longer be considered 'icing' but must be made an integral part of learning a language. This ties in directly with Leather's fourth research concern, namely, the 'transfer in pronunciation from L1': if we are to eradicate learners' 'accents' partially or nearly completely, more, or at least equal, emphasis must be placed on the suprasegmentals as on the segmentals.[4]

Leather's third and sixth research areas can be discussed together. The third deals with the 'factors involved in L2 phonological acquisi-

---

2 Cf., for example, Conrad (1991).
3 Cf. the most recent *ACTFL Oral Proficiency Interview Tester Training Manual* (1989).
4 Cf. van Els and de Bot (1987).

tion'[5] and includes questions such as the relationship between perception and production,[6] the importance of auditory feedback, and the different classes of sound patterns, e.g. consonantal, vocalic, and prosodic, which may call for different measures of articulatory and perceptual training.[7]

Further research on 'perceptual and articulatory training' is in fact Leather's sixth area, and he cautions that while perceptual training can change phonetic perception, it does not always permanently 're-tune' the perceptual system. Furthermore, the relation between articulatory activity and acoustic output may not be simple, i.e. speakers could learn to modify their articulatory output to within a good approximation of a target sound, but fine tuning to achieve the exact sound may be much more difficult (though possibly facilitated by perceptual training) (p. 208).[8] In addition, different classes of sounds are learned or acquired differently. Articulatory instruction depends upon orosensory perceptions, but sensory feedback is much greater for consonantal articulations (e.g. /θ/) than for vocalic ones (e.g. /œ/), and even less for a prosodic feature like voice pitch. Other researchers found that sensory perception played no part in the production of voice pitch, which might suggest that for pitch patterns the only approach is auditory perceptual training' (Mallard et al. 1978:210).

This leads directly to the seventh and last of Leather's research areas, namely 'instrumental aids,' which is also one of the focuses of this paper. Auditory self-perception aids like the record-replay facilities of language labs have existed for decades; but learners, who are required to monitor themselves, generally lack the phonetic criteria for critical listening. The situation can be remedied by real-time feedback, e.g. visual displays, about aspects which would otherwise remain below the threshold of discriminability. It is here that computers could play an increasingly important role.

2 The next decade: Communicative proficiency and discourse intonation. Recent scholarship and instructional materials that have appeared in the eight years since 1983 counter the state of the art described by Leather. Even the rationale for teaching pronunciation has changed. Gilbert (1984:1), in her handbook for teaching pronunciation and listening comprehension in English, for example, states very simply that 'there are two main reasons to teach pronunciation: Students need to

---

5 Cf. Leather (1983:202) who suggests, as with other areas of language pedagogy, 'advances in pronunciation teaching might well depend upon better understanding of pronunciation learning.'
6 Cf., e.g. Fox (1982), Broselow et al. in Ioup (1987).
7 Cf., e.g. de Bot (1981).
8 Cf. Molholt (1988) and Molholt and Presler (1986).

derstand and to be understood,' thus expressing the important link between pronunciation and comprehension instead of ignoring the situation as had previously been done.

The definition of the role of pronunciation in language has also changed. Research by Pennington and Richards (1986) and Pennington (1989b) emphasized the need to teach pronunciation with a 'top-down' approach, i.e. focusing on the rhythm and sentence melody of entire phrases or sentences as opposed to the 'bottom-up' approach of mastering single sounds or words. Discourse intonation, instead of only pronunciation, is beginning to be seen as a fundamental component of both listening comprehension and oral proficiency, as it serves to mark thought units, salient or new information, as well as to signal different types of conversational strategies. Students must be made aware of how intonation functions in language and must be given opportunities both to hear and to practice intonational patterns, so that they will comprehend better and be better communicators themselves.

In the 1980s, the field of ESL took the lead in reviving interest in pronunciation and in promoting the teaching of stress, rhythm, and intonation, whereas foreign language research seems to be lagging behind. For example, for the entire 10-year period from 1980-1990, there were only 3 articles in the *Modern Language Journal*,[9] 2 in the German pedagogical journal *Die Unterrichtspraxis*,[10] 2 in *The French Review*,[11] and 2 in *Hispania*[12] which dealt with pronunciation, and of the 9 total, 4 were on intonation.[13] Similarly, surveys of elementary German textbooks of the last decade also reveal very few treatments of intonation, and one can assume that it is not being taught explicitly in the classroom either.[14]

In contrast, however, to the dearth of both research and instructional materials for intonation in the foreign language classroom, there is greater research interest and more available materials for ESL. In the

---

9   Cf. McCandless and Winitz (1986), van Els and de Bot (1987), Chun (1988b).
10   Cf. Wipf (1985) and Chun (1988a).
11   Cf. Walz (1980) and Frommer and Weitz (1981).
12   Cf. Kelm (1987) and R. Brown (1990); Torreblanca (1988) is a theoretical article about pronunciation but not about practical applications.
13   In *Foreign Language Annals* 1980-1990, cf. Mantini (1980), Ecklund and Wiese (1981), Hieke (1981), Scanlan (1987).

For Chinese, available issues of the *Journal of Chinese Language Teachers' Association* were consulted. In 28 issues for the period 1966-1981, five articles on pronunciation were found: three dealt with tones (Ching 1971, Chen 1973, White 1981), one with segmentals (Chin 1972), and one with auditory perception and comprehension tests (Ching 1972).

14   In the last five years, two students in my graduate phonology seminars have surveyed several dozen elementary German textbooks. Copies of their papers are available on request. For Russian textbooks, a similar survey was done by Dennis Browne, Bates College, and presented at the MLA Meeting in 1989.

same 10-year period, for example, there were 11 articles in the *TESOL Quarterly* which dealt with some aspect of pronunciation; of the eleven, four dealt specifically with intonation.[15] Morley's 1987 collection of essays reflects focuses on 'working with pronunciation as an integral part of, not apart from, oral communication' and on 'the primary importance of suprasegmentals . . . and how they are used to communicate meaning, with a secondary importance assigned to segmentals . . .' (cf. Preface). In addition, the recent handbooks for teaching English pronunciation all include, if not specifically focus on, stress and intonation.[16]

Despite the fact that little is being done on intonation per se in foreign languages either theoretically or practically, the 1989 *ACTFL Oral Proficiency Interview Tester Training Manual* and the work by Byrnes (1987), Kramsch (1986), Lantolf and Frawley (1985), to name just a few, reflect in principle, the need for more research and applications to teaching.[17] With the OPI emphasis on *natural* conversation, much attention is given to the pragmatic and discourse aspects of speech, e.g. the negotiation of meaning, the importance of context, cultural and sociolinguistic competence, task- or goal-oriented activities.[18] In addition, the OPI manual outlines excellent *interviewer* strategies for eliciting speech, e.g. rephrased questions, hypothetical questions, prelude questions, polite requests, and intonation questions. It is this attention to the pragmatics of natural conversation that suggests we should also be teaching our students, the *interviewees*, to do this type of initiating and conversation management, well before they become OPI interviewers![19] Thus, we should now speak of sentence intonation and meaning instead of pronunciation, but the implementation of this change in focus has been slow both among teachers as well as testers.

---

15 Cf. Hill and Beebe (1980), Leahy (1980), Neufeld (1980), Flege (1981), de Bot and Mailfert (1982), Esling and Wong (1983), Temperly (1983), Acton (1984), Pennington and Richards (1986), Molholt (1988), and Brown (1988). Articles on pronunciation in other journals include: Tumposky (1982), Hieke (1981, 1984, 1985), Pritchard (1985), Pegolo (1985), and Boyle (1987).

16 Cf. Gilbert (1984), Pavlik (1986), Sheeler and Markley (1986), and English (1988) for American English; and Kenworthy (1987) and Bradford (1988) for British English.

17 The 1986 Guidelines mention pronunciation only very generally at the Novice and Intermediate levels, merely stating that it may be 'strongly influenced by the first language.' At the Advanced and Superior levels, intonation is said to be used to 'communicate fine shades of meaning' and as one means of using of interactive and discourse strategies, such as distinguishing main ideas from supporting information.

18 Cf. Chun (1990).

19 Cf. textbooks such as Fischer and Richardson (1989), *Wie, bitte?* for German, whose aims are to teach discourse strategy beginning at the elementary level. The topics they use all 'grew out of the functional syllabus for the book, which is squarely based on the *ACTFL Proficiency Guidelines*' (personal communication 1990).

Figure 1. Visi-Pitch displays of pitch of the French question *Qu'est-ce qu'il fait?*

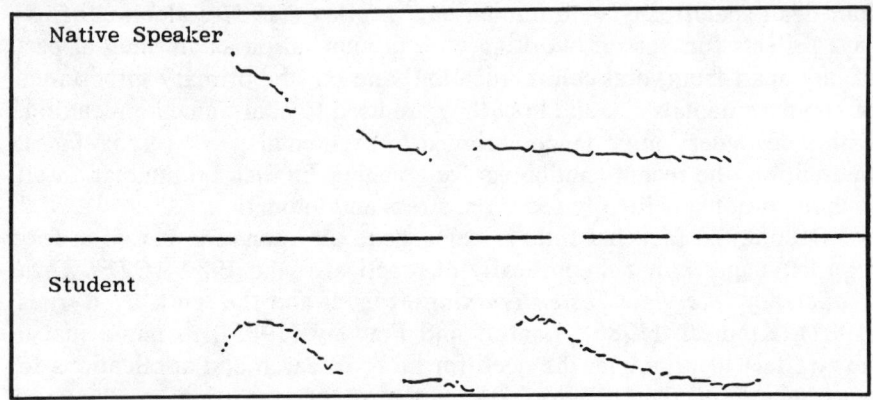

3 Use of computer technology and software for improving pronunciation and intonation. While the new emphasis on intonation and meaning has not yet shifted into practice, the situation for computer software has improved considerably. Leather had, in 1983, described the ideal computer-managed pronunciation training as one 'which makes use of synthetic as well as natural speech models, which processes learners' productions to provide visual displays of salient features together with an assessment of phonetic accuracy, and which leads the individual learner through a series of perception and production training activities selected according to ongoing performance, while simultaneously compiling a detailed record of progress for teaching supervision' (Leather 1983:212).[20] While these desiderata may have seemed to be just a 'wish list' in 1983, developments in hardware and software since then have addressed all of these features to varying degrees. Several of these capabilities are currently available commercially, and research is continuing on the effectiveness of such computer-assisted pronunciation tutors.

Computers have been utilized for providing learners with visualizations of their intonational patterns since the 1970s, but a recent development of the mid- to late-1980s is the increasing use of microcomputers and other hardware, such as Visi-Pitch.[21] With it students can see both a native speaker's pitch curve and their own simultaneously (Figure 1).[22]

---

20 Cf. also Underwood (1989) which describes a fictional HyperLang hypermedia system which is capable both of talking as well as understanding real spoken speech.
21 Cf. Abberton and Fourcin (1975), James (1976 and 1979).
22 Visi-Pitch can be purchased as a single unit including the computer or as a separate unit which can be interfaced with an MS-DOS PC. Available from Kay Elemetrics, 12 Maple Avenue, Pine Brook, NJ 07058, (201) 227-7760, 1-800-289-5297, Attention: Laurie Fischer.

For example, Fischer (1986a and 1986b) reports on the use of Visi-Pitch for teaching Chinese tones and French intonation, respectively, and Molholt (1988) used both the Visi-Pitch and a Speech Spectrographic Display for improving both the segmental as well as the suprasegmental phonology of Chinese speakers of English.[23]

For a more affordable price, students would be able to do the same thing with the Macintosh. The MacRecorder sound digitizer can be used in conjunction with Signalyze, for example, to produce and store intonation curves of native speakers and learners, as well as to display them next to each other (see Figures 2 to 4).[24] While no pedagogical software currently exists which automatically displays first the native speaker's utterance and then a student's attempt, each with a single keystroke, the technology is available and accessible, and it is up to us teachers to implement pedagogically sound intonational software.

Figure 2. Pitch curves made with *Signalyze* (speech digitized with *MacRecorder*). The Chinese nonsense word *aka*.

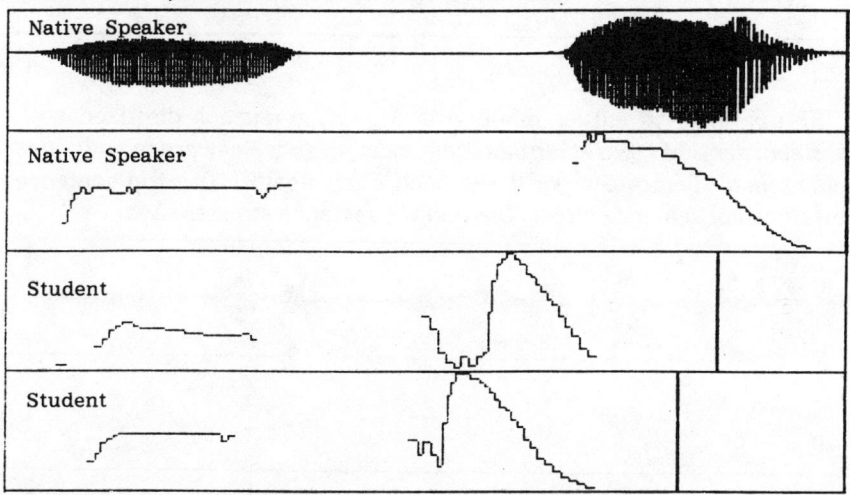

---

23 Software for more traditional pronunciation exercises, e.g. practicing vowels, consonants and common phrases or expressions, is also currently available. For example, the HyperGlot Software Co. markets Pronunciation Tutors for Chinese, French, German, Japanese, Russian and Spanish, all of which include digitized sound, and some of which include perception tests and/or graphics of the mouth, face, and tongue. HyperGlot's address: 505 Forest Hills Blvd., Knoxville, TN 37919; Telephone: 1-800-726-5087, 1-615-558-8270.

24 MacRecorder can be purchased from Farallon Computing 415-596-9000, FAX 415-841-5770. Signalyze is available from InfoSignal, Inc. FAX 206-525-7603. For a more extensive listing of other hardware and software products for both the Macintosh and the IBM-PC, cf. Chun (1989).

Figure 3. Pitch curves made with *Signalyze* (speech digitized with *MacRecorder*) of two Chinese sentences: *ta xian zai bu zai jia* 'He is not at home right now.' In the top sentence the stress is on the last two words 'at home'; the bottom sentence has normal sentence stress.

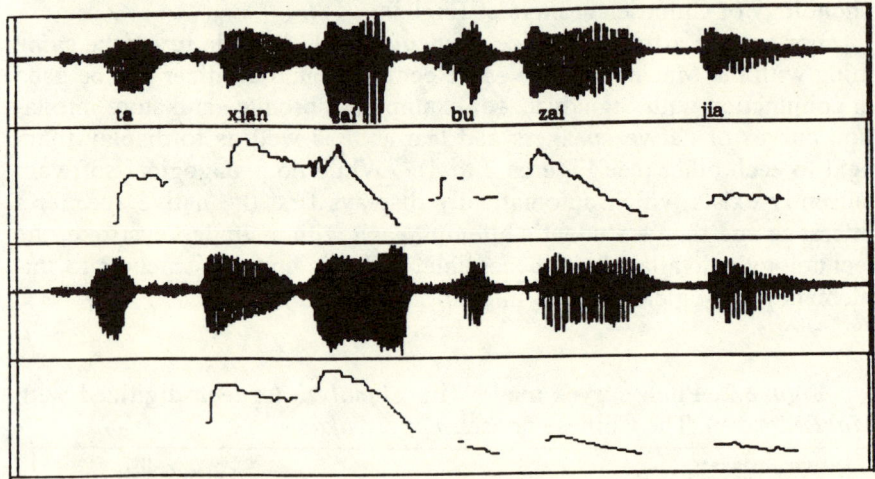

Figure 4. Pitch curves made with *Signalyze* (speech digitized with *MacRecorder*) of two German sentences: *Morgen werden wir uns wiedersehen* 'Tomorrow we'll see each other again'. The top sentence shows normal sentence stress; the bottom sentence stresses 'again'.

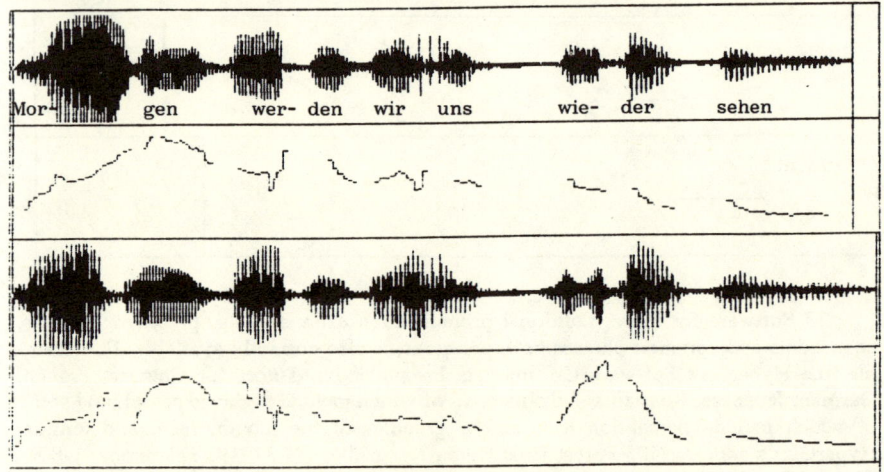

However, as Pennington (1989b) points out, there is still a need for further experimentation and research to determine the effectiveness of the various methods. One of the greatest advantages of using computer-assisted pronunciation and intonation tutors is that the computer serves both as a medium of instruction as well as a tool for research, i.e. a software program, while teaching pronunciation, can simultaneously keep detailed and thorough records of student performance and progress. Consequently, several recent studies on the effectiveness of visual feedback in teaching intonation and on the use of technology to develop new measures of speaking proficiency represent the type of ongoing research that must be done in addition to developing better and more efficient computer software.

De Bot's earliest work (1980 and 1981) warned against assuming that any type of feedback, no matter what form, would have a positive effect on the acquisition of pronunciation or on attempts to improve it. While experimental or instrumental measurements of intonation are an improvement over the impressionistic basis of traditional intonation teaching methods and handbooks, 'aspects of intonation which are physically and perceptually demonstrable, are not necessarily useful from a teaching point of view. Apart from this, methods making use of visualisation as an aid in intonation learning wrongly imply, that visualisation by itself is useful in teaching' (1981:39). It is thus necessary to ascertain whether or not students are as excited about such methods as researchers.

His 1982 study, however, showed that training in the perception of intonation did result in a statistically significant improvement in the production of English intonation patterns by both Dutch and French students. Subsequent studies using visual and audio-visual feedback with computers further corroborated his initial findings: the 1983 work showed that audio-visual feedback is more effective in intonation learning than auditory feedback, and the 1984 study with Weltens showed that 'feedback delay is not a critical factor when using a pitch visualizer for intonation teaching, but that the nature of the speech material [voiceless vs. voiced consonants, neutral vs. contrastive intonation] . . . does dramatically affect the quality of the visual feedback' (Weltens and de Bot 1984:79).

Pennington (1991:5) states that a further advantage of using computers in developing speaking/listening skills is the consistency of the feedback, 'eliminating the quirky views and behavior, the dogma, or the bias of a human judge as a source of feedback. The computer is just much fairer and more dependable than a human being, and more reliable.'

In addition to research on the effectiveness of audio-visual feedback from the computer, other studies have examined the possibility of using computers to evaluate speaking proficiency and pronunciation. For example, Molholt and Presler (1986) conducted a pilot study of the feasibility of computer-assisted evaluation of pronunciation and found that machine-generated scores of speech samples ranked the samples in the same order as trained human raters. Clark (1986) reported on a tape-mediated, 'semi-direct' test of speaking proficiency for English-speaking learners of Chinese. The test was designed to be scored and interpreted according to the ACTFL/ETS/ILR guidelines for proficiency tests. An interactive video project, TOPS or 'Test of Oral Proficiency Skills, was reported on by Lowe and Hughes (1990).[25] For the long term, this may remedy the implementation problems of switching emphasis to intonation but not being able to rate it.

Thus, the recent and rapid advances in computational linguistics make possible the use of computers for evaluation purposes, particularly in speech recognition. Consequently, even more corrective features of natural language may well be feasible in the not-too-distant future. The work available since 1983 allows us to suggest realistic directions for research and software packages in the near future.

4 Conclusions. First, the recent scholarship on the teaching of pronunciation indicates a trend toward incorporating meaningful, contextualized practice of sounds, rhythm and intonation into the broader domain of oral proficiency, as described in the 1989 *ACTFL Oral Proficiency Interview Tester Training Manual*. Learning to perceive and produce appropriate intonation is tied to comprehension and is needed to achieve cohesion and coherence in discourse. At the same time, while not necessarily explicitly building intonation practice into textbooks, authors are increasingly basing their materials directly on the ACTFL Guidelines, with the goal of providing students with opportunities to negotiate, to initiate and manage discourse, as well as to comprehend input from others. Therefore, we need to integrate pronunciation practice of both suprasegmentals and segmentals into these types of discourse activities, and perhaps into the Guidelines themselves, together with a feasible rating system.

Second, among others, Pennington (1989a) advocates the development of computer programs which provide this type of meaningful instruction in speaking and listening. Computers can both create environments which facilitate interaction as well as provide training in production and perception of speech. Citing the work of Chaudron (1985) and Richards (1986), Pennington stresses the need for language learning software to move to skill-based and task-based learning activities which not only offer users practice in listening comprehension but also elicit and practice specific types of interactions, language forms, sound contrasts, or nuances of meaning signalled by intonation.[26] In other words, she extends the definition of intonation to include context

---

25 Paper read at the ACTFL Annual Meeting, November 1990 in Nashville, TN.
26 Cf. also Piper (1986) and Young (1988).

and transactions, not only sentences. We must leave the concept of segmental pronunciation behind decisively as a teaching tool.

While the training of production and perception of speech may sometimes involve noninteractional formats, the goal of this decade's work should be to try, whenever possible, to use meaningful language. How can we implement this? When teaching intonation with the computer-generated visual displays of users' pitch curves, for example, the same sentence, using different intonations to express different pragmatic meanings, could be compared side by side by students. Similarly, visual images of such phenomena as linking, contraction, and other forms of reduction and phonological processes associated with fluent speech focus more on keeping meaningful units together than on getting individual sounds right.[27] That is, for those students who cannot correct their intonation by conventional aural stimuli, we can offer visual corrections and feedback in the form of pitch curves and emphasis or intensity curves to be matched.

Third, for the training of speech perception, listening comprehension tests as well as perception tests which test listening acuity or perceptual accuracy should also be increasingly computerized to improve our assessments of student performance. Automatic recordkeeping and scoring, for instance, would allow for individualized branching and pacing of the test for more differentiated testing. This recordkeeping capability of the computer would allow detailed tracking of the stages which learners pass through in acquiring oral and listening skills, e.g. by measuring the gradual changes in students' phonetic space or intonation contours over time. Providing individualized feedback and micro-tutors allows a much more sophisticated language learning pedagogy to emerge, which will ultimately feed into proficiency.

Thus, over the long term, the computer can ideally provide an almost self-contained system combining training, testing and research in the development of pronunciation and listening proficiency. 'Perhaps the most exciting possibilities combining language training, assessment and research involve two-person interactions which are both facilitated and analyzed by a computer' (Pennington 1989a:119), and it is in this direction, i.e. combining the teaching of pronunciation and discourse intonation with computer technology, that future research should proceed. Only if we integrate these functions into computer software will it be worth buying this technology. And only with this technology can we redefine the role of intonation in oral proficiency as the conclusion to more research on sophisticated speech-acts and sociolinguistic aspects of language than has been done before.

---

27 Cf. Hieke (1984 and 1985).

References

Abberton, Evelyn, and A. J. Fourcin. 1975. Visual feedback and the acquisition of intonation. In: Foundations of language development. Eric H. Lenneberg and Elizabeth Lenneberg, eds. 157-165. New York: Academic Press.
ACTFL Oral proficiency interview. Tester training manual. Heidi Byrnes, Irene Thompson, and Kathryn Buck, eds. NY: ACTFL.
Acton, William. 1984. Changing fossilized pronunciation. TESOL Quarterly 18.71-85.
Bot, Kees de. 1980. The role of feedback and feedforward in the teaching of pronunciation: An overview. System 8.35-45.
Bot, Kees de. 1981. Intonation teaching and pitch control. ITL Review of Applied Linguistics 52.31-42.
Bot, Kees de and Kate Mailfert. 1982. The teaching of intonation: Fundamental research and classroom applications. TESOL Quarterly 16.71-77.
Bot, Kees de. 1983. Visual feedback of intonation I: Effectiveness and induced practice behavior. Language and Speech 26(4):331-350.
Boyle, Joseph P. 1987. Perspectives on stress and intonation in language learning. System 15.189-195.
Bradford, Barbara. 1988. Intonation in context. Cambridge: Cambridge University Press.
Brazil, David, Malcolm Coulthard, and Catherine Johns. 1980. Discourse, intonation, and language teaching. London: Longman.
Broselow, Ellen, Richard R. Hurtig, and Catherine Ringen. 1987. The perception of second language prosody. In: Interlanguage phonology: The acquisition of a second language sound system. Georgette Ioup and Steven H. Weinberger, eds. Cambridge, Mass.: Newbury House.
Brown, Adam. 1988. Functional load and the teaching of pronunciation. TESOL Quarterly 22.593-606.
Brown, Richard. 1990. A maverick vowel: The notorious /e/ (schwa). Hispania 73.1158-1161.
Byrnes, Heidi and Michael Canale, eds. 1986. Defining and developing proficiency. In: Guidelines, implementations, and concepts. Lincolnwood, Ill.: National Textbook Co.
Byrnes, Heidi. 1987. Speech as process. Foreign Language Annals 20.301-310.
Chaudron, Craig. 1985. Intake: On models and methods for discovering learners' processing of input. Studies in Second Language Acquisition 7.1-14.
Chen, Shirley. 1973. The third tone and see-saw pairs. Journal of the Chinese Language Teachers' Association 8.145-149.
Chin, Yin-lien C. 1972. How to teach Mandarin retroflex and palatal sounds. Journal of the Chinese Language Teachers' Association 7.77-81.
Ching, Eugene. 1972. Chinese auditory perception and comprehension tests. Journal of the Chinese Language Teachers' Association 7.37-42.
Ching, Nora. 1971. A minor problem in tone sandhi. Journal of the Chinese Language Teachers' Association 6.41-57.
Chun, Dorothy M. 1988a. Teaching intonation as part of communicative competence: Suggestions for the classroom. Die Unterrichtspraxis 21.81-88.

Chun, Dorothy M. 1988b. The neglected role of intonation in communicative competence and proficiency. Modern Language Journal 72:295-303.
Chun, Dorothy M. 1989. Teaching tone and intonation with microcomputers. CALICO Journal 7:21-46.
Chun, Dorothy M. 1990. Teaching discourse intonation: Its effect on listening, comprehension, and oral proficiency. Paper presented at the AATG Annual Meeting, Nashville, Tenn.
Clark, John L.D. 1986. Development of a tape-mediated, ACTFL/ILR scale-based test of Chinese speaking proficiency. In: Technology and language testing. Charles W. Stansfield, ed. Washington, D.C.: TESOL.
Conrad, Bernd K. 1991. The relationship between empathy and pronunciation ability: A study of elementary-level college students of German. Ph.D. Dissertation. University of Texas at Austin.
Ecklund, Constance L. and Peter Wiese. 1981. French accent through video analysis. Foreign Language Annals 14.17-23.
Els, Theo van and Kees de Bot. 1987. The role of intonation in foreign accent. Modern Language Journal 71.147-155.
English, Susan Lewis. 1988. Say it clearly: Exercises and activities for pronunciation and oral communication. New York: Collier Macmillan.
Esling, John H. and Rita F. Wong. 1983. Voice quality settings and the teaching of pronunciation. TESOL Quarterly 17.89-95.
Fischer, Laurie B. 1986a. The use of Visi-Pitch in the analysis of Chinese language suprasegmentals. Unpubl. ms. Pine Brook, NJ: Kay Elemetrics Corporation.
Fischer, Laurie B. 1986b. The use of audio/visual aids in the teaching and learning of French. Unpubl. ms. Pine Brook, N.J.: Kay Elemetrics Corporation.
Fischer, William B. and Peter N. Richardson. 1989. Wie, bitte? New York: John Wiley and Sons.
Flege, James Emil. 1981. The phonological basis of foreign accent: A hypothesis. TESOL Quarterly 15.443-455.
Fox, R.A. 1982. Individual variation in the perception of vowels: Implications for a perception-production link. Phonetica 39.1-22.
Frommer, Judith G. and Margaret Collins Weitz. 1981. "Sound" learning: Using taped interviews in foreign language courses. The French Review 55.233-240.
Gilbert, Judy B. 1984. Clear speech: Pronunciation and listening comprehension in American English. Cambridge: Cambridge University Press.
Grover, C., D. Jamieson and M. Dobrovolsky. 1987. Intonation in English, French, and German: Perception and production. Language and Speech 30(3): 277-295.
Hieke, A. E. 1985. A componential approach to oral fluency evaluation. Modern Language Journal 69. 135-142.
Hieke, A. E. 1984. Linking as a marker of fluent speech. Language and Speech 17:343-354.
Hieke, Adolf E. 1981. Audio-lectal practice and fluency acquisition. Foreign Language Annals 14. 189-194.
Hill, Clifford and Leslie M. Beebe. 1980. Contraction and blending: The use of orthographic clues in teaching pronunciation. TESOL Quarterly 14(3).
Ioup, Georgette and Steven H. Weinberger. 1987. Interlanguage phonology: The acquisition of a second language sound system. Cambridge, MA: Newbury House.

James, Allan and Jonathan Leather (eds.). 1987. Sound patterns in second language acquisition. Dordrecht: Foris.

James, Eric. 1976. The acquisition of prosodic features of speech using a speech visualizer. IRAL 14(3):227-243.

James, Eric. 1979. Intonation through visualization. In: Current issues in the phonetic sciences. H. and. P. Hollien, eds. 295-301. Amsterdam Studies in the Theory and History of Linguistic Science, IV, Amsterdam: John Benjamins.

Kelm, Orlando R. 1987. An acoustic study on the differences of contrastive emphasis between native and non-native Spanish speakers. Hispania 70.627-633.

Kenworthy, Joanne. 1987. Teaching English pronunciation. London: Longman.

Kramsch, Claire. 1986. From language proficiency to interactional competence. Modern Language Journal 70.366-372.

Lantolf, James P. and William Frawley. 1985. Oral proficiency testing: A critical analysis. Modern Language Journal 69.337-345.

Leahy, Robert M. 1980. A practical approach for teaching ESL pronunciation based on distinctive feature analysis. TESOL Quarterly 14(2).

Leather, Jonathan. 1983. Second-language pronunciation learning and teaching. Language Teaching 16.198-219.

McCandless, Peter and Harris Winitz. Test of pronunciation following one year of comprehension instruction in college German. Modern Language Journal 70.355-362.

Molholt, Garry and Ari M. Presler. 1986. Correlation between human and machine ratings of test of spoken English reading passages. Technology and Language Testing, ed. by Charles W. Stansfield. Washington, D.C.: TESOL.

Molholt, Garry. 1988. Computer-assisted instruction in pronunciation for Chinese speakers of American English. TESOL Quarterly 22(1):91-111.

Morley, Joan (ed.). 1987. Current perspectives on pronunciation: Practices anchored in theory. Washington, D.C.: TESOL.

Neufeld, Gerald G. 1980. On the adult's ability to acquire phonology. TESOL Quarterly 14.285-298.

Pavlik, Cheryl. 1986. Speak up! Rowley, Mass.: Newbury House.

Pegolo, Catherine. 1985. The role of rhythm and intonation in the silent reading of French as a foreign language. Reading in a Foreign Language 3.313-327.

Pennington, Martha C. 1989a. Teaching languages with computers: The state of the art. La Jolla: Athelstan.

Pennington, Martha C. 1989b. Teaching pronunciation from the top down. RELC Journal 20. 20-38.

Pennington, Martha C. 1991. Interview with Martha Pennington. Athelstan Newsletter 2 p. 5.

Pennington, Martha C. and Jack C. Richards. 1986. Pronunciation revisited. TESOL Quarterly 20(2):207-225.

Piper, Allison. 1986. Conversation and the computer: A study of conversational spin-off generated among learners of English as a foreign language working in groups. System 14, 2:187-98.

Prator, Clifford H., Jr. and Betty Wallace Robinett. 1985. Manual of American English pronunciation. 4th edn. New York: Holt, Rinehart and Winston.

Pritchard, Rosalind M.O. 1985. The Teaching of French Intonation to Native Speakers of English. IRAL 23.117-147.

Richards, Jack C. 1986. Focus on the learner. University of Hawaii Working Papers in ESL 5.61-86.
Scanlan, Timothy. 1987. Improving fluency in spoken French through a study of native pause behavior. Foreign Language Annals 20.345-352.
Schaffer, Deborah. 1983. The role of intonation as a cue to turn taking in conversation. Journal of Phonetics 11:243-257.
Sheeler, William D. and R.W. Markley. 1986. Sounds and rhythm: Focus on vowels. New York: Regents.
Temperly, Mary S. 1983. The articulatory target for final -s clusters. TESOL Quarterly 17.421-436.
Torreblanca, Máximo. 1988. La pronunciación española y los métodos de investigación. Hispania 71.669-674.
Tumposky, Nancy Rennau. 1982. Activities for practicing stress and intonation. English Teaching Forum 20.15-18.
Underwood, John. 1989. Hypermedia: Where we are and where we aren't. CALICO Journal. 6.4:23-26.
Walz, Joel. 1980. An empirical study of pronunciation errors in French. The French Review 53.424-432.
Weltens, B. and K. de Bot. 1984. Visual feedback of intonation II: Feedback delay and quality of feedback. Language and Speech 27(1):79-88.
White, Caryn M. 1981. Tonal pronunciation errors and interference from English. Journal of the Chinese Language Teachers' Association 16.27-56.
Wipf, Joseph. 1985. Toward improving second language pronunciation. Die Unterrichtspraxis 18.
Young, Richard. 1988. Computer-assisted language learning conversations: Negotiating an outcome. CALICO Journal. 5, 3:65-83.
Yule, George. 1990. Review of Kenworthy, Wong, and Morley. System 18.107-111.

Teaching listening: Ends and means

Elizabeth Joiner
University of South Carolina

A listening event in an instructional context. Courtney sits down in front of a computer terminal and types French 2. On the screen is a description of the tools that will be at her disposal as she views, and listens to one of the programs whose titles are now displayed on the screen of a television monitor positioned next to the computer. She makes her selection, and the first frame of an Astérix cartoon immediately appears. At this point, Courtney may choose to scan through the entire transcription before viewing the program or to begin viewing and use the keyboard to call for the transcription, or the key words, of a given sentence at any time. Still other options will permit Courtney to select a slower, clearer narrative sound track to replace the rapid original dialogue; to ask for sentence-by-sentence play, in which case the video will pause until she requests the next sentence; or to relisten to one or several sentences by selecting the key that corresponds to the command 'go back N sentences.' When she is satisfied with her comprehension, Courtney will record in her listening journal what she has listened to and for how long, whether she liked it or not, and what she has observed about herself as a listener, including an account of which of the many options available to her she actually used. Courtney is not an imaginary student of the twenty-first century. This scene took place during the fall semester of 1990, when Courtney was enrolled in an intermediate-level, video-based course that I taught at the University of South Carolina; and both the 'Télédouzaine' videodisc and the software program, called the Listening Tool, were developed by Jim Pusack and Sue Otto at the University of Iowa.

Listening from the inside out. At first blush, the situation described above would not seem to be a normal listening experience, and, furthermore, there would seem to be very little of what we usually call teaching going on as the Listening Tool allows the student to operate in a completely exploratory mode. Nevertheless, this situation consists of a listener, a text, and a number of possibilities for interaction between the two. As we shall see later, it also embodies a number of widely-held beliefs about listening. In analyzing this sample act of listening, we must consider both what Samuels (1987:298-99) has called 'inside the head' and 'outside the head' factors. Such an approach makes it clear that listening is first and foremost a covert activity. Since Courtney had no task to perform and was not tested on the material that she listened to, my only way of knowing what went on inside her head during that specific occasion was to read her journal, and even then I was obliged to rely on her ability as a self-observer and self-reporter.

Although we probably know too little about the listener-learners in our classes, there are some general learner factors that are believed to affect the listening process. These include age (Byrnes 1984, Seright 1985), sex (Coakley and Wolvin 1986, Boyle 1987), background and experience (Long 1989, 1991), cognitive processing style and hemispheric specialization (Coakley and Wolvin 1986), attitude and motivation (Coakley and Wolvin 1986), and hearing acuity (Joiner 1986, Gilmor et al. 1989). Other factors such as anxiety or receiver apprehension (Meyer 1984, Bacon 1989) and time of day (Coakley and Wolvin 1986) might be expected to affect a listener's performance on specific occasions.

While we have for some years been aware of the factors mentioned above, some very interesting recent observations have been made about the listening abilities of language learners at both ends of the learning curve. One study (Sparks and Ganschow 1991) concludes that college students who experience severe difficulties learning a foreign language may have subtle native language problems, basically auditory in nature, which surface when they attempt to learn a foreign language.[1] Examining language learners at the other end of the spectrum, Schneiderman and Desmarais (1988) in an attempt to identify characteristics of individuals who achieve native-like competence in a second language after puberty, found that the two subjects of their case studies had a higher percentage of correct scores in the left rather than the right ear on two dichotic listening tests, indicating that they were not left-lateralized for either French or English. Yet another recent study linking native and foreign language listening is reported on by Feyten (1990 and in press), who found statistically significant relationships between native language listening ability and overall foreign language proficiency, foreign language listening comprehension skills, and oral proficiency skills.

'Outside the head' factors that affect listening have been identified by Samuels (1987) as discussion topic, speaker awareness of listener need, message clarity and context. Although these factors are more appropriately applied to two-way interactive listening, they are flexible enough to be loosely adapted to one-way reactive listening as well.

---

1 This conclusion finds support in the work on the relationship between listening and dyslexia done by Tomatis (1978) and by Vellutino (1979).

Courtney, for example, chose a text with which she would interact until she either was satisfied with her comprehension of it or lost interest. In a more normal situation, she would have been able neither to manipulate the text nor to access numerous 'helps' designed to make the text comprehensible to a nonnative listener; in this case, however, speaker awareness of listener need was compensated for, at least to some extent, by the Listening Tool. On the other hand, in contrast to what might have been the case in a conversational listening situation, Courtney did not have to cope with what we typically call spontaneous free speech with its redundancy, reduced and ungrammatical forms, pauses, false starts, hesitations and rephrasings (Richards 1983). Nor was she able to affect the oral message by participating in the situation as both listener and speaker.

All the programs on the 'Télédouzaine' videodisc are authentic texts, defined in this case as texts produced by native speakers for native speakers. While there is not universal agreement in the profession that the use of unedited, sophisticated, nonpedagogical texts is desirable, especially for the teaching of listening at the beginning level (Ur 1984, Dunkel 1986), authentic materials have been defended on a number of grounds. They typically are seen as more culturally rich and interesting (Gilman and Moody 1984), more likely to bring about attentive, motivated listening (Long 1991), more whole and complete both linguistically and culturally (Meyer 1984, Belasco 1981), and in general more facilitative of language learning than contrived and controlled pedagogical materials, which may sometimes actually inhibit comprehension by reducing the characteristic natural redundancy of oral texts (Byrnes 1984).

Depending on her choice, Courtney might have heard any of several types of oral language described by Byrnes (1984): the deliberate free speech of an interview, the oral presentation of a written text in the form of a newscast, or the oral presentation of a fixed, rehearsed script. In this instance, the *Astérix* cartoon that she began with was scripted in such a way as to reflect many of the features of oral language as described by Horowitz and Samuels (1987:9). Visuals, music and sound effects provided Courtney with numerous extralinguistic clues to meaning, and with these aids, she successfully constructed meaning from the stream of sound by actively employing strategies made possible by the computer. In fact, she wrote in her journal: 'I enjoyed the interactive video so much that I listened to all of the segments.'

This view of the listener as an active participant in the construction of text meaning has not always been widely accepted, nor has the complexity of processing oral language been fully appreciated. For years, listening and reading were referred to as passive language skills, and listening especially received little attention. Now, however, the effective listener is seen as an active comprehender who anticipates or predicts, monitors for discrepancies in messages and revises hypotheses accordingly, selects relevant and ignores non-relevant aspects of the message (Dunkel 1986), and makes inferences (Richards 1983), interprets and evaluates (Coakley and Wolvin 1990). In order to do this, the listener must first hear and attend to the acoustic signal, segment it in some meaningful way, and hold it in memory long enough to process it. Byrnes (1984:322) sees auditory processing as 'an interplay between all types of knowledge—phonological, lexical, structural, and semantic—where each knowledge source continuously has two-way access to every other source in the task of analyzing the sensory input'. Specialists in both second and native language listening (Newmark 1981, Gilmor et al. 1989) have emphasized the importance of attention and concentration during listening.

Current theory with respect to interaction between listener and text recognizes two processing styles: bottom-up (the listener builds up the message from information carried by the input) and top-down (the listener relies on contextual, semantic clues to predict message content). Top-down processing, believed to be the more efficient of the two styles (Conrad 1989), is closely associated with a priori knowledge, which may include scripts, or typical episodes that occur in specific situations (Richards 1983), and also text and genre schemata (Long 1989). Lack of comprehension may result from lack of an appropriate script, from not activating a known script, or from misapplying a script.

While the listening process has been variously described and defined in the native, foreign and second language literature, the interactive relationship between listener and text in one-way reactive listening and between listener and speaker in two-way conversational listening seems to be generally agreed upon.

Teaching listening in an 'information age'. Students like Courtney have grown up in an 'information age' in which they expect to obtain much information through their ears. Answering machines, cellular phones, car radios, books on tape, audiomagazines, and even 'Cliff's Cassettes—Companions for the Classics' permit and encourage us to surround ourselves with the sounds of language, wherever we may be. Sound is complemented by images not only in movies and on television but also in videotaped encyclopedias, yearbooks, and exercise tapes; and the videocassette recorder when combined with cable television and satellite, makes it possible for each of us to create what is in essence a personal television channel.

Although we have known since Rankin's 1926 study (cited in Coakley and Wolvin 1990), that listening is the central element in communication and information transfer, this essential skill does not yet occupy a central place in native, second, or foreign language instruction;

nevertheless, developments in recent years have helped to raise our professional consciousness concerning the importance of listening to, and comprehending, oral language. Several influential movements, each of which has contributed to our understanding of listening, can be identified. The communicative movement has taught us that the exchange of messages is fundamental to language use; the functional-notional approach has made us aware of the many real life purposes of both reactive and interactive listening (Guntermann and Phillips 1982); and the ACTFL Proficiency Guidelines have focused our attention on types of oral texts (Child 1987). A number of comprehension approaches have directed our attention to the important role of listening in language acquisition, to the necessity of providing contextual support for oral language, and to the possibility of signalling comprehension nonverbally. Finally, an information-processing view of listening and reading which emphasizes their similarities as receptive or comprehension skills has had considerable influence on the teaching of listening.

The influence of these movements, which themselves have drawn to varying degrees upon such fields as cognitive psychology, psycholinguistics, discourse analysis, linguistics, and sociology, has been felt in many aspects of listening instruction and at all levels of the curriculum. It is at the beginning level that the comprehension approaches have had the most impact, although their influence at other levels should not be overlooked. Even though these approaches do not consider listening an end in itself but rather as a means to the end of language acquisition, a brief update on them and on Krashen's closely-related Monitor Model is essential to any discussion of second and foreign language listening. Asher's Total Physical Response approach, introduced twenty-five years ago and widely used in second language teaching, is increasingly making its way into foreign language materials and classrooms, although usually as a technique rather than an approach; Winitz' self-in-structional, picture-based Learnables have now been with us for fifteen years and exist in six languages, and Terrell's *Dos Mundos*, which embodies his Natural Approach, has become one of the best-selling first-year Spanish textbooks. During recent years while Krashen has been refining and defending his Monitor Model (in press) and focusing on reading as a source of comprehensible input (1989, 1990), others have continued to develop and refine their approaches to comprehension-based instruction. Asher (in press) has extended what he has termed 'a brain-compatible instructional strategy' to new disciplines (science and mathematics) and new audiences (in prison and court schools); Terrell (1991) has reconsidered the role of grammar in comprehension-based learning and revised his method accordingly; and Winitz, drawing on experience derived from following college-level German students through four semesters of comprehension training (Winitz and Garcia 1986), is currently preparing a book in which he will describe an approach to intermediate instruction centered on the acquisition of vocabulary organized into semantic fields and on the comprehension of narratives and of conversational language (Winitz 1990). While still controversial, the comprehension approaches have proved to be both long-lived and adaptable.

Equally robust is the functional-notional approach to language instruction. Although the notions have in many cases been relegated to a less prominent place than the functions, certain principles and perspectives of this European approach have had a lasting effect on language teaching in the United States, especially in terms of needs assessment and curriculum and syllabus design. A listening course described by Richards (1983) illustrates many of the principles of functional-notional syllabus design. This article, a comprehensive treatment of second-language listening instruction, includes a model of the listening process, an analysis of the features of oral language, an assessment of learner needs, learner profiles based on diagnostic testing, a taxonomy of listening skills for both conversational and academic listening, a set of objectives based upon listening behaviors, and a description of appropriate teaching procedures and exercise types. A more recent publication by Richards (1990) brings together current perspectives on language functions and cognitive processes.

Like the functional-notional syllabus, the ACTFL Proficiency Guidelines (1988) attempt to reflect real-world purposes of language. Intended to measure language ability, they have also influenced curriculum design, materials, and methodology. An otherwise positive recent attempt to validate the Guidelines, using tests of French and of English as a Second Language based on the level descriptions, found that the area that exhibited the lowest level of validity in both languages was listening (Dandonoli and Henning 1990).

While the ACTFL Guidelines reflect a text-based approach to listening, a receptive skills approach derived from work in artificial intelligence focuses on the processing of information. Pairing the receptive or comprehension skills, which works especially well in cases of one-way reactive listening where technology permits the listener to relisten to an audio or videocassette, has lead us to the realization that comprehension normally is greater than production and that we may handicap learners if we allow the productive skills to 'drive' the curriculum.

The movements discussed above have contributed to our understanding and appreciation of listening as an important communication and informa-tion-getting skill by making us aware of various 'inside the head,' 'outside the head,' and interactive aspects of the listening process. We might legitimately wonder, however, just how this knowledge has been translated into listening instruction both in and out of classrooms.

Theory into practice: Listening in the classroom. If Courtney had viewed *Astérix* on a normal television set, she would have been able to understand very little of the dialogue, which would have continued relentlessly without regard for her needs as a listener; however, by using strategies made possible by the Listening Tool, she was able to achieve a level of comprehension that made her feel successful. Furthermore, her journal entry for that day contained an astute observation: 'I found out a very important factor in my listening abilities. If I listen word-by-word, trying to decipher each word as it goes by, I spend all my time concentrating on word and not sentence meaning. I found that when I relaxed a little and just kept on listening and watching, I was able to get most of the meaning.' What could have been at best mere exposure and at worst a demoralizing experience became, instead, a kind of discovery learning.

That exposure to oral language, while necessary, is not sufficient for the development of listening skills is now widely accepted. Krashen and other proponents of comprehension-based approaches have insisted that input must be made comprehensible and have described listening activities appropriate to various stages of language acquisition (Asher 1977, Terrell 1982, Nord 1981, Winitz and Garcia 1986, Belasco 1981). Richards (1983), using a needs-based approach to curriculum design, has identified numerous microskills which contribute to real-world conversational and academic listening; more recently, Morley (1990) has identified four design principles that underlie current listening instruction and Lund (1990) has proposed a taxonomy for organizing listening instruction based on the ACTFL Listening Guidelines. The question then is not whether listening should be taught but how best to provide students with both adequate opportunities for listening and focused listening experiences.

It goes without saying that second-language students have more possibilities for listening exposure than foreign language students and that students taught by one of the comprehension approaches or in a direct-method, immersion or content-based course will have more listening opportunities than those enrolled in a more traditional course of study. These considerations aside, oral input for most students is provided through teacher talk, classroom interaction, and recorded materials. A real problem with respect to teacher talk in the foreign language classroom is the wide range of linguistic ability of the teachers (Schulz 1991), most of whom are not native speakers of the language they teach. For this reason, foreign language teachers are particularly dependent upon recorded materials.

While specific listening courses and materials designed to develop listening as a separate skill have become more plentiful during the past decade in both second and native language listening (Morley 1990, Coakley and Wolvin 1990), specific listening courses remain rare in foreign language instruction, and audio and video materials are still most likely to exist in the form of supplements to basic or intermediate texts.

In recent years, foreign language teachers in search of materials capable of 'standing alone' have increasingly turned away from the traditional textbook publishers and to a variety of private and educational sources of authentic audio and video materials in the form of audiomagazines, radio programs and books on tape, videomagazines, foreign television programs recorded on videotape and videodisk, and satellite broadcasts.[2]

As the use of unedited authentic texts has increased, the teacher's role has become less one of serving as the primary source of oral input and more one of selecting appropriate and interesting texts and of facilitating comprehension by mediating between text and listener, not an easy task as there is still much that is not understood about which factors in an oral text may enhance or hinder comprehension. This lack of understanding is compounded by the fact that the interactivity of the listening process makes it almost impossible to consider text factors in the absence of learner factors. Nevertheless, native language listening specialists have attempted to isolate the features of oral texts that contribute to their 'listenability' (Rubin and Raforth, cited by Rhodes et al. 1990). The ACTFL Guidelines have proposed a hierarchy of texts, and foreign and second language teachers have identified factors that should be taken into account in the selection of audio and video materials (Morley 1990, Joiner 1990, Altman 1989). Recently, there have been indications that the profession is moving away from the naive assumption that video is automatically easier to understand than audio and taking a more analytical look at how television actually conveys information both visually and verbally (MacWilliam 1986, Rubin 1990). An interesting study in this regard, and one that attempts to relate text factors to listener/viewer factors, has been reported on by Long (1991), who asked students to 'think aloud' as they attempted to understand an authentic Spanish video.

Long's study makes use of a self-reporting technique in an attempt to make overt what is essentially a covert process, and it is precisely the covertness of listening that makes it so difficult to teach. Although some theorists refuse to include any type of response in their definitions of listening (Coakley and Wolvin 1986) and others contend that thinking about what has been heard is more important than any overt reaction (Bernhardt and James 1987), recommendations for procedures to be used in the teaching of listening almost always incorporate an observable response (Richards 1983, Morley 1990, Dunkel 1986, Lund 1990). Whereas in the past students might have demonstrated successful listening by correctly answering comprehension questions presented after the fact, it is now more likely that they will be given a task to complete

---

[2] For a list of sources of authentic foreign language materials, see Rogers and Medley (1988).

while listening and/or a follow-up activity that involves using information contained in the passage in some realistic way. This trend toward bringing classroom listening practice as close to real world listening as is possible is reflected by Lund (1990), who recommends that all aspects of listening instruction, including text, function and response should have a natural feel.

The ideal combination of authenticity of text, function and response meets its greatest challenge in the case of beginning language learners, who may experience extreme frustration when confronted by an authentic text. Nevertheless, the general view seems to be that even first-year students can achieve limited comprehension of unedited texts if they are provided with essential background material and given simple tasks to perform while listening (Meyer 1984, Richards 1983). The forms that such tasks may take are illustrated in a number of recent articles that contain descriptions of procedures designed to bridge the gap between authentic texts and beginning or intermediate listeners (Bacon 1989, Joiner et al. 1989, Robin and Leaver 1989). The prototypical listening activity that seems to be emerging consists of three phases, a pre-listening phase which focuses on script and schema activation, a listening phase accompanied by a task, and a post-listening phase to establish comprehension. The listening phase will probably include several successive passes through the oral text, and each pass may be accompanied by a slightly more difficult task to encourage increasingly complete comprehension (Richards 1983). In some cases, and especially with more advanced learners, a fourth phase that involves a realistic use of the information gained is included (Glisan 1988).

While empirical support for the efficacy of these procedures is not reported on, they do reflect current theory, and informal research concerning students' attitudes toward various task types has recently been presented (Eykyn et al. 1990). More controlled investigations currently underway will examine the relationship between task type and comprehension as measured by the immediate recall protocol, a procedure frequently used to measure reading comprehension which has been adapted for foreign language listening by James (1986). The protocol procedure involves having students listen to a foreign language text and write down in their native language everything that they can remember about it.

The use of the recall protocol to assess listening comprehension reflects a trend present in the majority of recent articles on listening. Drawing on first and second language reading theory, the authors of these articles focus on features shared by the two receptive skills (Glisan 1988). This tendency is evident in references to audio and video passages as texts, in the application of reading strategies such as skimming and scanning to oral passages, and in investigations into top-down and bottom-up listening modeled on previous research undertaken in reading.

While the comparison with reading has lead to many valuable insights, it has also resulted in relatively less interest in the characteristics that listening does not share with reading, namely sound perception, segmentation, and interaction.

In response to what he perceives to be an over-reliance on reading theory, Heike (1987) reminds us that the oral characteristics of language should not be ignored. Eschewing the common comparison of listening to reading, he uses the approach that listening is the mirror image of speaking in order to arrive at a number of strategies for teaching speech perception and segmentation. Although voices such Heike's and those of James and Leather (1987) and their collaborators call for a broader view of listening, it is likely that the profession will continue to capitalize on the similarities of the two comprehension skills and that listening instruction will reflect this comparison for some time to come.

Technology in listening instruction: From low to high tech. The present tendency to stress similarities between listening and reading has been made possible to a large extent by technology, which enables listeners to control fleeting aural material by stopping, rewinding, and relistening as often as they like. At the low-tech end of the spectrum are materials delivered by standard audio or video-cassette players; at the high-end are those requiring a work-station similar to Courtney's. Both low and high tech equipment can be used either in class for mass listening or outside of class for individual work. While teacher-mediated, in-class listening of the type described earlier has obvious advantages, it requires everyone to listen at the same time to the same material presented in the same way. At its best, this type of listening practice is clearly insufficient for, as Bacon (1989) has observed, college foreign language students probably have no more than nineteen hours of in-class listening per semester. For this and other reasons, extensive outside listening is seen to be essential by Morley (1984), who has provided numerous suggestions for creating self-instructional listening exercises.

Developments such as the walkman and vehicular cassette players make it possible for busy students to schedule listening practice at their convenience. As this already-common technology becomes even more accessible, the role of the language laboratory is becoming primarily one of supporting teaching, research, and materials development involving high tech equipment (Otto 1989). An exemplary use of technology to support teaching is LCEN, the Listening Comprehension Exercise Network, which distributes through BITNET or CompuServe a variety of exercises to be used with Russian news broadcasts downloaded from satellite (Robin and Leaver 1989). Another technology-based procedure that shows promise for the teaching of comprehension is the addition of foreign or second language captions to existing video materials (Garza

1989, ACTFL Newsletter 1991).³ The laboratory can also offer the possibility of expanding, compressing, and otherwise manipulating recorded speech through rate-alteration technology and of enhancing students' ability to perceive and produce target language sounds through a device known as the electronic ear (Vanthuyne et al. 1977, Gilmor et al. 1989).

In addition to supporting classroom teaching and research, state of the art laboratories provide students with audio and video equipment combined with computers in a variety of ways. A computer-controlled random access audio device described by Henry, Hartmann and Henry (1987, 1989) has permitted the creation of two innovative lesson types, both of which involve listening. The first of these requires the scripting and recording of a story with several possible plots and allows the students to determine the direction of the action by their choices; the second presents the student with a language sample and a number of instantly-available aids to comprehension. Similar lesson types can be delivered by a random-access videodisc player controlled by a microcomputer. Here, I will use the term 'interactive video' to refer to any lesson involving the use of such equipment, although purists reserve the term 'interactive' for multiple-branching programs. Brigham Young's 'Montevidisco' (Gale 1989), 'A Safe Affair' developed by Edna Coffin at the University of Michigan, and 'No Recuerdo' and 'Direction Paris' of MIT's Athena Language-Learning Project (1989) are examples of such multiple-branching programs, which provide a built-in purpose for listening and offer many options. 'Montevidisco,' for example, was designed to have 1,100 possible paths.

Multiple-branching video programs are far more costly and time-consum-ing to produce than programs developed around existing materials recorded on videodisc. Even though these materials are inherently linear in nature, they can be made more flexible by skillful authoring. For example, a program could be designed that would mimic the three-phase listening activity described earlier but would provide a wide choice of pre-listening information, tasks, comprehension aids and follow-up activities. Noblitt (1990), who prefers the term 'multimedia' to 'interactive video', has formulated a number of guidelines for would-be authors.

Because interactive video permits individualization and at the same time offers multiple meaning sources in the form of full-motion video, stills, audio, written text, and graphics, it has been greeted with enthusiasm by the profession. At this point much of the literature on this listen-

---

3 American teachers of English as a Second Language will no doubt want to take advantage of the new ruling requiring that television sets sold in America after July 1993 must include a computer chip that will provide closed-caption service at the push of a button.

ing tool consists of descriptions of projects (Eastmond and Mosenthal 1985, Smith 1989, Hughes 1989), but available research (Gale 1989) tends to support the early enthusiasm, and results of a three-year longitudinal study of interactive video in Spanish are expected this year from the United States Naval Academy (Fletcher 1990).

Research into listening: Findings and frustrations. The effectiveness of interactive video is only one of a number of listening-related topics investigated in recent studies (including more than a dozen dissertation studies since 1987) dealing with various aspects of second and foreign language listening. These investigations examine both reactive and interactive listening and include both empirical and ethnographic approaches to research. They have taken the form of laboratory experiments that necessitate especially designed pre-recorded oral texts (Conrad 1989, Rader 1990) and more pragmatically-oriented studies constructed to elicit unrehearsed exchanges between native speakers and non-native language learners (Pica et al. 1987, Kasper 1984). In the main, they have concentrated on listening comprehension rather than on the perception of sound, although this is not always the case.

Areas of investigation have included echoic memory (Greenberg and Roscoe 1988), long-term retention (Asher 1977), the relationship between the output of learners and the input of native speakers (Pica et al. 1989), features affecting the comprehensibility of foreigner talk (Pica et al. 1987, Kelch 1985), the use of advance organizers to enhance comprehension (Weissenreider 1987a, Mueller 1980), the segmentation of oral speech (Vogel and Winitz 1989), terminating devices (Andrews 1989), the effect of word order patterns on comprehension (Glisan 1985), the relative contribution of syntax and semantics to comprehension (Conrad 1989), differences in the approach to listening of natives and non-natives of varying ability levels (Vanderplank 1988, Conrad 1989), whether it is possible to process both form and meaning simultaneously at the lower levels of language instruction (VanPatten 1989), and whether even students with extensive language experience are capable of listening beneath the surface to detect the intended meaning of an utterance (Kasper 1984). A number of these studies conclude with recommendations not only for further research but also with implications for the classroom, such as Glisan's suggestion that students should engage in comprehension drills or Kasper's recommendation that instruction should move away from emphasis on the sentence and concentrate on the discourse-level features of language.

In addition to these empirical studies, there are a few ethnographic studies that attempt to understand listeners' strategies through case studies (Benson 1989) and other self-report and observational methods, including asking the students to think aloud while listening (O'Malley et al. 1989, Long 1991). Watson-Gegeo (1988) has discussed the principles of quality ethnographic work.

Research implies measurement, an area that remains problematic in foreign language listening. While native and second language researchers often compare groups and communicate the results of their studies on the basis of a standardized test whose reliability and validity are known to the profession, researchers in foreign language listening lack easy access to such instruments. The listening tests prepared by ACTFL for use in the previously-described validity study are not available commercially nor is the listening component of a test based on the ACTFL Guidelines developed at the University of Minnesota. Given the doubts concerning the validity of the Guidelines (Douglas 1988) and the lack of a widely-accepted standardized instrument compatible with present knowledge about listening, many foreign language researchers have adopted the recall protocol described earlier as a measure of listening. The use of this procedure to measure comprehension in English as a Second Language is less common since students do not typically share the same native language.[4] Given the numerous published tests for assessing various aspects of native language listening (Rhodes et al. 1990), the measurement area appears underdeveloped in both second and foreign language listening, and this represents a serious impediment to research.

In spite of a good deal of research activity in the area of listening, it remains a frustrating field of investigation. Researchers complain about the difficulty of deriving research hypotheses and about the fact that they must draw conclusions based on the outcomes of listening rather than directly observing the processes of listening. Casting doubts on the results obtained through highly-controlled laboratory studies inspired by reading research, Danks and End (1987) remind us that, while listening can be made to resemble reading through artificial means, laboratory conditions are not representative of listening in the real world.

Yet another area of frustration for the researcher is the fact that there are many competing definitions of listening. Suggesting that perhaps too much has been made of the search for the one perfect definition of listening, Witkin (1990), a specialist in native language listening, proposes defining listening as what a listener does and embracing a view of listening as a system composed of many interrelated and dynamically interacting parts or subsystems. This would permit the researcher to '. . . define the system under study as the individual listener, or as the total listening situation, including the occasion and the physical environment and its contents' (Witkin 1990:8). Witkin's approach has these obvious advantages: it emphasizes the listener, and it recognizes the covertness and the

---

4 The recall protocol should not be confused with the listening recall measure developed by Henning, Gary, and Gary for use with low-proficiency learners.

complexity of listening. At once, it reminds us that there is much that we do not know about listening and acknowledges that there are some things that we can and do know about the complex parts of an even more complex system.

The state of the art and beyond. It is customary in assessing the state of the art in a given field to speculate about emerging trends as well as to comment on the present state of affairs. Here are a few observations, which will be followed by a number of predictions.

Our present state reflects agreement on the part of the profession with respect to the important role played by listening in both second language acquisition and in real-world communication. Our accumulated knowledge concerning listening comprehension, though meager and somewhat short on empirical studies, reflects attempts to understand this complex process by identifying, naming, and classifying its components. We have defined and distinguished between reactive and interactive listening, between input and intake, between top-down and bottom-up processing, between oral and written language, and between authentic and pedagogical texts. We have also identified distinct types of listening skills, strategies, tasks, and purposes. Much of our present theory, many teaching practices, and some empirical investigations are the result of extrapolations to the emerging field of listening from the better established field of reading, a rapprochement that has been facilitated by the increased availability of audio and video equipment that permits our listening to become more like our reading than it actually is in most real life situations.

As we move into the future, second and foreign language teachers will approach the teaching of listening with more maturity and independence. Although we will continue to capitalize upon insights gleaned from comparing reading and listening, we will move toward a more contrastive approach that will examine listening as a unique skill, related to reading yet distinct from it. This shift in point of view, which is already evident in recent publications on native language listening and reading (Horowitz and Samuels 1987, Witkin 1990, Rhodes et al. 1990), will result in a renewed interest in listening as it functions in human interaction and in those aspects of listening most closely associated with sound such as perception, echoic memory, segmentation, and the prosodic and morphophonemic features of oral language.

As the aural aspects of listening comprehension are investigated in greater depth, we will turn to the fields of music, audiology, and acoustic phonetics for insights into sensory perception and sound analysis and to the fields of anatomy and neurophysiology for a better understanding of the differences between the visual and auditory systems that underlie reading and listening comprehension. Research conducted by Geschwind and Galaburda (1987), for example, has lead them to theorize that in thirty to thirty-five percent of the population the right rather than the left hemisphere is dominant for the processing of language.

Recent research linking first and second language listening ability will lead to increased cooperation between teachers and researchers in first, second, and foreign language listening as they attempt to identify the characteristics of very poor and very good listeners. The International Listening Association is a likely forum for an exchange of ideas among professionals from the three distinct but related fields.

The teaching of listening will become more research-based as reports from studies currently underway[5] are published and as new research is undertaken. The results of these studies will help teachers make more informed choices with respect to the selection of audio and video materials and to the types of schemata, tasks, and strategies that will best facilitate their comprehension. Complementing experimental studies will be numerous ethnographic studies based on interviews, questionnaires, thinking-aloud and observation. Questions raised by such studies will be formulated as hypotheses for more controlled investigations, including longitudinal ones. As research activity increases, it will be accompanied by a demand for valid and reliable listening tests, similar to those currently used to measure first-language listening.

As teachers of listening, we will continue to rely heavily on recorded materials and will turn to the fields of media arts, communication, and broadcast journalism in order to refine our knowledge of how meaning is conveyed by the audio and visual media. While interactive video is now available in only a few fortunate institutions, initiatives undertaken by CALICO and by the various microcomputer companies, coupled with an in-crease in the amount of material available on videodisc (Rubin et al. 1990) make it likely that this state-of-the-art technology will become more and more common over the next few years.

Return to square one. This last comment on interactive video brings us back to where we began with Courtney sitting down at her high tech work station. It is not only the sophisticated software and hardware that make this experience representative of the state of the art in the teaching of listening. In fact, the equipment, which might first attract an observer's attention, no longer represents cutting edge technology as the trend to one-screen rather than two-screen work stations continues. If we look beyond the technology and analyze this listening situation carefully, we will see that it involves an active listener engaged in interaction with

---

5 Irene Thompson and Joan Rubin, for example, are currently engaged in a three-year project which will examine the effectiveness of strategy training on listening comprehension in Russian at George Washington University.

an authentic video text. The fact that Courtney was asked to keep a listening journal reflects both our present interest in learner strategies and in ethnographic research. Finally, the fact that Courtney is alone at her work station focuses our attention on the importance of the individual in the listening process. Courtney's age, sex, interests, and prior knowledge are only a few of the factors that will contribute to her construction of a message from the text before her. Had another student sat down at the same computer terminal and viewed the same video passage with the same tools at her disposal, the experience would by no means have been the same. As Rivers (1980:16) has so well put it, there is meaning in the oral text, 'but *significance is in the mind of the listener*'. Neither state-of-the-art technology nor texts nor techniques should divert our attention from the role of learner factors in the active and interactive process of listening. As we seek to advance and develop the art of the teaching of listening, we should not overlook the important insights to be gained from becoming good listeners ourselves and listening to our students.

References

ACTFL proficiency guidelines. 1988. Hastings-on-Hudson, N.Y.: American Council on the Teaching of Foreign Languages.

Allison, Mary L. 1991. Closed-captioned TV is effective teaching tool. ACTFL Newsletter 3(2): 8-9.

Altman, Rick. 1989. The video connection. Boston: Houghton Mifflin.

Andrews, Barry. 1989. Terminating devices in spoken French. IRAL 27(3): 193-216.

Asher, James J. 1977. Learning another language through actions. Los Gatos, Calif.: Sky Oaks Productions.

Asher, James J. In press. Brain-compatible instruction for stress-free learning of second languages, mathematics, and science. In: R. Pelligrini and S. Pelligrini, eds. Psychology for correctional education: Facilitating human development in prison and court school settings. Chicago: Charles C. Thomas.

Athena Language-Learning Project. 1989. Cambridge, Mass.: Massachusetts Institute of Technoloby.

Bacon, Susan M. 1989. Listening for real in the foreign language classroom. Foreign Language Annals 22: 543-50.

Belasco, Simon. 1981. Aital cal aprene las lengas estrangieras, comprehension: The key to second language learning. In: Harris Winitz, ed. The comprehension approach to foreign language instruction. Rowley, Mass.: Newbury House.

Benson, Malcolm J. 1989. The academic listening task: A case study. TESOL Quarterly 23(3): 421-45.

Bernhardt, Elizabeth B., and Charles J. James. 1987. The teaching and testing of com-prehension in foreign-language learning. In: Diane W. Birckbichler, ed. Proficiency, policy, and professionalism in foreign language education. Lincolnwood, Ill.: National Textbook Company.

Boyle, Joseph P. 1987. Sex differences in listening vocabulary. Language Learning 37: 273-84.

Byrnes, Heidi. 1984. The role of listening comprehension: A theoretical base. Foreign Language Annals 17: 317-29.
Child, James R. 1987. Language proficiency levels and the typology of texts. In: Heidi Byrnes and Michael Canale, eds. Defining and developing proficiency: Guidelines, Implementations, and Concepts. Lincolnwood, Ill.: National Textbook Company.
Coakley, Carolyn G. and Andrew D. Wolvin. 1986. Listening in the native language. In: Barbara H. Wing, ed. Listening, reading, and writing: Analysis and application. Middlebury, Vt: Northeast Conference.
Coakley, Carolyn G. and Andrew D. Wolvin. 1990. Listening pedagogy and andragogy: The state of the art. Journal of the International Listening Association 4: 33-61.
Conrad, Linda. 1989. The effects of time-compressed speech on native and ESL listening comprehension. Studies in Second Language Acquisition 11(1): 1-16.
Dandonoli, Patricia, and Grant Henning. 1990. An investigation of the construct validity of the ACTFL Proficiency Guidelines and oral interview process. Foreign Language Annals 23: 11-22.
Danks, Joseph, and Laurel J. End. 1987. Processing strategies for reading and listening. In: Horowitz and Samuels, eds. 1987.
Douglas, Dan. 1988. Testing listening comprehesion in the context of the ACTFL Proficiency Guidelines. Studies in Second Language Acquisition 10: 245-61.
Dunkel, Patricia. 1986. Developing listening fluency in L2: Theoretical principles and pedagogical considerations. Modern Language Journal 70: 99-106.
Eastmond, J.N., and R. Mosenthal. 1985. The World Center for Computing's pilot videodisc project for French language instruction. CALICO Journal 2: 8-12.
Edasawa, Yasuyo, Osamu Takeuchi, and Kazako Nishizaki. 1990. Use of films in listening comprehension practice. IALL Journal 23(3): 21-32.
Eykyn, Lollie B., Elizabeth G. Joiner, and Polly B. Adkins. 1990. Accessing authentic audio: Learners' reactions to various pre-listening formats. Presented at the Northeast Conference, New York, April 1990.
Feyten, Carine M. 1990. Listening ability and foreign language acquisition: Defining a new area of listening. Journal of the International Listening Association 4: 128-42.
Feyten, Carine M. In press. The power of listening ability: An overlooked dimension in language acquisition. Forthcoming in the Modern Language Journal.
Fletcher, William H. 1990. Authentic interactive video for lower-level Spanish at the United States Naval Academy. Hispania 73: 859-65.
Gale, Larrie E. 1989. Macario, Montevidisco, and Interactive Digame: Developing interactive video for language instruction. In: Wm. Flint Smith, ed. Modern technology in foreign language education: Applications and projects. Lincolnwood, Ill.: National Textbook Company.
Garza, Thomas J. 1989. Watch your language: A study on the impact of captioned video in FL learning. ACTR Letter 14: 1-2.
Geschwind, Norman, and Albert M. Galaburda. 1987. Cerebral lateralization: Biological mechanisms, associations, and pathology. Cambridge, Mass.: MIT Press.
Gilman, Robert A., and Loranna M. Moody. 1984. What practioners say about listening: Research implications for the classroom. Foreign Language Annals 17: 331-34.
Gilmor, Timothy M., Paul Madaule, and Billie Thompson. 1989. About the Tomatis method. Toronto: The Listening Centre Press/Editions du centre de l'écoute.

Glisan, Eileen W. 1985. The effect of word order on listening comprehension and pattern retention: An experiment in Spanish as a foreign language. Language Learning 35: 443-72.

Glisan, Eileen W. 1988. A plan for teaching listening comprehension: Adaptation of an instructional reading model. Foreign Language Annals 21: 9-16.

Greenberg, Seth N., and Suzanne Roscoe. 1988. Echoic memory interference and comprehension in a foreign language. Language Learning 38: 209-19.

Guntermann, Gail and June K. Phillips. 1982. Functional-notional concepts: Adapting the FL Textbook. Washington, D.C.: Center for Applied Linguistics.

Heike, A.E. 1987. The resolution of dynamic speech in L2 listening. Language Learning 37: 123-40.

Henning, Grant, Norman Gary, and Judith Gary. 1983. Listening recall: A listening comprehension test for low proficiency learners. System 11(3): 287-93.

Henry, George M., John F. Hartmann, and Patricia B. Henry. 1987. Computer-controlled random-access audio in the comprehension approach to second-language learning. Foreign Language Annals 20: 255-64.

Henry, George M., John F. Hartmann, and Patricia B. Henry. 1989. FLIS: Random-access audio and innovative lesson types. In: Wm. Flint Smith, ed. 1989. Modern technology in foreign language education: Applications and projects. Lincolnwood, Ill.: National Textbook Company.

Horowitz, Rosalind and S. Jay Samuels. 1987. Comprehending oral and written language. San Diego: Academic Press.

Hughes, Helena. 1989. Conversion of a teacher-delivered course into an interactive videodisc-delivered program. Foreign Language Annals 22: 283-94.

James, Allan, and Jonathan Leather, eds. 1987. Sound patterns in second language acquisition. Dordrecht: Foris.

James, Charles J. 1986. Listening and learning: Protocols and processes. In: Barbara Snyder, ed. Second-language acquisition: Preparing for tomorrow. Lincolnwood, Ill.: National Textbook Company.

Joiner, Elizabeth G. 1986. Listening in the foreign language. In: Barbara H. Wing, ed. Listening, reading, and writing: Analysis and application. Middlebury, Vt.: Northeast Conference.

Joiner, Elizabeth G. 1990. Choosing and using videotexts. Foreign Language Annals 23: 53-64.

Joiner, Elizabeth G., Lollie B. Eykyn, and Polly B. Adkins. 1989. Skimming and scanning with *Champs-Elysées*: Using authentic materials to improve foreign language listening. French Review 62:427-35

Kasper, Gabriele. 1984. Pragmatic comprehension in learner-native speaker discourse. Language Learning 34: 1-20.

Kelch, Ken. 1985. Modified input as an aid to comprehension. Studies in Second Language Acquisition 7: 81-89.

Krashen, Stephen D. 1989. Language teaching technology: A low-tech view. In: Georgetown University Round Table on Languages and Linguistics 1989. Washington, D.C.: Georgetown University Press.

Krashen, Stephen D. 1990. How reading and writing make you smarter, or how smart people read and write. In: Georgetown University Round Table on Languages and Linguistics 1989. Washington, D.C.: Georgetown University Press.

Krashen, Stephen. In press. Comprehensible input and some competing hypotheses. In: R. Courchène and J. St. Johns, eds. Comprehension-based language teaching. Ottowa: University of Ottowa Press.

Long, Donna Reseigh. 1987. Listening comprehension: Need and neglect. Hispania 70: 21-28.

Long, Donna Reseigh. 1989. Second language listening comprehension: A schema-theoretic perspective. Modern Language Journal 73: 32-40.

Long, Donna Reseigh. 1991. What foreign language learners say they think about when listening to authentic texts. Unpublished.

Lund, Randall J. 1990. A taxonomy for teaching second language listening. Foreign Language Annals 23: 105-15.

MacWilliam, Iain. 1986. Video and language comprehension. ELT Journal 40(2): 131-35.

Meyer, Rene. 1984. Listen my children and you shall hear. Foreign Language Annals 17: 343-44.

Morley, Joan. 1984. Listening and language learning in ESL: Developing self-study activities for listening comprehension practice. Theory and Practice, No. 59. Washington, D.C.: Center for Applied Linguistics.

Morley, Joan. 1990. Trends and developments in listening comprehension: Theory and practice. In: Georgetown University Round Table on Languages and Linguistics 1990. Washington, D.C.: Georgetown University Press.

Mueller, Guenther. 1980. Visual contextual cues and listening comprehension: An experiment. Modern Language Journal 64: 335-40.

Murray, Janet H., Douglas Morganstern, and Gilberte Furstenburg. 1989. The Athena Language-Learning Project: Design issues for the next generation of computer-based language-learning tools. In: Modern technology in foreign language education: Applications and projects. Wm. Flint Smith, ed. Lincolnwood, Ill.: National Textbook Company.

Newmark, Leonard. 1981. Participatory observation: How to succeed in language learning. In: Harris Winitz, ed. 1981. The comprehension approach to foreign language instruction. Rowley, Mass.: Newbury House.

Noblitt, James. 1990. Multimedia and listening comprehension. In: Multimedia and language learning. McKinney, Texas: Academic Computing Publications, Inc.

Nord, James R. 1981. Three steps to listening fluency: A beginning. In: Harris Winitz, ed. 1981.

O'Malley, J. Michael, Anna Uhl Chamot, and Lisa Kupper. 1989. Listening comprehension strategies in second language acquisition. Applied Linguistics 10(4): 418-37.

Otto, Sue E.K. 1989. The language laboratory in the computer age. In: Wm. Flint Smith, ed. Modern technology in foreign language education: Applications and projects. Lincolnwood, Ill.: National Textbook Company.

Pica, Teresa, et al. 1987. The impact of interaction on comprehension. TESOL Quarterly 21: 737-58.

Pica, Teresa, et al. 1989. Comprehensible output as an outcome of linguistic demands on the learner. Studies in Second Language Acquisition 11: 63-90.

Rader, Karen E. 1990. The effects of three different levels of word rate on the listening comprehension of third-quarter university Spanish students. Unpublished dissertation, Ohio State University.

Rhodes, Steven C., Kittie W. Watson, and Larry L. Barker. 1990. Listening assessment: Trends and influencing factors in the 1980s. Journal of the International Listening Association 4: 62-82.

Richards, Jack C. 1983. Listening comprehension: Approach, design, procedure. TESOL Quarterly 17: 219-40.

Richards, Jack C. 1990. The language teaching matrix. Cambridge: Cambridge University Press.

Rivers, Wilga. 1980. Hearing and comprehending. English Teaching Forum 17(4): 16-19.

Robin, Richard M., and Betty Lou Leaver. 1989. The listening comprehension exercise network (LCEN). Foreign Language Annals 22: 573-84.

Rogers, Carmen Villegas, and Frank W. Medley, Jr. 1988. Language with a purpose: Using authentic materials in the foreign language classroom. Foreign Language Annals 21: 467-78.

Rubin, Joan, 1990. Improving listening comprehension. In: Georgetown University Round Table on Languages and Linguistics 1990. Washington, D.C.: Georgetown University Press.

Rubin, Joan, et al. 1990. A survey of interactive language discs. CALICO Journal 7(3): 31-47.

Samuels, S. Jay. 1987. Factors that influence listening and reading comprehension. In: R. Horowitz and S.J. Samuels, eds. Comprehending oral and written language. San Diego, Calif.: Academic Press.

Schneiderman, E.I., and C. Desmarais. 1988. The talented language learner: Some preliminary findings. Second Language Research 4: 91-109.

Schulz, Renate A. 1991. Second language acquisition theories and teaching practice: How do they fit? Modern Language Journal 75: 17-26.

Seright, Linda. 1985. Age and aural comprehension achievement in Francophone adults. TESOL Quarterly 19: 455-73.

Smith, Wm. Flint, ed. 1989. Modern technology in foreign language education: Applications and projects. Lincolnwood, Ill.: National Textbook Company.

Sparks, Richard L., and Leonore Ganshow. 1991. Foreign language learning differences: Affective or native language aptitude differences? Modern Language Journal 75: 3-16.

Terrell, Tracy. 1982. The natural approach to language teaching: An update. Modern Language Journal 66:121-32.

Terrell, Tracy. 1991. The role of grammar in a communicative approach. Modern Language Journal 75: 52-63.

Tomatis, Alfred A. 1978. Education and Dyslexia. Montreal: Les Editions France-Québec.

Ur, Penny. 1984. Teaching listening comprehension. Cambridge: Cambridge University Press.

Vanderplank, Robert. 1988. Implications of differences in native and nonnative speakers' approaches to listening. British Journal of Language Teaching 26: 32-41.

VanPatten, Bill. 1989. Can learners attend to form and content while processing input? Hispania 72: 409-17.

Vanthuyne, Gaston, José Debruyne, and Roger Schenkel. 1977. Utilisation de l'oreille électronique à effet Tomatis dans le cadre du cours d'anglais d'une première année de l'enseignement secondaire belge. Comines, Belgium: Athénée Royal pour Garçons et Jeunes Filles.

Vellutino, Frank. 1979. Dyslexia, theory and research. Cambridge, Mass: MIT Press.
Vogel, Deanie, and Harris Winitz. 1989. Word isolation and meaning in segmentation. Journal of Psycholinguistic Research 18: 473-84.
Watson-Gegeo, Karen Ann. 1988. Ethnography in ESL: Defining the essentials. TESOL Quarterly 22: 575-92.
Weissenrieder, Maureen. 1987a. Listening to the news in Spanish. Modern Language Journal 71: 18-27.
Weissenrieder, Maureen. 1987b. Understanding spoken Spanish: A course in listening. Foreign Language Annals 20: 531-36.
Winitz, Harris. 1990. Personal communication.
Winitz, Harris, and Paul Garcia. 1986. Teaching German to college students through the comprehension approach: A four-semester program of study. In: Vivian Cook, ed. Experimental approaches to second language learning. Oxford: Pergamon Press.
Winitz, Harris, ed. 1981. The comprehension approach to foreign language instruction. Rowley, Mass.: Newbury House.
Witkin, Belle R. 1990. Listening theory and research: The state of the art. Journal of the International Listening Association 4: 7-32.

Teaching languages communicatively: An examination of the presentation of phonology to first-year students of French

Pamela Kaleugher Levac
Georgetown University

Introduction. The following quotes are taken from the prefaces and instructor's guides in four textbooks of first-year French, published between 1988 and 1991 by four major foreign language publishing houses[1].

Interaction is based on tasks to be accomplished and on effective linguistic functioning in real situations (AL:xiii).

... active use of French for authentic communication is both the goal and the method of the course (CA:iii).

The approach ... is primarily communicative (RA:T5).

What matters most in the beginning language course is acquiring the ability to *use* the language studied to communicate basic needs and wishes in urgent, real-life, everyday situations (PA:iii).

Phrases such as 'effective ... functioning', 'authentic communication', and 'ability to use the language' are common to today's texts. One might assume that a solid presentation of the current phonological system of French would be an integral part of any text or program emphasizing communication, for without at least some knowledge of a language's phonological system, a student cannot hope to gain spoken communicative competence.

An examination of some aspects of the presentation of the French phono-logical system in the four texts referred to above is therefore the

---

1 The four texts examined in this study are: Bragger, Jeannette D., and Donald B. Rice. 1988. *Allons-y! Le français par étapes*, 2nd Edition. Boston: Heinle & Heinle; Sandberg, Karl C., Georges Zask, Anthony A. Ciccone and Françoise Defrecheux. 1990. *Ça marche! Cours de français communicatif*. New York: Macmillan; Brown, Thomas H. 1991. *Pas à pas*. New York: John Wiley and Sons; Walz, Joel and Jean-Pierre Piriou. 1990. *Rapports. Language, culture, communication*, 2nd Edition. Lexington, MA: D.C. Heath. They will be referred to throughout the study as AL (*Allons-y*), CA (*Ça marche!*), PA (*Pas à pas*) and RA (*Rapports*).

topic of this paper. The scope of this paper is limited to the vowel system of French, in accordance with the general conclusion in research that this is the greatest area of pronunciation difficulty for Anglophones (Clark 1967, Valdman 1961).

This paper is based on three questions that seem fundamental to any presentation of phonology. The author's explicit and implicit answers to these questions will be considered with regard to students' need to be able to generalize from explanations and examples in order to expand their knowledge to areas of the language not covered in a text. The three questions are:

How are the French vowel phonemes articulated?
How are these phonemes represented orthographically?
What are the linguistic contexts in which these phonemes can occur?

1 How are the French vowel phonemes articulated? It is generally said that the French vowel system, at its most complete, contains 16 vowel phonemes: 12 oral and 4 nasal. There is, however, disagreement among researchers as to the status of some of these vowels, for example, the mute 'e', the mid vowel pairs (/e/ - /ɛ/, /ø/ - /œ/, /o/ - /ó/),[2] the low back vowel /ɑ/ and the fourth nasal vowel /œ̃/ (Levitt 1970). In comparing the French and English vowel systems, we see that there are similar vowel phonemes in both English and French, and also vowel phonemes that are unique to French, such as the nasal vowels, and the high front rounded vowel /y/.

Once warned of the general articulatory characteristics of French, students could be given model words such as *father* for /a/, *feet* for /i/, *bet* for /ɛ/, or *food* for /u/ as starting points for 'anchoring' a French vowel phoneme. And the texts do use English as such to varying degrees. PA uses English in an introductory section to French pronunciation only to point out the difference between similar French and English sounds (PA:45). Otherwise, the French vowel phonemes are presented through familiar French model words, such as *merci, vous* (PA:45), *en, bon, vingt* (PA:87-88). RA uses English only to contrast comparable French and English vowel phonemes in a pronunciation section on vowel tension (RA:108) and in the presentation of /e/ (RA:250), otherwise giving French model words as guides for pronunciation. In CA, only brief pronunciation exercises are given in the text itself, in the form of short idiomatic phrases to be memorized and mimicked (CA:18). Students are referred to appropriate sections of the study guide and practice book for

---

2 Because of limited word-processing capabilities, the following phonetic symbols will be used:
French open o (e.g. bo̲nne): /ó/   French mute e (e.g. me̲): /ë/

explanations of phonemes occurring in some of the sentences. AL is the only text which relies systematically on English words to model French sounds. This could be misleading in the case of the phoneme /e/, where the model word given is English *fail* (AL:145). In this example, the sound of the vowel is clouded not only by a diphthong (which students are warned against) but also by the presence of a final dark (or 'velarized') 'l', making it very difficult to 'dissect' the French sound.

For the French phonemes that are not found in English, all texts give specific articulatory information, sometimes helpful, sometimes not. For the high front vowel /y/, the authors all present the sound as a combination of the tongue position for /i/ and lip rounding, either as for /u/, or as if one were about to whistle.

However, for the nasal vowels, in the Workbook accompanying AL, and in the Study Guide accompanying CA, students are given the following misleading information:

> French also has 3 nasal vowels; that is, the sound is pushed through the nose rather than through the mouth (AL, Workbook:6).

> A nasalized sound is produced by expelling the air through the nasal cavities instead of the mouth (CA, Study Guide:427).

Such articulatory information reminds us of the need for the instructor or a cassette tape to model the sound and complete the explanation.

PA is unique in that it presents the phonemes foreign to English by systematically building on French phonemes introduced in previous chapters, and combining previously learned tongue and lip positions. Figure 1 summarizes the combinations of phonemes.

Figure 1. Combinations of phonemes.

Tongue position +	Lip position =	New phoneme
/ɛ/	/ó/	/œ/ (PA:144)
/e/	/o/	/ø/ (PA:144)
/i/	/u/	/y/ (PA:45)

It would seem that this type of presentation would allow students to build on and combine previous knowledge, therefore providing them with more of a 'systematic' picture of the language, rather than dividing the language into discrete units and expecting students to piece things together on their own.

In answer to the first question about the articulation of French vowels, it can be said that the texts take a similar approach in their presentations: using English as an "anchor" for similar French phonemes, and giving articulatory information for those phonemes not found in English.

2 How are these phonemes represented orthographically? Once students have learned to pronounce the individual phonemes, they will need to know what is the orthographic representation for each of the phonemes. French, no less than English, is notorious for irregularities in its spelling system. However, there are many quite regular correspondences between sounds and letters and presentations from which students can generalize. Unfortunately, as can be seen in one text in particular, there can be a confusion between sound and letter which can muddle these regularities.

In AL, the phonological system is presented according to orthographic, not phonological, regularities. This leads to confusing terminology for the student, and a presentation from which generalizations cannot be made or can be made only with difficulty. The difficulties resulting from a presentation which moves from letter to sound instead of from sound to letter become evident, first in the initial presentation of the French vowel phonemes in the Workbook, and also in the chapter presentations. The following quote is from an exercise found in the first chapter of the Workbook accompanying AL. This exercise is designed to introduce students to the sounds of French.

Exercise 1. The sounds of French. The French equivalents of the five basic English vowels (**a, e, i, o, u**) are: /a/, /ë/, /i/, /o/, /y/. Listen and repeat...

There are in French, however, six other vowels that are close to these basic vowel sounds: /e/, /ɛ/, /ø/, /œ/, /ó/, /u/. Listen and repeat... (AL, Workbook:5)

If we examine this presentation carefully, we see that there is a hidden confusion between 'sound' and 'letter'. The student who looks at this exercise has been given the following definitions of 'vowel':

(1) *a, e, i, o, u*   'five basic English vowels'
(2) /a, ë, i, o, y/   'these basic vowel sounds'
(3) /e, ɛ, ø, œ, ó, u/   'six other vowels'

In reference to the 'five basic English vowels', the authors are talking about the five letters of the English alphabet which represent vowel sounds. They are equated to the pronunciation of these graphemes in the French alphabet, called 'these basic vowel sounds'. This may be misleading to students, especially in the case of the letter 'e' (e, é, è or ê), which in French has three possible phonemic realizations: /e/, /ɛ/ or /ë/. The choice of /ë/ as the 'basic' representation is made here because the alphabet letter 'e' is pronounced /ë/. However, some researchers do not even consider /ë/ to be a phoneme (Valdman 1976, Walter 1977). Furthermore, Valdman computes an 8.3% frequency of occurrence for the phoneme /e/ based on a running text of 25,000 consonant and vowel phonemes, which makes /e/ the most frequently occurring vowel phoneme. The phoneme /ɛ/ is given a frequency of 4.5%, and is the fourth most frequent (after /a/ and /i/). /ë/ is not listed on the chart. (Valdman 1976:65). A better definition of 'basic' might be frequency of occurrence among the phonemes of the language rather than pronunciation of the corresponding letter of the alphabet.

Another consequence resulting from the choice of basing the presentation on the alphabet instead of on regularities within the French vowel system is that similar vowels, such as /y/ - /u/ and /ó/ - /o/ are separated: /y/ and /o/ being presented as 'basic vowels' and /u/ and /ó/ as 'other vowels'. A student who has never had prior exposure to phonetics has learned, then, from this presentation, that a 'vowel' is either a sound, or a letter, or both.

Further confusion between sound and letter is evident in the pronunciation sections in each chapter of AL. For sounds with several orthographic representations, a presentation which moves from letter to sound can be confusing, especially if sound/letter correspondences are presented to the student in different chapters. Figure 2 contains a summary of the presentation of /o/ and the mid-vowels /e/ - /ɛ/ from AL.

Figure 2. A presentation based on orthography (AL).

/o/:	Chapter 5:	'au' pronounced as in *hope* (AL:132)
	Chapter 7:	'o' pronounced as in *go* (AL:171)
/e/ - /ɛ/:	Chapter 5:	'ai' in final position pronounced as in *wait* (AL:132)
		'ai' + oral consonant, proounced as in *melt* (AL:132)
	Chapter 6:	'é' pronounced as in *fail* (AL:145)
		'è, ê' pronounced as in *bed, belt* (AL:152)

For /o/, in Chapter 5, students learn that 'au' is like the vowel sound in *hope*. And in Chapter 7, students learn that the letter 'o' is like the vowel sound in *go*. The student is left to notice (or the instructor to point out) that /o/ can be spelled both 'o' and 'au'.

For /e/ and /ɛ/, in Chapter 5, the student learns that 'ai' in final position is like the vowel sound in *wait*, and that 'ai' followed by an oral consonant is like the vowel sound in *melt*. In Chapter 6 students are told that 'é' is like the vowel sound in *fail*, and 'è' and 'ê' are pronounced as in *bed* or *belt*. Here again, a student may not make the connection between 'ai' and accented or unaccented 'e'.

Clearly, such exercises do not allow a student to generalize or make broad conclusions from the information that is being given. Instead, an artificial separation of related points of the language may cloud the student's overall picture of French, leading him to conclude that there are no regularities in the language in areas where there is, in fact, a great deal of regularity.

3 What are the linguistic contexts in which these phonemes can occur? When presenting the vowel phonemes, all text authors give not only a list of possible orthographic representations of the sound, but rules for contexts in which the sound can or cannot be found. In examining these rules for contexts and also the words modeling the contexts, three potential problems are found. First, contexts are sometimes contradicted by words which the student is asked to pronounce in pronunciation drills directly following the explanation. Second, to correctly pronounce the practice words given, the student would need information that has not yet been presented. And third, the explanation given is much more detailed than necessary. Examples of each category will be discussed.

3.1 Contexts contradicted by words given in pronunciation drills. In AL, the authors state that 'in French, the letter *u* when not followed by another vowel or the consonants *m* or *n*, is always pronounced in the same fashion' (/y/), and give as practice words *vue* (/vy/), and *une* (/yn/) which contradict the preceding statement (AL:125).

In RA, the following rule for /o/ is given: 'You use the /o/ sound when the word ends in a vowel sound, the /ó/ sound when a pronounced consonant follows.' (RA:275) And students are asked to pronounce French *chose*, and English *propose* in which an /o/ sound is followed by a pronounced consonant in standard French dialects. The closing effect of final /z/ is mentioned for /ø/, however (RA: 299).

In the Study Guide accompanying CA, students are told that the final -er ending of verbs is silent. Two pages later we find the following rule: 'As you have learned, final -er is /e/: jouer. In all other positions, including final position, *r* is pronounced /r/.' (CA, Study Guide:432) Students are then asked to pronounce *raison, pourrais* and *cher*. Though the example of cher is not exactly a contradiction, because it is not a verb, and the rule does state that *r* is to be pronounced in final position, the fact that the presentation is on two separate pages, and the wording of the rule, may be confusing to the student. Instead of giving as an example of /r/ in final position a word which ends in -er, the point might have been made more clearly with an example word such as French *par* or *pour*.

3.2 Practice words which are beyond the student's current state of knowledge. In AL, the presentation of the nasal vowel phonemes is divided into three sections:

Les consonnes finales *m* et *n* (AL:90)
Les consonnes *m* et *n* au milieu d'un mot (AL:98)
Les consonnes *m* et *n* suivies de la voyelle *e* (AL:104)

But in the practice examples of the first section, where students have only been given rules for producing nasal vowels in word-final position, (AL:90) students are asked to pronounce *alle̅ma̅nd, appa̅rte̅ment, de̅main, ca̅nadien, ja̅mbon,* and *co̅mbien* (AL:90) words in which nasal and oral vowels are contrasted in non-final position. The explanation for such contexts is not provided for another eight pages.

3.3 Over-explanation. It is interesting, as an example of over-explanation, to compare the explanation of the contexts of nasal and oral vowels in two of the texts. The rules given in AL are, as mentioned above, found in three different sections:

(1) '... *m* and *n* are not pronounced at the end of a word. However, the presence of *m* or *n* frequently signals that the vowel preceding *m* or *n* is nasalized.' (AL:90)

(2) 'When *m* or *n* is followed by a consonant other than *m* or *n*, the preceding vowel is nasalized and the *m* or *n* is not pronounced... When *m* or *n* is followed by another *m* or *n* and when *m* or *n* falls between two vowels, the *m* or *n* is pronounced and the preceding vowel is not nasalized.' (AL:98)

(3) 'The presence of a mute *e* at the end of a word causes the preceding consonant . . . to be pronounced. In the case of *m* and *n*, pronouncing the consonant denasalizes the preceding vowel' (AL:104).

RA gives the following rule: 'The *n* or *m* must be pronounced if it is doubled . . . or followed by a vowel. . .' (RA:193). Instead of explaining every possible context, this rule only explains the places in which a nasal vowel is not found, leaving students to generalize that in all other contexts, a nasal vowel is found.

4 Conclusion. To conclude, if we return again to our original three questions, it is seen that the texts have a similar approach to describing the general idea of a 'French vowel' and to describing the articulation of the individual phonemes. But problems arise with an explanation of the orthographic representation of the phonemes and the contexts in which they occur. These problems seem to be related to a fundamental choice that the authors have made: to proceed from sound to letter, or from letter to sound. In AL, in particular, the entire presentation of phonology is based on orthography, which leads to numerous misunderstandings and explanations that do not clearly express the nature of the French vowel system. In CA, though much less information is provided on pronunciation than in the other texts, the presentation is not based on orthography. RA and PA have in common a presentation which introduces the phonemes according to common articulatory features, and then gives the orthographic representation for these sounds.

It seems that the one common factor to the potentially misleading exercises and examples cited above is that they do not allow the student to draw general conclusions which could then be applied to elements of the language not explicitly found in the texts. It is important to ask ourselves if the tasks we are demanding of our students are tasks which actually allow them to view language as a system, or if we are just giving them lists of rules which have no obvious relation to each other, nor to the language itself.

References

Bragger, Jeannette D., and Donald B. Rice. 1988. Allons-y! Le français par étapes, 2nd edition. Boston: Heinle & Heinle.
Brown, Thomas H. 1991. Pas à pas. New York: John Wiley and Sons.
Clark, J.L.D. 1967. Empirical studies related to the teaching of French pronunciation to American students. Cambridge, Mass.: Laboratory for Research in Instruction. Harvard Graduate School of Education.
Levitt, Jesse. 1970. The French vowel phonemes: some conflicting interpretations. Linguistics. 58. 38-51.
Sandberg, Karl C., Georges Zask, Anthony A. Ciccone, and Françoise Defrecheux. 1990. Ça marche! Cours de français communicatif. New York: Macmillan.
Valdman, Albert. 1961. Teaching the French vowels. Modern Language Journal. 45. 257-62.
Valdman, Albert. 1976. Introduction to French phonology and morphology. Rowley, Mass.: Newbury House.
Walter, Henriette. 1977. La phonologie du français. Paris: PUF.
Walz, Joel and Jean-Pierre Piriou. 1990. Rapports. Language, culture, communication, 2nd edition. Lexington, Mass.: D.C. Heath.

Language and communication:
A time for equilibrium and integration

Marianne Celce-Murcia
University of California, Los Angeles

Background. During the past fifty years, there have been several approaches to language teaching that have been influential in shaping our views of language and communication.[1] From the mid-1940s through much of the 1960s, the Audio-lingual Approach was dominant, e.g. Fries 1945, Lado 1964. This approach, based on Structural Linguistics and Behavioral Psychology, viewed language learning as habit formation and the language system (i.e. the phonology and grammar) as appropriate content for language instruction. Although the Cognitive Code Approach (Jakobovits 1968, 1970), inspired by Chomskyan Linguistics and Cognitive Psychology, challenged Audio-lingualism during the 1960s by viewing language learning as rule acquisition and hypothesis testing rather than habit formation, the focus of language instruction remained the phonological and grammatical systems of the target language. Thus while there was disagreement over the merits of the inductive learning-as-habit model of Audio-lingualism vis-à-vis the deductive learning-by-rules procedure associated with Cognitive Code, there was in fact agreement that the linguistic system of the target language constituted an appropriate curriculum for the foreign or second language classroom. Communication, when given any consideration, was generally thought of as something learners would be able to do after they had mastered the structures of the target language.[2]

By the mid-1970s there were two new approaches that challenged the linguistically-organized curriculum shared by Audio-lingualism and Cognitive Code: the Comprehension Approach and the Communicative Approach. In the Comprehension Approach (e.g. Winitz 1981, Krashen

---

1 These four approaches are not the only ones that have been influential during the 20th Century. For a brief but more comprehensive overview, see Celce-Murcia (1991b).

2 There were early precursors of the Communicative Approach such as Prator (1972), who in the early 1960s (Clifford Prator, personal communication) advocated a language pedagogy that moved from the manipulation associated with Audio-lingualism to activities focusing on communication.

and Terrell 1983), it was assumed that meaningful, comprehensible input was sufficient to trigger language acquisition; that is, by listening to and actively demonstrating comprehension of the target language, a learner would ultimately be able to produce that target language. In the Communicative Approach (Johnson and Morrow 1981, Littlewood,1981), which assumes that communication is the goal of foreign or second language instruction, meaningful activities that promote communication and meaningful tasks that promote learning are viewed as the keys to language acquisition and thus become the core of the language curriculum. Neither the Comprehension Approach[3] nor the Communicative Approach uses language structure as the major focus of language instruction. The Comprehension Approach explicitly states—and the Communicative Approach tacitly implies—that the acquisition of language structure will occur incidentally, as a by-product of practice involving comprehension-based or communication-based activities.

As we now know, the initial intuitive appeal enjoyed by both of these two major trends—each with its important variations—did not survive the test of time. Audio-lingualism and Cognitive Code did not produce competent communicators. More recently, the research has begun to show and the profession has slowly come to realize that the Comprehension Approach and the Communicative Approach—in spite of some of the impressive things they can accomplish—do not produce linguistic accuracy as an incidental by-product of fluency.

Taking stock. Why should we be surprised? As Schmidt (1990) points out in his review of learning theory, learners—and this includes language learners—tend to learn what they notice and internalize, and not to learn what they do not notice. Schmidt further elaborates that 'being taught' is not a simple one-dimensional notion; for learning to take place, the learner must pay attention to the learning objective, and the learner must then practice the objective so that it changes from being part of a controlled process to being part of an automatic process (McLaughlin 1987). Such noticing can proceed either consciously or unconsciously. In addition to attention (or noticing), Schmidt also discusses awareness or understanding, i.e. conscious recognition of a rule or principle. Such awareness, while perhaps not necessary to account for early stages of naturalistic language acquisition, may well be necessary

---

3 Actually, some comprehension-based teaching strategies such as Asher's Total Physical Response (1977) and Winitz' 'Learnables' (Winitz, n.d.) follow teaching sequences that are carefully controlled from a structural point of view. They contrast markedly with with the better-known Natural Approach of Krashen and Terrell (1983), which I am specifically referring to here in my discussion of curriculum in the comprehension-based approach.

to avert premature fossilization[4] and to engage the learner in effective error correction and language development in the later stages of language acquisition. Certainly, the long-term results that Higgs and Clifford (1982) have observed at the Foreign Service Institute would tend to confirm Schmidt's interpretation of learning theory as it relates to foreign and second language learning.

However, we also have other reasons not to be surprised that Audiolingualism and Cognitive Code did not produce learners who could communicate and that the Comprehension-based and Communicative Approaches have not necessarily produced language users who are accurate. Since 1980 we have used and referred to Canale and Swain's model of Communicative Competence (Canale and Swain 1980). This model posits four components for communicative competence:[5]

- Sociolinguistic competence (i.e. appropriacy): the speaker/writer knows how to express the message in terms of the person being addressed and the overall circumstances and purpose of the communication;
- Discourse competence: the selection, sequence, and arrangement of words and structures are clear and effective means of expressing the message;
- Linguistic competence (i.e. accuracy): the forms, inflections, and sequences used to express the message are grammatically correct;
- Strategic competence: the speaker/writer has effective means to compensate for any weaknesses shown in the above three areas.

Certainly, in many face-to-face communications, sociolinguistic appropriacy and discourse competence are more important than grammatical accuracy, provided that the grammar used is not inaccurate to the point of miscommunicating the speaker/writer's intended message; communication is the overriding concern in many such encounters. However, there are situations where grammatical accuracy is also very important, such as the academic writing of foreign and immigrant university students and the more formal verbal interactions of businessmen, professionals, and diplomats. Ideally, all four components of communicative competence should be well developed if a high level of proficiency in the target language is the learner's goal.

---

4 The term 'fossilization' comes from Selinker (1972), who in his landmark article on interlanguage describes as 'fossilized' those second language learners who plateau at some less than advanced stage of acquisition and are seemingly unable to progress any further in the acquisition of their second language.

5 This model builds on the work of the anthropological linguist, Dell Hymes (1972).

One language learning context that illustrates well what can happen when only some of the components of communicative competence have been addressed is the university-level composition class as it relates to foreign and immigrant undergraduate students who are non-native speakers of English. For many years now we have had large numbers of immigrant undergraduate students at UCLA[6] who are extremely bright and who understand their lectures and textbooks almost as well as native speakers; their comprehension of English is excellent. Yet when we examine their written work, it is clear that they have not mastered the English language in any true sense. It is also clear from our observations of these students that the 'rules' for producing language must be different in important ways from the 'rules' for comprehending language. Rules of pedagogical 'grammar', it appears, refer primarily to rules of production, and it is these rules that our students have not acquired.

In a relevant experiment McGirt (1984) found that forty percent of the undergraduate ESL composition students he studied had perfectly adequate top-down communicative writing skills but inadequate bottom-up language skills. He discovered this by correcting only the morphology and syntax in their compositions; as a result, their holistic scores moved from nonpass to pass when the two versions of their compositions (one version as written vs. the other with morphosyntax corrected) were evaluated by experienced composition teachers.[7] Schwabe (1989) surveyed the same population at the University of California, Davis, i.e., long-term resident, non-native undergraduate composition students, to get their assessments of why they were having problems with writing in English; four of the many revealing written responses that her survey elicited were the following, which I have not edited in any way:

- High school should teach more on grammar, sentence structures, vocabulary and idioms. They should make sure the students know the grammar pretty well before even make them write essay.
- My high school English teachers emphasized mostly on the English literatures, which we had to read the book in class, discuss what we read and answer the questions.
- Why didn't they let the non-native speaker reads other papers which a teacher consider it's a 'good' paper?
- An ESL person might be able to tell a grammer mistake in a sentence but not in a paragraph. I never knew how well I did if I

---

6 UCLA is not at all unique in this regard. Many public U.S. universities in large metropolitan areas face the same problems with the same population.

7 In McGirt's study (1984) 20% of the ESL writers had passing scores even without the morphosyntactic corrections, and the remaining 40% did not pass even with the corrections; i.e. their top-down skills were also inadequate.

wrote an essay. I first heard of adjective clause and subordinate conjugation in UCD.

It is obvious that language teaching professionals face many conflicts and dilemmas in language teaching. Our past experiences while less than completely successful have not, however, been fruitless; given that I believe we now know with greater assurance the general direction that we must take to facilitate more balanced and complete language learning in foreign and second language classrooms.

The current challenge. If we view communication and language as forming a continuum where top-down communication skills are at one end and bottom-up linguistic skills at the other, we can see that during the past 50 years or so language teaching can be represented as a swinging of the pendulum from a focus on language at one extreme to a focus on communication at the other. I would like to propose that what we now need is some balance and equilibrium; we need integrated approaches to language teaching which take into account and provide practice in both top-down communication skills and bottom-up linguistic skills. Depending on the needs and the level of proficiency of the learners, the proportion of top-down to bottom-up practices may vary at any given stage; however, we do need to deliberately work towards a balance and to stop deluding ourselves into believing that any significant and meaningful component of communicative competence will occur incidentally as a by-product of the learner attending to and practicing some other component.

The current challenge is to identify and develop promising integrated approaches to language teaching and to modify and improve them as needed so that both the learner's top-down communication skills and bottom-up linguistic skills are very carefully and deliberately nurtured. Since the learner's age, level of proficiency, and reasons for learning a foreign or second language will be major factors in developing any such approach (Celce-Murcia 1985), I would like to present two rather different example units to illustrate the solution I propose.

Sample 1: unit for beginning-level pupils (ages 10-12).[8] With beginning-level pupils (ages 10-12) it is important to spend time eliciting or generating vocabulary related to a particular topic or task so that the word-store brought to the foreground can be used to practice structures and to perform activities relevant to the topic. For example, in a begin-

---

[8] I am indebted to Elite Olshtain (personal communication), who has worked extensively with this learner population, for most of the ideas that I exploit in this first sample unit.

ning-level ESL/EFL class each pupil can generate a family tree (following the model of the teacher, who presents first). Then by learning a few kinship terms, the possessive adjective *my*, and the three present-tense forms of the copula *be (am, are, is)*, pupils will be able to introduce their families to the class:

*I am Antonio. My father is José and my mother is Ana.
My two sisters are Maria and Anita. My brother is Jorge.*

Depending on the needs of individual students, it may be necessary to introduce a few more kinship terms so that the pupils can introduce grandparents or other relatives who form part of their immediate family unit. Such additional vocabulary can be introduced as the need arises.

A subsequent activity has the whole class working together to generate master lists under three activity headings:

(1) Things I like to do when I have time.
(2) Things I have to do every day.
(3) Things I do occasionally.

The first heading elicits activities like: go to the beach, play football, watch television. The second heading includes things like: make my bed, study, do the dishes. The third will contain activities like: visit my grandmother, go to the movies, write a letter. The teacher can help generate the vocabulary for the lists, as needed, and can make sure that the short verb phrases written on the chalkboard or the overhead projector are grammatically and lexically accurate. At this point each pupil will generate his own short list, selecting at least two items from the three master lists created in class. Working with a partner, the pupil will write two sentences that describe what he and his partner do everyday using the information in the individually-generated lists (and, of course, using the simple present tense):

- *Every day I make my bed, study, and do the dishes.*
- *Every day Sergio walks his dog and practices the piano.*

These sentences will then be read aloud to the class for comprehension and retelling or summarization by others. Similar activities will be carried out using the information generated for the other two activity lists to further reinforce the simple present tense.

As a more challenging communicative activity, the pupils will draw on all the material they have generated while doing this unit to write a simple letter introducing themselves to a pen-pal (ideally a real person who will respond), thus incorporating the target vocabulary and structures into a larger piece of communication. This activity includes learning about the format of an informal letter and organizing ideas into a coherent and interesting text as well as reinforcing much of the vocabulary and structures that the pupils have practiced during the unit.

However, this should not be the end of the unit. As a final stage the teacher should present to the class data that the pupils themselves have generated, with the data grouped according to each structure being taught (copula *be*, simple present tense).The teacher directs the pupils to come to some kind of grammatical generalization in their own words about each structure. Finally, the teacher might give the pupils the formal rule for each structure and let them compare it with the rule they themselves have generated. If useful, the students can also work at correcting some of their own errors involving the structures they have covered in the unit.

According to Elite Olshtain (personal communication), who has used this type of approach to teach grammar within a communicative framework to beginning-level learners, the approach requires the learners to take risks and to be more responsible for their own learning. It also requires that the teachers know the materials and the grammar thoroughly and that they be flexible in responding to what the learners generate. They must also be good classroom managers so that all practice (individual, pair, small group, whole class) is carried out efficiently and productively.

Sample 2. Unit teaching intermediate ESL/EFL adults to complain. For learners who have mastered the basic structures and some vocabulary, it is often useful to view language in larger functional units such as speech acts. My second sample unit comes from the work of Hawkins (1985), who developed this unit to teach the complaint 'script' (Schank and Abelson 1977) to intermediate-level ESL/EFL students in an oral communication class at UCLA. The basic complaint script, according to Hawkins, involves two goals: to call attention to objectionable behavior and then to change that behavior. The two goals present the learner with a dilemma since s/he must strike a delicate balance and be polite yet assertive in calling attention to the objectionable behavior in order to get the person responsible to change his/her behavior.

Hawkins' objective was to get the predominantly foreign learners in her class to respond effectively and appropriately to six oral prompts describing situations designed to elicit complaints.[9] For example:

(1) You take a morning off from work to go to the doctor because of a serious medical problem that is causing you pain. For two hours you

---

[9] The example prompt and the six target prompts used by Hawkins in her unit were taken from research by Schaefer (1982) on the complaint speech act.

sit in the waiting room. During your wait, you periodically check with the woman at the desk to find out why you haven't been called in to the examination room. She keeps telling you that the doctor will be with you 'in a few minutes'. At 11:00 a.m., you approach her for the fifth time and she looks up and says, 'Don't worry, the doctor will be with you in just a few more minutes. I'll call your name when it's your turn.'

Prior to any instruction, Hawkins had her students respond to the six target prompts she had selected for the four-part unit. Then as the first step, each student had to record and transcribe one American English native speaker as s/he responded to the same six target complaint prompts. Second, the students were introduced to a discourse framework—based on the seven components identified by Schaefer (1982)—for analyzing the complaint data they themselves had produced and the data they had elicited from native speakers:

(2) **Seven typical complaint components:** (some components may be missing or reordered in any given complaint)

1. Opener (O): utterance which initiates the complaint;

2. Orientation (OR): utterance that provides the addressee with information about the complainer's identity and/or intent in initiating the complaint;

3. Act Statement (AS): utterance which identifies the trouble source;

4. Justification (J):
   a. of the Speaker (JS): an utterance by the complainer that explains why s/he is personally making the complaint;
   b. of the Addressee (JA): an utterance by the complainer that offers a reason for the addressee's having committed the wrong ('maybe you didn't have time, but . . .');

5. Remedy (R): utterance that calls for an action to rectify the wrong;
   a. Threat (T): a type of remedy in which the complainer states an action s/he will execute depending on what the addressee does (e.g. '. . . or I'll take my business elsewhere');

6. Closing (C): an utterance made by the complainer at the end of the complaint to conclude his/her turn;

7. Valuation (V): an utterance by the complainer that expresses his/her feelings about either the addressee or the wrong that's been committed. (Usually this is found with other components, e.g. with Act Statements: 'This pizza is terrible. Please bring us another.')

As another part of step two, Hawkins showed the students how the framework could help them not only to understand complaints but also to segment and classify the native-speaker data they had collected. She used examples like (3a, 3b), which provide a complaint generated in response to the prompt in (1) along with an analysis of the sample complaint:

(3a) **Sample complaint:** 'Well, I've been waiting two hours. I know the doctor might have gotten tied up, and that it's not your fault; but this is ridiculous. I've already taken three hours off from work, and I really have to be back at noon. Could you please see what you can do? If I can't get in to see the doctor in the next ten minutes, I'll have to leave and simply schedule another appointment or find another doctor. Thank you.'

(3b) **Sample analysis:**
O: Well,
AS: I've been waiting two hours.
JA & V: I know the doctor might have gotten tied up, and that it's not your fault, but this is ridiculous.
JS & V: I've already taken three hours off from work, and I really have to be back at noon.
R: Could you please see what you can do?
R & T: If I can't get in to see the doctor in the next ten minutes, I'll have to leave and simply schedule another appointment or find another doctor.
C: Thank you.

For the third step of the unit Hawkins had her students work in small groups to analyze the data from their own complaints, which they had produced during the preliminary exercise, in addition to the data they had elicited from their native speaker consultants. They then recorded the information they discovered on tally sheets provided by the instructor so that they could display clearly the similarities and the differences between the complaints produced by native speakers and their own complaints.

In the fourth and final phase, the groups came together as a whole to combine their results. There was a class discussion about what native speakers do when they complain and what the students—as non-native speakers—had done, how and why their verbal behaviors might differ, and what is—and what is not—likely to be an effective complaint if one is interacting with Americans.

At this stage, Hawkins found it desirable to draw special attention to the syntactic correlates of the remedy component in complaints because many of the students had failed to notice on their own that the modal auxiliaries *would* and *could* are more polite and appropriate forms to use in a request or suggestion expressed as a remedy than *will* or *can*.

Hawkins then administered a unit test that consisted of the class responding to the same six complaint prompts she had used in the preliminary exercise. Approximately three and one-half weeks had elapsed between the preliminary exercise and the unit test. (They had been working on other activities in class in addition to the work on complaints.) The students' responses from the preliminary exercise and the unit test were then rated by a native speaker of English who owns a business in the Los Angeles area and has to deal with complaints on a daily basis. The rater scored the complaints on a scale of 1 to 10 (10 being a very effective complaint and 1 being a totally ineffective complaint, with 5 being a complaint of average effectiveness). The data were scrambled and the rater did not know which of the data were pre-treatment and which were post-treatment. A statistical analysis using the sign test indicated that there was a positive change ($p<.01$) in the effectiveness of the students' complaints following the instruction, which had consisted largely of data collection, discourse analysis, and awareness-raising activities rather than simply a great deal of communicative practice with situations that would trigger complaints.

Comparing the two sample units. The first sample unit for young beginning-level pupils gives, on the one hand, a great deal of emphasis to bottom-up language practice since these learners need to familiarize themselves with the relevant vocabulary and grammar before they can apply it to a communicative task. On the other hand, in the second unit for intermediate-level adults in an oral communication class, the instructional focus is on the top-down sociolinguistic and discourse features of the complaint as speech act. At the end of the unit the instructor highlights one linguistic feature that is important to the speech act that the students have not noticed on their own. In both units the teacher helps to draw learner attention to salient features of language and communication and to achieve an appropriate balance between the two, given the needs and the level of the learners. In both units the learners are responsible for much of their own learning and the teacher is a highly knowledgable facilitator.

Integrated approaches for more advanced learners. Instead of continuing with more specific examples, I shall now turn to more

---

10 Hawkins (1985) included this step in her unit on complaints only retrospectively. She decided after the fact that her students' improvement would have been even more striking had she included some meaningful focus on this form-function correspondence, which had gone undetected by most of her students.

general descriptions of integrated approaches to language teaching that support the development of both top-down and bottom-up language skills. At the high intermediate and advanced level, university students can benefit from the type of genre analysis suggested by Swales (1990), whereby, for example, they learn the rhetorical features of the research article in the sciences with its familiar introduction-method-results-discussion format. In this approach some contextualized attention is also given to the salient and frequent linguistic features typical of the genre under study (e.g. tenses, logical connectors, and structures like the passive voice and anticipatory-*it* constructions).

Such students are also ready to benefit from an integrated approach such as content-based language teaching. (See Snow 1991; and Brinton, Snow, and Wesche 1989). In such an approach the content of an academic course such as introductory psychology or anthropology provides the basis for a very focused type of language learning experience whereby the related (or 'adjuncted') ESL class allows the students to develop skills that enhance their understanding of the language and content relevant to the academic course as well as improve their performance on the tasks required by the academic course. The philosophical similarity to the English-for-specific-purposes movement is obvious (See Johns 1991).

Another alternative that seems quite traditional, yet is not at all so, is the use of literature as content for language teaching. This type of language course has been promoted by Stern (1991), among others, and it is a far cry from the traditional view of teaching ESL/EFL learners to read, comprehend, and appreciate literature for its own sake. In the literature-as-content approach, appreciation of a particular literary selection is but one aspect of a more elaborate methodology. Selection of literature should be based on learner accessibility and enjoyment, and literature can be viewed broadly as including fairy tales, folk tales, and children's stories as well as the more usual selections from poetry, drama, and fiction. For example, using the poem 'Mending Wall' by Robert Frost, Stern describes how the ESL/EFL teacher can develop a series of related activities for intermediate-level students that focus on vocabulary, grammar, reading, writing, cultural content, and a variety of oral language skills. According to Stern, the teacher should select those language development activities that are most appropriate for their particular students and the works being read. All the activities in the unit should be sequenced to complement and build upon each other.

Yet another type of approach that seems fruitful is experiential language learning (Eyring 1991), where the life experiences that the learners bring with them as well as the experiences that the language class itself initiates offer opportunities for meaningful language practice and language development. For example, tasks and projects that encourage language learners to interview experts, conduct surveys, gather and synthesize information of interest to them can be highly motivating and stimulating. This is particularly true when some sort of tangible product emerges. For example, ESL pupils at one elementary school have published a school newspaper; secondary-level learners have done research on other countries and have sponsored a travel fair for their school; Eyring (1988) has had university-level ESL composition students at UCLA form groups to research and report on topics of their own choosing (the groups chose a range of fairly controversial topics including Chinese gangs in Los Angeles, surrogate motherhood, UCLA student attitudes toward homosexuality, and the current activities of the Ku Klux Klan).

In this approach, once the information has been gathered and is being prepared for presentation, the teacher has an excellent opportunity to focus on language features within a richly communicative context. In some cases, it may also be necessary for the teacher to do some specific language instruction at various stages to prepare students to gather information successfully and to present or write up their findings.

Conclusion. The preceding suggestions should all be implemented in such a way that both top-down communication skills and bottom-up linguistic skills can be practiced and developed by the learner. This is what should occur under ideal circumstances. However, in the real world, it is easy for a language teacher (or a language program) to misinterpret or subvert these suggestions in such a way that top-down skills are emphasized to the exclusion of bottom-up skills, or vice versa. Achieving the necessary integration and balance between language and communication is not simple, but it is necessary if we are going to help learners achieve optimal language development. Effective teachers will need to be well trained in discourse analysis and in the lexico-grammar of the target language, on the one hand, and integrated methodologies, materials, and curricula on the other. In addition, they will need to have skills in classroom management as well as a personal teaching style that promotes positive and productive classroom socialization.

If language and communication are complex, then language learning and language teaching are also highly complex undertakings. The poet Carl Sandburg once said, 'Slang is language that takes off its coat, spits on its hands, and goes to work'.[11] Using Sandburg's metaphor as inspiration, I would like to suggest that language pedagogy is ideally the application not only of linguistics, but also of learning psychology and social anthropology and that to improve language pedagogy practitioners of

---

11 This quote is from Esar (1989:175).

these disciplines should take off their coats, spit on their hands, and work together.

From linguistics we must draw on the language descriptions we need to carry out effective language awareness and discovery procedures in our classes; we must also draw on knowledge about developmental grammar sequences (e.g. Pienemann 1984) and universal grammar in order to make our accuracy-based instruction optimally productive.[12] From psychology we get a variety of learning theories, ranging from social to connectionist to neuro-anatomical ones, that we need to be aware of to fully understand and facilitate the process of language learning, since different theories may well account for different aspects of the learning process. From social anthropology we must draw on existing knowledge of the social and cultural factors that shape various discourse genres in the source and target languages of our students; we also need to understand and use appropriately the social and cultural forces that obtain in the foreign/second language classroom. In other words, those of us concerned with language pedogogy should seek to discover and apply how language, mind, and socio-cultural forces can come together optimally in the teaching and learning of both language and communication.

References

Asher, J.J. 1977. Learning another language through actions: The complete teachers' guidebook. Los Gatos, Calif.: Sky Oak Productions.

Brinton, D., M.A. Snow, and M.B. Wesche 1989. Content-based second language instruction. New York: Newbury House.

Canale, M., and M. Swain 1980. Theoretical bases of communicative approaches to second language teaching and testing. Applied Linguistics 1.1:1-47.

Celce-Murcia, M. 1985. Making informed decisions about the role of grammar in language teaching. TESOL Newletter, 29.1:4-5.

Celce-Murcia, M., ed. 1991a. Teaching English as a second or foreign language. 2nd ed. New York: Newbury House.

Celce-Murcia, M. 1991b. Language teaching approaches: An overview. In: Celce-Murcia 1991a, 3-11.

Esar, E., ed. 1989. The dictionary of humorous quotations. New York: Dorset Press.

Eyring, J. 1988. Project work in the ESL writing course: A case study. Unpublished Ms., University of California, Los Angeles.

Eyring, J. 1991. Experiential language learning. In: Celce-Murcia 1991a, 346-359.

Fries, C.C. 1945. Teaching and learning English as a foreign language. Ann Arbor: University of Michigan Press.

---

12 In other words, making a student practice and attend to a structure before s/he is developmentally ready to, 'notice' it and integrate it into his or her evolving system is not optimal use of teaching time and effort.

Hawkins, B. 1985. Complaints: Nonnative speakers learn from native speakers. Paper presented at the Second Language Research Forum, Los Angeles.
Higgs, T.V. and R. Clifford 1982. The push toward communication. In: T.V. Higgs, ed., Curriculum, competence, and the foreign language teacher. 57-79. Lincolnwood, Ill.: National Textbook Company.
Hymes, D. 1972. On communicative competence. In: J.B. Pride and J. Holmes, eds., Sociolinguistics: Selected readings. 269-293. Harmondsworth, England: Penguin Books.
Jakobovits, L. 1968. Implications of recent psycholinguistic developments for the teaching of a second language. Language Learning 18:89-109.
Jakobovits, L. 1970. Foreign language learning: A psycholinguistic analysis of the issues. Rowley, Mass: Newbury House.
Johns, A.M. 1991. English for specific purposes ESP: Its history and contributions. In: Celce-Murcia 1991a, 67-77.
Johnson, K. and K. Morrow, eds. 1981. Communication in the classroom. London: Longman.
Krashen, S. and T. Terrell. 1983. The natural approach. Hayward, Calif.: Alemany Press.
Lado, R. 1964. Language teaching: A scientific approach. New York: McGraw-Hill.
Littlewood, W. 1981. Communicative language teaching: An introduction. Cambridge: Cambridge University Press.
McGirt, J.D. 1984. The effect of morphological and syntactic errors on the holistic scores of native and non-native compositions. Unpublished MATESL thesis, University of California, Los Angeles.
McLaughlin, B. 1987. Theories of second language acquisition. London: Edward Arnold.
Olshtain, Elite. Personal communication.
Pienemann, M. 1984. Psychological constraints on the teachability of language. Studies in second language acquisition, 62, 186-214.
Prator, C.H. 1972. Development of a manipulation-communication scale. In: H.B. Allen and R.N. Campbell, eds., Teaching English as a second language: A book of readings. 2nd ed., 139-144. New York: McGraw-Hill.
Schaefer, E. 1982. An analysis of the discourse and syntax of oral complaints in English. Unpublished M.A. thesis in TESL. UCLA.
Schank, R.C. and R. Abelson 1977. Scripts, plans, goals, and understanding: An inquiry into human knowledge structures. Hillsdale, N.J.: Erlbaum.
Schmidt, R. 1990. Input, interaction, attention, and awareness: The case for consciousness raising in second language teaching. Keynote address at the 10th ENPULI Conference, Rio de Janeiro, July 30-August 3, 1990.
Schwabe, G.T. 1989. UC ESL Students' Evaluation of their High School English instruction. Appendix E of English as a Second Language at the University of California: A Report to UCUPRE from the ESL Subcommittee. G. Gadda (LA), R. Scarcella (I), J. McKay (B), W. Megenney (R), G.T. Schwabe (D), M. Celce-Murcia (LA), Chair. UC Systemwide Aca-demic Senate Report, Jan. 17, 1989.
Selinker, L. 1972. Interlanguage. IRAL 10: 219-231.
Snow, M.A. 1991. Teaching language through content. In: Celce-Murcia 1991a, 315-328.

Stern, S.L. 1991. An integrated approach to literature in ESL/EFL. In: Celce-Murcia 1991a, 328-346.
Swales, J. 1990. Genre analysis and its applications. Cambridge: Cambridge University Press.
Winitz, H., ed. 1981. The comprehension approach to foreign language instruction. New York: Newbury House.
Winitz, H. n.d. The Learnables. (Materials for teaching the initial comprehension phase of several languages including: English, Spanish, German, French, Japanese, Hebrew, etc. Available from International Linguistics Corp., 401 89th Street, Kansas City, MO 64114.)

Instructional balance:
From theories to practices in the teaching of writing

Ann Raimes*
Hunter College, City University of New York

It is difficult to examine exactly where we are now in the teaching of writing without also examining where we have been. And when we look at trends and movements in the teaching of writing in the last twenty years, we see more controversy than commonality. The plural forms in my subtitle—theories and practices—represent the diversity in the field and, at the same time, the current state of the art in writing pedagogy. It's important to recognize that the variety in our field is more fundamental than mere procedural ways of following the same approach (Richards and Rodgers 1986). Rather, each new approach to come along is quite distinct, reflecting its own set of assumptions about language, literacy, and the roles of writer, reader, subject matter, and textual form.

Balanced and unbalanced stances. To examine the present state of the art in teaching writing, we need to examine not only what we do and say we do but also what assumptions underlie the actions and statements of teachers and theorists. To do that, a framework is helpful, and I am going to borrow one from Wayne Booth, who, in an early influential article on writing, 'The rhetorical stance', discusses the importance of maintaining 'a proper balance' among the elements involved in communication: the subject itself, the audience, and the speaker or writer (1963:141). He suggests that the main goal of writers is this balance, this rhetorical stance, free from 'corruptions', or what he calls 'unbalanced stances' (141). In adopting Booth's framework to examine what we do as teachers, I propose to categorize approaches to teaching writing in terms of four elements that can be valued—or overvalued—in instruction and informed by research: the *form*, that is, the linguistic and rhetorical conventions of the text; the *writer* and the writer's ideas,

---

* The author wishes to thank Karen Greenberg, Kate Parry, Ruth Spack, and Vivian Zamel for their helpful comments on earlier drafts of this paper.

experiences, feelings, and composing processes; the *content* or subject matter; and the *reader*, specifically the expectations of the academic audience. A balanced stance, while it necessarily exhibits a principled 'governing philosophy' in relation to those four elements (Raimes 1987a:39), maintains a balance by taking all four elements into account. An unbalanced stance values one or more of the four elements at the expense of the others. This warps instruction and, I suggest, leads to contentiousness that is not always productive.

I think I can best illustrate what I mean by instructional balance if I contrast it with four current unbalanced stances that emerge from uncritical dedication to one approach or from an extreme reaction to a previous approach. I will describe the theoretical and research bases for each of the four approaches to teaching writing, and then, taking a cue from Booth, I will suggest a metaphor for each extreme stance that characterizes how an overzealous reliance on one element to the exclusion of others can so drive the governing philosophy of instruction that curriculum, materials, and methods are affected.

A form-focused approach. A form-focused approach to teaching writing is one that those of us who have been in the field for twenty years or more know very well. It is based on what Hill and Parry (1989), following Street (1984), call an 'autonomous model of literacy'; one that sees text as standing on its own independent of writer and reader. And certainly, imitation and manipulation of model texts used to dominate L2 writing instruction and theory (e.g. Pincas 1962, Paulston 1972). Almost the only composition textbooks available in the 60s and early 70s were books of guided and controlled composition (e.g. Kunz 1972, Paulston and Dykstra 1973). Our job as teachers then was to make sure our students did not make errors as they transformed or imitated given texts.

The concern for formal features of a text extends to rhetorical form as well as to grammatical accuracy. Kaplan's 1966 article is so well-known as to be popularly referred to as the 'doodles article' (Kaplan 1987:9); it has been even further familiarized by a typographical error calling it his 'noodles article' (Shen 1989:463). This article introduced the concept of 'contrastive rhetoric', which in turn generated pedagogic prescriptions intended to keep first language interference at bay and to prescribe clear formats for writing a 'linear' composition in English (Kaplan 1966:4). So we asked our students to copy models and pour their content into a given rhetorical form, like *Jell-O* into a mold. Twenty-five years later, contrastive rhetoric research has yielded interesting information about the structure of other languages (e.g. Tsao 1983, Eggington 1987, Ostler 1987), but has not moved in the direction of providing innovative approaches to instruction. And, in fact, the intent of contrastive rhetoric research is 'not to provide pedagogic method', but rather to provide teachers and students with knowledge about how the links between culture and writing are reflected in written products (Grabe and Kaplan 1989:271).

Instructional approaches rarely exist in a vacuum. They are supported by research. Researchers inform a form-focused approach when they look at and count textual features such as the number of passives or the number of pronouns (Reid 1990). Or they look at discourse-level textual features, such as the way introductions are structured (Scarcella 1984) or the way Japanese prose is organized (Hinds 1987). The large-scale International Association for the Evaluation of Educational Achievement (IEA) Study of Written Composition, codifying tasks and collecting students' writing at the end of compulsory schooling in 14 different countries, has developed the most comprehensive data base for cross-cultural text-based information (Purves 1988). In the teaching of writing, the largest body of research exists in this area of the examination of formal and grammatical structures in texts.

The copyeditor's stance. With a large body of empirical research and with many years of tradition to support a form-focused approach, an unbalanced stance can develop. Obviously, most teachers of L2 writing will pay attention to rhetorical form and linguistic accuracy. However, when this attention is not balanced as just one part of the whole complex process of the production of a text for a reader, and when there is a too-heavy privileging of the formal properties of the text, that is, of its linguistic correctness and rhetorical conventions, this is what I call the copyeditor's stance. This consists of downplaying the relationship between reader and writer and the truth value of the information in the written text, in favor of concentrating on formal features. We adopt this stance and favor the copyediting functions when we prescribe an organizational pattern, provide a model, and correct errors. When students are taught by a teacher with a copyeditor's stance, they worry mainly about meeting formal expectations. They edit prematurely; the interest or logic of their ideas is not something they spend time on. They end up producing a five-paragraph theme, often organized and grammatically accurate, but empty of life, voice, and originality. We have all read many products of students who have suffered from such an imbalance. We can barely stay awake beyond the first sentence, e.g. 'In this essay I will explain three reasons why teachers should insist on punctuality.'

A writer-focused approach. There is more to writing and to researching or teaching writing than the form and language of the text. Influenced by L1 writing research in the 1970s, teachers and researchers developed an interest in the writing process—that is, in what writers actually do as they write. This led to writer-focused approaches in the classroom, characterized by journals (Peyton 1990, Spack and Sadow 1983), invention (Spack 1984), students' choice of topics and attention to content before form (Zamel 1976, 1982, Raimes 1987a). Teachers began to allow time and opportunity for drafts and revisions, for feedback not only from the teacher but from other students as well. In a model of literacy that began to shift from autonomous to 'ideological' (Street 1984) or 'pragmatic' (Hill and Parry 1989), teachers and researchers began to emphasize the communication and negotiation that goes on between writer and reader in the writing and interpretation of a text, recognizing the 'ideological and therefore culturally embedded nature of [the social practices of reading and writing]' (Street 1984:2). The processes of reading, writing, and learning became important in the classroom. Now, teachers often ask students to think through issues by means of writing about them, to practice generating and revising ideas through the act of writing, and to read, discuss, and interpret texts, including each other's.

In addition, research on the cognitive processes of writers who write in L1 and L2 has burgeoned to inform and support a writer-focused approach, commonly called a 'process approach' (Zamel 1983, Jones and Tetroe 1987, Raimes 1985, 1987b, Cumming 1989; for a summary, see Krapels 1990). However, since the studies are mostly case studies, their small number of subjects limits generalizations. Despite the growing body of research, we are justly warned that the 'lack of comparability across studies impedes the growth of knowledge in the field' (Krapels 1990:51).

The therapist's stance. In the field of L2 writing, an acceptance of a new model of literacy that includes writer, reader, and text in communicative interaction has greatly affected the literature in our field and our classroom practices. Again, though, an overemphasis on the writer's role at the expense of the other elements has given rise to a second unbalanced stance, one that I will call the therapist's stance. This consists of the extreme position of valuing the writer's voice, openness, sincerity, and originality in a framework of personal writing above any notions of audience, context, of content, or accuracy. In L1 writing, Faigley has pointed out how much of Coles and Vopat's book *What makes writing good* (1985) actually stresses values of honesty and sincerity above all other considerations (1989). This stance is revealed in textbooks that ask students only to write about personal experiences and opinions not based on readings, and that make no mention of grammatical accuracy (Cramer 1985); it is revealed in programs that adopt and mandate what is perceived as a 'new' process approach but that merely substitute prescriptions about process for prescriptions about form. When program guidelines or an individual teacher's syllabus actually mandates personal experience topics, three drafts for every piece of writing, no grammatical correction, and the use of freewriting, for example, a therapist's stance might well be at work.

Critics of a process approach often mistakenly label this extreme position as 'the Process Approach' (Johns 1990a, her capitals) saying that it 'fails to give students an accurate picture of university writing' (Johns 1990a:1). They complain, too, that it has been 'miscast as a complete theory of writing' (Horowitz 1986a:141). The other side of the debate, however, observes that 'the casting agents are not the advocates of process but its detractors' (Liebman-Kleine 1986:785). And indeed, the excesses of writer-focused approaches are alluded to and criticized as if there were no balanced stance available or adopted. Proponents of English for Academic Purposes (EAP) and English for Special Purposes (ESP)—for ease I'll call both EAP—frequently criticize the type of writing that goes on in process classrooms, questioning whether an inductive approach prepares students for academic tasks or essay examinations (Horowitz 1986a) and characterizing a process approach as mere 'humanistic therapy' (Horowitz 1986c:789). Such a characterization might be apt for the unbalanced therapist's stance, but it errs in assuming that the extreme position is representative of the approach in general.

A content-focused approach. The new, enthusiastically-received process approach hit some sort of nerve in our profession. The focus on the writer and the writer's processes was such a big shift in the approach to teaching writing that it was seen by some as narrowly excluding any attention to content, form, and reader. With a writer-focused approach being mistakenly seen as synonymous with a therapist's stance, reaction was swift and on two fronts as new emphases—on content and/or on the reader's demands—were proposed. Such is the pace of movements in the field of teaching writing that the ink could hardly have been dry on some of the articles explaining the theoretical basis of a process approach when May Shih labeled it 'traditional' (1986) and proposed in its place a content-based approach—one that had in fact already been proposed in 1979 by Mohan. Teachers using this approach opt to use the subject matter of the fields outside English that the ESL students are studying, sometimes attaching an ESL course to a 'content' course in the adjunct model (Snow and Brinton 1988) or grouping language and content courses (Benesch 1988). In this approach, language is developed as students communicate about the subject matter of other courses they might be taking. In these language classes, learners get help with 'the language of the thinking processes and the structure or shape of content' (Mohan 1986: 18).

This pedagogical approach has its own body of research that informs and nurtures the theoretical base. Studies include analysis of types of writing, mainly technical writing (Selinker, Todd-Trimble, and Trimble 1978), examination of student writing in content areas (Selzer 1983, Jenkins and Hinds 1987), and surveys of the content and tasks L2 students can expect to encounter in their academic career (Horowitz 1986b, Bridgeman and Carlson 1983).

The butler's stance. Subject matter (that is, what students read and write about) is, of course, important in both pedagogy and research, but when ESL/EFL teachers value the subject matter of other disciplines at the expense of the content inherent in our field and at the expense of writer, reader, and language form, they adopt what I will call a butler's stance. 'Uncomplaining, unobtrusive service' is their motto—as the butler in *The Remains of the Day* knows only too well (Ishiguro 1989). They see language courses as service courses, in service of the larger academic community. Language courses, for them, have no intrinsic subject matter. They question the use of language, culture, and especially literature as a main component of language study and turn instead to business, engineering, and other courses (Horowitz 1990). Such an instructional stance is suggested in theoretical literature in which ESL instruction is seen as a service to 'prepare students to handle writing assignments in academic courses' (Shih 1986:617). A statement like this one: 'The language or composition course itself *simulates the academic process* (e.g., mini-lectures, readings, and discussion on a topic lead into writing assignments)' (Shih 1986:617; my italics) positions language and composition courses outside academia, with no academic process of their own. Spack, in turn, has criticized this extreme stance, arguing that 'the English composition course is . . . a humanities course' (1988:46) and that 'L2 English composition teachers should focus on general principles of inquiry and rhetoric' (1988:29).

A reader-focused approach. A fourth focus for teaching and research, and one that surfaced almost simultaneously with the focus on content (both of them apparently in opposition to what was perceived as the nonacademic bent of a process approach) is a focus on the audience or reader. It is interesting to note here that attention to audience was, in fact, first brought to the fore as a feature of a process approach, with teachers attempting to respond to ideas before accuracy, though not always with success according to Zamel (1985). Group work broadened the concept of audience from the one teacher to the many peers. English for Academic Purposes (EAP) focuses on the reader, too, though not as an individual but as the representative of a larger context, like a specific discipline, or academia generally. The concept of 'socialization into the academic community' (Horowitz 1986c:789) has gained attention in the theory of teaching writing. In L2 instruction, an EAP approach addresses this by having English teachers deal with the requirements and demands of faculty from other disciplines.

Research supports this classroom focus with surveys of faculty expectations (Johns 1981), examinations of the expectations of academic readers with regard to genres (Swales 1990), and definitions of the basic skills of writing transferable across the various disciplines (Johns 1988).

The sergeant major's stance. The unbalanced stance which comes from an overvaluing of the audience and the conventions of a discourse community I call the sergeant major's stance. Since this is the latest stance to have appeared, and thus the least examined, I will examine its features in detail. While a reader's expectations are emphasized, the reader is frequently a generalized construct, not a real reader, but one reified from an examination of academic assignments and texts. This, I suggest, along with the butler's stance, represents not a new and newly principled approach to teaching writing, but rather a return to the autonomous model of literacy, in which academic tasks and texts are seen as fixed, stable, and determinate, and, according to Johns, 'purged of personal meaning' (1990a). Teachers in an EAP context analyze the requirements and demands of the discourse community and translate them into activities geared to produce appropriate products. In an unbalanced stance, once the goals are established, the worth of those goals is seldom questioned. They are presented more for imitation than for critical analysis.

Unbalanced stances are frequently characterized by prescriptions both in the classroom and in the language used by theorists. In an article relating L1 to L2 composition theories, for instance, the reader in academic discourse is described as an initiated expert, one who is 'all-powerful' (Johns 1990b:31). In this context, a teacher who emphasizes the conventions of the discourse community will begin with 'the rules of discourse' in the community (Johns 1990b:32), since academic faculty 'insist that students learn to "talk like engineers," for example, surrendering their own language and modes of thought to the requirements of the target community' (33). The language used here—'power', 'rules', 'surrender'—reveals the bias. It is evidently political language, as is the very choice of terms used in the same article to characterize three composition theories: one (the process approach) is referred to tellingly as a 'camp' (1990b:25,30), while the other two categories merit the more dignified labels of 'views', 'groups', or 'approaches'.

The language used by theorists to discuss their approaches can yield interesting information about balance or imbalance when given such a close reading. In an article discussing the expectations of the academic audience, Reid (1987) presents the problems involved in helping nonnative speakers deal with the considerations of purpose and audience.

Solutions are reported prescriptively, with six uses of 'should' and twelve of 'must' in only five short paragraphs. For example: 'Students should have ample opportunity to practice the highly structured contexts of academic tasks.' 'Teachers must gather assignments from across the curriculum, assess the purposes and audience expectations in the assignments, and present them to the class' (Reid 1987:34). Here the reader and the content appear to be emphasized at the expense of the writer, since what the student brings to the class in terms of composing processes and rhetorical knowledge of texts is largely discounted. The model of literacy is an autonomous one. Presentation of text forms for conveying meaning is emphasized, not the interaction of writer, reader, and text in negotiating meaning.

An unbalanced sergeant major's stance values the demands of the academic discourse community and makes three assumptions:

(1) that a clearly defined, stable academic discourse community exists, with a fixed construct of language and rhetoric;
(2) that its requirements are fixed and should not be negotiated or challenged;
(3) that academic writing is what students need to learn and what English teachers know how to teach.

Peter Elbow, however, has challenged the notion that academic writing is necessarily good writing and that it is important for students' future lives (1991). Since, he says, 'the use of academic discourse often masks a lack of genuine understanding' of how a principle works, students should be able to write about a subject 'not using the lingo of the discipline' (137). Elbow even takes the position that there is so much variation that we 'can't teach academic discourse because there's no such thing to teach' (1991:138), meaning, of course, that there is no one definable discourse, even within one discipline. In addition, Faigley and Hansen have pointed out how English teachers have difficulty evaluating writing in another discipline since they do not necessarily know 'how that discipline creates and transmits knowledge' (1985:148).

With an increasing number of immigrants as college students in ESL classrooms (and fewer as short-staying foreign students) we, too, need to question the role and function of academic writing. Land and Whitley have pointed out that when we 'require our ESL students to share and reproduce in their writing our world view' we are situating them within our sociopolitical context, demanding assimilation. Such instruction they call 'composition as colonization' (1989:289). And Patricia Bizzell sees the academic community as synonymous with the 'dominant social classes' and so has recommended that we find ways to give students 'critical distance' on academic cultural literacy (cited in Enos 1987:vi).

These theorists, and many others, suggest that even if a discourse community can be characterized, it should not be a repressive outside force, setting immutable standards that the individual must meet. It is a two-way street. Not only the student but also the community has to adjust in a process of negotiation. When a reader-focused approach gives way to the sergeant major's stance, the view of the community is usually a one-sided one, stressing a clear and unified community with unquestioned standards. Joseph Harris, however, warns us that 'instead of presenting academic discourse as coherent and well defined, we might be better off viewing it as polyglot, as a sort of space in which competing beliefs and practices intersect with and confront one another. One does not need consensus to have community' (1989:20).

The term *polyglot* seems useful to language teachers, and I want to recommend it as representative of the current state of our art underlying all the controversy and unbalanced stances. Polyglot. Varieties of beliefs, practices, and emphases undeniably exist. So what does a balanced stance entail? It's not a merging of the unbalanced stances but a principled approach that recognizes the fundamentals in all our theories and practices. Despite the evidence that there are practitioners who are locked into an unbalanced stance, we can also find evidence of balance, particularly in the recognition and inclusion of process-based principles in both content-based and reader-based approaches (Shih 1986, Johns 1986, Swales 1987) and in the attention paid to audience demands and the requirements of academic content in writer-focused approaches (Hamp-Lyons 1986, Spack 1988). A balanced approach recognizes that the four elements—the form of the text, the writer, the content, and the reader—are not discrete entities to be emphasized and reduced to prescriptions. Rather, they are fluid, interdependent, and interactive. Writers are readers as they read their own texts. Readers are writers as they make responses on a written text. Content and subject matter do not exist without language. The form of a text is determined by the interaction of writer, reader, and content. Language inevitably reflects subject matter, the writer, and the writer's view of the reader's background knowledge and expectations. Recognition of these principles and their application in the classroom will help us find instructional balance.

References

Benesch, Sarah, ed. 1988. Ending remediation: ESL and content in higher education. Washington D.C.: Teachers of English to Speakers of Other Languages.
Booth, Wayne C. 1963. The rhetorical stance. College Composition and Communication. 14.139-145.

Bridgeman, Brent, and Sybil B. Carlson. 1983. Survey of academic writing tasks required of graduate and undergraduate foreign students (TOEFL Research Report No. 15). Princeton, N.J.: Educational Testing Service.
Coles, William E., and James Vopat. 1985. What makes writing good. Lexington, Mass.: D.C. Heath.
Cramer, Nancy Arapoff. 1985. The writing process: 20 projects for group work. Rowley, Mass.: Newbury House.
Cumming, Alister. 1989. Writing expertise and second language proficiency. Language Learning. 39.81-141.
Eggington, William G. 1987. Written academic discourse in Korean: Implications for effective communication. In: Writing across languages: Analysis of L2 text, ed. by Ulla Connor and Robert B. Kaplan. 153-168. Reading, Mass.: Addison Wesley.
Elbow, Peter. 1991. Reflections on academic discourse: How it relates to freshmen and colleagues. College English. 53.135-155.
Enos, Theresa. 1987. A sourcebook for basic writing teachers. New York: Random House.
Faigley, Lester. 1989. Judging writing, judging selves. College Composition and Communication. 40.395-412.
Faigley, Lester, and Kristine Hansen. 1985. Learning to write in the social sciences. College Composition and Communication. 36.140-149.
Grabe, William, and Robert B. Kaplan. 1989. Writing in a second language: Contrastive rhetoric. In: Richness in writing: Empowering ESL students, ed. by Donna M. Johnson and Duane H. Roen. 263-283. New York: Longman.
Hamp-Lyons, Liz. 1986. No new lamps for old yet, please. TESOL Quarterly. 20.790-796.
Harris, Joseph. 1989. The idea of community in the study of writing. College Composition and Communication. 40.11-22.
Hill, Clifford, and Kate Parry. 1989. Autonomous and pragmatic models of literacy: Reading assessment in adult education. Linguistics and Education. 1.233-283.
Hinds, John. 1987. Reader versus writer responsibility: A new typology. In: Writing across languages: Analysis of L2 text, ed. by Ulla Connor and Robert B. Kaplan. 141-152. Reading, Mass.: Addison-Wesley.
Horowitz, Daniel M. 1986a. Process, not product: Less than meets the eye. TESOL Quarterly. 20. 141-144.
Horowitz, Daniel M. 1986b. What professors actually require: Academic tasks for the ESL classroom. TESOL Quarterly. 20.445-462.
Horowitz, Daniel M. 1986c. The author responds to Liebman-Kleine. TESOL Quarterly. 20.788-790.
Horowitz, Daniel M. 1990. Fiction and nonfiction in the ESL/EFL classroom: Does the difference make a difference? English for Specific Purposes. 9.161-168.
Ishiguro, Kazuo. 1989. The remains of the day. New York: Knopf.
Jenkins, Susan, and John Hinds. 1987. Business letter writing: English, French, and Japanese. TESOL Quarterly. 21.327-349.
Johns, Ann M. 1981. Necessary English: A faculty survey. TESOL Quarterly. 15.51-57.
Johns, Ann M. 1986. The ESL student and the revision process: Some insights from schema theory. Journal of Basic Writing. 5.70-80.
Johns, Ann M. 1988. The discourse communities dilemma: Identifying transferable skills for the academic milieu. English for Specific Purposes. 7.55-60.

Johns, Ann M. 1990a. Process, literature, and academic realities: Dan Horowitz and beyond. Handout for paper presented at Annual TESOL Convention, San Francisco, March 1990.
Johns, Ann M. 1990b. L1 composition theories: Implications for developing theories of L2 composition. In: Second language writing: Research insights for the classroom. ed. by Barbara Kroll. 24-36. New York: Cambridge University Press.
Jones, C. Stanley, and Jacqueline Tetroe. 1987. Composing in a second language. In: Writing in real time: Modeling production processes. ed. by Ann Matsuhashi. 34-57. Norwood, N.J.: Ablex.
Kaplan, Robert B. 1966. Cultural thought patterns in intercultural education. Language Learning. 16.1-20.
Kaplan, Robert B. 1987. Cultural thought patterns revisited. In: Writing across languages: Analysis of L2 text. ed. by Ulla Connor and Robert B. Kaplan. 9-20. Reading, Mass.: Addison-Wesley.
Krapels, Alexandra. 1990. An overview of second language writing process research. In: Second language writing: Research insights for the classroom. ed. by Barbara Kroll. 37-56. New York: Cambridge University Press.
Kunz, Linda. 1972. 26 steps: A course in controlled composition for intermediate and advanced ESL students. New York: Language Innovations.
Land, Robert E., and Catherine Whitley. 1989. Evaluating second language essays in regular composition classes: Toward a pluralistic U.S. rhetoric. In: Richness in writing: Empowering ESL students. ed. by Donna M. Johnson and Duane H. Roen. 284-293. New York: Longman.
Liebman-Kleine, JoAnne. 1986. In defence of teaching process in ESL composition. TESOL Quarterly. 20.783-788.
Mohan, Bernard A. 1979. Relating language teaching and content teaching. TESOL Quarterly. 13.171-182.
Mohan, Bernard A. 1986. Language and content. Reading, Mass.: Addison-Wesley.
Ostler, Shirley E. 1987. English in parallels: A comparison of English and Arabic prose. In: Writing across languages: Analysis of L2 text. ed. by Ulla Connor and Robert B. Kaplan. 169-185. Reading, Mass.: Addison-Wesley.
Paulston, Christina Bratt. 1972. Teaching writing in the ESOL classroom: Techniques of controlled composition. TESOL Quarterly. 6.33-59.
Paulston, Christina Bratt, and Gerald Dykstra. 1973. Controlled composition in English as a second language. New York: Regents.
Peyton, Joy Kreeft, ed. 1990. Students and teachers writing together: Perspectives on journal writing. Alexandria, Virginia: Teachers of English to Speakers of Other Languages.
Pincas, Anita. 1962. Structural linguistics and systematic composition teaching to students of English as a foreign language. Language Learning. 12.185-194.
Purves, Alan. C., ed. 1988. Writing across languages and cultures. Newbury Park: Sage.
Raimes, Ann. 1985. What unskilled ESL students do as they write: A classroom study of composing. TESOL Quarterly. 19.229-258.
Raimes, Ann. 1987a. Why write? From purpose to pedagogy. English Teaching Forum. 25.4.36-41.
Raimes, Ann. 1987b. Language proficiency, writing ability, and composing strategies: A study of ESL college student writers. Language Learning. 37.439-468.

Reid, Joy. 1987. ESL composition: The expectations of the academic audience. TESOL Newsletter. 21.34.

Reid, Joy. 1990. Responding to different topic types: A quantitative analysis from a contrastive rhetoric perspective. In: Second language writing: Research insights for the classroom. ed. by Barbara Kroll. 191-210. New York: Cambridge University Press.

Richards, Jack C., and Theodore S. Rodgers. 1986. Approaches and methods in language teaching. Cambridge: Cambridge University Press.

Scarcella, Robin C. 1984. How writers orient their readers in expository essays: A comparative study of native and nonnative English writers. TESOL Quarterly. 18.671-688.

Selinker, Larry, Mary Todd-Trimble, and Louis Trimble. 1978. Rhetorical function shifts in EST discourse. TESOL Quarterly. 12.311-320.

Selzer, Jack. 1983. The composing processes of an engineer. College Composition and Com-munication. 34.178-187.

Shen, Fan. 1989. The classroom and the wider culture: Identity as a key to learning English composition. College Composition and Communication. 40.459-465.

Shih, May. 1986. Content-based approaches to teaching academic writing. TESOL Quarterly. 20.617-648.

Snow, Marguerite Ann, and Donna M. Brinton. 1988. The adjunct model of language instruc-tion: An ideal EAP framework. In: Ending remediation: ESL and content in higher education. ed. by Sarah Benesch. 33-52. Washington D.C.: Teachers of English to Speakers of Other Languages.

Spack, Ruth. 1984. Invention strategies and the ESL college composition student. TESOL Quarterly. 18.649-670.

Spack, Ruth. 1988. Initiating ESL students into the academic discourse community: How far should we go? TESOL Quarterly. 22.29-51.

Spack, Ruth, and Catherine Sadow. 1983. Student-teacher working journals in ESL freshman composition. TESOL Quarterly. 17.575-593.

Street, Brian. V. 1984. Literacy in theory and practice. Cambridge: Cambridge University Press.

Swales, John. 1987. Utilizing the literatures in teaching the research paper. TESOL Quarterly. 21.41-68.

Swales, John. 1990. Genre analysis: English in academic and research settings. Cambridge: Cambridge University Press.

Tsao, Fen Fu. 1983. Linguistics and written discourse in English and Mandarin. Annual review of applied linguistics 1982. ed. by Robert B. Kaplan. 99-117. Rowley, Mass.: Newbury House.

Zamel, Vivian. 1976. Teaching composition in the ESL classroom: What we can learn from research in the teaching of English. TESOL Quarterly. 10.67-76.

Zamel, Vivian. 1982. Writing: The process of discovering meaning. TESOL Quarterly. 16.195-210.

Zamel, Vivian. 1983. The composing processes of advanced ESL students: Six case studies. TESOL Quarterly. 17.165-187.

Zamel, Vivian. 1985. Responding to student writing. TESOL Quarterly. 19. 79-101.

Looking at and towards the future in French textbooks

Nadine O'Connor Di Vito
Georgetown University

Introduction. Over the past few years, we have seen a radical change in the presentation of the target language in textbooks. With applied linguistic research showing the importance of the various communicative functions and social contexts in which native speakers use language, current textbook authors have responded with an increasing amount of communicatively-oriented texts. We see more and more textbook chapters designed around functions of language and focussing particular contexts of language use. And, along with a more functionally-defined framework, current textbooks generally offer much more of a context for various grammar exercises than previous texts. But are these textbook transformations enough?

No one would deny the importance of functional and communicative goals and contextualized grammar exercises. But are the communicative functions and contextualized exercises which showcase textbook grammar reflective of the contexts in which native speakers use the grammar? The bottom line is: Do our textbooks represent the target language as it is used by native speakers? And do the explanations, exercises, and activities in our textbooks help our students to understand and assimilate these native speaker usage rules?

This study addresses these questions by examining how future tenses and future time are presented in 19 beginning and intermediate French foreign language textbooks, and then comparing this presentation with real native speaker use.

1 Textbook presentation of future time and future tenses.[1] First of all, we should note that there exist two specific future tenses in French, the simple future (SF) and the immediate future (IF):

---

1 Throughout this paper, I will be translating the French simple future by the English 'will do something' and the French immediate future by the English 'am going to do something', although I am not suggesting that the functions of these tenses are equivalent in the two languages.

(1a) Simple future: *Non, je n'épouserai que toi.*
                        'I'll only marry you.'
(1b) Immediate future: *Je vais la formuler de la façon suivante.*
                        'I'm going to state it in the following way.'

In the 19 beginning and intermediate French textbooks examined in this study, I found that discussion of future time always centers around the differences between the immediate future and the simple future.[2] Although a few textbooks note that clear-cut distinctions between these tenses are sometimes difficult to make, almost all of the textbooks state the basic difference to be one of temporal proximity.[3] The generally accepted explanation is that the immediate future refers to the 'not too distant' future, and the simple future refers to a 'more remote' future period, and that it is always used after certain conjunctions (*quand, lorsque, dès que, aussitôt que*).

Given these explanations, we would expect textbooks to highlight temporal distinctions in their examples and exercises, by focussing the immediate future in near future contexts and the simple future in more remote future contexts. However, this is not what we find. Instead, we see textbook examples in which the simple future is used to refer to the near future and the immediate future is used in remote future contexts, as well as exercises which ask students to merely transform the immediate future into the simple future or which present a variety of future contexts, both near and remote, in which the student is expected to practice exclusively one or the other tense. We might note, as well, that these examples and exercises often ignore any possible spoken-written or thematic distinctions in tense use:

(2a) *Que mangerons-nous au dîner ce soir?*
     'What will we eat for dinner tonight?'
     (*Fenêtre ouverte*, p.190)

(2b) *Modèle: Qu'est-ce que tu vas faire après la classe?*
     Model: 'What are you going to do after class?'
        J'irai en ville...
        'I'm going downtown...'
        (*Allons-y*, p. 387)

---

2 The following textbooks were examined: *Allons-y!; Ça marche!; Chapeau!; Découverte et création; En route; L'essentiel de la grammaire française; Fenêtre ouverte; Franc-parler; Grammaire française; A guide to contemporary French usage; Interactions; Invitation; Mise au point; Quoi de neuf?; Qu'est-ce qui se passe?; Rendez-vous; Thème et Variations; Traits d' union; Vous y êtes!* References at the end of this paper.

3 A few textbooks mentioned no functional differences at all between these two tenses.

In example (2a), the simple future is used in a near future context. In (2b), the immediate future is found in a textbook model sentence with the simple future used as a possible response in the model answer.

The only real distinction apparent in many textbooks is that the immediate future is presented as a sort of stepping stone to the simple future. Since the simple future is consistently presented after the immediate future with similar exercises, students can only infer that the immediate future is only for beginning level speakers and that native speakers use primarily the simple future.

Besides the temporal proximity distinction, some textbooks offer a few more remarks concerning tense use. For example, one textbook notes that the immediate future is 'common', and two mention that it is frequently used in conversation. Three textbooks note that the present tense is also 'possible' when referring to the future. However, what are students to make of such explanations? What do 'common' and 'possible' mean? One textbook notes that 'it is the speaker who distinguishes' among these tenses, but based on what criteria?

Given these ambiguous and contradictory explanations and exercises presented in our textbooks, we could not possibly expect our students to know, either explicitly or implicitly, when these different tenses are appropriate in various future contexts, even though such knowledge is essential to the acquisition of native-like competence in French.

2 This study. We can only address the question of appropriate use by looking at the contexts in which French native speakers use these different tenses to refer to future time. In order to accomplish this goal, I examined use of the simple future, the immediate future, and the present tense in approximately 1,300 clauses referring to future time. These clauses reflect a variety of spoken and written French contexts, from official correspondence to informal conversations. All contexts reflect speech used and understood by educated French native speakers. For example, the magazines examined are literate magazines, such as *L'Express* and *Le Point*, and the informal speech reflects conversations with nine different university-educated French native speakers.[4]

Given the fact that particular conjunctions are often associated with the simple future, let us first examine these conjunctions. There were no examples of *aussitôt que* in the data, but in the 38 examples of complex sentences with the other three conjunctions (*quand, lorsque,* and *dès que*), all of the verbs in the dependent clause were in either the simple future or the future perfect:

---

4 These sources of authentic spoken and written French data are part of a much larger corpus which I am examining in order to discover various grammatical relationships within and across diverse French genres.

(3a) *aussitôt que* - no examples found
(3b) *Dès que* j'aurai des précisions à vous transmettre...
'As soon as I will have specifics to send you....'
(3c) *Quand* je serai grand...
'When I will get big....'
(3d) *Lorsque* tu les auras vues...
'When you will have seen them....'

Since no immediate future or present tense was used in these contexts, we will accept them here as obligatory contexts for use of the simple future or future perfect, and exclude them from the present analysis.

3 Data analysis. In examining the native speaker data, we can first note that the typical temporal distinction between the immediate and simple future is certainly not a categorical rule for native speakers. Although there is no accepted definition of near and remote future time, most books mention use of the immediate future with such adverbs as *today, tomorrow, this week,* and *soon.* Even using this relatively restricted categorization of the near future, we find many examples of the simple future in these contexts in the data:

(4a) *Je serai à Poitiers avant minuit.*
'I'll be in Poitiers before midnight.'
(detective novel)
(4b) *C'est vendredi que je vous posterai le courrier annoncé.*
'On Friday I'll send you the aforementioned information.'
(formal correspondence)

Also, if we take the distant future to refer to some undefined remote time in the future, or a future month or year, we find a good number of examples of the immediate future in these contexts in our data, which again contradicts the notion of a temporal distinction between the tenses:

(5a) *L'année prochaine je vais travailler dans une école maternelle.*
'Next year I'm going to work in a school for infants.'
(informal conversation)
(5b) *Cabourg va reconstituer, dans la dernière semaine d'août...*
'Cabourg is going to reorganize, in the last week of August....'
(magazine)

It must also be noted that, in many instances, no temporal grounding for the sentence could be found at all. Therefore, not only does native speaker use often contradict the notion that temporal proximity governs the selection of future tenses when temporal adverbs are present, but the frequent lack of temporal grounding makes it virtually impossible to use temporal proximity as a criterion to distinguish among these tenses.

Also, if we examine the overall distribution of these tenses in the native speaker data, the idea of a temporal distinction alone is again put into question. We cannot ignore the fact that the simple future is nearly the only tense used to refer to future time in official correspondence, while it is found in only 36% of the examples in informal conversations, as indicated in Table 1.

Table 1. Tense use to refer to the future in spoken and written French

Context	SF	IF	Pres	N =
Official correspondence	88%	6%	6%	85
Magazines	83	14	3	197
Folklore	73	23	4	224
Informal letters	73	20	8	116
Television news	73	15	12	125
Detective novels	64	18	18	217
Conference speech	38	60	2	132
Informal conversation	36	39	26	236

If we consider evolutionary trends in tense use, we might hypothesize reasons for this range in frequency of the simple future from official correspondence to informal conversations. Use of the simple future began to decrease in favor of the immediate future and then the present tense in colloquial speech as early as the 14th century (Price 1971). This erosion of the simple future in spoken French has continued into the 20th century (Wales 1983). Therefore, we should not be surprised at its decline not only in informal speech, but in formal speech and even in some written contexts. Rome was not built in a day; neither should we expect the replacement of the simple future by the immediate future and now the present tense to be realized in all written and spoken contexts at the same time. Rather, we should expect these tenses to become the new norm in certain contexts before others, gradually extending their functions until fully grammaticalized in the language.

Assuming such an evolutionary pattern, we will consider our different discourse contexts as synchronic pieces of a diachronic picture. In the highly rule-governed official correspondence, we will examine the few non-simple future examples to find those contexts most vulnerable to the trend toward use of the immediate future and present tense. On the other end of the continuum, we will examine the relatively few examples of the simple future in informal conversations to see what pockets of resistance to change remain. Using these two extremes as functional guidelines and the discourse contexts inbetween as intermediary stages of the decline of the simple future, we will discuss the basic differences between contemporary use of the simple future and its challengers, the immediate future and the present tense.

4 Immediate future and present tense in official correspondence. In official correspondence, the simple future appears to be the accepted norm in referring to future events. Although only three of the ten examples where the immediate future or present tense were used reflect any type of near future context, eight of these ten sentences indicate 'personal involvement' or 'psychological immediacy':

(6a) *Dès que ma première ébauche de planning sera faite, je vous l'envoie.*
'As soon as my first schedule draft will be done, I send it to you.'
(6b) *Vous serez en fait trois conférenciers. Ma collègue ici va parler d'une des nouvelles de Marguerite de Navarre.*
'In fact, you will be three speakers. My colleague here is going to talk about one of the short stories of Marguerite de Navarre.'

In sentence (6a), there is no indication about when that first schedule will be finished, only that the writer will send it immediately upon completion. As for example (6b), although the simple future is used throughout the letter, in this one sentence where the writer mentions that one of her fellow colleagues will participate in a future colloquium, the immediate future is used. Therefore, although no clear temporal proximity is noticeable, personal involvement or psychological immediacy in these and the other examples reflecting the immediate future and the present tense is evident.

5 Simple future in informal conversations. With respect to informal conversations, approximately a third of all of the relatively few simple future examples are concentrated in discussions about three topics: life after death, life when one becomes middle-aged or old, and life after the speakers get their university diplomas. What is striking about these three topics is that they are all types of situations which are, if not completely hypothetical, definitely difficult to speak of with any assurance. These are all cases for the imagination: no one knows what is waiting for us after death, nor what our life will be like in a different generational phase, and any student in the French school system would admit that actually obtaining a university diploma is not something to be taken for granted.

If we examine particular linguistic expressions in these informal conversations, the notion of a certain linking between the simple future and a feeling of uncertainty or personal detachment is strongly reinforced. Although the simple future is found in only 36% overall in these conversations, its frequency is considerably higher in clauses containing the adverbs, *peut-être* and *un jour*, in expressions of the type, *On verra*, and in if-then clauses, as indicated in Table 2.

Table 2. Use of the simple future in informal conversations.

Context	SF usage	N =
Overall	36%	236
peut-être/un jour	90%	10
On verra, etc.	78%	9
si present, then future	59%	29

An example demonstrating use of the simple future and the immediate future to highlight differences in personal involvement and certainty about the future can be seen in the following spoken excerpt in which one of the speakers talks about her plans for the upcoming year:

(7a) *L'année prochaine je vais travailler dans une école maternelle.*
 'Next year I'm going to work in a school for infants.'
(7b) *mais je continuerai quand-même mes études à la Fac...*
 'but I'll still continue my studies at the university...'
(7c) *j'aurai non seulement le temps,*
 'I'll not only have the time,'
(7d) *mais j'aurai surtout la motivation.*
 'but I'll have above all the motivation.'
(7e) *J'aurai-je vais avoir de l'argent...*
 'I'll have-I'm going to have money.'

In (7a), the speaker has definitely decided to work in a pre-school, and has used the immediate future. As for having the time and the motivation to continue with school (7b, 7c, 7d), those plans can only be viewed as tentative. Here, she uses the simple future. But the job she will have is a paying job, so she will definitely have money (7e). In this sentence, the speaker begins to use the simple future, but changes to the immediate future. So, although all of the actions and conditions described will take place during the same future time period, the speaker employs different tenses to reflect different degrees of certainty regarding various aspects of that future period.

Thus, we have found that the simple future is still the norm in the highly structured language of official correspondence, with the immediate future and the present tense used primarily to emphasize personal involvement in or attachment to certain future events. In informal conversations, at the other end of the continuum, we find high personal involvement to be the norm, with the simple future used primarily to indicate uncertainty or personal detachment to particular future events.

6 Tense use in other discourse contexts. As for the discourse contexts between the two ends of the future tense continuum shown in Table 1, it is not surprising that political and cultural articles show future tense use similar to that of official correspondence. Although articles do not contain as much formulaic language as formal correspondence, they reflect little, if any, conversational speech, and generally attempt to transmit a well-informed, objective, personally detached account, or opinion. In such contexts, we would expect the simple future to be most firmly anchored.

On the other end of the continuum, we find similar percentages of the simple future in conference speech and informal conversations. Again appealing to speaker-listener relationship as a possible explanation for tense use, we find that these two spoken contexts have much in common. Despite the fact that there is not a true conversation between speakers and their audiences, a good speaker often makes remarks specifically for the audience's benefit. In all of the recordings analyzed, there were obvious attempts to involve the audience in the talk by shifting intonation patterns, telling jokes or directly addressing the audience through questions or remarks.

As for the discourse contexts in the middle of our continuum, where the simple future is clearly losing ground but not as rapidly as in conference or informal speech contexts, we have a mixture of discourse characteristics. In fairy tales, we have written conversational speech, but it is often highly formulaic and stylized with little attempt to portray any realistic relationships among the oftentimes non-human characters in the stories. In informal letters, there is little dialogue, but since the relationship between the writer and the reader is of prime importance, personal involvement in the speech is high. In television news, although featuring the spoken language, the reporter and the audience have little to do with each other, with personal detachment and objectivity highly valued. And, finally, in detective novels, we find a great deal of both description and dialogue, as in fairy tales. However, the involvement of the reader in the relationships developed among the various characters in detective novels is essential to the success of the story. In these novels, of course, we find less simple future than in fairy tales.

7 From a temporal to an aspectual system of tense use. In short, these data support the claim that the French language is moving away from a purely temporal distinction among the tenses used to refer to the future (Harris 1978, Wales 1983), and suggest an evolution toward a more aspectual system of tense use. The more personal involvement found in the discourse, the more immediate future and present tense we will find, with detachment or uncertainty highlighted by the simple future. On the other hand, the more formalized and uncertain the discourse context and the more detached the speaker is from his or her audience, the more we will find the norm to be the simple future. One very common type of discourse in which these factors favoring use of the simple future are quite evident is weather reporting, as indicated in Table 3.

Table 3. Use of the simple future in written weather reports.

Context	SF	IF	Pres	N =
Written weather reports	86%	6%	9%	287

Weather reports are always a monologue, reflect a high percentage of stock expressions and all too often reflect pure guesswork concerning even immediate weather forecasts:

(7) Sur la France, le temps sera très mitigé: localement il y aura des éclaircies, mais souvent le ciel sera très nuageux, voire même par endroits entièrement gris et brumeux. Des chutes de neige se produiront par-ci par-là. (*le Monde, 5 février 1991*)

'Throughout France, the weather will be very mild: locally there will be clearings, but often the sun will be very cloudy, even completely grey and hazy in some places. Snowfalls will occur here and there.'

8 Pedagogical implications and conclusion. Although more research is clearly needed to understand the functional distinctions between the immediate future and the present tense, the native speaker data presented here strongly suggest a radical change in the way the simple future and the immediate future tenses are explained and practiced in French foreign language texts. First, students should be made aware that the simple future is primarily used to indicate detachment or uncertainty in contexts where personal involvement is high, such as in conversations and in spoken contexts where there is an audience. It should be mentioned that, in such contexts, the immediate future and the present tense are normally used to indicate future events. On the other hand, in contexts where a conversational rapport is absent, as in most written genres as well as in spoken news and weather reporting, teachers should indicate that the simple future is the norm, with the immediate future and the present tense used primarily to highlight personal involvement or psychological immediacy.

Foreign language teachers have come a long way in contextualizing grammar exercises. However, contextualization is meaningless unless it truly reflects the way native speakers use the language. In this paper, we have examined how French native speakers use the present, the immediate future and the simple future to refer to future time and have discussed the pedagogical implications of these findings for the teaching of French as a foreign language. Of course, my hope is that such research will become part of a general framework for looking toward the future not just in French textbooks, but in all foreign language teaching and curriculum development.

References

Balas, Robert, and Donald Rice. 1984. Qu'est-ce qui se passe? Boston: Houghton Mifflin. 2nd ed.
Batchelor, Ronald Ernest, and M. H. Offord. 1982. A guide to contemporary French usage. Cambridge/New York: Cambridge University Press.
Bragger, Jeannette D., and Donald B. Rice. 1988. Allons-y! Boston: Heinle & Heinle.
Cadart-Ricard, Odette. 1990. Fenêtre ouverte. NY: Macmillan.
Dietiker, Simone R., and Gérard Burgère. 1984. Franc-Parler. Lexington: D. C. Heath.
Dineen, David A., and Madeleine Kernen. 1989. Chapeau! John Wiley.
Hagiwara, M. Peter, and Françoise de Rocher. 1989. Thème et Variations. NY: John Wiley. 4th ed.
Harris, M. 1978. The evolution of French syntax: A comparative approach. London: Longman.
Hester, Ralph, Gail Wade, and Gérard Jian. 1988. Traits d'union. Boston: Houghton Mifflin.
Hoffmann, Léon-François. 1973. L'essentiel de la grammaire française. NY: Charles Scribner's Sons.
Jarvis, Gilbert A., Thérèse M. Bonin, Donald E. Corbin, and Diane W. Birckbichler. 1988. Invitation. NY: Holt, Rinehart & Winston.
Jian, Gérard, and Ralph Hester. 1990. Découverte et création. Boston: Houghton Mifflin. 5th ed.
Muyskens, Judith A., Alice C. Omaggio, and Claudine Chalmers. 1986. Rendez-vous. NY: Random House. 2nd ed.
Ollivier, Jacqueline. 1978. Grammaire française. NY: Harcourt Brace Jovanovich.
Parmentier, Michel A. 1989. Mise au point. Toronto: Holt, Rinehart & Winston.
Phillips, June K., Francine M-V. Klein, and Renée N. Liscinsky. 1988. Quoi de neuf? NY: Random House. 3rd ed.
Price, Glanville. 1971. The French language: Present and past. London: Edward Arnold.
Sandberg, Karl C., Georges Zask, Anthony A. Ciccone, and Françoise Defrecheux. 1990. Ça marche! NY: Macmillan.
St. Onge, Susan, Katherine Kulick, and David W. King. 1991. Interactions. Boston: Heinle & Heinle. 3rd ed.
St. Onge, Susan S., and Robert M. Terry. 1986. Vous y êtes! Boston: Heinle & Heinle.
Valdman, Albert, Marva A. Barnett et al. 1986. En route. NY: Macmillan.
Wales, M.L. 1983. The semantic distribution of *aller* + infinitive and the future tense in spoken French. General Linguistics 23.1. 19-28.

Consensus and divergence on the content, role, and process of teaching grammar

Diane Larsen-Freeman
School for International Training

Introduction. With the invitation extended to me to speak at the Round Table this year was the request that I present a paper on the state of the art in teaching grammar. In order to comply with this request, I found it helpful not only to reflect on what the nature of the state of the art currently is, but also from where it came. Thus, before addressing what is, the paper will briefly review what was, beginning with the middle of this century. Moreover, in order to get a fuller picture of 'what was' occurring in grammar teaching, it was helpful to consider what was attracting attention in the related disciplines of linguistics, psychology, and language acquisition at the time. Following the historic review and the discussion of the state of the art in grammar teaching today, the paper will conclude by suggesting ways in which the evolution of grammar teaching can contribute to the related disciplines.

Antecedents of modern grammar teaching practice. The prevailing school of linguistic thought in the United States at mid-century was descriptivism or structuralism (see Figure 1 on page 263). Structural linguists based their work on the assumption that grammatical categories should not be established in terms of meaning, but rather in terms of the distribution of structures. The structural framework of English, as analyzed by Fries (1952), for example, 'is made up of four major "form classes" and fifteen groups of function words. These constitute the "structural signals" which convey grammatical meaning in a sentence' (Allen and Widdowson 1975:53).[1]

The dominant school of psychology at the time was behaviorism, in which learning was seen as conditioning, brought about through repetition, shaping, and reinforcement. This characterization of learning con-

---

[1] It would be beyond the scope and purpose of this paper to treat any school of thought completely. Selected references have been offered for those interested in learning more.

tributed to the perception of language as verbal behavior and to language acquisition as habit formation, involving the shaping of new verbal behavior through repetition and differential reinforcement (Skinner 1957). The challenge of acquiring a second language was compounded by the learners' having to overcome the mother tongue habits already acquired.

These views in linguistics and psychology influenced the development of language teaching practice. Grammar teachers attempted to inculcate grammar inductively in their students through the use of manipulative drills and sentence-level pattern practice.[2] The syllabus consisted of a sequence of linguistic structures with the forms ordered according to ascending linguistic difficulty. To the greatest extent possible, errors were to be prevented to avoid bad habits being established. Any errors that were committed were to be corrected immediately.

A clear challenge to structural linguistics and to language learning as a form of conditioning was issued by Chomsky (1959, 1965) through an appeal to what Sampson (1980) terms Chomsky's 'linguistic rationalism'. Chomsky's transformational-generative grammar posits the existence of a deep structure which determines the semantic interpretation of a sentence and a surface structure that determines the phonetic form of sentences. The two are linked by a set of transformational rules. It is the learners' task, through utilization of processes such as hypothesis formation and testing, to abstract the rules from the language input to which they are exposed. First language learners, and possibly second language learners as well, are thought to be aided in this process by a language acquisition device or an innate disposition to process linguistic data.

One way these views of language and learning were translated into teaching practice was through the importance ascribed to sentence-based linguistic rules. The rules were presented both inductively and deductively to learners, and class exercises were intended to give learners ample practice with applying the rules. The role of errors was vastly different from this perspective on the acquisition process: Errors were seen as inevitable byproducts of learners' hypothesis-testing and as something from which both teachers and students could learn.

In a later iteration of the view of language acquisition as rule formation, the process was depicted less as a conscious one of learners' figuring out the rules, and more one of 'creative construction', which referred to a 'subconscious process by which language learners gradually

---

2 Any such cursory survey as this results in simplification of the issues. Fries, who is deservedly credited with being the driving force underlying these grammar teaching practices, should not be labeled a behaviorist. Fries, however, did characterize the first of a two-stage process of language learning as one of habit formation. The second stage existed to foster in learners an ability to communicate and to understand on a deeper level. For further elaboration see P. Fries 1989. I thank Ed Anthony (personal communication) for clarifying Fries' position.

organize the language they hear, according to rules they construct to generate sentences' (Dulay, Burt and Krashen 1982:11). A consequence of this depiction of language acquisition was that grammar was not dealt with explicitly in the classroom. Rather, a learner's mastery of the grammar would emerge if the learner were provided with 'comprehensible input' (Krashen 1985). Thus, negotiation for meaning was the central activity with little attention given to grammatical forms. Errors might be left uncorrected, as long as the meaning of what the learner was attempting to communicate was understood.

The challenge to the Chomskyan notion that the task of linguists should be to construct sentence-level models of linguistic competence came about in the work of anthropological and sociolinguists in the United States (e.g. Hymes 1972) and functional linguists in Britain (e.g. Halliday 1973), who emphasized language as an instrument of communication. Hymes put it as follows:

We have then to account for the fact that a normal child acquires knowledge of sentences not only as grammatical, but also as appropriate. He or she acquires competence as to when to speak, when not, and as to what to talk about with whom, when, where, in what manner. In short, a child becomes able to accomplish a repertoire of speech acts, to take part in speech events, and to evaluate their accomplishments by others. (Hymes 1972:277-8)

Although no formal theory of learning was associated with this view of language, one could reasonably characterize the model of learning which subsequently developed as 'experiential', i.e. learning by doing. In learning languages this would be taken to mean learning to use language by using language; perhaps Hatch's (1978) views of second language acquisition (SLA) would be most closely aligned with this perspective on language acquisition. According to Hatch, 'one learns how to do conversation, one learns how to interact verbally and out of this interaction, syntactic structures are developed' (1978:409). Hence, we might term the process by which languages are acquired 'interactionism'.

This view of language and of learning was manifest in the Communicative Approach, in which role-playing and problem-solving tasks were used as vehicles to the acquisition of specific functions. The emphasis in this approach was on language use with little overt grammar teaching and with tolerance for error commission equal to that just discussed. Successors to functional syllabi, which adhere to the same principles of language and learning, are today's procedural and content-based syllabi, in which students are engaged in accomplishing certain tasks or investigating certain content, and thus attend only peripherally to structures.

Figure 1. Historic review of grammar teaching and related disciplines since mid-century.

Psychology (Theory of Learning)	(Second) Language Acquisition	Grammar Teaching	
	Descriptive / Structural Linguistics		
Behaviorist (Learning by conditioning: repeating, shaping, reinforcement)	Habit formation	Structural sequence: FORM	(1)
		Grammar presented inductively	(2)
		Drills/Pattern practice	(3)
		Errors prevented/corrected	(4)
	Transformational-Generative Linguistics		
Rationalist (Sampson 1987) (Learning by figuring out)	I. Rule formation (hypothesis formation/testing)	I. Grammar presented deductively	(2)
		Rule-based exercises	(3)
		Errors inevitable	(4)
	II. Creative construction	II. Comprehensible input: MEANING	(1)
		Grammar not presented	(2)
		Errors uncorrected	(4)
	Sociolinguistic / Pragmatic Linguistics		
Experiential (Learning by doing)	Interactionism	I. Functional sequence: USE	(1)
		Problem-solving & role-playing	(3)
		II. Procedural/Content-based: USE	(1)
		Tasks	(3)
	Discourse Analysis / Contextual Analysis Linguistics		
		Teach grammar in context	(3)
		Use authentic texts	(3)
	Government-binding Linguistics		
Nativist (Larsen-Freeman & Long 1991) (Not 'learning'?)	Parameter-resetting	Selection of grammar points	(5)
		Negative evidence	(4)
		Consciousness raising & the challenge principle	(2)
Cognitive (Information-processing) (Learning by automatization & restructuring)	I. Controlled vs. automatic processing	I. Controlled → free	(3)
	U-shaped behavior	Understanding of backsliding	(4)
	II. Processing constraints on developmental order	II. Rationale for sequencing	(5)
Connectionist ('empiricist', Sampson 1987, Gasser 1990; 'associationist', Lachter & Bever 1988; 'environmentalist', Larsen-Freeman & Long 1991) (Learning by rote & by analogy?)	Acquisition of 'connection strengths'	What are we already doing? (Ney & Pearson 1990)	(5)

Key: (1) – Content (4) – View of errors
     (2) – Role
     (3) – Process (5) – Issues

Roughly synchronic with the emphasis on language use was the recognition that sentence-level grammar rules were inadequate and that what was needed was information about how language was structured at the suprasentential or discourse level. With the advent of the interest in discourse analysis,[3] a particular approach to grammatical analysis, namely contextual analysis, was born. Contextual analysis requires researchers to examine an authentic corpus and to extract from it fully contextualized tokens of the structure being analyzed (Celce-Murcia 1980). Such an approach has helped to shed light on old grammatical conundrums in English like the alternation between *going to* and *will* or *used to* and *would* in past habitual discourse (Celce-Murcia 1990). It has also provided justification for the long-standing practice of presenting grammar in context, and using authentic, or at least semi-authentic, instructional materials whenever possible.

The next major linguistic theory to have evolved is what Chomsky (1987) has called 'the second major conceptual shift' in linguistics: government-binding (GB) theory. In this version of Chomskyan linguistics, language is not so much simply a system of rules, but rather a system of 'parameters and principles'. The system of principles and parameters constitutes the universal grammar (UG) with which all humans are endowed. All that is required of experience is to 'set the switches' on the parameters in keeping with the particular language of the environment. Because this theory purports to explain learning through positing an innate faculty, Larsen-Freeman and Long (1991) have classified GB theory as nativist. In fact, one could argue that really very little 'learning' is called for at all. As Chomsky himself has noted, 'once the [switches] are set, the system functions' (1984:25). For L1 acquisition to take place, then, all that would seem necessary are environmental 'triggers'.

One question which remains has to do with the accessibility of UG to second language learners and how these learners proceed to reset those parameters of the second language which differ from the first. This question is essentially a reformulated version of one posed during the period when structural linguistics reigned; namely, what is the nature of the influence of the L1 on L2 acquisition and does this influence result in there being different processes in L1 and L2 acquisition? White (1983), for example, has noted that while the typical acquisition route for a given structure in L1 acquisition proceeds from the use of unmarked forms to marked ones, the initial stages of SLA are likely to show the

---

3 What is being discussed here, of course, is the evolution of mainstream thinking. Certainly the structuralists, and others before them, recognized that a cohesive structure existed above the level of sentence. It was not until the 1970s, however, that discourse analysis received much attention in modern linguistic research.

effect of the first-language parameter, and thus marked forms may appear in learner interlanguage before unmarked ones.

The pedagogical implications of this view are by no means clear; however, one could imagine looking to GB theory for guidance in selecting certain points for instruction (see Belasco 1985). For example, Rutherford and Sharwood Smith (1985) observe that certain principles of UG remain constant for all language learners and therefore need not be considered actively in a pedagogical grammar (Larsen-Freeman 1990).

Another area of SLA research that has been encouraged by GB theory has to do with the role of negative evidence in the acquisition/learning process (Tomasello and Herron 1988; Carroll and Swain 1991). The so-called logical problem of language acquisition, the absence of negative evidence afforded L1 acquirers (the form of their L1 production is allegedly not corrected), has been a compelling argument for proposing a highly developed innate language faculty. What kind of negative evidence second language learners receive and to what advantage, if any, are questions which have important implications for SLA theory as well as for language pedagogy.

The restoration of grammar to center-stage in linguistics had reverberations in language pedagogy as well. For instance, Rutherford and Sharwood Smith (1985) offered grammatical 'consciousness raising', rebutting those who would ban grammar from L2 classrooms, and Larsen-Freeman (1991) proposed the 'challenge principle'. Underlying both these constructs is the assertion that a judicious focus on form can be of value, acknowledging all the while that focusing on form can be handled through many different means.

Another theory of learning which has had some impact on grammar teaching is a cognitive, information-processing approach. Acquiring a second language is seen to involve:

> a process whereby controlled attention-demanding operations become automatic through practice. . . . In addition, however, there are qualitative changes that occur as learners shift strategies and restructure their internal representations of the TL. (McLaughlin 1987:125)

Thus, two processes—automatization and restructuring—are central to cognitive theory. The former offers theoretical justification for the widely accepted pedagogical practice of initially employing controlled exercises, which gradually give way to freer activities as learners' performance becomes more fluent. The second concept, restructuring, helps to explain the commonly observed U-shaped phenomenon characteristic of SLA. Initial practice leads to improved performance as skills become automatized; further practice, however, sometimes results in attendant decrements in performance as learners reorganize their internal grammars. Once the restructuring has taken place, performance improves again as the new skills become automatized. Explanations such as these should console grammar teachers who commonly report 'backsliding' in students' performance subsequent to assumed mastery.

Another stream of SLA research from an information-processing perspective has led to significant findings regarding developmental orders which have been discovered in learners' interlanguage. Work by Pienemann and his associates has established that the speech-processing strategies available to learners determine what the learners are currently capable of comprehending, thereby acting as constraints on development. This observation also led Pienemann (1984) to claim that speech-processing strategies constrain what is learnable, hence what is teachable, at any one time and to suggest the futility of attempting to teach beyond a learner's current processing level. Pienemann's contribution, in other words, was to specify what previous knowledge or skills learners needed in order to be able to master new material. One obvious consequence of further work of this sort would be to have a principled means of sequencing items in a grammatical syllabus.

The final theory to be considered in this synopsis is one with no linguistic counterpart, although some linguists contend its implications for linguistics are great (Sampson 1980). Connectionism or 'parallel distributed processing' (PDP) represents a new approach to the study of mental activity based on the idea of neural networks and distributed representation. PDP theorists hold that learning is based on the processing of input, but that this processing does not lead to the accrual of rules. Rather, connections in complex neural networks are made and subsequently strengthened or weakened based upon the frequency of the pattern in the input. The networks produce what looks like rule-governed behavior, but which is simply a reflection of the connections formed on the basis of relative strengths of various patterns in the input (Larsen-Freeman and Long 1991).

Rumelhart and McClelland (1987) describe a two-phase process: The performance of the model in Phase 1 essentially amounts to rote learning. In the second phase it appears to be more analogy-based, leading to generalizations. Ney and Pearson (1990) have suggested that this description could easily apply to grammar textbooks which make use of exercises designed to initially encourage rote learning, followed by exercises which push students to make generalizations about the language. If this is the case, perhaps PDP will result in affirming current practice rather than challenging it. Clearly, at this point it is too early to tell.

State of the art in teaching grammar. When one switches from a diachronic to a synchronic perspective, what is striking is the extent to which current pedagogical practice is an aggregation of the many different views reflected during the latter half of the twentieth century. In terms of the content of grammatical instruction (all the items labeled **(1)** in the right column of Figure 1), it is commonly accepted, although not always explicitly acknowledged, that the *form, meaning*, and *use* of structures must be considered when teaching grammar (Larsen-Freeman 1991). For example, teachers today recognize that it is insufficient to teach the form and meaning of the passive voice in English without helping their students to understand when to use it (versus the active voice) as well. Thus, the current definition of the content of grammar instruction has expanded over the years by incorporating trends from different evolutionary stages.

As for the more fundamental question, the role of grammar in the L2 classroom (items(2) in the right column of Figure 1), there is perhaps more divergence of views. There are certainly some methodologists who subscribe to the view that explicit focus is unnecessary (Krashen and Terrell 1983); others would find such an omission irresponsible, given that language teachers should attempt to accelerate the acquisition of a second language, not merely to emulate the rate of natural L2 acquisition (Larsen-Freeman and Long 1991). Perhaps in the notion of consciousness raising resides a resolution to the divergence of views:

> Consciousness raising is intended to embrace a continuum ranging from intensive promotion of conscious awareness through pedagogical role articulations on the one end, to the mere exposure of the learner to specific grammatical phenomena on the other. (Rutherford and Sharwood Smith 1988:3)

The raising of students' consciousness regarding L2 grammar would seem to be a sufficiently inclusive notion to be able to embrace all views on the role of explicit grammar teaching, from those who would advocate a deductive or inductive presentation of grammatical rules to those who would suggest that no explicit grammar rules be given at all. There is still some question, however, as to whether the definition is broad enough to satisfy those who prefer a more 'natural' approach.

As for the process of teaching grammar (items labeled **(3)** in Figure 1), it can be seen that teachers of grammar have again demonstrated their willingness to learn from a variety of different viewpoints, as previously shown with regard to the content of grammar instruction. Teachers of grammar today make use of drills and pattern practice,[4] rule-based exercises, and tasks that are of a problem-solving and role-playing

---

4 They are more likely to be meaningful today, however, and are often introduced in the guise of games.

nature, and which are discourse-based. Moreover, most grammar teachers would sequence the activities in the order just given, i.e. following the guideline of moving from controlled activities to freer ones. The desirability of teaching grammar in context and using authentic materials is also commonly acknowledged.[5]

There is still a divergence of thinking with regard to how errors should be treated (items (4) in Figure 1), however, and this has resulted in some confusion among teachers who have been told to correct/not to correct errors or to correct only certain errors. The means of correcting errors has also generated much discussion among those holding differing points of view. Perhaps current research on the role of negative evidence will provide helpful information in sorting out the various options. Schachter (1986), for instance, has suggested that various forms of negative evidence are helpful to learners, including such indirect means as signaling a failure to understand or requesting a clarification. These types of negative evidence are indirect in that the teacher does not explicitly state that the learner's production is wrong. As with the notion of consciousness raising, the concept of 'giving students feedback' on their L2 production (including the fact that what they produced was accurate) might be broad enough to encompass divergent views with regard to error correction, although as with consciousness raising, it is also biased in implying that some sort of explicit attention to the learner's grammatical production is beneficial. This practice is not uniformly endorsed nor supported by what little empirical research has been conducted to date (Carroll and Swain 1991).

In addition to the role of negative evidence in SLA, other issues requiring further investigation (items (5) in Figure 1) have to do with:

- Selection of which grammatical points to include in instruction: Are there certain principles/parameters for which it makes more sense to include instruction than others? If we focus our energies on teaching marked forms in the L2, can we assume that learners will acquire unmarked forms by implication (Gass 1982) or by positive transfer from the L1 (Eckman 1977)?
- Sequencing of grammatical points: Can a developmental order based upon speech processing constraints serve as a pedagogical sequence? Are learners truly unable to acquire something unless it is presented at a particular stage in their acquisition? Is sequencing necessary at all?

---

5 It should be recognized that by saying all of these principles and practices are accepted today, I am not claiming that they are always put into practice. Certainly individual teachers vary in the degree to which they hold the principles or attempt to realize certain of these practices.

- Connectionism: What are the implications of connectionism for grammar teaching, if any? Is the theory neo-behaviorist or not (Gasser 1990)? If it is, is there a way we can learn from its insights without losing what we have gained from the last time that behaviorism was the prevailing theory?

These three areas of research, I submit, would all be suitable candidates for an SLT research agenda, something I called for at last year's Round Table. There is much that remains to be learned about the teaching of grammar which would enhance the state of the art.

Closing remarks. One cannot help but notice that there is more consensus around the teaching of grammar today than there is with regard to linguistic theories and theories of learning. At the risk of oversimplifying, let me observe that the pattern in the grammar teaching field seems to be one of subsuming ideas from previous evolutionary trends rather than discarding old ideas and replacing them with new ones, as is the case with linguistic and psychological theories. To be sure, as we have seen, there are contentious areas in grammar teaching today, and new ideas have been introduced to the field as a challenge to extant practice; however, when we view the state of the art in current practice, the degree to which grammar teaching has assimilated what has come before is noteworthy.

I do not believe that the eclecticism stems merely from the pragmatic bent of teachers. I think it can also be attributed to the fact that teachers confront the complexity of language, learning, and language learners every day of their working lives in a more direct fashion than any theorist does. This experience reinforces in teachers the conviction that no single perspective on language, no single explanation for learning, and no unitary view of the contributions of language learners will account for what they must grapple with on a daily basis.

Perhaps it would behoove applied researchers to move the locus of their work to the classroom from the beginning, rather than concentrating their efforts solely on determining the applicability of insights from linguistic and learning theories to classroom practice. A complementary approach, at least, would be to look at successful grammar teaching and work backwards from it in order to account for its success. After all, a theory of learning or SLA will ultimately have to explain what occurs in the classroom, so does it not make sense to start there?

On a matter related to starting our inquiries in classrooms, it is worth pointing out that many of the items in the right column of Figure 1 did not originate as insights from linguistics, psychology, or language acquisition. The desirability of providing L2 learners with feedback (negative evidence), the issue of beginning with exercises which are tightly controlled and then moving to those which are more communicative (controlled → automatic), and the readiness of learners to acquire certain structures before others are notions long known and widely accepted by grammar teachers. As Chomsky recently said:

> People who are involved in some practical activity such as teaching languages, translation, or building bridges should probably keep an eye on what's happening in the sciences. But they probably shouldn't take it too seriously, because the capacity to carry out practical activities without much conscious awareness of what you're doing is usually far more advanced than scientific knowledge. (Chomsky 1988:180 in Ney and Pearson 1990:474)

While I might dispute the suggestion that teachers carry out their activities without much conscious attention to what they are doing, I would concur that at times it seems as if practitioners are ahead of theorists. I would hope, however, that the two would not see each other as competitors, but rather as informing and being informed by each other in such a way that mutual benefit and respect obtain. In this way, we are all winners.

References

Allen, J.P.B., and H. G. Widdowson. 1975. Grammar and language teaching. In: J.P.B. Allen and S. Pit Corder, eds. Papers in applied linguistics. London: Oxford University Press. 45-97.
Belasco, Simon. 1985. Toward the identification of a core grammar in L2 acquisition. Studies in Second Language Acquisition. 7.1:91-8.
Carroll, Suzanne, and Merrill Swain. 1991. Negative evidence in second language learning. Paper presented at the Second Language Research Forum, February.
Celce-Murcia, Marianne. 1980. Contextual analysis of English: Applications to TESL. In: Diane Larsen-Freeman, ed. Discourse analysis in second language research. Rowley, Mass.: Newbury House. 41-55.
Celce-Murcia, Marianne. 1990. Data-based language analysis and TESL. In: James E. Alatis, ed. Georgetown University Round Table on Languages and Linguistics 1990. Washington, D.C.: Georgetown University Press.
Chomsky, Noam. 1959. Review of *Verbal behavior*. Language. 35:26-58.
Chomsky, Noam. 1965. Aspects of the theory of syntax. Cambridge, Mass.: MIT Press.
Chomsky, Noam. 1984. Changing perspectives on knowledge and use of language. Unpublished manuscript. Cited in Flynn 1985.
Chomsky, Noam. 1987. Kyoto lectures. Unpublished manuscript. Cited in James Ney and Bethyl Pearson 1990.
Chomsky, Noam. 1988. Language and problems of knowledge. The Nicaraguan lectures. Cambridge, Mass.: MIT Press.

Dulay, Heidi, Marina Burt, and Stephen Krashen. 1982. Language two. New York: Oxford University Press.
Eckman, Fred. 1977. Markedness and the contrastive analysis hypothesis. Language Learning. 27.2:315-30.
Flynn, Suzanne. 1985. Principled theories of L2 acquisition. Studies in Second Language Acquisition. 7.1:99-107.
Fries, Charles. 1952. The structure of English. New York: Harcourt Brace.
Fries, Peter. 1989. Fries' views on psychology: His nonmechanical view of human behavior. In: William Norris and Jeris Strain, eds. Charles Carpenter Fries: His 'oral approach' for teaching and learning foreign languages. Washington, D.C.: Georgetown University Press. 11-20.
Gass, Susan. 1982. From theory to practice. In: Mary Hines and William Rutherford, eds. On TESOL '81. Washington, D.C.: TESOL. 129-39.
Gasser, Michael. 1990. Connectionism and universals of second language acquisition. Studies in Second Language Acquisition. 12.2:179-99.
Halliday, Michael. 1973. Explorations in the functions of language. London: Edward Arnold.
Hatch, Evelyn, ed. 1978. Second language acquisition: A book of readings. Rowley, Mass.: Newbury House.
Hymes, Dell. 1972. On communicative competence. In: J.B. Pride and J. Holmes, eds. Socio-linguistics: Selected readings. Harmondsworth: Penguin Books. 269-93.
Krashen, Stephen. 1985. The input hypothesis: Issues and implications. New York: Longman.
Krashen, Stephen, and Tracy Terrell. 1983. The natural approach. New York: Pergamon.
Lachter, Joel and Thomas Bever. 1988. The relation between linguistic structure and associative theories of language learning: A constructive critique of some connectionist learning models. Cognition. 29:195-247.
Larsen-Freeman, Diane. 1990. Pedagogical descriptions of language: Grammar. Annual Review of Applied Linguistics. 10:187-95.
Larsen-Freeman, Diane. 1991. Teaching grammar. In: Marianne Celce-Murcia, ed. Teaching English as a second or foreign language. 2nd ed. New York: Newbury House. 279-96.
Larsen-Freeman, Diane, and Michael Long. 1991. Introduction to second language acquisition research. Essex: Longman.
McLaughlin, Barry. 1987. Theories of second-language learning. London: Edward Arnold.
Ney, James, and Bethyl Pearson. 1990. Connectionism as a model of language learning: Parallels in foreign language teaching. Modern Language Journal. 74.4:474-82.
Pienemann, Manfred. 1984. Psychological constraints on the teachability of languages. Studies in Second Language Acquisition. 6.2:186-212.
Rinvolucri, Mario. 1984. Grammar games. Cambridge: Cambridge University Press.
Rumelhart, David, and James McClelland. 1987. Learning the past tense of English verbs: Implicit rules or parallel distributed processing. In: Brian MacWhinney, ed. Mechanisms of language acquisition. Hillsdale, N.J.: Lawrence Erlbaum. 195-248.
Rutherford, William, and Michael Sharwood Smith. 1985. Consciousness raising and universal grammar. Applied Linguistics. 6.3:274-82.
Rutherford, William, and Michael Sharwood Smith, eds. 1988. Grammar and second language teaching. New York: Newbury House.

Sampson, Geoffrey. 1980. Schools of linguistics. London: Hutchinson.
Schachter, Jacquelyn. 1986. Three approaches to the study of input. Language Learning. 36.2:211-25.
Skinner, B.F. 1957. Verbal behavior. New York: Appleton-Century-Crofts.
Tomasello, Michael, and Carol Herron. 1988. Down the garden path: Inducing and correcting overgeneralization errors in the foreign language classroom. Applied Psycholinguistics. 9:237-46.
White, Lydia. 1983. Markedness and parameter setting: Some implications for a theory of adult second language acquisition. Paper presented at the University of Wisconsin-Milwaukee Linguistics Symposium, March.

Writing in foreign language classrooms: Process and reality

L. Kathy Heilenman
University of Iowa

It has been ten years since the publication of Claire Gaudiani's (1981) guide to what was essentially process-oriented writing in foreign language (FL) classrooms. Basing her analysis on what has since become widely known as process-oriented writing theory,[1] Gaudiani set forth a rationale and a step-by-step plan for the implementation of writing-as-thinking, collaborative writing, peer-editing groups, journal writing, and grammar in the service of meaning. The next ten years, while seeing the growing acceptance and extensive development of process-oriented writing in native language composition programs and English as a Second language (ESL) instruction, saw no such wide-scale movement in FLs. Little was written about writing in general and even less about process-oriented writing in particular (see Barnett 1989, Dvorak 1986, and Magnan 1985 for exceptions). Further, although it is impossible to assert with any pretense to empirical certainty, my own experience as a foreign language teacher, teacher-trainer, and materials developer, during those same years, indicates even less innovation in actual classroom practice.

Is process writing and all it implies, then, simply unthinkable in FL classrooms? Are the conditions inherent in FL teaching so different from those found in native language composition and ESL programs that pedagogical insights developed in the latter are untenable in the former? Or, is it simply a question of time? Will the present relative lack of interest change to curiosity, investigation, and adaptation, and will process-oriented approaches to writing be integrated into foreign language instruction?

---

1 By a process-oriented writing or approach, I refer, in a rather generic way, to those theoretical and practical perspectives on writing that emphasize its complex, non-linear, idea-generating, and communicative nature. Although my own personal preference tends toward the social constructionist view of process (Johns 1990), I do not mean here to so limit the use of the term process-oriented writing or approach (see Silva 1990 for an historical overview of writing theory in ESL).

FL versus ESL classrooms. There are very real differences in the realities of teaching English as a native or second language and teaching English, or any other language, as a foreign one.[2] Beyond the fact that FL programs operate under the obvious disadvantage of providing the quasi-totality of language input for their students, there are other differences. FL programs tend to have a larger percentage of students at less advanced levels, to have shorter sequences of study, to be staffed by non-native speakers, and to operate relatively independently of other academic disciplines. These factors combine to make writing, in the sense of composing, a minor component in the overall fabric of instruction (cf. Katz 1988).

Writing in the sense of expressive writing or writing-as-thinking has traditionally been seen in both FL and ESL programs as most appropriate at advanced levels of instruction, with earlier years being given over to speaking, listening, some reading, and the study of grammar. That writing which is done at early levels has tended to focus on writing down or transcribing rather than on writing about or composing. Omaggio (1986:221), for example, advises the use of 'process-oriented composing tasks' only at the Advanced and Superior levels of proficiency as defined by the ACTFL/ETS writing scale (Omaggio 1986: Appendix 1). Similarly, Bowen, Madsen, and Hilferty (1985:253), in an ESL context, recommend 'Writing with a Purpose' and 'Full Expository Prose' as the predominant tasks for learners at the high intermediate to advanced levels (levels that presuppose a vocabulary of between 1,000 and 3,600 words along with a basic command of the language). Given, then, that the majority of FL instruction in the United States concerns beginning to low-intermediate levels (i.e. two years of high school or the first year or two of college), the pedagogy as well as the research generated in native language composition and college-level ESL classrooms has quite literally had little or no applicability in FL instruction.

This situation has been compounded by the fact that formal FL instruction in the United States is effectively terminated after the third, or sometimes, fourth year of college instruction, even for those relatively few students who continue beyond whatever obligatory courses exist. There is, in other words, no real FL equivalent of the ESL 'freshmen composition' course found at many universities. The FL close equivalent,

---

[2] There are equally obvious differences between language instruction provided by bilingual programs and that found in FL programs. Similarly, there are differences between the language instruction usually provided children and that provided adults. Here, however, I limit the discussion to language instruction provided adults who are native speakers of the language, second language learners (i.e. learning the language in an area where that language is spoken), and FL learners (i.e. learning the language in an area where that language is not spoken). For further discussion of problems in terminology, see Stern (1983).

the so-called 'advanced composition and conversation' course usually found at the the third-year level, tends to focus on the study of grammar and on writing as a product produced to sanction that study. In addition, as pointed out by Gutiérrez (1990), these courses are generally staffed by literary specialists with little or no exposure to the pedagogical and experimental literature. To sum up, writing as practiced in FL classrooms, has been neglected in favor of the other skills and has largely been viewed as a means of practicing language or of making learning concrete through the writing of exercises or tests. Writing in the sense of creating meaning has not typically been seen as part of the FL teacher's job description.

Another salient difference between ESL instruction and that in FLs concerns staffing. The dominant language of most FL departments is English; the same holds true for most ESL programs. This reflects the fact that FL programs in the United States are largely staffed by native speakers of English as are ESL programs. This simple demographic fact translates, however, into, potentially, very different levels of control over the language taught. Teachers for whom the language taught is a second language maintained within a first language English context are likely to be less confident dealing with writing in rhetorical terms (concern with intent, audience, etc.) than are teachers who are native speakers of English. In this respect, it is important to point out that the vast majority of research and pedagogical writing issuing from composition and ESL scholars implicitly assumes native-speaker-like competence on the part of instructors. Instructors are urged, for example, to respond to student journal writing with their own journal entries, typed and distributed as 'examples of the writing processes and products of native speakers' (Lucas 1990:104). These same instructors are encouraged, as well, to react to student writing as would a competent reader of the target culture. Many FL teachers, well aware of the fact that they are not native speakers of the languages they teach, understandably shy away from these types of demands, fraught as they are with questions of teacher fallibility and loss of face. The implication here is not that all FL teachers are less than competent users of their second language, nor to say that all ESL instructors are models thereof. I myself am a competent user of French and a native speaker of English. I have also dealt with student writing in both languages. As a native speaker of English, reacting to ESL student writing, the question of my qualifications to do so, that is to act as a reader and evaluator in a rhetorical sense, was never an issue. As a second language user of French, however, that very issue, my competence, colored my teaching as well as my reaction to student writing. There were two choices: admit to my own rhetorical limits and model competent, second language problem-solving behavior (using authentic materials as models along with dictionaries, grammars, divergent thinking, and any nearby native speakers) or restrict myself (and my students) to a definition of writing largely reduced to the correction of surface error (see Green and Hecht 1985 and Takashima 1987 for a discussion of the issues involved). I chose the first alternative but not without a great deal of anxiety—and this after extensive teaching experience and with the full knowledge of how dishonest the second response would have been. It is easy to sympathize, then, with the agonies of other non-native teachers of writing who ask themselves if they are indeed competent to correct, much less teach, free composition and who answer that question in the negative (Takashima 1987). Finally, FL programs tend to exist in spite of, not because of, the outside world. Although the world may indeed be getting smaller, it remains likely that beyond the classroom, FL students will not be called upon to write with any degree of expertise.[3] The writing of compositions and essays in the FL becomes, then, a rather sterile exercise designed to prepare those few students who will continue beyond the obligatory courses to courses where writing about literature or perhaps civilization will be required. Instructors of native language and ESL composition courses, on the other hand, are assured an eventual if temporally limited audience for their students. These students will be asked to write, and to write effectively, in other academic areas. This, of course, brings its own panoply of problems (how to define academic discourse(s), to what extent composition courses are responsible for introducing students to discipline-specific discourse, how to accomplish this, and so on [e.g. Belcher 1990, Spack 1988]). Nevertheless, these connections to more or less immediate accountability do provide an external motivation that is usually lacking in the FL context.

Writing in FL classrooms—the traditional view. Writing, in the sense of composing, has been largely exempt from the communicative demands the 1970s and 1980s placed on speaking, listening, and to a lesser extent, reading. Writing, in FL classrooms, particularly at lower levels, is and has been primarily a 'handmaid' (Rivers 1981:293) or 'support' (Magnan 1985, Omaggio 1986) skill. Writing, in the sense of creating meaning, has been most noticeable by its absence (Nerenz 1979) or by its use to apply and practice grammatical knowledge (Dvorak 1986).

Further, when writing as composing is discussed by FL educators, this discussion takes place largely within the framework of a linear,

---

3 Of course the same can be said for speaking. Chastain (1988) however, points out that students are as likely to be required to write to native speakers as they are to speak to them.

sequenced, product-centered, and form-driven view of language.[4] This view of language learning, or perhaps, more accurately put, language teaching as applied to writing, has a long tradition. Over 100 years ago, in 1880,[5] the International Phonetic Association declared that writing, when it was introduced, should proceed from 'reproduction of thoroughly familiar reading texts' to 'reproduction of narratives produced by the teacher,' to 'free composition' (cited in Stern 1983:89). Forty years later, we find Harold Palmer ([1921] 1964:74) insisting on the necessity of drill work before free work, and invoking the specter of mother tongue interference if such a progression were not rigorously followed:

> If the student has not been put through a proper course of drill-work, all his efforts at free work will be based on the most unnatural and vicious of processes—conventional translation from the mother tongue.

Then, to skip ahead another forty years or so, we find Nelson Brooks (1960), writing from the audio-lingual perspective of the early 1960s, recommending that writing instruction follow a strict sequence, beginning with transcriptions of what learners knew how to say during the first two years, and moving to highly structured activities (e.g. summaries, directed compositions, rewriting of texts, and imitation) in years three and four.

Similar advice, although frequently couched in more communicative terms, is present in more contemporary pedagogical works. Rivers (1981:291) calls for the tracing out of 'the steps by which this skill [writing] can be progressively mastered,' while contending that early, unguided practice is the cause of weakness in advanced classes. She goes on to state (306-307) that:

> A great deal of uncorrected writing is merely a waste of time and energy. Inaccuracies and misconceptions become firmly fixed in the students' mind and are difficult to eradicate at a later date (Rivers 1981:306-307).

---

4 I do not mean to disparage the work of the people referred to, but rather to make evident the basic incompatibility of the positions expressed with process-oriented approaches. Along with Lange (1990:103), I do not see what he terms the 'scientific-technical' (here called, sequenced, linear, and form-driven) as necessarily misguided or inherently evil. Again echoing Lange (1990), I do view it, however, as basically limiting and, in the case of writing, insufficient, for the majority of students.

5 The examples given here are meant to be illustrative, not conclusive. They were chosen largely because they were at hand, which may or may not indicate their relative importance in the history of FL teaching.

Rivers is not alone in her recommendations. Concern with sequenced practice, avoidance of the L1, and eradication of error continue to be echoed in articles and handbooks. The ACTFL/ETS Writing Guidelines, as currently written, emphasize sentence-level skills, concentrating on spelling, punctuation, grammatical accuracy, and lexical exactness while largely ignoring such areas as organization, audience, or creativity (Dvorak 1986, see Herzog 1988 for discussion). Omaggio (1986), taking the ACTFL/ETS Guidelines as a basis, has produced a 'sequenced approach' to writing that moves from controlled activities through guided writing to free writing. And, to give only one example, Terry (1989:43), in an article detailing several interesting writing activities for beginning and intermediate FL learners defines his goals as 'practice for the development of writing as a true communicative skill and . . . the ability to use a correct, well-structured target language as a communicative vehicle for effective self-expression.' He then outlines six writing activities, four of which are focused on form (past tenses, future time, and the subjunctive).

Finally, a concern with error has been and remains pervasive. To paraphrase Dvorak (1986:148), writing about writing in FL terms means, to an overwhelming extent, writing about error, its prevention and remediation. To cite only a few examples, Reschke (1990) discusses the global assessment of writing, not as a substitute for the correction and evaluation of errors, but rather as a way to increase student writing without a subsequent increase in teacher workload. Articles by Hendrickson (1980), Lalande (1982), and Sempke (1984) albeit with different conclusions, all look at teacher reaction to error and its effect on students' subsequent performance. Further, it appears that any discussion of how to teach writing must, obligatorily, be followed by recommendations for correction strategies (e.g. Pilarcik 1986, Walker 1982 among others).

Thus, within the traditional approach, learning how to write in a FL means learning how to produce sentence-level, error-free text within a progression of tasks and under conditions of careful guidance. The concerns of process-oriented writing, recursiveness, writing-to-know, and effectiveness vis-à-vis audience, are irrelevant. Further, several of the issues currently discussed within a process-oriented paradigm pose knotty problems to FL instruction, especially when that instruction is conceived of in a linear, sequenced, form-based fashion which attempts to eliminate or at least minimize the role of students' L1.

Issues in teaching/learning writing. A process-oriented approach to writing is, in essence, antithetical to the traditional approach outlined above. At best, it can, as Omaggio (1986) suggests, be appended to a program of sequenced, form-based instruction that assumes a certain level of linguistic competence before serious attention to writing-as-creating-meaning can be envisaged. There are several issues here, One way of looking at these issues is to borrow Fulkerson's (1990) description of the elements that a complete theory of composition must encompass. His model has four parts: (1) an axiological component or definition of what constitutes good writing, (2) a procedural component describing the means by which learners can attain the end defined by the axiological component, (3) a pedagogical component or description of the means teachers can use to help learners achieve that end, and (4) an epistemology or assumption(s) as to what constitutes knowledge.

Of axiologies and pedagogy. According to Fulkerson (1990), composition theory in the 1980s reached a kind of consensus on this issue: good writing is rhetorically effective and the criteria by which such writing is to be judged are the responses of its readers. FL instruction, on the other hand, has continued to see good writing primarily in terms of correctness. That is, in Fulkerson's terms, FL pedagogy has espoused a formalist axiology. Good compositions tend, overwhelmingly, to be syntactically and morphologically correct ones (Barnett 1989, Dvorak 1986).

At present, as elements of process-oriented writing are beginning to infiltrate FL instruction, teachers are being encouraged to look beyond formal correctness to rhetorical effectiveness. As Fulkerson (1990) points out, however, axiology, procedure, pedagogy, and epistemology are logically independent of one another and can combine in ways that are either theoretically congruent and maximally effective or, on the other hand, contradictory and dissonant. Such is quite likely to be the case as FL instruction makes the transition (assuming it does) from writing-as-product to writing-as-process. Here, many potential problems stem from embracing one axiology but using the tenets of another for teaching and evaluating (e.g. valuing writing as a rhetorical event but evaluating the results as a formal product). In other words, embracing a new axiology means more than changing names. It requires more than simply using peer-groups to critique essays or having students write multiple drafts, and keep journals. Such a change also requires a fundamental rethinking of what it means to learn to write in a foreign language.

Cosmetic changes and paradigm shifts. The same intellectual and social climate that worked toward paradigm instability in composition (Hairston 1982), has had similar effects in FL instruction. The communicative view of language as socially-mediated, culturally-embedded learning has called into question the rote learning of rules and the memorization of conjugations. The movement toward proficiency has caused teachers to look more closely at actual outcomes measured in more global terms. In addition, research in second language acquisition has raised questions about the efficacy of overt grammar teaching and language taught as product rather than process (Swaffar 1991). As a result, FL classrooms and materials have become, at least, cosmetically more communicative and more process-oriented.

The changes that have been effected, however, can be seen as more in the nature of ad hoc adjustments, aimed at patching the cracks and preserving the traditional paradigm, than as considered and substantial changes in the way FLs are taught (here, see Lange 1990 for a discussion of curricular perspectives). Raimes' (1983) description of ad hoc solutions in the field of ESL is equally valid for FLs. FLs also have grammar explanations masquerading as functions, drills pretending to be communication (cf. Walz 1989), and, in the case of writing, grammar study and error correction disguised as drafts, journals, and peer-editing. My point here is that changing names and adopting techniques is not equivalent to rethinking assumptions. Process-oriented writing may well make its way into FL classrooms. My prediction, however, is that writing will continue to be taught, if at all, in much the same manner as before.

This is the place, perhaps, to point out that in the fields of composition and ESL, as well, there are those who see the world in terms of politically correct pedagogy accompanied by very little actual change. The activity of the past 20 years, from this point of view, is seen as having amounted to little more than busy work for academics. Fulkerson (1990), in a discussion of composition theory in the eighties, points out that a defense of formalism, the position that the only good writing is correct writing, has been conspicuously absent from professional journals since at least 1979. Nevertheless, as he puts it (Fulkerson 1990:412), 'we [have] had plenty of evidence of its classroom existence.' In a similar vein, Gungle and Taylor (1989:235) call an essentially linear concept of the composition process, 'a ghost still hovering in English as a second language (ESL) writing classes,' and Hamilton-Wieler (1988) contends that the post-shift paradigm represented by process-oriented writing is simply not present in the pre-shift classrooms of the vast majority of English teachers.

Issues in writing for FL classrooms. In this context, then, I foresee three major areas of difficulty in the application of process-oriented approaches to writing in FL classrooms. The first of these is error. It is probably correct as Leki (1990:59) argues, that 'an element of prescription is necessary' in responding to second language writing. There are, however, numerous studies indicating that laborious error correction by teachers does little but assuage guilt and produce feelings of a job well done (e.g. Robb, Ross, and Shortreed 1986, Sempke 1984, Zamel 1985). Teachers, it would seem, could better spend their time responding to larger issues of rhetorical import and reserving concerns with surface error to the more appropriate arena of the editing of the final draft (Raimes 1979).[6] This type of shift, however, requires first, that more time be accorded writing instruction; and, second, that teachers feel themselves competent to respond to rhetorical issues—both conditions that tend to be less common in FL classrooms than in composition and ESL ones.

The second area of concern is whether writing skill can be or should be separated from linguistic skill. Research attempting to tease apart these two variables indicates, that, at least for learners with a certain degree of linguistic competence, the two are indeed different (Cumming 1989, Cumming 1990a, Doushaq 1986, Kroll 1990). Doushaq, for example, (1986) compared compositions written in L1 (Arabic) and L2 (English as a foreign language) by university level students. Results indicated that good writing in one language was related to good writing in the other. Further, compositions written in Arabic by English majors were judged the most coherent, while those written in Arabic by Arabic majors were found to be least coherent, a finding that Doushaq attributes to the training in writing provided by the English but not by the Arabic department. This would seem to indicate that FL students who have already developed writing expertise need only develop a corresponding linguistic expertise to be successful. Conversely, students whose linguistic performance is adequate may produce poor writing due to a lack of writing skills (Cumming 1990a). A further implication is that writing expertise can be developed in an L2 as well as in an L1. It should be noted, however, that these issues are complex, that the studies done thus far have been primarily correlational in nature, and that there has been little or no research involving low proficiency L2 learners. Given that the majority of FL learners are at low or intermediate levels, generalizing results found for fairly advanced ESL and EFL students to FL students may be questionable. Further, the low correlations between L1 writing and L2 writing found by Carson, Carrell, Silberstein, Kroll, and Kuehn (1990) may indicate that we are dealing with issues of general (writing)

---

6 Fathman and Whalley (1990) have produced research indicating that feedback on grammar produced significant improvement in grammatical correctness while feedback on content did not. There are several problems, however, in applying this finding to teacher response to student writing in general. First, the comments were given to a final draft. It is possible that such comments on early drafts may prematurely restrict L2 writers to issues of surface form. Second, the content comments, as Fathman and Whalley point out, were less precise than the grammatical ones and thus more difficult for students to apply during a rewrite. Third, rewriting was done during thirty minutes in class, a period of time that would seem to encourage attention to more easily repaired errors of form than to infelicities of content. Their study, nevertheless, does provide evidence that L2 students can correct errors under certain conditions.

versus local (language specific) expertise that are quite complex (see Carter 1990 for discussion).

Finally, a third and potentially very volatile issue concerns the use of L1 in L2 composing. The basic question here is how effectively learners can compose in a second language. Although the evidence is somewhat mixed (see Jones and Tetroe 1987, Krapels 1990 for overviews and discussion), the majority of studies indicate that learners do use their L1 in composing and that doing so is beneficial. Lay (1982), for example, noted that the Chinese learners she studied translated key words into Chinese, apparently, in order to access various cognitive schemata. Similarly, Kozue and Cumming (1989), after studying the composing processes of intermediate students of Japanese as a FL, conclude that expecting students to function in a FL while engaged in a cognitively demanding task such as composing, is unrealistic and even counterproductive. Finally, Friedlander (1990), working with Chinese learners of English, found that, when topic-area knowledge was in the L1, writers were helped by the use of translation. He concludes: 'Writers would thus lose little by writing in their first language and then translating into English at the appropriate time for their emerging texts'(Friedlander 1990:124). This is, of course, heresy for most FL teachers who have been insisting since time immemorial that students not write out their compositions in English and then translate them. Even Gaudiani (1981) who was an early supporter of process-oriented writing for FLs and who advocated the use of both L1 and L2 in the composition classroom, balked at this, calling it 'the translation trap' (Gaudiani 1981:50) More recently, Dvorak (1986:156), another proponent of process-oriented writing for FL classrooms has skirted the issue, suggesting that: 'while one does not want to seem to suggest that students be allowed to write in English and then translate, the concept of a bilingual first draft, or bilingual brainstorming should be explored.' Thus, as Atkinson (1987) has suggested, the use of students' L1 may be appropriate and even beneficial in certain contexts. The problem, of course, is negotiating the contexts.

Thus, three issues, response to error, the development of writing expertise versus linguistic expertise, and the use of students' L1, all pose significant problems for FL instruction as traditionally conceived. Although a full consideration of each of these areas is beyond the scope of this paper, nevertheless, the outlines of a response can be suggested. This response is, of course, an unavoidably personal one. It reflects my knowledge, my values and my presuppositions. It can be generalized to others only insofar as my biases and my reading of the relevant literature are shared.

First, in regard to errors, I find Shaughnessy's (1977:12) definition of mechanical errors (the L1 analogue of L2 grammar mistakes) to be helpful. Shaughnessy views such errors as:

unintentional and unprofitable intrusions upon the consciousness of the reader . . . demand[ing] energy without giving any return in meaning . . . [and] shift[ing] the reader's attention from where he [sic] is going (meaning) to how he [sic] is getting there (code).

This definition raises the question of error to a rhetorical plane and establishes the relevant criterion for evaluation as reader reaction, rather than a putative ideal, native-speaker-written product (Kroll 1990). The significance of errors, then, is relative. They are important only insofar as they irritate readers and take attention away from the message—and the better the message, the less likely readers are to note the errors.[7]

The question of separating writing instruction in a general sense from the type of instruction found in FL classrooms concerns both responsibility and opportunity—responsibility to do more than teach structure and vocabulary and opportunity to go beyond form to function. My own view is that it is possible to treat learning to write, in the sense of composing, and learning a foreign language, in the sense of acquiring linguistic knowledge and ability, as separate areas of instructional endeavor. It is certainly possible to develop a high level of oral expertise in a first, second, or third language without, at the same time developing literacy skills in these languages. The question, however, is not that of possibility; it is one of desirability. Ignoring the teaching of writing as composing, in the FL classroom is tantamount to reducing the use of writing to a convenient means of verifying student performance in other realms. This, I would contend, is a waste of resources and an unnecessary compartmentalization of instruction. Further, and perhaps most importantly, writing in the sense of creating meaning, has the potential of providing students with the opportunity of reflecting upon their language learning and working out problems in lexicon and structure as well as in organization and voice, all within the context of their own, and not someone else's meaning.

My perception of how languages are learned favors a whole language approach (Freeman and Freeman 1989) within which language is seen as best learned as a whole rather than piecemeal. From this point of view, sequences of activities from lower-level to higher-level, from drill to use, or from memorization to thought (cf. Resnick 1987) do not provide a sufficiently rich context for either first or second language acquisition. Writing, or more properly, composing, within a whole language approach has the potential of integrating language and content (Swain and Lapkin

---

7 This is not the forum for a full discussion of error severity relative to context. It is, however, important to note that native speakers of a language appear to be more tolerant toward written error than do language teachers or non-native speakers (Green and Hecht 1985, Santos 1988).

1989) as well as that of helping learners to acquire, as well as to extend their control of the L2 (Cumming 1990b).

And finally, there is the issue of native language use. There are, as Friedlander (1990) suggests, at least two perspectives one can employ. If, as is often the case, teachers ask students to write about experiences encoded in their L1, it is unreasonable to expect them to retrieve those experiences in their L2. On the other hand, if teachers want students to avoid their native language, provision will have to be made for providing them with the linguistic and other experiences required. This may involve integrating writing about a topic into reading, talking and listening about that same topic in such a way that writing becomes an integral part (as opposed to the last assignment) in an ongoing process of learning (see Cortese 1985 for an example). This would require teachers to provide what Ammon (1985:82) has called 'rich activities'—that is, activities that give learners opportunities to be exposed to, to reflect on, and to produce L2 discourse. Within this context, L1 use is likely to be minimized without being prohibited.

Toward a conclusion. Two possibilities come to mind as appropriate quasi-conclusions. First, an exhortation to all those involved in foreign language instruction to subscribe to Phillips' (1989) action agenda for the nineties and to join in using whatever force may be necessary to eject formal grammar study from the central place it currently occupies in our classrooms (Lalande 1990). If we were to turn our backs on our 'lifelong loyalty to the organization of the grammatical syllabus', as Phillips (1989:11) puts it, then process-oriented writing would be a welcome newcomer to our shores.

On the other hand, there is the reality of classrooms (Cummins 1989), the cyclicity of methods and approaches (Pennycook 1989), and the overwhelming inertia that opposes change. Is it in any way reasonable to expect process-oriented writing to make headway against bottom-heavy programs with relatively few advanced students, a tradition of writing-down-correctly rather than writing-about-with-meaning, and the reluctance of non-native speaking teachers to deal with rhetorical concerns? Probably not. My realistic expectation is that there will be isolated attempts to import the theory along with the technology but that, for the most part, only the technology—the techniques—will have any lasting effect. Nonetheless, I am planning on being among those making the isolated attempt and I am also planning to join Phillip's (1989) action squad. You have to keep trying.

References

Ammon, Paul. 1985. Helping children learn to write in English as a second language: Some observations and some hypotheses. The acquisition of written language: Response and revision, ed. by Sarah Warshauer Freedman (65-84). Norwood, N.Y.: Ablex.
Atkinson, David. 1987. The mother tongue in the classroom: A neglected resource? ELT Journal. 41. 241-247.
Barnett, Marva A. 1989. Writing as a process. French Review. 63. 31-44.
Belcher, Diane. 1990. The case for teacher-student/author conferencing in field-specific writing by graduate students. TESOL Newsletter. 24 (August). 11-12.
Bowen, J. Donald, Harold Madsen, and Ann Hilferty. 1985. TESOL techniques and procedures. New York: Newbury House.
Brooks, Nelson. 1960. Language and language learning. New York: Harcourt Brace.
Carson, Joan Eisterhold, Patricia A. Carrell, Sandra Silberstein, Barbara Kroll, and Phyllis A. Kuehn. 1990. Reading-writing relationships in first and second languages. TESOL Quarterly. 24. 245-266.
Carter, Michael. 1990. The idea of expertise: An exploration of cognitive and social dimensions of writing. College Composition and Communication. 41. 265-286.
Chastain, Kenneth. 1988. Developing second language skills: Theory and practice. Orlando, Fla.: Harcourt Brace Jovanovich.
Cortese, Giuseppina. 1985. From receptive to productive in post-intermediate EFL classes: A pedagogical experiment. TESOL Quarterly. 19. 7-23.
Cumming, Alister. 1989. Writing expertise and second-language proficiency. Language Learning. 39. 81-141.
Cumming, Alister. 1990a. Expertise in evaluating second language compositions. Language Testing. 7. 31-51.
Cumming, Alister. 1990b. Metalinguistic and ideational thinking in second language composing. Written Communication. 7. 482-511.
Cummins, Jim. 1989. The sanitized curriculum: Educational disempowerment in a nation at risk. In: Richness in writing: Empowering ESL students, ed. by Donna M. Johnson and Duane H. Roen (19-38). New York: Longman.
Doushaq, Mufeeq H. 1986. An investigation into stylistic errors of Arab students learning English for academic purposes. English for Specific Purposes. 5. 27-39.
Dvorak, Trisha. 1986. Writing in the foreign language. In: Listening, reading, writing: Analysis and application. ed. by Barbara H. Wing (145-167). Middlebury, Vt.: Northeast Conference on the Teaching of Foreign Languages.
Fathman, Ann K. and Elizabeth Whalley. 1990. Teacher response to student writing: Focus on form versus content. In: Second language writing: Research insights for the classroom, ed. by Barbara Kroll (178-190). Cambridge: Cambridge University Press.
Freeman, Yvonne S. and David E. Freeman. 1989. Whole language approaches to writing with secondary students of English as a second language. In: Richness in writing: Empowering ESL students, ed. by Donna M. Johnson and Duanne H. Roen (177-192). New York: Longman.

Friedlander, Alexander. 1990. Composing in English: Effects of a first language on writing in English as a second language. In: Second language writing: Research insights for the classroom, ed. by Barbara Kroll (109-125). Cambridge: Cambridge University Press.

Fulkerson, Richard. 1990. Composition theory in the eighties: Axiological consensus and para-digmatic diversity. College Composition and Communication. 41. 409-429.

Gaudiani, Claire. 1981. Teaching writing in the foreign language classroom. Washington, D.C.: Center for Applied Linguistics.

Green, Peter S. and Karlheinz Hecht. 1985. Native and non-native evaluation of learners' errors in written discourse. System. 13. 77-97.

Gungle, Bruce W. and Victoria Taylor. 1989. Writing apprehension and second language writers. In: Richness in writing: Empowering ESL students, ed. by Donna M. Johnson and Duanne H. Roen (235-248). New York: Longman.

Gutiérrez, John R. 1990. Overcoming anarchy in the advanced language class. ADFL Bulletin. 21. 41-45.

Hairston, Maxine. 1982. The winds of change: Thomas Kuhn and the revolution in the teaching of writing. College Composition and Communication. 33. 76-88.

Hamilton-Wieler, Sharon. 1988. Empty echoes of Dartmouth: Dissonance between the rhetoric and the reality. Writing Instructor 8. 29-41.

Hendrickson, James M. 1980. The treatment of error in written work. Modern Language Journal. 64. 216-221.

Herzog, Martha. 1988. Issues in writing proficiency assessment: Section 1: The government scale. In: Second language proficiency assessment: Current issues, ed. by Pardee Lowe Jr and Charles W. Stansfield (149-177). Englewood Cliffs, N.J.: Prentice-Hall.

Johns, Ann M. 1990. L1 composition theories: Implications for developing theories of L2 composition. Second language writing: Research insights for the classroom, ed. by Barbara Kroll (24-36). Cambridge: Cambridge University Press.

Jones, Stan and Tetroe, Jacqueline. 1987. Composing in a second language. Writing in real time: Modelling production processes, ed. by Ann Matsuhashi (34-57). Norwood, N.J.: Ablex.

Katz, Anne. 1988, Issues in writing proficiency assessment: Section 2: The academic context. In: Second language proficiency assessment: Current issues. Pardee Lowe, Jr and Charles W. Stansfield, eds. (1178-201). Englewood Cliffs, N.J.: Prentice-Hall.

Kozue, Uzawa and Alister Cumming, 1989. Writing strategies in Japanese as a foreign language: Lowering or keeping up the standards. Canadian Modern Language Review, 46. 178-94.

Krapels, Alexandra. 1990. An overview of second language writing process research. Second language writing: Research insights for the classroom, ed. by Barbara Kroll (37-56). Cambridge: Cambridge University Press.

Kroll, Barbara. 1990. What does time buy? ESL student performance on home versus class compositions. Second language writing: Research insights for the classroom, ed. by Barbara Kroll (140-154). Cambridge: Cambridge University Press.

Lalande, John F. II. 1982. Reducing composition errors: An experiment. Modern Language Journal. 66. 140-149.

Lalande, John F. 1990. Inquiries into the teaching of German grammar. Unterrichtspraxis. 23. 30-41.
Lange, Dale L. 1990. Sketching the crisis and exploring different perspectives in foreign language curriculum. New perspectives and new directions in foreign language education, ed. by Diane W. Birckbichler (77-109). Lincolnwood, Ill.: National Textbook.
Lay, N. 1982. Composing processes of adult ESL learners: A case study. TESOL Quarterly, 16, 406.
Leki, Ilona. 1990. Coaching from the margins: Issues in written response. Second language writing: Research insights for the classroom, ed. by Barbara Kroll (57-68). Cambridge: Cambridge University Press.
Lucas, Tamara. 1990. Personal journal writing as a classroom genre. Students and teachers writing together: Perspectives on journal writing, ed. by Joy Kreeft Peyton (99-123). Alexandria, VA: Teachers of English to Speakers of Other Languages.
Magnan, Sally Sieloff. 1985. Teaching and testing proficiency in writing: Skills to transcend the second-language classroom. Proficiency, curriculum, articulation: The ties that bind, ed. by Alice C. Omaggio (109-136). Middlebury, Vt.: Northeast Conference on the Teaching of Foreign Languages.
Nerenz, Anne. 1979. Utilizing class time in foreign language instruction. Teaching the basics in the foreign language classroom: Options and strategies, ed. by David P. Benseler (78-89). Lincolnwood, Ill.: National Textbook.
Omaggio, Alice C. 1986. Teaching language in context: Proficiency-oriented instruction. Boston, Mass.: Heinle & Heinle.
Palmer, Harold E. 1964 (1921). The principles of language study. London: Oxford University Press.
Pennycook, Alastair. 1989. The concept of method, interested knowledge, and the politics of language teaching. TESOL Quarterly. 23. 589-618.
Pilarcik, Marlene A. 1986. Creative writing as a group effort. Unterrichtspraxis. 19. 220-224.
Phillips, June K. 1989. From talk to action: An essential for curricular change. Defining the essentials for the foreign language classroom, ed. by Dave McAlpine (1-13). Lincolnwood, IL: National Textbook.
Raimes, Ann. 1979. Anguish as a second language? Remedies for composition teachers. In: Learning to write: First language/second language. Arriva Freedman, Ian Pringle, and Janice Yalden, eds. (258-272). New York: Longman.
Raimes, Ann. 1983. Tradition and revolution in ESL teaching. TESOL Quarterly. 17. 535-552.
Reschke, Claus. 1990. Global assessment of writing proficiency. Realizing the potential of foreign language instruction. Selected papers from the 1990 Central States Conference. ed. by Gerard L. Ervin (100-111). Lincolnwood, Ill.: National Textbook.
Resnick, Lauren B. 1987. Education and learning to think. Washington, D.C.: Academy Press.
Rivers, Wilga M. 1981. Teaching foreign-language skills. 2nd ed. Chicago: University of Chicago Press.
Robb, Thomas, Steven Ross, and Ian Shortreed. 1986. Salience of feedback on error and its effect on EFL writing quality. TESOL Quarterly. 20. 83-93.
Santos, Terry. 1988. Professors' reactions to the academic writing of nonnative speaking students. TESOL Quarterly. 22. 69-90.

Sempke, Harriet D. 1984. Effects of the red pen. Foreign Language Annals. 17. 195-202.
Shaughnessy, Mina P. 1977. Errors and expectations: A guide for the teacher of basic writing. New York: Oxford University Press.
Silva, Tony. 1990. Second language composition instruction: developments, issues, and directions in ESL. Second language writing: Research insights for the classroom, ed. by Barbara Kroll (11-23). Cambridge: Cambridge University Press.
Spack, Ruth. 1988. Initiating ESL students into the academic discourse community: How far should we go? TESOL Quarterly, 22. 29-51.
Stern, H. H. 1983. Fundamental concepts of language teaching. Oxford: Oxford University Press.
Swain, Merrill and Sharon Lapkin. 1989. Canadian immersion and adult second language teach-ing: What's the connection. Modern Language Journal. 73. 150-159.
Takashima, Hideyuki. 1987. To what extent are non-native speakers qualified to correct free composition? A case study. British Journal of Language Teaching. 25. 43-48.
Terry, Robert M. 1989. Teaching and evaluating writing as a communicative skill. Foreign Language Annals. 22. 43-54.
Walker, Ronald W. 1982. Text manipulation techniques and foreign language composition. Unterrichtspraxis. 15. 232-239.
Walz, Joel. 1989. Context and contextualized language practice in foreign language teaching. Modern Language Journal. 73. 160-168.
Zamel, Vivian. 1985. Responding to student writing. TESOL Quarterly. 19. 79-101.

Linguistics, language pedagogy, and teachers' technical cultures

Robert C. Kleinsasser
Memphis State University
Sandra J. Savignon
University of Illinois at Urbana

At the close of the 1950s few American foreign language (FL) teachers had even heard of applied linguistics, let alone guessed the impact that this new field was about to have on their profession. The application of linguistic theory to foreign language teaching was soon to bring dramatic changes to classroom methods, materials, and testing. The 'New Key' in language teaching, as it came to be known, would be a systematic, principled approach based on some of the best current descriptions of language and language behavior.

The story of applied linguistics and FL teaching in the United States has its beginning in the 1960s, when audio-lingual theories of language learning changed the nature of language classrooms around the country. In the decades since those early years, theories of language and language behavior have evolved. Subsequent research into the nature of language acquisition has brought with it new insights and raised further questions. What has not changed, however, is the concern for a systematic, principled approach to teaching, that is to say, teaching practice grounded in theory. Along with their ESL colleagues, FL teachers look to applied linguistic research for insight and innovation in curriculum, methods, and evaluation.

Or do they? The representation of a language teaching profession looking for guidance to linguistic theory and, more recently, second language acquisition (SLA) theory is flattering to those linguists and applied linguists who presume to offer their insights. However, the implications of linguistic and applied linguistic research for language teaching are often unclear, or require a full appreciation of the complex nature of learning and contexts of learning before they can be understood. SLA research only recently has begun to focus on language learning in classroom settings, moreover. Classroom language learning was the focus of a number of studies in the 1960s and early 1970s (e.g. Scherer and Wertheimer 1964, Smith 1970, Savignon 1972). However,

L2 classrooms were not a major interest of the SLA research that rapidly gathered momentum in the years that followed. The full range of variables present in educational settings was an obvious deterrent. Other difficulties included the lack of well-defined classroom processes to serve as variables and lack of agreement as to what constituted learning "success." Confusion of form-focused drill with meaning-focused communication persisted in many of the textbook exercises and language test prototypes that directly or indirectly shaped curricula. Not surprisingly, researchers eager to establish SLA as a worthy field of inquiry turned their attention to more narrow, quantitative studies of the acquisition of selected morphosyntactic features.

Recent initiatives include the analysis of activity or task-based curricula. Researchers are looking at classroom language events, breaking them down into units of analysis with a view to establishing a typology of tasks that teachers frequently use. Since tasks determine the opportunities for language use and for the interpretation, expression, and negotiation of meaning, their systematic description constitutes the first step in establishing a relationship between task and learning outcomes.

Teacher preparation and expectations are another part of the overall picture. Surprisingly little systematic inquiry has been conducted into language teacher perceptions and practices. Anecdotal evidence suggests, however, that FL classrooms around the U. S. today do not, in the main, reflect the communication based, proficiency orientation widely promoted in teacher conferences and workshops throughout the 80s. The discrepancy between what we say and what we do can be seen in textbooks. Publishers talk about negotiation of meaning, sociolinguistic competence, and whole language; however, their learner materials continue to offer a familiar four skills program of listening, speaking, reading, and writing, with token inclusion of a few cultural clichés. Innovation is blocked, they say, by market place demands. Creative authors are pressed to conform.

Similarly, teachers in training note the discrepancies between what they learn in methods courses about the importance of opportunities to interpret, express, and negotiate meaning and what they often observe in foreign language classrooms. The following comments excerpted from the observation reports of a group of foreign language teacher education majors tell the story:

> The chairs in both classes were arranged in straight parallel rows set up so that they faced the teacher.
> It was obvious that the focus of the course was on the form of the language rather than on the function. Class time was spent on doing exercises out of the textbook as well as filling in the blanks on worksheets.

As in the first year class, all grammar explanations occurred in the L1. Whether it was review or a new lesson, English prevailed. In a third year class, I had hoped to see more extensive use of Spanish.

The fourth year class was similar to the first year class in the amount of French that was used. All student and teacher talk was in English. (Savignon 1991:40-41; for discussion of similar findings in English as a foreign language classrooms, see Savignon 1990)

Yet there do exist classrooms in which language is used to convey meaning and learners develop the rudimentary communicative skills they need for continued language study and experience. Classroom teachers can be found who experiment with and adopt communicative, experiential approaches to teaching, teaching based on current SLA theory. The key to understanding how curricular innovation happens lies not with linguistic theory or SLA research, but with an understanding of teachers' technical cultures and how they develop. The following first-person account by Robert Kleinsasser, an FL teacher turned educational researcher, looks at the technical cultures of foreign language teachers in a selected sample of U.S. secondary schools.

* * *

My interest in looking at the technical cultures of FL teachers emerged from my experience as a classroom teacher of German followed by advanced study in linguistic theory, SLA, and educational research. From a liberal arts and sciences perspective, I became familiar with precepts for elaborating communicative (or proficiency) goals—the ideas of grammatical, sociolinguistic, discourse, and strategic competencies (Canale and Swain 1980, Savignon 1983). Courses in education contributed to my knowledge base regarding learner styles of learning and teacher styles of teaching, highlighting the diversity in strategies of both learning and teaching. From both disciplines, I also heard the importance of the classroom context. The linguistic perspective emphasized the importance of an 'acquisition rich environment' wherein opportunities for second language (L2) use are a priority. The educational perspective emphasized the importance of a 'learning enriched environment', a context for learners and teachers that supports, encourages, and nurtures the acquisition of knowledge.

Once into my studies, I was given the assignment of supervising FL teacher education undergraduates going out to language classrooms for the first time. The differences in classroom/school contexts were striking. Teachers in training were often placed in contexts that bore little resemblance to environments that are either language acquisition or learning enriched. Student teachers were often bewildered, moreover, because they had not been taught how to teach directly from a textbook. The realities of teaching were remarkably different from the ideas and innovations to which they had been introduced in their language methods and education courses.

I began searching the literature for help in understanding the enormous inconsistencies between knowledge and practice. I found little evidence regarding FL classroom contexts and even less research in FL education that actually considered the perceptions and environments of FL teachers. Indeed, after reviewing ten years of the ACTFL Annual Bibliography (1977-1987), Bernhardt and Hammadou (1987:293) concluded that the research base in FL education was comprised essentially of the perceptions of FL 'educators'. 'Up until now, the field has relied on the discussions among experienced foreign language educators about the educational needs of foreign language teachers as the experts have perceived them, rather than on the principled collection of data and information'. Typical teachers' perceptions of their workplace along with their instructional habits were a vital missing piece of the knowledge base.

The importance and relevance of this perspective is undeniable, as Clark (1979:31) emphasizes: 'Teachers and students are seen as purposive agents whose thoughts, plans, perceptions, and intentions influence their behavior. The social context in which teaching and learning take place is considered an important source of explanation for classroom phenomena'. Additionally, recent research completed in elementary and middle schools suggests that teachers' perceptions of their work, and the school conditions in which these perceptions are embedded, determine in no small way what students actually learn (Ashton and Webb 1986, Rosenholtz 1989). Moreover, educational change literature strongly recommends that any attempt at change consider teacher beliefs, teaching strategies, and teaching materials (Fullan 1991).

In short, what this means for second language education is that the improvement of the United States' scandalous incompetence in second languages requires consideration of what it is like for teachers to teach in schools. In essence, to influence the state of the art, proponents of educational reform must first come to terms with the current state of that art. Those who are interested in developing and maintaining language acquisition and learning enriched environments must first get to know the current conditions of classrooms, staffrooms, and schools. This is no small task.

A promising theoretical notion in understanding teachers' perceptions of their workplace is 'social organizational thought'. Perrow (1986:11) contends that "organizations are tools for shaping the world as one wishes to shape it". Consequently, the existence of the organization is defined by its participants; in the case of FL teaching this means that

FL teachers define their job according to their school (and district) and the degree of autonomy that that school (and district) accords them in developing their instructional programs. In order to understand second language teachers' definitions of their organization, their 'perceptions' and behaviors must be gathered and analyzed. These perceptions and behaviors can serve as data to define and describe teachers' 'technical cultures', the processes designed to accomplish an organization's goals and determine how work is to be carried out (Dornbusch and Scott 1975; Perrow 1967 1986; Thompson 1967). Using survey and interview data, Rosenholtz' (1989) sociological model of inquiry begins to reveal technical cultures of elementary schools through teachers' perceptions. However, survey and interview information uncover only 'perceptions' of teacher work environments, they do not document teacher 'behavior'. It is important to note that technical cultures mirror what the organization 'does' rather than what it professes to be. Direct observation is needed, therefore, to more clearly describe the context in which FL teachers find themselves.

A strategy that can aid in understanding and documenting FL teachers' technical culture, then, is 'triangulation'—the use of three or more differing collection strategies to affirm and articulate the validity of evidence each produces. By using multiple measures, it is possible to concentrate on the point at which a series of independent, indirect, and perhaps weak indicators converge to minimize their separate errors and maximize their overall validity (Williamson, Karp, Dalphin, and Gray 1982). Surveys, interviews, and micro-ethnographic observations were the three types of strategies I chose to gain a better understanding of the technical cultures in U.S. secondary school FL programs (Kleinsasser 1989). The interviews documented FL teachers' perceptions of their environment by allowing them to answer open-ended questions about their work. The micro-ethnographic observations documented FL teachers' behavior during class periods, in particular the interaction(s) with students during class and also FL teacher interaction(s) with colleagues in the school building. The survey documented FL teacher perceptions of their working conditions.

FL teachers in the four midwestern American high schools included in the study revealed two distinct types of technical cultures. One certain and nonroutine, the other uncertain and routine. The labels of certainty/uncertainty and routine/nonroutine serve to distinguish between varying teaching technical cultures. An understanding and clearer explication of these specific terms will emerge in the observations that follow.

The greatest difference between the two technical cultures of these FL teachers was the extent to which they collaborated. Uncertain/routine teachers tended to define their particular culture individually and separately from their co-workers. Offering little evidence of collaboration and cohesiveness, they appeared to see their work environment as isolated, accepting sole responsibility for instructional duties as the normal state of affairs. When teachers talked to other teachers in the school, they relied heavily on topics unrelated to school, class, and student issues. An example of this isolation is related by a French teacher:

> There isn't a foreign language department. I never talk to the members of the foreign language department cause they do not happen to be in my prep period by design. So you never talk to members of your department. You talk to the people with whom you happen to share [the same] prep period that I have. So, it's not ever. Do I ever talk to people in the foreign language department, the answer is no. There are three separate persons who go their separate ways and never the three shall meet.

In contrast, certain/nonroutine teachers talked to each other concerning school and instructional issues. They tended to interact for purposes of problem solving, resolution, and garnering fresh ideas. Resolution is used here in the sense of improved instructional practice that helps students learn, that alleviates classroom boredom, and that allows teachers to learn and grow with their colleagues, not only within the FL department but within the school as well. In these environments, teachers defined their reality by what they did in their schools, and this allowed them to work together for their own benefit as well as for their students' learning. Although teachers in certain/non-routine technical cultures ran into classroom and school problems almost daily, they felt they could do something about them. Rather than supporting an almost fatalistic sense of defeat that prevailed in schools with an uncertain/routine technical culture, their school's context provided a variety of avenues for successes. This ethos was exemplified by a Spanish teacher when asked, 'What are the most typical things you talk about with your colleagues?'

> Well, with other foreign language teachers, I think sometimes, it's you know, we discuss we wish we had more opportunity to get new ideas, try to get new ideas from each other. Someone in my particular field, a lot of time we just talk about what are you doing in class and do you have any ideas for me and I might offer suggestions. And if it's other faculty in general within the school it might be about the kids or just day to day, you know, events that are going on in school.

Collaboration is but one of the variables that aid in classifying and documenting technical cultures. Other variables such as parent involvement, positive feedback, goal setting, cohesiveness, managing student behavior, and teachers' learning opportunities are also important contributors (see the Appendix for descriptions of these variables). Space does not allow for further elaboration of these topics here. Suffice it to say, both quantitative and qualitative data concerning these variables further help describe the foreign language teaching environments in which instructors find themselves. What readily emerges from the data is that the greater the manifestation of these variables, the greater the teacher 'certainty' about a technical culture; the less these variables are manifested, the greater the teacher 'uncertainty' about a technical culture.

The more certain a technical culture could be classified, the more nonroutine teachers acted in their workplace. The more uncertain a technical culture could be classified, the more routine teachers acted in their workplace.

Discrete point, grammar centered topics, and vocabulary activities provided the basic focus observed in uncertain/routine technical cultures. Vocabulary memorization, verb conjugations, verb tense, and adjectives, along with direct translations, were the major themes for all classroom activities. In fact, typical vocabulary presentations had the instructor say the word with the class responding chorally; sometimes one to three students were then individually selected to repeat the same word. Completing textbook pattern drills and teacher-made worksheets, students sat at their desks and teachers called on them in row order. Typically, if the student's response was correct, the teacher would go on to the next student; if it was incorrect, the teacher would either give the correct response or recurrently call on the two or three particular individuals who always seemed to know the correct response. Finally, when grammatical structures were introduced, it was not at all uncommon to hear both teacher and student reading grammar points, word for word, directly from the textbook. Relying solely on themselves, it was not surprising that many teachers in uncertain technical cultures used the book exclusively for exercises and activities. Teachers' isolation shaped what they planned to accomplish in their classrooms and the textbook appeared to be these teachers' best colleague.

Examples from observations in two separate uncertain/nonroutine environments are revealing:

> The class completed three exercises from the book. The students responded in row order, one student was not paying attention and the teacher asked him if he was lost. He was, so she went to the next person. The major task was verb conjugations. Then the teacher said for tomorrow they had to write out exercises 5, 6, and 7. These were the exercises they had just completed in class. (German 1)
>
> The teacher presented grammar points. He read the grammar explanation directly from the book. Then the teacher asked the students to translate the Spanish sentence to English and he did quickly note

that yesterday's handout that he gave might explain it better than the book. Then he went on to the next exercise. The class completed this exercise in row order. The class went over the verb *tener* on page 220. When that was done, the teacher handed out a worksheet. He told them that this worksheet was similar to a test and the more practice the student got, the more practice on whether they should choose the imperfect or preterit tense of the verb form they would have. The teacher then gave the assignment which was to complete activities 6 and 7 (which were just completed in class) and a short worksheet. (Spanish 3)

Activities in certain/nonroutine technical cultures were strikingly different. They included students writing a play about a roman wedding, in Latin, first year French students reading French newspapers, and students designing and completing scavenger hunts in Spanish. Although teachers in nonroutine technical cultures did complete controlled practice exercises, they also involved their students with other language learning experiences. Learners and teachers used their new language for communication. Students in these schools spoke to each other and their teachers in Spanish, Latin, and French before and after class periods. In fact, Spanish students in one school talked to each other in Spanish after school while working on their foreign language fair. And the students were at different instructional levels! At no time was this type of language use evident in the uncertain/routine schools. Students in nonroutine technical cultures seemed motivated to use their second language with their classmates and teachers as a means of communication.

The practice and translation exercises that supplemented other more communicative activities were personalized and/or contextualized. For example, in a Spanish 1 class students read and translated a selection dealing with basketball. Afterward, the teacher asked questions about the school's basketball team and games, allowing learners to use the same vocabulary but in a context that involved the students' school environment. Not relying strictly on book exercises and explanations, nonroutine teachers attempted to overcome classroom tedium and boredom. They took language teaching one step further by using the new language in the classroom and making sure that learners themselves had the opportunity for self expression.

Teachers in certain/nonroutine schools randomly selected students to respond to a much greater extent than in uncertain/routine schools. What is interesting is that the clear majority of students were called on and actively participated. Furthermore, in many classes it was not unusual for students to raise their hands and assist the instructor in explaining a point for a student having difficulty or an exercise that started out to be a teacher-student-teacher response pattern and ended as a group activity—everyone working together to complete and understand the task at hand. Most of the time the bell rang for the period to end, but students would be too involved in the activity, not realizing how quickly time passed. Unlike students in the uncertain/routine schools who spent the last few minutes of their class piling their books and talking to each other in English, students in certain/nonroutine classrooms used the second language and appeared to be continually active in their second language acquisition process. Teachers in certain/nonroutine technical cultures have a story to tell that differs from that heard from teachers in uncertain/routine technical cultures. The following remarks are taken from interview and observation data:

> I think that within every class period, every day, every level, you need to do a variety of things. Sometimes you don't get them all done, because of the 50 minute limitation. But you need to hit at least two every day. I do only Spanish with third and fourth year [students]. But I don't hesitate to refer back to English. That may be a problem, but I make the conscious decision of keeping the students with me so they understand my instructions, instead of staying in the language. (Spanish Instructor)
>
> During the translation exercise the students told the teacher that she could translate and they would tell her if she was wrong. She took them up on their challenge and it was quite amazing how all students got involved in listening to her translate and see if she would do something wrong. And they were checking with her on some of the words she chose for translation, instead of some of the ones they chose. (Latin 1)
>
> First the teacher had the class do a book exercise that involved a review of verb conjugations. Then the teacher presented three more new verbs. It was a very lecture oriented presentation. Not using the book, the teacher would talk about the verb, say the verb, write it on the board, and then give some examples of how to use the verb. After the examples, the students got involved with the teacher and tried to come up with other examples. All of the students did take out pieces of paper and were writing the examples offered by both teacher and classmates. (Spanish 2)

What the data begin to show is that besides routine versus nonroutine pedagogical practice, foreign language teachers' use of the L2 in the two (technical) cultures also varies. The routine environment reveals heavy teacher reliance on controlled practice, whereas the nonroutine situations reveal teacher tendencies to incorporate communicative practice to a greater extent, occasionally incorporating real language use. The data suggest certain/nonroutine teacher emphasis on language use as well as on language form, whereas uncertain/routine teachers emphasize language form, or usage, to the exclusion of language use. Thus, the notions of routine and nonroutine are further elaborated by the FL teachers' task conceptions of language form and language use.

We begin to see some interchanges in the typology: some foreign language teachers' particular task conceptions of certainty fit with their classroom behaviors of nonroutineness, other foreign language teachers' particular task conceptions of uncertainty fit with routine behaviors. Two distinct technical cultures emerge: one where teachers work together with colleagues and learners and one where teachers work by themselves; one where teachers think all learners can acquire a second language and one where teachers suspect that some students have no foreign language learning ability; one where learners have the opportunity to use the second language for communication, and one where students spend class time talking about the foreign language grammar in English; one where the learners, teachers, parents, administration, and community together shape a successful learning environment and one where teachers individually define their idiosyncratic classroom situations.

The situations in which foreign language teachers find themselves are real. Many of their pedagogical and linguistic ideas are determined by the environment in which they participate daily. Many of their day-to-day decisions rely on practice with little theory. Uncertain/routine technical cultures are theoretically exclusive. This should come as no surprise, for as Hargreaves (1984) suggests, classrooms are culturally exclusive of formal theory. Yet, surprisingly, in certain/nonroutine technical cultures there are notions of communicative language teaching (bits and pieces of linguistic, sociolinguistic, second language acquisition, and education theories). This type of technical culture may not exclude theoretical notions altogether, but provide a context that seeks to uncover what theoretical notions have to offer. As educational restructuring efforts in the U.S. seek to change rules, roles, relationships, and results, the concept of technical culture may help to define current rules, roles, relationships, and results. Additionally, for linguistics, second language acquisition theory, and other disciplines to influence FL instruction, certain/nonroutine environments will need to be developed and nurtured and uncertain/routine cultures modified.

* * *

We have much yet to learn about the nature of language and language development. Our quest for principles and parameters has only just begun. Yet few would argue that our understanding of the collaborative nature of meaning making is not far richer today that it was a quarter of a century ago. The study of language, i.e. *linguistics*, continues to broaden. As questions of situated language use continue to be raised, specially trained ethnographers have come to replace the native speakers that were once the authority on how language worked. And *applied linguistics* has emerged as a young and, not surprisingly, occasionally irreverent field of inquiry.

Drawing on current understanding of second language acquisition both inside and outside the classroom, language teaching methodologists now offer a view of the language learner as a partner in learning; they encourage learner participation in communicative events and self-assessment of progress. In keeping with second language acquisition theory, methodologists advise learners to take communicative risks and to focus on the development of learning strategies. Valued as are the reasoned proposals of linguists, applied linguists, and second/foreign language teaching methodologists, however, exploration of the potential of communicative language teaching cannot proceed without the involvement of classroom teachers. Teachers have intimate knowledge of the teaching context. They are needed on research teams to help frame the questions to be addressed as well as to interpret the outcome for methods and materials.

Teaching contexts vary widely. The experience of a secondary school teacher of English in San Juan differs from that of a teacher in Osaka or Marseille. And these experiences differ, in turn, from those of teachers of Spanish, Japanese, or French in Houston, Pittsburgh, or Des Moines. While considerable attention has been directed to 'linguistic' contexts of learning and to comparative/contrastive analyses of individual languages, the instructional context itself has been neglected. In our quest for the improvement of language teaching, we have overlooked the language teacher. Exploration of the technical cultures operating in instructional settings, of teachers perceptions of what they do and why they do it, holds promise for understanding the frequently noted discrepancies between theoretical understanding of second/foreign language acquisition and classroom practice. The constraints of language classrooms are real. Tradition, learner attitudes, teacher preparation and expectations, and the instructional environment in general all contribute to and support teachers' technical cultures. Recommendations for methods and materials must take into account this reality. For them to do so, researchers, curriculum developers, and teachers will have to work together. Teamwork between linguists, methodologists and classroom teachers offers the best hope for the elaboration and diffusion of language teaching methods and materials that work, that encourage and support learners in the development of their communicative competence.

Appendix

Social organizational thought. The existence of any organization is defined by its participants in a particular work environment. The environment heavily influences what the worker decides or decides not to do.

Organizations are tools for shaping the world as one wishes it to be shaped (Perrow 1986).

Technical culture. The processes designed to accomplish an organization's goals (Perrow 1967, 1986; Thompson 1967).

Encompasses the nature of activities to be carried out in performing an organization's tasks and embodies the procedures, knowledge and skills related to attaining organizations goals. In essence a technical culture determines how work is to be carried out (Dornbusch and Scott 1975).

The technical culture of education rests on abstract systems of beliefs about relationships among teachers, teaching materials, and pupils; but learning theories assume the presence of these variables and proceed from that point (Thompson 1967).

Figure 1. Typology. With parameters of certain, uncertain, routine, and nonroutine outside the square, the space in the boxes represents the extent to which an organization's technical culture is certain/routine, certain/nonroutine, etc.

	Routine	Nonroutine
Certain		
Uncertain		

Triangulation. The use of three or more differing collection strategies to affirm and articulate the validity of evidence each produces. These multiple measures make it possible to concentrate on the point at which a series of independent, indirect, and perhaps weak indicators can converge to minimize their separate errors and maximize their overall validity. (Williamson et al. 1982)

Description of variables (Kleinsasser 1989)

Teacher certainty: Strength of teachers' beliefs in their own instructional skills and students' learning potential.

Teacher cohesiveness: Feelings of temporal, physical, or psychological separation from other teachers and principal.

Teacher collaboration: Extent to which teachers engage their colleagues in requests for and offers of assistance about the substance of teaching.

Teacher evaluation: Frequency, objectivity, and clarity of evaluation as well as duration of supervisor's classroom observation.

Faculty goal setting: Goal directedness or task orientation of faculty and principal activity.

Management of student behavior: Presence of rules for student conduct and how consistently those rules are applied.

Parent involvement: Extent to which parents are involved in their children's learning.

Teachers' learning opportunities: Degree of teachers' experimentation with new ideas in the classroom and their opportunities for learning new teaching strategies and skills.

References

Ashton, P. T., and R. B. Webb. 1986. Making a difference. New York: Longman.
Bernhardt, E., and J. Hammadou. 1987. A decade of research in foreign language teacher education. Modern Language Journal, 71, 289-299.
Canale, M., and M. Swain. 1980. Theoretical bases of communicative approaches to second language teaching and testing. Applied Linguistics, 1, 1-47.
Clark, C. M. 1979. Five faces of research on teaching. Educational Leadership, 37, 29-32.
Dornbusch, S. M., and W. R. Scott. 1975. Evaluation and the exercise of authority. San Francisco: Jossey-Bass.
Fullan, M. 1991. The new meaning of educational change. New York: Teachers College Press.
Hargreaves, A. 1984. Experience counts, theory doesn't: How teachers talk about their work. Sociology of Education, 57, 244-254.
Kleinsasser, R. C. 1989. Foreign language teaching: A tale of two technical cultures. Unpublished doctoral dissertation, University of Illinois at Urbana-Champaign.
Perrow, C. 1967. A framework for the comparative analysis of organizations. American Sociological Review, 32, 194-208.
Perrow, C. 1986. Complex organizations: A critical essay. 3rd ed. New York: Random House.
Rosenholtz, S. J. 1989. Teachers' workplace. New York: Longman.
Savignon, S. J. 1972. Communicative competence: An experiment in foreign language teaching. Philadelphia: Center for Curriculum Development.
Savignon, S. J. 1983. Communicative competence: Theory and classroom practice. Reading, Mass.: Addison-Wesley.
Savignon, S. J. 1990. Communicative language teaching: definitions and directions. In: J. E. Alatis, ed., Georgetown University Round Table on Languages and Linguistics 1990: Linguistics, language teaching, and language acquisition: The interdependence of theory, practice and research. Washington, D.C.: Georgetown University Press.
Savignon, S. J. 1991. Research on the role of communication in classroom-based foreign language acquisition: On the interpretation, expression, and negotiation of meaning. In: Barbara F. Freed, ed., Foreign language acquisition research and the classroom. Lexington, MA: D. C. Heath.
Scherer, G., and M. Wertheimer. 1964. A psycholinguistic experiment in foreign language teaching. New York: McGraw-Hill.
Smith, P. 1970. A comparison of the cognitive and audio-lingual approaches to foreign language instruction: The Pennsylvania foreign language project. Philadelphia: Center for Curriculum Development.
Thompson, J. D. 1967. Organizations in action. St. Louis: McGraw-Hill.
Williamson, J. B., D. A. Karp, J. R. Dalphin, and P. S. Gray. 1982. The research craft: An introduction to social research methods. Boston: Little, Brown.

Metacognitive strategies in L2 writing: A case for task knowledge

Anita L. Wenden
York College, City University of New York

Purpose of the study. This is an exploratory study which sought insight into the following relatively unexplored questions regarding the use of metacognitive strategies in the regulation of a writing task: (1) What mental operations or procedures are involved in the implementation of each of the metacognitive strategies? (2) In the course of completing a writing task, what kind of task knowledge is required for the execution of each of the metacognitive strategies? And (3) What insight does the study of metacognitive strategies shed on the use of cognitive strategies?

Definitions

METACOGNITIVE STRATEGIES are mental operations or procedures which learners use to regulate their learning. The cognitive literature (e.g. Brown et al. 1983) refers to three main kinds of metacognitive strategies named in terms of the function that they serve and that are applicable across all kinds of learning tasks, i.e. planning, monitoring, and evaluating. In the literature, terms such as regulatory skills, cognitive control, self-regulation and self-direction also refer to the functions of these three metacognitive strategies.

TASK KNOWLEDGE refers to what learners need to know about the tasks teachers set for them (e.g. 'revise your composition') or the tasks they set for themselves (e.g. 'I want to practise my pronunciation') in order to accomplish them successfully. Task knowledge is one category of metacognitive knowledge—the stable, statable, if sometimes inaccurate, knowledge which learners have stored in long term memory regarding learning.

The cognitive literature (Flavell and Wellman 1977; Flavell 1979, 1981a) and the literature in second language learning (Wenden 1987, 1991; Breen 1987) describe one or more of the following dimensions of task knowledge: knowledge of the purpose and nature of the task, knowledge of whether the task requires deliberate learning, and knowledge of task demands, which includes knowing (a) what resources (including knowledge) are necessary to complete the task, (b) how to go about completing it, and (c) whether the task is hard or easy.[1]

COGNITIVE STRATEGIES are mental operations or steps used by learners to learn new information and apply it to specific learning tasks. Based on the view of human learning put forth by information processing scientists, these strategies may be used at any one of the four following steps of learning: (a) selection of what is to be learned, (b) comprehension of the selected information, (c) storage, and (d) retrieval of what has been comprehended.[2] Cognitive strategies are task specific.

Rationale. Thus far, research on learner strategies has focused on identifying, defining, and classifying strategies, distinguishing learners primarily on the basis of the number and range of strategies they use, and determining which strategies are used for which tasks (e.g. Wenden and Rubin 1987, Cohen 1990, O'Malley and Chamot 1990). It has not really addressed the relationships between the main classes of strategies nor looked at the role task knowledge plays in the regulation of a learning task.

The scant research done on metacognitive knowledge has classified learners' beliefs and knowledge about their language learning process, including task knowledge (Wenden 1982, 1983; Horowitz 1987), but has not attempted to see how task knowledge relates to the use of metacognitive strategies in the performance of a particular task. In her research on comprehension strategies used by L2 readers, Block (1986) identified ten general strategies used by L2 readers to comprehend and to monitor their comprehension. Of the ten, two, in fact, refer to the use of task knowledge: rhetorical knowledge (strategy 2) and world knowledge (strategy 6). Moreover, the description of strategy six notes the relationship of task knowledge to other aspects of the reading process. However, because the focus of the report is on strategies, the significance of this information is not fully exploited.

In a study conducted at the University of Notre Dame, Holec (1987) examined both how language learners self-direct their learning and the quality of skill learners brought to the planning and to the evaluation of the learning activities necessary to meet particular linguistic needs. The study also showed how skills changed and improved over time. However, in assessing the skill change, the researchers made no reference to task knowledge nor to the mental procedures involved in planning and evaluation. O'Malley and Chamot (1985a, 1990) in their research have

---

1 See Wenden (1991) for a more complete description of each of these dimensions.
2 The names of these processes or stages vary slightly depending on which version of the information processing theory writers may adhere to. See, for example, the discussion in O'Malley and Chamot (1990).

consistently distinguished metacognitive from cognitive strategies but they have not looked at how these interact in the performance of a learning task. Their most recent taxonomy of learning strategies (1990:137-139) includes seven metacognitive strategies—four of which refer to planning processes, one to monitoring, one to self-evaluation and one, 'problem identification', to a dimension of task knowledge. To my knowledge, however, they have not, so far, attempted to determine the particular mental operations that constitute the metacognitive strategies nor studied the task knowledge required for their implementation.

As regards the research on writing processes in L1 and L2, Cohen's 1990 summary of this research describes nine strategies (or processes) used by effective writiers, but planning is the only metacognitive strategy that is explicitly mentioned. Moreover, no mention is made of research on task knowledge. In her review of the process research in L1 writing, Stein (1986) criticizes this lack, noting specifically that while the research has alerted us to the importance of accessing knowledge at every point in the writing process, no explicit description has been made of how knowledge interacts with process strategies and what types of knowledge are necessary to construct a coherent text.

While no systematic research has been done on the areas outlined by the research questions, the use of metacognitive strategies and the application of knowledge demands relevant to a task have been noted in recent learner strategy research as a factor for explaining the ineffectiveness of otherwise strategically active learners (Vann and Abraham 1990) and as a characteristic of effective learners (O'Malley and Chamot 1990). The importance of these two factors for successfully navigating one's way through a learning task is further corroborated by research in other areas.

Literature on expert learners notes that it is their domain specific knowledge and their knowledge of how to organize their approach to a problem that distinguish them from novices (Anderson 1985). In their review of the literature on L1 reading, Baker and Brown (1984a) list the following aspects of task knowledge as a prerequisite for both self-regulation and effective reading, i.e. knowledge of the active nature of reading, knowledge of basic strategies for reading and remembering, knowledge of the simple rules of text construction, knowledge of the importance of using background knowledge. Research on L2 reading based on schema theory (e.g. Johnson 1982; Carrell 1983 and 1987) has illustrated how readers' comprehension can be influenced by the extent of their familiarity with the content and rhetorical structure of a text (both examples of task knowledge).

Included in Stein's review and critique of the research on knowledge and process in the acquisition of writing skills in an L1 are reports on the results of several research projects that have demonstrated that writing deficits are also due to a writer's lack of declarative knowledge about different dimensions of the writing task rather than a lack of processing strategies. In her state of the art review on writing research, Connor (1987) includes reports on how instructional strategies adapting methods from text analysis to teach students how to use thetorical knowldege in writing or revising their writing had positive results. Finally, in research on unskilled L2 writers (Raimes 1985), factors listed as determining whether or not a writer is skilled are examples of task knowledge (i.e. language proficiency, knowledge of L1 and L2 writing) and cognitive control (i.e. self-evaluation of L1 and L2 writing).

Procedures

Subject and task. Eight students of ESL were required to write a composition at the computer and to introspect as they wrote. That is, they were expected to observe themselves in the process of writing and to reveal the process that went on before writing, during pauses that punctuated the writing, and just after they had written something. The composition was typical of the type they would have to write in order to pass from the ESL sequence into the regular English sequence (see Appendix 1 for the list of topics). The eight subjects, all enrolled in an ESL course that met nine hours weekly, were taking undergraduate courses in a senior college. They had scored from 76-86 on Michigan's English Language Placement test and were considered high-intermediate.

Training. The composition was written at the computer after a two to four-hour orientation and practice session which had familiarized the students with the word processing program they would be using. Students who could not type were also introduced to a typing program and encouraged to develop facility at the keyboard.

There was no advance training in introspection. At the outset of the session, students were given a list of topics to choose from. Having chosen a topic, they were asked to start writing and to report what they were thinking as they wrote. The first part of the session clarified what was intended by this request. In the case of four of the students, the request presented almost no problem. They introspected almost spontaneously, without too much prompting on my part. Others needed more prompting, but eventually contributed more spontaneously. Yet others needed prompting all the way through.

Prompting included questions such as 'what's happening?' 'what were you thinking when you did that?' and was sometimes followed by further probes when it was deemed necessary to determine that student responses were actual accounts of their thinking and not justifications or inferences. Otherwise, interventions were intended to clarify and/or verify what they had said or done.

Length of session. The first session lasted two hours. A second appointment was made for one student who had not finished and for two others who wished to revise their first draft. These second appointments also lasted two hours. In those instances when students did not decide to revise spontaneously, I asked them if they felt the composition was ready to hand in. Except for one, who said she would have revised it if it had been a pen-in-hand assignment, the others felt there was no need for further revision.

Recording procedures. As students wrote, I copied what they wrote and noted all observable behaviors in brackets at the point in the sentence where they occurred. When students paused, made changes, reread, if they did not choose to spontaneously report what they were thinking/had just thought, I asked. Their responses were tape recorded and numbered. That is, when the student stopped reporting, I spoke the number of the response into the tape recorder (i.e. #1, 2, 3 . . .) and also noted the same number at the point in the sentence where the report was made. The recorded reports for each sentence were transcribed and the notes of the observed behaviors included at the appropriate places.

Data analysis. First, statements in each transcript that referred to planning, evaluation, and monitoring were so coded, and references to different kinds of task knowledge were labelled. Cognitive strategies that learners reported using were also identified. The coded statements were then translated into a list of verbal and nonverbal behaviors (Appendix 2) and the list was used as a basis for a second more detailed coding. This second coding defined both the metacognitive and cognitive strategies in behavioral terms and refined the initial set of categories developed to identify the various kinds of task knowledge. Categories of metacognitive knowledge other than task knowledge that had been referred to were also noted. (See Appendix 3 for a brief excerpt from a coded transcript.)

Descriptive profile of metacognitive strategies in writing. The profiles of each of the metacognitive strategies to be presented here are based on a summary of the data analysis of the three most successful writers.[3]

---

3 The compositions of these writers received the highest rating for development and language use from five instructors who regularly taught and assessed compositions of students at this level.

Planning

Operations/procedures that constitute the planning strategy. Planning consisted of two distinct operations: KNOWLEDGE RETRIEVAL and DECISION MAKING.[4]

Knowledge retrieval. Writers had to access the knowledge they had available for the task at hand. Reference to the fact that they were engaged in this operation was made when learners said, 'I'm thinking . . .', 'I'm looking for . . .', and variations thereof. Such statements were sometimes accompanied by nonverbal behavior, such as a pause or looking up, or by the description of a strategy that was used to help elicit the knowledge.

Writers engaged in knowledge retrieval before writing and while writing. Before writing, knowledge was an essential part of the decision-making process regarding what they would write about and how. While writing, the need for knowledge retrieval followed upon a decision about how to implement some aspect of their rhetorical plan or to revise. Sometimes it occurred as writers sought the criteria they needed to evaluate what they had written.

Decision making. At the outset of writing, decision making followed upon knowledge retrieval. Writers made decisions about their rhetorical plan: what to write about, what their views were on the topic, how to support their views and how to present this information, both rhetorically and linguistically. As writers proceeded with the development of their overall rhetorical plan, they further decided to utilize strategies when obstacles to knowledge retrieval were encountered, and after evaluating what they had written, decided whether or not they would revise, and if so when (immediately or later), to what extent, and how.

Evidence of the decision making related to rhetorical plans was made when writers announced what they intended to do. Decisions about strategies usually included the actual choice of the strategy to be utilized. Sometimes decisions that followed upon evaluation were verbalized. Others were inferred from the behavior that accompanied a verbalized evaluation, i.e. writers deleted, changed, added.

---

4 These two operations are similar to procedures generally referred to as 'determining objectives' and 'selecting resources (or methods and materials)' in definitions of planning in the cognitive literature (cf. Wenden 1987 for a review) and the literature of self-directed learning (cf. Holec 1981).

Planning and task knowledge. In the planning of their writing task, learners had to access and make decisions about three kinds of task knowledge: world knowledge, rhetorical knowledge, and linguistic knowledge.

World knowledge. Learners had to decide what to write about. This meant accessing their world knowledge about the suggested topic(s) and the knowledge of the beliefs and values they held about the topic they chose to write about. The following sets of questions, explicitly or implicitly stated in the writers' reports, outline the world knowledge that the three writers reported needing to write on the topic of illegal immigrants.

Choosing and structuring a topic. 'What shall I write about?' i.e. which of these topics am I sufficiently familiar with to select? 'What do I think about this topic?' i.e. What is my opinion?

e.g. 'I was thinking before of the topic . . . 'I was thinking about the title. I decided it's a big problem and my idea is I don't have . . . you know that I think they don't have to go back to their native countries.'

Developing and specifying ideas. 'What can I say to show that. . .? . . . to support this idea? . . . to develop this point in my thesis? What more can I add? What facts can I give to support my example? What other examples can I add? What can I say to explain? What's a related idea? . . . a more appropriate idea?'

e.g. 'I'm thinking how hard they work . . . I'm trying to find something with their work . . . something that really . . . you know generally they try to improve their personal benefits but without understanding, they also help the American society, the people, and everything.'

Rhetorical knowledge. Having decided on the topic and their views about it, writers were faced with the question of how to translate their mental representation into appropriate rhetorical form. To do this, they had to draw upon their knowledge of written discourse—of what they knew about how to organize an essay.

The following sets of questions, which outline the dimensions of rhetorical knowledge they reported using, show how writers moved back and forth from a broad focus on the whole composition, to a narrow focus on a single paragraph and to a narrower focus yet on single ideas within the paragraph that needed development:

Overall plan. 'How shall I organize this? How many points should I include in my thesis statement? Which ideas from my thesis need elaboration? Which one of these ideas do I discuss first, second, next? Where does this idea fit best? How do I start? What shall I say in my introduction? When is it appropriate to conclude? What kind of information goes into the conclusion?'

e.g. '... but I'm going to give first why is the problem and then I'm going to ... uh ... you know the against, the plus and the against, but my opinion, I will try to support my opinion.'

e.g. 'I don't really like ... I could put this one (i.e., the sentence she's just written) in the last one ... I was thinking this one could be to make the conclusion, but not there.'

Paragraph plans. 'How do I go about writing a paragraph? How do I start? With a general idea? or a specific idea? How can I present my main idea? How many ideas have to be developed in a paragraph?'

e.g. 'So I have to write a topic, no, a main sentence, main idea in the first paragraph ... Now I think this is the main sentence. Now I'm going to describe how this sentence works.'

Specifying techniques. 'How do I develop and/or specify ... ? Should I add a fact? ... an example? What kind of information is needed?'

e.g. 'So I will give facts to support my first main point.

Linguistic knowledge. Learners also needed appropriate grammar and vocabulary to translate their ideas and selected rhetorical plans into written prose.

The following sets of questions outline the dimensions of linguistic knowledge they reported needing:

Words. 'What word(s) can I use to be exact? ... emphatic? ... sound English? that means...? Which of these two words should I use?'

e.g. 'I'm thinking for a verb ... which one is better, .. is the best?'

Grammar. 'What's the grammar rule that applies in this instance? How do I apply this grammar rule?'

e.g. 'I'm thinking *operation* can be plural or singular?'

Grammar and vocabulary. 'How can I express my idea?'

e.g. '... Now I'm trying to put it in the way I'm thinking ... I have the idea in my mind but I can't express what I want to say.'

Planning and cognitive strategies. There were times when the writers were unsure about how to implement some aspect of their writing task or when they had difficulty retrieving the knowledge they needed. In such cases, they reported (or were observed) using five different kinds of strategies depending uon the nature of the problem. The selection of these strategies called upon another dimension of task knowledge—knowledge about which strategies might work (best) for that particular problem.[5]

Clarification. Clarification strategies were used by the three writers when they were unclear about (a) the implications of the writing task or of the ideas they had chosen to express, (b) the application of a relevant rule—to determine which of two alternatives would be better, and (c) the thematic coherence between ideas. To clarify they used one of the following strategies:

- self-questioning
- hypothesizing
- defining terms
- comparing

Retrieval. The following retrieval strategies were used primarily to elicit 'world knowledge':

- rereading aloud or silently what had been written
- writing in a lead-in word or expression (e.g. first ...)
- rereading the assigned question
- self-questioning
- writing till the idea would come
- summmarizing what had just been written (in terms of content or of rhetoric)
- thinking in one's native language

---

5 There is an overlap in the definition of strategic knowledge and task knowledge. Flavell lists strategic knowledge as a third category of metacognitive knowledge, i.e. learners' knowledge of which cognitive strategies to use for a given task. At the same time, knowledge of 'how to do a task', one aspect of task demands, includes knowing which strategies to use to complete it. Thus strategic knowledge is, in fact, a form of task knowledge.

The following strategies were used to retrieve 'linguistic knowledge':

- circumlocute (when they were looking for a word)
- write the same sentence several times changing it each time; then take the most correct.

Resourcing. When they were unable to retrieve the linguistic knowledge they needed, learners sought information from an outside source:

- ask researcher
- refer to a dictionary

Deferral. The writers also reported deferring the attempt to change/rewrite with the intent of returning later.

Avoidance. Writers gave up attempts to write about an idea they could not express and moved on to the next point. In the case of specific words and expressions they could not retrieve, they did not change their original version.

Evaluation

Operations/procedures that constitute evaluation. As implemented by the three writers, evaluation included three operations. (1) Writers reviewed what had been written, i.e. they reread either the single word, sentence or a longer piece of discourse. (2) They determined the criteria for evaluation, i.e. they verbalized the criteria used to assess their work. (3) They applied the criteria to their work, verbalizing their assessment. Sometimes steps (2) and (3) were combined, i.e. the criteria were made explicit in the writers' assessment.

Task knowledge and evaluation. In order to evaluate what they had written, L2 writers had to access and apply the following kinds of task knowledge: message knowledge, rhetorical knowledge, and linguistic knowledge.

Message knowledge. Message knowledge refers to the learners' understanding of what they want to say—of their views on the topic they are writing about. Message knowledge is the outcome of the planning process described earlier. Moreover, as writing process research has shown (see Zamel 1983, Raimes 1985), this particular category of knowledge changes as a writer proceeds through the writing task.

As illustrated in these three case studies, learners called upon their message knowledge to evaluate the 'acceptability' of what they had written. The following questions, implicitly or explicitly stated in their reports, show how the writers approached this evaluation: 'What do these ideas sound like? Do I like these ideas? Is this idea OK?'

e.g. 'I like the ideas, but I don't like the place . . .'

The next set of questions, also taken from the writers' reports, shows how message knowledge was used to determine the correspondence between the writer's intent and the written product: 'Is this what I want to say? Is my idea there? Is this an exact expression of my idea? Does this fit my meaning?'

e.g. Having completed a third paragraph (with difficulty), the writer says, 'Now my idea is expressed.'

Rhetorical knowledge. As noted in the discussion of planning, rhetorical knowledge refers to what learners know about how to organize and develop their ideas. Without rhetorical knowledge, learners cannot decide how best to present their ideas. Rhetorical knowledge is also drawn upon to evaluate their writing. The following sets of questions indicate how the three categories of rhetorical knowledge described earlier (i.e. knowledge of overall plans, paragraph plans, specifying techniques) were used to evaluate the appropriateness and adequacy of their writing:

Appropriateness. 'Is my supporting information appropriate? . . . my main idea sentence?'
Having just written the main idea sentence of a paragraph, the writer checks to see if it is related to his main thesis:

e.g. 'Before giving my example, I thing this [is] the main statement of this paragraph and it's the same thing, it's a part of the main (referring to his thesis sentence) . . .'

Adequacy. 'Is my main idea sufficiently developed? . . . is this paragraph? . . . this point? . . . the introduction? Were the ideas clearly written?'

e.g. 'I know this is not correct . . . because I know I have to explain why they have . . . they help American society and in what way. It's not enough to put the sentence without saying anything . . .'

Linguistic knowledge. In evaluating what they had written, the three writers drew upon their acquired knowledge of language structure and vocabulary. The following sets of questions outline how linguistic knowledge was used to determine the accuracy and appropriateness of their writing.

Accuracy. 'Is what I've written grammatically correct?' Writers had questions about the accuracy of inflection, word order, tense, punctuation.

> e.g. 'If I write 'present tense' here, the next sentence [he means 'clause'] must also be 'present/future tense' so . . .[he looks at his sentence] . . . here is 'present tense', here is 'present tense' also . . . OK.'

Appropriateness. 'Is my choice of words appropriate?'

> e.g. 'The idea it's OK, but . . . it's not the right way to say it.'

Evaluation and cognitive strategies. Verification was the only cognitive strategy utilized by these three writers to facilitate the evaluation process. That is, whenever they were uncertain as to the accuracy or appropriateness of their evaluations, they either checked their dictionary or asked the researcher for verification.

Monitoring

Operations/procedures that constitute monitoring. When monitoring, writers engaged in one of the following two mental operations: (1) problem recognition, or (2) problem assessment. The mental operation most often made explicit by the three writers was problem recognition. They acknowledged that they were having a problem executing some aspect of the task either in general terms (e.g. 'I'm not sure, I'm confused.') or in specific terms (e.g. 'I've got the idea but I want to write words . . .') The second operation of the monitoring strategy, referred to less often, was an assessment of the cause of the problem (e.g. '. . . I can't concentrate. It's a difficult topic. We've never discussed this before.').

Monitoring and task knowledge. While task knowledge was essential to the execution of planning and evaluation, it was a requisite for monitoring ONLY when writers assessed the cause of the problem they encountered, at which time they referred to some aspect of task knowledge as an explanation.[6] On the other hand, knowledge was the 'outcome'

---

6 In seeking reasons to explain the problems they encountered, learners also considered person knowledge, i.e. their own personal reactions to the task as well as the level of knowledge they brought to it.

of problem recognition. That is, recognizing that they were having difficulty provided writers with insight into the quality and extent of their knowledge and skills vis-à-vis some aspect of the writing task. This kind of knowledge is referred to as 'person knowledge' in the literature.

Monitoring and cognitive strategies. The previous definition of monitoring, based on the data provided by the three case studies, suggests that it is not relevant to look for cognitive strategies used to facilitate monitoring. That is, problem recognition, the first procedure that constituted monitoring, points to the need to use a strategy, and the other procedure, problem assessment, should provide information that would guide the choice of strategy. The data corroborated this assumption— writers did not report using cognitive strategies to facilitate monitoring but did report decisions to use a cognitive strategy and/or the actual deployment of one following upon a reference that they were monitoring (i.e. experiencing difficulty). In other, equally frequent cases, however, the monitoring that preceded the deployment of the cognitive strategy had to be inferred. The writers reported using the strategy but did not make explicit the fact that it was in response to a perceived difficulty.

Significance. What is the significance of this analysis? What does it illustrate regarding the use of metacognitive strategies in the accomplishment of a writing task, and more specifically, about its relationship with task knowledge and cognitive strategies? The following are some of the insights that the case studies bring to light for further systematic study.

The centrality of task knowledge. Focusing in on the steps involved in planning, monitoring and evaluation highlighted the following important functions of task knowledge in regulating a writing task:

Task knowledge is a requisite for the regulation of a writing task. One of the mental operations that define each of the metacognitive strategies requires knowledge retrieval. The writers needed world knowledge, rhetorical knowledge, and linguistic knowledge to plan, i.e. to make decisions about what they would write and how. To evaluate, they required rhetorical, linguistic, and message knowledge as a basis for the criteria against which they measured the quality of their written product. While planning and evaluation required knowledge 'to do' the task, when monitoring, the retrieved knowledge was used to assess the particular reason for the difficulty the writers experienced completing it.

Task knowledge was a prerequisite for the use of cognitive strategies. For writers who became aware that they were having a problem, the decision to use a cognitive strategy was based on two dimensions of task knowledge. First, writers had to know that there was a *need* to use the strategies—that they could/should use them to deal with the problem. Secondly, they needed to know *which* strategies would be appropriate to deal with that particular problem.

The role of metacognitive and cognitive strategies. While the functional difference between metacognitive and cognitive strategies has been acknowledged in the taxonomies derived from earlier research, the analysis of these case studies suggests a hierarchical relationship between the two which, to date, has not been acknowledged.

Metacognitive strategies are directly responsible for the execution of a writing task. Planning involves making decisions about what is to be done and the selection and coordination of the resources necessary to implement the plans—planning moves the task ahead. Evaluating involves determining the quality of the written product—evaluation means looking back to determine the need for revision and change. Finally monitoring provides oversight on the whole process noting when and why it is being prevented from moving ahead. It identifies the presence of obstacles.

Cognitive strategies, on the other hand, are used to deal with the obstacles encountered along the way. They are auxiliary strategies that aid in the implementation of the metacognitive strategies. As noted in these case studies, cognitive strategies facilitated planning and evaluation. They helped with knowledge retrieval; they enabled the writers to clarify the knowledge they wished to use to implement their rhetorical plans and to verify the knowledge used to evaluate what they had written. The use of cognitive strategies followed upon and depended on both monitoring and planning. Monitoring yielded awareness of a difficulty—the need for a cognitive strategy, and the decision to use one and the choice of one appropriate to deal with the problem was a part of the planning process. In contrast to the metacognitive strategies, the function of cognitive strategies are narrower in scope.

The relationship between cognitive strategies and task. The research referred to earlier has already noted that cognitive strategies are task specific, i.e. that certain tasks elicit the use of certain strategies. Looking at the use of cognitive strategies from the vantage point of a productive task, such as writing, provides further insight on the relationship between task and cognitive strategy. First of all, the type of strategy chosen will depend on which of the various processes or stages of learning (as defined by information processing theorists) predominate in the doing of that particular task: selecting, comprehending, storing, or retrieving knowledge.[7] In a writing task, stored knowledge must be accessed, as illustrated in the three case studies, so retrieval strategies were used frequently. Secondly, whereas in a receptive task, clarification and verification are used to assure efficient storage, in a productive task, they can be used to ensure appropriate application or use. The purpose of the strategy will vary depending on the kind of task it facilitates.

The specificity of metacognitive strategies. Metacognitive strategies have been described as general learning skills—transferrable across all types of learning tasks and, therefore, not task specific (cf. Brown et al. 1983). Of course, it is true, that whatever one learns, it is necessary to plan, evaluate, and monitor and that the execution of these strategies will probably entail similar mental operations across tasks. However, the task knowledge necessary for the implementation of each metacognitive strategy is task specific. For that reason, it may be said that in their implementation, metacognitive strategies are also task specific.

At the same time, the categories of knowledge used by the three writers suggest that there are levels of specificity in the task knowledge required for a writing task. In the writing of the 'compositions' that are requirements in ESL classes (such as the one written by the students in this study), world knowledge will vary accordingly. Rhetorical knowledge would not be quite as variable—the changes depending on whether students were expected to write expository prose, informal essays, or subject-based term papers. Except for lexical knowledge which will vary depending on the composition topic, linguistic knowledge is constant—the grammar of the language does not change with the nature of the writing task.

Conclusion. In this concluding section, suggestions regarding what these insights imply for future research on learner strategies and for the application of this research in learner training will be offered.

A new research paradigm. The present paradigm used to research learner strategies is strategy-focused. Researchers have sought to identify the different kinds of strategies that learners report using; but metacognitive knowledge has been ignored, specifically the task knowledge required to perform these strategies. In cases when the use of task knowledge is noted, it has been coded as a strategy (e.g. Block 1986:472; O'Malley and Chamot 1990:139). Moreover, while the functional differences between metacognitive strategies and cognitive strategies are recognized, they have, otherwise, been treated as equals.

---

7 See Rubin 1989 for a taxonomy of strategies that is based on these processes.

Finally, the research has used a discrete approach to collecting and analysing the data. That is, relationships between the two kinds of strategies (i.e. the metacognitive and cognitive strategies) and between the strategies and task knowledge in the actual performance of a task have not been examined. Rather, the objective has been to identify and classify strategies and improve taxonomies that are then used for learner training and research separate from the task that generated their use.

This paradigm has been useful and, perhaps, was even necessary in the development of the field of learner strategies. As noted earlier, it has documented the fact that L2 learners used strategies, classified them, and had begun to note differences between effective and ineffective learners. However, in the more recent research a certain dissatisfaction with this approach has been noted (cf. Vann and Abraham 1990). Perhaps, therefore, we should consider an alternative model, one that approaches the research integratively rather than discretely.

An integrative approach to the research would mean, first of all, approaching it from the perspective of how learners regulate their learning of a particular task: how are the metacognitive strategies used? when? what cognitive strategies do they bring into service to help do the task and why? what task and/or person knowledge accompanies their use? That is, the relationships between these aspects of cognition need to be established. Moreover, in the coding and analysis, knowledge should be distinguished from strategies. Secondly, task-based strategy-knowledge networks should be developed. These networks could be organized according to different types of language learning tasks and outline the task knowledge as well as the cognitive strategies necessary to the regulation of the task. Finally, a special emphasis should be placed on research based on ill-defined or complex tasks that are not highly specified in terms of problem definition or solution.[8]

A broadened perspective on ineffective learners. The centrality of task knowledge in the use of metacognitive strategies suggests that it is a factor to take into account in trying to understand why some learners are ineffective depite the fact that they use strategies. This is a conclusion already made by research referred to earlier. Stein (1986) pointed out that the lack of research on the knowledge base needed for writing has resulted in incorrect assump-tions being made in the diagnosis of the causes of poor writing. In their analysis of two unsuccessful learners,

---

8 Yussen (1985) contrasts ill-defined tasks with puzzle-solving tasks. The former, he notes, are not so specified in terms of problem definition and solution. See Vann and Abraham (1990) for a framework for analysing task demands that suggests one way of identifying the complexity of a task—i.e. whether or not it is ill-defined.

Vann and Abraham (1990) noted that in order to pinpoint reasons why otherwise active learners were not successful, the range of strategies they used needed to be complemented with an analysis of task demands to see whether or not their strategies were appropriately chosen.

The writers in this study illustrate another way in which a lack of task knowledge can affect learner performance. Though they were very 'active writers' involved in planning, evaluating, and monitoring, they were not 'successful' writers in the sense that their writing lacked a mature and sophisticated development of ideas and evidenced a fair number of problems with syntax and word choice (see Appendix 4 for the composition of one of the writers). To a large extent, this was due to an inadequacy of the knowledge-resources demanded by the task. Their store of acquired world, rhetorical, and linguistic knowledge was insufficient.

It is important, therefore, that the task knowledge that learners actually report using be taken into account in seeking to understand why they are ineffective at some tasks some of the time. For, even if they plan, evaluate, and monitor their learning and deploy cognitive strategies to deal with problems, if their task knowledge is inadequate, their use of strategies may be inappropriate and their final product will make them appear 'ineffective'.

Alternative for learner training. First of all, learner training should be based on tasks that particular groups of learners need to do to achieve lan-guage proficiency. The content should be determined by the language learning needs of the learners. Moreover, learner training syllabi and the activities that implement the syllabi should include (a) the task and person knowledge, and (b) the appropriate cognitive strategies necessary for the effective regulation (i.e. the planning, evaluation, and monitoring) of these specific tasks. Learner training should be integrated.[9] Secondly, to date learner training has focused on developing learner facility in the use of cognitive strategies. These objectives should be expanded to include activities that will help learners develop proficiency in the use of metacognitive strategies in regulating broader-based and more ill-defined learning tasks (such as writing and reading).

---

9 See Wenden 1991 for activities and planning instruments intended to guide an integrated approach to learner training.

Appendix 1. Composition topics

The following statements express opinions about women's and men's roles, technology, immigration, success, retirement. Choose one and decide whether you agree or disagree with what is stated. Support your opinion with reasons and examples. Give your composition a title.

1. Many people believe that certain types of jobs are men's jobs and others are women's jobs.
2. Modern technology has made our lives easier and more enjoyable. However, it has not solved the major problems of society. It has created more.
3. Everyone, regardless of the person's health, should be forced to retire at 65.
4. In order to be successful in the United States, it is important that you make as much money as you can.
5. Illegal immigrants should be returned to their native countries. The United States should not have to help them.
6. Why do people steal?

Appendix 2. Taxonomy of behaviors

Letter and letter/number combinations used for coding reflect the order in which the behaviors were identified.

Non verbal:

pause	b	change/add/replace	h/i
reach for dictionary	d-3	write lead in word of a sentence	j
put quotes around word or sentence	d-4	look up	k
use words from assignment sheet in text	d-5	reread assigned question	l
reread silently	g-s	move cursor	l-1
delete	f	gesture/facial expression	m

Retrospect: Writers refer to acquired, stable knowledge about their writing process based on past experience and tell researcher (not included in the analysis).

Verbal:

Think aloud:

Relatively unedited commentary by writer; thinks through idea/rule application	c	*Self-observe:* Writers observe their own process and report say 'I'm thinking' or a variant thereof	a
verbalizes and evaluates	e	report on personal and task constraints just assessed	o-1
rereads auditorializing	g-a	report that they're evaluating	p
verbalizes a decision (writing plan; strategy)	n	say they're thinking in NL/translating	r
guesses	q	says 'I'm reading.'	g-a1
reads outloud while typing	s	says he's comparing/analyzing	y
articulates criteria used to evaluate	t	*Ask:*	
asks self a question	v	Asks researcher for information without explanation	d
summarizes what's just been done	w	asks researcher for information by paraphrasing	d-1
make a statement assessing the cause of an experienced obstacle	(o)	asks researcher for verification	d-2

Appendix 3. Excerpt from a coded transcript

The left-hand column lists the metacognitive strategy, the mental operation, the kind of knowledge, and (when relevant) the cognitive strategy. The right-hand column includes the excerpt from the sentence being coded together with the letter that identifies the behavior. What the student has written is in *italics;* what he reports is in single quotes. The interviewer questions and/or probes are written in CAPITAL letters.

Starts his first sentence, *'In order to live in the US . . .'*

Planning: knowledge retrieval/WK	pause - **b** YOU STOPPED? 'looking for ideas' - **a**
Decision making:RK Decision making: RK	YOU JUST STARTED WITH THIS SENTENCE? I started with the general sentence. I put one fact. You know I put something is not in this (points to what he's written. .) - **n** MAIN STATEMENT? Yes I have to write my own introduction - **n**
Knowledge retrieval: WK/LK evaluation/ appropriateness: RK	YOU HAVE THE IDEA OR ARE YOU LOOKING FOR WORDS? both continues writing *'. . . you have to make as much money as you can'* pauses - **b** 'must be sure what I'm gonna put is right' - **e** 'because everything is based on that' - **t**

RK = rhetorical knowledge   **WK** = world knowledge   **LK** = linguistic knowledge
See Appendix 2 for an explanation of the coding letters (**e, t** . . .).

Appendix 4. Sample composition: 'Illegal Immigrants'

One of the biggest problems that exists today in the U.S.A. is the problem of the "ILLEGAL IMMIGRANTS." Thousands of people of different nationality enter every day in the U.S. and that makes the citizens very confused to wonder if all those new people should be stay or returned to their native country.

American people believed that the most of the illegal immigrants are criminals or they have a bad past and this unfortunately is true. They believe that when they come in the new country they try to do the same things and they have the same hobbies.

The biggest immigrant's number is also uneducated people who try to find any kind kind of job and they don't offer anything in the American cociety. They don't pay taxes, they don't vote and in other words they don't participate in the Amerikan way of life.

On the other hand now the illegal immigrants, affraid and incalculable left their poor country trying to find a new life, a better "tomorrow" for their children and their family. They came here and they work very hard with all the news and strange situations trying to unsterdant how the things are going on the "new homme" and what the new society exept for them.

Usually all those immigrants work harder that the American trying to satisfy their felings for leaving. They try to take a education and they also try to educate their children make a better family and finally a better society.

Nowdays the number of the illegal immigrants which according to the population' statistics is respectable size not helped by the American government. However they don't either caused them difficulties. Sometimes looks that immigrants live in their world.

Nobody also has the right to say in all those people what they have to do and if they have to stay or live the country.

References

Anderson, J.R. 1985. Cognitive psychology and its implications. 2nd ed. New York: Freeman.
Baker, L., and A. L. Brown. 1984a. Cognitive monitoring in reading. Understanding reading comprehension. ed. by J. Flood. 21-44. Newark, Del.: International Reading Association.
Block, Ellen. 1986. The comprehension strategies of second language readers. TESOL Quarterly. 20:463-494.
Breen, M. 1987. Learner contributions to task design. Language learning tasks. Lancaster practical papers in English language education. ed. by C.N. Candlin and D. Murphy. London: Prentice-Hall International.
Brown, A., J. D. Bransford, R. Ferrara, and J. C. Campione. 1983. Learning, remembering, and understanding. Carmichael's manual of child psychology. ed. by J. H. Flavell and E. M. Markham. 77-166. New York: Wiley.
Carrell, P. 1983. Three components of background knowledge in reading comprehension. Language Learning. 33:183-207.
Carrell, P. 1987. Content and formal schemata in ESL reading. TESOL Quarterly. 21:461-482.
Cohen, Andrew. 1990. Language learning: Insights for learners, teachers, and researchers. New York: Newbury House.
Connor, Ulla. 1987. Research frontiers in writing analysis. TESOL Quarterly. 21:677-696.
Flavell, J. H. 1979. Metacognition and cognitive monitoring: A new area of cognitive developmental inquiry. American Psychologist. 34. 906-911
Flavell, J.H., and H. M. Wellman. 1977. Metamemory. Perspectives on the development of memory and cognition. ed. by R. V. Kail, Jr. and J. W. Hagen. N.J.: Erlbaum Associates.
Flavell, J.H. 1981a. Cognitive monitoring. Children's oral communication skills. ed. by P. Dickson. New York: Academic Press.
Holec, H. 1981. Autonomy in foreign language learning. Council of Europe Modern Language Program. Oxford: Pergamon.
Holec, H. 1987. The learner as manager: Managing learning or managing to learn. Learner strategies in language learning. ed. by A. Wenden and J. Rubin. 145-157. London: Prentice-Hall International.

Horowitz, E. 1987. Surveying Student Beliefs about Language Learning. In A. Wenden & J. Rubio (eds.) Learner Strategies in Language Learning. London: Prentice Hall International.
Johnson, P. 1982. Effects on reading comprehension of building background knowledge. TESOL Quarterly. 16:503-516.
O'Malley, J.M., A.U. Chamot, G. Stewner-Manzanares, and L. Kupper. 1985a. Learning strategies used by beginning and intermediate ESL students. Language Learning. 35:21-46.
O'Malley, J. Michael, and Anna Uhl Chamot. 1990. Learning strategies in second language acquisition. New York: Cambridge University Press.
Raimes, A. 1985. What unskilled ESL students do as they write: A classroom study of composing. TESOL Quarterly. 19:229-258.
Rubin, J. 1989. How learner strategies can inform language teaching. Proceedings of LULTAC. ed. by V. Bickley. Institute of Language in Education. Department of Education. Hong Kong.
Stein, Nancy. 1986. Knowledge and process in the acquisition of writing skills. Review of research in education. ed. by E. Z. Rothkopf. 13:225-258.
Vann, Roberta, J., and Roberta G. Abraham. 1990. Strategies of unsuccessful language learners. TESOL Quarterly. 24:177-198.
Wenden, A. 1982. The Processes of Self-Directed Learning: A Study of Adult Language Learners. Unpublished doctoral dissertation. Teachers College, Columbia University.
Wenden A. 1983. The Process of Intervention: Review Essay. Language Learning 33 (1) 103-121.
Wenden, A. 1987. Metacognition: an expanded view on the cognitive abilities of L2 learners. Language Learning. 37:573-597.
Wenden, A., and J. Rubin. 1987. Learner strategies in language learning. London: Prentice-Hall International.
Wenden, A. 1991. Learner strategies for learner autonomy. London: Prentice-Hall International.
Yussen, S.R. 1985. The role of metacognition in contemporary theories of cognitive development. Metacognition, cognition, and human performance. Volume 1: theoretical perspectives. ed. D.L. Forrest-Pressley, G. E. McKinnon, T. G. Waller. 253-283. New York: Academic Press.
Zamel, V. 1983. The composing processes of advanced ESL students: Six case studies. TESOL Quarterly. 17:165-187.

Social attitudes: The key to directing the evolution of grammar teaching

Sally Sieloff Magnan
University of Wisconsin-Madison

Introduction. Few would argue with either of the following two points: (1) that one of the greatest controversies in foreign language teaching today concerns the place of grammar in our classrooms, and (2) that social and political attitudes affect foreign language teaching. This paper examines the interaction of these two notions. How have shifting American social attitudes helped define new directions for teaching grammar? In what ways do these same attitudes deter us from putting innovative theoretical ideas into practice? How can a better understanding of American social attitudes help direct the evolution of grammar teaching in the future?

The grammar teaching controversy. The grammar teaching controversy stems from the naturalistic versus tutored debate. The basic positions are clear. Believers in naturalistic acquisition generally support Krashen's (1981) now well-known belief that comprehensible input is both necessary and sufficient for at least early language learning and that explicit teaching of grammar offers, at best, a monitor of performance and, at worst, an affective barrier to naturalistic acquisition. Their suggested shift away from grammar as the dominant focus and organizing feature of foreign language teaching has clearly influenced a variety of communicative approaches, where direct and explicit grammar instruction have now assumed somewhat peripheral positions in courses designed around activities and toward functional goals (Terrell 1991).
Scholars and teachers on the tutored side of the debate caution against completely removing grammar from the classroom, based on concerns that inaccurate forms might fossilize (Higgs and Clifford 1982), on professional beliefs that, in an adult classroom setting, language acquisition needs concentrated, structured practice in a progressive sequence from learning to communication (Omaggio 1986, McLaughlin 1990), and especially on growing evidence that some grammar instruction can facilitate learning (Long 1983, Chaudron 1988). As Garrett (1986) has pointed out, this debate hinges on a traditional

definition of grammar as consisting of morphological paradigms and freestanding lexical and syntactic features. As our research and our teaching begin to focus less on traditional grammatical paradigms and more on the processes that learners use to communicate, we open up possibilities for cross-fertilization of ideas between these two seemingly contradictory viewpoints.

Indeed, advocates of naturalistic approaches have recognized the necessary roles of grammar in acquisition for some learners: to lower the affective filter for learners with low tolerance for ambiguity and with a desire to focus on form and to accelerate the acquisition process in later stages by changing how learners process input (VanPatten 1989, VanPatten 1991, Terrell 1991, see also Rutherford and Sharwood-Smith 1985 and Long 1983). According to Terrell (1991:62), 'grammar instruction is seen as an aid to the learner in the acquisition process by making certain grammatical forms more salient and thereby aiding the learner to establish correct meaning-form connections.' Clearly, it would be unfair today to claim that scholars and teachers associated with the naturalistic side of the debate are totally opposed to grammar instruction. And it would be equally unfair not to acknowledge the massive impact that naturalistic arguments have had on what might be considered traditional grammar-based instruction.

Over the past two decades the desire and ability to incorporate into our courses more authentic input, more learner-directed communicative activities, and a broader cultural perspective have helped us implement suggestions made in the early 1970s and 1980s: to teach for communication first (Savignon 1972), to lighten the grammatical load, especially in our beginning courses (Valdman and Warriner-Burke 1980), and to make culture the message of instruction (Strasheim 1981). Although, as Schulz (1991) points out, our textbooks lag far behind our theoretical desires, they too have evolved: shortening and sometimes reshaping grammatical sequences and presentations, reducing rote drill in favor of contextualized and personalized activities, and attempting to present and practice language in terms of its communicative function.

Our sometimes fiery professional debate over what grammar is and where it fits into our classrooms has indeed influenced our teaching. But our evolution has not yet become the revolution that many foreign language educators advocate; it has spread slowly and not far enough. Between the two sides of the naturalistic vs. tutored debate and in their compromises there remain fundamental uncertainties. Why is our acceptance of change growing? How can we direct that change? For answers, we might look beyond the theoretical debate and its practical applications to social factors that influence American education in general and foreign language teaching in particular.

The importance of social and political attitudes. McKay and Wong (1988) remind us that, although we recognize the profound impact of social and political attitudes on foreign language teaching, we often fail to consider them when developing theories of second language acquisition and classroom teaching practices. In their survey of articles in TESOL and foreign language journals between 1974 and 1987, McKay and Wong found relatively few articles concerned with how language teaching and learning fit into the larger society, especially in comparison with the number of articles about pedagogical techniques and psycholinguistic and second language acquisition theories. Their conclusion reflects, unfortunately, the predominant vision of foreign language teachers today: that teaching is 'primarily a matter of understanding psycholinguistic processes in the individual learner and devising effective classroom techniques in accordance with these processes' (McKay and Wong 1988:386).

While we have made major advancements in learning theory and important related changes in classroom practice, we have not given adequate consideration to social attitudes: values that provide a climate for discovery and innovation, beliefs that compel us to see how language functions in society and what we can give to students through language, pressures that make us think about what we are doing and direct change. In this paper, I will consider American social attitudes about who is to learn foreign languages and under what circumstances, the purposes of foreign language instruction, and the selection of linguistic norm. I draw my examples from French, leaving it to you to consider the impact on teaching in your own languages.

Promoting change: Belief in more democratic and more positive educa-tion. Before educational change can occur, teachers must be receptive both to adopting new ideas and to relinquishing the old. Modern efforts to make American education more democratic and more positive have altered our instructional climate. In so doing, they may have provided a key stimulus compelling us to reconsider the role of grammar in foreign language classrooms.

Over the past few decades our student population has changed dramatically. Compared with the 25% of high school graduates who attended college thirty years ago, nearly 60% went on to college by 1988 (Forrest 1987, U.S. Department of Commerce 1988). Of these students, two-thirds did not have to concentrate on academic courses in high school and thus many received less rigorous academic preparation than 'college prep' students of the past (Sedlak, Wheeler, Pullin, and Cusick 1986). And in both high school and college, many more students now hold at least part-time jobs that divide their priorities between work and school: the increase in high school, from 22.6% of females and 33% of males in 1960 (Sedlak, Wheeler, Pullin, and Cusick 1986) to 76% of all senior in 1988 (McCartan 1988), and the increase in college, 62% of all students in 1990 (Hexter 1990).

In response to this democratization of education, our student body in foreign language classes has grown and diversified at both the college and high school levels. No longer reserved for an elite intellectual group, foreign language classes welcome learners of diverse linguistic backgrounds, aptitudes, and motivations: students without a solid analytical knowledge of grammar, students who speak different varieties of English or for whom English is a second language, students with learning styles that appear incompatible with traditional language teaching methods, students who want to be in a language class and students who do not. As Erickson and Strommer (1991) point out, the old sorting strategy of 'educate the best, shoot down the rest' is no longer tenable in light of our national need to educate an increasingly heterogeneous society. In foreign languages, as in all of American education, our philosophy is changing: it is now the educational system that should adjust to the student, not the student who should adjust to instructional expectations.

As American education is becoming more democratic, it is also becoming more positive. Research revealing the essential role of motivation (Gardner and Lambert 1972) and affective factors in learning (Horwitz 1990) supports the beliefs that students learn more through positive motivation than through correction and that we should design activities to build success rather than to separate the able from the unable.

This national social evolution toward more democratic and more positive learning leads us to ask many difficult questions:

- Since students' ability to use grammar correctly in communication develops slowly and at an uneven pace (Magnan 1989), does the practice time needed for grammar detract too much from development of communicative skills?
- If emphasis on rote learning and strict application of rules makes foreign languages less accessible to students not oriented to analysis (Ehrman and Oxford 1990), are we justified in defining grammar as morphological paradigms to be memorized and syntax as rules to be applied?
- Given that most older adolescents value multiplicity and subjective knowledge over right or wrong 'truth' (Kurfiss 1988), does focusing on paradigmatic grammar create a learning climate that is incompatible with the dominant developmental stage of many of our students?
- Is the explicit and rigorous correction generally associated with an emphasis on grammatical accuracy more harmful to developing

positive self-concepts and motivation to learn than it is beneficial to achievement?
- Since people tend to retain negative impressions from language learning experiences (Horwitz 1988), does having viewed language as model rather than language as meaning make parents reluctant to support foreign languages when advising their children or making choices for their schools?

Answers to these questions probably lead many teachers away from traditional grammar teaching. For others, being receptive to change comes more from an instinct for survival: grammar-based classes may be unpopular, and unpopular classes give teachers lower student evaluations and make it hard to maintain enrollment in upper-level programs.

If maintaining a pedagogical focus on grammar leads us to so many questions and frustrations, why has the communicative teaching evolution not accelerated to a revolution? Many important questions remain largely unanswered. To what degree is proficiency associated with grammatical control? What if incorrect forms become fossilized in student speech? Is our teaching somehow less rigorous if its outcome is less testable by the fixed rules offered in grammar? In order to truly benefit from the current social climate and shape the evolution of foreign language teaching, we need to free ourselves from these fears. This liberation will come only through research and by uncoupling two prevalent beliefs: that the primary role of education is to maintain intellectual standards and that, in language, these high standards are epitomized by orthoepic grammatical accuracy.

Today our profession faces immediate demands for more democratic and more positive instruction, while it lacks a single proven communicative approach where self-expression is always valued and valid and where acquisition always culminates in sophisticated linguistic control. Encouraged by research, experiments in classroom applications, and especially social pressures, many teachers now seem receptive to leaving behind traditional paradigm-based notions of grammar teaching and searching for alternative possibilities for presenting language. For many instructors, the alternative of choice is an eclectic curriculum: not because it reflects their preferred theory of second language learning, but because it offers an expedient rationale toward a solution for an immediate, complex problem. In order to move beyond eclecticism as a convenient default option until something more unified and proven comes along, we need to look more deeply into the social attitudes that prompted this choice.

Is this scenario depressing? Quite the contrary! It can be exciting to realize how society, from which language comes, can influence what foreign language teaching is to become.

Directing the evolution: American pragmatism and focus on self.
While our belief in democratic and positive education encourages us to look beyond grammar for new approaches to teaching, the current pragmatic and self-directed orientation of American youth help determine what these new approaches will be. A 1985 Gallup poll provides insights into why Americans value college: 52% to get a job and another 18% to earn a higher income. This pragmatic economic focus reflects a change in attitudes over the past two decades: in 1967, 44% of first-year college students held financial well-being as an essential or very important goal of their college experience; by 1989, the number of students with this goal had risen to 75% (Erickson and Strommer 1991).

Looking for an organizing focus to succeed grammar in basic foreign language curriculum, teachers find success with teaching approaches that appear compatible with the pragmatic perspective of Americans today: emphasis on functional language use, especially in the sociocultural contexts of travel and business situations. The move toward everyday language use in situation has been encouraged by developments in Teaching English as a Second Language and—ironically— even by the English Only movement, which attempts to mandate English for such daily language needs as reading street signs and understanding telephone messages. As some Americans hope to ban other languages in the U.S., others learn from their arguments where foreign languages are needed for basic survival and seek out opportunities to build their foreign language study around these situations. Both views relate to American pragmatism and focus on self: the isolationism of *Speak like me to live with me* and the survival instinct of *Give me what I most need to get by*.

Upon closer examination, these apparently related social attitudes— pragmatism and focus on self—may actually be in conflict. Students want to learn the language of everyday use. They also appreciate the self-confidence they experience in talking about themselves. Attempting to respond to these desires, teachers often personalize lessons by shaping them around students and how they use language in their daily lives. Students thus learn to ask about food, shelter, and transportation, but not to interpret the sociocultural content of the situation. They talk about *Me* and *my life in the U.S.*, rather than about *You* and *your life*. Will this focus on self make them more comfortable with first-person verbs than with second- or third-person verbs? Will this, in turn, lead them to talk mostly about themselves with people of the other cultures? Will such limitations on their communicative ability contribute to the stereotype of the egocentric American? Rather than teaching communicative competence are we, unknowingly, growing a new breed of 'ugly American?'

Indeed, tendencies to talk too much about oneself may well be perceived as impolite in many countries, such as France, where, in comparison with the U.S., conversations tend to focus more on institutions and concepts and less on individuals. For example, the French are more hesitant to ask directly for someone's name: people may talk on several occasions without exchanging first or sometimes even last names. Yet, from the first day students in an American French class spend most of the period directly asking classmates, *Commment vous appelez-vous?* 'What's your name?' and beginning interactions with *Bonjour, je m'appelle* . . . 'Hello, my name is. . .'. Such activities appeal to students because they focus on the students themselves and on their perceived need for communicative strategies. But they foster American habits and attitudes rather than build French ones; and ironically, their social need produces an asocial result.

Classroom testing presents another problem. In refocusing our teaching toward the communicative purpose of language, we must also refocus our tests. Following the model of Omaggio (1986), the profession is replacing discrete point, isolated, or sentence-length grammar items with more divergent and global items, where grammar items are contextualized in paragraphs that give cultural information or tell stories. Such items are designed so that students must process meaning as well as form, in hopes that students will learn the cultural information and enjoy the story while taking the test.

Criticizing contextualized items in teaching exercises, Walz (1989) challenges their naturalness and efficiency. While it may, at first, seem unnatural for students to imagine themselves as characters in fictitious situations, this kind of projection of self may be a necessary step to entering into another culture, to understanding that culture, and eventually integrating into it. While contextualized grammar items may appear inefficient in terms of space and time, we must remember that they also test reading with a focus on the meaning of key vocabulary items.

In light of how social values often determine student reactions to curriculum, perhaps we should be concerned less with how natural and efficient contextualized test items may be and more with how students feel about them. Pragmatism may work at cross purposes. Do students prefer contextualized grammar items because they simulate travel or business situations better than discrete-point grammar tests? Or do they view the testing exercise simply as getting the right answers as directly as possible, making context in a grammar test superfluous? Underlying this dilemma is the fact that we are still in the beginnings of our instructional evolution: we need to work toward abandoning paper and pencil tests all together and evaluating students performing actual tasks in the target culture. If we are to meet our students' expectations for functional and communicative instruction, we must change traditional expectations for paper and pencil testing in order to make testing compatible with our teaching goals.

Toward a revolution: Valuing and understanding different language norms. Before we can truly revolutionize how we introduce grammar to our students, we must determine which linguistic norm or norms are appropriate for instruction. If we are teaching adolescents, should we teach language appropriate to this age group or teach the language of the adults that our teenagers are soon to become? Since students are likely to use the foreign language as tourists, should we teach language most typical of the streets and stores? If our students envision careers in international business, should we direct them toward more educated, sophisticated norms? Should we recognize that, regardless of their goals, our students will probably always be marked as foreigners and allow them to use features characteristic of foreigner talk? Or, on the contrary, should we adopt a pedagogical norm that is pleasing, or at least not irritating, to native speakers of the target language?

Even more basic than these questions is 'Should we adopt one norm or many?' Traditionally, of course, we have opted for one norm, the orthoepic standard. Based on the conventional assumption that education means aspiration to a higher socioeconomic level and on the traditional practice of using the literary canon to present language to students, this prestigious standard seemed appropriate and practical. However, modern authors, such as Queneau and Camus in French, have violated our expectations for literary language, and we have become more informed about language varieties of different target language countries around the world.

A first move from a prescriptive standard toward descriptive norms has already taken place. We find expressions taught for local color (Québécois *dîner* for the midday meal and *souper* for the evening meal), textbooks that take into account language change (allowing *des* 'some' before plural adjectives preceding nouns and the subjunctive with *après que* 'after'), and some shifting toward pedagogical norms (teaching reduced but common forms like *Comment tu t'appelles?* 'What's your name?' and promoting use of 'easier' forms like *est-ce que* before 'more difficult' forms like inversion). Although more closely approaching the reality of multiple and flexible norms than is the orthoepic standard, this newly evolving pedagogical norm is still mainly prescriptive. Too often its deviations from the orthoepic standard are based more on perceptions of student abilities than on realities of native language use. We are still chasing a single teachable standard, just an evolving one. If we want to describe rather than prescribe to students, we should consider offering students a series of norms representing the fluidity of the many continua for language use in different cultural, social, political, and economic contexts.

Teaching several norms, however, also poses serious problems from both pedagogical and social perspectives. From the pedagogical point of view, teachers may not be familiar enough with different norms to be comfortable teaching them. Learners may become confused by multiple forms of expression and mix features of different norms inappropriately or use them in inappropriate situations. From the social point of view, it would be unnatural for teachers and students to assume the personae of native speakers from different geographic regions and socioeconomic groups. Indeed, students may hesitate to use language norms of a native social group that is not equivalent to their own: for example, upper middle class students who are told to assume working class norms. And if they did so, their use of this unfitting norm might be interpreted as parody, much like teachers who talk like their teenage students may appear laughable or yuppies who adopt the new trend of wearing blue collar working clothes may be criticized as condescending.

Extended to a foreign culture, such parody could have disastrous consequences. Whereas people may tolerate or even be amused when native speakers deviate from social norms, the range of acceptable language may be narrower for foreigners: native French speakers may be quite irritated, for example, when an obviously well-off American French student in France talks like an immigrant Algerian worker. When entering a new and uncertain situation, it is generally considered better to err through better manners or better dress than necessary, rather than to underestimate the expectations of the situation. Hence, when choosing a norm for foreign language study, high standards may be more appropriate than sometimes lower ones.

Are we not then back to the neutrality of a single norm resembling the orthoepic standard? Our modern technology offers us another option. Consider the possibility of students learning to understand and appreciate a series of norms for reception only. As we work with satellite television, video, and short wave for native audiences, we can no longer realistically edit or gloss the input as we routinely do with printed texts. As students will need to receive the language as it is used naturally, their pragmatic orientations will encourage them to broaden their concept of norm. By giving students wider parameters for reception and acceptance than for production, we can incorporate the notions of multiple norms into our teaching without risking as many of the problems associated with teaching multiple norms for active use. We do not ask our students, or teachers, to be linguistic chameleons, changing social affiliations with each role play. But we demand that students come to terms with the diverse realities of language and, through language, we give them insights into the diversity of cultures and of cultural interactions.

An advantage of such an approach—beyond the obvious advantage of better developing students' ability to understand native speakers—is that, by focusing on the multiplicity and fluidity of language norms, we can raise the intellectual level and cultural content of even our basic language courses. We can teach students how ideology affects language and how sometimes ideological or political views about the status of a particular language arise in response to issues unrelated to language (Heath 1981). We can also show them how language can, in turn, affect ideology: by educating our students and ourselves about the hidden messages of social and linguistic interactions, will we not reshape our own ideological views?

Through the democratization of American education we have improved our understanding of and tolerance for different norms of English. We can help extend this attitude to other cultures by diversifying the language notions we experience with our students: register distinctions, such as between the orthoepic, formalized *Qu'est-ce que cela?* 'What is that?' and the informal, highly common *C'est quoi ça?* 'That's what?'; situational constraints, such as questions to ask and not to ask when meeting neighbors for the first time; social conventions, such as polite ways to receive a compliment or decline an invitation; and, the communicative effects of making *faux-pas* that violate these expectations. If we believe that social and political understanding builds acceptance of differences, surely linguistic understanding will do the same. In teaching students to understand and appreciate sociolinguistic differences, we are educating them beyond words and phrases of another language. Foreign language teaching becomes an agent of social change as we give direction to how social attitudes will evolve in the future.

Conclusion. It's a truism to say that language takes its life from society. But don't we too often fail to consider the impact of social notions when planning pedagogical innovation? I have argued that social pressures have deeply influenced how we view grammar and teach it in American classrooms today. Our desires to make education more democratic and positive may have made us more receptive to change. Increasing pragmatism and focus on self probably made us more enthusiastic about functional, situational, and personalized approaches. As our current social attitudes are leading us away from grammar teaching based on morphological paradigms and normative syntactic rules to be memorized and applied, they are exposing sensitive social areas involving group identity and language norms. In so doing, social change offers us new and exciting challenges: to teach more authentic language and to develop a deeper understanding of how people interact, both among members of the same culture and when people of different cultures come into contact.

Kramsch (1989) has argued that it is economic and political forces, not humanistic ones, that currently promote foreign languages. While developing language acquisition theories and appealing pedagogical techniques, we must not overlook the effect of social attitudes that subtly influence what we teach and what and how students learn. How we teach foreign language grammar may well have evolved because our social attitudes toward human culture and learning have evolved. More democratic, individualistic, pragmatic, and worldly, we are coming to a new understanding of intercultural communication. Yet, the greatest opportunity lies ahead: the challenge of bringing students to greater linguistic and social sophistication that will contribute to their intercultural understanding. Only true progress toward this goal will allow our evolution of teaching grammar to take on revolutionary dimensions.

References

Chaudron, Craig. 1988. Second language classrooms. Cambridge: Cambridge University Press.

Ehrman, Madeline and Rebecca Oxford. 1990. Adult language learning styles and strategies in an intensive training setting. MLJ. 74. 311-27.

Erickson, Bette LaSere, and Diane Weltner Strommer. 1991. Teaching college freshmen. San Francisco: Jossey-Bass.

Forrest, A. 1987. Managing the flow of students through the higher education system. National Forum: Phi Kappa Phi Journal. Fall 1987. 39-42.

Gallup, A. M. 1985. The seventeenth annual Gallup Poll of the public's attitudes toward the public schools. Phi Delta Kappan. 67. 35-47.

Gardner, R. C. and W. E. Lambert. 1972. Attitudes and motivation in second-language learning. Rowley, Mass.: Newbury House.

Garrett, Nina. 1986. The problem with grammar: What kind can the language learner use? MLJ. 70. 133-48.

Heath, S. B. 1981. English in our language heritage. Progress in language planning: International perspectives, ed. Charles A. Ferguson and S. B. Heath, 87-105. Berlin: Mouton.

Hexter, H. 1990. Students who work: A profile. Research briefs. 1,2:1-6.

Higgs, Theodore V., and Ray Clifford. 1982. The push toward communication. Curriculum, competence, and the foreign language teacher, ed. by Charles J. James, 57-79. Lincolnwood, IL: National Textbook.

Horwitz, Elaine K. 1988. The beliefs about language learning of beginning university foreign language students. MLJ. 72. 283-94.

Horwitz, Elaine K. 1990. Attending to the affective domain in the foreign language classroom. Shifting the Instructional Focus to the Learner, ed. Sally Sieloff Magnan, 15-33. Middlebury, Vt.: Northeast Conference.

Joseph, John E. 1988. New French: A pedagogical crisis in the making. MLJ. 72. 31-41.

Kramsch, Claire. 1989. New directions in the study of foreign languages. ADFL Bulletin. 21, 1. 4-11.

Krashen, Stephen. 1981. Second language acquisition and second language learning. Oxford: Pergamon Press.

Kurfiss, J. G. 1988. Critical thinking: Theory, research, practice, and possibilities. ASHE-ERIC Higher Education Report No. 2. Washington, D. C.: Association for the Study of Higher Education.

Long, Michael H. 1983. Does second language instruction make a difference? TESOL Quarterly. 17. 359-82.
Magnan, Sally Sieloff. 1989. Do spoken French and grammatical control improve with course work? French Review. 63. 16-27.
McCartan, A. M. 1988. Students who work: Are they paying too high a price? Change. Sept./Oct. 11-20.
McKay, Sandra Lee and Sau-Ling Cynthia Wong. 1988. Language teaching in nativist times: A need for sociopolitical awareness. MLJ. 72. 379-88.
McLaughlin, Barry. 1990. Another look at aptitude. Keynote address at RP-ALLA 90. October, 1990. Columbus, Ohio.
Omaggio, Alice C. 1986. Teaching language in context: Proficiency-oriented instruction. Boston, Mass.: Heinle & Heinle.
Rutherford, William and Michael Sharwood-Smith. 1985. Consciousness raising and universal grammar. Applied Linguistics. 6. 274-82.
Savignon, Sandra. 1972. Communicative competence: An experiment in foreign language teaching. Philadelphia: The Center for Curriculum Development.
Schulz, Renate. 1991. Bridging the gap between teaching and learning: A critical look at foreign language textbooks. Challenges in the 1990s for college foreign language programs, ed. Sally Sieloff Magnan, 167-81. Boston: Heile & Heinle.
Sedlak, M. W., C. W. Wheeler, D. C. Pullin, and P. Cusick. 1986. Selling students short: Classroom bargains and academic reform in the American high school. New York: Teachers College Press.
Strasheim, Lorraine A. 1981. Language is the medium, culture is the message: Globalizing foreign languages. A Global approach to foreign language education, ed. Maurice W. Conner, 1-16. Lincolnwood, Ill.: National Textbook.
Terrell, Tracy. 1991. The role of grammar instruction in a communicative approach. MLJ. 75. 52-63.
U. S. Department of Commerce. Bureau of the Census. 1988. High school completion rates and enrolled-in-college participation rates of 18-to-24 year-olds by race/ethnicity, 1976 to 1988. Current Population Reports. Series P-20.
Valdman, Albert, and Helen Warriner-Burke. 1980. Major surgery due: Redesigning the syllabus and texts. Foreign Language Annals 13. 261-70.
VanPatten, Bill. 1989. What should Portuguese language teaching do about grammar? Proceedings of the National Conference on Portuguese Language Teaching and Testing, Dale Koike and A. Simes, eds. Austin: University of Texas. 25-42.
VanPatten, Bill. 1991. The foreign language classroom as a place to communicate. Foreign language acquisition research and the classroom, ed. Barbara Freed, 54-73. Lexington, Mass.: D. C. Heath.
Walz, Joel. 1989. Context and contextualized language practice in foreign language teaching. MLJ. 73. 160-8.

Ann, Bert, Carla, Derek, and Oakley's Thesis

Earl W. Stevick
Independent researcher

Introduction. About ten years ago, I had the opportunity to interview seven people, each of whom had in some way been exceptionally successful as an adult learner of foreign languages. More recently, I have been using transcripts of those interviews with my students in classes on Language Learning at UMBC and in Barcelona, as well as with a number of workshops in this country and abroad. The reaction to these interviews has been quite positive, apparently for two reasons: (1) The seven gifted learners are quite different—sometimes dramatically different—from one another. (2) The interviews are long enough and full enough so that readers have the feeling that they have come to know the seven gifted learners almost personally.

And so, a year ago, I decided to ask my current batch of students to answer two pairs of questions about the first four of these seven learners. The first pair of questions was, 'Which of these four people do you personally, as a language learner, find it easiest to identify with, and why?' The second pair was, 'Which of the four do you find it most difficult to identify with, and why?' The replies of that group and of their successors this past semester are what I would like to report on to you today.

Oakley's Thesis. Which brings us to Oakley's well-known Thesis. Oakley's Thesis, or rather its converse, is a concise formulation of what may be one of the most important principles in the history of the language teaching profession down through the ages. The thesis itself, of course, in its original statement, was *Anything you can do, I can do better*, and its classic restatement was *I can do anything better than you*. The Converse of Oakley's Thesis, which is what we're interested in today, is *Anything I can do, you can do too, although probably not as well*, or perhaps *Whatever I can't do or enjoy, you won't be any good at either*. There has been some research that indicates that students learn best from teachers whose styles are consistent with their own. (See, for example, Hartnett 1985.) It may also be true that teachers teach best in styles that they can relate to intuitively, and that they teach much less well in styles that deep-down just don't make sense to them as learners.

And that is why I asked my students for their reactions to the interviews with Ann and Bert and Carla and Derek. These two groups, totaling about 50 people, consisted almost entirely of practicing teachers, many of them with a fair amount of time in the classroom, and most of them with significant experience of learning and using one or more foreign languages. To the extent that these 50 are representative of the profession as a whole, their reactions may suggest to us both some prospects and possibly some caveats with regard to the various methodologies of language teaching.

So let me just take the next eight minutes in order to summarize briefly the data that my respondents were working with. (The transcripts my students had read are in Stevick 1989.) As you listen, you may want to keep in mind the same questions that I asked them: 'Which person is easiest, and which is hardest, to identify with as a learner, and why?' You can either answer the questions for yourselves, or you can try to predict the rather clear results that I obtained from my questions.

Ann. The first of the four gifted learners was Ann, a dignified, well-educated woman married to a senior military officer. She was studying Norwegian. Some of the facts that the readers learned about Ann were:

(1) She was good with sounds—both at reproducing sounds and at identifying regional and foreign accents. In order to remember how certain words were to be pronounced, she sometimes made up her own phonetic symbols rather than using the phonemic transcription that was provided in her textbook.

(2) When, in a small hotel in India, Ann was subjected to what she called a 'torrent of sound' in a totally unknown language, she was unflustered, and coolly went about sorting out recurring bits of sound and meaning.

(3) Ann was convinced that she had a knack for communicating with small babies, and even with the zebras and rhinoceroses in the zoo.

(4) A few dozen hours into the study of Norwegian, Ann overheard a conversation between two native speakers of that language, and understood essentially all that they said. (The accuracy of her understanding was later verified by a third party.) Ann's success here was evidently due to rapid and skillful top-down processing plus her knowledge of a few common words.

(5) During our interview, Ann happened to overhear a comparable conversation between two speakers of a totally unrelated language. She again had a very strong sense of understanding everything. In this case, her understanding was totally wrong, but it had clearly been reached by the same top-down processing that she had used in the earlier conversation.

(6) Ann's only significant failure in language study had been in a second-year college course where she had been required to memorize long lists of uncontexted vocabulary every night.

Bert. Bert, the second learner, was a middle-grade official in his thirties. He talked about his earlier experiences with the study of Chinese, a language in which he had become exceptionally proficient. Some of the things that the readers remembered about Bert were:

(1) He had had a year of university Chinese some years before going to Taiwan.

(2) In the first part of his program in Taiwan, most of Bert's time was spent sitting across the table from his tutor, 30 hours a week, repeating words and lists of sentences, and being corrected. He called this 'the natural way' of learning a second language.

(3) Bert believed that for mastering grammar, the best way was through intensive drills so as to 'burn the patterns into the brain'.

(4) Later in his training, Bert was given the same series of textbooks that Chinese-speaking children used in their schools. He took the books home, studied them, left them at home, and then came to class and discussed them with his tutor.

(5) Still later, Bert spent much time in activities that required paraphrasing from Chinese into English, but little or no time in anything that involved translation between English and Chinese. He felt that this accounted for much of his practical proficiency in speaking.

(6) Bert was concerned to get the segmental phonemes and of course the tones of Chinese words right. He was not, however, interested in getting the nuances of pronunciation right so as to avoid having a foreign accent. 'After all', he reasoned, 'my skin is white and my nose is big, so nobody is going to take me for a Chinese anyway'.

Carla. The third interviewee, Carla, was a secretary in her late twenties. She had picked up Portuguese in Brazil and German in Germany, both to the S-2+ level, with virtually no formal instruction. At the time of our interview, Carla was taking further training in German. Some of the facts that readers learned about Carla were:

(1) The oral testers in both Portuguese and German reported that although Carla's language was only at the S-2+ level, her overall way of communicating almost left them with the feeling that they were dealing with a native speaker.

(2) Carla had had a brief and happy experience in self-initiated learning of Japanese from a fellow worker in a factory.

(3) Carla's view of how she had succeeded in Portuguese and German was that she just 'threw herself into' life as it was being lived by

speakers of the languages, just saying whatever came to her, without thinking or analyzing.

(4) Carla was having considerable difficulty and discomfort in her present German course, both linguistically and emotionally. This was a traditional audio-lingual course which was built around mastery of dialogs and drills, and which insisted on correct endings for verbs, nouns, and noun modifiers. The fact that Carla was already able to express her thoughts effortlessly and fairly correctly in her "own" German had no value. She was required to learn to express the thoughts in the textbook, in the exact words of the textbook.

(5) For Carla, the very idea of thinking about 'why' she should use one ending and not another was intimidating, yet she repeatedly expressed regret that she had not been taught in this way from the beginning.

Derek. The last of the four was Derek, a fairly senior official about 50 years old. He had been highly successful overseas with both German and Russian. The language he was studying at the time of the interview was Finnish, which as you may know has tremendously complex paradigms both for nouns and for verbs. About Derek, readers seemed to remember:

(1) He claimed to have derived great benefit from writing the paradigms out numerous times, not just copying them mechanically, but trying to arrange them in more and more economical, systematic, illuminating ways. Once he was satisfied with a formulation, Derek put the paradigm aside and seldom or never looked at it again.

(2) Derek volunteered the information that he placed great value on drills, and that he rated teachers according to how limp and exhausted they left him at the end of a drill session.

(3) Derek had accumulated for himself and made use of a stockpile of little words and phrases that held conversations together, or bought time, or indicated transitions between successive parts of the discourse.

(4) Derek emphasized the importance of having the meaning of forms vividly in mind while he was practicing them. To this end, he had invented for himself an imaginary brother to talk about during conversation practice—a rather flamboyant brother who did all sorts of things that Derek himself would never have done.

(5) In German and Russian, Derek's pronunciation was good enough so that he was sometimes mistaken for a child of native-speakers.

Student reactions. Before we go on, readers may want to record for themselves their own guesses as to the reactions of my students.

The answers to the Who? questions are very brief and also very clear-cut. The learner far and away most identified with was Derek, at 63% of the vote, with Carla, Ann, and Bert bringing up a distant second, third, and fourth. And the one least identified with was Carla, at 52%, followed by Ann, Derek, and Bert. Derek was also the learner who received the largest total number of comments (105), followed by Carla (62), Ann (55), and Bert (21).

Six responses. The really interesting question of course is not Who? but Why? That is to say, of the facts that readers had retained about the four learners, which did they respond to, and how did they respond to them? We don't have time today to answer these questions in detail, but I'd like to share with you six that came out most clearly.

1 Derek's homemade charts of the noun and verb morphology drew 41 comments—twice as many as its nearest competitor. Of those 41 comments, 36 (88%) were favorable. That is, the teacher respondents to the questionnaire were saying that this was an activity in which they felt that they as learners could identify with Derek.

'I, too, create charts for studying or stockpiling grammar. Even though the Russian charts had been done by the instructor, I still found it necessary to construct a chart so that it would be mine'.

'In high school, I too had to work out the grammar and vocabulary my own way'.

'The act of making charts leaves me with a visual image and the same "physical feeling" Derek describes, of pieces plopping into place'.

'Making a table of the forms is something I would never do'.

2 Two other topics in the comments on Derek were closely related to the charts. They were his need to see structure in what he was doing, and his belief in the value of mechanical drills. The favorable comments on these topics were respectively 86% and 82% of the total.

'We have to learn languages in the way we learn other things as adults, and there is more method and more system'.

'I feel comfortable speaking a foreign language only when I know how the linguistic system works'.

3 A closely related topic, found in the Carla comments, was the fact that she went ahead and spoke before she had developed any idea of the structure of Portuguese or German. Ninety-four percent of the comments on this (16/17) cited it as a reason why the respondents could not identify with Carla.

'Even when I pick up a language outside the classroom, I spend time organizing the language in my head and figuring out the rules of grammar before venturing to speak. The rules and paradigms give me something with which I can compare new information'.

4 Carla's statement that she just 'threw herself into' the life of the country was frequently quoted by respondents. That, plus their references to her fearlessness and their own fearfulness about making mistakes, accounted for a total of 21 comments, 81% of which said that this was a way in which they were not like Carla.

'I'm not courageous enough to learn by hearing the conversation of those around me, and throwing myself into their lives'.

'Unlike Carla, I do think about language, and I care about making mistakes'.

5 The value of mechanical drills was mentioned a total of 16 times in the comments on Bert and Derek. Of these, 11 (69%) were favorable.

'I enjoy repetition and rote memorization of vocabulary and systematic information'.

'Both Derek and I use drilling as an opportunity to discover what we have and haven't learned'.

'Like Derek I find that drills help me to lock patterns into place, to make the forms more automatic. I must have an awareness of structures and usage rules combined with intense practice to incorporate new forms into my skills'.

'When I have worked with repetition I find myself going through the motions but not really focusing on the material'.

6 Finally, 25 comments on Ann, Bert, and Derek touched on the value of near-native accuracy in pronunciation. Of these, 20 (80%) either identified with Ann or Derek for trying to have a good accent, or they disapproved of Bert for not caring about one.

'I share Ann's ear for accent'.

'I want to sound as much like the native speaker as I can. I also have fun mimicking accents'.

'Learning pronunciation is just as important as learning grammar'.

'I had the most difficulty with Bert's attitude toward pronunciation. I would not be comfortable accepting my own poor pronunciation'.

'Like Bert, I would not feel intimidated by having a foreign accent if I were understood easily enough'.

Some comments on the responses. These, then, were the most conspicuous results that showed up when I tabulated the results of my assignment. I need hardly point out that although I used something that could be called a questionnaire, and although my results are expressed in terms of numbers, this was not a piece of scientific research, but only an informal exploration. For that reason, it cannot give us any answers or even suggest any answers. I do think, however, that it can suggest an uncomfortable question.

For just suppose that these fifty respondents are at least fairly representative of public school FL and ESL teachers in this country. What kind of composite image do we get from the six findings that I've just reported to you?

To me, this composite is of a person who very much needs structure—who is active and creative within that structure, but who still demands it. The extreme manifestations of structure in a language class are, of course, tables of forms and mechanical drills, both of which received overwhelming support from these teachers when they were thinking of themselves as learners. In fact, they are quite uncomfortable without the social support of the classroom (as contrasted with 'throwing themselves into' everyday life among foreigners), and without the linguistic support of knowing how the language works before they try to speak it.

Even their attitude toward foreign accents contributes to this image. Thirty or forty years ago, pronunciation was seen as the indispensable basis for all else in language study. Nowadays, it receives little or no overt attention in most language courses. Some methodologists seem to believe that pronunciation will take care of itself in the course of general exposure to the language; others assume that for most people nothing can really be done about pronunciation after the age of puberty anyway; still others see concern for accurate reproduction of the standard pronunciation of prestigious monolinguals as elitist, as a relic of colonialism, and as a means by which a ruling oligarchy expresses and perpetuates its power (Loveday 1982). If this is the case, then the clear trend among the respondents to my little questionnaire seems to be very conformist.

The apparent concern of these teachers, when they think of themselves as learners, for structure and paradigms and drills raises questions for methods such as the Natural Approach and TPR, which de-emphasize the overt and serious study of grammar. It also raises questions for methods such as the Silent Way and Community Language Learning, which do not have a clearly specified and organized, explicit syllabus. In the overall strategy of communicative language teaching as outlined by Brumfit (1979), there are four basic steps: (1) the teacher selects some practical task; (2) the students try to do that task; (3) the teacher presents whatever new language turns out to be needed; and finally (4) the students practice the new language—if necessary. Here again, I suspect my composite teacher-as-learner will feel quite uneasy. On the other hand, an overall teaching strategy that seems to fit the composite image I have sketched for you is the five-step outline of Hammerly (1985:90): (1) identify a new item, to find out how it sounds and looks; (2) reproduce the new item, either overtly or covertly; (3) understand what the item does, and how it relates to other items; (4) manipulate the new item, first in a mechanical way and then meaningfully; (5) apply the new item, putting in into real or realistic use. Note that I am not recommending or rejecting any of the approaches I have mentioned here, but only pointing out their apparent relationship to a composite image derived from the responses of 50 teachers to my questionnaire.

Finally, how ought we to interpret this composite if it does turn out to be valid? I can think of four ways: (1) Maybe it's just an artifact of the Audiolingual Era during which many of the respondents probably had their first language training. (2) Maybe it's a linguistic manifestation of Original Sin, to be regretted but impossible to do away with. (3) Maybe it's regrettable but can also be done away with, in the words of the Dudley J. Trudge College for Teachers *Fight Song,* 'through good education'. (4) Maybe it's none of the above. Maybe it's just a fact that we have to work with. That would be my guess.

References

Brumfit, Christopher. 1979. Communicative language teaching: An educational perspective. In: The communicative approach to language teaching, edited by C. J. Brumfit and K. Johnson, Oxford: Oxford University Press. 183-191.
Hammerly, Hector. 1985. An integrated theory of language teaching and its practical consequences. Blaine, Wash.: Second Language Publications.
Hartnett, Dayle Davidson. 1985. Cognitive style and second language learning. In: Beyond basics, edited by Marianne Celce-Murcia. Rowley, Mass.: Newbury House. 16-34.
Loveday, Leo. 1982. The sociolinguistics of learning and using a non-native language. Oxford: Pergamon.
Stevick, Earl W. 1989. Success with foreign languages: Seven who achieved it, and what worked for them. Hemel Hempstead: Prentice Hall.

An analysis of text in video newscasts:
A tool for schemata building in listeners

June K. Phillips
Tennessee Foreign Language Institute

Statistics as to the numbers of hours children and young students spend in front of television sets bombard us periodically in news reports; debates as to the educational benefits of television versus its stultifying effect on creative thinking rage without solution; recent data on the amount of time citizens spent watching CNN during the recent Persian Gulf Crisis, War, or "Storm" indicate that significant numbers of adults receive more messages via the tube than through the written word. For better or worse, television is here to stay for monolinguals and for those hoping to access information from other languages.

Second language learners in the target culture have often found television programs to be an additional opportunity for listening, one that can proceed in solitude and at will. For the less proficient person, it relieves the tension and frustration associated with too much immersion and coping; for the more proficient, it challenges and expands upon the routine when used selectively. For those learning languages in native cultures, television offers one more context, one more delivery system for multiple voices, multiple perspectives on real world events, and with the advent of videotape, multiple opportunities for listening.

Television is not, however, a panacea for the introduction of authentic listening materials into the classroom nor is it a complete system for language learning. There are various ways in which television can enhance language instruction and, unfortunately, ways it which it can mask real learning by providing the spectacle of son et lumière but in the absence of meaning. A viable pedagogy for listening comprehension targets learners' needs and expectations within specific contexts and for specific purposes. One of those contexts is video newscasts for adult learners who have an interest in and a familiarity with the content of world events. Using this source of authentic listening materials effectively requires drawing upon existing research in listening comprehension and upon instructional experimentation with learners.

With advances in satellite transmission and video recordings, oral documents are now as readily available for foreign language learners as they have been for second language learners. Regular video offerings, such as news broadcasts, are especially attractive to adults wishing to maintain or improve language proficiencies within a content base. A subset of this group consists of foreign language teachers. "Tuning in" for news by highly proficient language users who automatically process meaning does not require instructional intervention, and these listeners derive linguistic benefits and an international perspective from the content of the programs. The larger audience of intermediate to advanced language users profits from some assistance with the comprehending process.

The question then, for researchers, for teachers, and for motivated learners themselves, is, broadly, how to facilitate the interactive process of listening and, narrowly, how to do so within the range of video newscasts which is an increasingly international delivery system and one in which national and cultural underpinnings play significant roles.

Within the range of listening contexts, television or videotaped materials occupy but a short span. Yet in the realm of instructional materials, they expose learners to a variety of speakers dealing with global content in a rich cultural environment. These factors both enhance and inhibit meaningfulness. Obstacles include the absence of opportunities to negotiate meaning as occurs with face-to-face communication. When the source is a live telecast, retrieval of meaning is difficult, especially in cases of initial false hypotheses which necessitate making drastic adjustments. Finally, the linear delivery places strains on the listener's ability to remember while processing information. Of course, with the prevalence of video-recording and interactive formats, nonlinear movement through a text may proceed as it does with written passages.

In seminars and workshops with teachers and in talking with adults wanting to use television as a means of improving language comprehension, it is evident that simply watching repeatedly on one's own has some benefits. Misunderstandings do occur, some messages remain opaque, but successive viewings do engender message elaboration on familiar subjects and topics of general interest. Assisting the learner with prepared materials may not be worthwhile because the "shelf life" of the broadcast is so short. Nothing gets old faster than yesterday's news.

Relevant research on listening. Second language pedagogy and research in the study of reading as an interactive process (Swaffar, Arens, and Byrnes 1991) have benefited from a symbiotic relationship in that the research findings have endorsed many instructional practices (Phillips 1990). For example, studies in receptive language learning have largely supported approaches that sought to facilitate comprehension of authentic documents through prereading activities that activate schemata. Research has also illuminated the fluid mediating role that teachers play in helping readers assign meaning.

As one searches the literature for listening comprehension theories or practice, one finds that theoretical studies in second language listening are few and research studies in ESL far surpass those in foreign languages for English-speakers. (See Long 1989 for a review of relevant L1 listening comprehension research and Joiner in this volume for an excellent overview of theory and practice in listening.) In addition to discussions of reading and of listening as separate entities, there is also a trend toward grouping the receptive skills under a single rubric. The temptation is great to attempt transferability in both research design and classroom practice, and in many instances the commonalties have permitted prelistening and prereading approaches to parallel one another effectively. The direction of influence is definitely one in which successful reading practices have been transferred to listening rather than the contrary (Glisan 1988, Liskin-Gasparro 1990).

Certainly, renewed interest in receptive skills has also been sparked by the adoption of pragmatic and functional goals within the larger paradigm of communicative language learning which in turn cultivates the use of authentic materials in teaching. The movement toward greater integration of documents from target cultures is well underway, although one cannot yet assert that stilted, unnatural, and contrived language input has been banished from the view of language learners. At the same time, the commercial market and the world of mass communication have inundated language teachers with ample resources should they chose to exploit them with learners.

A review of the research in listening comprehension and a survey of instructional support materials for video materials reveal that the ties between the two are not as strong as is evidenced in reading. Those linkages which do exist draw as heavily from the more extensive literature in the reading domain than from listening itself. Investigators do tend to assume that listening, like reading, is an interactive process. The listener is a "maker of meaning," one who constructs the factual and inferential meaning of the oral document. In the world of video, significant amounts of meaning are rendered by the visual element where, if the medium is not the message (to paraphrase McLuhan), it is often a major portion of it.

Two compatible theoretical models for the listening (and reading) comprehension process are script theory and schema theory. Script theory assumes that certain events activate a "script" in the head which serves as a framework upon which the discourse can be hung. While the theory applies to other skills, the focus here is on listening. Listeners match this perceived script with reality as heard and viewed. When good matches occur, meaning is confirmed; when mismatches occur, the script must be revised to reach intended meaning. Scripting is a listener device that operates on an organizational level as well as on a content one. Scripts work best in routine events; they break down in novel contexts. This last factor has import for video newscasts since these are highly predictable scripts in terms of text organization.

Among the studies with script theory are two that provoke ideas for application to video broadcasts. A study by Arnold and Brooks (1976) was conducted with second-graders and fifth-graders in native language (English) to assess the effect of videotext with "content clarifying" visuals versus the "talking head." The content was a fantasy story. Results showed that comprehension in fifth graders was enhanced by the accompanying visuals, yet they did not serve to facilitate understanding with the second graders. The researchers concluded that younger students did not benefit perhaps because their "fairy tale" schemata was not developed fully enough for that textual aid to be effective. Making implications from this study to that of television for adults may seem farfetched, but the role of visuals and combinations of visuals will be an element to analyze with video broadcasts.

A study done with second language learners, specifically English-speaking students of German (Mueller 1980) shows that the helpfulness of visual cues is inversely related to proficiency levels. Listening comprehension of beginning students was helped when visual contextual cues were provided as script activators, but more proficient students were not. The researcher concluded that their greater linguistic abilities required less stimulation by other factors. This would appear to be an implicitly logical assumption when one peruses television in languages one does not understand well. Even minimal comprehension does not occur with the unadorned broadcasts from Middle Eastern television, whereas the more graphically and visually presented western-style programs convey a fair amount of meaning by triggering background knowledge through visual cues.

Schema theory has illuminated the crucial role of background knowledge and the necessity for active cognitive structuring by the comprehender, and thereby furnished the theoretical foundations for the efficacy of prereading, previsioning, and prewriting heuristics and related activities. Schema theorists have identified two types of schemata in language acquisition, textual schemata, and content schemata. The preponderance of research and instructional implications in second or foreign languages has dealt primarily with the influence of content background and less often with textual schemata. Weissenreider (1987) did testify to the significance of both in a study of intermediate and advanced students of Spanish with newscasts. Since most of the students were journalism majors, they brought knowledge of the newscasting process to the listening comprehension tasks. Weissenreider attributes their understanding to interplay among textual schemata, content schemata (because the programs contained familiar themes), and effective listener strategies. In terms of the latter, ongoing research in metacognition demonstrates that strategy training does advance comprehension and is indeed a tool that can be learned (Carrell 1985, 1989).

Textual frameworks in videobroadcasts. Comprehension of any text, oral or written, depends upon a constellation of factors. Materials currently on the market, as well as teacher-designed plans, seek to provide instructional support for video by drawing heavily on previsioning activities which exploit prior knowledge and on a series of linguistic tasks to elaborate meaning. Not much has been done with the fact that textual schemata in video news is configured in predictable ways and is limited in formats. It was hypothesized that describing the most common frameworks would be a useful prelude to assessing their potential as tools for language users working independently with contemporary materials. It might also be practicable for teachers when preparation time is at a premium.

Initial global analyses were done in three languages with follow-up experimentation in French and Spanish. All broadcasts were taken from those available on the SCOLA (Satellite Communicaitons for Learning) network. If newscasts are narrowed to particular channels or programs, presentation styles become even narrower, thus more predictable and beneficial. A detailed analysis of two French channels, TF1 and Antenne 2 uncovered peculiarities of the two networks which could be used to predict which station was reporting in the absence of logo or prior information (Challe and Noaro 1984).

One of the first dimensions investigated was the effect of the visual element on comprehension. After all, while the visual should be utilized to its fullest to aid comprehension, the language learners' purposes go beyond deriving meaning in the absence of language! Thus, a goal of the listening exercise is to distinguish in the equation that meaning achieved without benefit of language from that derived explicitly from language. This presumes that the hypothetical listener has bi-directional objectives of "learning to listen" and "listening to learn."

As a first step, one can identify a number of characteristics of a given news program and arrange them diagonally in terms of their contribution to meaning of visual to verbal elements (see Figure 1). Note that this representation does not reflect order of presentation during a broadcast nor does it represent any hierarchy of comprehensibility to nonnative speakers. Within any one segment, it was possible to identify several subtexts. What was especially interesting was that over a number of days, stability in organization of the segments and in their order of presentation was evident.

Weather forecasts. Let us take as an example the weather forecasts. In German, French, and Spanish, listeners could relate weather conditions in terms of global concepts in every case without the sound. All three cultures used maps, familiar symbols for rain, snow, sun, and those isobars that are more or less informative depending on one's ninth-grade science class. However, the organization among the three was quite different.

The French program consistently visualized what was said with deliberately orchestrated graphics, gestures, and speech. Somewhat in a Willard Scott mode, the listener was carefully drawn into an overview of climatic conditions, temperatures in key cities which were enumerated on the map, followed by a chart showing conditions for the next few days.

The following types of video text were found in 30-minute broadcasts from FRG Heute, GDR Aktuelle Kamera, Mexico ECO, France A2/TF1, Canada L'Info, and Argentina. The types occur on a continuum which extends from items where the visual element dominates to items where the language and content dominate.

Figure 1. Broadcast video text characteristics.

Visual element dominates: →
Standard features:
    Weather Reports
    Ads
    Sports Reports
    Business Charts and Graphs
        Soft news
            Music
        Human Interest Stories
            News
                Anchor headlines + graphic
                Anchor + graphic + footage
                      Footage = action scenes
                              = file background
                              = expert interviews
                              = street interviews
                    Short documentaries
                        Commentary / Editorial
                        Discussions
                          ↔ **Language and content dominate:**

The ECO program from Mexico, because of its manner of presenting visuals and speech was much more difficult to follow. The match-up of visual and speech was not done in tandem. One viewed maps of the southwestern U.S., Mexico, South America, and Europe. Each segment stressed different information, so textual schemata established for Mexico did not carry to its southern continent. Background music was added which further distracted the nonnative listener by rendering speech less distinct. The map remained still with symbols in place, but the discussion went into much greater detail.

For South America, temperatures on the map were in Celsius but were given orally in Fahrenheit. Each day's world weather followed the same procedure (although the music did change).

The German report was distinct from the others but standard for future broadcasts. It contained a highly visual element, but rather than beginning with the simple visual, it started with a "talking head" lecture of approximately 80 seconds. This was followed by radar maps across which the forecaster's pointer aimed. Finally, the familiar graphics (gray clouds, raindrops) appeared and temperatures popped up as they were enunciated. Naturally, in the comprehension process, it is artificial, if not impossible, to separate language, content knowledge from text formats, but the analysis attempted to do just that in order to see if textual outlines which could carry over into future segments were identifiable. Weather forecasts proved to repeat their sequence as did many other news segments.

A brief rundown follows of some of the observations that mark the text formats that provide the framework for subsequent broadcasts:

Advertisements. The task of viewing advertisements in a purposeful way would only require understanding the product being advertised and its heralded advantages. That purpose was achieved for the most part without language. However, the ads often offered listening opportunities beyond the immediate real world goal. To that end, classification of text formats was useful and included: stories in themselves with a loose connection to the product; stories built around the product; testimonials to the product; combinations of visual, musical, and verbal images that evoked the product. Voices ranged the spectrum from the speech of small children to adults; register and articulation represented professional speakers and actors, and style could be colloquial to seductive. Ascertaining the textual framework of the advertisement prepared the listener for deriving specific meanings which may or may not have much to do with the product. It should be noted that this analysis serves a very different purpose than Lund's (1990) taxonomy of functions and responses for listening exercises with advertisements.

Soft news and human interest stories. These segments demonstrated the most variability and their essential textual schemata resembled most closely that of a story grammar. The interview format of question/answer was another identifiable "script" used regularly in these segments. For instance, ECO (Mexican channel) would intersperse a half-hour broadcast with songs and finally an interview with an entertainment group. On U.S. television, series such as ABC's American Agenda or Person of the Week would be of this type. Reporters' speech was standard but interviewees displayed varied speech styles, including regional and foreign accents; slang or in-group language was often used.

Hard news. Repeated viewings of news reveals that the delivery systems are more complex than first envisioned. Each time it appeared as though the text outline was visible, it became clear that another layer was waiting to be peeled back. Some of the breakouts include: anchor person giving headlines with a graphic "over the shoulder"; anchor + window with footage; footage consists of the action scenes being described by the anchor, reporter, or voice-over; "file" footage provides background with varying immediacy to message; reporter interviews experts; reporter interviews "people-in-the-street." By reflecting on these many configurations, one can begin to see how information on the textual arrangement can interact with content. Standard speech dominates most segments; the street interviews contain speech patterns which deviate most from the norm.

Commentary or editorials. On all the newscasts viewed in this initial study, this category was totally language-oriented with no support from graphics or other visuals, and delivered with minimal use of gestures. In most instances, outside clues were restricted to an introduction to the commentator by an anchor person and a fit with a topic that had preceded the editorial or that had dominated the news on that day.

Implications for understanding. The analysis of the textual organization of these newscasts was undertaken to see whether an awareness of the frame-works common to the medium would be helpful to the second language listener. The importance of the contribution of prior knowledge and topic familiarity is not being bypassed, but it is hypothesized that when textual formats are predictable as scripts, this additional element up front might be facilitating and self-generating during future episodes. To this point, the analysis has shown that for specific languages and program series, one can classify the great majority of televised segments as fitting a pattern or combination of patterns. Cases of nonconformity are few.

An interesting revelation of the analysis was that preconceived notions of difficulty for listeners were adjusted, because the combination of formats and speakers highlighted factors not previously apparent. There was no strict hierarchy of texts. As with reading, topic familiarity, background knowledge, and interest compensated for predicted text levels. Neither the presence or absence of visual clues predict comprehensibility, for recognition of the framework seemed to render that less of a factor. For example, most newscasts contain a segment that involves interviewing people on the street for reactions. Typical structure includes: Reporter asking the same question (with minimal variation); edited responses which fall into categories of pro/con/no opinion. The question/answer format is not complex, although the fact that longer responses are often crudely edited means that lead-in thoughts are absent and shared assumptions and inferences may be lost. Listeners also realize that they will hear a variety of accents and speech patterns for short periods. Consequently, what is a seemingly simple exchange, in reality, becomes more complex. At the same time, once those background factors are accepted into the scheme, this information can be used to further the understanding of actual content and ultimately to form reactions to meanings expressed. (See Appendix 1 for an interview segment in Spanish.)

On the other hand, the discourse of editorials generates a very distinct set of expectations. Listeners anticipate a well articulated argument where every word counts. In essence, the editorial is an oral presentation of a written document. Syntax is complex, vocabulary is scholarly, delivery is crisp. In French, the analysis showed a preponderance of clearly enumerated discourses in the pattern of 'I took away from the discussion three impressions . . . The first, . . . My second reflection . . Third remark finally . . .' This logical outline with its forcefully enunciated 'first, second, third' permits the listener to develop the framework of the argumentation on the initial listening. Comprehension then becomes a process of 'filling-in the outline.' A further useful stylistic device is that of parallel structures in the heart of the commentary such as '. . .the same refusal . . . the same precaution . . . the same determination . . .' (See Appendix 2 for the complete text in French.)

This researcher conducted an introspective experiment with textual schemata in a language in which she possesses an intermediate-level oral proficiency. In preparation for a trip to a Spanish-speaking country, she began to view newscasts from SCOLA and to listen to cassette tapes of radio programs. With the TV segments, she reproduced the frameworks identified for segments of interest. Subsequently, she listened several times before drafting recalls of the meanings derived. Finally, because she also wanted to be able to identify the language phrases that conveyed the meaning, she scripted key parts of the texts heard. The use of the text outline as an initial activity enabled a degree of understanding and provided a systematic way of processing and reprocessing so that comprehension was elaborated.

A second case to experiment with the deliberate identification of textual schemata occurred during the 1990 Fall term. A high school Spanish teacher, newly returned to teaching, was enrolled in a graduate course in second language acquisition. As her independent research project, she proposed to improve her own listening skills and strategies. She diagnosed herself as a poor listener and as someone who had never had opportunities to listen to authentic materials in Spanish. She kept a journal of the materials she used as sources for listening, of the strategies she applied in listening, of the numbers of times she listened to documents. With video newscasts, she tried the approach of text identification prior to dealing with the content of the newscasts. She did this with free listening, i.e., newscasts for which she had no supporting materials, and also with video segments which were accompanied by learning materials. In both cases, she concluded that she achieved greater comprehension with the assistance of textual schemata generating activities.

Applications to instruction. While a follow-up to the analytical stage, anecdotal evidence is premature to envisioning an instructional role in listening comprehension. One would have to discover whether a concentrated effort to lead listeners' to attend to potential text organization does have benefits. How much time must be spent in developing recognition of the various text formats peculiar to a network, and is that time well spent? How proficient must the listener already be for this tool to be valuable? What happens when the target culture formats differ greatly from that of the native culture (which was not the case in those studied here)? Does this schema activator have an advantage in that the listener, after initial practice, can draw upon it for independent listening because of its stability and finiteness.

Conclusion. As we move forward in second-language acquisition research and in pedagogical implications from interactive models for processing meaning, listening processes will warrant more attention. Video is a powerful tool; it is also a real world informational system. Consequently, in the classroom, it need not be dedicated solely to instructional support, but it can serve as a source of meaningful content to students and to adults. Whatever progress can be made in rendering live material more accessible to learners advances not only their language learning, but also continually updates their international perspectives on world events. At its worst, television numbs and inhibits thinking; at its best, it is a means of providing students and adult language users with insights into target cultures, with broader perspectives of their own, and experiences with international events as interpreted by the international press and the global citizenry it serves.

Appendix 1. Broadcast segment from ECO (Mexico) on SCOLA (August 27, 1990).

A. Framework identification.

Listener outlines segments using visuals and language segments understood on the first listening.
- Introduction to the story by the anchorwoman.
- Introductory remarks by correspondent on the scene.
    Correspondent relates story over action footage.
    Correspondent interviews two people.
        First interviewee faces camera and gives well enunciated, seemingly practiced response.
        Second interviewee responds in a more spontaneous fashion (*side view*).

B. From schemata to language script.

Within the framework, the listener, moving from gist to words and phrases to sentences so that the actual scripts were elaborated to a point where comprehension was achieved but short of dictation. Example below is from an interview segment and is not corrected for spelling or grammar. Context is the governor's race in Illinois.

Correspondent:—¿Qué traje el candidato Edgar para la communidad hispana?
Woman interviewee:—Bueno, traje un record de trabajar bastante duro para la communidad hispana como secretario del estado. Y traje bastantes planes muy importantes para nuestra communidad que sea elegido el gobernador del estado de Illinois. Alguna de las cosas que ha mencionado hoy son muy claras es que el tendrá bastantes personas hispanas in posiciones claves en su administración.
Man interviewee: En Illinois, no todo, en Chicago hay alrededor un millión y media de hispano-americanos . . . es un potencial ya lo político que ya no puede ignorar. . .

Appendix 2. Broadcast as a commentary. Delivered by Albert du Roy for Antenne 2, relayed by SCOLA on 20 August 1990.

A. Framework identification.

The context is one in which news coverage revolved around debate in the French parliament on the commitment of French forces to the Gulf. The anchorperson makes a transition to the commentary. Listener identifies the following framework from a clearly enunciated, full face delivery:
- J'ai retiré . . . trois impressions . . . La première est que . . . Ma deuxième réflexion est que . . . Troisième remarque enfin . . .
    Quelques questions graves . . . trois exemples . . .

B From schemata to language script.

With each additional listening, the learner can use this outline to elaborate the text segments understood. The full script is as follows (underscores identify initial framework):

J'ai retiré du discours <u>trois impressions</u>. <u>La première est que</u> sur le fond la position de la France est approuvée par tous: Même refus de toute concession. Même soucis de nier à Saddam Hussein le droit de parer le sud contre le nord, les pauvres contre les riches, les arabes contre les autres. Même espoir d'une solution pacifique. Même détermination s'il faut l'accourir à la force. Ça n'exclut évidemment pas les divergences. Les uns considèrent que la position française a évolué quand les autres disent qu'elle a flotté. Certains se demandent si les moyens militaires dans le Golfe sont adaptés à la situation. D'autres s'inquiètent devant la France entrainée dans une opération qui aura pour but, non pas de libérer Kuwaït mais de renverser le régime irakien. Mais ces divergences ne portent pas sur l'essentiel.

Ma deuxième réflexion est que décidément on ne reformera pas nos parlementaires. La séance était calme mais certains ont quand-même saisi la moindre occasion pour chaouter un peu, qui le gouvernement, qui l'opposition, comme s'il fallait à tout prix, faire l'étalage de quelques désaccords.

Troisième remarque enfin: Quelques questions graves pour l'avenir en étaient évoquées. Trois exemples: après le conflit, les Nations Unies se montreront-elles aussi fermes pour faire appliquer leur résolution pour Israël dans les territoires occupés? Ne faut-il pas moraliser le commerce des armes? Ne faut-il enfin créer une défense européenne commune? Ces questions divisent chacune de nos familles politiques. Je suis curieux de savoir si le crise passé on les débordera sérieusement.

References

Arnold, D.J. and P.H. Brooks. 1976. Influence of contextual organizing material on children's listening comprehension. Journal of Educational Psychology 68:711-16.
Carrell, Patricia. 1985. Facilitating ESL reading by teaching text structure. TESOL Quarterly 19:727-52.
Carrell, Patricia. 1989. Metacognitive awareness and second language reading. Modern Language Journal 73:121-34.
Challe, Odile and Pierre Noaro. 1984. Décoder le journal télévisé. Paris: BELC.
Glisan, Eileen W. 1988. A plan for teaching listening comprehension: Adaptation of an instructional reading model. Foreign Language Annals 21:9-16.
Joiner, Elizabeth G. 1991. Teaching listening: Ends and means. In: Georgetown University Round Table on Languages and Linguistics 1991. Washington, D.C.: Georgetown University Press.
Liskin-Gasparro, Judith. 1990. A four-stage approach to teaching listening comprehension. Paper presented at Northeast Conference on the Teaching of Foreign Languages, New York City.
Long, Donna Reseigh. 1989. Second language listening comprehension: A schema-theoretic perspective. Modern Language Journal 73:32-40.
Lund, Randall J. 1990. A Taxonomy for teaching second language listening. Foreign Language Annals 23:105-15.
Mueller, Guenther. 1980. Visual contextual cues and listening comprehension: An experiment. Modern Language Journal 64:335-40.
Phillips, June K. 1990. Research : teaching :: Sin : confession—An analogy for the times. In: Georgetown University Round Table on Languages and Linguistics 1990. Washington, D.C.: Georgetown University Press.
Swaffar, Janet K., Katherine M. Arens, and Heidi Byrnes. 1991. Reading for meaning. An integrated approach to language learning. Englewood Cliffs, N.J.: Prentice-Hall.
Weissenrieder, Maureen. 1987. Listening to the news in Spanish. Modern Language Journal 71:18-27.

In search of a sense of place:
The state of the art
in language teaching methodology

Heidi Byrnes*
Georgetown University

Introduction and statement of problem. Our professional dialogue regarding language teaching methodology is burdened by major and seemingly insurmountable interpretive differences. These pertain to what are considered to be optimal or even superior methodologies. They apply as well to the use of specific terms; for instance, the term 'communicative language teaching', or the 'incorporation of grammar'. And, finally, they extend to actual teaching practice that is taken to be a manifestation of a particular methodological stance.

Claims, counter-claims, and variant beliefs persist, even though attempts to establish lasting superiority for one method over another have ultimately remained inconclusive (Chastain and Woerdehoff 1968). They endure although we have known for some time that methodological purism probably does not exist in teaching practice in any case (Swaffar, Arens, Morgan 1982). And mutually exclusive assertions linger, even though we know that intellectual agreement on the desirability of a certain approach in no way guarantees its consistent realization in practice. It is fair to say, for example, that there are probably as many actualizations of the communicative or form-centered classroom as there are classrooms.

As a consequence, the usefulness of the concept of 'methodology' is, at the very least, seriously undermined, at worst, utterly discredited.

So, shall we abdicate the responsibility of having to create an optimal learning environment? Shall we proceed on the assumption that one approach is as good as the other? I believe that we cannot. However, it is

---

* For its support of the preparation of this paper, I wish to acknowledge the National Foreign Language Center, Washington, D.C., for the award of a Mellon Fellowship during the spring semester of 1991. Thanks also to Janet Swaffar and Katherine Arens for their reading and comments on ealier drafts of this paper.

abundantly clear that a meaningful continuation of our search is possible only under the following conditions:

- we must find a higher level of abstraction for discussing pedagogy than that of classroom activities or tasks, or even the concept of methodology;
- we must take a diachronic long-range view of pedagogy, rather than a purely synchronic one;
- we must be willing to evaluate, with a critical look, assumptions underlying our pedagogy, as well as likely future results; and, finally,
- we must place our pedagogy in the larger context of American education, in terms of its goals and issues, content, and structures.

I realize that all of these conditions make my observations considerably less safe. But I do not equate that riskiness with futility. In fact, if our look at language teaching is to go beyond simple description, such an expanded, though less certain perspective is imperative. Perhaps it can lead us to a sense of place and an appreciation of the state of the art in language teaching methodology.

Some basic premises for examining pedagogical intervention. To assure a broad enough scope, two fundamental points must be clarified at the outset. One pertains to the instructional goals we impute to variant methodologies, and, by extension, how we value or disallow the means being used to reach them. The other refers to what options exist for structuring intervention into otherwise unguided language learning. Intervention is, after all, the essence of language teaching. Teachers manipulate in three ways: through selection (what to teach), through sequencing (when to teach it), and through error correction (how to improve learner language).

As for the first point, instructional goals, I consider it crucial to assume that any kind of language instruction aims to create competent users of the language. In other words, no matter what particular areas of language use are emphasized (e.g. speaking, listening, reading, writing), and, perhaps even more importantly, no matter how their development is nurtured in the instructional setting (e.g. through memorization, through dialogues, through role plays, through inductive or deductive grammar-focused approaches, through extensive or intensive reading), the ultimate instructional goal is always to allow learners to be fully functional in the language, or, at least, not to bar them from becoming fully functional should the need arise.

This seemingly common-sense requirement has been violated entirely too often. As a result we often treat unfamiliar approaches with a grand gesture of dismissal, a treatment that then allows us to ignore their premises about the human capacity to learn a non-native language. For example, many today believe that audio-lingualism aspired only to produce fully functional robots, completely disregarding such work as Robert Lado's *Language Testing* 1961, with its emphasis on functional ability and language as an instrument of communication. Similarly today, some argue that communicative approaches aspire to creating abominably flawed speakers who can successfully talk themselves out of most any situation, or that functional approaches are essentially non- or even anti-academic, limiting learners to look, in perpetuity, for train stations or restaurants. Such casual dismissal serves only short-term territorial claims. Over the long term, belittling what have to be taken as honest attempts to enhance learning, keeps us from dealing seriously with the complex issues surrounding language acquisition and, perhaps, even from improving instruction.

The second point, the options that exist for structuring intervention into otherwise unguided language learning, ties in with the first. Any formal language teaching assumes that there are aspects about language as a formal system, about its use, or about how it is learned that are central, pervasive, generalizable; therefore, they can provide a suitable, perhaps even preferred basis for language teaching and learning. Foreign language teaching is a form of intervention with the purpose of optimizing learning, by capitalizing on the inherent differences between second and first language learning. Whether that intervention is through selection and sequencing of instructional materials and strategies, or whether it is through intervention to improve learner language, it is invariably informed by explicit or implicit understandings about a preferred locus and modus of intervention. For both the 'where' and the 'how' of intervention, a theory of second language learning and teaching really has only two possible bases. One is linguistic in the broad sense of the word, encompassing form and use, the other is psychological. Both influence each other and together they engender favored classroom activities. For example, it is hard to imagine audio-lingualism without Bloomfieldian structuralism, or cognitive approaches without the work of Ausubel (1963) and Ausubel, Novak, and Hanesian (1978).

It seems to me that the foregoing contradictions in theory and professional practice justify the position I will take in the rest of the paper. Over the past three decades, the bases for methodological intervention have changed dramatically; at the same time, the consequences of these changes for instruction have not always been fully appreciated, not fully implemented, and their benefits not fully reaped. Why? First, change has led to the existence of a multiplicity of approaches that are being advocated side by side. Second, and as a direct result, it has brought about a confused state of affairs in language classrooms. Researchers like

Bernhardt (1990) have noted that instructional activities seem to have a life of their own. In her words, 'regardless of time frame, theoretical framework or theory . . . the instructional activities suggested are almost identical. That is, there seems to be a canon of teaching procedures that supersedes theory and research' (p. 280). One can hardly escape the resulting anomaly: diverse instructional options represented by equally diverse theoretical insights are being honored more in the breach than in the observance.

To work ourselves out of this thicket, I propose to look at the underlying assumptions regarding language and language learning in three areas. To clarify the significance of the three realms for instructional practice, I will, in each case, connect them to the historical manifestations they assumed in the classroom. The three areas are: (1) formal linguistic features, (2) features of language use which, for ease of reference, I term sociolinguistic features, and (3) features of knowledge application. In addition, each one of these can be seen from two perspectives, as a generalized, idealized, though contextualized version, and as a variable, context-sensitive, individuated version.[1] The terms *langue* and *parole* refer to this distinction, as does our differentiating between presumed cultural universals for language use and culture-specific features; and in the area of knowledge application, we recognize general aspects of human learning and human behavior and individual learner cognition and intent.

Each perspective, the generalized as well as the specific, comes with its own set of advantages and disadvantages. Generalizability permits maximum rule coverage, thereby aiding acquisition. Language instruction targets a form which, presumably, will be recognized by the native interlocutors, and is least obtrusive, perhaps even acceptable to the largest number of them. On the downside, basing intervention on maximal generalizability risks fostering a false sense of sameness between the two languages, thereby encouraging inappropriate transfer of semantic structures. Learners with general formulae for ordering a meal may indiscriminately apply this ability whether the meal is being ordered in a bistro or in a first class restaurant. In some cases, the resultant language can be perceived as stilted, formal, hyper-correct, perhaps even elitist.

In large measure, generalizability comes at the expense of space for the learner's direct emotional, volitional, and cognitive involvement, a

---

[1] With the term *contextualized* I want to indicate that generalized language occurs within and depends for its meaning on a context of situation which provides the larger frame of reference. By *context-sensitive* I mean that a specific communicative event is played out in response to an intricate network of factors, whether they arise from the specific setting or from the individual players who perform specific verbal actions within it.

restriction that, to some, is justified by the safety which it provides. I believe it is fair to say that both teachers and learners are basically aware that real people in the other culture do not interact according to the language model presented in class. But both parties are willing to suspend disbelief for the presumed pedagogical advantage of generalizability.

Highly contextualized and individuated models of language, by contrast, focus on the idiomaticity of language use in a specific setting, with specific speaker intentions, an emphasis that creates an air, some might say, illusion, of authenticity, cultural sensitivity, and speaker involvement. Within a very restricted area, learners come close to native-like language use, if one considers only its surface performance attributes. However, precisely because learners could not be given the freedom of choosing their own speaker intentions, they also did not engage in the kind of encoding process that is really the critical precursor to successful performance in the infinitely varied circumstances of real life communication. Role playing a well-scripted emergency situation is not the same as functioning independently and decisively under emergency conditions. Moreover, especially for adult learners with an analytical bent, a particularistic approach can lead to considerable anxiety and uncertainty for the following reasons: there is relatively little data or time for determining what in the separate, perfectly instantiated communicative events is generalizable and what is not. As a result, learners can feel extremely frustrated. Such frustration may even damage motivation if the meticulously staged communicative exchanges are of minimal personal interest to the learners to begin with. Who cares, after all, whether I can describe to someone else, how I tie my own shoe laces!

Language pedagogy arising from linguistic bases. Let us begin our look at the three areas of possible intervention with area one, aspects of language. Here, a pedagogy whose bases of intervention are the formal characteristics of language encompasses the majority of teaching practice, both past and present. The basic assumption is that the inherent rule-governedness of various aspects of language provides the most powerful enhancement for learning in an instructed setting and, ultimately, in attaining communicative competence.

(1) A form-based pedagogy. The more traditional version of this pedagogy focuses on language form, overlaid on restricted use. For example, since irregular verbs must eventually be learned, as many indicative forms of *go* are seeded into a dialogue, with minimal concern for its message. From the standpoint of learning psychology, one assumes that learners should first learn a limited number of unequivocal form-meaning relationships; e.g. every present tense form of *be* has only one meaning. One expects that learners, through extensive opportunity for use and their own intuition as users of language, will ultimately apprehend that *be*, like the vast majority of words in a language, has a whole range of contextually specified meanings, from truth value of a current event (e.g. *he is here*) to meanings about the future (*he's coming later*), to ontological givens (e.g. *the earth is round*).

The critical issue is whether learners can, in fact, bridge that gap. For advocates of a language-based pedagogy the distinction between a language-based ability to perform tasks or a use of language driven by speaker intentions has negligible value for explaining learners' ultimate chance for achieving competence in the language, particularly if instruction encourages iterative skill-getting- skill-using phases (Rivers 1988). There are plenty of learners raised in the most rule and form-governed environments who, when immersed in the target language culture, were quite capable of making the shift. As a consequence, these advocates can interpret the need for an immersion component more as a function of the short sequences of instruction available to most American learners than as an inherent flaw of enlightened form-based pedagogy.

However, those skeptical about the value of a form-based pedagogy see too few communicative opportunities, given the restrictions I mentioned. To them, the need for a period of immersion in the speech community becomes further proof that the critical leap to meaning- and intentionality-focused use of language is largely impossible with such a pedagogy.

These criticisms of form-based pedagogy have been further aggravated, by a marked shift toward functional abilities as the goal of language instruction, and by new theoretical positions about language. Over the past two decades, these developments have exploded the field of language pedagogy. From an era of methodological orthodoxy we have moved to one approaching anarchy, with the possibility that instructional intervention may become random.

(2) A socially grounded pedagogy. The second option, a socially-grounded pedagogy, represents a shift in our understanding of the essence of language. This shift can be characterized as moving from a concern with the static systemicness of language forms to a focus on dynamic interaction. A new kind of systematicity emerged, this one socially derived. But the system for language in use is immensely more complex than form-based systemicness. Form-based systemicness, within which structuralism had flourished, was unidimensional. It defined norm and variation, acceptable standard and non-permissible deviant form, once and for all. A socially-grounded pedagogy, on the other hand, confronts teachers with the multi-dimensional norms and variations that characterize use.

If a multi-dimensional view of language is to inform teaching practice and language learning, then our pedagogy must incorporate the immensely complex rules of language use. Yet, this very rule complexity threatens to overwhelm both teachers and learners. As we have seen, teachers have struggled with the complexity of this issue in several ways. Some respond with the equivalent of a pedagogical *laissez-faire* attitude where anything goes; others seek a delicate balance between the social construction of language, the learners' individual expressiveness, and, to a lesser extent, the formal requirements of language.

Whatever response is chosen, the task of teaching non-native languages has become even more formidable than we have always known it to be. Even so—or precisely for that reason—pedagogy cannot abdicate its responsibility for constructing new guidelines for the conduct of non-native language classrooms. What, then, are our current options?

An indirect pedagogy for language learning. Let me begin with those who view pedagogical intrusion with suspicion. The current intellectual climate favors assigning a significant function to the learners as they face the data to be learned. Any learning seems better described by emphasizing learners' active and creative engagement, their desire to solve problems, their ability to organize, imagine, infer, than by characterizing it as a type of rote receivership of pre-packaged materials.

In foreign language pedagogy such thinking manifests itself in numerous ways. Specific instances are an emphasis on the presumed greater effectiveness of incidental learning over intentional learning (Bransford 1979), learning by problem solving, the natural approach to language learning (Krashen and Terrell 1983); the distinction between learning and acquisition (Krashen 1981); the extremely limited function of conscious learning as summarized in the Monitor Hypothesis (Krashen 1977); the Input Hypothesis (Krashen 1985). Even such concepts as the order of acquisition of certain morphemes (Krashen and Terrell 1983) and learnability and teachability (Pienemann 1984) which seem to indicate that learners are impervious to teaching unless their own language development is just at the right stage, show a strong affinity to this indirect stance. In their respective ways all of the foregoing attribute only scant effectiveness to pedagogical intrusion.

Thus, compared to earlier methodological approaches, the indirect view privileges learners socially and, to some extent, intellectually. At the same time it underplays the complexity of language learning by seeing teacher-learner interactions as:

(1) superfluous except to provide input;
(2) ineffectual since too many rules overload the learners, and

(3) inappropriate since the descriptive validity of rules does not in any way guarantee for them psychological validity (Garrett 1986).

A focus on social settings. Another option for capturing the social basis of language in the classroom for the purposes of language learning is to center it around a specific context which is socially embedded, culturally derived, and situationally specified (e.g. Morley 1987, Kramsch 1991, Rivers 1989). Partner and group work are advocated to a degree and in ways unknown in audio-lingualism, for example (Long and Porter 1985, Pica and Doughty 1985).

These contexts can be set up in two ways: as cultural universals (e.g. ordering food at a restaurant, arranging a meeting with someone) or as communicative acts in specific cultural contexts (e.g. meeting a young woman to whom one was recently introduced who is of a certain social position which requires strict observance of acceptable standards of venue and time). In either case, pedagogical intervention consists of selecting communicative contexts or stipulating the tasks learners are to negotiate. For all their seeming naturalness and authenticity both variants have serious drawbacks.

Let me exemplify: instruction presents a language context (e.g. family, school, social interactions) either as a cultural universal (any school, anywhere) or as a cultural specific (the lycée in a Paris suburb), as normed language for a particular setting (*langue*), or as one of numerous options related to cultural variables (*parole*). When students talk about things they like about a generic school, their performance necessarily lacks sensitivity to the language requirements inherent in culture-specific settings. Conversely, when materials present highly specific negotiation scenarios (e.g. requesting class notes from a close friend, or a relative stranger), students practice speech acts without generating their own cognitive intent and the strategies to realize that intent. They learn to play a role, but not necessarily how to encode or generate that role. They learn behaviors, but not sensitivity about how different linguistic techniques achieve different objectives.

Ironically, while the non-interventionist rejects most pedagogy as interference, seemingly solving the whole problem in that fashion, the reality for most teachers is that the social basis for second language learning has increased pedagogical insecurity with regard to an acceptable basis for classroom conduct. This insecurity is perhaps best observed in the difficulty we have in deciding on how to deal with learner errors. In order to identify our teaching as meaning-focused and socially-attuned, many of us are extremely ambivalent about error correction, frequently offering diffuse and contradictory signals to the learners regarding the focus of our intervention, on meaning or on form. If corrections are on an effective exchange of information (i.e. stress on cognitive processing variables) we feel that students will fail to master the formal features of the language. If corrections are based on specific cultural situations, they necessarily deal only with the *parole* of that situation (i.e. sociolinguistic settings), leaving a potentially critical gap regarding the larger conventions of *langue*. In sum, whether one attempts to capture the social basis of language through a non-interventionist or a pedagogically activist stance becomes largely irrelevant in the face of contradictory practice in error correction (Swain and Lapkin 1989).

A similar dilemma occurs with regard to standardized language testing, which, by and large, continues to assess *langue* and not *parole*. Moreover, that *langue* is tested without regard to students' background or interests. Whether they are of national or local-institutional origin, placements exams in effect ignore such key variables as temporary language loss due to lack of practice, unfamiliarity with subject matter, or inadequate command of specialized grammar terminology and item types. Consequently, most language programs really cannot afford to encourage more than token sociolinguistic features of language use. Presumptions about relationships between language processing, social milieu, and cognitive processing are invalidated in light of the official performance expectations. Standardized testing on a national level has, for all intents and purposes, preempted the many possibilities for other forms of testing in the individual classroom.

Developing a new basis for intervention. To summarize, recent pedagogy has had difficulty finding coherent ways to make learners full partners in the second language acquisition process. How can students progress from incomplete command of the language to an understanding of how situationally motivated *parole* is related to the more general *langue*. Our search for a new basis for intervention must acknowledge that language **exists for** the conveyance of meanings and that language learning **proceeds through** the conveyance of meanings.

There are numerous challenges inherent in such a stance. The central issue is, of course, the assertion that one can and should be teaching language without using language as the basis of decision-making about language use. A second consideration is that, in order to be maximally effective from the pedagogical standpoint, the new basis for intervention must possess a systematicity that facilitates learning a language, even while it is not itself focused on language. The critical question is: how can pedagogy converge with psychology and linguistics in a way which is focused on the learner and intervenes in terms of more than just the system of language?

Knowledge-based approaches offer examples of research and classroom practice that has grappled with this challenge:

(1) Current knowledge application or content-based programs seem to speak most directly to learners' background knowledge as well as interests. Apparently such approaches capitalize on the results of psychological research showing that comprehension is more readily associated with content knowledge than it is with linguistic knowledge. By providing extremely rich input for learners, on more than a linguistic level, one can enhance learners' ability to produce appropriate output as well. Language learning for special purposes, a particularly important field for adult learners, is perhaps the best known example for this approach.

(2) Similarly, a content-based approach which emphasizes learner styles and strategies aims to have learners become aware of the process of learning, and empower them for success (O'Malley and Chamot 1990, Oxford 1990). At the same time, because the information and reasoning are the classroom focus, responsibility for successful learning is shifted from the teacher to the learner. That shift entails taking seriously both the motivational and cognitive forces that drive learners, whatever the goals they pursue, and continuously tending to their cognitive growth.

(3) The particular suitability of content-based instruction for language learning derives from the fact that learners are taught to correlate a relatively limited number of major organizational patterns (e.g. enumerative, additive, contrastive, illustrative) with possible linguistic manifestations (Chamot and O'Malley 1987, Swaffar, Arens, and Byrnes 1991). They learn to do so in line with a coherent rationale for processing textual meaning, one which simultaneously exploits insights from linguistics, learning psychology, and second language acquisition research. In this fashion, conceptual competence and linguistic competence can be gradually and mutually enhanced.

Conclusion. If designed in terms of knowledge application, content-based programs integrate three major aspects of second language acquisition: social contexts, cognition, and processing strategies of second language learners. Such efforts suggest that foreign language pedagogy may become less distinct from native language instruction than it was in the past, when programs focused on second language acquisition *per se*. Approaches that have already gained prominence in native language instruction are increasingly being incorporated into non-native instruction with the most conspicuous examples being reading and writing instruction (Carrell 1987, Cumming 1989, Flower and Hayes 1984, Raimes 1983, Swaffar 1991).

As a consequence, language teaching can now connect with the larger discussion in education. The potential exists for language teaching methodology to discard odious associations with simple-minded teaching and learning skills, thus substantiating claims that it has always made about its humanistic provenance.

A pedagogy for knowledge applications presents a unique opportunity for language learning to be mainstreamed into the curriculum. By rigorously following through with an interpretation of language learning in terms of content learning, the insidious marginalization of language teaching and learning might be overcome.

It is too early to say whether content-based programs can capture the imagination of teachers and learners and, more importantly, to what extent, they can fulfill their inherent promises toward enhanced language learning.

Even so, for instructed language learning, there is every indication that knowledge applications or performance programs in the sense of Wesche (1991) are the way to join learner and teacher in optimal language acquisition. Content-based instruction is the only realm where learners and teachers can potentially be evenly matched and evenly engaged. Inherently, neither language form nor socio-cultural conventions of use can allow learners the equal access which is at the heart of full learner participation and which, in turn, is at the heart of the critical motivation to learn the language. Since cognition is best stimulated through comprehensive engagement with content, subject-matter suggests itself as an appropriate micro-environment for presenting foreign language *parole*. Through the teacher's consistent efforts in relating *parole* (a content area) to *langue* (the vehicle for acquiring content) students are given the opportunity, ultimately, to attain communicative competence in the original sense of that term. Only by drawing on all three aspects of language use, formal language, sociolinguistic appropriateness, and knowledge applications can the foreign language teacher and the learner harmonize their intentions and learn language to learn.

References

Ausubel, D. 1963. The psychology of meaningful verbal learning. New York: Grune and Stratton.

Ausubel, D., J. Novak, and H. Hanesian. 1978. Educational psychology: A cognitive view. 2nd. ed. New York: Holt, Rinehart, and Winston.

Bernhardt, E.B. 1990. Knowledge-based inferencing in second language comprehension. In: Georgetown University Round Table on Languages and Linguistics 1990. Washington, D.C.: Georgetown University Press. 271-84.

Bransford, J. 1979. Human cognition. Learning, understanding and remembering. Belmont, Calif.: Wadsworth.

Carrell, P. L. 1987. Content and formal schemata in ESL reading. TESOL Quarterly 21:461-81.

Chamot, A.U., and J.M. O'Malley. 1987. The Cognitive Academic Language Learning Approach (CALLA): A bridge to the mainstream. TESOL Quarterly 21:227-49.
Chastain, K.A., and F.J. Woerdehoff. 1968. A methodological study comparing the audio-lingual habit theory and the cognitive-code learning theory. Modern Language Journal 52:268-79.
Cumming, A. 1989. Writing expertise and second-language proficiency. Language Learning 39:81-141.
Flower, L., and J.R. Hayes. 1984. Images, plans, and prose. The representation of meaning in writing. Written Communication 1:120-60.
Garrett, N. 1986. The problem with grammar: What kind can the language learner use? Modern Language Journal 70:133-47.
Kramsch, C. 1991. The order of discourse in language teaching. In: B.F. Freed, ed. Foreign language acquisition research and the classroom. Lexington, Mass.: D.C. Heath. 191-204.
Krashen, S.D. 1977. Some issues relating to the monitor model. In: H. Brown, C. Yorio, and R. Crymes, eds. On TESOL '77. Teachers of English as a Second Language.
Krashen, S. D. 1981. Second language acquisition and second language learning. Oxford: Pergamon.
Krashen, S.D. 1985. The Input Hypothesis. London: Longman.
Krashen, S.D. and T.D. Terrell. 1983. The Natural Approach. Hayward: Alemany Press.
Lado, R. 1961. Language testing. New York: McGraw-Hill.
Long, M.H., and P.A. Porter. 1985. Group work, interlanguage talk, and second language acquisition. TESOL Quarterly 19,2:207-28.
Morley, J. 1987. Current directions in teaching English to speakers of other languages: A state-of-the art synopsis. TESOL Newsletter 21.2, April 1987.
O'Malley, J.M., and A.U. Chamot. 1990. Learning strategies in second language acquisition. New York: Cambridge University Press.
Oxford, R.L. 1990. Language learning strategies: What every teacher should know. New York: Newbury House.
Pica, T., and C. Doughty. 1985. Input and interaction in the communicative language classroom: A comparison of teacher-fronted and group activities. In: S.M. Gass and C.G. Madden, eds. Input in second language acquisition. Rowley, Mass.: Newbury House 115-32.
Pienemann, M. 1984. Psychological constraints on the teachability of languages. Studies in Second Language Acquisition 6:186-214.
Raimes, A. 1983. Techniques in teaching writing. Oxford: Oxford University Press.
Rivers, W.M. 2nd. ed. 1988. Teaching French: A practical guide. Lincolnwood, Ill.: National Textbook Co.
Rivers, W.M. 1989. Ten principles of interactive language learning and teaching. Occasional papers of the National Foreign Language Center at the Johns Hopkins University. Washington, D.C.
Swaffar, J.K. 1991. Language learning is more than learning language: Rethinking reading and writing tasks in textbooks for beginning language study. In: B.F. Freed, ed., Foreign language acquisition research and the classroom. Lexington, Mass.: D.C. Heath. 252-79.
Swaffar, J.K., K. Arens, and M. Morgan. 1982. Teacher classroom practices: Redefining method as task hierarchy. Modern Language Journal 66:24-33.

Swaffar, J., K. Arens, and H. Byrnes. 1991. Reading for meaning: An integrated approach to language learning. Englewood Cliffs, N.J.: Prentice Hall.

Swain, M. 1990. Second language testing and second langauge acquisition: Is there a conflict with traditional psychometrics? In: Georgetown University Round Table on Languages and Linguistics 1990. Washington, D.C.: Georgetown University Press. 401-12.

Swain, M., and S. Lapkin. 1989. Canadian immersion and adult second language teaching: What's the connection? Modern Language Journal 73,2:150-59.

Wesche, M. 1991. Performance testing for job-related assessment. Paper delivered at the symposium "Testing and evaluating: Feedback strategies for improvement of foreign language learning." National Foreign Language Center. Washington, D.C., February 4-5, 1991.

Second-language learning:
Engaging, simulating, and converting

Kenneth Chastain
University of Virginia

Introduction. Some of us have been engaged in second-language learning for longer than we may like to contemplate. We have moved hopefully through the years and the evolving cycles of alluring alternative approaches attempting to stay abreast of all that is new and good. We have embraced innovative proposals and incorporated them into our classroom repertoire only to have them replaced regularly by subsequent promises. We have taught according to grammar-translation tenets, audio-lingual techniques, cognitive approaches, and, more recently, proficiency guidelines.

Some of us feel that we are wiser now than when we began teaching in the unenlightened age of grammar translation. Of course, this is an opinion that we readily grant to ourselves in spite of the skepticism of our younger colleagues who typically believe that we have become cynical and that we suffer from a severe case of hardening of the intellect. In this assessment there may be a grain, or even several grains, of truth, but I do maintain that having experience, experience being labeled by the term *old timer*, does give us the necessary perspective that enables us to analyze more fully where we are in our quest for higher levels of language proficiency among our students.

For the 'old timers' and the 'young timers' here let me describe briefly some of the ideas that have been touted during my years in second-language teaching.

At one time we were told that learning a foreign language, or any other subject for that matter, was really quite simple. All one had to do was to put on a record, place a speaker under one's pillow, turn on the record player, go to sleep, and let one's subconscious do the hard part—learn the language. That approach certainly has a compelling appeal. Many of us want to learn so many things. The only obstacle preventing us from doing so is the time and energy required to acquire the knowledge that we desire. If learning were so easy, the world would be full of Solomons, and I would be asleep making a relaxed effort to join the group.

Lest you succumb to the temptation to snicker at such foolishness and to dismiss the idea completely let me remind you that there is a more modern version. In fact, I think that all in all I much prefer it to having a potentially uncomfortable speaker under my pillow. The newer approach recommends a slightly altered format. The students recline in soft, easy chairs and listen to soothing baroque music while they receive the language they are to learn. From my point of view, this arrangement is preferable to the older one because students have the opportunity to listen to some good music before they drift off into oblivion.

During another phase we were offered a new approach that would solve all the difficulties with which we had struggled for so many years. If we would follow the suggestions proposed by the adherents of these new insights, our students would become the bilinguals we had always sought. An even more impressive aspect of this innovation in second-language teaching was that any student could learn by the system because intelligence was not a factor. (An oft-cited study was one in which a researcher taught French to a group of idiots, morons, and imbeciles via this method, which proved the irrelevance of intelligence, as contended.) In fact, students did not even have to understand what they were saying. (Another researcher taught students language patterns taken out of a meaningful context, took the students at the end of the instruction period to the country of the foreign language, and found that they functioned very well.) All they had to do was to submit to the techniques utilized in the classroom and the language laboratory, to repeat after the master voice, and to practice the pattern drills to the point of automatic, non-thoughtful response.

Another unique solution to the problems students have learning second languages is the total physical response approach. Now that is a title befitting a Madison Avenue ad and deserving of serious consideration. It has appeal. It creates an image, one that implies action, and results. What could be more simple than acting out the instructor's commands? No one gets bored; no one gets frustrated. Everyone learns; everyone retains the material for long periods of time. Anxiety is lessened and achievement is increased. I am convinced. Just tell me what to do.

Of course, for a quiet person like me an even more alluring title attracts my attention. If any approach is the one for me, it must be the silent way. An approach based on using wooden blocks, directing the class with a pointer, and remaining silent while the students use their powers of perception to comprehend the structural patterns under consideration appears to be a perfect fit for my personality. Remaining silent suits my natural inclination, and placing the responsibility for learning on the students seems to be a justifiable orientation.

I hasten at this point to express my apologies to all of you. Surely, at least a few of you are faithful followers of and firm believers in one or more of the approaches that I have treated in a somewhat frivolous manner. Please forgive me. My intent was not to denigrate any particular set of teaching tenets but to prepare you for the main focus of my comments.

One of our past mistakes is that we have continued to pursue the illusory objective of finding an easy way to learn second languages. There is no method that is so inherently perfect that all students will be totally consumed by an intense desire to learn that language, that all will perform all the homework and classroom activities effortlessly and correctly, and that all will become fluent in the language. While experience prevents my being so foolish as to think that I have the perfect approach to unveil today, I do hope to convince you that any set of effective classroom teaching-learning activities must include the three processes given in the title of this presentation: engaging, simulating, and converting.

Engaging

Definition. What do I mean by engaging? Imagine this situation. I am in a car. The motor is running, and I want to go from point A, my home, to point B, the university. To make the car move I must transmit the energy being produced by the engine to the wheels, and to do that I must engage the clutch. When the clutch is engaged, the car moves, and I continue on my way until I arrive at the university.

A similar situation exists with students in our classes. The students may be in class, but they may not be attending to the learning process. Being in class is not synonymous with being engaged. Being physically present is not the same as being mentally present and active. As the poet said, 'Stone walls do not a prison make nor iron bars a cage.' Students can leave class almost at will. Their mind can carry them away to any place or any time whenever they wish, and the glazed look in the eyes that we instructors dislike so much is irrefutable evidence that such travel occurs with disturbing frequency. A particularly astute and perceptive high school art teacher told me once of an experiment that he had conducted with his students. One day in the middle of an explanation of a particular type of art he asked, without changing the tone of his voice, 'Would all of you who are listening please raise your right hand.' Well, he was astounded. He vowed that he would never ever make that mistake again. The result was just too humiliating.

Of course, the analogy between a car with the motor running and students with brains emitting brain waves has obvious limitations. Surely, both have to be engaged to accomplish goals. However, cars are nonliving, mechanical devices. Human beings engage the clutch to move the car toward the goal that they have chosen. The car has no goal of its own. The motivation, the goal, and the engaging are exterior to the car.

On the other hand, students are living, thinking, feeling human beings. They each have an amazingly capable and active brain. They have the ability to engage, to disengage, or not to engage as they see fit. They have the free will to learn or not to learn. They are influenced by exterior forces, but they are not controlled by them. With regard to engaging in the learning process theirs is a responsibility rather than a requirement. For them engaging is an internal rather than an external process.

The importance of engaging. Clearly, students who are not engaged are not learning. As much as we may yearn for that dream approach in which students absorb language without conscious effort and persistence, we are doomed to failure by the inherent qualities of the learning process. The term 'passive learning' is an oxymoron. By definition learning is and can be only an active process, and the implication of active is that students must be engaged in completing the learning tasks and achieving their goals. Cognitive processes are involved whether they employ inductive or deductive reasoning, and these processes require that students be actively engaged. Wittrock (1980: 398) stresses the active nature of the learning process saying, 'The research on the brain and its cognitive processes emphasizes the generative nature of learning and the reciprocal interplay between environmental events and the learner's generative cognitive processes.' In order to learn, students must attend to relevant information, comprehend it, organize it, rehearse it, prepare it for storage, and subsume it into their cognitive network for long-term storage, placing it in the appropriate schemata and thereby facilitating future retrieval.

Physical changes in the brain result from the electrical and chemical processes that occur during learning. These processes are active, and they require active participation by the students. For example, in order to learn, students must focus their attention on what they are to learn. First, they must arouse their attention and focus it on the material or task at hand. Second, they must activate their attention with the purpose of giving a response. Third, they must concentrate on maintaining their attention until they have completed the learning task. (Wittrock 1980)

Meaningful learning is an example of a learning model that requires active engagement by students. As defined by Ausubel (1978), meaningful learning requires active participation in the learning process. In order to understand new material students must activate the information that they already have stored in their cognitive network. After recalling all relevant background knowledge, they must seek to relate it in their own way to the new material to be learned. And finally, they must prepare the new information for storage in such a way that it will be available for retrieval.

The principal component affecting learning is not the teacher, the method, the instruction, the materials, nor the class, but the students.

'The key factor in learning is not what teachers think but what *students* think, because it is the students' *thought processes* that determine whether learning is taking place. Researchers have been exploring the relationship between teachers and instruction on the one hand and students' thought processes and learning on the other. They hypothesize that teaching influences student cognition and that cognition leads to learning. According to Wittrock (1980:297) 'the distinctive characteristic of the research on students' thought processes is the idea that teaching affects achievement through student thought processes.' Thus, the evolving theoretical framework supports a model in which teachers and instruction play an indirect rather than a direct role in learning. Until the students use information to generate meaning that they can store in their cognitive network, learning does not occur, no matter how much time they have spent in class or how many notes they have taken.' (Chastain 1988:163)

Some classroom applications. Although students are ultimately responsible for engaging in the learning process and therefore for learning, instructors can do much to foster their engagement. Normally, instructors choose course content, arrange it, present it, choose activities, arrange them, and provide feedback on students' performance. At what point or points in this teaching-learning sequence can they incorporate procedures that will result in a larger number of students being engaged for longer periods of time? When they choose content and arrange it, they should always analyze the learning task so as to sequence the materials to build from the old to the new, i.e. to proceed from the known to the unknown. When they present new material, they should include an activity or activities in which students recall what they already know so that it will help them learn this material more easily and more completely. When they choose activities, they should select those that require some type of product from the students. (This is especially true if the students work in groups. After the activity, members of the groups should have to give oral or written evidence that they did indeed accomplish the assigned task.) When they give students feedback on their work, they should be conscious of the need to establish the connection between students' efforts and achievement, i. e., to demonstrate to them the need to engage themselves in the learning process.

The examples given in the preceding paragraph lead to the following general principles related to engaging. First, instructors should describe the learning process so that students with misconceptions will revise their image of how to learn. Second, they should make students aware of the cause-and-effect relationship between the amount of time they are engaged in learning and their achievement. Third, they should choose learning tasks that require students' engagement for successful achievement.

An example of what not to do would be the audio-lingual recommendation that students copy each line of the dialogue four times. An example of a more appropriate task would be to ask students to study a given sentence describing a member of one's family and to give them the assignment of writing a similar type of sentence about each member of their family. Fourth, they should choose procedures that require that students be engaged. For example, if instructors always repeat in the native language all important information, there is little incentive for students to listen to what they say in the second language. Another would be to form a habit of asking students about the recitations of their classmates as a means of encouraging them to attend to all that is said in class. Fifth, they should choose objectives that require engaging. If students know that by the end of the chapter they must be able to know something that they do not know at the beginning or to give evidence of having achieved some skill that they did not have at the beginning and that the instructor will hold them responsible for that material, they will have to engage in the learning process to complete the objectives successfully. Sixth, they should give all students clear and helpful feedback on their performance, i.e. on their engagement as well as their achievement. Most students need assistance in monitoring their learning, especially in a second language, and instructors should make improved metacognitive skills for each student one of their priorities.

Simulating

Definition. Simulating involves completing the actions of the real activity without actually performing it. During basic training soldiers learn to fire weapons. However, providing that type of training for such a large number of people in relatively close quarters is potentially very dangerous, and the officers in charge are fully aware of the hazard. In order to lessen the possibility of a fatal error, they require that all soldiers simulate firing several times before they proceed to the real thing with live ammunition. That is, all recruits must practice each step several times prior to putting ammunition in the weapon and shooting at the target. This preparation makes the trainees, as well as the trainers, feel much more comfortable and relaxed, improves the safety record, and raises the resultant scores.

Simulating in second-language classes has exactly the same purpose and potentially a similar effect. Having students participate in practice in which they have to simulate the same types of mental processes that they would be using if they were actually communicating even though they are not seems to be a justifiable activity. (This is an hypothesis that requires empirical support. One can well imagine students' being able with the appropriate preparation and activities to engage directly in converting activities, thereby bypassing the traditional intermediate simulation practice. Too, data on different types of learners may reveal that simulation is helpful for some second-language students but not others. Certainly, children do seem to practice some aspects of language and to enter directly at certain stages into the converting process to achieve communication goals.)

The importance of simulating. Time-wise practice probably continues to be one of the two dominant activities in most second-language classes. (The other would be grammatical explanation.) Texts contain a large number of exercises and drills designed to help students learn grammar and vocabulary and to give them control over both. Teachers devote a significant portion of class time to doing these exercises and drills. Students expend much effort to complete them successfully. In fact, they spend so much time and energy on them that often they have little time for converting practice. Based on observations of the activities of 864 foreign-language classes at the middle and high school levels, Nerenz (1979) concluded that the teachers and the students were involved in communication activities only 0.4 percent of the time. Clearly, both theorists and practitioners have an obligation to question that dominance and to study its effects on the amount of class time available for communication activities.

In this presentation my interest lies not with the amount of class time students spend doing all these exercises and drills, as important as that topic certainly is, but with the type of mental processing that is taking place while students are doing them. What is happening? Are students actually simulating the same type of mental processing that they will need later to convert their thoughts to language in order to communicate in that language with someone else? Regarding exercises, Hosenfeld's (1976) descriptions of students' thoughts as they completed exercises lead to the conclusion that they are not. In her study students often did not read the directions nor the entire sentence. Instead, they looked for the clue to solve the linguistic puzzle presented by the exercise. Their goal was to supply the correct form. They were not processing language in the normal sense at all. With regard to drills, Lightbown (1983) states, 'some researchers have suggested that pattern practice involving memorized dialogues or 'mechanical' drills is actually processed by the brain in a different way from the way in which language for communication is processed, and that only the latter processing actually leads to real language acquisition.'

Although contextualized drills are currently in vogue, a careful examination of the content and format reveals that they share the basic weaknesses of earlier audio-lingual pattern drills. (In an insightful analysis Walz (1989) identifies seven problems with contextualized drills.) Basically, they are 'set-ups' formulated to ensure correct student responses. Authors do attempt to place the drill in some believable situation which the students can understand and to which they can relate. However, the format is such that students tend to focus their attention much more on finding the clue or pattern in order to respond correctly than on simulating real language processing. The result is that students complete the drills without simulating real language processing and without enhancing to any significant degree their ability to communicate in the language.

Some classroom applications. If students need to do exercises and drills, and they may not, they should do only those that require simulation of the same types of mental processing necessary for communication. Developing these types of practice materials will come about only as a result of questioning what students do now in class and as a result of contemplating the way they must think in order to complete simulation materials successfully. Given the creative intellects active in our profession and the variety of possibilities, I hesitate to predict what types of simulation practice we may develop. However, I would like to suggest that they must have at least three basic characteristics. The students must understand the meaning, they must choose among possible alternative responses, and they must tell the truth as they see it when they respond. Instructors can improve the materials they are currently using in class by altering the exercises and drills to incorporate these three basic principles and by themselves creating others.

An activity in which students learn to answer yes-no questions can serve as an example of how these three principles can be incorporated into the class. The instructor begins by telling the students to listen to the questions and to answer them truthfully. Then, he ask a series of questions similar to the following:

> Hi, what are you doing? Are you breathing? Are you thinking? Are you swimming? Are you sitting? Are you walking?
> What do you (all) normally do in class? Do you speak English? Do you write compositions? Do you listen to tapes? Do you watch movies? Do you catch a bus? Do you eat breakfast?

A written activity might be similar to the following:

Possessive	Noun	Verb	Adjective
My	*father*	*is (not)*	*tall*
	mother		*short*
	sister		*slender*
	brother		*heavy*
			good-looking

Converting

Definition. One of the meanings of the verb convert is to change or to transform something into another form. For example, my wife can change an unappetizing accumulation of left-overs into the most delicious vegetable soup that I have ever tasted. On her birthday I convert an ugly glob of flour, sugar, shortening, vanilla, salt, baking powder, and milk into quite a tasty cake, which she regards as a treat and I regard as a miracle. An artist turns a few flowers and greens into a beautiful bouquet. Mozart transformed a few simple notes into an enchanting melody.

Language, too, is a product of converting. For example, let's consider what is happening at this very moment. I am talking to you, and you are converting my words to thoughts. If I were really talking rather than giving a presentation, I would be converting my thoughts to language which in turn you would be converting from language to thoughts. Of course, at the end when you ask questions or make comments, you, the producer, will be converting your thoughts to language and I, the receiver, will be converting your language to thoughts. That is, utilizing our knowledge of English sounds, morphemes, words, and syntax we can manage this complex conversion process in a remarkably efficient and effective manner.

The importance of converting. Converting is central to communication. The essential process in the verbal exchange of information is the conversion of thoughts to language or vice-versa. I can not read your thoughts, and you can not read mine. If I want to share my thoughts with you, I must put them into language comprehensible to you, and you must do the same for me. Messages are not exchanged by osmosis. Both parties must participate actively in the process to ensure its successful completion.

Practice in converting is also central to second-language learning. The thesis is simple. If students want to learn to communicate in a language, they must practice conversion. They can no more take a set of grammar rules and a list of vocabulary and convert their thoughts into that language than they can begin with knowing the position of all the notes on a piano and play a Bach sonata. They surely must know the components of language, but they must know them in a functional and usable fashion. In order to acquire this facility to use language to convert their thoughts, they must have opportunities to participate in activities in which they are required to convert language to thoughts, i. e., to express their own ideas and feelings.

Some classroom applications. Converting involves the self expression of ideas, but the implications for classroom activities requiring students to convert thoughts to language and vice-versa are much broader. What are the essential characteristics of converting activities? Obviously, they include meaning and choice, the principles associated with simulating. In addition, they entail at least four others: understanding the context, expressing one's own ideas, having as a purpose the exchange of information, and sending the message to someone else. At this stage in the teaching-learning sequence instructors do not tell students what to say. Students must express their own thoughts. Instructors must, however, provide the input needed to stimulate the students' thoughts so that they will have something to say and to give them the vocabulary and structures that they may need during the exchange. Too, they can suggest a purpose for the activity and establish a format in which conversion will seem natural and necessary.

Two suggestions for activities that meet the criteria presented in the preceding paragraph are DiPietro's open-ended scenarios (1983,1987) and Horwitz' class-participation role-plays (1985).

In open-ended scenarios students interact in social situations similar to those they might encounter in the real world, and they have to create the language needed to function in that situation. The format is simple, but potentially effective. First, the instructor describes a scene for the students. For example, you are at a party near the university where you are an exchange student, and you have just met a student from that university. You want to meet and to talk with native speakers. Although the other student does not want to be offensive, it is obvious that he/she has a rather negative attitude toward Americans. Second, the students in the class divide into two groups, one to anticipate what the American might say and to prepare to play that role and the other to think of what the native speaker might say and to prepare to play that role. Third, each group chooses one student to play the role assigned to their group, and the two do the scene, pausing if they need help to ask the other members of their group how to say something or for ideas of what they might say. Fourth, afterward, all the students discuss what was said and explore what the two speakers might have done or said to have improved the exchange.

In role-plays with student participation instructors can employ a variety of approaches to avoid situations in which some students perform while others take advantage of the opportunity to pay little or no attention to what is occurring. In order to turn these typically passive students into active participants, Horwitz recommends audience feedback, role switching, voting, instant replays, cultural discussions, and audience direction. She also suggests group role-plays such as press conferences and class soap operas.

Conclusion. Theory and practice in second-language teaching and learning are richer than ever. We have a wide variety of approaches from which to select. All have their proponents and their attractive features. Fortunately, most of us enjoy the liberty of being able to incorporate into our own classes those techniques that best fit our experience and our beliefs. However, if we want our students to develop the ability to communicate, we must emphasize three essential processes: engaging, simulating, and converting.

References

Ausubel, David. 1968, 1978. Educational psychology: A cognitive view. New York, Holt, Rinehart and Winston.
Celce-Murcia, Marianne. 1985. Making informed decisions about the role of grammar in language teaching. TESOL Newsletter, 19:1,4-5.
Chastain, Kenneth. 1987. Examining the role of grammar explanation, drills, and exercises in the development of communication skills. Hispania, 70:160-166.
Chastain, Kenneth. 1988. Developing second-language skills: theory and practice. San Diego: Harcourt Brace Jovanovich.
DiPietro, Robert. J. 1983. Scenarios, discourse, and real-life roles. In: J. W. Oller, Jr. and P.A. Richard-Amato, eds. Methods that work: A smorgasbord of ideas for language teachers. Rowley, Mass.: Newbury House. 226-238.
DiPietro, Robert. J. 1987. Strategic interaction: Learning languages through scenarios. Cambridge: Cambridge University Press.
Horwitz, Elaine. K. 1985. Getting them all into the act: Using audience participation to increase the effectiveness of role-play activities. Foreign Language Annals. 18:205-208.
Hosenfeld, Carol. 1976. Learning about learning: Discovering our students' strategies. Foreign Language Annals. 9:117-129.
Lightbown, Patsy. M. 1983. Exploring relationships between developmental and instructional sequences in L2 acquisition. In: J. W. Seliger and M. H. Long, eds. Classroom oriented research in second language acquisition. Rowley, Mass.: Newbury House. 143-217.
Morton, F. Rand and Lane, Harlan. L. 1961. Techniques of operant conditioning applied to second language learning. (An address to the International Congress of Applied Psychology. Copenhagen.)
Nerenz, A. 1979. Utilizing class time in foreign language instruction. In: D. P. Benseler, ed., Teaching the basics in the foreign language classroom: Options and strategies. Skokie, Ill.: National Textbook. 78-89.
Walz, Joel. 1989. Context and contextualized language practice in foreign language teaching. The Modern Language Journal. 73:160-168.
Wittrock, M. C. 1980. Learning and the brain. In: M. C. Wittrock, ed., The brain and psychology. New York: Academic Press, 371-403.

The shifting sands of bilingual education

Linda Schinke-Llano
Millikin University

The state of the art of bilingual education is, in the United States at least, reminiscent of one of the ubiquitous framed sand paintings found at summer art fairs. Tip the painting one way, and the effect is positive; tip it another, the effect is negative. Certainly, recent literature abounds with writings both critical of and supportive of bilingual education programs. Given the number of pages already devoted to the alleged advantages and disadvantages of bilingual education, the purpose of this paper is neither to summarize in great detail nor to reanalyze past studies. Rather, incorporating findings from the recently completed longitudinal study conducted by Ramirez, Yuen, and Ramey (1991), I will argue that the potential effectiveness of any bilingual education program (and, thus, the state of the art of bilingual education in general) is a function of (1) the degree to which the program design and curriculum adhere to principles of L1, L2, and content area acquisition; (2) the availability and quality of resources, both human and material, to facilitate the desired program; and (3) the congruence among parental, community, and national goals.

In its most recent incarnation in the United States, bilingual education was begun in 1967 with the passage of Title VII of the Elementary and Secondary Education Act (ESEA). Since their inception, bilingual education programs throughout the country have been controversial, for what is at issue is not only how children learn best, but what it is that they should learn, and specifically in what language they should learn. Given the small number of well constructed, methodologically sound studies conducted during the first decade of program implementation (see Zappert and Cruz 1977 and Dulay and Burt 1978 for critiques of early studies), as well as the contradictory nature of their results (see Ramirez, Schinke-Llano, and Bloom 1984 for a summary of results), it is not surprising that several reports and studies severely criticize bilingual education. The first negative report to have widespread impact is the 1977 book *Language, ethnicity, and the schools* by Noel Epstein who concludes that there is no evidence for the educational effectiveness of bilingual education. The second is the 1978 American Institutes for Research

(AIR) report which states that students in Title VII Spanish bilingual programs perform lower in English than their non-Title VII counterparts and equivalently in mathematics. Finally, there is the Baker and de Kanter report commissioned by the U.S. Department of Education to investigate transitional bilingual education (TBE) which finds that 'no consistent evidence supports the effectiveness of TBE' (1981b:50).

Also not surprisingly, these negative reports have all drawn criticism. Epstein's conclusions, for example, are based largely on interviews with legislators and administrators (Ramirez et al. 1984). Further, the AIR study includes large numbers of English-dominant and English monolingual students in experimental groups (Dulay and Burt 1979). Finally, the Baker and de Kanter study relies greatly on 'unexamined' programs, i.e. programs which bear the label 'bilingual', but which in actuality are not (Krashen 1991). Willig (1985), in her meta-analysis of the Baker and de Kanter study, concludes among other things that the better the evaluation design, the greater the likelihood that bilingual education shows a positive effect (see also Willig 1981-82).

It must not be forgotten, of course, that as the controversy over the effectiveness of bilingual education continues in the United States, other countries utilize this form of instruction as well. Although it is not in the scope of this paper to provide a review of bilingual education on an international level, suffice to say that the research results vary as well. On the subject of bilingual education in Ireland, Scotland, Wales, and England, for example, Baker reports that '... from the little research that exists, it seems reasonable to conclude that bilingual education is not detrimental' (1988:77). In contrast, bilingual education as practiced in Canada (i.e. language immersion for language majority students rather than for language minority students) has provided us with a wealth of studies attesting to its efficacy in the areas of L1 and L2 acquisition, content skills development, and social-psychological growth (see Genesee 1987 for a summary; see also Schinke-Llano and Ramirez 1984, Schinke-Llano 1985, and Schinke-Llano 1990). Even the successes are somewhat problematic, however. When compared with native speakers of the target language, immersion students do not demonstrate native-like performance in speaking and writing (Genesee 1978, Harley 1979, Spilka 1976), and they need six to seven years to reach native-like proficiency in listening and reading (Swain and Lapkin 1982).

Into this realm of conflicting views comes the latest study to impact opinion of bilingual education in the United States. The 'Longitudinal study of structured English immersion strategy, early-exit and late-exit transitional bilingual education programs for language-minority children' is a federally funded eight-year long (four years of data collection) study conducted by Ramirez, Yuen, and Ramey of Aguirre International (1991). The study evaluates the progress of Spanish speaking students in math, oral English, and English reading in three different program types: structured immersion (in which English is used 94.3% to 98.6% of instructional time and Spanish is used for clarification); early-exit (in which instruction in English increases from two-thirds of the time in kindergarten to 100% of the time in fourth grade); and late-exit (in which instruction in English increases more slowly from 40% in kindergarten to 60% in fourth grade, with all students remaining in the program through sixth grade regardless of English language ability).

Results show that limited English proficient (LEP) students improve in math, language and reading in all three treatments at a rate greater than or equal to comparable students in the general population. Thus, in the case of the late-exit program, it is obvious that instruction in Spanish does not impede progress in either subject matter or English development, a fear often expressed by opponents of bilingual education. On the contrary, of the late-exit groups studied, the one that was most at risk and that also received the most native language instruction demonstrated an accelerated growth curve (Ramirez 1991). (Note that a decelerated growth curve is the norm in the mainstream student population.) However, those late-exit students who were transitioned abruptly into English at the second grade experienced slower growth rates than those students whose transition was more gradual. Nonetheless, those same opponents of bilingual education will likely be encouraged by the finding that no differences are reported in math, reading, or language between those students in structured immersion programs and those in early-exit TBE programs. Interestingly, it is important to note that students remained in these programs longer than expected; further, while 72% of the students in the early-exit program had been reclassified by the end of four years, only 66% of those in the structured immersion had—a finding not in keeping with the basic program definitions. Other findings include that parents of children in late-exit programs are more involved than the other two groups of parents (a fact undoubtedly attributable to the strong use of the home language) and that teachers in the late-exit programs have stronger Spanish language skills, possess more advanced training, and assign more homework than do the teachers in the other two types of program. Finally, in another similarity among the three programs that is particularly relevant to our discussion here, Ramirez et al. report that 'teachers in all three programs offer a passive language learning environment, limiting student opportunities to produce language and develop more complex language and thinking skills' (1991:8).

Thus, in answer to the question, 'Does bilingual education work?', it is obvious that some earlier studies have replied 'yes', while others have replied 'no.' Most recently, with the publication of the results from the longitudinal study, the answer appears to be 'yes,' especially late-exit programs whose students experience a gradual transition into English in the earlier years of the program. Given the fact that the federal government has already requested that the National Academy of Sciences review the study (Miller 1990), it is also obvious that we have not yet heard the final verdict on bilingual education. Given our lack of closure on the subject, perhaps a different strategy would be appropriate to help us define the state of the art of bilingual education. A more productive course may be to examine what we do know about language and concept development and to determine whether bilingual education can provide the requisite features.

In short, I argue that bilingual education is an effective means of educating LEP students if, and only if, several criteria are met. First, the program must provide a language environment facilitative of second language acquisition; that is, the language environment must provide optimal input (Krashen 1981, 1982), negotiated interaction (Long 1980, 1981), and comprehensible output (Swain 1985) in a non-threatening way. Next, since we know that the first language serves as the basis for second language development and that literacy skills transfer from one language to another (Cummins and Swain 1986), and since we know that students abruptly transitioned into instruction in L2 experience slowed growth curves (Ramirez et al. 1991), the program should provide both basic and advanced literacy development in L1 (Krashen 1991). Also, since content area knowledge is best developed through procedural as well as declarative knowledge and through metacognitive as well as cognitive strategies (O'Malley and Chamot 1990), the program should provide for these factors as well, regardless of whether the instruction is taking place in the students' L1 or L2.

While it is essential for a bilingual program to adhere to the principles of L1, L2, and content area acquisition just mentioned to be considered successful, a second criterion must be met as well. Resources, both material and human, must be available in sufficient quantity and quality. Krashen (1991) argues for the importance of a print-rich environment in both L1 and L2, especially for the kinds of students enrolled in U.S. bilingual programs. As discovered in the Significant Bilingual Instructional Features (SBIF) study, effective bilingual teachers exhibit a congruence between the intent of the instruction and its organization and delivery; they use active teaching behaviors (such as monitoring and feedback), as well as the students' L1 and information from the students' home culture to enhance lessons; and they integrate English language development and content skills (Tikunoff 1983). And, as already indicated, teachers must break away from the mold of teacher dominated discussions and focus on interaction that facilitates critical thinking and higher order problem solving.

Even if learning principles are followed and appropriate resources are present, bilingual education programs will most likely not succeed—

or at least be perceived as not succeeding—if the third, and perhaps most important, criterion is not met. There must be a congruence among parental, community, and national goals regarding the education of LEP students. Fishman and Lovas (1970), Spolsky (1978), and Paulston (1980) have repeatedly reminded us not to view programs in isolation from their sociolinguistic context. In our desire, however, to prove or disprove the efficacy of particular bilingual education programs or of bilingual education in general, we have repeatedly done exactly that.

In sum, I argue that the effectiveness of bilingual education—and, as a result, the state of the art of bilingual education—is a function of the degree to which programs adhere to principles of first and second language acquisition and of content acquisition; the availability and quality of resources, both human and material, to facilitate the programs; and the congruence among parental, community, and national goals. Ideally, I believe that all three criteria can be met; if they are, bilingual education can and will be effective. Realistically, however, I believe that the third criterion, that of congruence of goals, is problematic, at least in the United States. Clearly, the lack of congruence of goals for the education of LEP students accounts for the continually shifting picture of bilingual education that we have been receiving for the past quarter of a century. Only if those goals are rectified will the effects of bilingual education programs be perceived as positive rather than negative.

References

American Institutes for Research. 1977-78. Evaluation of the impact of the ESEA Title VII Spanish/ English bilingual education program. Vol. III: Year two impact data, educational process, and in-depth analyses. Washington, D.C.

Baker, Colin. 1988. Key issues in bilingualism and bilingual education. Clevedon, England: Multilingual Matters, Ltd.

Baker, Keith, and Adriana de Kanter. 1981a. Summary report of a review of the literature on the effectiveness of bilingual education. Washington, D.C.: U.S. Department of Education, Office of Planning, Budget, and Evaluation.

Baker, Keith, and Adriana de Kanter. 1981b. Effectiveness of bilingual education: A review of the literature. Washington, D.C.: U.S. Department of Education, Office of Planning, Budget, and Evaluation.

Cummins, Jim, and Merrill Swain. 1986. Bilingualism in education. New York: Longman.

Dulay, Heidi, and Marina Burt. 1978. Why bilingual education? A summary of research findings. 2nd ed. San Francisco: Bloomsbury West.

Dulay, Heidi, and Marina Burt. 1979. Bilingual education: A close look at its effects. NABE News, 3 (1).

Epstein, Noel. 1977. Language, ethnicity, and the schools: Policy alternatives for bilingual-bicultural education. Washington, D.C.: George Washington University, Institute for Educational Leadership.
Fishman, Joshua, and J. Lovas. 1970. Bilingual education in sociolinguistic perspective. TESOL Quarterly 4.215-222.
Genesee, Fred. 1978. A longitudinal evaluation of an early immersion school program. Canadian Journal of Education 3.31-50.
Genesee, Fred. 1987. Learning through two languages: Studies of immersion and bilingual education. Rowley, Mass.: Newbury House.
Harley, B. 1979. French gender rules in the speech of English-dominant, French-dominant, and monolingual French-speaking children. Working Papers on Bilingualism 19.129-156.
Krashen, Stephen D. 1981. Second language acquisition and second language learning. Oxford: Pergamon.
Krashen, Stephen D. 1982. Principles and practice in second language acquisition. New York: Pergamon.
Krashen, Stephen D. 1991. The case against bilingual education. Speech presented at the Fourteenth Annual Statewide Conference for Teachers of Linguistically and Culturally Diverse Students, Oak Brook, Ill. February.
Long, Michael. 1980. Input, interaction, and second language acquisition. Unpublished Ph.D. dissertation, UCLA.
Long, Michael. 1981. Input, interaction, and second language acquisition. Annals of the New York Academy of Sciences. 379.259-278.
Miller, Julie A. 1990. Native-language instruction found to aid L.E.P.'s. Education Week. October, 31.
O'Malley, J. Michael, and Anna Uhl Chamot. 1990. Learning strategies in second language acquisition. Cambridge: Cambridge University Press.
Paulston, Christina Bratt. 1980. Bilingual education: Theories and issues. Rowley, Mass.: Newbury House.
Ramirez, J. David. 1991, March. Personal communication.
Ramirez, J. David, Linda Schinke-Llano, and Gilda Bloom. 1984. The characteristics and effectiveness of transitional bilingual education programs. Mountain View, Calif.: SRA Technologies.
Ramirez, J. David, Sandra Yuen, and Dena Ramey. 1991. Executive summary/final report: Longitudinal study of structured English immersion strategy, early-exit and late-exit transitional bilingual education programs for language-minority children. San Mateo, Calif.: Aguirre International.
Schinke-Llano, Linda. 1985. Foreign language in the elementary school: The state of the art. Englewood Cliffs, N.J.: Prentice Hall Regents.
Schinke-Llano, Linda. 1990. Can foreign language learning be like second language acquisition? The curious case of immersion. In: Second language acquisition—Foreign language learning, ed. by Bill VanPatten and James Lee, 216-25. Clevedon, England: Multilingual Matters.
Schinke-Llano, Linda, and J. David Ramirez. 1984. Programmatic and instructional aspects of language immersion programs. Mountain View, Calif.: SRA Technologies.
Spilka, I. 1976. Assessment of second language performance in immersion programs. Canadian Modern Language Review 32.543-61.

Spolsky, Bernard. 1978. A model for the evaluation of bilingual education. International Review of Eduction 24.347-60.
Swain, Merrill. 1985. Communicative competence: Some roles of comprehensible input and comprehensible output in its development. Input in second language acquisition, ed. by Susan Gass and Carolyn Madden, 235-53. Rowley, Mass.: Newbury House.
Swain, Merrill, and Sharon Lapkin. 1982. Evaluating bilingual education: A Canadian case study. Clevedon, England: Multilingual Matters.
Tikunoff, William, ed. 1983. Significant bilingual instructional features study. San Francisco: Far West Laboratory.
Willig, Ann. 1981-82. The effectiveness of bilingual education: Review of a report. NABE Journal 6:1-19.
Willig, Ann. 1985. A meta-analysis of selected studies on the effectiveness of bilingual education. Review of Educational Research 55:269-317.
Zappert, Laraine, and B. Roberto Cruz. 1977. Bilingual education: An appraisal of empirical research. Berkeley: Bahia, Inc.

Normative language and language use: The separate implications for instructional practices and materials

Janet Swaffar
University of Texas at Austin

The influence of normative language and language-use positions in FL education. In the past decade, increasing numbers of North American and European scholars have challenged the notion that the language an L2 learner can reasonably be expected to use bears much resemblance to that language's normative standard. 'Telegraphic language', 'structurally reduced speech', 'interlanguage' are all terms that suggest interim speech is necessary and is necessarily imperfect. Not only are errors of all kinds natural, but, given appropriate exposure to increasingly complex communication, a degree of self correction seems to occur naturally. Huebner cites evidence that points to a common developmental evolution of grammaticality among L2 learners. Thus, fifteen-year longitudinal German studies suggest 'word-order rules required for standard German can be located along a developmental dimension, which all learners of German as a second language must pass through if their language is to approximate that of the target group... Furthermore, the acquisition of the word order rules at each successive stage can be ranked according to their cognitive complexity...' (Huebner 1981:157).

As Huebner cautions, however, these findings have limited pedagogical implications about what structures to teach, since it is not feasible to group learners by acquisitional stage. More important, findings revealed that 'acquirers even at relatively early stages can produce extended texts, albeit imperfect ones' (Huebner 1981:163). L2 learners can engage in discourses to discuss issues, even though the language they use is structurally reduced. Current thinking is not that structurally reduced performance in classroom settings fixes fossilized language usage, but rather that a mix of communicative freedom and corrective procedures enables learners to develop more complex usage (Lightbown 1983). The strict normative view is that errors must all be confronted at the same time. The use-oriented view attempts to balance errors against developmental and affective factors—to reward degrees of improvement.

This difference—judging learning based on invariant norms versus appropriate learner development—is nowhere more evident than in American assessment tools. Influenced by our tradition in standardized testing, the American educational community stresses the assessment of a student's language product. Until recently, FL testing has been objective and hence it largely disregarded the language learner's cognitive processes (Shih 1986). Regardless of classroom emphases, then, evaluation in FL has stressed performance measured against a linguistic rather than a cognitive standard, an emphasis on conditioned responses (automaticity), rather than measuring how well a student uses an FL to learn.

Restructuring the L2 paradigm in the light of normative/language-use differences. When trying new combinations of tasks, teachers refer increasingly to 'eclectic approaches.' That terminology confuses more than it clarifies. Depending on one's definition, an eclectic approach can have two very different implications. On the one hand, eclectic can imply a learner-responsive flexibility. When, on the other hand, eclectic means tasks are implemented ad hoc rather than as integral to overall learning or are implemented without sensitivity to learners and their environment, inconsistency results. Without consistent implementation, it is next to impossible for teachers to set reasonable learning priorities. As Byrnes (1991) has noted elsewhere in this volume, a teacher has only three options for intervention: selecting materials, sequencing those materials, and addressing improvement in student communication.

The chief problem with eclecticism is that it is, by definition, unsystematic. Normative and use-oriented views necessarily use similar materials in different ways. The two standards necessitate different learning sequences and different concepts about how to improve student communication. For example, to offset the absence of prescribed learning sequences to teach basic skills, a language-use pedagogy must recycle or spiral language by reframing speech acts and contexts in which that language is used. Otherwise, students lack sufficient exposure to the underlying systemicness of a non-prescribed language system.

The two standards result in entirely different classroom implementation. For example, a normative sequence would ask adult learner Maria to learn a word list and answer content questions about an L2 version of Cinderella assigned for one class hour. A use-oriented program would commence with ten minutes of one class on comprehension (e.g. completing a semantic map of Cinderella), arrange textual information in a logical pattern a second day (a list of problems Cinderella faces matched against solutions), and then assign a discussion or a short essay about Cinderella as a negative role model for women (she needs fairy godmothers, runs away instead of explaining, etc.). In subsequent weeks the fairy tale might be read again and compared to a modern version with similar themes.

Aside from learning sequences, another hazard in eclectic approaches is unsystematic, inappropriate testing. For example, Maria may well learn vocabulary automatically by thinking about it and using it to express her ideas, but nonetheless fail to perform well on tests with word lists (Slobin). Learning modes are related to focus of attention. Spending time on memorizing vocabulary lists with external motivation to test well probably will yield more vocabulary learning of word definitions—but not necessarily of their meaning function in context (Schneider and Shiffrin (I) 1977, Shiffrin and Schneider (II) 1977).

Random eclecticism, then, suffers from a confounding of normative/language-use premises. Briefly these are summarized below:

Normative premises and resultant practices:
(1) Reading and writing abilities are predicated on normed linguistic competence rather than age or literacy of students. Mechanics precede use in functional settings in L2 as in L1.
(2) Language competency (accurate use of form or understanding of grammar function) precedes presentation of content, i.e. L2 accuracy is developed independent of students' intellectual maturity, cultural background, and interests.
(3) If confronted with students who have a variety of exposures to the FL, such teachers pretest language competence, then evaluate and place accordingly.

Language-use premises and resultant practices:
(1) Eight-year-olds cannot generally produce complex sentences in any language. Age factors among literate students affect how teachers access student cognition. Teachers cannot expect them to encode (conceptualize) language they cannot decode (replicate), e.g. the language of authentic texts chosen must reflect students' cognitive development.
(2) In courses emphasizing content, language learning is tested as a subset of learning about content, e.g. questions in English, but based on FL knowledge and answerable in English or FL without penalty for purely formal errors.
(3) When FL accuracy is emphasized as well, accuracy in L2 will not weigh more heavily than accurate learning about content. Even when emphasizing language, use-oriented teachers will present and evaluate specific content, e.g. reading and writing ability is not a question of linguistic skill in isolation.
(4) Students who have interrupted exposure to the FL need work in reactivation rather than remediation. They should be placed on the basis of post-tests subsequent to brief, but intensive exposure to language use in functional situations.

The curricular impact of these distinctions, is readily seen in Figure 1,

Figure 1. Curricular impacts of differing 'eclectic approaches'

Educational Activity / Focus	Normative premises & practices	Language-use premises & practices
Language loss placement	Pre-test, re-take language courses	'Refresher' courses followed by post-test
Linguistic competency vocabulary & grammar rules	L2 basic 2,000 vocabulary & rule mastery, L2 remedial work in sentence level exercises & drill	Concrete & personal applications of language illustrate rule learning, L2 real world use (diary entries, memos, letters)
Socio-linguistic, pragmatic & discourse competency situational functions (open-ended into which variables are filled) register, efficiency, student control, etc.	Must be preceded by automaticity through rule & vocabulary over learning	Automaticity results from functional language use in affectively interesting & purposeful content (no rules transfer without clear situational functions, e.g. classes of examples)
Content learning respective role of high and low culture learning in sequence	Wait until linguistic competence is in place before real use (linguistic overlearning precedes application) generally normative or high culture only	Analogizing personal (low culture) & general (high or standard) culture, cognitive overlearning rather than linguistic overlearning—analogical reasoning situationally bound
Testing two definitions of achievement and proficiency	First—normative usage (linguistic proficiency); then— multicultural variation (plural content achievement), possibly particular L2 culture (in a single program such as German for engineers)	First—functional use (tangible achievement in the sense of a speech act), second functional social use in particular L2 culture (disciplinary proficiency—German for engineers), third evolving individuals norms for L2 culture
Curricular objective for educated FL use	High-level cognitive usage serves social & personal needs as defined by the dominant culture's self image	High-level cognitive usage serves social & personal needs as redefined by the disciplinary community or interest group

which helps us to pinpoint the difficulties students confront in randomly eclectic programs. In short, we must align time on task and testing with what we teach. Use-oriented tasks and normative testing (or the reverse) will frustrate all concerned. Thus, language-use emphasis must also account for linguistic accuracy as one aspect of personal empowerment in FL learning. But that is a point on the continuum rather than a necessary precondition. Whether a program is normative or use-oriented, to avoid frustrating students, classroom modality and reward systems from K-16 must reflect stages in either the right or middle column in Figure 1.

To be sure, few professionals would espouse one of the two positions in either column to the exclusion of the other. But, as I have tried to suggest above, that is precisely why curricular problems occur. Although evident in multiple guises, two clear poles do exist. Conflicting programs will short-circuit one another. On one side are programs and goals predicated on the need for language mastery before language use. In other words, an unspecified amount of work on language itself—whether on grammar rules (formal features), vocabulary (for recognition or recall) specific skills (speaking, writing), or normative functional abilities (negotiation, information gathering under a generic set of circumstances)—precedes subject-matter instruction in that foreign language.

On the other side, immersion and interdisciplinary programs try to use the L2 to learn information about other disciplines. How can clear thinking about the normative/language-use question lead to more effective curricular planning? Before addressing this issue, consider the extent to which the normative standard for language learning dominates thinking in American education to the virtual exclusion of use-oriented features in college and graduate school programs.

The basis for rethinking a coherent language sequence. The difference between a departmental use of either a language-first or a content-based approach is the difference between teaching and testing skills in generic situations and teaching and testing problem-solving in specific cultural situations (Dannerbeck 1987, Klein 1986). Without a consistent theoretical framework, no consistent pedagogical direction is possible. Polarity at beginner-, intermediate-, and advanced-level FL programs originates in confusion about normative and use-oriented positions. Equally important, such polarity inhibits analyses of our pedagogical practice. The claim that students need linguistic rules is not the same thing as the claim that teaching linguistic rules fulfills this need.[1]

---

1 For example, Chastain and Woerdehoff's 1968 work on the cognitive code principle is often cited as evidence in behalf of teaching structural rules in isolation. It can also be construed as revealing how rules affect cognitive processing. Normative arguments overlook the fact that grammars represent only one among many cognitive interactions involved in successful communication (Huebner 1981).

People with fears about 'fossilization', or 'repetitive error patterns in language structure' (Higgs and Clifford 1982:67) fail to consider studies in interlanguage research. Studies such as those cited in Faerch and Kasper (1983) suggest errors occur as part of the learning process. Similarly, acquisition research that compares an accuracy-first approach with a communicative emphasis suggests that initial classroom focus on form inhibits language learning and language production (Vigil 1987). Significantly, Carroll's 1967 research, one basis for Higgs and Cliffords's conclusions, reveals measurable gains for those FL majors who started training in high school over those who began in college—when instruction in high school was conducted in the foreign language and when students used the FL in class (Carroll 1967:136-137).

Figure 2. Secondary and lower-division trends: Materials/Sequencing/ Correction.

Normative standard	Language-use standard
Materials: Culturally neutral dialogs: overlearning normed words and structures	*Materials:* Culturally familiar texts: overlearning social structures (personalized speech acts in real-world contexts)
Sequence & expectations: Separate skill emphasis in short expository texts (1-2 pages), sentence-level exercises (fill in the blanks, dehydrated sentences, sentence gambits, substitutions,etc.): success measured by formal correctness (a grammaticality standard)	*Sequence & expectations:* Integrative use (mixed skills) in longer texts with content focus, or developed plot structure (novels and plays as outside reading for macro-ideas or practical applications), supersentential practice: success measured in effective performance in particular social and occupational settings, increasing capacity to edit one's own speech or writing (an evolving accuracy standard)
Vocabulary lists to be memorized for active use—largely cued by translation or decoding in the L2	Distinction between actively used and situationally comprehended words—vocabulary learning focuses on words essential to messages understood and cued in L2 context

Secondary schools and lower division college programs, in part due to the influence of research and performance testing efforts such as the ACTFL Proficiency Guidelines, have begun to teach skills in terms of cognitive capabilities. The two lists in Figure 2 reveal another reason why FL instruction in colleges and universities are gradually recognizing the need to become increasingly language- and audience-specific. Spanish students need to understand subjunctive usage much earlier and more actively than German students, for example. The relative importance of subjunctive in placement should differ accordingly. On the other hand, placement defined only in a linguistic dimension overlooks the fact that students not taught in or responsive to focus on form find themselves beginning a type of language study entirely different from the one to which they have been previously exposed. Secondary school instruction probably stressed self-expression in casual conversation, factual reports. and describing familiar people, places, and events. Post-secondary programs and their testing must offer these same activities with familiar settings and content or recognize that they are making unfamiliar, multiple demands on learners' cognitive processes.

Using a content (non-normative) sequence would actually prepare students for the expanded purview of upper-division work in a department in a manner more conducive to continued language study than is currently the case. If both upper- and lower-division programs worked with parallel subject-matter emphases, redundancy would ease students' transition to advanced courses from more elementary work.

The lists in Figure 3 illustrate the emergent features of upper-division programs. Compared to characteristics of FL departments a decade ago, it suggests a far greater orientation toward functional language use in a range of social settings.

Figure 3. Upper-division programs.

Non-normative syllabi	*Curricular changes*
(1) Literature as part of cultural values: — popular culture, — multi-media options, — intertextuality rather than formal genre, — thematic rather than period emphases	(1) Student-generated analysis of various messages and message modes assessed on the basis of content clarity, communicative as well as linguistic intelligibility
(2) Pragmatic use of language in: — culture tracks — careers — study abroad — content courses	(2) Larger role, in student evaluation as well as curricular practice, for successful transfer of FL knowledge to other disciplines and real world activities

Assignments that focus on the connection between word order and speaker intent help students become sensitive to distinctions in form as signals for distinctions in meaning. In German, for example, when speakers use adverbial markers for emphasis, word order changes result: *Heute kommt er* rather than *Er kommt heute*. The implications in this shift are similar to those in English. *Today he's coming* suggests an exception; *He's coming today*, a confirmation of anticipated events. By linking language to realizations of social meaning, students start learning to learn not only language or facts in isolation, but their strategic realization as messages.

These same precepts apply to our graduate training. As already noted at the outset of this paper, coherence is perhaps the single most glaring omission in most graduate programs. The diversity of fields in today's literary studies illustrates what happens when curricula change and departments fail to see the broader classroom implications of those changes: we add new topics courses without rethinking the pattern of total course offerings. In the past twenty years the once relatively narrow spectrum of positivism, intellectual history, and text-immanent criticism has expanded into over a dozen competing critical theories.

In the absence of coherent pedagogy about how to learn and apply these theories, the sheer breadth of demands placed on graduate students is rapidly leading to confusion about standards for competence. Are students learning literature or a critical mode, linguistics or language? Without a pedagogy for our broadened scope of studies, theories of literature and linguistics (reader response, translation as reception, semiotics, post-structuralism, deconstruction, structuralism, text-linguistics, phenomenology, feminist criticism) are frequently perceived as unrelated to high school or undergraduate teaching.

Yet, as Figure 4 suggests, more recent literary theories share presumptions about literature as an artifact that reflects its cultural setting, a document that arises out of a particular time and place.

Figure 4. Graduate programs in linguistics applied to literary theory.

Linguistic theory	Literary theory
— speech acts	— reader response (sociological)
— discourse theory	— intertextuality (surface/subtextual)
— supersentential	— reader response (phenomenological)
— (meta-) cognitive	— deconstruction (text-external)
— pragmatic	— author intentionality (text-immanent)
— semantic	— literary sign systems (cultural artifact)
— generative-transformational	— unmasking textual ambiguities, their implications
— psycholinguistics	— affective reader response (text-linguistics)
— sociolinguistics	— stylistic analysis of surface features
	— anthropological analysis of social features

Current graduate programs in cultural geography, dialect studies, colonial literatures, women's studies, and minority studies all illustrate this point. Given applications of these theories, prior learning about a period's social, political, economic, geographic, and scientific background renders literature from such an era more comprehensible to readers—theories about how cultural artifacts work automatically prescribe assumptions about what is learnable and worth learning.

The new options are considerably more extensive than the old ones, thereby implying a diffuse focus. Those options can, however, also be viewed as frames for textual interpretation. Iser's (1981) and Scholes' (1985) reader-response theories are directly applicable to classroom teaching, as are text-linguistics or semiotics. If such studies are linked to creation of reading and writing assignments that reflect these theories, this activity could serve a dual purpose. Graduate students could see direct connections between, for example, theory in text-linguistics and their own classroom teaching. They could use explicit applications to teach a particular poem in first semester Spanish.

After choosing a poem that presents appropriate features, the teacher would, for instance, ask students to look for shifts in usage such as pronoun substitution or unusual word order that signals shifts in meaning—foregrounding particular topics in the poem (an interpretive activity) by identifying grammar features (a language learning activity). A graduate program that made various theoretical applications a consistent feature in its teaching at all levels would link research and teaching as learning strategies. Potentially, a dual focus would enhance language skills of graduate and undergraduate students, since, presumably, all participants would use the L2 to think out and implement interpretive assignments.

In addition to interpretive applications from literary theory, advanced undergraduate and graduate courses also need to teach students how to apply linguistic methodology to reading and interpretation of FL literature (Fleishman 1986:11-12). Without such practice in turning theories into applications, graduate students are effectively cut out of advanced levels of professional dialogue in any of the graduate specialty fields.

Figure 4 sums up these expanded demands by exemplifying graduate studies in FL linguistics, relating linguistic and literary theories in current graduate programs so as to suggest ways in which they could reinforce one another in practical pedagogy. The comparison illustrates the degree to which linguistic programs in most foreign language departments could, if desired, begin to join forces with literary analysis. The same precepts could readily be expanded to include transfers to acquisition theory or teaching culture. For example, pedagogical discussions of universal grammar are founded on premises about teaching language acquisition (a teaching-linguistics link [Cook] 1988). Similarly, semioticians explore many of the same text features as post-structuralists (a linguistics-cultural studies link). College language departments must develop programs to make these links explicit. Only then can post-secondary departments 'come to grips with our academic and intellectual identity and the increasingly diversified agenda of responsibilities' (Gay-Crosier 1967:4).

Even more important, only then can multicultural knowledge empower our citizenry. Individual differences between cultures are rarely, in themselves, informative because they appear random and incomprehensible. Only if Americans can identify the interrelated personal and public, the economic, social, and political systems that create those differences, both at home and abroad, can we become culturally literate. Cultural literacy is, after all, the ability to dispel stereotypes by identifying the differentiated but comprehensible realities that mold human values and behaviors. The power of recognizing cultural systems is the power of taking the first step toward addressing our own problems and those of other nations (Lunsford, Moglen, and Slevin 1990).

References

American Council on the Teaching of Foreign Languages. 1986. ACTFL Proficiency Guidelines. Hastings-on Hudson. NY: ACTFL Materials Center.
Byrnes, Heidi. 1991. In search of a sense of place: The state of the art in language teaching methodology. Georgetown University Round Table on Language and Linguistics 1991. Washington, D.C.: Georgetown University Press.
Carroll, John. 1967. The foreign language attainments of language majors in the senior year: A survey conducted in U.S. colleges and universities. Cambridge, Mass.: Graduate School of Education, Harvard University. [ED 013 343].
Chastain, Kenneth D. 1970. A methodological study comparing the audio-lingual habit theory and the cognitive code-learning theory: A continuation. Modern Language Journal 54. 257-66.
Chastain, Kenneth and Frank J. Woerdehoff. 1968. A methodological study comparing the audio-lingual habit theory and the cognitive code-learning theory. Modern Language Journal 52. 268-79.
Cook, Vivian J. [1988] 1989. Chomsky's universal grammar: An introduction. Worcester: Blackwell.
Dannerbeck, Francis J. 1987. Adult second-language learning: Toward an American adaptation with a European perspective. Foreign Language Annals 20. 413-19.
Faerch, Claus and Gabriele Kasper, eds. 1983. Strategies in interlanguage communication. New York: Longman, 1983.
Fleischman, Suzanne. 1986. Getting Calliope through graduate school? Can Chomsky help? or, the role of linguistics in graduate education in foreign languages. ADFL Bulletin 17. 9-13.
Gay-Crosier, Raymond. 1967. Reshaping foreign language programs: Implications for department chairs. ADFL Bulletin 19. 3-7.
Higgs, Theodore V., and Ray Clifford. 1982. The push toward communication. In: Curriculum, competence, and the foreign language teacher. Skokie, Ill.: National Textbook. 57-79.
Huebner, Thomas. 1981. Trends in European SLA research and some implications for the American foreign language classroom. In: Foreign language acquisition research and the classroom. Barbara F. Freed, ed. Lexington, Mass.: D. C. Heath. 155-169.
Iser, Wolfgang. 1981. The act of reading. Baltimore: Johns Hopkins University Press.
Jarvis, Gilbert A. 1991. Research on teaching methodology: Its evolution and prospects. In: Foreign language acquisition research and the classroom. Barbara F. Freed, ed. Lexington, Mass.: D. C. Heath. 295-306.
Klein, Wolfgang. 1986. Second language acquisition. Cambridge: Cambridge University Press.
Lightbown, Patsy M. 1983. Input, interaction, and acquisition in the SL classroom. In: Classroom oriented research in second language acquisition. Herbert W. Seliger and Michael Long, eds. Rowley, Mass.: Newbury. 217-43.
Lunsford, Andrea A., Helene Moglen, and James Slevin. 1990. The right to literacy. New York: The Modern Language Association.

Schneider, Walter and Richard M. Shiffrin. 1977. Controlled and automatic information processing: I: Detection, search, and attention. Psychological Review 84. 1-55.

Scholes, Robert. 1985. Textual power: Literary theory and the teaching of English. New Haven / London: Yale University Press.

Shiffrin, Richard M., and Walter Schneider. 1977. Controlled and automatic information processing: II. Detection, search, and attention. Psychological review 84. 127-90.

Shih, Mary. 1986. Content approaches to teaching academic writing. TESOL Quarterly 20. 617-48.

Slobin, Dan Isaac. 1978. A case study of early language awareness. In: The child's conception of language. In: A. Sinclair, R. Jarvella, and W. Levelt, eds. Berlin: Springer.

Vigil, Virginia Dorothea. 1987. Authentic text in the college-level Spanish I class as the primary vehicle of instruction. University of Texas dissertation.

X-raying the international funny bone:
A study exploring differences in the perception of humor across cultures

Genelle G. Morain
University of Georgia

I have taught a class on intercultural understanding for twenty years. During the course I try to sensitize students to the many dimensions of culture which they would encounter if they were to become a part—even temporarily—of another society. My students know that people in other cultures eat different foods, speak different languages, and get married, harried, and buried in different ways. But one of the hardest things for them to grasp is that people in other cultures laugh in the special way their cultures have taught them to laugh. To illustrate this point I would mount a dozen cartoons clipped from American magazines around the walls of the room and ask students to rank them from the most amusing to the least amusing. While the American students bickered good naturedly over the humorous merits of the cartoons, the international students were reluctant to participate, explaining that they did not even understand what the cartoons were about. Their distress provided a lead-in to a discussion of *Cultural literacy* (Hirsch 1987) and the view that without a knowledge of the shared referents of any group, one is shut away from full participation in that group.

Last year I decided to explore in a more systematic way some of the problems international students have in appreciating American humor. I selected the single frame cartoon as the genre for the study and chose *The New Yorker* magazine as the source because its cartoons are drawn by a variety of American cartoonists and represent a range of artistic styles. The content of these cartoons is aimed at a literate adult audience and is free of racial, sexual, or scatological overtones which might prove offensive to some participants.

As a first step, a content analysis of all cartoons appearing in *The New Yorker* for 1990 was conducted. The method used is derived from Raskin's script-based semantic theory (Raskin 1985); the *script* of Raskin's theory is '. . . a cognitive structure internalized by the native speaker and it represents the native speaker's knowledge of a small part of the world . . . certain routines, standard procedures, basic situations, etc.' (Raskin 1985: 81). For Raskin, the text of a verbal joke is compatible with two different scripts which overlap partially or fully on the text. The two scripts must be opposite in some special way, e.g. actual situation/non-actual situation; normal state of affairs/abnormal state of affairs; plausible situation /implausible situation, etc. (Raskin 1985:111). It is the oppositeness of the two overlapping scripts which produces the humor. Many jokes, according to Raskin, contain a trigger which activates the switch from one script to another. This semantic script-switch trigger (Raskin: 114) usually relies on either ambiguity or contradiction.

While Raskin's theory was formulated to deal with short verbal texts, other writers have used his script-based idea to analyze humor in advertising (Allen 1988), humor in puns (Marino 1988), and humor in cartoons (Hofstadter and Gabora 1989). For his cartoon analysis, Hofstadter uses the term *frame* instead of script. When elements of two forms are brought together by a cartoon viewer in such a way as to create a new, hybrid situation, that new situation is called a 'frame blend' (Hofstadter and Gabora 1989:420). An example cited from W. B. Park's *Off the Leash* series blends animal and human frames (Hofstadter and Gabora 1989:426). Park depicts a pig-feeding frame in which a dozen fat hogs are seen guzzling swill from a trough. As a farmer approaches, bearing two buckets of fresh slop, one porker raises his snout and calls imperiously, 'Garcon!'—thus introducing a French-restaurant frame which enables the startled viewer to create a frame blend (pig feeding and French restaurant) which produces the humor. Although Hofstadter's frame blends work well with cartoons, this study retains Raskin's script terminology.

In order to determine what kinds of scripts occur in *The New Yorker* cartoons, a team of three—the researcher and two graduate assistants—analyzed every cartoon in the 1990 issues, searching for whatever categories might emerge. Ultimately the categories were refined as follows:

AREAS OF CULTURE WITH WHICH ONE MUST BE FAMILIAR IN ORDER TO UNDERSTAND THE CONTENT OF CARTOONS FOUND IN *THE NEW YORKER* MAGAZINE, 1990:

A. THE SOCIAL WORLD:
 1. Couples and kids: friends, spouses, parent/child, pets; entertaining, interacting, domestic scenes.
 2. Restaurants, bars, and clubs.
 3. Popular culture: fashions, fads, trendy things (yard sales, Ninja Turtles, diets, health clubs, etc.)
 4. Social expectations: stock characters of a stereotypical nature (hippie, old maid, punk rocker, used car salesman, etc.);

patterned social behavior (standing in line, bride throwing bouquet, tuna casserole as a family, not a 'company,' dish, etc.); defined social roles and role reversal; 'typical' city life/rural life scenes.
5. Entertainment: TV, movies, theater, recreation, travel, sports, show biz from an audience perspective.

B. THE WORKING WORLD:
1. Business and technology: office life, machines in the workplace, etc.
2. Politics and government: national and international (recent or contemporary).
3. Professions: doctors and hospitals, teachers and schools, lawyers and courts, pharmacists, librarians, engineers, etc.
4. Other work: blue collar workers, hairdressers, sales persons, show biz folks (chorus girls, actors, musicians) from the worker's perspective.

C. THE LANGUAGE WORLD: Word play, folk say (The early bird catches the worm), puns, slang, gestures and other body language.

D. THE INTELLECTUAL WORLD:
1. History.
2. Literature: all genres, both written and oral.
3. Art and architecture.
4. Music and dance.
5. Science, nature, ecology.
6. Philosophy, religion, psychology.

E. ANY OTHER WORLD: visual gags, fantasy, etc.

Once the categories of culture content had been designated, we analyzed the cartoons in every other issue of the 1990 series to see what percentage of scripts fell into which category. Of the 1,067 scripts analyzed, by far the largest proportion (53%) fell under the heading of The Social World; 16% of the scripts were assigned to The Working World; 12% to The Language World; 15% to The Intellectual World; and 4%—mainly visual gags—to Any Other World. The scripts of the twelve cartoons selected for the study represented approximately these same percentages.

One other factor entered into the choice of the final cartoons—that of degree of difficulty. A pilot study involving a class of 26 graduate and undergraduate students, both American and international, obtained responses to 20 cartoons and provided information as to the degree of perceived difficulty. The final selection of 12 cartoons included some judged to be easy, some difficult, but the majority were considered of medium challenge.

The cartoons were assembled into a response packet which included a page of instructions, a page with a sample cartoon and responses, and 12 individual response sheets, one for each cartoon. The packets were distributed to two classes of American students: an undergraduate class with 24 students and a graduate class of 13 (N=37). Another group of packets was distributed to international students attending the American Language Program at the University of Georgia; the 45 students participating in the study represented 21 foreign countries and were distributed across five levels of English language proficiency as determined by evaluation measures at the American Language Program. The students had been in the United States for periods ranging from six weeks to one year.

The questionnaire was structured to elicit responses in two areas: appreciation of the cartoon (I think this cartoon is Very Funny, Moderately Funny, Not Funny); and comprehension of the humor involved. To check comprehension, respondents were asked if they understood the point of the cartoon. If they said 'Yes', they were asked to explain what the point was. If they said 'No', they were asked to specify what kept them from understanding. A sample cartoon and responses were presented for discussion by the instructors who administered the questionnaires. Responses of both groups—the American and international students—were tallied and compared.

Because the international students had been in the United States a relatively short time, in-depth interviews concerning responses to the packet and to American humor in general were conducted with six international graduate students who had been in this country for several years. These students represented Chinese, French, German, Japanese, and Korean cultures. Finally, an American graduate student and an American professor were also interviewed.

In tallying the responses, the appreciation measure involved a straightforward commitment to either liking the cartoon or not liking it. Responses of Very funny and Moderately funny were lumped together as a positive response for the final tally. The comprehension measure was more complicated. It was tallied as a 1 if the respondent claimed to understand it and the written explanation of the point indicated that he/she in fact did understand. It was tallied as a 2 if the respondent claimed to understand, but the written explanation revealed a misunderstanding. It was tallied as a 3 if the respondent said he/she didn't understand and the explanation reinforced that perception. It was tallied as a 4 if the respondent said he/she didn't understand, but the explanation indicated that actually the student had grasped the point. The 1s and 4s were totaled to arrive at the percentage of students who understood the joke; the 2s and 3s were totaled to arrive at the percentage of students who did not understand the joke. For the purposes of this study, understanding the joke meant that the respondent seemed to have been aware of both scripts and their connection.

Some interesting conclusions may be drawn regarding the responses of this particular group of students to the twelve *New Yorker* cartoons.*

(1) American and international students agreed more closely on the cartoons they found to be Not Funny than they did on those they found to be Funny. For the Americans the overwhelming favorite, understood by 100% of the group and rated Funny by 95%, was the cartoon based on miscommunication (See Cartoon 1). The international response was lukewarm—only 54% found it Funny, and 54% did not understand it. A student from Germany who rated it Very Funny provide this rationale: 'The woman probably stutters or something so has to write out his (sic) discontentment with husband.'

Cartoon 1.

"*If something is bothering you about our relationship, Lorraine, why don't you just spell it out.*"

	Funny	Not Funny	Understood	Not Understood
American:	95%	5%	100%	0%
International:	54%	46%	46%	54%

Cartoon by Eric Teitelbaum © 1990 The New Yorker Magazine, Inc.   Reprinted by Special Permission.   All Rights Reserved.

---

*For the purposes of this paper, I focus the discussion on six of the cartoons: the two rated most humorous by the American students; the two rated most humorous by the international students; and the two rated least humorous by both groups. G.G.M.

The runner-up favorite of the Americans was difficult for 91% of the international students to understand (See Cartoon 3). A respondent from Japan summed it up: 'I know these vocabularies' meaning, but I can't find the point.' A student from Indonesia fretted, 'The chicken shouldn't take this place. It should be outside.' On the other hand, a student from Saudi Arabia marked it Very Funny and wrote, 'Yes, I understand this cartoon. This man married a checken (sic).'

Neither of the top two choices of the Americans was included among the top four preferences of the international students.

The favorite cartoon of the international students was the third choice of the Americans (See Cartoon 2). The cartoon involves a Business and Technology script and a visual gag. A Korean student expressed delight with the cartoon: 'Just the scene makes me funny.' And a positive thinker from Turkey explained, 'They don't make paper copy. They made friends copy.'

Cartoon 2.

"My God, there's been a terrible accident in our Chicago office!"

	Funny	Not Funny	Understood	Not Understood
American:	79%	21%	97%	3%
International:	81%	19%	37%	63%

Cartoon by Charles Barsotti © 1990 *The New Yorker* Magazine, Inc. Reprinted by Special Permission. All Rights Reserved.

The runner-up favorite of the international students was ranked third from the bottom on the American list (See Cartoon 4). The cartoon brings together a *Social expectations* (urban street scene) script opposed to a *Science* (evolution) script. Seventy-three percent of the international students understood this cartoon—making it the best understood of all the cartoons for the foreign respondents. American respondents were prone to be snappish in their evaluations: 'Evolution, but I don't think it's funny.' The international group, on the other hand, were appreciative—even philosophical—like the Japanese student who mused, 'Who is our first parents? I thought that my ancestor is a microbe. Where did it come?'

Cartoon 3.

"*Why do* you *think you cross the road?*"

	Funny	Not Funny	Understood	Not Understood
American:	83%	17%	91%	9%
International:	49%	51%	9%	91%

Cartoon by Arnie Levin © 1990 *The New Yorker* Magazine, Inc. Reprinted by Special Permission. All Rights Reserved.

The two groups were in closer harmony on cartoons which they did not find amusing (See Cartoon 5). Least liked and least understood by both groups was the cartoon depicting King Canute of Britain, who used the fact that he could not stop the rising of the tides to demonstrate to his courtiers that no sovereign has unlimited powers. The second script evokes the contemporary political scene in which George Bush's promise of 'No new taxes' proved to be equally impotent. Comments from both groups indicated that the reference to Canute's vow was completely baffling; and many foreign students failed to catch the allusion to the political campaign promise.

Cartoon 4.

	Funny	Not Funny	Understood	Not Understood
American:	57%	43%	88%	12%
International:	74%	26%	73%	27%

Cartoon by P. Steiner   © 1990 *The New Yorker* Magazine, Inc.   Reprinted by Special Permission.   All Rights Reserved.

The runner-up in the 'Not Funny category' for both groups (See Cartoon 6) juxtaposed a script depicting the classic frieze—a decorated horizontal architectural form—in opposition to a script depicting the modern law enforcement agent who bursts into a crowded room, draws a weapon, and shouts 'Freeze!' The pun on the word *frieze* was unrecognized by many respondents.

(2) A second conclusion drawn from the responses is that the international students frequently marked a cartoon as Funny even when they did not understand it. American respondents were less inclined to do this. An Indonesian student marked the 'Frieze' cartoon 'Moderately Funny' and commented, 'People act in opera.' A Korean who found the cartoon Funny explained simply, 'Picture is about Jesus.'

In response to the Canute cartoon, a Cameroonian who found it Moderately funny conjectured: 'Maybe they were praying or something traditional and now they must pray in order not to die by waves.' A Colombian who rated the cartoon as Very Funny provided this explanation: 'King is take a shower in the Canute's vow. He is very happy.'

In describing the Fax machine cartoon (Cartoon 2), a Venezuelan respondent marked it Moderately Funny, then added a grim commentary: 'Meny (sic) work murder the people.' And for an Indonesian student who rated it Very Funny the rationale was, 'Person in picture wear wrong tie.'

Cartoon 5.

	Funny	Not Funny	Understood	Not Understood
American:	6%	94%	0%	100%
International:	29%	71%	2%	98%

Cartoon by J.B. Handelsman © 1990 *The New Yorker* Magazine, Inc.   Reprinted by Special Permission. All Rights Reserved.

Cartoon 6.

Cartoon by Eldon Dedini   © 1990 *The New Yorker* Magazine, Inc.   Reprinted by Special Permission. All Rights Reserved.

(3) A third conclusion drawn from the response analysis is that where comprehension is concerned, a knowledge of the cultural referents contained in the cartoon is essential if one is to perceive the two scripts

of a cartoon and the connection between them. On all twelve cartoons a number of international students (an average of 26%) were confident they had understood the point of a cartoon, when, in fact, they had not. In eight out of twelve of the cartoons, an average of 6% of the Americans felt they had understood the point, but had not. It seems possible to experience a humorous response to a cartoon when perceiving only one of the two scripts; or indeed, from merely being amused by the expression on a face or by some other element of the cartoon design. A Chinese respondent marked Cartoon 1 as 'Very Funny' and wrote, 'Don't understand, but unknown object makes it funny.'

The final stage of the study involved in-depth interviews with six graduate students who had been in the United States for several years. Surprisingly, their responses to the cartoons were at much the same level of comprehension as those of the international students who had been in this country a relatively short time, a fact which underscores the difficulty of understanding another culture's humor. One of the students, however, understood eight out of twelve cartoons; another understood seven.

Without exception, the six students made the point that of all the aspects of culture which they are struggling to acquire, humor is the most difficult to understand. A French respondent said, 'For me, humor is the hardest part of the culture—especially when it refers to something from your childhood background that everyone else has experienced . . . If you are able to understand the humor, you can consider yourself bilingual.' This statement seems to echo Edward Hall's contention that . . .'if you can learn the humor of a people and really control it, you know that you are also in control of nearly everything else' (Hall 1959/1973: 52).

The German respondent explained, 'I get most of what has to do with contemporary America—the 80's and 90's. But some situations I don't get . . . mostly allusions to the wonderful 50's and 60's, and any time when it has to do with growing up in the United States—behavior in high school, for instance. Childhood games, pastimes, and stories are sufficiently different that they don't go across cultures readily.'

One Chinese student talked about the struggle to absorb American humor: 'I try to read some American cartoons like *Peanuts*. They are hard to understand. It turns out to be serious reading—so I gave it up. Words are a language barrier. Humor in daily conversation with American friends, that's easier. But I miss a lot of the humor in class. Chinese professors keep lectures serious. Professors who use humor would be considered not very good lecturers.'

Coming through these interviews with compelling urgency was the emotional impact of not being able to share the humor of their cultural surroundings. These informants are not insecure adolescents. They are all mature and sophisticated members of the academic community. Yet with one voice they spoke of the alienation they experience when humor passes them by:

'If you are in a situation and understand one joke, that encourages you. If you don't understand, and everyone else laughs, you may get discouraged. You feel isolated. You have to mask your ignorance.'

'If I don't get a joke, I pretend that I get it so I don't look stupid. Then later I ask someone to explain.'

'I don't understand American jokes. Nine out of ten I don't understand. Everyone is laughing. I feel dumb. I feel, oh, I will never be in this group. I feel apart.'

Such comments underscore the fact that the emotional impact of being left out of a humorous exchange which binds everyone else together severely erodes one's sense of belonging. It is obvious that international students feel keenly the need to acquire a more dimensional understanding of American humor.

In the language teaching profession humor has never been perceived as a sufficiently vital element of culture to merit the struggle of teaching it. But humor is an integral part of culture and, according to Apte, '. . . can be a major conceptual and methodological tool for gaining insights into cultural systems' (Apte, 1985: 16). Some preliminary suggestions for incorporating a study of humor into the foreign language curriculum on a systematic basis are as follows:

1. Provide students with authentic examples of humor—cartoons, puns, quips, jokes, anecdotes, folktales, advertisements, the introductory course on to the completion of their studies.
2. Enrich the culture content with the addition of as much of the 'childhood experience' as possible to help supply those currently missing cultural referents. The rich lore of childhood—riddles, rhymes, taunts, songs, stories, games, holiday observances, superstitions—has enough color and verve to merit a place in the high school and college class, not just in the FLES classroom.
3. Teach students the conventions of humor in the target culture: the institutionalized patterns of humor; the situations, objects, behaviors, and characters that members of a culture consistently joke about; the functions that humor performs in the society; the joking relationships approved by the culture; the buffoons, numskulls, and clowns that figure in oral and literary tradition; the personalities of contemporary comedy; and the social situations where joking is expected/ tolerated/ taboo (Ziv 1988).

4. Teach high school and college students a workable technique for analyzing humor (script/frame/schema theory) to enable them to explore a joke with greater sophistication.
5. Give students performance opportunities where they share a variety of humor genres from the target culture with their classmates and other audiences.

It is possible that sustained exposure to the many facets of humor, coupled with systematic teaching about the nature of humor throughout the entire language learning sequence, can have both cognitive and affective outcomes of a significant and positive nature.

References

Allen, Nancy. 1988. Semantics and Madison Avenue: Application of the semantic theory of humor to advertising. Humor: International Journal of Humor Research 1-1. 27-38.
Apte, Mahadev L. 1985. Humor and laughter: An anthropological approach. Ithaca and London: Cornell University Press.
Hall, Edward T. 1959/1973. The silent language. Garden City, New York: Anchor Press/Doubleday.
Hirsch, E.D., Jr. 1987. Cultural literacy: What every American needs to know. New York: Houghton Mifflin.
Hofstadter, Douglas and Liane Gabora. 1989. Synopsis of the workshop on humor and cognition. Humor: International Journal of Humor Research. 1-1. 27-38.
Marino, Matthew. 1988. Puns: The good, the bad, and the beautiful. Humor: International Journal of Humor Research. 1-1. 39-48.
Raskin, Victor. 1985. Semantic mechanisms of humor. Dordrecht: D. Reidel Publishing.
Ziv, Avner, ed. 1988. National styles of humor. New York: Greenwood Press.

The Input Hypothesis: An update

Stephen D. Krashen
University of Southern California

Introduction. There have been a number of hypotheses concerning the causes of language acquisition, or, rather, the environmental ingredient or ingredients that act on the language acquisition device to produce language acquisition.

(1) The INPUT HYPOTHESIS states that we acquire language by understanding messages, that 'comprehensible input' (CI) is the essential environmental ingredient in language acquisition. Comprehensible input is necessary for language acquisition, but is not sufficient. The acquirer must be 'open' to the input, i.e. have a low Affective Filter (Dulay, Burt, and Krashen 1982). Also, the input needs to contain 'i+1,' an aspect of language that the acquirer has not yet acquired but that he or she is ready to acquire.

(1a) The READING HYPOTHESIS is a special case of the Input Hypothesis. The Reading Hypothesis claims that comprehensible input in the form of reading also stimulates language acquisition.

(2) The SIMPLE OUTPUT HYPOTHESIS (SO). This hypothesis claims that producing language, speaking or writing alone, without feedback or interaction, will result in language acquisition. I am not sure if any professional has proposed this hypothesis for speaking, but it is at least implicitly supported by those who recommend free writing as a means of developing literacy.

(3) The SKILL-BUILDING HYPOTHESIS (SB), or the 'Learning becomes Acquisition' hypothesis. This hypothesis, long an assumption of applied linguistics, claims that we acquire language by first consciously learning individual rules or items, and then, through output practice, often in the form of drills and exercises, we make these rules 'automatic.' This hypothesis has also been referred to as the 'Interface Hypothesis'.

(4) The OUTPUT PLUS CORRECTION HYPOTHESIS (OC). According to OC, we acquire language by trying out new rules or items in production. If we receive negative feedback, we alter our hypothesis about what the rule is or what the new vocabulary word means, or how it is spelled. Negative feedback can come in several forms, including explicit correction.

(5) The COMPREHENSIBLE OUTPUT HYPOTHESIS (CO). According to CO, we acquire new language when we attempt to produce a message, but our conversational partner (or reader) has trouble understanding us. When we experience communicative failure, we adjust our output and try a new version of the rule or item we are acquiring (Swain, 1985).

Pica (1988) helps clarify the distinction between OC and CO: In Output plus Correction, the output is comprehensible but not grammatical. In Comprehensible Output, the output is neither grammatical nor comprehensible.

I have argued that comprehensible input results in 'acquired' competence, represented subconsciously in the brain, while SB and OC result in 'learned' competence, represented consciously in the brain (Krashen 1981a, 1982). The status of competence gained by SO has not been clearly specified. According to Liming (1990), CO results in 'learned' competence.

Methods are often combinations of the hypotheses. Natural Approach rests on the Input Hypothesis, but allows some SB and OC (Krashen and Terrell 1983). Traditional form-based language teaching is usually a combination of SB and OC, with some CI (sometimes included inadvertently). 'Communicative' language teaching appears to be a combination of CO and CI. 'Whole language' seems to be a combination of CI, SO, and CO.

In this paper, I argue that only the Input Hypothesis is successful in accounting for the data in language acquisition and in the development of literacy. Specifically:

(1) Only comprehensible input is consistently effective in increasing proficiency; more skill-building, more correction, and more output do not consistently result in greater proficiency.
(2) Methods with more comprehensible input consistently win in method comparison research.
(3) Output and error correction do not exist in great quantity. Thus, strong versions of hypotheses that depend on output and correction cannot be correct. (A strong version of a hypothesis insists that there is only one path to acquisition.)

(4) Clear gains and even high levels of proficiency can take place without output, skill-building, error correction, and comprehensible output. Each time this has occured, acquirers had obtained comprehensible input. High levels of proficiency cannot take place without comprehensible input.

1 Only comprehensible input is effective in increasing proficiency. More comprehensible input clearly results in more language acquisition. Those with more exposure to a second language tend to show more proficiency in it (Krashen 1982, 1985a),[1] and those who say they have read more or who live in a more print-rich environment show better development of literacy-related aspects of language (Krashen 1985b, 1989).*

Correlations between LOR and second language acquisition, and between reading/living in a print-rich environment and literacy development are typically quite modest (usually between .2 and .3 for the latter; see Krashen 1988, for a review). One reason for this is that the relationship might not be linear. In both cases, there is good evidence that improvement declines with greater amounts of exposure; in other words, the relationship is logarithmic (for second language acquisition, see Wahlberg, Hase, and Pinzur-Rasher 1974; for literacy development, see Greaney 1980 and Anderson, Wilson, and Fielding 1988).

A similar phenomenon might be present at lower levels of proficiency. If acquirers rely only on the informal environment, or readers read only authentic texts, progress at first may be slow, since very little of the input will be comprehensible. As acquirers make more progress, the input becomes more comprehensible, and the acquisition curve becomes more linear, until it flattens out again at the advanced level. Figure 1 portrays this relationship as a logistic curve (see e.g. Mendenhall and Sincich 1989).

What this means, on a practical level, is that 'exposure' is primarily of benefit to the intermediate acquirer. For second language acquisition, living in the country helps most when the acquirer already understands at least some of the language. It will bring the acquirer to the point where he or she can use the language comfortably in ordinary situations, but improvement may slow down or cease after a time, since ordinary 'conversational' input will no longer contain i+1.

---

* Krashen's comprehensive additional commentaries on the several aspects of current hypotheses on language acquisition may be found at the end of this paper. The five notes are on pages 424 through 426. EDITOR

Figure 1. Informal exposure and language acquisition.

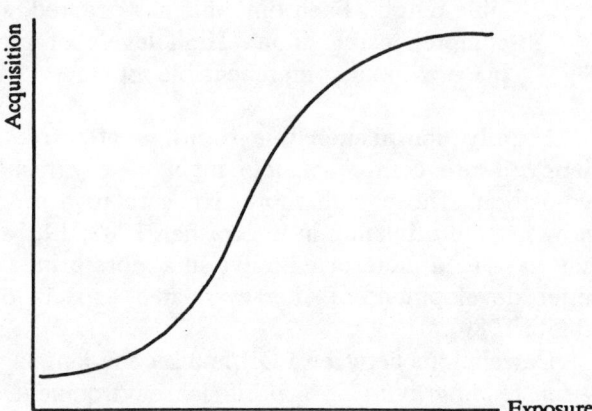

Similarly, light free reading helps when the acquirer can already understand at least some print. It will not, in itself, produce high levels of literacy, but will bring the acquirer to the point where at least some complex texts are comprehensible.

The acquisition curves for conversational type input and printed input are probably similar in shape, but the former may begin earlier, flatten earlier, and not rise to as high as level as the latter (Figure 2). This could explain Freed's results (Freed 1990). Freed studied college students in a 'study abroad' summer program. She reported that the more 'interactive' contact the less advanced students had, the more they improved. This was not the case for more advanced students. For these students, there was a tendency for more interaction to be associated with less improvement.

The pattern was reversed for 'noninteractive contact' (e.g. reading). While there was a tendency for more noninteractive contact to be associated with greater gains for more advanced students, greater noninteractive contact clearly meant lower gains for less advanced students.

Freed's interpretation is that interactive exposure, since it was probably mostly casual, contained i+1 for less proficient students but not for advanced students. In other words, those 'who have more or less mastered the language of daily activities profit less . . . from oral/social interaction' (Freed 1990:473). The noninteractive input was probably more demanding, often beyond the i+1 of less proficient students but suitable for the more advanced students. The lines on Figure 2 indicate these two groups. Note that line (a), representing the lower proficiency group, intersects the conversational input line while it is at a steep slope, but intersects the printed input line while it is still flat. The reverse is true for line (b).

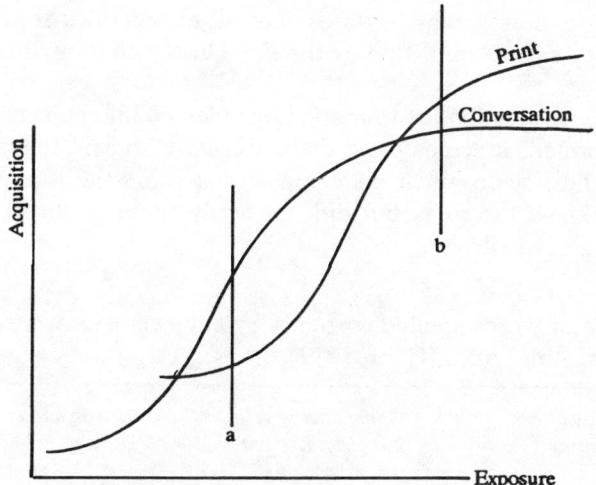

Figure 2. Exposure to conversational and printed input.

There are other possible explanations for 'length of residence' and print environment findings in terms of rival hypotheses, but they are strained (Krashen, in press).

For hypotheses rivaling the Input Hypothesis, evidence is either negative, contradictory, or absent.

More skill-building seems to result in more second language acquisition. Those who have engaged in more formal study generally show higher levels of language proficiency. I have argued, however, that it is not the skill-building aspect of class that has an impact; rather, it is the fact that classes, sometimes despite their best efforts, supply at least some comprehensible input (Krashen 1981a). There are few cases of pure skill-building in the literature, but the ones that exist strongly suggest that skill-building alone is a hopeless way of trying to acquire a language. See, for example, Diller's description of Gouin's efforts to acquire language by conscious study alone (Diller 1971).

Vocabulary teaching programs also appear to show results, but the effects are superficial; pre-teaching vocabulary of a passage does not have a consistent effect on the comprehension of the passage (Mezynski 1983). Direct teaching of grammar has no effect on reading and writing ability (Krashen 1984; Hillocks 1986).

Direct teaching of spelling has, at best, modest results (research reviewed in Krashen 1989). Cook (1912) provides an excellent demonstration of the effects of learning rules on spelling performance. In his study, remedial college freshmen and high school freshmen and seniors who had studied spelling rules the previous semester were given a 50-word spelling test exemplifying common spelling rules. After taking the test, subjects were asked to write all spelling rules they consciously used while spelling the words, noting which words they used the rules for, and to write all rules they saw exemplified by the list, but which they did not think of while writing.

Table 1 presents Cook's results for four spelling rules. While no statistical tests were performed, it seems clear that subjects who said they applied spelling rules did not do much better on words using the rules than those who either knew the rules but did not apply them or those who did not know the rules at all.

Table 1. Percentage of words spelled correctly by subjects who were aware and unaware of spelling rules (Cook 1912).

Rule:	Conscious of rule while writing	Conscious of rule but did not use it while writing	Unconscious of rule
ie/ei:			
UNIV:	79%	71%	73%
	87	87	86
Final e:			
HS:	82	78	82
UNIV:	87	94	88
Final y:			
HS:	74	67	73
UNIV:	94	96	91
Final C:			
HS:	78	72	75
UNIV:	88	87	84

Even though the students had just studied the rules, many could not recall them (Table 2). Of those who did recall rules, the version they gave was often much simpler than the version they were recently taught:

> Curiously enough, most of the collegians who cited a version of the *ie/ei* rule as consciously used relied upon the word 'Alice' and other mnemonic devices which gave a clue to only one or two of the 11 words (relating to the *ie/ei* rule) . . . No (high school) freshman cited the rule as recently taught, but four had it almost correct . . . Three (high school) seniors gave the rule substantially as taught, but nearly all the others who cited anything gave a version of something taught in earlier years, the 'Alice' rule, etc. The rule seems more likely to stick as first learned . . . " (Cook 1912:322).

Table 2. Number of students conscious of spelling rules (Cook 1912).

Rule	High school	University
ie/ei:	31/69 (45%)	30/70 (43%)
Final *e*:	52/69 (75%)	29/70 (41%)
Final *y*:	29/69 (42%)	31/70 (44%)
Final *C*:	42/69 (61%)	34/70 (49%)

Explanation of rules:

ie/ei: '*i* before *e* except after *c*, or when sounded like *a*, as in *neighbor* and *weigh*.' (Cook 1912:317)

Final *e*: 'Final *e* is dropped before a sufffix beginning with a vowel; but it is retained (1) when the suffix begins with a consonant, (2) when a word in *-ce* or *-ge* suffixes *-able* or *-ous*, (3) to keep the pronunciation of a word constant, (4) to maintain the identity of a word.' (Cook 1912:317)

Final *y*: 'Final *y* after a consonant changes to *i* before all suffixes not beginning with *i*; final *y* after a vowel is usually retained.' (Cook 1912:317)

Final *C*: 'Monosyllables and words accented on the last syllable, ending in a consonant after a single vowel, double that consonant before a suffix beginning with a vowel, unless the suffix changes the accent.' (Cook 1912:318)

The data in Tables 1 and 2 also indicate that high school students knew some rules better than the college students did. The college students, however, performed better on the test, confirming that conscious rule knowledge makes little contribution to spelling competence.

The Simple Output, Output plus Correction, and Comprehensible Output hypotheses all require language production. A few studies appear to show that more output results in more acquisition (Hillerich 1971 (spelling); Clarke 1988 (spelling), Lokke and Wykoff 1948 (composition), Brière 1966 (ESL composition)). Brière, however, did not have a control group, and his subjects (ESL students) had other sources of input inside and outside of class. Also, differences in Lokke and Wykoff's study were very small. Many more studies show that increasing output makes no difference (see Table 3).

In addition, Hillocks (1986), after an extensive review that included unpublished dissertation research, found no significant effect for free writing on writing quality.

Similarly, Gradman and Hanania (1991) found that while the 'extracurricular reading' was a strong predictor of TOEFL scores among the

Table 3. Studies showing increasing output makes no difference

Study	L1/L2	Measure
Dressel et al. 1952	L1	composition
Sutton & Allen, 1964[a]	L1	composition
Arnold, 1964	L1	composition
Varble, 1990	L1	writing; mechanics, content[b]
Ely, 1986	L2	oral, written[c]
Burger, 1989	L2	cloze, comp., LC, dict., transl.

a. Described in Hunting (1967)
b. No difference in mechanics in grade 2 and 6 and for content in grade 6. For grade 2, more writing resulted in better writing content.
c. Voluntary class participation correlated significantly with performance on a test of oral fluency for first quarter college Spanish students (r=.4) but not for second quarter students (r=.02) and correlations between voluntary participation and performance on measures of oral and written correctness were small and not significant.

international students (r = .53), extracurricular writing did not correlate with TOEFL performance and extracurricular speaking only correlated with one part of the test (listening comprehension; r = .20). Neither writing nor speaking survived a multiple regression analysis, while reading was the best predictor of TOEFL performance.

In fact, one study even found that more production, in the form of speaking in class, resulted in less acquisition of grammar (Ellis 1988); students who were called on more made less progress. As Ellis notes, this may be due to teachers' requiring weaker students to 'practice' more.

Several studies strongly suggest that more correction does not mean better language acquisition. A number of classroom studies have failed to show that error correction has any impact (for first language, Brandenberg 1919; Arnold 1964; for second language, Cohen and Robbins 1976; Semke 1984; Robb, Ross, and Shortreed 1986). When error correction has an effect in the classroom, the impact is modest, and the effect occurs where acquisition/learning theory predicts it will occur: On discrete-point form oriented measures and with students who have done a great deal of conscious learning (my interpretation of Lalonde 1982; Cardelle and Corno 1981; Ramirez and Stromquist 1979). In informal situations, error correction also seems to have little effect (Brock, Crookes, Day, and Long 1986).

The only study I know of that suggests a clear impact for error correction is Lightbown and Spada (1990), who reported that 'focus on the code,' which consisted nearly entirely of correction and teachers' reactions to student requests for help 'seems to have been effective in some cases, and less so in others' (Lightbown and Spada 1990:443) for 10 to 12 year old Francophone students in an intensive ESL course. Focus on the code had, according to Lightbown and Spada, a clear impact on avoidance of the 'there has/there is' error on an oral picture description task, and a less spectacular but clear effect on correct production of the *-ing* morpheme, and correct adjective/noun order. Focus on form did not, however, influence correct production of the *-s* plural ending, and students in a class with very little focus on form performed quite well on a test of listening and reading comprehension.

Some researchers have simply assumed the effectiveness of error correction. When correction fails, they simply call for more, or more consistent correction. More likely, language acquisition simply does not work that way.

There has been no research that I know of that shows that more comprehensible output results in more language acquisition, although it can be argued that studies showing a relationship between interaction/length of residence and second language acquisition are consistent with the comprehensible output hypothesis.

2 Methods with more comprehensible input consistently win in method comparison research. To my knowledge, CI-based methods have never lost a second-language method comparison study. CI-based methods have been shown to be superior in beginning second language acquisition when tests are communicative, and at least as effective when tests are form-based (Bushman and Madson 1976; Voge 1981; Asher 1988; Hammond 1988; Lightbown, in press). At the intermediate level, studies have shown sheltered subject matter teaching to be very effective (see Krashen, forthcoming, for a review).

In first language development, comparison studies have also shown that classes containing more CI in the form of stories read outloud to children and free reading (e.g. sustained silent reading) are more effective than traditional skill-building approaches, when the treatments are allowed to run for a sufficient length of time (Krashen 1985b, 1989).

Table 4. Effectiveness of in-school free reading programs.

Duration	Results: Tests of reading comprehension		
	Positive	No difference	Negative
Less than 7 months	8	8	3
7 months - 1 year	11	4	1
Greater than 1 year	7	2	0

Table 4 presents a summary of the effectiveness of sustained silent reading and self-selected reading programs for developing reading comprehension; this table is an up-dated version of one appearing in Krashen (1988). I have added the results of two successful sustained silent reading studies (Langford and Allen 1983, Holt and O'Tuel 1989).

Also, results of 'read and test' studies of vocabulary acquisition have suggested that picking up words from reading is more efficient in terms of words acquired per minute than are traditional intensive vocabulary learning programs, if the goal is a knowledge of the word deep enough to aid in reading comprehension (Nagy, Herman, and Anderson 1985).[2]

A possible counter-argument to such results is the claim that method comparison studies are meaningless, since we do not know exactly what is going on in these classes. It is true that in some cases we must simply rely on a broad, descriptive term, such as 'Natural Approach,' 'TPR' or 'sheltered subject matter teaching.' The results are so consistent, however, so robust, that they cannot be easily dismissed.

McLaughlin (1987) and Krahnke (1985) have another objection. They argue that since all teaching methods have at least some comprehensible input, the Input Hypothesis justifies all methods. It is true that all methods provide some comprehensible input, but this fact does not justify all methods. Some methods supply more comprehensible input than others, and the research confirms that those that provide more comprehensible input are more effective.

3 Output and error correction do not exist in great quantity.

> I thought the answer (to how we learn to write) must be that we learn to write by writing until I reflected upon how little anyone writes in school, even the eager students, and how little feedback is provided... No one writes enough to learn more than a small part of what writers need to know... (F. Smith 1988:19).

It is likely that people simply do not produce enough language to support strong versions of the Simple Output, Output plus Correction, or Comprehensible Output hypotheses. This appears to be true for oral output in second language classes, and for written output, both in class and outside of class.

Swain (1988) notes that student oral output is relatively rare in immersion classes. For grade six classes, for example, there were only about two student turns per minute, with nearly half 'of minimal length' and only 14% 'sustained' (longer than a clause). Instead of concluding that output may not have a direct role in language acquisition, Swain recommends more output, assuming that it has a function. We must, however, ask how the students achieved their impressive level of competence without extensive output.

The small amount of data I have been able to find on how much people write suggests that they do not write very much. Confirming Smith's statement, writing in school appears to be infrequent. Applebee, Langer, and Mullis (1986) asked students how many essays and reports they had written over six weeks for any school subject. Only 18.6% of the fourth graders wrote more than ten, while only 7.8% of the eleventh graders wrote more than ten. Writing outside of school is also not frequent: the eleventh grade group did the most out-of-school writing, but only 17.4% kept diaries, 37.3% said they wrote letters to friends, and 74.8% said they wrote notes and messages at least weekly (Applebee et al. 1986).

Research by Rice (1986) allows us to make at least a crude comparison of writing and reading frequency. Rice probed reading and writing behavior of several groups, and I present one of them (high verbal adults) as a representative example. These subjects reported 15.1 hours per week in 'total reading,' but only two hours per week in writing (1.9 hours for 'short writing' and .1 hours for 'long writing'). Assuming even a very slow reading rate (200 wpm) and a very fast writing rate (typing at 60 wpm), this still means that people deal with far more words in reading than in writing (a ratio of 25 to 1). More likely, the true ratio is more like 150 to 1. Considering the complexity of the system that is to be acquired, this data severely weakens the case for writing as an important source of language acquisition. (Evans and Gleadow 1983 made similar estimates of reading and writing frequency.)

Error correction is also rare, both in the informal environment and in the classroom. Chun et al (1982) reported that very few errors made by non-native speakers of English were corrected by their conversational partners (about 9%), and of those, many consisted of filling lexical gaps. Obanya's informal acquirers of Yoruba (Obanya 1976; see Note 1, *this paper*) reported that they did not rely on correction; only 5.6% of the sample said they used trial and error (mistakes and correction) as a strategy for acquisition of Yoruba. Liming (1990:12), a strong believer in the effectiveness of correction, found that 'negative evidence was not readily available' in the informal environment and concluded that acquirers need to aggressively seek out correction and other forms of negative input.

Classroom studies give similar results. Allen, Swain, and Harley (1988) reported that only 19% of the errors made by grade six immersion students were corrected, and Cathcart and Olsen (1976) found that the community college and university ESL teachers they surveyed averaged only 6.3 corrections per class.

There is relatively little data on the frequency of comprehensible output. Pica (1988) reported that beginning language acquirers (ESL) modified their spoken output 31% of the time in response to interlocuters' signals of non-comprehension in a way that made the utterance closer to correct English, while intermediate acquirers did so 51% of the time (Pica et al. 1989). Cumming (1990) examined think-aloud protocols of second language writers, hypothesizing that instances in which writers appeared to be attending to both form and meaning at the same time are potential instances of language acquisition, according to the Comprehensible Output hypothesis. His analysis revealed that about 30% of the verbal reports made by second language writers in his sample were of this kind (p. 490).[3] While these studies confirm that comprehensible output exists, whether it is frequent enough to account for much of language acquisition depends on how much output people produce.

4 Clear gains and even high levels of proficiency can take place without output, skill-building, error correction, and comprehensible output. Each time this has occured, acquirers had obtained comprehensible input. High levels of proficiency cannot take place without comprehensible input. In previous papers (Krashen 1989), I documented cases of language acquisition without instruction (skill-building and output plus correction). It can be argued that in all cases in which this took place, comprehensible input was available and utilized.

The most compelling cases are the 'read and test' studies mentioned earlier, studies in which subjects were able to acquire measurable amounts of vocabulary and spelling knowledge from just a few exposures to target words in a meaningful text (sometimes only one exposure)(see e.g. Nagy, Herman, and Anderson 1985; other studies are reviewed in Krashen 1989). In read and test studies, acquisition occurs without skill-building, correction, or output. Even though gains in vocabulary knowledge are modest after only one exposure, Nagy et al. argue that given enough reading, modest gains are more than enough to account for vocabulary growth; the same may be true of spelling (Krashen 1989).[4]

Little or no output, skill-building, error-correction, and comprehensible output takes place in certain comprehensible input-based language teaching methods (e.g. Natural Approach, TPR, sheltered subject matter teaching) and in reading, yet they result in clear gains in proficiency. Kessler and Quinn (1984) report a case of progress in second language acquisition for a high school student from a combination of informal exposure and comprehensible input-based instruction.

In a number of case histories, it appears quite likely that high levels of second language proficiency were obtained without instruction, from informal means alone (see e.g. J.P. in Krashen 1985a; also Dittmar 1981). Indeed, many if not most cases of advanced second language proficiency throughout the world may be of this kind. Such cases make certain rival hypotheses unlikely (skill-building) but could be interpreted as support for comprehensible output, since the acquirers interacted with native speakers (but see the case of Schliemann, discussed below).

There is good evidence that reading alone can result in high levels of literacy development. Those with large vocabularies typically credit reading with having helped them (Smith and Supanich 1984), and those who write well report having read more than less competent writers (research reviewed in Krashen 1984). Also, there are impressive case histories that strongly suggest that reading alone is enough.

Richard Wright grew up in an environment where reading and writing were disapproved of by family members; his grandmother actually burned the books he brought home, 'branding them as worldly' (Wright 1966:142).

Wright became interested in reading and in hearing stories at an early age, thanks to a schoolteacher, a boarder at his home, who told him stories from novels.

Wright struggled to gain access to reading material. He delivered newspapers only so that he could read them, and used an associates' library card to take books out of a library that was restricted to whites.

In agreement with the Input Hypothesis, Wright credits reading with providing his language development:

> I wanted to write and I did not even know the English language. I bought English grammars and found them dull. I felt that I was getting a better sense of the language from novels than from grammars. (Wright 1966:275)

While Richard Wright depended, to a great extent, on fiction. Malcolm X, on the other hand, credited non-fiction with his literacy development.

As he describes in his autobiography, Malcolm X had early success in school. He was, in fact, president of his seventh-grade class. His life in the streets, however, 'erased everything I'd ever learned in school' (Malcolm X 1964:154). As a prisoner, in his early 20s, his literacy level was low. He describes his first attempt to write a letter to Elijah Mohammed:

> At least twenty-five times I must have written that first one-page letter to him, over and over. I was trying to make it legible and understandable. I practically couldn't read my handwriting myself; it shames even to remember it. My spelling and grammar were as bad, if not worse (p. 169).

The change came in prison:

> Many who hear me today somewhere in person, or on television, or those who read something I've said, will think I went to school far beyond the eighth grade. This impression is due entirely to my prison studies (p. 171).

These 'prison studies' consisted largely of reading. Building his vocabulary at first the hard way, by studying the dictionary, Malcolm X became a dedicated reader:

> ... in every free moment I had, if I was not reading in the library, I was reading on my bunk. You couldn't have gotten me out of books with a wedge... (p. 173).

Like Richard Wright, Malcolm X specifically gives reading the credit:

> Not long ago, an English writer telephoned me from London, asking questions. One was, 'What's your alma mater?' I told him, 'Books.' (p. 179)

These case histories are not hard data. Stories like these, however, are not uncommon, and it is difficult to imagine other sources for the literacy development that took place.

Acquisition without comprehensible input? It has been claimed that second language acquisition can take place without comprehensible input, that there are "well-documented" cases in which high levels of proficiency have been attained by conscious learning alone (McLaughlin 1987; Brumfit 1984).

Horner (1987) argues that Heinrich Schliemann was such a case:

> There is also the case of auto-didacts like Heinrich Schliemann, a German who mastered English in six months in Amsterdam by writing essays, having them corrected, and memorizing them while working as an office boy. (Jahn 1979:340).

This is Horner's entire discussion of Schliemann, and, reading it, one gets the impression that Schliemann acquired English solely by writing essays, having them corrected, and memorizing the corrected versions. Not so. Jahn (1979) states that Schliemann did a number of other things as well: He studied with a native speaker of English every day for one hour, 'read out loud for extended periods of time' (Jahn 1979:273) and attended two church services in English every Sunday. He not only memorized his own corrected essays, but he also memorized other English writing (he claimed to have memorized *The Vicar of Wakefield* and *Ivanhoe* (see Ludwig 1932:63), and stated that he only needed three readings to memorize a text. He averaged about 20 pages daily, a considerable amount of input (Ludwig 1932).

Schliemann devoted every spare moment to language study, reading and memorizing while on errands and while waiting in line. Jahn estimated that in six months Schliemann was exposed to about 1,350 hours of English, the equivalent of seven years of formal study.

To be sure, Schliemann's methods were not, according to the Input Hypothesis, the most efficient. If, however, he understood what he read out loud, his corrected essays, and the texts he memorized, and even partly understood the sermons he heard, he obtained a great deal of comprehensible input, enough to attain at least a reasonable level of proficiency in English.

Of course, it would be impossible to investigate every proposed instance of second language acquisition without comprehensible input. But at least this famous case is not such an instance.

Some affective evidence. It must be more than coincidence that those aspects of instruction that students find the most anxiety-provoking are those found to be ineffective: error correction and forced output (Young 1990; Loughrin-Sacco, Bommarito, Sweet, and Beck 1988; Horwitz, Horwitz, and Cope 1986; for a report of the devasting affective effects of negative feedback, see Taylor and Hoedt 1966). Often, experts advise the use of activities that will soften the blow of error correction and forced speaking, such as positive 'self-talk,' reading passages outloud in groups, and relaxation exercises. These proposals, however, deal with the symptoms and not the cause of anxiety. The real cure, as Horwitz et al. (1986) point out, is to change the class. In my view, this means dropping error correction in communicative activities, and not requiring students to produce language that is beyond their acquired competence. This is the procedure Natural Approach follows (Krashen and Terrell 1983).

On the other hand, the activities that students report to be the least anxiety provoking or non-anxiety provoking seem to be very effective in encouraging language acquisition, such as silent reading (for adult foreign language, see Young 1990; for first language free reading, see Schwartzenberg 1962; and for hearing stories (Walker and Kuerbitz 1979; Mason and Blanton 1971; Wells 1985; Elley 1989).

While not everything that is enjoyable is good for you, it may be the case that activities that are good for language acquisition are not anxiety-provoking and those that are painful are not effective. It is possible that 'no pain, no gain' does not apply to language acquisition.[5]

Notes

1 Day (1985) is an apparent counterexample. For his subjects, university students in an intensive ESL program, there was no significant relationship between amount of contact with native speakers and proficiency. There are several possible reasons for this outcome: As Day noted, the duration of the treatment was short (six weeks). Also, there may not have been enough variation in proficiency among the subjects (the standard deviation for the 28 item cloze test was only 2.85), and Day used post-test scores in his analysis, not gains (Day also performed a multiple regression controlling for level in the ESL program and found similar results; it could be argued that level is only a crude estimate of initial competence, however; see also Day, 1984).

An earlier study of the effects of exposure missed in my previous reviews is Obanya (1976), who reported that immigrants to Ibadan who had been there longer reported more competence in Yoruba; 60% of these acquirers had been in Ibadan for six years or more. When asked what their strategies were for developing competence in Yoruba, nearly 70% said it was from communication ('mixing freely with Yorubas,' 40.2%; 'merely listening to conversations' and 'repeating,' 28.8%). While 'repeating' does not fit the Input Hypothesis, the other strategies clearly do.

For a spectacular case of literacy development resulting from enriching the print environment with magazines, see Rucker (1982).

Despite the striking consistency of 'length of residence' studies, it has been claimed that they teach us nothing. McLaughlin (1987:40) states that in order to demonstrate that research on exposure supports the Input Hypothesis, one would have to 'provide some way of determining what is comprehensible input for a given learner'. Such a view excludes the LOR studies as evidence for or against any hypothesis, and allows only 'laboratory' studies as evidence.

2 A number of method comparison studies are 'impure,' that is, methods are compared that are a mixture of hypotheses. I present here some of these comparisons, analyzing the methods in terms of the combinations of hypotheses. In every case, the method containing significant amounts of comprehensible input is on the winning side:

Study	Results
Beginning L1:	
Hagerty, Hiebert and Owens (1989)	IH+SO+CO > SB+CO
Intermediate L1:	
Holt and O'Tuel (1989)	IH+SO > SB+OC
Beginning L2:	
N. Davies (1983)	IH+SB > SB
Beretta and A. Davies (1985)	IH+CO > SB+OC
Thomas (1987)	IH+CO > SB+OC

Several studies claim to support form-based language teaching, but a close analysis shows this is not the case. Spada (1987) found little difference in achievement between intensive intermediate ESL classes that were more form-based (i.e. 'focussed on grammar'; p. 144) and those that were more function-based ('focussed on meaning'; p. 144). The function-based classes made better gains in listening, but there was no difference on a number of other tests. Spada also presented evidence suggesting that more explicit focus on "discourse activities" resulted in greater gains on a test of discourse, but differences were very small (raw data in Spada 1986). Spada (1986) reported that students who did more form-based activities benefited more from informal contact with native-speakers, but significant results were found only for grammar and writing performance, and not on a number of other measures; only three comparisons were significant out of a total of 28 (see her tables 7 and 8).

Harley (1989) provided grade six French immersion students with eight weeks of special instruction on the *imparfait/passé composé* distinction. Her experimental groups averaged 11.9 hours of work on this comparison, while control groups did less than half that amount. Experimental students performed significantly better on two out of three measures, but differences on one measure (the cloze test), while significant, were small (less than 3%), and delayed post-testing done three months later revealed no significant differences among the groups.

3 The nature of the episodes in Cumming's study makes it unlikely that they play a major role in language acquisition. Cumming reports that very few of the thinking episodes involved conscious reasoning about form and meaning at the same time, and even fewer dealt with form alone (less than 2%). Most of the episodes were simply writers' searching for the right word or searching for L1 equivalents. The latter is the familiar strategy of falling back on the first language when competence is lacking in the second language (Newmark, 1966).

4 The results of one read and test study appear to be contrary to the Input Hypothesis. In Scott (1988), intermediate college French students were presented with one of two different approaches to the relative pronoun and the subjunctive. The 'explicit' group received six short (ten minute) lessons. In each lesson, one relative pronoun or aspect of the subjunctive was explained, followed by five model sentences illustrating the rule. The implicit group received no explanation, but instead heard the target language in an episode of a story 'designed to hold their attention' (p. 16) for ten minutes per day for six days. Each episode contained either 25 uses of the relative clause or 15 uses of the subjunctive. After reading each episode, the teacher checked comprehension by asking questions, and reread the story in the last session. Implicit students were not told they were being exposed to a particular structure.

As is typical with intermediate students, these target structures were not new: 'All subjects acknowledged through informal questioning that they had previously studied these two elements of French grammar' (p. 15).

Scott's results show that the explicit group made greater gains on a written test (fill-in-the-blank), but not on an oral test (also form-focussed; students were asked to answer questions using a particular form). Scott noted also that this modality difference is consistent with the Monitor Hypothesis, since subjects had less time on the oral test to apply conscious rules.

With the wisdom of hindsight, I would like to claim that the Input Hypothesis does not predict that the implicit group should do better. First, there is a good chance that both target structures were beyond these students' i+1—while both structures may be learnable, they may not be acquirable at this stage (Scott (1991:103) also notes that the subjunctive ' . . . is perhaps one of the latest acquired structures for students of French'; for evidence that the Spanish subjunctive is acquired late, see Terrell, Baycroft, and Perrone 1987; Stokes 1988; Stokes and Krashen 1990). Thus, even if the stories were comprehensible, acquisition might not occur.

Second, there is reason to suspect that the subjects in the implicit group were not focussing on meaning very much. Recall that they heard the same story three times, twice during the lesson and then again in the last session.

Scott also suggested that the treatment may have been too short for acquisition to have taken place and that the format of the tests may have given the explicit group an advantage, since the tests were form-focussed and even used grammatical terminology (e.g. 'Fill in the blank with the correct relative pronoun,' p. 21).

Scott does not mention whether test scores were adjusted for guessing. If so, her results suggest that some acquisition did in fact take place in the implicit group. For the subjunctive, for example, the implicit group made a 13% gain (2.63/20), for relative pronouns a 2% gain (.47/20); not bad for one hour of input. These gains are, in fact, surprising, considering the problems discussed above. If acquisition of grammar works anything like acquisition of vocabulary, these modest gains might be enough; Nagy et al. (1985) have estimated that gaining only 5% of the meaning of an unfamiliar word each time it is encountered in context is enough to account for much of vocabulary acquisition, several thousand words per year for school children who do a moderate amount of reading. The increment seen here was much smaller, but it could be enough, given sufficient input.

('Acquired' gains showing up on a form-based test is not contrary to current theory, which predicts that both 'learned' and 'acquired' competence can be reflected on a form-based test, but only acquired competence will be applicable to communicative tests (Krashen 1981b). Students who have 'acquired' but have not 'learned' will be at a disadvantage on form-based test items that are late-acquired.)

5 Additional evidence that CI-based activities are less anxiety-provoking are findings that students in CI-based classes report more confidence for future success in acquiring the target language (Voge 1981), and are more interested in continuing second language acquisition (Lafayette and Buscaglia 1983).

References

Allen, P., M. Swain, and B. Harley. 1988. Analytic and experiential aspects of core French and immersion classrooms. Bulletin of the Canadian Association of Applied Linguistics. 10. 59-68.

Anderson, R., P. Wilson, and L. Fielding. 1988. Growth in reading and how children spend their time outside of school. The Reading Research Quarterly 23. 285-303.

Applebee, A., Langer, J., and I. Mullis. 1986. The writing report card. Princeton, N. J.: Educational Testing Service.

Arnold, L. 1964. Writer's cramp and eyestrain: Are they paying off? English Journal 53. 10-15.

Asher, J. 1988. Learning another language through actions: The complete teacher's guidebook. Los Gatos, Ca.: Sky Oaks Productions.

Beretta, A. and A. Davies. 1985. Evaluation of the Bangalore Project. ELT Journal, 39/2. Reprinted in Prabu, N. 1987. Second Language Pedagogy. Oxford: Oxford University Press. 144-153.

Brandenburg, G. 1919. Some possibly secondary factors in spelling ability. School and Society 9. 632-636.

Brière, E. 1966. Quantity before quality in second language composition. Language Learning 16. 141-51.

Brock, C., G. Crookes, R. Day, and M. Long. 1986. The differential effects of corrective feedback in native speaker-nonnative speaker conversation. In: Talking to Learn: Conversation in a Second Language, ed. R. Day. New York: Newbury House. 229-236.

Brumfit, C. 1984. Communicative methodology in language teaching. Cambridge: Cambridge University Press.

Burger, S. 1989. Content-based ESL in a sheltered psychology course: input, output, and outcomes. TESL Canada 6. 45-59.

Bushman, R. and H. Madsen. 1976. A description and evaluation of Suggestopedia: A new teaching methodology. In: On TESOL '76. Eds: J. Fanselow and R. Crymes. Washington, D.C.: TESOL. 29-39.

Cardelle, M. and L. Corno. 1981. Effects on second language learning of variations in written feedback in homework assignments. TESOL Quarterly 15. 251-274.

Cathcart, R. and J. Olsen. 1976. Teachers' and students' preferences for correction of classroom conversation errors. In: On TESOL '76. Eds. J. Fanselow and R. Crymes. Washington, D.C.: TESOL. 41-53.

Chun, A., R. Day, N. Chenoweth, and S. Luppescu. 1982. Errors, interaction, and correction: A study of native-nonnative conversations. TESOL Quarterly 16. 537-547.

Clarke, L. 1988. Invented versus traditional spelling in first graders' writings: Effects on learning to spell and read. Research in the Teaching of English 45. 281-310.

Cohen, A. and M. Robbins. 1976. Towards assessing interlanguage performance: The relationship between selected errors, learner's characteristics, and learner's expectations. Language Learning 26. 45-66.

Cook, W. 1912. Shall we teach spelling by rule? Journal of Educational Psychology 3. 316-325.

Cumming, A. 1990. Metalinguistic and ideational thinking in second language composing. Written Communication 7. 482-511.
Davies, N. 1983. The receptive way to active learning. System 11. 245-248.
Day, R. 1984. Student participation in the ESL classroom or some imperfections in practice. Language Learning 34. 69-102.
Day, R. 1985. The use of the target language in context and second language proficiency. In: Input in second language acquisition, ed. S. Gass and C. Madden. New York: Newbury House. 257-271.
Diller, K. 1971. Generative grammar, structural linguistics, and language teaching. New York: Newbury House.
Dittmar, N. 1981. On the verbal organization of L2 tense marking in an elicited translation task by Spanish immigrants in Germany. Studies in Second Language Acquisition 3. 136-164.
Dressel, P., J. Schmid, and G. Kincaid. 1952. The effects of writing frequency upon essay-type writing proficiency at the college level. Journal of Educational Research 46. 285-293.
Dulay, H., M. Burt, and S. Krashen. 1982. Language Two. New York: Oxford University Press.
Elley, W. 1989. Vocabulary acquisition from listening to stories. Reading Research Quarterly 24. 174-187.
Ellis, R. 1988. Investigating language teaching: The case for an educational approach. System 16. 1-11.
Ely, C. 1986. An analysis of discomfort, risktaking, sociability, and motivation in the L2 classroom. Language Learning 36. 1-25.
Evans, P. and N. Gleadow. 1983. Literacy: A study of literacy performance and leisure activities in Victoria, B.C. Reading Canada 2. 3-16.
Freed, B. 1990. Language learning in a study abroad context: The effects of interactive and noninteractive out-of-class contact on grammatical achievement and oral proficiency. Georgetown University Round Table on Languages and Linguistics 1990. Washington, D.C.: Georgetown University Press. pp. 459-477.
Gradman, H. and E. Hanania. 1991. Language learning background factors and ESL proficiency. Modern Language Journal 75, 39-51.
Greaney, V. 1980. Factors related to amount and type of leisure time reading. Reading Research Quarterly 15.337-357.
Hagerty, P., E. Hiebert, E., and M. Owens. 1989. Students' comprehension, writing, and perceptions in two approaches to literacy instruction. In: Cognitive and social perspectives for literacy research and instruction: 38th yearbook of the National Reading Conference. Eds. S. McCormick and J. Zutell. Chicago, Illinois: National Reading Conference. 453-459.
Hammond, R. 1988. Accuracy versus communicative competency: The acquisition of grammar in the second language classroom. Hispania 71. 408-417.
Harley, B. 1989. Functional grammar in French immersion: A classroom experiment. Applied Linguistics 10. 331-359.
Hillerich, R. 1971. Evaluation of written language. Elementary English 48. 839-42.
Hillocks, G. Jr. 1986. Research on written composition: New directions for teaching. Urbana, Ill.: ERIC

Holt, S. and F. O'Tuel. 1989. The effect of sustained silent reading and writing on achievement and attitudes of seventh and eighth grade students reading two years below grade level. Reading Improvement 26. 290-297.

Horner, D. 1987. Acquisition, learning and the Monitor: A critical look at Krashen. System 15. 339-349.

Horwitz, E., M. Horwitz, and J. Cope. 1986. Foreign language classroom anxiety. Modern Language Journal 70. 125-132.

Hunting, R. 1967. Recent studies of writing frequency. Research in the Teaching of English 1. 29-40.

Jahn, J. 1979. A self-motivated and self-directed second language learner: Heinrich Schliemann. Modern Language Journal 63. 273-276.

Kessler, C. and Quinn, M. 1984. Second language acquisition in the context of science experiences. Paper presented at the 18th annual convention of Teachers of English to Speakers of Other Languages, Houston, Texas, March 6-11, 1984.

Krahnke, K. 1985. Review of The Natural Approach: Language Acquisition in the Classroom. TESOL Quarterly 19. 591-603.

Krashen, S. 1981a. Second language acquisition and second language learning. New York: Prentice Hall.

Krashen, S. 1981b. Letter to the editor. Language Learning 31, 217-221.

Krashen, S. 1982. Principles and Practice in Second Language Acquisition. New York: Prentice-Hall.

Krashen, S. 1984. Writing: Research, theory and applications. New York: Prentice-Hall.

Krashen, S. 1985a. The input hypothesis: Issues and implications. New York: Longman.

Krashen, S. 1985b. Inquiries and insights. Menlo Park: Alemany Press.

Krashen, S. 1989. We acquire vocabulary and spelling by reading: Additional evidence for the Input Hypothesis. Modern Language Journal 73. 440-464.

Krashen, S. (in press). Comprehensible input and some competing hypothesis. In: Comprehension-based language teaching. Eds. R. Courchène and J. St. John. Ottawa: University of Ottawa Press.

Krashen, S. and T. Terrell. 1983. The Natural Approach: Language Acquisition in the Classroom. Menlo Park: Alemany Press.

Lalonde, J. 1982. Reducing composition errors: An experiment. Modern Language Journal 66. 140-149.

Langford, J. and E. Allen. 1983. The effects of U.S.S.R. on students' attitudes and achievements. Reading Horizons 23. 194-200.

Lafayette, R. and M. Buscaglia. 1983. Students learn language via a civilization course—a comparison of second language classroom environments. Studies in Second Language Acquisition 7. 323-342.

Lightbown, P. (in press). Can they do it themselves? A comprehension-based ESL course for young children. In: Comprehension-Based Language Teaching. Eds. R. Courchène and J. St. John. Ottawa: University of Ottawa Press.

Lightbown, P. and N. Spada. 1990. Focus on form and corrective feedback in communicative language teaching: Effects on second language learning. Studies in Second Language Acquisition 12. 429-448.

Liming, Y. 1990. The comprehensible output hypothesis and self-directed learning: A learner's perspective. TESL Canada 8. 9-26.

Loughrin-Sacco, S., E. Bommarito, W. Sweet, and A. Beck. 1988. Anatomy of an elementary French class. Paper presented at the Symposium on Research Perspectives in Adult Language Learning and Acquisition, Ohio State University, October 21, 1988.
Lokke, V. and G. Wykoff. 1948. 'Double writing' in freshman composition—an experiment. School and Society 68. 437-439.
Ludwig, E. 1932. Schliemann: Geschichte eines Goldsuchers. Berlin: Paul Zsolnay Verlag.
Mason, G. and W. Blanton. 1971. Story content for beginning reading instruction. Elementary English 48. 793-796.
McLaughlin, B. 1987. Theories of Second-Language Learning. London: Edward Arnold.
Mendenhall, W. and T. Sincich. 1989. A Second Course in Business Statistics: Regression Analysis. San Francisco: Dellen.
Mezynski, K. 1983. Issues concerning the acquisition of knowledge. Review of Educational Research 53. 253-279.
Nagy, W., P. Herman, and R. Anderson. 1985. Learning words from context. Reading Research Quarterly 20. 233-53.
Newmark, L. 1966. How not to interfere with language learning. International Journal of American Linguistics 40. 77-83.
Obanya, P. 1976. Second language learning out of school. ITL: Review of Applied Linguistics 31.15-26.
Pica, T. 1988. Interlanguage adjustments as an outcome of NS-NNS negotiated interaction. Language Learning 38. 45-73.
Pica, T., L. Holliday, N. Lewis, and L. Morgenthaller. 1989. Comprehensible output as an outcome of linguistic demands on the learner. Studies in Second Language Acquisition 11. 63-90.
Ramirez, A. and N. Stromquist. 1979. ESL methodology and student language learning in bilingual education schools. TESOL Quarterly 13. 145-158.
Rice, E. 1986. The everyday activities of adults: Implications for prose recall, part I. Educational Gerontology 12. 173-186.
Robb, T., S. Ross, and I. Shortreed. 1986. Salience of feedback on error and its effects on EFL writing quality. TESOL Quarterly 20. 83-95.
Rucker, B. 1982. Magazines and teenage reading skills: Two controlled field experiments. Journalism Quarterly 59. 28-33.
Schwartzenberg, H. 1962. What children think of individualized reading. The Reading Teacher 16. 86-89.
Scott, V. 1989. An empirical study of explicit and implicit teaching strategies in French. Modern Language Journal 73. 14-22.
Scott, V. 1991. Response to Schloter. Modern Language Journal 75, 103-104.
Semke, H. 1984. The effects of the red pen. Foreign Language Annals 17. 195-202.
Smith, F. 1988. Joining the Literacy Club. Portsmouth, N. H.: Heinemann.
Smith, R. and G. Supanich. 1984. The vocabulary scores of company presidents. Chicago: Johnson O'Connor Research Foundation, Technical Report 1984-1.
Spada, N. 1986. The interaction between type of contact and type of instruction: Some effects on the L2 proficiency of adults learners. Studies in Second Language Acquisition 8. 181-199.

Spada, N. 1987. Relationships between instructional differences and learning outcomes: A process-product study of communicative language teaching. Applied Linguistics 8. 137-155.

Stokes, J. 1988. Some factors in the acquisition of the present subjunctive in Spanish. Hispania 71. 705-10.

Stokes, J. and S. Krashen. 1990. Some factors in the acquisition of the present subjunctive in Spanish: A re-analysis. Hispania 73. 805-806.

Swain, M. 1985. Communicative competence: Some roles of comprehensible input and comprehensible output in its development. In: Input in second language acquisition. Eds. S. Gass and C. Madden. New York: Newbury House. 235-256.

Swain, M. 1988. Manipulating and complementing content teaching to maximize second language learning. TESL Canada 6. 68-83.

Taylor, W. and K. Hoedt. 1966. The effect of praise upon the quality and quantity of creative writing. Journal of Educational Research 60. 80-83.

Terrell, T., B. Baycroft, and C. Perrone. 1987. The subjunctive in spanish interlanguage: Accuracy and comprehensibility. In: Foreign language learning: A research perspective. Eds: B. VanPatten, T. Dvorak, and J. Lee. New York: Newbury House. 19-32.

Thomas, J. 1987. Comparing traditional and communicative approaches to the teaching of French. Applied Linguistics Interest Section Newsletter (TESOL), 9,1: 7-8.

Varble, M. 1990. Analysis of writing samples of students taught by teachers using whole language and traditional approaches. Journal of Educational Research 83. 245-251.

Voge, W. 1981. Testing the validity of Krashen's input hypothesis. Paper presented at the International Congress of Applied Linguistics, Lund, Sweden, 1981.

Wahlberg, H., K. Hase, and S. Pinzur-Rasher. 1974. English acquisition as a diminished function of experience rather than of age. TESOL Quarterly 12. 427-437.

Walker, G. and I. Kuerbitz. 1979. Reading to preschoolers as an aid to successful beginning reading. Reading Improvement 16. 149-154.

Wells, G. 1985. Language development in the preschool years. Cambridge: Cambridge University Press.

Wright, R. 1966. Black boy. New York: Harper and Row.

X, Malcolm. 1964. The autobiography of Malcolm X. New York: Ballintine Books.

Young, D. 1990. An investigation of students' perspectives on anxiety and speaking. Foreign Language Annals 23. 539-553.

A look at foreign language testing in the secondary schools: The state of the art in 1990

Rebecca M. Valette
Boston College

Introduction. The 1980s have witnessed a significant rise in foreign language enrollments as the result of a renewed national interest in international business needs, together with expanded language offerings at the secondary school level and increased college entrance requirements. During this decade, significant professional energies were committed to the development of the ACTFL Proficiency Guidelines and the dissemination of Oral Proficiency Interview (OPI) techniques. This paper presents a very modest attempt to ascertain what impact these changes have had in the area of foreign language testing and assessment in American secondary schools, to determine where we stand in 1990, and to indicate some directions for future development. The basic research for the study consisted of two parts: (a) a survey of state foreign language supervisors who were invited to describe local testing practices and to express their future testing needs; and (b) an analysis of published tests currently used at the secondary school level in this country. The emphasis was on Spanish, French, and German, with occasional reference to Italian, Modern Hebrew, and Latin.

The supervisor survey. In June 1990, a testing questionnaire was mailed to all state supervisors and coordinators (see Appendix 1). A follow-up mailing was sent out in December. The results of the 37 completed questionnaires will be referred to throughout this paper. Certain supervisors suggested the names of teachers in their areas who were exploring new testing techniques, and an effort was made to contact these people for further information.

Test analyses. The original proposal included a study of all published language tests currently in use. There was no problem in obtaining copies of tests administered by the College Board and by the various language organizations. However, examples of tests and assessment procedures developed by publishers to accompany current teaching materials were received only from D. C. Heath, Heinle & Heinle, Houghton Mifflin, and EMC.

Part I. Brief historical background.

A. The standardized language tests of the 1960s.
The heightened national interest in foreign languages in the 1960s together with the availability of substantial public monies stimulated the publication of several major standardized tests: the Carroll-Sapon *MLAT (Modern Language Aptitude Test)* (1959) and *EMLAT (Elementary Modern Language Aptitude Test)* (1967), the *Pimsleur Language Aptitude Battery* (1966), the *MLA Cooperative Foreign Language Tests* (1963) in French, German, Italian, Russian, and Spanish, and the *Pimsleur Modern Language Proficiency Tests* (1967) in French, German, and Spanish. These tests represented the joint efforts of the applied structural linguists and the psychometricians. (For a review of the history of language testing in the United States and a description of the state of the art in in 1968, see Valette 1969.) The standardized language tests of the 1960s were revolutionary in their emphasis on 'good language habits' as reflected in the following guidelines:

- The language used should reflect natural contemporary usage.
- Only correct forms should appear in test items.
- Vocabulary and structures should not be tested in isolation but rather in sentence or paragraph context.
- Translation should be avoided.
- Test items should not mix English and the target language.
- The four skills (listening, speaking, reading, and writing) should be tested separately.

(1) The standardized aptitude batteries. In the 1960s, language aptitude scores had been used both in a prognostic sense (to predict whether a student was likely to be a successful language learner) and a diagnostic sense (to determine whether a student might need additional help with some aspects of the course.)

By 1990, however, the Supervisor Survey (Appendix 1, Part C, qq. 7, 8) indicated that standardized aptitude tests were no longer being used. Those schools which were selective in determining who could study a foreign language would generally use other more readily available criteria such as IQ scores and grade point averages. The supervisors themselves generally felt that all students should be encouraged to study a foreign language and that, therefore, there was not a strong need to develop new aptitude measures.

(2) **The standardized four-skill achievement tests.** In the 1960s and early 1970s, school systems used the Pimsleur and MLA Coop language achievement tests to evaluate their programs and develop local norms. It was gradually discovered, however, that these standardized tests had two drawbacks. First, items often tended to exhibit a vocabulary bias, that is, the selection of a correct answer to a question would depend on knowing a specific word or expression. Secondly, the listening-speaking-reading-writing division reflected the format of the student's response and did not always correspond to a testing of language 'skill'. For example, a 'listening test' might include items focussing on specific linguistic features (such as sound discrimination or the ability to match a spoken sentence with its corresponding written form) as well as recorded selections to test the skill of listening comprehension. A reading test might contain multiple-choice vocabulary and grammar items as well as excerpted passages to evaluate the skill of reading comprehension.

As the euphoria of the 1960s, with its generous financial support from the U.S. Government, gave way in the mid 1970s to falling language requirements and declining enrollments, the erosion of federal monies meant that the MLA Coop Tests were not revised, and no new standardized tests were developed.

By 1990, according to the Supervisor Survey, these four-skill standardized tests had fallen into disuse (Appendix 1, Part C, qq. 7, 9). In fact the majority of the supervisors indicated either that they were unfamiliar with the tests or that they felt the tests were not administered in their states at present. Eight supervisors felt that these tests might still be given in a few of their districts.[1]

B. The 1980s and the Oral Proficiency Interview. The 1980s witnessed the emergence of the ACTFL Proficiency Guidelines and Oral Proficiency Interview which were adapted from the proficiency rating scale and the oral interview test that had been elaborated over the previous three decades by the Foreign Service Institute and the Defense Language Institute (see Sollenberger 1978). The most important modifications in the guidelines consisted in (a) the inclusion of categories for listening and writing (and culture, in the preliminary version) and (b) in the development of expanded descriptors for the bottom end of the rating scale, that is Novice (Low, Mid, High) and Intermediate (Low, Mid, High) which correspond to 'O' and '1' on the Interagency Language Roundtable (ILR) scale.

---

[1] In a personal communication, Renate Donovan, Coordinator of Foreign Languages, indicated that the written portion of the MLA Coop test is part of the admission requirement for Honors 3 courses in the Spring Branch (TX) Independent School District.

The administration of oral proficiency interviews requires the availability of certified OPI testers. Only three states (Iowa, Illinois, and Louisiana) currently maintain a file of qualified testers and sponsor OPI training programs (Question 5). As of February 1991, there were only 376 certified OPI testers in the United States, many of whom taught at the university, rather than the secondary school level.[2]

(1) Use of the OPI for teacher certification. The second part of the Supervisor Survey (Appendix 1, Part B, q. 4) asked to what extent the OPI was used for teacher certification. None of the states responding require current secondary teachers to take the OPI, although Vermont will institute a minimum requirement of Intermediate High effective in the year 2002. As for new secondary teachers, several states have made the OPI part of their certification requirements. The District of Columbia requires that candidates demonstrate oral proficiency at the Advanced level. Vermont will require the Intermediate High level for certification as of 1995. For French certification, Louisiana requires either two semesters of study abroad or the score of Intermediate High on the OPI. Wisconsin also requires a 'certified' immersion experience for new teachers and recommends the score of Intermediate High. As of fall 1991, Texas is requiring that prospective teachers of French and Spanish demonstrate oral proficiency at the 'advanced level' on the new tape-mediated Texas Oral Proficiency Test (TOPT) (see Stansfield et al. 1990). In Colorado, certain districts recommend that both current and prospective teachers demonstrate oral proficiency at the Advanced level.

(2) Use of the OPI in secondary school programs. Through the Supervisor Survey it was possible to identify only one school district that has administered oral proficiency interviews with trained OPI testers. In Pittsburgh, several hundred students of French, German, and Spanish in the 12-year International Studies Program have been tested at the fifth, eighth, and twelfth grade levels. The results were used for program assessment.[3]

Part II. The situation in the 1990s: Nationally published tests. The nationally published language tests administered in the United States fall into three general categories: (a) the standardized tests administered by the College Board, (b) the tests developed for the annual contests sponsored by the professional language organizations, and (c) the textbook-related tests prepared by language publishers.

---

[2] Personal communication, ACTFL office, February 15, 1991.
[3] Personal communication from Thekla Fall, Director of Foreign Language Education, Pittsburgh Public Schools.

A. **Standardized tests administered by the College Board.** College-bound secondary school students, especially those with three or more successful years of language study, are frequently encouraged to take the College Board Achievement Tests (offered in Spanish, French, German, Italian, Latin, and Modern Hebrew) and Advanced Placement Tests (offered in Spanish, French, and German Language; and Spanish, French, and Latin Literature). The Educational Testing Service has released the following statistics for 1990 (Table 1):

Table 1. Results of 1990 College Board Achievement Tests

Achievement test	Number of students	Mean score
Spanish Achievement	31,609	544
French Achievement	22,449	539
German Achievement	2,977	569
Italian Achievement	667	575
Latin Achievement	3,338	548
Modern Hebrew Achievement	526	637

Advanced placement test	Number of students	% '3' or higher
Spanish Language AP	11,284	64.0%
Spanish Literature AP	3,231	78.0
French Language AP	10,635	66.2
French Literature AP	1,723	67.3
German Language AP	2,465	69.5
Latin: Vergil	1,888	64.4
Latin: Catullus/Horace	552	67.0

Although the College Board Achievement and Advanced Placement Tests are only taken by 1 to 2% of the students studying foreign languages in the United States,[4] their content and testing formats have a significant influence, or 'washback' effect, on the curriculum not only at the advanced levels of instruction but also at the beginning and intermediate levels. It is, therefore, useful to determine precisely what these tests are measuring.

(1) The College Board Achievement Tests. The College Board Achievement Tests are one-hour multiple-choice tests that provide standardized scores on scale from 200 to 800. In order to assure the

---

4 Based on the incomplete enrollment responses to the Supervisor Survey and rough extrapolations of ACTFL 1985 enrollment statistics, it would appear that the approximate 1989-90 foreign language enrollments in U.S. public secondary schools are more or less on the order of: Spanish—3,000,000; French—1.500,000; German—350,000; Latin—150,000.

comparability of scores from one test administration to the next, all items are carefully edited, pretested and statistically analyzed, a process that stretches across several years. For this reason, the format of the tests changes very slowly. In spring 1990, it was proposed that a video-based listening comprehension portion be incorporated into the Spanish Achievement Tests on an experimental basis, but this option was found to be too costly. There are, however, definite plans to include an 'authentic' audio-taped listening comprehension section in the French Achievement Tests, effective fall 1992.

The Achievement Tests in the modern languages use predominantly the types of items that characterized the standardized tests of the 1960s: contextualized vocabulary and grammar completion items, and reading passages with comprehension questions. The items are written entirely in the foreign language, there is no translation, and no incorrect forms are used.

> COMMENT: *It is interesting to note that the only test which reflects the new professional emphasis on authentic language use is the Italian Achievement Test which has a reading comprehension section based on contemporary realia.*

The Latin Achievement Test, on the other hand, focuses heavily on grammar forms, language analysis, and translation. Some items ask the students to switch between English and Latin in the same sentence, a test format which was dropped in the modern languages twenty-five years ago.

> COMMENT: *Although the test description states that 'the best preparation for the test is the gradual development of competence in sight-reading Latin' (ETS 1990e:22), the sample items contain no general reading comprehension questions of the type found in the modern language achievement tests. (The reading passage entitled 'A wicked governor' is accompanied by seven questions, 3 asking for close translations of specific phrases and 4 asking for the grammatical analysis of single words (pp. 23-24). There is not a single question asking, for example, why Metellus is thought to be 'wicked'.)*

(2) **The Advanced Placement Examinations.** The Advanced Placement Examinations (ETS 1990a, 1990b, 1990c) allow students to obtain college credit and/or advanced placement for qualifying secondary school work. The exams, which last about 2 1/2 hours, consist of a multiple-choice portion and a free-response section. They are scored on a five-point scale: 5 - extremely well qualified; 4 - well qualified; 3 - qualified;

2 - possibly qualified; 1 - no recommendation. In order to obtain a total grade of 3, for example, students must perform acceptably on the free-response section and must also answer correctly about 50 to 60% of the multiple-choice questions.

The Advanced Placement Language Examinations. The AP Language exams test the four skills of listening, speaking, reading, and writing. The format varies slightly from language to language:

Section I: Multiple Choice

LISTENING
- A: Student hears a statement and selects the appropriate rejoinder (*printed*) [French]
- B: Student hears a dialogue and selects the correct responses (*printed*) to spoken questions [French, Spanish, German]
- C. Student hears a short lecture followed by spoken questions and selects the correct responses (*printed*) [Spanish, German]
- D. Student hears an exchange between two people and selects the appropriate rejoinder (*printed*) for the the first speaker. [German]

READING
- A. Student completes a sentence with the appropriate vocabulary item. [Spanish, German]
- B. Student completes a sentence with the appropriate grammatical form. [Spanish, German]
- C. Student indicates which of 4 underlined words in a sentence is grammatically incorrect. [Spanish]
- D. Student reads a passage followed by multiple-choice questions. [French, Spanish, German]

Part II. Free Response

WRITING
- A. Student completes a sentence with the appropriate form of a suggested verb. [Spanish]
- B. Student fills in blanks in a paragraph with the appropriate form of a suggested word. [Spanish, French]
- C. Student completes a sentence with the appropriate missing word: sentence cloze format. [French]
- D. Student fills in blanks in a paragraph with the appropriate missing words: paragraph cloze format. [German]

E. Student writes a 200 word essay on a given topic. [French, German, Spanish]

SPEAKING
A. Students responds on tape to recorded questions or instructions. [French, German, Spanish]
B. Student recounts a story indicated by pictures. [French, German, Spanish]

COMMENT: *The Advanced Placement language tests require students to demonstrate their command of vocabulary and grammar as well as their ability to function in the four skills. Given the present professional interest in natural language use, it might be appropriate to include some authentic listening selections, such as announcements in a railroad station or actual radio broadcasts.*

The Advanced Placement Literature Examinations. The AP Literature exams are correlated to a reading list distributed at the beginning of the year. The Multiple Choice section contains reading items based on literary selections. The Free Response section asks students to write a literary essay and to analyze a poem or short literary selection.

COMMENT: *The Advanced Placement Literature Examinations seem to correspond well to the syllabus and the description of the course.*

(3) The Comprehensive Russian Proficiency Test (CRPT). The Comprehensive Russian Proficiency Test (ETS 1990e) is a new test which has been developed to assess the listening, reading, writing, and speaking proficiency of secondary school and university students of Russian. It consists of four sections:

- LISTENING. Student hears a variety of thematically-linked recorded Russian texts (newscasts, conversations, etc.) and answers multiple-choice comprehension questions in English. (15 minutes: 22 items).

- READING. Student reads a variety of passages and realia (advertisements, tickets, etc.) and answers multiple-choice comprehension questions in English. The shorter selections test the examinee's ability to extract factual information, while the longer texts measure comprehension and analysis skills. (30 minutes: 40 questions).

- WRITING. Students completes free-response exercises of varying lengths and formats (30 minutes: 40 questions).

- SPEAKING. Student responds to taped questions and statements in a simulated conversation (approximately 15 minutes).

For each section there are five possible scores which correspond to the ACTFL proficiency levels of Novice, Novice-High, Intermediate, Intermediate-High, and Advanced. The manual provides a chart which translates the raw scores in listening and reading to the corresponding proficiency levels. The writing and speaking texts are rated holistically. Tables are provided for listening and reading which show the percentage of examinees at each of the proficiency levels according to number of years of study.

COMMENT: *This type of test would be most welcome for the more commonly taught languages.*

B. Tests developed by the professional organizations. Annual secondary school contests based on specially prepared national tests are sponsored every spring by the major language associations. In 1990, these examinations were taken by the numbers of candidates listed in Table 2.

Table 2. Language Students Taking 1990 Contest Examinations

Spanish		French		German		Latin	
I	25,134	FLES	3,480	2 Native	632	Intro	7,268
II	23,310	01	12,226	2 Non-native	8,370	I	32,295
III	17,591	1	16,724	3 Native	509	II	19,788
Advanced	13,227	2	22,031	3 Non-native	5,220	III Prose	5,851
		3	16,008	4 Native	427	III Poetry	2,068
		4	9,230	4 Non-native	2,997	IV Prose	938
		5	3,180			IV Poetry	2,697
						V	552
TOTAL:	79,262		82,879		18,155		71,457

Because of the significant numbers of students taking the contest examinations, these tests often have a 'washback' effect on the curriculum. (The Level 2 tests in each language are analyzed below.) It might be advisable for the test committees of the four associations to meet together to compare examination formats and approaches. Given the current interest in natural language use, the three modern language tests designers might wish to consider including more 'proficiency-type' items, such as listening to phone messages or recorded announcements and reading realia such as ads, train schedules, and movie programs.

(1) **The AATSP National Spanish Examinations.** The 1990 National Spanish Examinations were administered during the first two weeks of March. Each level of the National Spanish Examination is a one-hour multiple-choice test consisting of 30 listening items presented on cassette, followed by 50 reading items. The Level 2 test consists of seven parts with the following item types:
- A. Student hears a description and selects the appropriate picture. [10 items]
- B. Student hears questions about an illustrated accident scene and selects the appropriate answer (*printed*). [5 items]
- C. Student hears an exchange between two people followed by a question identifying the scene or summarizing the content; the student selects the appropriate answer (*printed*). [10 items]
- D. Student hears a longer dialog followed by spoken questions; for each one, student selects the correct answer (*printed*). [5 items]
- E. Vocabulary completion items in sentence context. [18 items]
- F. Grammar completion items in sentence context. [20 items]
- G. Reading comprehension passages with corresponding questions. [12 items]

COMMENT: *The listening portion of the test is quite natural and is recorded by very welcoming voices. Each dialog or question is read only once, as would be the case in 'real life'. This does, however, introduce a significant memory factor into Part D which contains longer listening passages. In the written portion, 35% of the items measure control of vocabulary and structure.*

(2) **The AATF National French Contest.** The 1990 AATF National French Contest was given between during the first part of March. Each test of the National French Contest contains 80 multiple choice items. The first part (20 minutes) contains from 34 to 38 listening items which are presented via audio cassette. The second part (40 minutes) consists of 42 to 46 reading items.

The Level 2 test consists of eight different item types:
1. Student hears a statement and selects the appropriate picture. [8 items]
2. Student hears a conversation and identifies the setting by selecting the appropriate picture. [7 items]
3. Student hears a word or phrase and selects the corresponding (*printed*) text. [6 items]

4. Student hears a question and selects the appropriate response (*printed*). [5 items]
5. Student hears a longer dialog followed by spoken questions; for each one, student selects the correct answer (*printed*). [12 items]
6. Grammar completion items in sentence context. [20 items]
7. Reading comprehension passages with corresponding questions. [14 items]
8. Sentence completion items on cultural topics (in French). [8 items]

COMMENT: *All the listening questions are read twice in the French test. This minimizes the memory factor for the longer dialogue (section 5). The two readings may also be necessary for sections 1 and 3 where the emphasis is often on minimal sound distinctions (elle le lui donne vs. elle les lui donne; j'en veux vs. Jeanne voit). Because of its content and occasionally its use of adult voices to portray children, the listening section tends to sound artificial. Of the modern languages, the French test is the only one to include a section on culture.*

(3) **The AATG National German Examinations.** In 1990, the AATG examinations were administered during the first three weeks of January. Each level of the National German Examination contains 100 multiple-choice items. During the first 20 minutes, an audio cassette presents 40 listening items. The students then have 40 minutes to complete 60 reading items. The contest results are published together with item analyses for each test.

The Level 2 test consists of six parts with the following item types:
A. Student hears a question selects the appropriate answer (*printed*). [17 items]
B. Student hears an exchange between two people and selects the appropriate rejoinder (*printed*) for the first speaker. [17 items]
C. Student hears a longer dialog followed by spoken questions; for each one, student selects the correct answer (*printed*). [6 items]
D. Student reads the description of a situation and selects the appropriate remark. [25 items]
E. Grammar completion items in sentence context. [25 items]
F. Reading comprehension passages with corresponding questions. [10 items]

COMMENT: *Of all the contest examinations, the German tests are the most effective in stressing natural language usage. All the listening items are scripted in a meaningful and idiomatic conversational style. The items of Part D are particularly effective in incorporating a variety of vocabulary and structures within real-life contexts. Only one-fourth of the items (Part E) measure control of elements of language.*

(4) The ACL /NJCL National Latin Exam. Clearly it is the Latin contest that is the most influential of the language association tests since it touches the highest proportion of students enrolled in that language. In 1990, the National Latin Exam was administered in the second week of March. Each 35-minute exam contains 40 multiple-choice questions: 20 on grammar, 15 on mythology, culture, history and derivatives, and 5 passage-based reading comprehension items. The Latin V exam is somewhat different in that it consists of several passages accompanied by 40 multiple-choice questions covering comprehension, grammar, historical background, and literary devices. In all of the Latin exams, the discrete multiple-choice section intermingles a wide variety of item types. The reading passages are accompanied with both general and specific comprehension items, generally formulated in English.

COMMENT: *In its approach, the Latin test is the most atomistic of the language contests. The first 35 questions are discrete items, intermingling topics and formats. Students may be asked to translate an English word in an English sentence, an English word in a Latin sentence, a Latin word in a Latin sentence. They may be told to complete a Latin sentence with a Latin word, or an English sentence with an English word, or an English sentence with a Latin phrase. The last 5 questions refer to a single passage, but exhibit the same mix of item styles.*

C. Textbook-Related Tests. The published tests which have the widest impact on secondary students are clearly those developed by publishers to accompany their textbooks. These are sometimes labeled as follows:

(a) 'achievement' tests, that is tests which measure how well the students have mastered the material (grammar, vocabulary) and the skills developed in the corresponding lessons;

(b) 'pro-chievement' tests, that is 'achievement' tests whose items are presented in a 'proficiency' or real life context;

(c) 'proficiency' tests, that is tests in which students demonstrate 'natural' language use, in understanding 'authentic' materials and/or in expressing themselves in an open-ended format.

The labels, however, may be misleading, for one publisher's 'achievement' test may contain 'pro-chievement' and 'proficiency' segments, while another publisher's 'proficiency' test may have many 'achievement' items. It is important, therefore, to look beyond the titles of textbook-related tests to determine what they are actually measuring.

As a part of this study, the major foreign language publishers were all invited to submit samples of their published testing programs. The following materials were received:

(1) Houghton Mifflin: Tests to accompany *German Today 2* (fourth edition). The testing program for *German Today, 2* (Putnam and Kent 1989) consists of a student test booklet, a teacher guide, and test cassettes with the listening materials. One original feature is the pre-test for each lesson, a cognitive worksheet which helps review what the students have learned about the structure of the language. Each lesson test consists of five sections:

- Listening Comprehension: sound/symbol recognition and short passages.
- Reading Comprehension/Vocabulary: discrete vocabulary items plus reading comprehension questions based on pictures, paragraphs, and/or realia.
- Writing/Structure Skills: directed writing activities.
- *Land und Leute*: multiple-choice culture items in English.
- Composition: varied formats such as directed paragraphs and open-ended sentence composition.

The teacher guide provides instructions for nine types of speaking test items, including suggestions for oral interviews using Proficiency Cards.

COMMENT: *Although at first glance one might consider these to be straight 'achievement' tests (the pre-test and the Writing/Structure sections are definitely grammar-based), closer analysis reveals that for each skill there is also a 'proficiency-type' component. In the Listening and Reading sections of each test there is usually one 'natural' situational segment, such as a conversation, an informational paragraph or a written notice, accompanied by meaningful comprehension checks. In the Composition section students write about daily life topics, and the scoring system is clearly proficiency-oriented. As mentioned above, the suggestions for the speaking tests include guidelines for evaluating oral proficiency.*

(2) Heinle & Heinle: Tests to accompany *On y va*. The *On y va* testing program consists of a Testing Manual (Bragger 1989) and three sets of tests, one for each level (Kline 1989, Cook 1989, Cole and Miller 1989), which contain quizzes for each lesson (or *étape*), chapter tests and unit tests. All tests have three main parts:

- Listening Comprehension: oral cues with written responses.
- Writing/Grammar: written grammar items as well as guided paragraphs.
- Reading Comprehension: a variety of reading types (passages, articles, realia) followed by short-answer questions. In addition, the chapter and units tests have a culture section and also provide situation cards for testing oral expression.
- Oral Expression. In Level One, students answer interview questions or perform in pairs using situation cards. In Levels Two and Three, students are asked to perform skits or respond to more challenging questions. The Testing Manual (Bragger 1989) describes the philosophy of the testing prgram and presents a variety of alternate testing formats and scoring systems.

COMMENT: *On y va comes with a well-written Testing Manual. The tests themselves offer a wide range of item types evaluating both grammar and vocabulary as well as language use. The situation cards are novel in that they assign different roles to two or three students who participate in a conversational exchange.*

(3) **EMC: Tests to accompany:** *Deutsch aktuelle, Le Français vivant, and ¡Mucho gusto!* All of these EMC language programs include a student testing component which consists of a student test booklet, a teacher guide, and audiocassettes containing listening comprehension items. The level one test booklets in German and French (Kraft 1991, Hopen 1991) and the level one and two test booklets in Spanish (Brett 1988a, 1988b) contain a listening test and a written test for each lesson, plus end-of-semester listening and written achievement tests. The listening tests consist of five sections which vary in format from lesson to lesson: logical/illogical statements, questions on short passages, vocabulary comprehension, spot dictation, etc. The writing tests consist of a wide variety of short-answer items measuring control of grammar and vocabulary. Each of the French tests end with a short section on culture.

The testing component for the Spanish level three *Somos así* (Funston et al. 1991) is somewhat more extensive, comprising 40 lesson tests, 10 chapter tests, and 2 achievement tests. There is also more variety in the items types. Some of the listening tests contain longer dialogues, such as phone conversations. Some of the written tests contain reading comprehension passages and some end with compositions on daily life topics.

COMMENT: *The EMC tests, with their combinations of various types of short-answer and multiple-choice questions, are easy to administer and score. They offer the teacher a practical achievement battery for assessing how well students have mastered the lesson content. (The classroom teacher may want to develop additional 'proficiency-type' tests, especially in the area of speaking.)*

(4) D.C. Heath: *Spanish for Mastery* **Proficiency Testing Kits.** In addition to an achievement testing program containing lesson quizzes, unit tests and end-of-semester test, each with listening and writing sections, *Spanish for Mastery 1* and *2* also are accompanied with Proficiency Testing Kits (Carrera-Hanley and Valette 1990a, 1990b). Each kit contains an audio cassette and four copymaster booklets (listening comprehension, speaking, reading comprehension, writing) with ten unit tests for each skill. Scoring criteria for the speaking and writing tests focus on the communication of meaning. The four sections are constituted as follows:

- LISTENING TESTS: Five short recorded dialogues, statements or announcements, each followed by a general comprehension question. Each selection is preceded by an 'advanced organizer' which sets the context.
- SPEAKING TESTS: For each unit, the kit provides a student scoring sheet together with 14 different conversation/speaking cards. Each student responds to two cards from each of the following categories:
    (a) *Situaciones:* Students answer four questions related to a real-life situation;
    (b) *Tienes la palabra*: Students make three comments on a suggested topic.
- READING TESTS: Ten comprehension questions based on four or five selected realia or reading selections.
- Writing Tests: Five or six open-ended activities, such as writing short notes, lists, and brief descriptions.

COMMENT: *These 'proficiency-type' tests let students show how well they can understand and express themselves in spoken and written Spanish. A distinctive feature of the open-ended speaking and writing items is that possible answers are suggested for less creative students who might have difficulty thinking how to respond. The reading tests make heavy use of various types of authentic realia.*

Part III. The situation in the 1990s: Testing initiatives at the state and local level. Of the states that responded to the Supervisor Survey, only three (New York, Texas, and Vermont) require all secondary school students to take a foreign language. Two other states (California and Illinois) have cluster requirements in which a foreign language is one of several options. Eleven states offer some sort of 'honors' diploma for which foreign language study is required (Georgia, Hawaii, Indiana, Kentucky, Louisiana, New York, Rhode Island, South Carolina, Texas, Utah, and Vermont). Typically these requirements are expressed in terms of 'seat time'—usually two years. Only one state, New York, administers special tests to determine whether standards have been met. The Kentucky Commonwealth Diploma Program requires the successful completion (with a grade of C) of four Advanced Placement courses, one of which must be a foreign language. In addition to the coursework, students must take AP exams in three of these subjects and attain a minimum composite score (6 in 1990-91, 7 in 1991-92, 8 in 1991-93).

A. State-developed assessment materials. Of the 29 state supervisors who responded to the survey, 9 indicated that their state was developing its own instruments to measure proficiency.

(1) New York: Foreign Language Examinations. New York is the only state which administers an annual testing program. As a logical outgrowth of its new curriculum guides in Latin and modern languages (New York 1987a, 1987b), New York has developed new Second Language Proficiency Examinations corresponding to their Checkpoint A (for one unit of Regents credit) and have modified the format of the Regents Comprehensive Examinations (for three units of Regents credit) which correspond to their Checkpoint B.

New York Second Language Proficiency Examinations. The Second Language Proficiency Examinations are intended primarily for eighth-grade students who have completed two units of study and have reached the learning outcomes of Checkpoint A of the new state syllabus (New York 1988). The examinations, which are offered in French, German, Italian and Spanish, evaluate the four language skills, as follows:

- Speaking 30% (assessed prior to the written examination):
    Classroom performance (10%).
    Oral test consisting of 4 communication tasks (20%).

- Listening Comprehension 40% (based on a script read by the teacher); the context for each excerpt is set in English):
    Multiple-choice questions in English (20%).
    Multiple-choice questions in the second language (10%).
    Multiple-choice questions based on pictures (10%).

- Reading Comprehension 20% (based on realia):
    Multiple-choice questions in English (12%).
    Multiple-choice questions in the second language (8%).

- Writing 10% (based on English instructions):
  Writing notes (6%).
  Writing lists (4%).

COMMENT: *All parts of the French test which were analyzed (New York 1990) focus on communication. The only weakness of the battery is that the listening portion is read by the teacher (thus reducing both its validity and its reliability). The actual format of the listening portion, however, reflects realistic language-use in that for each segment the context is described and the student is instructed what to listen for.*

New York Foreign Language Regents Examinations. Effective in June 1991, the Regents Comprehensive Examinations in modern languages includes a formal speaking test comprising to 24% of the total score. The test consists of two separate conversational situations in which the student is expected to make six comprehensible and appropriate utterances (New York 1989). Also effective in 1991, the Latin examination includes an oral reading test and a dictation. (Actual tests were not available for analysis.)

(2) Indiana: Model Proficiency Tests. The State of Indiana is developing tests in French, German and Spanish based on the learning outcomes stated in the Indiana proficiency guides. These are not presently intended to be used as instruments for statewide assessment but rather as models for classroom teachers. There will be six tests per language: three forms for Level One (end of first year) and three forms for Level Two (end of second year).

The first form of the German test (Bartz 1990), which was prepared for field testing, contains the following sections:

- Part I. Reading and Writing. Mixed-skill reading and writing activities based primarily on maps, art, and realia.
- Part II. Listening. Multiple-choice listening comprehension items based on a recording:
  (a) understanding commands
  (b) understanding a conversation about reserving rooms
- Part III. Listening and Speaking. A variety of guided speaking activities based on taped instructions and/or questions and visual cues; student responses are recorded.

COMMENT: *This test focuses on meaningful language use. The adaptation of the SOPI (Simulated OPI) format for Part III allows for group administration in a language laboratory and thus economizes classroom time.*

(3) Colorado: Proficiency Sample Project. The state of Colorado has developed the Proficiency Sample Project to encourage a statewide sampling of Beginner and Mid-Level assessments of speaking, listening, reading and writing. The descriptive booklet (Apodaca 1990) contains clear guidelines for the test items and innovative flowcharts for rating student performance.

COMMENT: *This grassroots approach to developing proficiency benchmarks for secondary students in schools across the state is worthy of serious study and might well offer a model for a nationwide assessment program.*

(4) Virginia: Standards of Learning Program. The Virginia Standards of Learning (SOL) provide a comprehensive framework for integrating curriculum and assessment in Levels I through IV of French, Spanish, and German. Coordinators and teachers throughout the state worked together to develop comprehensive resource materials (Virginia 1988). Part I contains detailed objectives and strategies closely aligned with the ACTFL Guidelines. Part II consists of an extensive compendium of assessment guidelines and sample techniques for evaluating course objectives.

COMMENT: *This guide constitutes an excellent assessment handbook for classroom teachers.*

B. Testing initiatives at the local level. Many individual school districts across the country are developing their own testing guidelines and/or assessment procedures. The following is a sampling of such initiatives.

(1) Missisquoi Valley Union High School (VT): Portfolio Assessment of Writing Proficiency. Missisquoi Valley Union has been developing a proficiency-based curriculum derived from the ACTFL guidelines. In particular, the program contains a clearly elaborated portfolio assessment of writing proficiency complete with student and teacher guidelines. The portfolio program, which is introduced in the second year of language study, allows students to see their improvement and take pride in the development of their writing skills.

(2) Pittsburgh (PA): Proficiency-oriented district-wide final exams. The Pittsburgh Public Schools are in the process of developing district-wide final exams which at the lower levels include, among other things, a speaking section using thematic questions, a contextualized grammar section, and a writing sample.

(3) Richardson (TX): Texas Essential Elements Test Specifications and Items. The Richardson Independent School District has developed a guide to help teachers certify whether students have mastered the Texas Essential Elements (Maples 1990). Sample testing procedures are correlated with the Level 1 Certification Items (which include specific grammar concepts as well as vocabulary themes, cultural topics and communication skills).

(4) Ysleta (TX): Foreign Languages Testing Brochure. The Ysleta Independent School District has distributed to all teachers a brochure containing sample proficiency-oriented testing techniques (Calk 1990) which includes a six-weeks test format adapted from the OPI model: I. Warm-up (listening), II. Level Check (language: grammar and vocabulary), III. Probes (open-ended speaking and writing questions), IV. Wind-down (Reading).

(5) Fort Worth (TX): Advanced Placement Tests. The Fort Worth Independent School District has developed a credit-by-examination system based on 'advanced placement' tests for Levels I and II in French, German, and Spanish (Lowry et al. n.d.). These tests, which include grammar in context, reading, listening, writing, speaking and culture, are designed for students who have learned the language outside of class (for example, through residence abroad) and wish to be placed in a higher course. The test allows them to earn credit for their prior study. It can also be taken by students who want to try again to earn credit for a course they have failed.

Part IV. Looking to the future.

A. Testing needs as perceived by State supervisors. The last two pages of the Supervisor Survey focussed on clarifying current testing needs and defining future directions. Of particular interest are the open-ended responses to Questions 12 -15 which are included in Appendix 1, Part D.

(1) Possible usefulness of new machine-scored standard language tests. When the state supervisors were asked (Appendix 1, Part C., qq. 10 and 11) whether they felt there was a need for new machine-scored language tests with up-to-date norms, 10 indicated that this was a definite need for such tests, 12 felt that such tests could be useful but that the main thrust in their state was toward oral proficiency testing, and 15 responded that they were turning away from norm-referenced standard tests.

When asked to rank the types of machine-scored language tests according to usefulness, the supervisors recorded their preferences as follows:

(1) Standard tests of listening proficiency, correlated to the ACTFL Guidelines.
(2) Standard tests of reading proficiency, correlated to the ACTFL Guidelines.
(3) Standard tests of linguistic accuracy, correlated to the ACTFL Guidelines.

Of much less interest were:

(4) Tests similar to the College Board Achievement Tests, but designed for first and second year students.
(5) Tests similar to the listening and reading sections of the MLA Coop Tests, with new items and new norms.

(2) Limited Need for New Aptitude Measures. When asked whether they thought there was a need for a different type of language aptitude test (Appendix 1, q. 8), 29 supervisors responded in the negative. Those who felt that some sort of new aptitude instrument would be useful offered the following suggestions:

- A set of criteria or an aptitude profile which could be established using data already collected for other purposes (Illinois).
- New aptitude tests reflecting current theory and research in second-language acquisition and proficiency (Maine, Texas).
- An oral-proficiency-oriented aptitude test designed for native speakers of Spanish (New Mexico).

(3) Definite need for practical classroom tests and other assessment techniques to evaluate language proficiency. The greatest testing need appears to be practical and efficient classroom assessment instruments to evaluate language proficiency across the four skills. For busy teachers, ease of administration and ease of scoring are paramount concerns.

(4) Concern about the 'washback' effect of outside language tests. In various ways, state supervisors indicated their awareness of the 'washback' effect of outside language tests on the curriculum. They expressed their concern over the negative 'washback' effect generated by the placement tests and procedures at some colleges and universities, fearing an overemphasis on structure at the expense of fluency. They were concerned that the single-skill College Board Achievement Tests placed too great an emphasis on grammar and vocabulary control. The Advanced Placement language tests, on the other hand, were credited with a more positive 'washback' because of their four-skills approach and opportunity for self-expression.

The state supervisors expressed mixed feelings about the contests sponsored by the language associations (see Appendix 1, Part D, q. 15). Since participation in these tests is voluntary, those who find that they do not meet local curricular objectives can simply choose not administer them. Clearly the tests would meet with the approval of more supervisors if they were to adopt a greater 'proficiency' orientation.

B. National testing needs identified by the 1989 ACTFL priorities conference. In November 1989, ACTFL sponsored the second National Conference on Professional Priorities. The Committee on Testing and Assessment, chaired by Suzanne Jebe and Manuel Rodriguez, discussed the position paper by Henning (1990) and the reactions by Shohamy (1990), Stansfield (1990), Lange (1990) and Valette (1989) as a preliminary to formulating a preliminary list of testing priorities (ACTFL 1989:10). Although many of the concerns expressed related to testing research, there was an expression of concern for needs of teachers at the secondary school level.

- We must validate the ACTFL/ETS Guidelines for adolescent learners.
- We must more clearly define our testing purposes in relation to various assessment procedures (observation, informal evaluation, self-assessment, classroom tests, standardized tests, etc.).
- We must analyze the tests currently available and develop new tests that reflect the purposes of language use and assessment.
- We should research into the 'washback' effect that our tests have on teaching and learning.
- We must prepare teachers and future teachers to understand the assessment process and their role in it.
- We must explore the role of technology in language assessment, for example the use of computerized test banks, simulated oral proficiency testing, and comprehension tests based on video segments.

C. The 1996 National Assessment of Educational Progress (NAEP). Preliminary studies are underway to determine whether foreign languages will be included in the 1996 National Assessment of Educational Progress. In December 1989, the National Assessment Governing Board (NAGB) adopted a policy to include non-mandated subject areas such as arts and foreign languages in the next NAEP which is scheduled for 1996. In the initial feasibility study concerning the assessment of foreign languages, Roeber and Fisher (1990:17-19) explore three possible options:

(1) **Instructional assessment.** Instructional assessment is simply a statistical survey set up to determine to which extent elementary and secondary school students have the opportunity to learn languages and what percent of the students avail themselves of this opportunity.

(2) **Population Proficiency Study.** In a Population Proficiency Study, all students taking an exam in a mandated subject matter area (such as mathematics) would be asked to fill out a form indicating how much language instruction they have received, and then to answer a few written questions in the foreign language(s) they have studied.

(3) **Student Proficiency Study.** The Student Proficiency Study is an actual language test to sample the student's cultural awareness and 'authentic' language proficiency across the four skills, probably with reference to the ACTFL guidelines. The Student Proficiency Study would obviously yield the most useful information, but it is also the most complex and expensive type of assessment to carry out.

COMMENT: *It might be worth exploring the possibility of developing proficiency benchmarks on the 100-500 scale used for the other NAEP assessment areas (cf. Mullis et al. (1990:14, 17). If the assessment of speaking proficiency proves to be too expensive, it might still be possible to have language-specific proficiency tests in listening, reading, and writing. Roeber and Fisher have defined the assessment requirements of each of these three options and suggest that the NAGB convene a planning group of language and measurement specialists to prepare a more detailed prospectus. The inclusion of foreign languages as a new subject area in the 1996 National Assessment of Educational Progress would definitely have an important impact on the profession.*

Conclusion. This brief overview of the current situation in foreign language testing has demonstrated that while there is a renewed interest in language teaching, there is a definite need for new assessment instruments readily accessible to teachers across the country. A great deal of creative work is being done—by certain education centers, by certain states, by certain school districts, by certain publishers—but it is difficult for an individual practitioner to gain access to this material. It is hoped that this paper will help language teachers become more aware of the state of the art in language testing and guide them in addressing present and future needs.

GURT '91 postscript. As this paper was going through many versions, I was haunted by a feeling of uneasiness, which I subsequently discovered was shared by the authors of several other foreign language state-of-the-art papers. Part of this could be traced to the realization that most foreign language students in the United States study a second language for only a few years often with teachers who are not themselves fluent, whereas ESL students benefit not only from longer sequences with native or near-native teachers, but are also motivated to attain real-life proficiency. But the problem ran deeper. As I studied the various tests we use to assess foreign language attainment in this rather artificial and academic environment, it slowly became apparent that the underlying problem was that while we as a profession were beginning to recognize the complexity of second language acquisition, in the area of testing we were still very much in the four-skills testing mode of the 1960s with a premium on the cognitive aspects of language such as 'logical thinking' and 'problem solving'. What the profession requires is a new way to analyze current language tests with a clearer focus on what we want to assess and how to do so effectively. This, however, must be left to another paper.

Appendix 1: Survey on the state of the art in language testing.

Completed surveys were received from the following state supervisors or their representatives:

Arizona: Robert Sosa
California: Fred Dobb
Colorado: Mary Apodaca
Delaware: Rebecca H. Scarborough
District of Columbia: Marion Hines
Florida: Gabriel M. Valdes
Georgia: Greg Duncan
Hawaii: Anita Bruce
Iowa: Paul D. Hoekstra
Illinois: Paul T. Griffith
Indiana: Walter Bartz
Kansas: Maria C. Collins
Kentucky: Anthony L. Koester
Louisiana: David G. Beste
Maine: Donald H. Reutershan, Jr.
Maryland: Dorothy V. Huss
Massachusetts: Kathleen Riordan
Michigan: Terry Peterson
Montana: Duane Jackson

Nebraska: Mel Nielsen
Nevada: Holly Walton-Buchanan
New Jersey: Paul Cohen
New Mexico: Margo Chávez-Charles
New York: Paul E. Dammer
North Dakota: Valorie Babb
Oklahoma: Al Gage
Pennsylvania: Larrie H. McLamb, Jr.
Rhode Island: Virginia M. C. da Mota
South Carolina: Lucinda L. Saylor
South Dakota: Connie Colwill
Texas: Robert LaBouve
Utah: Joan D. Patterson
Vermont: Jessica Turner
Virginia: R. Marshall Brannon
Washington: Joe Dial
Wisconsin: Frank M. Grittner
Wyoming: Paul O. Soumokil

Questionnaire on the State of the Art in Language Testing (July 1990)

Note. This is a brief summary of responses. The answers do not always add up to 37 since respondents sometimes did not answer every question.

Part A. Background information.
1. *Enrollment statistics (provided separately).*

2.a. *Does your state have a foreign language requirement for high school graduation?*
    for all students?   (4) yes   (23) no
    for certain categories of students?   (12) yes   (24) no
2.b. *Which test (if any) is used to assess whether this requirement has been met?*
    (1) local test   (1) AP test

3. *Does your state have a foreign language entrance requirement for state institutions of higher education:*
    state universities?   (16) yes   (17) no
    state colleges?   (7) yes   (29) no
    If yes, please describe:
        (15) two years high school credit (1) one year high school credit

Part B. ACTFL Proficiency guidelines.
4. *State certification and the Oral Proficiency Interview (OPI)*
a. Are all current secondary language teachers required to take the OPI?
    (0) yes   (37) no
b. Does the state recommend that all current secondary language teachers take the OPI?
    (1) yes   (36) no

c. Are all new secondary language teachers required to take the OPI as part of their certification requirements?
    (5) yes   (32) no
d. Does the state recommend that all new secondary language teachers take the OPI as part of their certification requirements?
    (1) yes   (36) no

5. *Training of OPI Testers*
a. Does your state sponsor the training of OPI Testers?
    (5) yes   (32) no
b. Do you keep a file of qualified OPI testers from your state?
    (6) yes   (31) no

6. *Other proficiency measures*
a. Is your state developing its own instruments and tests to measure proficiency?
    (11) yes   (25) no
b. Are certain school districts in your state developing their own instruments and tests to measure proficiency?
    (11) yes   (26) no

Part C. Standardized tests.
7. The 1960s saw the development of several batteries of standardized language tests. For each test below, indicate your familiarity with the instrument and whether or not you believe it is still used in your state. Please use the following scale:
    1 - I am not really familiar with this test.
    2 - I know this test, but I do not believe it is used in our state at present.
    3 - This test may still be used in some school districts.
    4 - This test is still used in a majority of the school districts.
    5 - This test is recommended for use in all school districts.

	1	2	3	4	5
MLAT (Carroll-Sapon Modern Language Aptitude Test):	15	19	2	-	-
EMLAT (Carroll-Sapon Elementary Modern Language Aptitude Test):	20	14	2	-	-
Pimsleur Aptitude Test:	7	19	11	-	-
MLA Coop Tests (forms LA, LB: lower):	8	20	8	-	-
MLA Coop Tests (forms MA, MB: middle):	7	22	6	-	-
Pimsleur Achievement Tests:	11	19	6	-	-

8. *Language aptitude.*
a. To what extent are language aptitude tests used in your state?
    (0) Most districts use aptitude tests to determine who may take a foreign language.
    (0) Most districts use aptitude tests for placement to determine which 'track' is appropriate for a given student.
    (12) Most districts do not use aptitude tests; decisions as to who should take a language and/or which class is appropriate for a given student are made on the basis of other information such as IQ scores, GPA, etc.
    (25) All students are encouraged to study a foreign language, aptitude tests are not generally used and there is generally no tracking.
b. If you use an aptitude test, which one do you use and how effective is it?
    no answers
c. Do you find there is a need for a different type of language aptitude test?
    (5) yes   (29) no

9. *If your state does not give standardized language skills tests, did you once use the following tests in the past?*
   MLA Coop tests: (6) Yes, we used to give them. (28) No, we never gave them.
   Pimsleur tests: (5) Yes, we used to give them. (32) No, we never gave them.

10. *Do foreign language teachers and administrators in your state feel there is a need for new machine-scored standard language tests with up-to-date norms?*
   (10) Yes, definitely. If such tests were available, we would want to use them.
   (11) Yes, such tests could be useful, but our main thrust is oral proficiency testing.
   (15) No, we are turning away from norm-referenced standard tests.

11. *What type of new machine-scored language tests do you feel are most needed? Rank in order of preference, with '1' being the highest preference. Leave a blank next to tests you feel are not needed. (average ranking indicated below)*
   (5) Tests similar to the MLA Coop and Pimsleur Tests (listening and reading sections), but with new items and new norms.
   (4) Tests similar to the College Board Achievement Tests, but appropriate for first and second-year students
   (1) Tests of listening proficiency, related to the ACTFL guidelines
   (2) Tests of reading proficiency, related to the ACTFL guidelines
   (3) Tests of linguistic accuracy (vocabulary and structure), related to the ACTFL guidelines

   Part D. Future testing needs (open ended section: responses summarized).

12. In the area of foreign language testing, what is the greatest need that should be addressed in the next decade?
   (a) practical classroom instruments to evaluate language proficiency
       - tests to assess performance in listening, speaking, reading, writing [and culture] (13)
       - practical speaking/oral proficiency tests that are affordable, efficient to administer, and easy to score (7)
       - guidelines for creating student portfolios with samples of speaking and writing ability (1)
   (b) encouragement of a positive 'washback' effect: being sure that the tests are measuring what we want teachers to teach and students to learn.
       - development of college placement tests that assess language use rather than simply knowledge of grammar and vocabulary (7)
       - research into the effects of tests on teaching (1)
   (c) development of national language tests and standards
       - a national consensus on a common body of what to assess (1)
       - nationally standardized language tests (proficiency, prochievement, and achievement) (2)
       - criterion-referenced language tests corresponding to specific points in the elementary/secondary curriculum, e.g. Grade 5, Grade 8, Grade 11 (2)
       - tests for state-mandated programs (at specific points or levels in the curriculum) (1)
   (d) restructuring schedules to allow course time for meaningful communication testing (1)

13. *If you had a testing 'wish list', what would it contain?*
   (a) performance-based tests of listening, speaking, reading and writing (6)
       - computerized item banks (3)
       - oral proficiency tests that are easy to administer (3)
       - tests that incorporate authentic documents (2)
       - formative tests for on-going assessment (1)
   (b) modified proficiency guidelines and corresponding tests
       - new proficiency guidelines should be established for elementary school and secondary school students (2)
       - tests should be developed that correspond to proficiency benchmarks (2)
   (c) in-service training
       - free workshops in OPI

- workshops on performance-based testing (2)
- workshops on non-paper/pencil forms of assessment: portfolios, observations, interviews (2)
- workshops on using tests to promote positive learning outcomes (2)

14. *If you were hiring a new teacher, what would be his or her ideal background in the area of language testing?*
 (a) training in proficiency and performance-based testing (12)
 - coursework in second-language testing and measurement (8)
 - OPI training (6)
 - familiarity with ACTFL guidelines (4)
 - ability to analyze tests and 'washback' effect (3)
 - knowledge of non paper/pencil forms of assessment (2)
 - training in the administration of oral classroom tests (2)
 - awareness of the limitations of multiple-choice tests (1)
 (b) excellent command of the language and knowledge of the culture (3)
 (c) flexibility in teaching and testing with the aim of promoting learning for students of all abilities and interests (2)

15. *Are there other testing areas you would like to comment on?*
 (a) Textbook publishers should offer:
 - tests that evaluate proficiency and language use (3)
 - computerized test banks with alternate items (2)
 - oral testing kits (1)
 (b) New tests are needed to measure cultural patterns and realities (1)
 (c) College Board Advanced Placement language tests . . .
 - should be praised for the positive 'washback' effect on good teaching practices (2)
 - should be more skills-oriented (1)
 (d) College Board Achievement Tests should be less grammar-based and should measure language proficiency (3)
 (e) Language association (AAT) tests received mixed comments:
 - AAT tests are heavily based on knowledge of grammar and vocabulary, and should focus more on language use (2)
 - AAT tests are counter-productive because of negative 'washback' (1)
 - AATF tests should come with norms like the AATG and AATSP tests (1)
 - AATF tests can be used as a year-end achievement test (1)
 - AATSP is a good test (1)
 - all AAT tests should be eliminated, except German (1)

References

AATF. National French Contest. 1990. Long Beach, N.Y.: AATF.
AATG. National German Examinations. 1990. Cherry Hill, N.J.: AATG.
AATSP. National Spanish Examinations. 1990. Newark, Del.: AATSP.
ACL/NJCL. National Latin Exams. 1990. Mt. Vernon, Va.: ACL/NJCL.
ACTFL. 1989. 1989 ACTFL National Priorities Conference: Summaries of Priority Proceedings. Yonkers, N.Y.: ACTFL.
Apodaca, Mary et al. 1990. Proficiency Sample Project. Denver: Colorado Department of Education.
Bartz, Walter H. et al. 1990. German Test. Level 1. Form A. Indianapolis: Indiana Department of Education.
Bragger, Jeannette. 1989. On y va! Testing Manual. Boston, Mass.: Heinle & Heinle.
Brett, Robert J. 1988a. ¡Mucho gusto! Test Booklet. St. Paul, Minn.: EMC Publishing.
Brett, Robert J. 1988b. ¡Qué gusto! Test Booklet. St. Paul, Minn.: EMC Publishing.
Calk, Linda. 1990. Foreign Languages Testing Brochure. Ysleta, Tex.: Ysleta Independent School District.
Carrera-Hanley, Teresa, Rebecca M. Valette and Jean-Paul Valette. 1990a. Spanish for Mastery 1, Proficiency Testing Kit. Lexington, Mass.: D.C. Heath.
Carrera-Hanley, Teresa, Rebecca M. Valette and Jean-Paul Valette. 1990b. Spanish for Mastery 2, Proficiency Testing Kit. Lexington, Mass.: D.C. Heath.
Cole, Charlotte and L. Floy Miller. 1989. On y va! Troisième Niveau Testing Program. Boston, Mass.: Heinle & Heinle.
Cook, Kathleen. 1989. On y va! Deuxième Niveau Testing Program. Boston, Mass.: Heinle & Heinle.
Educational Testing Service (ETS). 1990a. Advanced Placement Course Description: French, May 1991. Princeton, N.J.: College Entrance Examination Board.
Educational Testing Service (ETS). 1990b. Advanced Placement Course Description: German, May 1990. Princeton, N.J.: College Entrance Examination Board.
Educational Testing Service (ETS). 1990c. Advanced Placement Course Description: Spanish, May 1991, May 1992. Princeton, N.J.: College Entrance Examination Board.
Educational Testing Service (ETS). 1990d. Advanced Placement Program: National Summary Information. Princeton, N.J.: College Entrance Examination Board.
Educational Testing Service (ETS). 1990e. Taking the Achievement Tests 1990-91. Princeton, NJ: College Entrance Examination Board.
Funston, James F., Eric G. Narváez and Alejandro Varbas Bonilla. 1991. Somos así: Test Booklet. St. Paul, Minn.: EMC Publishing.
Henning, Grant. 1990. Priority Issues in the Assessment of Communicative Language Abilities. Foreign Language Annals 23 (5): 379-384.
Hopen, Dianne B. 1991. Le français vivant 1: Test Booklet. St. Paul, Minn.: EMC Publishing.
Ingram, David E. 1990. The Australian Second Language Proficiency Ratings (ASLPR). In John H.A. L. de Jong, ed., Standardization in Language Testing. AILA Review 7: 46-61.
Kline, Rebecca. 1989. On y va! Premier Niveau Testing Program. Boston, Mass.: Heinle & Heinle.

Kraft, W. S. 1991. Deutsch aktuell 1: Test Booklet. St. Paul, Minn.: EMC Publishing.
Lange, Dale L. 1990. Priority Issues in the Assessment of Communicative Language Abilities. Foreign Language Annals 23 (5): 403-407.
Lowry, Annette et al. [n.d.] Advanced Placement Test: French I. Fort Worth, Tex.: Fort Worth Independent School District.
Maples, Fran. 1990. Teacher Certification of Mastery of Essential Elements. Richardson, Tex.: Richardson Independent School District.
Mullis, Ina V. S., Eugene H. Owen, and Gary W. Phillips. 1990. America's Challenge: Accelerating Academic Achievement: A summary of findings from 20 years of NAEP. Washington, D.C.: U.S. Department of Education.
New York State Education Department. [1987a]. Latin for Communication: New York State Syllabus. Albany, N.Y.: New York State Education Department: Bureau of Foreign Languages Education.
New York State Education Department. [1987b]. Modern Languages for Communication: New York State Syllabus. Albany, N.Y.: New York State Education Department: Bureau of Foreign Languages Education.
New York State Education Department. 1988. New York State Second Language Proficiency Examinations in Modern Languages: An Introduction. Albany, N.Y.: New York State Education Department: Bureau of Foreign Languages Education.
New York State Education Department. 1989. Regents Comprehensive Examinations in Modern Languages; Teacher's Manual for Part 1: Speaking. Albany, N.Y.: New York State Education Department: Bureau of Foreign Languages Education.
New York State Education Department. 1990. New York State Second Language Proficiency Examination: French. Albany, N.Y.: New York State Education Department: Bureau of Foreign Languages Education.
Putnam, Constance E. and Clifford J. Kent. 1989. Tests to accompany *German Today, Two*, 4th ed. Boston, Mass.: Houghton Mifflin.
Roeber, Edward D., and Thomas H. Fisher. 1990. Assessment in the Arts and Foreign Languages: A Proposal for the National Assessment Governing Board. [Unpublished paper]
Shohamy, Elana. 1990. Language Testing Priorities: A Different Perspective. Foreign Language Annals 23 (5): 385-394.
Sollenberger, Howard E. 1978. Development and Current Use of the FSI Oral Interview Test. In: John L. D. Clark, ed. Direct Testing of Speaking Proficiency: Theory and Application. Princeton, N.J.: ETS.
Stansfield, C. W. 1990. Some Foreign Language Test Development Priorities for the Last Decade of the Twentieth Century. Foreign Language Annals 23 (5): 395-401.
Stansfield, Charles W. , Dorry Mann Kenyon, Ricardo Paiva, Fatima Doyle, Ines Ulsh, Maria Antonia Cowles. 1990. The Development and Validation of the Portuguese Speaking Test. Hispania 73 (3): 641-651.
Valette, Rebecca M. 1969. Directions in Foreign Language Testing. New York: MLA/ERIC.
Valette, Rebecca M. 1977. Modern Language Testing, 2nd ed. New York: Harcourt.
Valette, Rebecca M. 1989. Reaction Paper: ACTFL Priorities Conference, Testing Section. [Unpublished paper, Boston, Nov. 16, 1989]
Virginia Department of Education. 1988. Introduction to the Standards of Learning, Modern Foreign Languages: Resource Materials. Richmond, Va.: Virginia Department of Education, Division of Research and Testing.

Content-based instruction:
A method with many faces

Marguerite Ann Snow
California State University, Los Angeles

Introduction. The many faces of content-based instruction may be reflected in the following six scenarios:

Scenario 1:
Martha Ter Maat, Randy Cox, and Alice Tuan designed a 'Poster Skills' unit around the theme 'Science and Technology: East and West' for graduate ESL students from the Department of Biochemistry at USC. The culminating activity of the course is a simulated conference poster session in which the students present their posters and critique their own and their peers' presentations.

Scenario 2:
In Rome, EFL secondary school teachers, Anna Rita Tamponi and Daniela Sorani, developed a thematic unit on 'Wind'. The unit includes materials from social studies, science, poetry, and art and has both content objectives (e.g. advantages and disadvantages of wind power) and language objectives (e.g. comparing and contrasting).

Scenario 3:
ESL teacher, Jack Cousineau, designed a medical occupations unit for ESL students studying to be certified nurse assistants and medical front-office and back-office assistants at Baldwin Park Adult School. The unit focuses on the study skills the students need to cope with the reading and vocabulary in the medical occupations class.

Scenario 4:
In Barcelona, Catalan-speaking elementary school students ages 6 to 12 study *Plastica* 'Art', *Etica* 'Socialization', and *Sciencia* 'Science' in English. The science curriculum of these experimental schools centers around such themes as geometric concepts and scientific change.

Scenario 5:

At Thomas Jefferson High School in Los Angeles, ESL students are grouped into a four-hour core curriculum. ESL teacher, Eva Wegrzecka-Monkiewicz, works with the biology and U.S. history teachers to develop lesson plans and activities which integrate the three subject areas.

Scenario 6:

In Beijing, students from the Graduate School of the Chinese Academy of Social Science take courses in 'Academic English', minicourses in such topics as 'Intercultural communication' and 'American values and institutions', and a course taught by an American professor such as 'Microeconomics: Price determination in the United States economy,' 'The sociology of social rules,' or 'The United States and world politics'.

Content-based instruction: A definition. These six scenarios illustrate content-based instruction in both the ESL and EFL settings, at various grade levels (elementary through adult) and across proficiency levels (beginning through advanced). They represent programs which focus on a single skill or treat all skills including study skills and grammar, teach vocational skills or promote sophisticated academic English, and, reflect a variety of program configurations and models; some of the programs take place in the language class, others in the content class, still others in a learning resource center.

Although the content-based programs illustrated in the six scenarios reflect great diversity in their audience and objectives, they all share a common theoretical base. Content-based instruction rests on the premise that the second or foreign language is learned most effectively when used as the medium to convey informational content of interest and relevance to the learner. Content, historically in second and foreign language teaching, has been defined in a variety of different ways. In certain methods, for example, it has been synonymous with the teaching of grammar or with the study of literature. In content-based instruction, 'content' is defined as the integration of content learning with language teaching aims. More specifically, it refers to the concurrent study of language and subject matter, with the form and sequence of language presentation dictated by or, at least, influenced by the content material. This view of language learning removes the arbitrary distinction between language and content by assuming that language and content should not be separated. Mohan (1986:1) underscores this point: 'In subject matter learning we overlook the role of language as a medium of learning. In language learning we overlook the fact that content is being communicated'.

Content-based instruction: A method. Using the descriptive framework developed by Richards and Rodgers (1987) as a heuristic for understanding the elements of method and the criteria for determining what counts as a method, I will build a case for content-based instruction to be seen as not just orientation or philosophy about integrating language and content, but as a method of second and foreign-language teaching.

Three elements make up a method in the Richards and Rodgers framework: APPROACH, DESIGN, and PROCEDURE. APPROACH is defined as the assumptions, beliefs, and theories about the nature of language and of language learning that provide the theoretical foundation upon which teachers base their teaching. As teachers we are guided by fundamental beliefs about the nature of language and language learning.

DESIGN is the relationship of theories of language and learning to both the form and function of instructional materials and activities. There are four sub-elements to DESIGN: (1) A definition of the linguistic content and specification for the selection and organization of content; (2) a specification of the role of learners; (3) a specification of the role of teachers; and (4) a specification of the role of materials.

The third element in the Richards and Rodgers framework, PROCEDURE, consists of the classroom techniques and practices that are the consequences of APPROACH and DESIGN.

Content-based instruction satisfies the three elements of METHOD set out by Richards and Rodgers. The APPROACH of content-based instruction assumes a theory of language and of language learning in which language is the *vehicle* of instruction, not the *object* of instruction. Language teaching aims are inextricably tied to content teaching aims to create the prerequisite conditions for second language acquisition. The DESIGN of content-based instruction places a priority on the interests and needs of the learner and takes into account the eventual uses the learner will make of the language. It seeks to provide optimal conditions for second language acquisition by exposing learners to meaningful, cognitively demanding language usually presented in the context of authentic materials and tasks. These conditions are enhanced by PROCEDURE in content-based instruction which makes pedagogical accommodation to learner proficiency levels and skills through a variety of instructional techniques and practices. In sum, this combination of theoretical rationale and strategies for classroom implementation provides the basis for content-based instruction as a method of second and foreign language teaching.

Content-based instruction: A method . . . and more. In this section, the diversity of content-based instruction as reflected in the six scenarios will be illustrated in greater detail at the levels of DESIGN and PROCEDURE. The first element of DESIGN, the definition of the linguistic content and specification for the selection and organization of content, can be seen in the choice of content-based model. The scenarios provide illustrations of variations of three models of content-based instruction: Theme-based, sheltered, and adjunct (cf. Brinton et al. 1989). Theme-based languages classes, such as the "Wind" unit in Scenario 2, involve structuring the language class around topics or themes, with the content material rather than a linguistic syllabus dictating the course curriculum. Sheltered courses, like the Art and Science classes in Scenario 4, consist of content classes taught to second language students by subject matter specialists. In adjunct courses, students are concurrently enrolled in two linked courses (a language course and a content course) with the two courses sharing the content base and complimenting each other in terms of a coordinated curriculum. Scenario 5 at Jefferson High School is an example of an adjunct program at the secondary school level.

The 'Poster Skills' unit in Scenario 1 provides an example of how the selection and organization of content was determined in the theme-based course 'Science and technology: East and West'. In this setting, faculty in the Biochemistry Department encourage their students to submit posters at poster sessions of scientific conferences as an initiation into academic presentation making. The faculty had observed, however, that their ESL students were generally poor at interacting appropriately at poster sessions. For example, it is common for participants at poster sessions to pass by the displays and ask questions such as 'What do you think are the implications of your experiment?' or 'Where do you plan to go from here?' Many of the ESL students expected to stand silently next to their posters and were generally unprepared to respond to such questions and to engage in this kind of interaction which is typical of Western scientific poster sessions.

The theme-based course was designed by ESL teachers around the topics of AIDS, History of Science in China, and Asian Languages to make the students aware of the expectations of Western scientists and equip them with *all* the skills needed to perform well at a poster session. Their curriculum includes outlining and summarizing, reading and constructing graphics such as charts, graphs, tables, flowcharts, figure legends, and oral presentation skills such as asking and answering questions. This course is a good example, in my opinion, of perceptive teachers recognizing students' specific language needs and designing a content-based curriculum which prepares them to function effectively in their second language within the academic community of Biochemistry.

Other motivations for determining linguistic content in the DESIGN of content-based programs can be seen in the scenarios. In the experimental schools in Barcelona of Scenario 4, course designers had a hard time finding time in a packed curriculum for the teaching of English. The decision to offer content courses such as Art and Science in English was seen as an efficient way to meet both content and foreign language teaching objectives. One of the key objectives of the design of the content-based course at the Graduate School of the Chinese Academy of Social Sciences, described in Scenario 6, was to expose the Chinese students to native speakers of English and to the types of academic English and critical analysis skills typically required at an American university.

The second sub-element of DESIGN in the Richards and Rodgers framework is the role of the learner. Several of the scenarios illustrate different facets of the learner's role in content-based instruction. For example, in the 'Poster Skills' unit of Scenario 1, discussed in detail above, learners are seen as a members of the scientific community and the theme-based class is designed to prepare them to operate professionally within this milieu. In Rome, the EFL teachers of Scenario 2 were concerned about the 'intermediate plateau' their students seemed to hit. The teachers responded to learner needs by designing thematic units that add interest to the language class, thereby boosting motivation and extending their students' language skills toward higher levels of development.

The third sub-element, the role of the teacher in content-based instruction, is well exemplified by the adjunct program at Jefferson High School in Scenario 5. In this setting, ESL, History, and Biology teachers collaborate daily in four-hour blocks. An eight-week unit developed around the theme 'Culture and Human Behavior' reveals how the three teachers coordinate their respective roles and objectives. The History teacher traces the cultural roots of Hispanic populations and discusses cultural differences between the U.S. and Latin America. The Biology teacher covers the differences between human and non-human behavior and demonstrates how human behavior is culturally conditioned. In the ESL class, students work on critical reading skills throughout the unit using the readings of the History and Biology classes and learning the elements of paragraph and essay writing. The three teachers meet to coordinate the units, each striving to develop the second language skills of their ESL students through the subjects of History and Biology.

The role of instructional materials, the fourth sub-element of the Richards and Rodgers framework, provides a continuing profile of the variety of design elements in content-based instruction. In the 'Poster Skills' unit' in Scenario 1, the students read excerpts from *Scientific American* and *Far East Economic Review*, and watch a video on Chinese Science from the Public Broadcasting Service NOVA series. In the thematic unit on 'Wind' described in Scenario 2, students listen to a recording of Vivaldi's poem *Winter* and to his *Concerto in F minor 'Winter'*, comparing the two art forms in terms of sonority, rhythm, motion, feelings, images, and contrasts. The range of materials in these two settings illustrates the central role of authentic materials in content-based instruction. In both of these examples, creative teachers have adapted materials not designed for language teaching purposes to meet the objectives of their second or foreign language classes.

The six scenarios also illustrate the great variety of classroom techniques and practices, or PROCEDURE, of content-based instruction. The Biology and History teachers in Scenario 5 are charged with making the regular curriculum of these two cognitively-demanding subject areas comprehensible to low intermediate/intermediate ESL students. They use a variety of techniques 'to shelter' instruction and, thereby, accommodate to their students' developing language proficiency levels (cf. Richard-Amato and Snow, in press). These strategies include instructional activities such as brainstorming to activate students' background knowledge about a new topic, highlighting key vocabulary words and concepts, providing multiple examples, and controlling the pace of their presentations. The teachers also use the students' native language, Spanish, when appropriate, as a bridge to comprehension. Other instructional strategies include the extensive use of advance organizers and graphics to help students organize and synthesize difficult content material. For instance, using information from several reading sources, students complete a 'Cultural Analysis' chart containing three headings 'European English Culture', 'Northern Indian Culture(s)', and 'New England Culture(s)'. They then use the chart to write an essay comparing the three cultures along the dimensions of language, food habits, time, space, values, and customs.

The instructional techniques and practices used in several of the other settings further illustrate the PROCEDURE of content-based instruction. In Scenario 2, the 'Wind' unit is structured according to the Cognitive Academic Language Learning Approach (CALLA) (Chamot and O'Malley 1987). It includes learning strategy instruction as a major objective, in addition to language and content objectives (cf. O'Malley and Chamot 1990). Integral to the unit is teaching metacognitive strategies such as monitoring one's comprehension, cognitive strategies such as inferring meaning, and social affective strategies such as role-taking. In addition, cooperative learning activities are incorporated into the 'Wind' unit (cf. Kagan 1986). In one activity, students take the roles of 'note-taker', 'experimenter', 'phenomenologist', 'hypothesizer', and 'reporter' as they conduct an experiment on pressure and convection in the foreign language class. After the experiment, group members write up their sections based on their assigned roles and work together to produce a joint lab report.

In Scenario 4, the curriculum of the Catalan elementary school capitalizes on the hands-on, experiential nature of art, socialization, and science. In 'Plastica', students use English to learn to draw, paint, cut, and design. In 'Etica', they learn how to cooperate, share, and express their feelings in English. In 'Sciencia', they observe, describe, and measure in English as they master the scientific concepts of the thematic units.

Sheltered English, cooperative learning, learning strategy instruction, and the use of manipulatives are just some of the many instructional practices which fit well under the PROCEDURE of content-based instruction. Other techniques and practices which we typically associate with communicative language teaching such as role play, information gap, and journal writing are also right at home. The suitability of these techniques is, of course, determined by the proficiency level of the students and the goals of the program. In these six scenarios, the range of techniques spans from a Total Physical Response (TPR) activity with medical terminology for parts of the body in the medical occupations unit in Scenario 4 to the complex critical thinking skills required of the Chinese students in Scenario 6 who were asked in an essay to 'Discuss U.S. containment policy from an idealist point of view'. Clearly the techniques and practices just described are not unique to content-based instruction; the point is that they are compatible with the *approach* and *design* of this method.

Through these illustrations of actual ESL/EFL classes, I have attempted to demonstrate that content-based instruction offers a method for second and foreign language teaching which satisfies the three criteria proposed in the Richards and Rodgers framework. Its approach places a priority on content as a cornerstone in second language learning and teaching. The design of content-based instruction offers clear direction in terms of syllabus and curriculum design, the roles of the learner and teacher, and the role of instructional materials. Furthermore, the method takes full advantage of the vast array of instructional techniques and practices available in second and foreign language teaching.

Content-based instruction: Teacher training and evaluation. In the remainder of this paper, I will discuss activities in two other areas of content-based instruction which cannot be directly addressed by the Richards and Rodgers framework. I would like to suggest that a complete description of a method must also include a teacher training component and must address issues of evaluation.

Several conceptual frameworks have been proposed to provide the basis for teacher training and staff development in content-based instruction. Snow et al. (1989) proposed a framework in which language and content teachers work collaboratively to determine language teaching objectives. These objectives derive from two considerations: Content-obligatory language (language essential to an understanding of content material) and content-compatible language (language that can be taught naturally within the context of a particular subject and that students require practice with). This framework has been used as part of a comprehensive video tape series designed to train immersion foreign language teachers (Montgomery County (MD) Public Schools, 1990). Mohan's (1986) frame-work for determining the key knowledge structures inherent in subjects across the curriculum and identifying their graphic representations has been used as the basis for staff development in schools which serve language minority students in Vancouver, B.C. (Early et al. 1986).

Several teacher training and staff development projects have built on the collaborative nature of content-based instruction. The Cognitive Academic Language Learning Approach (CALLA), which was applied in Scenario 2 in the EFL context, was developed to provide a bridge between bilingual or ESL classes for limited English proficient students and mainstream classes in the U.S. In this model, language and content teachers work together to develop lesson plans which integrate science, mathematics, and social studies, with reading, writing, listening, and speaking activities. The lessons also provide students with learning strategy instruction. Through the mathematics/science project at the Center for Applied Linguistics, workshops have been set up for ESL/English teachers and math and science teachers to jointly develop lesson plans which integrate language and content instruction (Spanos 1989). The development of a video tape on interactive math and science teaching is one of the major outcomes of the project. In addition, a training manual for integrating language and content instruction and strategy sheets for mathematics, science, and social studies have been developed by for use in staff development (Short, Crandall, and Christian 1989).

The integration of language and content teaching raises many interesting evaluation issues which must also be addressed in a complete description of content-based instruction. Mohan (1986) points out that we must distinguish between language knowledge and content knowledge in content-based evaluation. Brinton, Snow, and Wesche (1989) underscore this concern pointing out that the 'what' of evaluation is not always so straight-forward in content-based instruction. One example of diagnostic assessment techniques is the 'Pre-Algebra Lexicon' which was designed to help math teachers determine their students' proficiency in the language of mathematics (Hayden and Cuevas 1990).

Content-based instruction: A research base. Consideration of evaluation issues and teacher training and staff development activities in content-based instruction has begun to establish an interesting set of research questions. Several areas of investigation offer fertile ground for research in content-based instruction. In recent work, Mohan (1990) calls for the investigation of knowledge structures and student tasks as a way to understand the relationship between language learning and content learning. This might include analysis of task discourse and lead to ways of developing 'language-sensitive' instruction to support content learning. A second promising area for research is identification of the special registers of the content areas. For example, Spanos et al. (1988) examined the ways language minority students use math language in mathematics and algebra problem-solving. Similarly, Spanos and Crandall (1990) discuss the language of physical science and biology and consider the instructional implications of academic language in all its linguistic and cognitive complexity. Clearly, this area holds promise for increasing our understanding of academic language demands and for its translation into effective instructional practices.

Another area for investigation deals with what Swain (1988:72) has called the 'interface of language and content teaching'. Using data from studies of Cantonese-speaking students learning English in Hong Kong and English-speaking students in French immersion programs in Canada, Swain (1988:68) makes the case that typical content teaching may provide *inadequate* conditions for second language learning and remarks that 'not all content teaching is necessarily good language teaching'. One role of the teacher, Swain suggests, is to help learners undertake the sort of form-function analysis needed to become effective users of the second or foreign language. Ways in which content teaching can be manipulated and complemented to capitalize on its language learning potential include providing a full range of input, not the restricted range characteristic of the classroom, providing extended opportunities for students to produce the second or foreign language, and giving feedback on their errors so they learn to attend to their language deficiencies. Swain reminds us that we cannot make assumptions that language learning in content-based instruction will occur automatically; careful consideration must go into the planning and delivery of instruction in content-based instruction programs. Research must illuminate the interface between language and content learning and teaching so as to broaden our understanding of the conditions which maximize the language learning benefits of content-based instruction.

Conclusion. The scenarios I have highlighted reflect six faces of content-based instruction; there are undoubtedly many others. Content-based instruction is more than a collection of models and programs. Underlying these seemingly diverse programs is a common theoretical foundation which guides curriculum and program design, defines the roles of teachers and learners, influences materials selection and development, and suggests a wealth of techniques and practices on an everyday basis in the content-based classroom. Content-based instruction extends the traditional boundaries of second and foreign language teaching, offering opportunities and challenges for teachers and learners in both second and foreign language settings. In short, content-based instruction is a method with many faces.

References

Brinton, D. M., M. A. Snow, and M. B. Wesche. 1989. Content-based second language instruction. New York: Newbury House/Harper Collins.

Chamot, A. U., and J. M. O'Malley. 1987. The cognitive academic language learning approach: A bridge to the mainstream. TESOL Quarterly. 21(3):227-249.

Early, M., C. Thew, and P. Wakefield. 1986. Integrating language and content instruction K-12: An ESL resource book. Victoria, BC, Canada: Publications Service Branch, Ministry of Education.

Hayden, D., and G. Cuevas. 1990. Pre-algebra lexicon. Washington, D.C.: Center for Applied Linguistics.

Kagan, S. 1986. Cooperative learning andsociocultural factors in schooling. In: California State Department of Education, Beyond language: Social and cultural factors in schooling language minority students. 231-298. California State University, Los Angeles: Evaluation, Dissemination and Assessment Center.

Mohan, B. A. 1986. Language and content. Reading, Mass.: Addison-Wesley.

Mohan, B. A. 1990. LEP students and the integration of language and content: Knowledge structures and tasks. Paper presented at the National Symposiumon Limited English Proficient (LEP) Students Research Issues, Office of Bilingual Education and Minority Languages Affairs, Washington, D.C.

Montgomery County (MD) Public Schools. 1990. Planning for instruction in the immersion classroom. Rockville, Md.: Office of Instruction and Program Development.

O'Malley, J. M., and A. U. Chamot. 1990. Learning strategies in second language acquisition. Cambridge: Cambridge University Press.

Richards, J. C., and T. S. Rodgers. 1987. Method: Approach, design, and procedure. In: M. H. Long and J. C. Richards, eds. Methodology in TESOL: A book of readings. New York: Newbury House. 133-157.

Richard-Amato, P., and M. A. Snow. in press. Strategies for content-area teachers. In: P. Richard-Amato and M. A. Snow, eds. The multicultural classroom: Readings for content-area teachers. New York: Longman.

Short, D., J. Crandall, and D. Christian. 1989. How to integrate language and content instruction: A training manual. Washington, D.C.: Center for Applied Linguistics.

Snow, M. A., and D. M. Brinton. 1988. Content-based language instruction: Investigating the effectiveness of the adjunct model. TESOL Quarterly. 22:553-574.

Snow, M. A., and M. Met, and F. Genesee. 1989. A conceptual framework for the integration of language and content in second/foreign language instruction. TESOL Quarterly. 23: 201-217.

Spanos, G. 1989. On the integration of language and content. Annual Review of Applied Linguistics. 10:227-240.

Spanos, G., and J. Crandall. 1990. Language and problem solving: Some examples from math and science. In: A. M. Padilla, H. H. Fairchild, and C. M. Valadez, eds. Bilingual education: Issues and strategies. Newbury Park, Calif.: Sage.157-170.

Spanos, G., N. Rhodes, T. C. Dale, and J. Crandall. 1988. Linguistic features of mathematical problem solving: Insights and applications. In: R. R. Cocking and J. P. Mestre, eds. Linguistic and cultural influences on learning mathematics. Hillsdale, N.J.: Lawrence Erlbaum. 221-240.

Swain, M. 1988. Manipulating and complementing content to maximize second language learning. TESL Canada Journal, 6,1:68-83.

Literacy, language, and multiculturalism

JoAnn Crandall
Center for Applied Linguistics

Introduction. During the late 1980s, a number of factors converged to create an unprecedented interest in adult literacy throughout the world, resulting in the designation of 1990 as International Literacy Year by the United Nations and during that same year, in the establishment of 'adult literacy and lifelong learning' as one of the six educational goals articulated by the President and the Governors in the United States. That goal stipulates that 'By the year 2000, every adult American will be literate and will possess the knowledge and skills necessary to compete in a global economy and exercise the rights and responsibilities of citizenship.'

Both economic and social reasons account for this renewed interest in adult literacy in the United States. A number of policy-makers have suggested that literacy and productivity are very closely linked and that the future economic health of the United States is tied to improving the skills of the American workforce (Chisman 1989, United States Department of Education and United States Department of Labor 1988). An early study, in this regard (*Workforce 2000*, Johnston and Packer 1987) predicted an increasing mismatch between the kinds of likely employment at the turn of the century and the profile of the workers who would be available to take those jobs. The study describes a shift from a manufacturing to a service-based economy, resulting in a need for increasingly complex literacy, numeracy, and problem-solving skills, and then identifies the prospective entry-level workforce as comprised increasingly of ethnic and racial minorities and women, many of whom are likely to have limited education, literacy, and English language skills needed to function in this workplace. A later study, *America's Choice: High Skills or Low Wages* (Commission on the Skills of the American Workforce 1990) defined the issue in even more depressing terms, identifying two alternatives for the future of employment in the United States: either high skills, high-productivity workplaces, where individuals with substantially increased skills will be engaged in stimulating, high-productivity jobs and sharing in the decision-making **or** routinized, low skills work requiring minimal literacy and decision-making skills and resulting in minimal wages. To choose the former will involve mounting a concerted language and literacy instructional effort and recognizing the importance of lifelong learning for all Americans; to choose the latter involves doing little or nothing.

Not everyone accepts the premise which underlies this economic argument, since it places the blame for reduced productivity on America's workers and ignores a host of other factors which contribute to undereducation and marginalization of individuals. Recognizing, however, the changing demography of the United States—with dramatic increases in ethnolinguistic minority populations, as evidenced by a 50% increase in the Hispanic population and more than a 100% increase in the Asian-American population between 1980 and 1990—these educators and researchers nonetheless promote expanded language and literacy instruction for personal growth and for empowering individuals to take more control over their lives in order to meet both personal and larger community goals (Kazemek 1988, Fingeret and Jurmo 1989). As Frances Kazemek puts it, literacy can lead to 'the liberation of people for intelligent, meaningful and humane action upon the world' (1988:466.)

Defining literacy. To a large extent, how we answer the need for increased literacy depends upon our views of what constitutes literacy, the purposes for which literacy is sought, and what is considered appropriate literacy instruction. While there is substantial agreement that the United States has a literacy problem, there is little consensus on what constitutes literacy or how many individuals are actually in need of literacy education. Estimates of illiteracy range from fewer than a million individuals to more than 60 million and estimates of the language minority population within those estimates range from 30% to 60% (Hunter and Harman 1985) Terms such as 'computer literacy' or 'cultural literacy' only complicate an already full dictionary of 'basic', 'functional', 'workplace', 'family', or other literacy terms used by researchers and practitioners to describe the kinds of skills and contexts in which literacy functions.

In general, it is clear that standards for literacy have increased and definitions of literacy have likewise become more complex. (A fuller discussion of this can be found in Crandall and Imel 1991.) Earlier definitions of literacy focus on the skills of reading and writing. There was a time in American history when being literate meant being able to write one's name. At other times, completion of four or six years of school or achieving a comparable grade-level equivalency on a standardized test of reading and writing skills has been considered evidence of adequate literacy. If one were to choose a sixth-grade level of education or the ability to read and write in English or one's own language as the basis, then only .5% of the American population would be considered "illiterate" (Irwin 1987). However, the increasing complexity of literacy demands has led Chall and a number of reading researchers (Aaron et al. 1990), to suggest that a twelfth grade level may be more accurate. If that were an appropriate definition, large numbers of the American adult population who have not completed high school would find themselves considered marginally illiterate. I should add, however, that one must view grade level equivalencies with caution since the current standard income tax form is reputedly written at an eighth grade level!

There is a growing recognition that the view of literacy as a set of autonomous reading and writing skills is not very descriptive or reflective of the ways people use literacy to accomplish tasks at home, at work, or in the community, within their lives. More recent attempts at defining or characterizing literacy place reading and writing skills into functional contexts and include computational, problem-solving, and interpersonal skills, focusing on ways that adults use literacy to accomplish tasks in the home, the community, and the workplace. This has led to increasingly contextualized definitions of literacy. An early attempt, in this regard, was made by the Adult Performance Level Project (APL) at the University of Texas (1975). It is intriguing to note that while the Council of Europe was characterizing how adults use language in context, identifying notions and functions, among other things, to produce a communicative syllabus, (van Ek 1975) the Adult Performance Level Project was identifying ways that adults use listening, speaking, reading, writing, computational, problem-solving, and interpersonal skills to function in American society—placing language and literacy skills in the contexts of employment, health and medical care, citizenship, and the like. The concept of 'functional literacy' owes its genesis to the APL, which led to the development at the Center for Applied Linguistics of competency-based curricula stipulating performance objectives and contextualized learning tasks (CAL 1983). However, it is also the APL which led to estimates of 'functional illiteracy' or 'functional incompetency' [sic] as high as 20 percent or 23 million adults.

It may not be necessary to point this out, but it is instructive to note that all of these definitions are based on sets of criteria to which nonliterate individuals had little input and that national surveys of literacy skills always assess literacy in English, a factor which certainly biases against accurate assessment of literacy levels of language minority individuals. Hunter and Harman (1985) rightly ask: 'Who but the person or group involved can really describe what "effective functioning in one's own cultural group" really means? How is a "life of dignity and pride" measured? The [real] question may be: Whose needs are served by generalized statistics about the population?'

There has been a limited attempt to reflect the wider range of literacy through the inclusion of prose, document, quantitative and other literacy tasks in formal literacy surveys such as the National Assessment of Educational Progress Young Adult Survey, but these are conducted only in English and reflect a majority cultural orientation (Kirsch and Jungeblut 1986).

In a secondary analysis of the National Chicano Survey, conducted by Wiley for his dissertation (1988, 1991), 'non-functional literacy rates,' while high among Chicanos surveyed, were 'far lower' when Spanish literacy was included in the analysis. In fact, as a number of ethnographic descriptions have demonstrated, those identified by surveys as functionally illiterate may in fact be functioning quite competently in their own communities (Fingeret 1983); and ironically, the impact of literacy upon those participating in literacy programs may create new roles and render traditional relationships dysfunctional. Also, those who appear to learn little in literacy classes may, in fact, be engaged in complex literacy practices in their own communities (Weinstein-Shr 1989).

Descriptions of workplace literacy programs, as well, have demonstrated that employees are often able to function much more effectively than literacy assessments might predict, since familiarity with context, predictable text formats, and the use of a number of productive strategies (oral support, routinization of literacy tasks) can reduce literacy demands (Crandall 1981). Boren (cited in Collins 1989:458) points out that while most of the adults in their union-based literacy programs for Hispanic workers in New York City (the Consortium for Worker Education) would be viewed as 'illiterate' or 'functionally illiterate' using 'traditional academic standards,' their 'storehouses of both information and experience' enable them to function effectively. As she puts it, 'We are talking about a "plurality of literacies" of which reading, writing, and speaking English is just one form'.

More recently, a number of individuals have suggested that literacy be viewed as a continuum, with adults continuing to acquire literacy skills to function in new contexts throughout their lives and recognizing that even the most literate individual may prove to be 'functionally illiterate' when faced with a text in a context with relatively little background information or experience to interpret it (e.g. a theoretical scientific or technical volume in an unfamiliar discipline). The best that one might be able to do in that scenario is to 'decode' the text, something which few would accept as 'functional literacy' or literacy adequate or appropriate to the task.

From an ethnographic perspective, literacy can be defined in terms of cultural practices acquired through participation in literacy events, rather than as a set of discrete skills that are learned and then applied to different tasks and settings. The distinction is an important one, because it suggests that while the most basic reading and writing skills may transfer across languages, the appropriate use of these in new contexts is a much more complex question. Is there transfer at a more than trivial decoding level or do different contexts, background information, role relations, expectations about appropriateness of language and literacy use require the acquisition of new practices in socially relevant situations and contexts?

The distinction is particularly important for bilingual adults, and not surprisingly, many of the ethnographic studies of literacy practices have focused on ethnic and linguistic minorities. The allocation of languages for literacy within bilingual communities is complex, and even very proficient bilinguals may find that they use different languages for different literacy practices or events (Ramirez 1990). For example, Wiley (1988, 1991) found that among Mexican-origin Americans, English language literacy showed a stronger association with income, but biliteracy, with employment. Biliteracy was also found to demonstrate a stronger relationship with voter registration and political participation than English language literacy.

Wallace (quoted in Ramirez 1990) points out that 'There will be kinds of reading and writing undertaken in order to maintain feelings of identity with one's own community, ethnic group and family, where readers are taking on what we might call "private" roles. Then there are more "public" roles to do with being a member of the wider society, for example as motorist, consumer, or taxpayer.' And experience with one language in a domain can preclude the use of the other or make it difficult to 'transfer.' Thus, for example, a bilingual may find it difficult to translate or complete a workplace form in a home language or to read or write informal notes in a second.

Adults engage in a wide range of contextualized literacy practices, in 'multiple literacies,' with different situations requiring different types of practices and few would disagree that the range of literate tasks and their complexity has increased for adults in the United States. Examples from the workplace are often cited as evidence. For example, in the past, an insurance query or claim would be addressed by a number of individuals: one might verify the name and policy number, another might manually seek out the file to provide basic information, while a third would be able to interpret the information and render a decision on coverage. Today, what used to be the work of several individuals is done by one clerk who receives the inquiry, calls up the information on the computer, interprets the caller's claim in light of that information, and then makes a decision.

Perhaps a more graphic example is that of today's assembly line, where in the past the majority of individuals were engaged in heavy labor, with little opportunity or necessity to interpret information. Today, with the use of computers and statistical process control, individuals are expected to read and interpret graphs, tables, and other complex, computer-generated information; to perform sophisticated calculations to determine whether changes need to be made; and then to communicate that information orally or in writing to co-workers.

Adult literacy instruction. Different views of literacy result in different instructional programs, affecting the purposes and goals for literacy, the content of the literacy instruction, and how literacy acquisition will be assessed. Programs may be offered in almost any imaginable setting in an attempt to serve adult learners where they live: in community centers, schools, libraries, churches, homes, shopping centers, workplaces, union halls, colleges, or correctional institutions. These programs may have dramatically different goals and instructional programs.

A major issue among literacy educators concerns the goals or purposes of literacy instruction: literacy for whom and for what? Those who link literacy with economic development are likely to create programs in which the focus is on helping adults to meet expectations of the wider community, in education (for example, helping adults to be able to pass a high school equivalency exam) or in the workplace (helping them to acquire the skills and knowledge required for successful functioning on the job). Those who view the role of literacy as 'the liberation of people for intelligent, meaningful and humane action upon the world' (Kazemek 1988:466) are likely to involve learners in the statement of goals and to create programs where the emphasis is on self-development.

Perhaps nowhere is this more clear than in programs for workers. 'Workplace literacy' programs are likely to help adults to acquire the specific skills and knowledge required of the workplace, focusing on tasks that are identified through literacy audits or needs assessments. 'Worker education' or 'workforce literacy' programs are likely to focus on a worker's personal development, addressing current workplace expectations but also the worker's future potential. Similarly, family literacy programs may teach English language and literacy to enable parents to help children with their homework and to improve their own educational prospects, or they may offer native language literacy to enable these parents to record and read traditional stories to their children and by enriching the literacy events in the home, contribute to their children's education.

Currently, there are two major approaches to adult ESL and literacy programs—competency-based and participatory. While these need not be mutually exclusive, in practice they may be so.

Competency-based programs are developed through needs assessments of the community and relevant settings within it, and through interviews and other assessments conducted with the individual learners. From this needs assessment, a variety of competencies with performance objectives are identified and a competency-based or task-based syllabus is developed, from which language and literacy teaching and learning activities are devised. In these programs, the context tends to define the content and much of it is actually pre-determined. For example, if the goal of the program is 'survival literacy,' an assumption may be made that most learners need to learn how to use public transportation, how to locate and obtain employment, how to access medical care and follow prescriptions, and the like; if the focus is on 'workplace literacy,' a task analysis or literacy audit of the workplace is conducted to identify how and why oral and written language and other skills are used in the workplace and learners are assessed in terms of how well they are currently functioning within these tasks and what kinds of competencies they still need to acquire.

Unfortunately, while the content may be 'evident' through needs assessments, in actuality, the community may have developed a number of ways of 'surviving' or functioning in identified contexts which can be accomplished without literacy or English language skills for each individual; what the learner may really be interested in is recording family histories and preserving folk tales before they are lost to the community. Likewise, rather than focusing on what the workplace demands of the worker, it may be that the worker is more interested in a program of educational development which addresses larger personal growth than that afforded by a pre-determined curriculum.

In response to this larger goal of empowering individuals to chart their own growth and to take more control over their lives, and with the influence of the theories of Paulo Freire (Freire 1970, 1973; Spener 1990) adult literacy programs have increasingly become more participatory or liberatory in nature, with learners participating in every aspect of the program design, from initial goal setting to decisions about the content of the program (Fingeret and Jurmo 1989; Auerbach 1989, 1990). Using a problem-posing approach, the curriculum and content for these programs evolves from discussions of learner concerns and the teacher becomes more of a facilitator for learners to accomplish their goals. Rather than a response to what adults 'need to learn,' the focus is on what adults bring with them to the educational program and where they want to go.

The above descriptions are, of course, necessarily simplistic; in actuality, programs are usually a blend of the two, with some of the initial content growing out of community needs assessments and the prior experience of the literacy providers, and when learners have become more of a community and are more willing to articulate their concerns and needs, the program becomes increasingly learner-centered. But the questions of whose literacy? for what purposes? in what languages? remain critical, as the following program differences illustrate.

Many reports document the relationship between family literacy and its consequences for children, linking the intergenerational transmission of illiteracy to children's underachievement in school. One particularly important study, by Sticht and McDonald (1989) has suggested that the single most important factor in the educational achievement of children is the mother's level of education. While this finding has led to increased support for family literacy programs, in which parents and children are engaged in language and literacy activities as part of a larger family education program, it has also led others to suggest that it unfairly places the blame for children's underachievement on the family, "ignoring the responsibilities of the school and society for the academic success of children" (Crandall and Imel 1991) As a result, different family literacy programs have been developed, reflecting different purposes and instructional content. In some, the focus is on ways in which parents can assist children with their homework, participate more in school activities, and otherwise support their children's formal education in the home. These programs are likely to include English language literacy and basic skills development for the parents. In others, the focus is on ways in which parents can use naturally occurring contexts in the home to support literacy; in these, the focus may be on learning to read appropriate stories, in either the first or second language and on taking advantage of the print-rich environment that surrounds them in the community.

A similar distinction occurs in workplace literacy and worker education/development programs. In 'workplace' programs, the focus may be on the kinds of language and literacy skills needed to function in specific jobs or in general employment contexts, whereas a worker education program may still be provided on the job site, but address the broader personal development concerns of participants as well. In others, even though the program is housed at a worksite, the program may be broadly learner-centered. For example, one large workplace program, supported by both labor and management in a number of worksites in Vancouver, offers a writing program with participant concerns addressed through the topics, readings, and discussions among participants. There is little focused attention to workplace documents, work-based tasks, or other demands of the workplace.

In theory, it is possible for programs to be both competency-based and participatory, to address both the larger community and its institutional requirements as well as the more personal goals of the individual learner, but in practice this is difficult. What is interesting to note is that there is often little relationship between the purposes and content of instruction and the types of learning activities involved. Participatory programs may use phonics or whole language techniques such as language experience stories, dialogue journals, process-based writing, or shared reading. So can and do competency-based programs. In general, the role of both reading and writing have increased substantially in literacy programs. That may sound like a tautology, but it is still possible to find literacy classes in which little authentic reading or writing is included and in which a prospective literacy instructor could report in a job interview that she did very little reading because she did not like to read very much!

What is critically affected by the choice of program is the assessment and program evaluation. Too often, participants in participatory programs find themselves assessed by standardized tests of basic skills (e.g. ABLE) or competency-based assessment systems (e.g. CASAS); even competency-based programs may find that commercially available assessment items bear little relationship to the program of instruction. Increasingly, programs are adding inventories of adult reading habits and preferences, self-reports of reading abilities and practices, writing portfolios which document literacy acquisition, dialogue journals, and audiotapes of oral reading to provide a more relevant (and valid) picture of individual achievement and to serve as the basis for program evaluation (Lytle and Wolfe 1989, Collins 1989, Auerbach 1990).

Central to the decisions about the content and purposes of literacy is the choice of language for literacy. It is a question which is only rarely asked in adult literacy programs, unless a sufficient number of individuals speak a common language other than English and instructors and other resources are available. Then the choice of first language literacy is possible, if the learners are so inclined. While there may be compelling reasons for adults to seek English language literacy as a means of achieving other life goals, it is also possible that contexts for first language literacy can and should be promoted, especially given at least some preliminary evidence of the role of first language literacy upon second language acquisition. Although there are a number of studies which demonstrate the benefits of mother tongue literacy for academic achievement of children in both the first and second language, there is only limited research on the effects of first language literacy on second language acquisition for adults, perhaps because of the difficulty of separating the effects of literacy and schooling. (See Scribner and Cole 1981, for their report on the Vai in Liberia, some of whom have acquired literacy outside school settings, for a fuller discussion of the issues.)

Program administrators frequently report that previous education is the single most important factor in predicting language gain among ESL literacy learners and the major factor they consider in initial placement. But what about literacy achieved outside of schooling? Robson (1981) had an opportunity to study Hmong adults in a refugee camp in Ban Vinai, Thailand. Hmong culture is principally an oral culture and Hmong people are preliterate (i.e. they speak a language which lacks a written system, or one which is not widely shared; Savage 1985). The Hmong language has only recently been written and previous literacy, if attained, was usually in Lao. Although the sample was small, Robson was able to study the differential effects of literacy and formal schooling, since she included in her sample groups exhibiting all four possibilities of presence or absence of literacy and formal schooling. While Robson found that literacy in any language (Hmong, Lao, or Thai) promoted acquisition of oral English, she also found that ability to read Hmong, among those individuals who had no formal schooling, enabled these individuals to perform as well as those who had previous formal education. Burtoff (1985) found similar results with Haitians in New York City.

These studies were concerned with language and literacy learned within a classroom context, and support the practices of many adult ESL literacy programs, who provide special ESL/literacy classes for adults who enter with minimal prior education and little or no literacy in their first (or second) language. Participants may remain in these classes with a special ESL/literacy focus for several months, since previous experience has shown that it will take these individuals substantially longer to progress through a beginning ESL program. Some of this is undoubtedly due to the expectation of adults to learn to read and write at the same time as they are acquiring a new language and to participants' lack of socialization into classrooms and schooling, but it may also be the case that literacy offers cognitive advantages to language learners and that those with prior literacy, especially in their first language, are able to progress much more rapidly in second language learning situations.

Some needed research. Before I close, I would like to outline some of the contributions which linguists and language educators can make to adult literacy research and practice.

(1) There is a need for both developmental literacy studies, analyzing the cognitive consequences or intellectual effects of literacy, and socio-cultural or functional literacy studies, which describe the ways that societies organize literacy activities, the functions of various languages in this regard, and the roles of the individuals involved. There is also a need for ethnographic studies of specific settings, analyzing the tasks and texts involved, the levels of literacy required, and the strategies that individuals use to compensate or reduce literacy requirements (something I attempted several years ago in an ethnographic analysis of literacy demands of clerical workers in a federal agency).

(2) There is also a need to describe the role of language and literacy in the negotiation of power and role relationships and to document the degree to which shifts in language and literacy skills result in changes in these relationships (Weinstein-Shr 1989).

(3) Additionally, linguists and language educators should conduct further studies of the effects of first language literacy, with or without formal education, upon second language oral and written language

acquisition, as well as studies which identify factors which affect adults' motivation to participate in mother tongue or second language literacy programs. (I might add that a major focus of our work at the Center for Applied Linguistics, as part of the National Center on Adult Literacy, will be biliteracy, especially the identification of learner and program characteristics for first language literacy, ESL literacy, or a combination of the two.)

(4) Evaluation studies are also needed, using a range of assessment instruments, including learner-generated, program-generated, and where appropriate for statistical comparisons, standardized measures. These evaluations need to document the factors which lead to enhanced literacy achievement.

Conclusion. The issues of content and purpose of literacy are critically important to bilingual learners and communities. Literacy is a powerful force which can profoundly affect the roles and relationships of an individual within the family and the immediate and wider communities. Individual adults have a role to play in setting their own goals, identifying the language of literacy, contributing to the content of the program, and assessing their own growth. We, as a profession, also have an important role to play in the process.

References

Aaron, I. E. et al. 1990. The past, present, and future of literacy education: Comments from a panel of distinguished educators, Part I. The Reading Teacher, 43, 4:302-311.

Adult Performance Level (APL) Project Staff. 1975. Adult functional competency: A summary. Austin: University of Texas. ED 114 609

Auerbach, E. 1989. Toward a socio-contextual approach to family literacy. Harvard Educational Review, 59,2:165-181.

Auerbach, E. 1990. Making meaning, making change: A guide to participatory curriculum development for adult ESL and family literacy. Boston: University of Massachusetts, English Family Literacy Project. Englewood Cliffs, N.J. and Washington, D.C.: Prentice Hall Regents/Center for Applied Linguistics, in press.

Burtoff, M. 1985. Haitian Creole literacy study. Final report submitted to the Haitian Centers Council, Inc. Washington, D.C.: Center for Applied Linguistics.

Center for Applied Linguistics (CAL). 1983. From the classroom to the workplace: Teaching ESL to adults. Washington, D.C.: Center for Applied Linguistics.

Chisman, F. P., ed. 1990. Leadership for literacy: The national agenda. San Francisco: Jossey-Bass.

Chisman, F. P. 1989. Jump start. The Federal role in adult literacy. Final Report of the Project on Adult Literacy. Southport, Conn.: Southport Institute for Policy Analysis. ED 302 675.

Collins, S. D. et al. 1989. So we can use our own names, and write the laws by which we live: Educating the new U.S. labor force. Harvard Educational Review, 59, 4:454-469.
Commission on the Skills of the American Workforce. 1990. High skills or low wages. Rochester, N.Y.: National Center on Education and the Economy.
Crandall, J. A. 1981. Functional literacy of clerical workers: Strategies for minimizing literacy demands and maximizing available information. Paper presented at the Annual Meeting of the American Association of Applied Linguistics, New York, N.Y., December 28. ED 317 796
Crandall, J. A. 1984. Adult literacy. In: Annual Review of Applied Linguistics, vol. 4, R. Kaplan, ed. Rowley, MA: Newbury House.
Crandall, JoAnn. 1988. The bottom line: Basic skills in the workplace. Washington, D.C.:U.S. Department of Education and U.S. Department of Labor.
Crandall, J. A., and S. Imel. 1991. Issues in adult literacy education. The ERIC Review. 1.2:2-9.
Fingeret, A. 1983. Social network: A new perspective on independence and illiterate adults. Adult Education Quarterly. 33, 3:133-146.
Fingeret, A. 1988. The politics of adult literacy education. Paper presented at the National Urban Literacy Conference, Washington, D.C., January 22. ED 292 053.
Fingeret, A. and P. Jurmo, eds. 1989. Participatory literacy education. San Francisco: Jossey-Bass.
Freire, P. 1970. Pedagogy of the oppressed. New York: The Continuum Publishing Corporation.
Freire, P. 1973. Education for critical consciousness. New York: Seabury Press.
Harman, D. 1985. Turning illiteracy around: An agenda for national action. New York: Business Council for Effective Literacy.
Harman, D. 1987. Illiteracy: A national dilemma. New York: Cambridge Book Company.
Hunter, C. S., and D. Harman. 1985. Adult literacy in the United States. New York: McGraw Hill.
Irwin, P. M. 1987. Adult literacy issues, programs, and options. Issue Brief. Washington, D.C.: Congressional Research Service. ED 317 794.
Johnston, W.B., and A. H. Packer. 1987. Workforce 2000: Work and workers for the 21st century. Indianapolis, Ind.: Hudson Institute.
Kazemek, F. E. 1988. Necessary changes: Professional involvement in adult literacy programs. Harvard Educational Review. 58.4:464-487.
Kirsch, I., and A. Jungeblut. 1986. Literacy: Profiles of America's young adults. Princeton: Educational Testing Service.
Lytle, S. L., and M. Wolfe. 1989. Adult literacy education: Program evaluation and learner assessment. Columbus, Ohio: ERIC Clearinghouse on Adult, Career, and Vocational Education. ED 316 665.
Ramirez, A. 1990. Literacy in a second language: Learners, languages, and texts. Paper delivered at the Third Gutenberg Conference on Literacy across Languages and Cultures, Albany, N.Y., March 2-3.
Robson, B. 1981. Alternatives in ESL and literacy: Ban Vinai. Asia Foundation Final Report.
Savage, K. L. 1985. Teaching strategies for developing literacy skills in non-native speakers of English. In: Adult literacy: Focus on limited-English-proficient

learners, D. Longfield et al., eds. Rosslyn, Va.: National Clearinghouse for Bilingual Education.
Scribner, S., and M. Cole. 1981. The psychology of literacy. Cambridge: Harvard University Press.
Spener, D. 1990. The Freirean approach to adult literacy education. Washington, D.C.: National Clearinghouse on Literacy Education.
Sticht, T. G., and B. A. McDonald. 1989. Making the nation smarter: The intergenerational transfer of cognitive ability. San Diego, Calif.: Applied Behavioral and Cognitive Sciences. ED 309 279.
van Ek, J. A. 1975. The threshold level in a European unit/credit system for language learning by adults. Strasbourg: Council of Europe.
Weinstein-Shr, G. 1989. From problem-solving to celebration: Discovering and creating meaning through literacy. ED 313 916.
Wiley, T. G. 1988. Literacy, biliteracy, and educational achievement among the Mexican origin population in the United States. Ph.D. dissertation. Los Angeles: University of Southern California.
Wiley, T. G. 1991. Literacy and the adult Mexican-origin population: What a biliteracy analysis can tell us. Journal of the Association of Mexican American Education. In press.

Soviet phraseology: Problems in the analysis and teaching of idioms

Maria Tarasevitch
Moscow State Linguistic University (Eastern Michigan University)

Phraseology is a relatively new branch of linguistics which attracts the attention of an ever increasing number of scholars. It is impossible to dwell upon all the varying and sometimes conflicting approaches to phraseology in Soviet linguistics in one paper, that is why I shall be concentrating on the concept elaborated at Moscow State Linguistic University which I have the honor of representing here.

It was a long time ago that linguists became aware of the existence in the language of special larger-than-word units: word-groups consisting of two or more words whose combination is integrated as a unit with a specialized meaning of the whole, e.g. mention of such language academicians F. I. Buslaev 1861, A. A. Potebnya 1862, and some others though they used different terms to denote them. The term *phraseology* was first used by the Swiss linguist Charles Bally (1905 and 1909) when he wrote about different types of word-groups that vary in the degree of stability from free word-groups to phraseological unities. He compared the latter with chemical substances which have a set of properties different from the properties of the elements that make them up.

The first attempt to study various word-groups on a scientific basis was made by the outstanding Russian linguist A. A. Shakhmatov (1925) and a few years later another linguist, Professor E. D. Polivanov (1931), pointed out the need to establish a branch of linguistics that would study the peculiarities of word-groups. However it was not until the 1940s that academician V. V. Vinogradov (1947) actually undertook such an investigation and suggested the first classification of phraseological units in the Russian language. Later years saw a remarkable rise in the interest in this new branch of linguistics and a further development of its theory.

To conclude this brief survey of the development of phraseology I have to mention the Soviet school of English phraseology which is connected with the names of N. N. Amosova (1963) and A. V. Kunin who is the author of several books on the theory of English phraseology (1970, 1972, 1986) and the English-Russian phraseological dictionary 1984. A. V. Kunin is a founder of a phraseological school as the advisor for about 80 doctoral dissertations on the subject.

At present, phraseology is defined as a branch of linguistics studying phraseological units (henceforth PUs), i.e. stable word-groups that are not based on the generative patterns of free word-groups and are characterized by a complexity of meaning. This definition sums up the basic criteria one should have in mind to determine whether a word-group is a PU; thus they show:

(a) stability of use,
(b) structural separateness,
(c) complexity of meaning, and
(d) the fact that they are not built on the generative pattern of free word-groups.

The criterion of the stability of use stands for the ready-made reproduction of PUs as language units known to the members of a language community and not the 'private property' of an individual. Structural separateness of PUs describes them as separately spelt language units—a feature that helps distinguish them from compound words. The complexity of meaning signifies the non-compositionality of phraseological meaning which is different from the sum total of the meanings of the components making up the PUs. The fourth criterion helps further differentiate stable and free word-groups: the latter can be freely made up in the flow of speech according to a set of patterns. For example, the verb *drink* is a part of a pattern *drink + n* (something that can be drunk) and one can safely predict that a name of any new drink will enter this pattern. There is no such regularity in phraseology where each unit is made up according to its own unique rule.

Of the four above-mentioned criteria only complexity of meaning allows some variability which enables us to differentiate between three groups of PUs which share all the other peculiarities, namely:

(a) idioms,
(b) semi-idioms, and
(c) phrasemes.

Idioms are PUs with the highest degree of semantic complexity. Their non-compositionality can be complete or partial, as the meaning of their components can be transferred fully, e.g. *kick the bucket*, or partially, e.g. *pay through the nose*.

Semi-idioms are a peculiar group of PUs that have two meanings: the first is usually terminological and thus more complicated than the sum of the literal meanings of its components and the second is a metaphorically transferred variant of the first, original meaning, e. g. *mark time,* (1) military: 'to stamp the feet as when marching but without moving forward', (2) 'to wait until further progress becomes possible'.

Phrasemes are characterized by the least degree of semantic complexity. The peculiarity of these units is that they retain the literal meaning of their components but the word-group as a whole has an extra, inferred semantic element which is added to the sum of the meanings of the components, e.g. *nod one's head* has the inferred meaning of 'agreement', or *yellow pages* that of a 'special part of a telephone book'.

These types of word-groups constitute the subject matter of phraseology which is one of the language universals since there are no languages that do not have PUs. PUs form a treasure trove in any language as they reflect the history, culture, and life of a people speaking this language and though some PUs are shared by many peoples and languages, e.g. Biblical PUs *the prodigal son* or *to cast pearls before swine*; there are many others that have distinct national character, e.g. American idioms: *to bury the hatchet*, or *the last of the Mohicans*.

Since PUs form an integral part of any language, they have to be considered for teaching and learning purposes. Theoretically, language students should be encouraged to study them both for understanding and usages since adequate and apt use of PUs undoubtedly is one of the characteristics of a native speaker or a person who has mastered a foreign language. Paradoxically, language teachers are not enthusiastic about including PUs in their teaching materials and, further, sometimes ask their students to refrain from using them. There are probably two reasons for this. One, ungrammatical use of PUs is relatively easy to overcome as grammatically correct speech is any teacher's aim in the first place and teachers devote a lot of time, effort, energy, and ingenuity to achieve it. The other reason is the frequent incorrect use of PUs. One can cope with that only if one can answer the question why students make mistakes in using the PUs they have learnt. Research suggests several reasons for such mistakes.

First, PUs name or describe a situation expressively and very often in an emotive way and the failure to appreciate and take into account the connotational aspect of meaning can lead to unfortunate mistakes. This peculiarity was proved by an experiment carried out at Moscow State Linguistic University. Two groups of Russian students with a good command of the English language—certified teachers of English and graduate students majoring in English—were given a list of PUs with dictionary definitions and asked to use them in sentences of their own. The subjects in the experiment were not familiar with the PUs on the list and had to rely on the supplied definitions. The otherwise identical assignments differed in the type of definitions with which the two groups were supplied. In one case these were plain statements of the denotational meaning; in the other the definitions contained elements that could help decipher the connotational aspect (e.g. the etymology of the image involved or various dictionary labels). The results of the experiment were dramatic: in the first group which had the denotational meanings of PUs 98% of the participants failed to use the PUs correctly while the other group carried out the assignment successfully.

Secondly, mistakes in the use of PUs occur as a result of ignorance of the cultural component of the meaning of a PU. If, for example, somebody comments on the progress of a good student saying that hardwork is *in his blood* meaning that it is characteristic of, or natural to, this person, the speaker may just get away with it. But he should be aware of the implied offense to the person's family if he uses the same phrase about a student who is cheating in his tests since the cultural component of the meaning of the PU *to be in one's blood* is that of a feature or quality received through heredity, because of family or ancestral association.

Thirdly, mistakes in the use of PUs result from the student's native language experience. Some languages have PUs that are based on similar or identical metaphors, but the different treatment of these images leads to the difference in meaning. For example, both the English and the Russian languages have the PU *to cross somebody's path*; but if in English it simply means 'to meet', its meaning in Russian is 'to outwit, to best somebody, to frustrate somebody's plans'.

Finally, PUs can change their initial meaning in the language. This may seem a contradictory statement. It is recognized that diachronically some PUs can and do change their initial meanings, e.g. *there is no love lost between them* used to mean 'that the people in question loved each other very much' but at present it means 'that they hate each other'. However, if we allow a possibility of semantic changes for PUs in speech would it not amount to the elimination of the criterion of stability which is most vital for the theory of phraseology? Such a statement is not strange for the semantic change implied should be treated in terms of variability of dialect, i.e. the change in the meaning of a PU depends on which person in the act of communication employs the PU.

There are no semantic changes in PUs used about a third person, but in the case of the two direct participants in the communication the meaning alters, depending on whether the unit is used by the speaker about himself or about the addressee. The derogatory or negative connotation of a PU lessens when it is used about the first person, e.g. if the person describes himself as *once a fool always a fool* he does not really mean that he is foolish, the remark is aimed at getting compassion, reassurance. The same PU used about the addressee—the second person— sounds different, its negative connotation, negative reaction to this person increases and the PU becomes insulting. In the case of PUs with positive connotation the change goes in the same direction: the connotation increases when such a PU, e.g. *an old hand,* is used about the second person, but when used about oneself the PU sounds ironical or joking, and if the speaker is not aware of it, he can make a bad mistake. The only possible way out of this difficulty is to point out to students the reasons for possible mistakes and to train them to remember the communicative aim of speech always, so that there is never any discrepancy between 'the aim of the utterance' and 'its form' in the effort to achieve successful communication.

References

Amosova, N. N. 1963. Osnovy angliyskoy frazeologii 'The fundamentals of English phraseology'. Leningrad.
Bally, Charles. 1905. Précis de stylistique. Geneva.
Bally, Charles. 1909. Traite de la stylistique française. Geneva.
Buslayev, F. I. 1861. Istoricheskiye ocherki narodnoy slovesnosti i iskusstva 'Historical essays of popular philology and art'. St. Petersburg.
Kunin, A. V. 1970. Angliyskaya frazeologya 'English phraseology'. Moscow.
Kunin, A. V. 1972. Frazeologya sovremennogo angliyskogo yazika 'Phraseology of the modern English language). Moscow.
Kunin, A. V. 1984. Anglo-russkiy frazeologicheskiy slovar' 'English-Russian phraseological dictionary. Moscow.
Kunin, A. V. 1986. Kurs frazeologii sovremennogo angliy-skogo yazika 'A course in modern English phraseology'. Moscow.
Polivanov, E. D. 1931. Za marksistkoye yazikoznaniye 'For Marxist language theory'. Moscow. Potebnya, A. A. 1862. Misl' irech. 'Mind and speech'. Zhurnal ministerstva narodnogo prosveshcheniya. St. Petersburg.
Shakhmatov, A. A. 1925. Sintaksis russkogo iuzyka 'Russian syntax'. Moscow.
Vinogradov, V. V. 1947. Ob osnovnykh frazeologicheskikh yedinits v russkom yazike 'On the principal types of phraseological units in the Russian language'. Akademik A. A. Shakhmatov (1864-1920). Moscow-Leningrad.

Shared knowledge

John M. Sinclair*
University of Birmingham, England

Introduction. It is my belief that a new understanding of the nature and structure of language will shortly be available as a result of the examination by computer of large collections of texts. This kind of study, which has been in progress for thirty years but is just becoming fashionable, is called 'corpus linguistics'. It began—almost simultaneously on both sides of the Atlantic, but independently—innocently enough, as a documentation exercise, both in the U.S.A. at Brown University in a study of the printed language of the year 1961, (Kuera and Francis 1967) and in the U.K. in a study of transcribed conversation, also in 1961 (Jones and Sinclair 1974). However, the view of language obtained from these studies is not the same as the generally received view of language, and gradually the effect is being felt within descriptive linguistics.

The first area to be strongly affected was lexicography (Sinclair 1985), and it is already clear that corpus evidence will become the foundation of virtually all lexicography in the future. There is important work showing in variation study, a vast subject in which the computer is clearly going to be central (Biber 1988).

Lexicography and variety study have traditionally remained on the fringes of language theory and description, while grammar and phonology have retained a central position, on high ground. The new evidence is just beginning to raise queries about the relation of grammar to meaning, and is supporting the growing movement towards functional grammars and lexicogrammars.

Corpus linguistics and language teaching. All this has no direct bearing on the way languages may be presented in a pedagogical context. It says nothing about the way languages are learned, and indeed most corpora in general use restrict themselves to the language of adult native speakers; their evidence simply does not concern interim states of language acquisition, whether the language is native, second, or foreign.

---

* Copyright © 1991 by J. M. Sinclair.

It is important to be clear about this, because the position of corpus linguistics can be seriously misrepresented. If it is associated with a particular approach to language pedagogy—particularly a behaviourist one, which is the most likely target—it can be ridiculed and its effect nullified.

Many spokespeople in language education are nervous about new evidence, about having to say new and different things about a language. Wherever methodology becomes dominant, as at present in ESOL and EFL, there is a natural tendency to avoid facing new information on the subject being taught because the teachers' concentration is on how to teach it and they tend to take for granted what it is that is to be taught. The balance in such cases is wrong, and important new knowledge can be hidden from teachers and students for a considerable time. For those who are fearful of new insights, the best way of dealing with uncomfortable material is to tie it to a discredited methodology and hope it will go away.

In the case of corpus linguistics, it would be a big mistake to ignore the growing evidence, because the evidence is fairly rapidly becoming available to the general public, to anyone who has a personal computer, and has only been limited by the technicalities of large capacity storage. With CD-ROM and similar storage media, it will become commonplace to have available on a domestic computer far more genuine information about a language than any existing set of reference books can provide. The students will put irresistible pressure on the teachers to respond to this evidence, and it does language teachers no service to conceal this prospect from them.

In fact, I hope to show that the new evidence offers to stimulate more exciting, interesting and creative teaching than the teaching based on scant evidence and relying too heavily on intuition. For a corpus linguist, this is an interesting prospect, but just a by-product, of the research.

The corpus as a sample of the language. One of the most serious misconceptions about the corpus-based study of language is that it is confining, restricting, or limiting in some way associated with texts gone by, rather than productive and new, exciting and interesting. This comment is only ever made by people who have not studied the evidence, because it is just not true. The myth began with theoretical posturings in the early sixties, arguing that since there was no limit to the number of different possible sentences in a language, then no corpus was an adequate sample of that language. This was no doubt true from a statistical point of view. But the further step—that therefore we should not bother studying any actual texts—did not follow from the premise, although it had an unfortunate effect on the work of linguistics and language teaching for several decades.

When corpora were small, there was always the possibility of accidental gaps; the more so when scholars were fairly inexperienced in building them. With thirty years' experience, there is a good chance that this factor is now small. But however big corpora get, there will always be two factors to be considered alongside the factual reports of what is in the corpus.

On the one hand, the principles of selection will never be wholly objective. Every corpus project will have a policy, and the evidence from the corpus will be affected by that policy. However, all scientific evidence is subject to this constraint, so I do not lose any sleep over it. One important point here is that if the make-up of corpora is to come under criticism, the grounds for debate should concern the design and selection of the corpus components, and not the results. It is bad sociolinguistic argument to criticise the corpus because you do not like what it tells you about the language.

Secondly, once the data is processed, and results are available, there is an enduring problem of how to interpret those patterns for which there is some evidence, but insufficient to make a conclusive case for significance. There are always going to be a large number of patterns for which there is still not enough evidence. There is some evidence but not enough on which to base firm and accurate statements.

This will not, unfortunately, apply only to a slender margin of data, a few per cent of doubtful cases, but to something like half of it—a very large proportion indeed. How does one assess a single occurrence of a word, when a word which occurs 100 times shows several unusual instances? Is the lone example a typical one or an untypical one? The only answer is to collect more examples until the initial pattern is reinforced or replaced by the additional examples. But by then you will have collected single instances of new rarer patterns, and so it goes on.

One response, then, to the initial criticism of a corpus as a sample is that any corpus is a good and valid sample *of some* aspects of language patterning, but not all. Moreover by studying the corpus it is possible to discover precisely what patterns it does exemplify adequately. The corpus then in a simple and direct sense, demonstrates its own validity.

Widdowson's criticism. I have changed the emphasis of what I am saying on this occasion in response to H. G. Widdowson's opening talk (*this volume*), in which he insisted on the rights of pedagogy to determine its own affairs. While paying due attention to the findings of corpus linguistics, pedagogy will not in any sense be bound by them.

I would like to say that I wholly endorse that position, and have said as much on many occasions. The way a language is taught is quite independent of the structure of the target language, even though the efficacy of the teaching is eventually measured by mastery of that language. That fact alone would suggest that pedagogics should be aware *in detail* of the state of knowledge about the language, but need not be bound by it.

I remember an Australian teacher of opera singers who came to England many years ago and horrified the establishment by his teaching method. He used to make his students lie down on the floor and put large weights on their chests. I believe it was effective, and it certainly did not replicate anything one would witness in an opera.

Although Widdowson and I, then, agree broadly about the independence of pedagogy from language evidence, I think that anyone who heard his talk would certainly think that he delivered a courteous but quite serious and sustained criticism of the relevance of corpus linguistics to language teaching. I only have my memory to draw on, but I do believe that he made at least three specific criticisms:

(1) One was that the evidence from texts was confining. I believe that he has modified his position on that since his talk, but it is a point frequently made and worth tackling.
(2) A second point was that any corpus had unpredictable gaps.
(3) He pointed out that people's intuitions about language are not coextensive with their usage, as evidenced by a corpus.

Productivity. The most effective answer to the first point I think is to throw it back as a challenge; to say that actual, real language text is exhilaratingly creative, marvellously unpredictable, wayward, unruly, quite incredibly productive. Compared with the delightful inventiveness of what ordinary people actually say and write, the language offered them in conventional text books and reference books is dull, unmotivated, deeply boring, and uninteresting. The language in action, when people are trying to get things done, is fascinating no matter how banal is the task being performed.

The only way to check this is to experience it. It is highly addictive and you get hooked in no time at all. Whatever the textbooks say, language users treat the regular patterns as jumping off points, and create endless variations to suit particular purposes. The variations are not random, but are rule governed, like the underlying patterns.

This poses a problem for applied linguistics, because it may not be a good idea to immerse learners in all this variation, without guidance and tools for evaluation. But it is worth knowing which rules of the language are productive and which are not; it could have a dramatic effect on the teaching.

Widdowson contrasted the external (e-language) and the internal (i-language). Of course they can be contrasted and kept apart; they can also be compared and related, since one is just the realisation of the other. E-language faithfully reflects i-language if you know the conventions that relate them.

Last year we published a grammar that contains a lot of productive rules (Sinclair and Fox 1990). These rules are not restrictive, they are not 'do not' rules; they are 'try this one' rules where you can hardly go wrong. There is an open-ended range of possibilities and you can try your skill in simply using, trying to say what you want to say. There are in fact a large number of such rules although they do not often appear in grammar books.

Here is one tiny one by way of illustration. If you want to state a field of reference for an adjective, e.g. important in or for politics, then you can make an adverb from the adjective *political* by adding *-ly*, for example, *politically important*. This is true of any classifying adjective like *political, aesthetic, biological, technical*; there are hundreds of them and there is no restriction; any one of these can be used productively as an adverb modifying another adjective and stating the field of reference. In addition, you can put the new adverb at the front of a clause in a thematic position and say *politically, it was quite important*.

Not only that, but you can add the word *speaking* to this and make it interactive; you can say *politically speaking, it was quite important*. All three possibilities are there in an open-ended way for any such adjective that is of a classifying nature. And this is typical of the kind of productive rule of which there are hundreds if not thousands. And these are leading us to rethink the way in which grammar can be offered to a user of a language.

Frequency. As to Widdowson's point about unpredictable gaps in corpora, I think I have more or less covered that. There are many reasons why some sorts of words are infrequent, and it is certainly a policy matter for the teacher as to how far frequency is allowed to influence the design of materials. The exigencies of the kinds of conversation one can have in a classroom, the material constraints of the environment, the design of the pedagogical approach—all these may suggest a different set of priorities from what is reported from a study of a cross section of the language in general.

On the other hand, Dave Willis, a most experienced teacher, trainer and materials writer, argues cogently in his new book *The Lexical Syllabus* (1990) for considerable attention to be paid to frequency matters.

In COBUILD lexicography, as I have explained in print, frequency is a key matter because it is inescapably important in any consideration of evidence. But other factors are also weighty, and quite often in the dictionaries the first sense given is not the most frequent one.

It seems that in most cases the use of a word as a contributor to multi-word phrasal units is more frequent than its stand-alone meaning. Language is just like that, and the competent learner has to master both aspects, the stand-alone meaning of a word which is usually the meaning whch comes first in the dictionary, and its phrasal, sometimes called partially delexical meaning as it occurs in naturally idiomatic expressions. To offer only one—no matter which—is to leave a large part of the learning to chance, and to inculcate a skewed model of the language in the learner.

The meaning *have* = 'possess' is much less frequent than its prominent place in traditional dictionaries suggests, and this also goes for several other common verbs. Many less frequent words are most commonly used in phrases, (e.g. *mean, bet*) yet in dictionaries we lead the entry with the concrete, familiar 'core' meaning. The reason is to do with the way a dictionary entry is structured, and with the overall policy of the dictionary. The important thing to note is that frequency is by no means the only criterion used.

Intuition about language. Widdowson's third main point concerns intuitions. Certainly one's intuitive ideas about language are not always supported by the facts. In cases of discrepancy or conflict, which do we choose? This is a very sensitive area for language teachers who rely, often very heavily, on their intuitions. If they are native speakers, they often rely almost totally on their intuitions, and will go against the printed statements in text books, thank goodness, on occasion in order to follow their intuitions. But if there is a difference, as there often is, between your view of the way a word or a phrase works and what actually happens, then which do you choose?

The answer, perhaps surprisingly, is both. There appears to be not so much a conflict but a systematic correlation between the language patterns of which we are normally aware, and those that are subliminal. If you ask someone the meaning of a word like *have* you are presenting the word in isolation. It is not surprising that you are likely to get a meaning of the word which does not anticipate any other choices around about.

Singular and plural. Let me give a small example—both innocent in its way and also far-reaching in its implications. What is meant by singular and plural in nouns? It is generally accepted that nouns can be countable, and that most of them have a singular and a plural form. There is the formal agreement with numerals and some determiners (such as *this/these, every, many*) and, when head of the subject group, with a present-tense verb. In reference to countable entities, the forms are in complementary distribution; and the decision between them depends purely on how many are being referred to.

The boy sat on the wall
The boys sat on the wall   [made-up examples]

It may be of interest, then, to know that there are some nouns that have both singular and plural forms, but those forms do not normally have the capacity to replace each other.

One such is the noun, *eye eyes.*

If we look at the patterning of each word form, we see that they are quite different.

The two things in your head you see with are your eyes.

However the word form *eyes* is mostly used in a figurative sense. If we look at the adjectives that are used, there are: *blue eyes, brown eyes, red eyes, protuberant eyes.* But also in numbers there are: *covetous eyes, critical eyes, disbelieving eyes, humorous eyes, hypercritical eyes, manic eyes.* These are the adjectives that deal with figurative meanings of the word *eyes*. And the remainder of its patterning is made up of a large number of familiar phrases, for example:

all eyes will be on
in the eyes of
through the eyes of
rolling their eyes

The singular *eye* hardly ever means the anatomical object except when talking about injury or handicap. It occurs in a large range of phrases and this is by far the majority usage:

something took the eye
keep an eye on something
(under) the watchful eye of
turn a blind eye (to)

Commonest of all in the material I have with me is the phrase *an eye for an eye*, strangely enough. It is a fixed phrase that obviously sticks. But with most phrases there are many variations and the variations are much more interesting than the regularities.

In the eye of the storm is complemented by an interesting use *in the eye of a historical process* which is a figurative expression. *A look in the eye,* a *twinkle in the eye,* a *gleam in his devilish old eye.* Things *attract the eye, take the eye,* and *disappoint the eye.* They can come *under the studious eye* of somebody, as well as *under the watchful eye* . There was a time when *eye teeth would have been donated for something*—a strong variation of the phrase. So the pattern of the word form *eye* is essentially phrasal.

This range of phrasal and figurative meaning is not just a fringe area or idiom, but is typical of the majority usage in the language. Patterns and meanings which you would inescapably have to teach if you were going to teach English to anybody.

It might be said that this kind of usage is predictable because people have two eyes and so the relationship between the two word forms is likely to be different from something that does not naturally occur in pairs. This is so. The singular is 'available' for wide idiomatic use because it is not much needed in its physical meaning. Similar things can be said about *arm, arms*, and no doubt other parts of the body that come in pairs.

The point is that the meaning affects the structure profoundly and this is, if you like, the principal observation of corpus linguistics in the last decade. Much current description of English and presentation of it in teaching do not allow for this.

I suggest you just do not use such items as *eye* and *eyes* prominently in presenting a choice between singular and plural, because that is something that will just have to be unlearnt. There is hardly any common environment between the two words.

The only common environment I have found in the hundred instances plucked at random is: *human* which can go with either *eye* or *eyes*.

The focus of my paper was originally to be on the importance of shared knowledge in the understanding of how language is used. I would like to address this topic now, building on the ground that we have covered.

There are four relevant kinds of shared knowledge. The first two concern the structure of the language, and the other two concern the way it is deployed in communication.

I contend that language teachers should be aware of all of them, and should take up an explicit professional attitude to each of them.

(1) Subliminal mastery of phraseology. This is the foundation of fluency, naturalness, idiomaticity, appropriateness, etc. The computers are beginning to offer it to all. There is a great mass of detail, and it needs to be pedagogically processed, prioritized, made available to the learner in an acquisition routine. But make no mistake—it is certainly now available.

If a language is described from an intuitive perspective, in terms of words and meanings and grammatical choices, then the detail appears to be uncontrollable, bewildering, and without limit. The job of learning a language looks to be formidable in the extreme, and the competent foreign speaker seems to be a person of immense talent and dedication. However, it is very likely that much of the apparent disorder is created by the perspective that is initially adopted. If in fact, words and meanings do not normally co-vary, but the common units of meaning are rather flexible multi-word units, then a more adequate description will so organise the detail that it largely falls in line with the meaning, and becomes easy, rather than difficult, to learn. If also, the grammatical choices turn out in the main to be also lexical choices, then a massive simplification can be expected. If on top of that, grammar is seen as a springboard for creativity rather than as an instrument of social discipline, the pleasure of teaching and learning can increase enormously.

To begin with, the new evidence will not be very well organised, because there are no ready-made frameworks for it. Language teachers should be in at the beginning, because there is a great deal to do to build this new information into a teaching programme. Some advance warning of the kind of information can be got from the COBUILD publications, Sinclair (1987, 1991), and ICAME publications. It should be noted, however, that these are just the tip of the iceberg, some refreshing additions to familiar presentations and arguments. During this year the Bank of English expects to increase its central reference corpus from 20 million words to over 200 million words, in order to get better information on word patterning for both dictionaries and grammars.

(2) Received information about grammar, lexis, etc. This is what the fuss is usually about—whether we teach these things or not, if so how; if not how are they acquired—how is accuracy acquired? I do not want to take up a position on that, except to say that the new evidence will make considerable changes in our received information. In particular it may make it more accurate. But on the whole I would say that it will come under very considerable revision over the next few years and is best left as it is in current language teaching practice.

(3) Strict linguistic inference (including textual inference). There is a general hypothesis about language in use, that if something is obvious it is optional. The more obvious it is, the less likely it is to occur, and the more marked for meaning is its occurrence.

For example, David Brazil (1985) has shown that, in intonation, it is not necessary to express a distinctive tone pattern when the information content of the phrasing is low. Martin Warren (forthcoming) has shown that if you take the relation between an utterance and its context seriously then you can predict that anything which can be retrieved from the context can be omitted from the utterance. And so he has some recordings of service encounters which do not sound like service encounters at all because the details of the transactions are not problematic to the participants and do not need to leave a trail in the discourse.

The effect of this kind of optionality on word occurrence was noted in pioneering work on vocabulary done in France some 35 years ago

(Gougenheim et al. 1956). It was pointed out that there are a number of words in people's use of language which are not very frequent but which are 'disponibile', i.e. available when they are needed. In syntax the same principle leads to major confusions, particularly because we still tend to look only at sentences and and not at wider contexts. For example, many verbs in English are notionally transitive—like *drive, read* . . . say, but the object can be dropped when it is obvious. There are problems of ambiguity here; for example a recent headline *Schoolgirls Saved in Fells Blizzard*. Presumably they were not putting money away against a rainy day.

I predict that the interplay between text and context will become a major field of research in the coming years—exactly what are the inferences that we can take from texts. More careful definitions of meaning and inference, and pragmatic studies to relate form and meaning more accurately, will contribute to a much clearer picture.

(4) Aspects of the culture, signalled nowhere in the text, but which just have to be known. This is a type of knowledge which is popular in comprehension exercises. It is in principle without limit, and its effect must be constrained by an adequate theoretical framework. At the very simplest there must be a hypothesis of a target reader; a person who shares enough cultural assumptions with the originator of the text to understand it in a broadly similar way to the way that we assume the author intended. If you are not a target reader the text is not going to help you understand and appreciate it; but it is not a language teacher that you need, in my opinion. Your need is for a general acculturation towards the position of the target reader.

Sometimes a text will signal a reference to this type of shared knowledge, without indicating what the point at issue is. For example, in my English if you invite some one to have a drink, the range of choice may include or exclude hot drinks and/or soft drinks. It depends on some signals in the phraseology, but mainly on the occasion, the time, and the company.

The short explanation of this kind of shared knowledge is that of the target reader hypothesis. Any text identifies its target readers, and an ideal target reader is someone who shares cultural assumptions with the writer. If you do not have access to them, you should not be reading the text. Your problem is not the English language, but the cultural assumptions of the originator of the text.

Thus a British English speaker like myself may quite often be bewildered by the cultural references of American English, even though he understands the U.S. variety almost perfectly. People, places, events, and particularly acronyms are difficult to put into an appropriate cultural framework. It is not incompetence in the language, but in the culture.

The grey area between a dictionary and an encyclopedia is a physical manifestation of the dividing line.

Shared knowledge and language teaching. The types of shared knowledge that are of immediate interest to language teachers are the first and the third. The first is the one that I have concentrated on because we have only just begun to uncover it, and, as I have tried to show, it is a major new source of evidence. It will probably gradually draw in the second type and the two will merge, because the distinction between conscious and subliminal knowledge is probably accidental. In order to merge, the two types will have to be made compatible, both in theory and description. The accurate description of the language will remove many of the mysteries that lurk between specific observations of language in use and the general rules which we tend to take for granted.

The third type of shared knowledge, the textual inference, is also of interest because we are just beginning to understand the nature of discourse, and to work out precisely where meaning is created. In its turn it will probably gradually merge with the fourth type as the more accurate description of the language will remove a lot of the semantic mysteries.

Conclusion. I have made it clear that corpus linguistics makes no demands on the methodology of language teaching. It is not geared to serving any particular method, and the current software is quite neutral.

However, there are implications:

(1) There is now no reason to offer a student, as a 'model' of English, some string of words that is not attested. Of course teachers will forever make up casual examples for an unforeseen classroom need—I am not talking about that. I am talking about where a teacher, a course book writer, a grammarian, or a lexicographer offers something, claiming that it is a reliable instance of English. If it is not attested then everyone beware! Speakers of a language, strangely enough, are very poor simulators of it.

(2) The frequency of words, structures, collocations, and the like is surely a factor to be taken into account in language teaching. I expect no more, but no less. It just cannot be ignored, because it is so distinctive. One glance at the evidence shows that it is quite inescapable. The skewness of the distribution of words, of structures, and of meanings in a language is quite remarkable, a phenomenon which leads to all sorts of new ideas about language teaching.

(3) The relation between the conscious impressions we have of language and subliminal usage is also vital information for the language professional. As a corollary to this it should not ever be necessary for students to 'unlearn' anything they have been taught. They cannot be

taught everything at once, and because our knowledge of the textual detail of language has been so vague, they have been taught half-truths, generalities which apply only in some circumstances. However, we now have the information on which accurate selection can be made. Students may have to unlearn some of their own projections and hypotheses, but that is a different matter from unlearning what has been authoritatively put forward as an accurate observation about the language.

(4) The productivity evidenced by real text is so remarkable that language teachers should wonder why it is not encouraged in the learning process. Here again, it is necessary to experience the true character of language in use. From my present perspective, it is a strange irony that some authorities on language teaching, like Widdowson, can urge and value creativity in the learning process, while keeping at arm's length the documentary evidence of its central role in everyday communication.

References

Bank of English: A major new corpus of British, American, and other native speakers' English. Details from: The Corpus Administrator, Bank of English, Westmere, 50 Edgbaston Park Road, Birmingham B15 2RX, U.K.

Biber, D. 1988. Variation across Speech and Writing. Cambridge: Cambridge University Press.

Brazil, D.C. 1985. The communicative value of intonation. Discourse analysis monograph no. 8. English Language Research, University of Birmingham.

COBUILD publications: Catalogue available from Harper Collins publishers. 77-85 Fulham Palace Road, Hammersmith, London W6 8JB

Fox, G. forthcoming. Context dependency and transitivity in English. In: Computers and Language ELR Journal No 4, University of Birmingham.

Gougenheim, G., A. Michea, and T. Rivenc. 1956. Le français fondamental. In: L'Elaboration du français élementaire. Paris: Didier.

ICAME: International Corpus Archive of Modern English. Information available from Professor Stig Johansson, Dept. of British & American Studies, University of Oslo, P. O. Box 1003. Blindern 0315 Oslo 3, Norway.

Jones, S., and J. M. Sinclair. 1974. English lexical collocations. Cahiers de lexicologie. Paris Institut des professeurs de français à l'étranger.

Kuera, H., and W. Francis. 1967. Computational analysis of present-day American English. Providence, Rhode Island: Brown University Press.

Sinclair, J. M. 1985. Lexicographic evidence. In: Ilson R., ed., Dictionaries, Lexicography, and Language Learning, Pergamon Press. (ELT Documents no 120).

Sinclair, J. M.,ed., 1987. Looking up. London: Collins.

Sinclair, J. M., and G. Fox. 1990. Collins COBUILD English grammar. London: Collins.

Sinclair, J. M. 1991. Corpus concordance collocation. Oxford: Oxford University Press.

Warren, M. (forthcoming). Towards a description of the features of naturalness in conversation. Ph.D. thesis. University of Birmingham.

Willis, J. D. 1990. The lexical syllabus. London: Collins COBUILD.

Second language teaching in Poland prior to the reform of 1990

Hanna Komorowska
University of Warsaw

1 Language teaching prior to the reform of 1990. Language pedagogy in Poland attracted social and academic attention in the seventies when English became widely—although informally—identified as an indispensable part of education that had been denied to Polish students under the age of 15 and limited to 10 percent of secondary and tertiary school students.

Until 1990 it was Russian that enjoyed the status of the first foreign language to be taken up in grade 5 of the primary school, i.e. at the age of 11. Obligatory instruction lasted throughout the primary and the secondary course of schooling irrespective of the type of post-primary education selected by the student. The total number of contact hours was always kept above the magic level of 600 considered to form the international communicative minimum.

A second foreign language became part of the curriculum in grade 1 of the secondary school, i.e. at the age of 15. Courses were being offered at full secondary schools of the lycée-type only. This meant that the teaching of English, French, and German covered no more than 18 percent of the age group. Typical courses of 350 hours (3 hours per week over 4 years) were, by far, below the communicative minimum. Some exceptions to the rule could be found among schools with an extended language program. Schools of this type, very few in number, offered 6 hours of instruction per week for a total of up to 800 hours that is double the length of the regular course. These, however, were available to no more than 2 percent of the age group for all the foreign languages in the school system. It is interesting to note that the minimum length of the Russian course was kept at the level of the maximum length of all the other courses.

Since 1982 optional courses of English, French, and German have been allowed in preterminal and terminal grades of the primary school, i.e. for children aged 13 to 15. The introduction of those courses brought about unexpected results: 25 percent of the age group took advantage of the opportunity, a near-miracle if one considers the teacher shortage.

Throughout the seventies and the eighties Polish society revealed an astonishing amount of parental determination as well as voting with the children's feet to show the inadequacies of education as it was offered by the state. To cite some statistics from the all-Polish research on secondary school-leavers—launched by the author of the present paper in 1978—two thirds of urban lycée leavers admitted having received private tuition in English for a period of over 2 years. The phenomenon grew more and more conspicuous in the eighties when hundreds of private language schools mushroomed all over the country advertising courses of various types and levels.

The analysis of statistical data pertaining to foreign language teaching in Poland until the year 1990 leads many foreign educators to believe that Polish students speak fluent Russian. This is, however, not so. Several reasons can be cited to explain this seemingly unusual situation.

Firstly, Russian as the first foreign language and the language obligatory for all was a political mandate related to international alliances rather than a means of international communication. Secondly, long 'dripping' courses of 2 contact hours per week with no clear-cut objectives yielded low educational attainment. Thirdly, teaching materials served ideological rather than communicative purposes, producing the famous boomerang effects. Fourthly, the quality of teaching was very poor, and there was no opportunity to counteract halo effects of students' and parents' negative attitudes toward the political system.

Poor effects, despite considerable time investment in the learning of Russian, access to English limited to one-tenth of the age group, the communicative minimum courses available to one student in a hundred, were factors forming the picture of FL teaching before the reform.

Statistics show an interesting reverse pyramid effect that totalitarian systems often produce within their schooling. In order to conceal the fact that educational, cultural, and political freedoms were denied to the population—activities considered undesirable from the point of view of the totalitarian government were being restricted to small fractions to the society rather than completely banned. A reverse proportion of needs on the one hand and activities aiming at the satisfaction of those needs on the other hand, therefore, occur as

- no one, out of 100 percent of primary school students, was allowed to take a regular English course;
- half of the lycée students took such a course; lycées, however, take not more than a fifth of the age cohort;
- the majority had access to a language course at college, tertiary education, however, embraces only 10 percent of the age group and offers short courses.

A propaganda effect was, therefore, successfully attained. Those who participated in international exchanges were likely to come from the small fraction of lycée or university graduates, which helped to preserve the façade of high quality in the educational system.

2 Research in applied linguistics and language teaching. In the situation as depicted above, language pedagogy in Poland was able to gain its status in the field of linguistics, but not in the field of educational sciences. In fact, it did gain its academic status as part of English-Polish contrastive projects. First degrees in the field were granted in the early seventies. A strong linguistic orientation was recommended partly to ensure high academic standards and partly to protect the field from the then-strong ideological bias of the educational sciences. Research concentrated on prognosticating success and predicting and counteracting interference errors as well as on assessing the value of particular language teaching methods in the Polish context. No learner-centered approach had a chance to develop due to the importance of the search for methods applicable to large-size classes.

Changes in the secondary school syllabus design and materials development were being introduced in an attempt to achieve an acceptable balance between the audiolingual and the cognitive approaches. The lack of radicalism typical of the seventies had its advantages for the practice of language teaching, although it seemed negative from the point of view of theory construction.

At the same time, a fair amount of research activity was undertaken at universities and curriculum development centers. In the seventies, research focused on teacher variables, while in the eighties learner variables were seen to prevail within diagnostic research designs.

A number of the advantages and disadvantages can be distinguished as connected with the above mentioned trends. Let us first turn to the teacher-oriented research of the seventies. Its definite advantage can be found in the very fact of starting disciplined reflection in the new field given so far to trial and error procedures. Implications and applications, however, remained limited as several factors operating in the country made it difficult to construct coherent theories and concentrate on innovative solutions. Such factors can be traced back to both sociopolitical and methodological spheres. Sociopolitical obstacles can be found in the incapability of the system to admit need or imperfection, let alone shortage or failure—incapability paradoxically accompanied by pressures to assist educational institutions through research and experimentation. As no educational difficulty stood a chance of being discussed in the open—the silent function of applied linguistic research was to compensate for the deficient educational system. In effect, lifebelts were then labelled as experimentation, which brought about distrust of research methodology.

Obstacles can also be sought in the methodological sphere. Inability to deal with confounded variables, emotional attachment to hypotheses, selective samples and a tendency to deal with easily measurable, rather than important, variables contributed to the loss of credibility of empirical research.

The situation changed considerably between the seventies and the eighties when the first large-scale diagnostic projects were launched which were oriented toward the learner and learner language. This meant transferring of emphasis from ad hoc improvements to the cause-result studies of mechanisms underlying language learning. More sophisticated sampling, improved apparatus, and more complex research designs were used—inviting broader generalizations and finer distinctions between factors. The typical pendulum-swing can, however, be noticed in the scarcity of research integrating teacher and learner variables. Problems posed by the nature of the discipline were still there; however, the most important of them caused:

- difficulty in using research instruments to measure effective variables as well as to assess the communicative value of learners' utterances;
- difficulty in assessing nonlinear developmental aspects of learner language;
- difficulty in controlling global variables; and,
- difficulty in assessing factors of non-verbal communication and group interaction.

3 The innovative activity of the eighties. The eighties in Poland brought about interest in research methodology, testing, and evaluation. Structural-notional syllabi, followed by first communicative materials, promoted interest in classroom techniques.

Innovative activities in the field of curriculum construction, syllabus design, and classroom methodology increased considerably. Small research projects, in partial fulfillment of M.A. or Ph.D. requirements, were often launched at universities. Large-scale national projects were practically non-existent. Innovative activity was definitely useful in the out-dated class-lesson system. Frequently, however, it failed to fulfill such basic methodological requirements as:

- not always did diagnostic research precede innovation;
- not always could innovation avoid fulfilling compensatory rather than improvement functions;

- not always did systemic innovation of the organizational type precede innovation in the field of teaching methodology;
- not always was the value of innovation assessed for specific contexts.

All the above led in many cases to the sorcerer's apprentice effect whereby research results were difficult to explain, account for, and replicate. The mushrooming of small-scale innovative projects in the Poland of the eighties had an important stimulating effect on the backwater school routine—the social value of innovation was, therefore, considered larger than the methodological one.

4 The 1990 reform of language teaching. 1989—the year of the implementation of the Polish Round Table debates of 1990—opened with the reform and promotion of language education in Poland. Action to be undertaken was designed by the Expert Committee for Foreign Language Education on the basis of a report on the state of FL teaching in Poland—completed in the fall of 1989 by the author of the present paper.

Russian lost its obligatory status, a choice of a foreign language was made possible, and a new language policy was implemented.

The guidelines for the educational policy of the nineties can be identified as tendencies:

- to promote one foreign language in primary schools;
- to promote two foreign languages in secondary schools;
- to recognize the value of English as a means of international communication;
- to encourage intensive training; and,
- to encourage early language start.

There was no movement to eliminate Russian from the curriculum; attention had, however, been drawn to the fact that emphasis should be relocated from inefficient, extensive teaching of Russian to well-focused intensive instruction geared to communicative purposes and provided for smaller groups of learners in combination with another foreign language.

The important goal was to promote one foreign language, preferably English, throughout the whole of the population and a second foreign language throughout at least 60 percent of the population.

The present state of foreign language teaching can be described as follows. The first foreign language becomes obligatory from age 11. Language choice is limited by the teacher shortage, but still in the first year of the reform as many as 32% take English, 22% German, 5%

French, and about 40% Russian. Percentages in urban areas are more favorable to western languages while in the rural regions, where the shortage of teachers is much more severe, Russian prevails. Many schools took advantage of the opportunity to introduce early language start. The second foreign language—whether English, German, French, Russian, or Spanish—becomes obligatory at the secondary school. In several big towns courses are being offered of less widely spoken languages as, for instance, Italian, Swedish, Hungarian, and Japanese. With the increase in the number of private schools, more intensive courses will be promoted that will implement new methodologies and offer a broader selection of languages. Innovation reached state schools in the form of new curricula that combined structural and functional criteria applicable to primary school language teaching. The relatively new communicative curricula worked out for secondary schools in the mid-eighties are being updated along the lines of The New Threshold Level of the Council of Europe.

5 The 1990 reform of the system of teacher training. Implementing the language reform would prove absolutely impossible without changes at the tertiary level aimed at increasing the number of teachers. Otherwise, a free choice of languages would remain but a legal possibility and paper freedom, with 1,800 teachers of English in a state school system now calling for at least 20,000.

At the moment of the implementation of the modern languages reform in February 1990, it was evident that the universities alone would not provide the 20,000 teachers thatPoland needs. English departments at ten universities altogether produce 300 graduates each year. A century would have passed by the time the desired number is achieved, or more, since academically trained graduates do not treat schools as workplaces where they can use their linguistic and literary background. Increasing the intake of students at universities did not seem worthwhile considering low social mobility indices. Moreover, it was clear that the university does not develop practical teaching skills as the system is based on a highly theoretical, one language-bound five-year M.A. course of linguistics and literature offered in a variety of departments of philology.

To solve problems connected with the demand for teachers of foreign languages, a new system of 3-year B.A. courses at newly-opened teacher training colleges was devised and implemented in October 1990. At that time, fifty colleges opened with 41 tracks for English, 19 tracks for French, and 13 tracks for German offering courses for a total of 1,500 students of English, 400 students of French, and 400 students of German. Efforts are now being put into the opening of a Spanish and an Italian college as well as into increasing the intake of students.

Seven large universities, each with a university college, function as regional centers to provide supervision and assistance to smaller colleges in the area, thus forming clusters of five to nine regional institutions.

The existence of a relatively large number of colleges is due to local community pressure to establish a teacher training center for the region and to decision making at the national level based on the awareness of low social mobility levels which do not guarantee teachers for smaller places even if a bigger intake is planned for large university towns.

Colleges offer intermediate to advanced language courses as they take secondary school graduates who have completed a 4-year language course and passed a highly selective entrance exam. Colleges, therefore, are not viewed as a channel for the retraining of teachers of Russian. Since no restrictions have been introduced regarding age or profession exercised before entering the college, the teachers of Russian can become college students according to regular procedures.

Within the curriculum framework for the 3-year course of 24 hours per week, colleges offer instruction through the medium of the foreign language. Typically 60 percent of the time is devoted to language enrichment, 20 percent to teacher training, 10 percent to education for democracy through language and culture classes, 5 percent to history of the language and its varieties, and 5 percent to a compact course on the history of literature. It is assumed that, from the time planned for practical language teaching, 60 percent will be content-based. During the remaining 40 percent of the time, language skills are to be developed so as to present simultaneously methods and techniques of language enrichment. Self-, teacher-, and peer-observation thus developed will be more regularly employed later during practice teaching periods in schools and at FLT methodology classes at college. Cross-curricular activities are recommended to bridge the development of integrated language skills of college students with the development and maintenance of teaching skills.

Colleges are formed under two different legal acts. Colleges situated in the university structure operate under the higher education act, while colleges in non-university towns situated within the structure of Local Educational Authorities operate under the school act. The former enjoy more freedom in terms of course content and syllabi; the latter are obliged to follow central guidelines. LEA colleges can only be established on the condition that assistance and supervision of a university department or of a university college will be provided. Assistance can take the form of joint entrance and diploma examinations, workshops, and summer courses as well as study visits by the affiliated college staff to universities and consultancy visits by the university staff to colleges.

The new teacher training system is expected to pave the way for new forms of teacher training in subject areas other than that of modern languages. The new system will implement educational reforms as qualified teachers will be provided in sufficient numbers. New teachers are likely to become agents of change beneficial to a system where asking a question can still be viewed as undermining the teacher's authority. Modern language teaching methodology is of immense help here as it has long been acquainted with the values of interpersonal communication, free flow of information, and learner-centered education.

6 Future activity: research and teaching practice. Language pedagogy of the nineties has to concentrate on the implementation of language reform as well as of the new system of teacher training. Once fundamental organizational and curricular problems have been solved, it will be time to focus attention on both the 'know how' of language teaching and teacher training and dissemination of experience into other educational areas.

As far as research in applied linguistics and language teaching is concerned, the situation calls for nation-wide research and development activity, mass media support for language teaching and teacher training as well as for all the logistic support for the language reforms. The second line of research of great significance for the country is connected to the problem of personality growth through language with FL learning as a means to promote critical thinking, negotiation, and cooperation. This bridges the practice of language teaching with broader educational values, a principal aim for a country at the very beginning of a long road toward learning how to function as a democracy.

Greek diglossia to Greek dimorphia:
A new dilemma for linguists and teachers

Elli Doukanari*
Georgetown University

Introduction. Ferguson, in his classic 1959 paper, describes diglossia as a language situation in which two or more varieties of the same language coexist. Other researchers extend Ferguson's original concept of diglossia to different languages and/or styles. Among others, Fishman (1967), Fasold (1984) and Britto (1986) provide discussions on this issue. This paper follows Ferguson's notion of diglossia as the coexistence of two varieties of the same language, where one, the Low variety, is the acquired 'natural' language, and the other, the High variety, is a superposed variety. This language situation was shared by several speech communities, among them Arabic, Swiss German, Haitian Creole, and Modern Greek. In 1976, the Greek government abolished diglossia and established the Low variety, Demotikí, as the official language. In this study, I provide evidence that elements of the High variety, Katharévousa, still exist in contemporary Greek as the language has moved from the state of diglossia to the state of monoglossia; and I address linguistic and pedagogical problems which exist in the current language as a result of diglossia.

Greek diglossia. The two varieties involved in Greek diglossia were Katharévousa and Demotikí. Katharévousa, literally the 'puristic language', was the variety artificially created by juxtaposing the archaic Greek with the vernacular of the nineteenth century. It was taught formally and was what Ferguson refers to as the High variety which was used for written and the most formal spoken situations. Katharévousa had been established as the official language of the Greek state since 1830 and continued to be the official language of Greece until 1976. Demotikí, literally meaning the 'language of the people', was the vernacular which 'naturally' evolved over a period of

---

* This paper is dedicated to the memory of my loving friend and classmate ALKIS IACOVIDES who lost his life prematurely in an automobile accident in June 1991.

I would like to acknowledge the following: Dean James E. Alatis, of the Georgetown University School of Languages and Linguistics, who has referred me to useful literature and has kindly lent me all his valuable books on the Greek language and diglossia that helped to make this study possible, John J. Staczek and Nadine O'Connor Divito for their valuable comments and constructive discussions, and Stavros Tsarouchas, the educational consultant at the Greek Embassy in Washington, D.C., for his constructive discussions and reference to valuable books.

many centuries from Ancient Greek. It was the language first acquired by a child at home and what Ferguson refers to as the Low variety, which was used in everyday conversations. Demotikí also included the regional dialects. Among others, the following provide more detailed information on Greek diglossia and its historical evolution: Hatzidakis (1915), Thomson (1960), Peridis (1965), Mandilaras (1972), Babiniotis (1979), Karanikolas (1979), Browning (1969, 1982) and Mackridge (1987).

In addition to the different situations in which each variety functioned, there were differences between Katharévousa and Demotikí in terms of phonology, morphology, lexicon, and syntax. It is important to understand, however, that the distinction between Katharévousa and Demotikí was not absolute. The two varieties could more adequately be represented on a continuum with extreme Demotikí on one end, and extreme Katharévousa on the other. Various hybrids, intermediate varieties emerged, using an admixture of Katharévousa and Demotikí to different degrees, as indicated in Figure 1.

Figure 1. Continuum of Katharévousa and Demotikí.

```
                    Hybrids
       Demotikí                    Katharévousa
       <----------------------------------------------->
```

Some of these hybrids reached the status of being defined formally. For example, one hybrid was called Miktí 'Mixed', another Kathomilouméni 'vernacular, colloquial'. Browning (1982) describes Mirambel's (1937) distinction of five different degrees of the Greek language which overlap.

Given the diglossic situation in Greece, the LANGUAGE QUESTION (Which variety would it be most appropriate to recognize and establish as the 'official' language of Greece?) became more and more of a political issue. The Demotikí variety became associated with the political Left, and the Katharévousa variety became associated with the political Right.

In addition, there were also linguistic and pedagogical problems associated with diglossia:

- Educators were unable to design a program appropriate to teach Katharévousa.
- Because of its complexity, only highly educated people could master Katharévousa and that was usually achieved by a thorough study of Ancient Greek and Katharévousa by the individuals themselves.
- Teachers had to spend a lot of time ˚explaining in Demotikí the material that had been previously presented in lectures and textbooks in either Katharévousa or Miktí 'Mixed'. Therefore, a lot of valuable teaching time was spent explaining language rather than content.

- Many people, especially the less educated, had difficulty understanding even the newspapers, although most of the language of the press did not use pure Katharévousa, but an admixture of the two varieties.
- People from regions who spoke a dialect (e.g. Greek Cypriots), had to learn both standard Demotikí (Athenian Greek) in order to be able to communicate with Greeks from other regions, and Katharévousa in order to understand among others, official documents, political speeches, and newspapers.
- To compensate for communicative problems which arose in diglossia, a lot of uncodified and unstable intermediate varieties (hybrids) emerged, as previously mentioned; this created other problems. Individuals used their own admixture of the two varieties. As Lampsas (1975:6) put it, 'there were as many mixed languages as there were Greeks' [my translation]. These mixed varieties were unacceptable to a lot of people because they were considered vulgar.
- It was not uncommon for a person to use Katharévousa or Demotikí inappropriately and to become an object of ridicule (Ferguson 1959). That is, a person might use one of these varieties in a situation where it would not be socially appropriate for that variety. For example, a person might use Demotikí in a formal speech, or Katharévousa in an ordinary conversation.
- Since Katharévousa was mostly associated with the written language and Demotikí with the spoken, a significant distinction between spoken and written was created. Of course in every language there is a distinction between the spoken and written modes, but in Greek, the gap was great. Pappageotes and Macris (1964) made a distinction between the different degrees of spoken and written, indicating the difficulties encountered when using the Greek language.
- The problems were not only limited to native speakers but also affected foreign students learning Greek. In most textbooks (e.g. *Spoken Greek* by Kahane et. al. Book One 1976, and *Demotic Greek* by Bien et al. 1972), it was considered necessary to include a statement explaining that foreign students learning Demotic Greek could not be quaranteed that they would be able to understand the language of the newspapers, courts, university lectures etc. [my emphasis].
- Another problem also identified by Ferguson (1959) was transcription. When citing words from Greek to English, the question was which variety to use. If words were cited in Demotikí, which Demotikí variety should be chosen since Demotikí included the standard (Athenian Greek) with the regional dialects.

- Spelling was another problem. Katharévousa spelling was relatively consistent, but there was not a generally accepted orthography for Demotikí.

In 1976, in an attempt to abolish diglossia and its linguistic, educational, and political problems, the Greek government decided that the official language of education and state should be the language of the people. Therefore, the government declared Demotikí as the official language, abolishing Katharévousa. The Demotikí variety, according to the Greek law, should be based on Triandafyllidis' Grammar and be rendered free from 'vulgarisms' (Law 309, 1976).

Today we would expect, since we have monoglossia (only one variety), that there should not be any problems related to diglossia. But linguists and educators still face another dilemma. Recent studies show that the Greek language is still affected by the diglossia of the past, and there is a significant degree of Katharévousa elements in the language. The following sections demonstrate the occurrence of Katharévousa elements in contemporary Greek, and address linguistic and pedagogical problems existing in the language as a result of the previous state of diglossia.

Evidence of Katharévousa elements in contemporary Greek. In a theoretical study, Philippaki-Warburton (1980) arrives at the conclusion that in the Greek language today, a large number of words still retain their phonotactic rules in Katharévousa and do not adjust to the phonotactic requirements of Demotikí. For example, Katharévousa allows only for voiceless consonant cluster combinations such as stop + stop and fricative + fricative. In Demotikí, these clusters become fricative + stop; e.g. the Katharévousa πτ /pt/, κτ /kt/, χθ /xθ/, become φτ /ft/, χτ /xt/, χτ /xt/ respectively. In addition to these Demotic consonant clusters, today's language still includes the Katharévousa clusters /pt/, /kt/, /xθ/. Example 1 demonstrates this point.

Example 1 Consonant clusters in contemporary Greek:
KATHARÉVOUSA: πτ /pt/   DEMOTIKÍ: φτ /ft/
πταίω /ptéo/ 'it is my fault'--> φταίω /ftéo/ 'it is my fault'

πτηνό /ptinó/ 'fowl'-->   πτηνό /ptinó/ 'fowl'
                            φτηνό /ftinó/ 'cheap'

In Example 1, the word /ptéo/ meaning 'it is my fault' changes to /ftéo/ in Demotikí, retaining its meaning; the Katharévousa consonant cluster /pt/ becomes /ft/ in Demotikí. However, a large number of words retain their Katharévousa phonotactic rules rather than become assimilated to Demotikí. For example, the word /ptinó/ 'fowl', still exists in Demotikí, and retains its Katharévousa phonotactic rules. This may be attributed to the fact that another word with the Demotic consonant cluster /ft/, the word /ftinó/, already exists in Demotikí and means 'cheap'. Another interpretation is that the word /ptinó/ has been adopted by Demotikí as a technical term. According to Browning (1982:62) 'the more technical the term, the more likely is it to be taken over from Katharévousa to Demotic without morphological change.'

Kazazis (1976) reports that Greek writers and poets of the older generation use more Katharévousa elements in their casual speech than in their formal speech and written work. That is, they somehow 'go out of their way' to use more pure Demotikí in their careful language. Paradoxically, this indicates a REVERSE PURISM towards Demotikí, which resembles the purism in the past leading towards Katharévousa. We know from the history of the Greek language that Katharévousa was the 'pure' language devoid of linguistic elements from the vernacular. Greek writers and poets today try to use a pure form of Demotikí devoid of Katharévousa elements, which does not exist in their actual casual speech. However, the younger writers do not reflect the phenomenon of reverse purism. According to Kazazis, these writers include Katharévousa elements in their written work similar to the actual spoken language. When Katharévousa was the official language, the writers and poets were the first to attempt to write in Demotikí, in order to accustom their readers to seeing Low forms in writing. Since Demotikí is now established, the younger generation of writers does not need to fight for Demotikí the way its predecessors did.

Identifying the need for more data-based research to describe the language situation in Greece today as it has been affected by diglossia, I conducted a diachronic and synchronic study of the language of the Athenian newspaper *Kathimerini* (Doukanari 1989). By applying quantitative measures, I found that in 1988, twelve years after the establishment of Demotikí as the official language of Greece, even though Demotikí is more predominant, a significant amount of Katharévousa elements seem to have been adopted by the modern Greek language.

Example 2 demonstrates my point by the use of the word η κυβέρνηση /i kivérnisi/ 'the government', in the nominative and genitive cases of the Old Third Declension Feminine Nouns.[1]

---

[1] By Old Third Declension Nouns, I mean nouns which in Katharévousa follow the third declension. In Katharevousa, the declension of nouns is classified according to their endings, e.g. third declension nouns include masculine, feminine, and neuter nouns whose nominative case ends in α, ι, υ, ω, ν, ρ, ς, ξ, ψ. In Demotikí, the classification is based on the grammatical gender of nouns, i.e. all masculine nouns constitute the first declension, feminine nouns the second declension, and all neuter nouns the third declension. Since the basis of classification is different in the two varieties of Greek and since in my 1989 study the identification of nouns is based on the endings of masculine and feminine nouns, I call the noun forms mentioned here 'Old Third Declension Nouns' in order to avoid confusion.

Example 2 Old Third Declension feminine nouns.

KATHARÉVOUSA:	DEMOTIKÍ:	Language today:
	Nominative	
ἡ κυβέρνησ-ις	η κυβέρνησ-η	η κυβέρνησ-η
/i kivérnis-is/	/i kivérnis-i/	/i kivérnis-i/
	Genitive	
τῆς κυβερνήσ-εως	της κυβέρνησ-ης	τηςκυβερνήσ-εως/ -ης/
/tis kivernís-eos/	/tis kivérnis-is/	/tis kivernís-eos/ -is/

In Katharévousa, the nominative case of these nouns ends in -ις /-is/, e.g. ἡ κυβέρνησ-ις /i kivérnis-is/. In Demotikí, the nominative case ends in -η /-i/, e.g. η κυβέρνησ-η /i kivérnis-i/. In the language of the Greek press today, the nominative case ends in /-i/. This means that the Katharévousa nominative ending /-is/ has given way to its Demotic counterpart /-i/. The genitive cases, however, show a different picture. The genitive case in Katharévousa ends in -εως /-eos/, e.g. τῆς κυβερνήσ-εως /tis kivernís-eos/. In Demotikí, it ends in -ης /-is/, e.g. της κυβέρνησ-ης /tis kivérnis-is/. But according to these findings, today's language of the press includes both Katharévousa and Demotikí Old Third Declension Noun genitive endings, with Katharévousa endings predominating. Therefore, it appears, that the Katharévousa genitive ending /-eos/ still persists in the Greek language today.

Table 1 depicts the percentages of the nominative and genitive cases in Katharévousa and Demotikí. This distribution shows the persistence of the Katharévousa genitive endings in the language of the press in 1988.

Table 1. Distribution of the nominative and genitive case endings of Old Third Declension nouns in 1988 *Kathimerini* newspaper articles.*

	% Demotikí	% Katharévousa
Nominative case endings	100	0
Genitive case endings	28	72

*Nominative endings = 83   Genitive endings = 94

In the nominative case, Demotikí is used exclusively. In the genitive case however, 72% of the endings are still in Katharévousa. This ties in with Babiniotis'(1976 and 1979) claims that the modern Greek language is not pure Demotikí but a synthesis of the two varieties, Demotikí and Katharévousa. This phenomenon, according to Babiniotis, is called dimórphia. That is, the modern Greek language consists of elements from both varieties, which are selected and synthesized, not randomly mixed. However, dimorphia should not be confused with *Miktí* the 'Mixed' hybrid that occurred in the diglossic times of the Greek language. *Miktí* is a fortuitous mixture of Katharévousa and Demotikí, while dimorphia according to Babiniotis (1979:15) is a synthesis based on 'the more general structural principles that govern languages during the various phases of their evolution.' Browning (1982) further states that Miktí was used by speakers and writers who had difficulty using 'pure' Katharévousa whereas the Greek language today is used unselfconsiously.

Triandafyllidis' Grammar is the official grammar of Demotikí according to Greek law. In the 1988 edition of this grammar, the paradigm for the Old Third Declension Feminine Nouns is similar to what appears in Example 2, under the heading Demotikí. Triandafyllidis' Grammar (1988) does not include the Katharévousa genitive endings in the paradigm, although it states that these endings may occur in the modern Greek language. But as it has already been demonstrated, the Katharévousa genitive endings, at least in the language of print journalism, appear more frequently (72%) than their Demotic counterparts (see Table 1). Therefore, the Katharévousa genitive ending /-eos/, which is the most frequent, should also appear in the paradigm. That is, both Katharévousa genitive and Demotic genitive endings should appear in the paradigm as illustrated in Example 2, under the heading, *Language Today*. A paradigm of this kind exists in the *Synchronic Grammar of the Modern Greek Koine* written by Babiniotis and Kontos (1967), and in the readjusted grammar (KEME 1986) based on the *Small Modern Greek Grammar* by Triandafyllidis (1949).

It is important not to confuse the *Neoelliniki Grammatiki-Anaprosarmogi tis Mikris Neoellinikis Grammatikis tou Manoli Triandafyllidi,* literally 'Modern Greek Grammar-Readjustment of the Small Modern Greek Grammar of Manolis Triandafyllidis (KEME 1986), with the larger version of the original grammar, called *Neoelliniki Grammatiki-Anatyposi tis Ekdosis tou OEΔB (1941) me Diorthoseis* 'Modern Greek Grammar-Reprint of the Edition of OEΔB (1941) with Corrections' (Triandafyllidis et. al. 1988). The readjusted small grammar (KEME 1986) is a revised version of the Small Modern Greek Grammar (Triandafyllidis 1949) which was a concise and simplified version of the original grammar (1941) written by Triandafyllidis to be used in public schools. The small grammar (KEME 1986) has been revised to better reflect the contemporary linguistic and educational reality. Triandafyllidis' Grammar (1988), however, is only a reissue of the original grammar published in 1941, a more bulky version than the small grammar. Except for the revision of stylistic and typographical errors and an appendix of the revised orthographic system, this 1988 version does not readjust to today's language, but remains in its 1941 original form.[2] The 1941 Triandafyllidis' original grammar

---

[2] For more detailed discussions on the nature, and/or the evolution of Triandafyllidis' *Grammar* see Foris (1976), Tombaidis (1976), G. Babiniotis and P. Kontos (1967), and Triandafyllidis et al. (1988).

represents the language of the late 1930s which was then intended to be descriptive. But it appears to be prescriptive for at least some aspects of today's language. This, of course, is a conclusion reached not only from Example 2, but also one based on other data (Doukanari 1989) and on previous reports from other researchers such as Babiniotis and Kontos (1967), and Philippaki-Warburton (1980). Triandafyllidis'(1988) grammar, the larger version, may be seen today as an ideal model frozen in time. Therefore, it needs further revision to describe better the language used today, both spoken and written, so that linguists and educators who need more detailed information than what the small grammar (KEME 1986) provides, will use a more extensive version that describes the contemporary linguistic reality.

Katharévousa elements are also observed in official documents. Example 3 demonstrates occurrences of Katharévousa lexicon, phonology, morphology, and syntax. For grammatical references and differences between Katharévousa and Demotikí, the following were consulted: Alexiou (1982), Economou (1989), Eleftheriades (1985), Householder (1974), Triandafyllidis (1986, 1988), and Tzartzanos (1954). For word etymology and Katharévousa vocabulary, Andriotis (1990), Dangitzis (1984), and Kyriakopoulos (1969) were used as references.

Example 3 presents one sentence taken from a letter written by an education official in 1989 to Greek educators in the United States (Text A Sample), and three sentences taken from a 1990 article from an official government newspaper which specifies university rules (Text B Sample). These samples illustrate that an abundance of Katharévousa elements still occur even in official documents.

In Example 3, Katharévousa elements are underscored in both the Text A and Text B Samples. A word-for-word translation (gloss) is provided for each line of text, which is then followed by an idiomatic translation.

Example 3. Sampling of Katharévousa elements in recent official Greek documents.

1 Η <u>ακριβής θεματολογία</u> του σεμιναρίου <u>θα καθορισθεί</u>
The <u>exact thematology</u> the-(gen.) seminar-(gen.) <u>will-be determined</u>
'The exact topic of the seminar will be determined

2 μετά από τις προτάσεις των <u>συναδέλφων</u>,
after from the proposals the-(gen. pl.) <u>colleagues-(gen. pl.)</u>
following the suggestions of our colleagues

3 οι <u>οποίες</u> παρακαλώ να σταλούν εγκαίρως
the <u>which</u> I-request to be-sent promptly
which I request to be sent promptly

4   στο γραφείο μας.
    to-the office our
    to our office.'

Text B Sample.

5   Ο Πρόεδρος του Συμβουλίου <u>συγκαλεί</u>
    The President the-(gen.) Executive-Committee-(gen.) <u>calls</u>
    'The President of the Executive Committee calls

6   τις συνεδριάσεις του και <u>προεδρεύει των Συνεδριάσεων</u>
    the meetings it-(gen.) and <u>presides the-(gen. pl.) Meetings-(gen. pl.)</u>
    the meetings and presides over the Sessions

7   του Συμβουλίου στις <u>οποίες παρίσταται.</u>
    the-(gen.) Executive-Committee-(gen.) at-the <u>which is-present.</u>
    of the Executive Committee at which he is present.'

8   Σε περίπτωση <u>απουσίας</u> του Προέδρου από
    In case <u>absence-(gen.)</u> the-(gen.) President-(gen.) from
    'In case of the President's absence from

9   <u>οποιαδήποτε συνεδρία</u> ο Αντιπρόεδρος ή σε περίπτωση
    <u>whichever meeting</u> the Vice-president or in case
    any meeting, the Vice-president or in case

10 <u>απουσίας</u> του Αντιπροέδρου, μέλος
    <u>absence-(gen.)</u> the-(gen.) Vice-president-(gen.) member
    of the Vice-president's absence, a member of the

11 του Συμβουλίου <u>εκλεγόμενο</u> προς τούτο,
    the-(gen.) Executive-Committee-(gen.) <u>elected</u> to this
    Executive Committee elected for this (purpose)

12 <u>προεδρεύει της συνεδρίασης.</u>
    <u>presides the-(gen.) meeting-(gen.)</u>
    presides over the session.'

    . . .

13 <u>Αποτελεί</u> δευτεροβάθμιο όργανο <u>κρίσεως</u>
    <u>Constitutes</u> second degree instrument <u>judgment-(gen.)</u>
    'It constitutes a second degree instrument of judgment

14 και δευτεροβάθμιο πειθαρχικό συμβούλιο.
    and second degree disciplinary committee.
    and a second degree disciplinary committee.

In Example 3, Katharévousa elements (underscored) constitute about one third of the text. This is an indication that the occurrence of Katharévousa elements in the language of official documents is significant. In a qualitative discourse analysis of the official newspaper and the educator's letter, we can observe examples of Katharévousa phonology; e.g. the verb θα καθορισθεί /θa kaθorisθí/ 'will be determined' (line 1), includes the Katharévousa consonant cluster σθ /sθ/ instead of its Demotic counterpart στ /st/. This confirms Philippaki-Warburton's (1980) findings that Katharévousa consonant cluster combinations such as voiceless fricative + fricative still occur in today's language.

The occurrence of Katharévousa morphology is also observed in official documents; e.g. the word κρίσεως /kríseos/ 'of judgment' (line 13) has the Katharévousa genitive ending /-eos/ instead of the Demotic ending /-is/, e.g. κρίσης /krísis/. This is in agreement with my previous findings (Doukanari 1989), that the Katharévousa genitive ending of Old Third Declension Nouns still occurs, to a significant degree, in today's language.

Among the underscored Katharévousa elements in Example 3, there is also evidence of Katharévousa syntax; e.g. in the phrase προεδρεύει των Συνεδριάσεων /proeδrévi ton sineδriáseon/ '(he) presides over the Sessions' (line 6), the noun των Συνεδριάσεων /ton sineδriáseon/ is in the genitive plural form. This is constructed according to the Katharévousa syntactic rules instead of the Demotic. Although the genitive case exists in Demotikí, it is often avoided, especially in its plural form. According to Triandafyllidis' Grammar (1988), paragraph 521(ζ) states that the use of the genitive in Demotikí is very restricted and is replaced by the accusative, usually accompanied by a preposition. In paragraph 524, Triandafyllidis' Grammar adds that although in the written language the use of the genitive appears to be more necessary than the spoken, it is not correct to violate the rule of the genitive when it can be replaced with other means that the modern Greek language has adapted. I have used this as a criterion to classify the genitives as either Katharévousa or Demotikí. That is, if it is possible for the genitive in question to be easily replaced by another means in Demotikí, but in the actual data it is not replaced, I consider the case form here to be a Katharévousa element. In Example 3 (line 6), the phrase προεδρεύει των Συνεδριάσεων /proeδrévi ton sineδriáseon/ '(he) presides-over the-(gen.) Sessions-(gen)' appears in the genitive case, even though it could very easily be substituted by the Demotic structure προεδρεύει στις Συνεδριάσεις /proeδrévi stis syneδriásis/ '(he) presides at the meetings' where the genitive could be replaced by the accusative accompanied by the preposition σε /se/ which combined with the article τις /tis/ 'the', becomes στις /stis/ 'at the'. Therefore, based on Triandafyllidis' Grammar (1988), the use of this Katharévousa syntactic structure violates the rules of Demotikí since it violates the rule of the genitive which, in this case, could be replaced with another means that the modern Greek language has employed. This is another indication that at least the written language is not Demotikí in its grammatical sense.

In Example 3, there is also evidence of Katharévousa lexicon; e.g. απουσίας /apusías/ 'of absence' (lines 8 & 10). In addition, this lexical item is in the genitive form, which in this context σε περίπτωση απουσίας /se períptosi apusías/ 'in case of absence' (lines 8 & 10), constitutes a Katharévousa syntactic characteristic since it has violated the rule of the genitive as mentioned previously. That is, although this syntactic structure could have been replaced by the possible Demotic expression σε περίπτωση που απουσιάζει /se períptosi pu apusiázi/ 'in case that (he) is absent', it is not replaced here, but instead a genitive construction is used. It is often possible, that linguistic categories overlap; e.g. in lines 8 & 10, by a more microscopic analysis of the text, we can find occurrences of Katharévousa lexicon. Looking at the lexical item as it occurs in a larger context, we can observe occurrence of Katharévousa syntax.

In Example 3, we have seen occurrences of Katharévousa phonology, morphology, syntax, and lexicon. These are the more obvious and unquestionable Katha-révousa elements. But as has already been mentioned, there exist a whole series of hybrids of Katharévousa and Demotikí which are not easily determined, creating a dilemma for the researcher. For example, it may be argued that the noun του Συμβουλίου /tu simvulíu/ 'of the Executive Committee' (line 5) could be classified as a Katharévousa element since, in etymological lexicons, it is listed as a Katharévousa word. The reason that this word /tu simvulíu/ has not been classified here as a Katharévousa element, is based on three criteria:

(1) the Katharévousa noun το Συμβούλιον /to simvúlion/ 'the Executive Committee', even though it has been adopted from Katharévousa as a lexical item, has adjusted to Demotic morphology by deleting the final ν /n/ in the nominative case, το Συμβούλιο /to simvúlio/;

(2) although in line 5, /tu simvulíu/ is in the genitive form, this genitive is not classified as a Katharévousa occurrence because in this case, it is not replaceable by other Demotic means. This is based on Triandafyllidis' (1988) statement that the genitive may be used in instances where the modern Greek language has not employed another means to express it. In this context, /o próedros tu simvulíu/ (line 5), the genitive /tu simvulíu/ indicates attribute. This is based on the classification of the genitive in the *Syndaktiko tis Neas Ellinikis* 'Modern Greek Syntax' (KEME 1985); and,

(3) since the genitive ending of this word is similar in both Katharévousa and Demotikí, it is not obvious whether the writers of these documents have in mind here the Katharévousa nominative ending or the Demotic. This example indicates the need for researchers to state explicitly the criteria based on which they classify an element as Katharévousa or Demotic, because different criteria may result in different conclusions. When the distinction between the two varieties is not clear-cut, research on diglossia becomes very

difficult. This may be a reason why not many data-based studies exist on Greek diglossia.

It is important to note that the examples above are not given to show that I disagree with what appears on these documents, but to enhance my point that certain Katharévousa elements have been adopted by the modern Greek language and may occur even in official documents. This is more an indication of actual language use rather than of Katharévousa interference. The examples serve also as a practical instance to indicate a way that qualitative analysis could be applied, in order to investigate diglossia and dimorphia as well as to emphasize the difficulties encountered when conducting research on diglossia and its implications.

Triandafyllidis' Grammar (1988:100, note 3) makes reference to the abundance of lexicon borrowed from Katharévousa, stating that even though Katharévousa lexical items, in some cases, harm the homogeneity of the language, in other cases, they have abundantly enriched the Greek language. A large number of words which are used in everyday conversations have either been transferred to the language from Ancient Greek via Katharévousa or are vocabulary which was created by Katharévousa. Names of people, numbers, months, colors, still keep their Katharévousa counterparts. Many signs on stores and street addresses are still in Katharévousa. That all these elements have been adopted by the modern Greek language is not surprising, since Demotikí has always been tolerant of several Katharévousa elements. Katharévousa has been around for over 150 years and has influenced the Greek language to a great extent. This issue has to be kept in mind when we design educational materials for both native and non-native learners of Greek. Linguists and teachers must keep in mind that parents and teachers who have experienced Katharévousa will transfer aspects of this language to the next generation. Language teaching materials should include both Demotikí and their Katharévousa counterparts if they still exist to a significant degree in the Greek language.

The dilemma. We know that the official language of Greece is Demotikí. The question is: What kind of Demotikí? There are two main interpretations assigned to it: (1) Demotikí in its literal sense, which means the language of the people; and, (2) Demotikí in its grammatical sense, which is based on Triandafyllidis' Grammar (1941). According to Philippaki-Warburton, the first interpretation of Demotikí develops and changes constantly whereas the second has remained static (Philippaki-Warburton 1980). When the Greek Law established Demotikí based on Triandafyllidis' Grammar as the official language of Greece, it became confusing because Demotikí based on Triandafyllidis' Grammar (1941, 1988), although it undoubtedly has a lot of advantages, does not always faithfully reflect the actual language used by people. As a result, linguists and teachers now face a new dilemma. Which Demotikí do we teach? If we teach Demotikí based on Triandafyllidis' Grammar, we may be introducing a variety of language which is not necessarily the language of the speakers. If we teach Demotikí in its literal sense, based on the language of the people, there is a need for the creation and revision of pedagogical grammars, lexicons and teaching materials. Therefore, there is a need for more data-based quantitative and qualitative studies of spoken and written language to describe the actual state of language in Greece. Since the language today is not 'pure' Demotikí, some researchers suggest that it should be given a different name. Babiniotis (1979) prefers to call today's language *Modern Greek Koine (MGK)* rather than Demotikí. Browning (1982) suggests that to avoid confusion, perhaps it should be called *Standard Modern Greek (SMG)*.

A number of problems we had with diglossia recur in the Greek language today, appearing in different forms: One problem is reverse purism that Kazazis (1976) has observed. In formal situations (spoken and written), people may tend to use more Demotikí than their actual conversational language which may be an indication that a pure form of Demotikí is somehow enforced [my emphasis].

Another problem is Katharévousa interference: As we know, Katharevousa was used in formal situations. Today, formal situations call for standard Demotikí, not Katharévousa. I have observed, however, that people, especially of the older generation, in certain formal situations where standard Demotikí is required, still use Katharévousa elements that have not even been adopted by the modern Greek language. As a result of Katharévousa interference, there is still a lot of inconsistency in spelling. People confuse standard Demotikí with Katharévousa, in addition to the confusion that takes place between standard Demotikí and the dialects.

Another problem is the fact that important literature was written in Katharévousa or Miktí. How do we teach this literature to our students? If we translate it, we lose originality and linguistic nuance. If we teach the actual literary piece, we need to teach it through the language in which it is written, Katharévousa. Of course, Katharévousa is still taught in Greek public schools as an object of study, not as the medium of instruction. But how do we teach it even as an object of study so that students will better understand literature written in Katharévousa? Students are first introduced to Katharévousa in the *gymnasio* which corresponds to American middle school. During those three years of education, the students gradually become acquainted with Katharévousa through readers, and through explanations concerning Katharévousa given by the teacher. Following the *gymnasio*, the students attend three years of high school, what is called the *lykeio*, where they continue to be taught Katharévousa through readers, in combination with grammatical explanations. Therefore, even though diglossia is eliminated, students still have to learn Katharévousa in order to better understand important literature written in the past, based on that variety. Of course, the ideal method to teach the literature written in Katharévousa should not be to teach that literature as a language text, but rather to teach it mainly for its didactic humanistic values. Similarly, Sifakis (1976), suggests that the literary work of classical Greeks should be taught for its didactic humanistic values. This is based on the Ancient Greek scholars' philosophy that human virtue (*aretí*) is to be human as much as possible; and the way to achieve that is through παιδεία /pedía/ 'the cultivation of human virtue'. Whether the approach to teaching literature written in Katharévousa in public schools is effective and satisfactory in promoting cultivation of the human virtue still needs to be investigated. Moreover, the identification of specific problems that teachers and students encounter when studying literature written in Katharévousa still needs to be thoroughly investigated.

An important issue concerning contemporary Greek, which is indirectly related to diglossia, is the fact that the New Testament is written in *Hellenistic Koine*, the language used between the 3rd century b.c. to the 4th century a.d. Even though Demotikí is the direct descendant of *Koine*, to many people, Katharévousa appears to be closer to the language of the New Testament. The question is, do we translate the New Testament into Demotikí or not? The Greek clergy believes that we should not translate it. But, even when we had diglossia and Greeks were more familiar with Katharévousa, people still had difficulty understanding the language of the New Testament. One can imagine how much more incomprehensible it is today and will be in the future.

There are also problems which concern teachers and students of Greek as a foreign language. One of the problems is teaching materials. Some older teaching materials do not always represent the actual language. More contemporary materials are inconsistent in their use of Katharévousa elements adopted by today's language, especially in cases of paired vocabulary items existing in contemporary Greek. For example, in *Ellinika Tora* /eliniká tóra/ 'Greek Now' (D. Dimitra and M. Papaheimona 1987:31), a textbook intended for adults learning Greek as a foreign language, the first time that the spelling of numbers is given, the number εφτά /eftá/ 'seven', which includes the consonant cluster /ft/, is listed in its Demotic form. Its Katharévousa counterpart επτά /eptá/, including the consonant cluster /pt/ is not given. In this case, the Katharévousa counterpart should also be listed since it is still used abundantly in the modern Greek language. On the same page of the textbook, the opposite happens with the numbers οκτώ /októ/ 'eight' and εννέα /enéa/ 'nine'. These numbers are listed in Katharévousa but their Demotic counterparts οχτώ /ohtó/ and εννιά /enyá/ respectively are not listed. On page 51 of the same book, the first part of the number επτακόσιες /eptakóshes/ 'seven hundred' includes the Katharévousa consonant cluster /pt/ and not /ft/. The students have already been introduced to /eftá/ on page 31 but not /eptá/. It becomes confusing for the students and necessary for the teachers to explain this inconsistency. On page 71, however, both the Katharévousa and Demotic counterparts of the numbers 'seven', 'eight', and 'nine' are listed. This procedure could have been followed on page 31, the first time that the spelling of these numbers appeared in the book, so that confusion might be avoided.

In instances where teaching materials do not mention both forms of paired vocabulary items which exist in contemporary Greek, I would suggest that the teachers explain from the beginning the coexistence of both counterparts. Even the most elementary students who have been exposed to the Greek language have heard either or both forms of the numbers just mentioned. I have always had many students, both adults and children, who inquire why, for example, they have learned from another book, another teacher or their Greek friend that the number 'seven' is pronounced /eptá/ and not /eftá/ or vice-versa. Students always want to be reassured that it is acceptable to use the form they previously heard or learned. In the case of paired vocabulary items, it is more meaningful for the students to be introduced from the beginning to both forms of a word appearing together in the same lesson, rather than learn each form in separate lessons. Providing the students with only one form of a certain word (either its Katharévousa or Demotic form) is usually more confusing.

In teaching Greek as a second or foreign language, I find it useful during the first lesson, at all levels, to provide a simple brief introduction to the particularities of the Greek language. Part of that introduction is to briefly explain Katharévousa and Demotikí and to reassure the students that in cases where the textbook gives only one form, the teacher will provide the other. One of the pedagogical benefits of such an introduction is that the students are prepared in advance with an overview of the Greek language, part of which is how the language has been influenced by diglossia. This helps them to cope more easily later on with the specific problems related to diglossia. One may argue that it is not necessary to make students aware of diglossia since it belongs to the past. I believe that diglossia constitutes an important landmark in the history of the Greek language. Fortunately for some and unfortunately for others, it has enriched the Greek language with an abundance of Katharévousa elements. Diglossia became associated not only with linguistic factors, but also with political, social, and psychological issues which are still be reflected in the Greek culture today. The linguistic and social reality is that students of all levels will encounter, at a certain stage, traces of Katharévousa in the Greek language. Even students at the beginning level will see store signs and street addresses in Katharévousa and will come across Katharévousa and Demotic word couplets such as /eptá/ - /eftá/ 'seven', /anδréas/ - /andréas/ 'Andrew', /ianuários/ - /yenáris/ 'January', /lefkós ínos/ - /áspro krasí/ 'white wine'.

Another problem for researchers is how to identify and classify Katharévousa and Demotic elements, a problem that also existed with diglossia. Elements which fall on the extreme ends of the continuum may be clearly identified as Katharévousa or Demotic. But certain elements, especially those positioned at the intermediate points along the continuum, are not always easy to determine. This problem was illustrated above through the analysis of official documents. The researcher was faced with the dilemma whether certain elements would be classified as Katharévousa or Demotic.

This may be why the lists of Katharévousa and Demotic elements provided by researchers such as Householder (1974) and Alexiou (1982) are not exhaustive. How can we define dimorphia in its entirety since we have not yet been able to define diglossia in its entirety? Philippaki-Warburton (1980) and Browning (1982) point out that the synthesis of Demotikí and Katharévousa is done unselfconsiously by native speakers. If this is indeed the case, perhaps we do not need to study the language as two distinct systems, Katharévousa and Demotikí, but rather to describe the actual language in its entirety as an autonomous system.

The Greek language today, at a transitional stage from diglossia to monoglossia, is confronted by two important issues. First, it indicates dimorphia, a synthesis of the two varieties based on systematic structural patterns. Second, the Greek language indicates Katharévousa interference which gives an impression of a mixed language, a haphazard mixture of the two varieties rather than a synthesis. That is, certain Katharévousa elements not adopted by today's language are still used, especially by people of the older generation. Elements attributed to Katharévousa interference are more likely to disappear with time. But there is also the possibility that if these interfering elements occur frequently, they may be adopted at a later stage in the evolution of the Greek language, in a way similar to that by which other elements have already been adopted, thereby constituting dimorphia.

The fact that Katharévousa elements have been adopted by today's language has already been addressed by researchers. However, it is important that the issue of Katharévousa interference also be addressed so that dimorphia, which is synthesis based on a process of natural selection, would be distinguished from the mixed language phenomenon where Katharévousa elements not adopted by today's language are still used as an arbitrary mixture of the two varieties.

Second, for researchers who want to investigate Katharévousa interference as it relates to, or as it differs from dimorphia, and for those who want to investigate the quantity and quality of elements borrowed from Katharévousa, it is necessary to study the Greek language as two separate systems: Katharévousa and Demotikí.

In summary, I would like to suggest the necessity for two different kinds of data-based linguistic research to describe the language today, depending on what we want to investigate: (1) to examine the actual language as an autonomous entity, as one system, and (2) to examine the language as the coexistence of two distinct systems, Demotikí and Katharévousa. The latter is even a more complicated task, since Katharévousa and Demotikí differences are not always clear-cut.

These are only a few of the problems associated with the transition from diglossia to dimorphia. It is important to note that the present study, by addressing these problems, neither suggests, nor favors a return to diglossia. The study rather draws attention to the actual state of language used by native speakers, so that a standard Greek language will be more adequately described by linguists, taught by educators, and learned by both native speakers and non-native learners. By abolishing diglossia, the Greek language has now become more comprehensible in its formal spoken and written registers even to the less educated Greeks. According to Karanikolas, with diglossia, children, although not linguistically and intellectually mature, were forced to use two forms of language, one in school and one in their interpersonal relationships. This led not only to linguistic anarchy, but also to unorganized thought (Karanikolas 1976). Understanding television and radio news reports, newspapers, official documents and educational materials, without much struggle to find the meaning in the complex grammatical constructions that Katharévousa prescribed, represents an advancement toward the human virtue (*aretí*) that the Ancient Greek scholars aimed at when teaching their students.

Conclusion. This study has provided evidence that the Greek language today is not pure Demotikí in its grammatical sense as stated by the Greek law. It is Demotikí in its literal sense, 'the language of the people', which is a synthesis of Demotikí and Katharévousa with Demotikí predominating. This phenomenon that Babiniotis (1976 and 1979) defines as dimorphia calls for further data-based studies to describe appropriately the actual state of language, and for the revision of grammars, lexicons, and educational materials. The study also addresses some of the linguistic and pedagogical problems today as they relate to diglossia and views the awareness of these problems as an incentive to solve them rather than an omen. By addressing problems that result from diglossia, this study intends to make linguists and teachers more aware of the new situation.

From the perspective of the interdependence of linguistics and language pedagogy, linguistic studies in the past have given us a picture of diglossia and its problems and implications for language teaching. Recent studies have shed light on the dimorphic nature of the Greek language today. Future linguistic research will further describe the new dimorphic language situation and the pedagogical implications for contemporary Greek.

References

Alexiou, M. 1982. Diglossia in Greece. In: W. Haas, ed. Standard languages: Spoken and written. 156-192. Manchester: Manchester University Press.
Andriotis, N. P. 1990. Etymologiko lexiko tis koinis Neoellinikis. Thessaloniki: Institouto Neoellinikon Spoudon.
Babiniotis, G. 1976. Realismos kai outopia stin glossa. Kathimerini newspaper, August 3, 4, 5, 7.
Babiniotis, G. 1979. A linguistic approach to the language question in Greece. Byzantine and Modern Greek Studies. 1-16. Oxford: Basil Blackwell.
Babiniotis, G., and P. Kontos. 1967. Synchroniki grammatiki tis Koinis Neas Ellinikis. Athens: G. Babiniotis and P. Kontos.
Britto, F. 1986. Diglossia: A study of the theory with application to Tamil. Washington, D.C.: Georgetown University Press.

Bien, P., J. Rassias, and Ch. Bien. 1972. Demotic Greek. Hanover: The University Press of New England.
Browning, R. 1969. Medieval and Modern Greek. London: Hutchinson.
Browning, R. 1982. The Greek diglossia yesterday and today. International Journal of the Sociology of Language. 35:49-68.
Dangitzis, K. 1984. Etymologiko lexiko tis Neoellinikis. Athens: Vassiliou.
Dimitra, D., and M. Papaheimona. 1987. Ellinika Tora 1+1 'Greek Now 1+1'. Athens: Ekdoseis Ammos.
Doukanari, E. 1989. From diglossia to dimorphia: A diachronic and synchronic study of the language of the press in Greece. Unpublished manuscript.
Economou, M. 1989. Grammatiki tis Archaias Ellinikis A' Lykeiou. Athens: Organismos Ekdoseos Didaktikon Vivlion.
Eleftheriades, O. 1985. Modern Greek: A contemporary grammar. Palo Alto: Pacific Books.
Fasold, R. 1984. The sociolinguistics of society. Oxford: Basil Blackwell.
Ferguson, C. A. 1959. Diglossia. Word, 15, 325-340.
Fishman, J. A. 1967. Bilingualism with and without diglossia; Diglossia with and without bilingualism. Journal of Social Issues. 2:29-38.
Foris, V. D. 1976. Parousiasi tis 'Neoellinikis grammatikis': Provlimata. Eisigiseis: I Archaia Elliniki grammateia apo metafrasi, I Neoelliniki glossa kai grammateia. 301-310. Athens: KEME, Ministry of Education and Religion, Greece.
Hatzidakis, G. N. 1915. Syntomos istoria tis Ellinikis glossis. Athens: I. N. Sideri.
Householder, F. W. 1974. Studies in Modern Greek for American students: III Greek Triglossia. Bloomington: Indiana University Linguistics Club.
Kahane, H., R. Kahane, and R. L. Ward. 1976. Spoken Greek, Book One. Ithaca: Spoken Language Services.
Karanikolas, A. S. 1976. Ta nea ekpaideftika metra i simasia tous kai proypotheseis gia tin epityhia. Eisigiseis: I Archaia Elliniki grammateia apo metafrasi, I Neoelliniki glossa kai grammateia. 13-21. Athens: KEME, Ministry of Education and Religion, Greece.
Karanikolas, A. S. 1979. The evolution of the Greek language and its present form. In: J. E. Alatis and G. R. Tucker, eds. Georgetown University Round Table on Languages and Linguistics 1979. 78-85. Washington, D.C.: Georgetown University Press.
Kazazis, K. 1976. A superficially unusual feature of Greek diglossia. In: S. S. Mufwene, C. A. Walker, and S. B. Steever, eds. Papers from the Twelfth Regional Meeting Chicago Linguistic Society. 369-375. Chicago: Chicago Linguistic Society.
KEME. 1985. Syndaktiko tis Neas Ellinikis: Voithima gia ton daskalo. Athens: Organismos Ekdoseos Didaktikon Vivlion.
KEME. 1986. Neoelliniki grammatiki. Anaprosarmogi tis Mikris Neoellinikis Grammatikis tou Manoli Triandafyllidi: Vivlio gia ton daskalo. Athens: Organismos Ekdoseos Didaktikon Vivlion.
Kyriakopoulos, D. 1969. Orthographikon kai ermineftikon lexikon tis Ellinikis glossis. Athens: I. Sideris.
Lampsas, I. 1975. Tetraglossia: Os pote? Kathimerini newspaper. p. 6. April 23.
Mackridge, P. 1987. The Modern Greek language. Oxford: Oxford University Press.
Mandilaras, B. G. 1972. Studies in the Greek language. Athens: B. G. Mandilaras.
Mirambel, A. 1937. Les états de langue dans la Grèce actuelle. Conférences de l'Institut de Linguistique de l'Université de Paris 5.
Pappageotes, G. C., and J. Macris. 1964. The language question in Modern Greece. Word, 20 (3), Special publication 5:53-59.
Peridis, M. 1965. I Elliniki glossa kai i simerini morphi tis. Athens: M. Peridis.
Philippaki-Warburton, I. 1980. Greek diglossia and some aspects of the phonology of common modern Greek. Journal of Linguistics, 16:45-54.
Sifakis, G. M. 1976. Klasiki philologia kai anthropistiki paideia: Alitheies kai parexigiseis. Eisigiseis: I Archaia Elliniki grammateia apo metafrasi, I Neoelliniki glossa kai grammateia. 25-39. Athens: KEME, Ministry of Education and Religion, Greece.

Language awareness:
The common ground between linguist and language teacher

Leo van Lier
Monterey Institute of International Studies

Introduction. There's an old joke which is probably told in every introductory philosophy course. It goes like this:

What is mind?
　No matter.
What is matter?
　Never mind.

I have taken the liberty of adapting that joke to the topic of my presentation. If we ever have introductory Educational Linguistics courses, perhaps this adapted version might have a place in them. Here it is:

What is theory?
　Practically irrelevant.
What is practice?
　Fine, in theory.

There is a perennial debate in our field between the theoretical and research side on the one hand, and the applied or practical side on the other. (For recent contributions to this debate see *Issues in Applied Linguistics*, vol. 1, no.2. and Larsen-Freeman 1990.)

In this paper I will not review the various proposed delimitations of the domains of theoretical and applied concerns, and the one- or two-way flow of scientific traffic between them. Rather, I want to argue the need for a closer collaboration between two particular fields which in recent times have had less contact than might be deemed desirable or necessary.

The two fields are linguistics and education, particularly language education, and my thesis is that it makes sense, for a number of reasons, for linguists to become more actively involved in education, and for educators to study linguistics. In this way, a fruitful link between theoretical and applied concerns in linguistics can be re-established.

Thomson, G. 1960. The Greek language. Cambridge: W. Heffer.
Tombaidis, D. E. 1976. I anaprosarmosmeni Neoelliniki grammatiki. Eisigiseis: I Archaia Elliniki grammateia apo metafrasi, I Neoelliniki glossa kai grammateia. 311-322. Athens: KEME, Ministry of Education and Religion, Greece.
Triandafyllidis, M. 1941. Neoelliniki grammatiki (tis Demotikís). Athens: Organismos Ekdoseos Sholikon Vivlion.
Triandafyllidis, M. 1949. Mikri Neoelliniki grammatiki. Athens: Organismos Ekdoseos Didaktikon Vivlion.
Triandafyllidis, M., K. Lakonas, Th. Stavrou, A. Tzartzanos, V. Vafis, and N. Andriotis. 1988. Neoelliniki grammatiki (tis Demotikís). Anatyposi tis ekdosis tou OEΣB (1941) me diorthoseis. Thessaloniki: Institouto Neoellinikon Spoudon.
Tzartzanos, A. A. 1954. Grammatiki tis Neas Ellinikis glossis (tis aplis Katharévousis). Athens: K. Kakoulidis.

In promoting a close link between linguistics and education, the first priority is teacher education (both pre-service and in-service), for reasons which I hope to make clear in this paper. Currently, language courses play only a minor role in teacher education, a situation which, especially given the present-day communicative demands of classrooms, schools, and the world beyond, constitutes a serious shortcoming in the professional preparation of teachers. Although the situation is perhaps less acute in the U.K. than in the U.S.A., Mitchell and Hooper 1990 report serious inadequacies in language education in British teacher training establishments as well.

I will first list some of the reasons for an educational linguistic enterprise. Next, I will give an overview of the history and principles of Language Awareness. Finally, in the last part of the paper I will give some practical examples of Language Awareness activities for teacher education.

1 Reasons for a role for linguistics in education.

1.1 Role of consciousness in language learning. The psycholinguistic analysis of learner performance which replaced error analysis (and contrastive analysis before that) has led to a richer picture of what language learning is and what it involves, and more importance is given to the role of consciousness and focussed attention in language learning. At the same time, the once-banished field of contrastive analysis has now re-emerged under the title of crosslinguistic influence.

In a parallel development, more detailed descriptive studies of classroom interaction have painted an increasingly rich picture of language use by learners in classrooms, and this is providing fresh insights into the dynamics of language and learning in language classrooms.

Finally, SL researchers in areas ranging from universal grammar to connectionism are reaching a consensus that, for older students and adults at least, negative feedback of one sort or another is beneficial. This negative feedback is most prominently given by way of an overt focus on language, though this is not by any means limited to grammar drills or explanations. In general terms, cognitive science strongly suggests a central role for LANGUAGE AWARENESS in language learning. In order to facilitate this awareness in their students, teachers themselves need to be more aware of the uses of language in their professional life and in the socio-cultural world in which their students live. To enable teachers to cope with these demands, their metalinguistic knowledge and skills may need urgent attention.

1.2 Language policy and the curriculum. There have been regular calls for consistent language policies across the school curriculum from a number of quarters, on a number of occasions. In Great Britain, for instance, the Bullock Report (DES 1975), the Swann Report (DES 1985), and the Kingman Report (DES 1988) all made such calls. OISE has adopted a general language policy (OISE 1984), the Australian Government has just produced a discussion document on a national language policy (Literacy and Language Task Force 1990), and the European Community is considering a number of guidelines in preparation for 1992 (for recent surveys, see Corson 1988, 1990).

In 1986 the University of Southampton founded a Centre for Language in Education, directed by Professor Chris Brumfit. This Centre is unique in Great Britain (and probably elsewhere), for its explicit focus on the study of language in education. In his inaugural address Brumfit proposed the following 'language rights' for British school children:

1. Development of mother tongue or dialect;
2. Development of competence in a range of styles of English for educational, work-based, social, and public life purposes;
3. Development of knowledge of the nature of language in a multilingual society, including some basic acquaintances with at least two languages from the total range of languages available in education or in the local community;
4. Development of a fairly extensive practical competence in at least one language other than their own. (Brumfit 1990:10).

In the U.S.A. such national policies or guidelines are not generally available,[1] with the result that most practitioners just have to get on with their job using the courage of their convictions, often in the face of factional bickering that tends to be more counterproductive than constructive. The lack of general guidelines for language education has also led to a number of distinct reform proposals. Although many of them are based on excellent ideas and practices, in today's fragmented and unconcerted educational market place such reforms run the danger of having only a shortlived and superficial impact. To gain full advantage of such innovative practices as whole language, experiential learning, cooperative learning, critical thinking, and so on, a national policy giving carefully articulated language guidelines across the curriculum, is clearly advantageous. Now is the right time for doing so, since a number of

---

1 This is in spite of several calls for such policies, e.g. Tucker's (1986) proposals for a 'language competent' American society, and the integrative efforts of several organizations, most notably CAL (Center for Applied Linguistics) and, from 1985-1989, CLEAR (Center for Language Education and Research). Unfortunately, such work has so far not captured the attention of U.S. policy makers in the way that it has elsewhere, as discussed in this paper. Nor has Language Awareness been considered in detail as a pedagogical option.

countries across the world are engaged in similar efforts, and excellent opportunities for international discussion and collaboration therefore present themselves.

1.3 The multicultural, multilingual nature of modern education. Classrooms in most countries are, for better or for worse, becoming increasingly mixed in terms of the ethnic, cultural, and linguistic backgrounds of the students. To understand some of the depth of this change, it is useful to think back to the days we, today's educators and academics, were inside the classrooms in our respective countries, as children. I think that the overwhelming majority of us found ourselves together with kids who were pretty much similar to ourselves, in terms of race, religion, native dialect, and so on. Now it is clear that for our children this is, by and large, not the case. Homogeneous classrooms of the sort that were common only twenty years ago, are now few and far between. We may regard this as an asset, or as a catastrophe. The fact is, we do not know whether it is one or the other, so long as we fail to take control of the situation, and work with it rather than run from one emergency to the next. A solid language policy across the curriculum will surely not solve all current problems at a stroke but, given the centrality of language in education (indeed, in the world at large, as is becoming increasingly clear), it is the most likely focal point at this juncture for producing a concerted restructuring in an increasingly disconcerted and depressed institution.

It would be easy to continue enumerating reasons for a closer involvement of linguists in the affairs of education, but I must proceed. It should be possible to arrive at a clear national language policy by proposing some basic principles which reflect broad agreement across different political and social groups. For example, here are three principles which might form a reasonable starting point (I have based them on the Australian principles, but adapted them to the American setting):[2]

1. All US residents should attain and maintain competence in a range of contexts in spoken and written forms of English, and should be provided with adequate support and opportunities to do so;
2. The learning of languages other than English should be substantially increased to enhance educational outcomes and communication both within the USA and internationally (thus changing Bullock's famous slogan to 'Two Languages for Life');
3. Maintenance of native languages should be encouraged since it is in the interest of both (1) and (2) above, and it enhances the

---

[2] The similarities between these guidelines and the proposals of Tucker (1986), which I unfortunately did not have available at the time of my first draft, are obvious.

self-esteem and full development of the individual. It is also crucial for preserving the minority family, especially when first-language loss can mean the breakdown of communication between parents and children (Wong Fillmore 1991).

2 Language awareness

2.1 History and principles of Language awareness. In Great Britain the need for more consistent and systematic language education was brought sharply into focus by the government report *A Language for Life* (also known as the 'Bullock Report 1975'), and reiterated by subsequent reports (Swann 1985, Kingman 1988). This need was most often expressed in the form of calls for a language policy 'across the curriculum' (see above). One of the results of the increased focus on language was an interest in general language courses, often called LANGUAGE AWARENESS courses, or GENERAL LANGUAGE courses (the GLC courses in Australia, see Quinn and Trounce 1985).

In the early 1980's The British Centre for Information on Language Teaching (CILT) and the National Congress on Languages in Education (NCLE) set up a working party on Language Awareness which made a number of recommendations (Donmall 1985) and encouraged the piloting of language awareness courses, first in seven 'core schools', subsequently in many more (a full list is appended to Donmall 1985).

The Language Awareness Working Party (LAWP) agreed on the following simple definition of Language Awareness:

> Language Awareness is a person's sensitivity to and conscious awareness of the nature of language and its role in human life. (Donmall 1985:7).

Donmall et al. give a number of suggestions and reasons for Language Awareness courses. In general they claim that heightened language awareness

> ... may be expected to bring pupils to increase the language resources available to them and to foster their mastery of them, to develop the sensitivity and level of consciousness they bring to their experience of language in everyday school and social contexts and eventually to improve their effectiveness, for example, as citizens, or as consumers, and in their working life. (1985:7).

Returning for a moment to the Bullock Report *A Language for Life*, it proposes three factors that relate to Language Awareness (see Hawkins 1987 for a discussion). All three stress the role of the teacher in this enterprise and in fact, as we shall see, teacher preparation turns out to be the linchpin in successful Language Awareness Development. The three proposals mentioned in the Bullock Report are:

1. Responsibility of all teachers for language across the curriculum.
2. The inclusion of language education in the initial training of all teachers.
3. The restoration of 'adult time' to children cheated of it by home circumstances.

Hawkins points out, however, that the issue of HOW to deal with language in the classroom is treated with great ambivalence in Bullock. On the one hand, the report calls for explicit and systematic attention to language, on the other hand it abhors the 'teaching of grammar'. The latter sentiment is echoed by Donmall et al., who hasten to assure their readers that Language Awareness does not mean a return to 'grammar grind' (1985:8), and that 'it is time to exorcise the ghost of grammar past' (1985:25). It is acknowledged, however, that some explicit attention to language, hence some talk *about* language, is inevitable. How this is to be done is by no means clear, though some of the Language Awareness courses reviewed in the next section provide some initial ideas.

Some further light on the complexities of Language Awareness Development is shed by a report on early Australian efforts to implement Language Awareness courses (often called General Language Courses, or GLC). Quinn and Trounce (1985) show how the Australian Language Awareness movement peaked in 1976 and declined steadily after that (though a smaller number of successful programs continued). They suggest three main reasons for the decline, and these reasons need to be given serious thought by those of us who wish to implement Language Awareness development in the U.S.A. and elsewhere. Briefly, the reasons identified are:

1. The Language Awareness courses made demands on teachers for which they were ill-prepared.
2. It was difficult to justify the Language Awareness courses to curriculum planners and other educational decision makers.
3. The courses were not successfully adapted to the increasing population of Limited English students.

As I have suggested, a number of convincing arguments can be put forward for a more systematic educational language policy across the curriculum, both in language classes and in other subject areas. However, experience so far has shown that such a policy is fraught with problems. It is therefore essential to study the different possibilities for dealing with language in the schools very carefully. In this endeavour, linguists and educators can and must work in collaboration with one another.

In the next section we shall look at some models and pilot applications of Language Awareness in Great Britain.

2.3 Language Awareness courses. One of the most fully worked out programs for Language Awareness is set forth in Hawkins 1987. This book, which is especially addressed to teachers, provides a number of arguments for the inclusion of Language Awareness courses in schools, particularly at the secondary level. We have already alluded to several of these arguments (many of which find their origin in the Bullock Report), and others that are of general relevance will be added as we go along.

In the second part of his book Hawkins describes seven small topic books designed for 11 to 14 year-olds. The titles of these books (published by Cambridge University Press) indicate the thematic organization of the program:

Get the message!
Spoken and written language
How language works
Using language
How do we learn languages?
Language varieties and change
Comparing languages: English and its European Relatives

In these books informal descriptions of a number of topics in linguistics are given, with many illustrations and examples, as well as activities and project topics. These books are well worth studying if we propose to introduce Language Awareness courses in the U.S.A., even though there are a number of respects in which they can be significantly improved upon. In particular, one might object that Hawkins's program still treats language as a store of knowledge that needs to be TRANSMITTED. It is likely that we will need to transcend the transmission model if we want Language Awareness to succeed. However, as a pioneering efforts the series must be applauded.

Sinclair (Donmall 1985) isolates six crucial features of language and offers them as organizing content for Language Awareness courses. These are:

1. Productivity
2. Creativity
3. Stability and change
4. Social variation
5. How to do things with language
6. The two-layered code

Corson (1990) builds on the well-known distinction between 'knowing how' and 'knowing what' and gives useful blueprints for each of these two aspects. He subsequently extends the notion of Language Awareness to CRITICAL LANGUAGE AWARENESS, under which heading he identifies three major categories of issues:

1. Promoting social awareness of discourse.
2. Promoting critical awareness of variety.
3. Promoting consciousness of and practice for change.

It is clear that this perspective has much in common with the currently very popular CRITICAL THINKING (Costa 1985) and PRACTICAL INTELLIGENCE (Sternberg et al. 1990) courses. Indeed, critical thinking and everyday reasoning build upon an awareness of language and language use.

Stubbs (in Carter 1982) divides language content areas into six blocks, and in each block looks at language from three points of view: Textual Analysis TX, Language Variation LV, and Language Planning LP.

The six language content blocks that Stubbs proposes are:

1. Styles of language
2. Native language learning
3. Dialects and codes
4. Multilingualism
5. Written language and literacy
6. Literary language

Finally, Donmall (1985) contains detailed descriptions of several actual Language Awareness programs in different schools in Great Britain. Particularly interesting is a report from a school in Southall (written by Jean Brewster) which illustrates language awareness work in a primary school context. One of the closing comments in this report refers to the problem of teacher education (p. 207):

> . . . most teachers remain relatively unaware of the nature and function of language learning and teaching. It is vital therefore that teacher education should include initial and in-service courses covering these features so that teachers can more effectively enhance their own awareness of language and thereby that of their pupils.

Note that the lack of teacher preparation was also cited by Quinn and Trounce as a major reason for the decline of GLC courses in Australia. It seems reasonable, therefore, to concentrate our efforts at the teacher education level before we make wholesale recommendations for the implementation of Language Awareness courses in the public schools.

2.4 Language Awareness in teacher development. Language Awareness Development for teachers (LAD, to borrow an acronym) does not primarily consist of linguistics or grammar courses, though I do not wish to imply that it would make such courses superfluous for language teachers. All teachers need some form of language education, though not all need the specialized linguistics training of language teachers. What would an effective and innovative LAD look like?

Let us begin with two quotes from Halliday (1982:13). These quotes, though somewhat lengthy, give us a solid platform to begin our discussion of LAD. First, as to the relevance of linguistics for teachers, and a methodological recommendation:

> I would like to reject categorically the assertion that a course of general linguistics is of no particular use to teachers. I think it's fundamental. But I don't think it should be a sort of watered down academic linguistics course. It should be something new, designed and worked out by linguists and teacher trainers together.

Further, Halliday's stern admonition to those who would reject theory and insist on immediately useful 'practical' things only:

> ... we should beware of thinking that every subject exists simply to serve the needs of education. There is a tendency for educators to demand an immediate pay-off: if we can't apply these ideas directly here and now in our teaching, then we don't want anything to do with them. This attitude passes for a healthy pragmatism: we're practical people with a job to do, no time for the frills. In fact it is simply mental laziness—a refusal to inquire into things that may not have any immediate and obvious applications, but which for this very reason may have a deeper significance in the long run. Most of linguistics is not classroom stuff; but it is there behind the lines, underlying our classroom practices, and our ideas about children, and about learning and reality.

Most teacher trainers will sympathize with Halliday's tirade, even though many teachers may not. However, if we make an accommodation between the first Hallidayan quote and the one below it, we will naturally mellow the latter while at the same time fleshing out the former. What I mean is that, when we look for innovative ways to encourage teachers' development of Language Awareness, we will find that an EXPERIENTIAL approach, drawing on teachers' experiences with language in their professional as well as in wider social contexts, will be most beneficial. Further, we will draw on RELEVANT and AUTHENTIC data sources, that is, spoken and written language which directly relates to teaching and learning in classrooms. Thirdly, we will design activities that challenge the teachers' intellectual powers and give them CHOICES for drawing on various professional interests and knowledge bases.

If such criteria, and others like them, are applied in the design and execution of LAD courses, it is my experience that the theory/practice confrontation evaporates almost instantaneously. It becomes obsolete, being replaced by exploration and discovery.

Before giving some concrete suggestions, let us look briefly at the ideal place of Language Awareness in the school curriculum, so that the focus and purpose of Language Awareness Development courses for teachers can be seen more clearly.

2.5 Language Awareness in the school curriculum. Eric Hawkins (1987:2) makes a useful distinction between a **horizontal** and a **vertical** curriculum. The horizontal curriculum is synchronic, a timetable of subjects and slots, planned by the principal and hung on the wall. The vertical curriculum is diachronic, the cumulative experiences and learning processes of the students as they progress in their scholastic careers. We thus have a distinction between breadth and depth, or attention to language as spread over the various classrooms (across the curriculum, as recommended in Bullock 1975), and as embedded deep inside the students' learning experiences. Although this distinction is of necessity somewhat imprecise, it is very useful for avoiding a narrow role—or having no role at all—for language education. Such a narrow role would be implied in quadrants A, B, and C of the semantic wheel in Figure 1.

Figure 1. Semantic wheel.

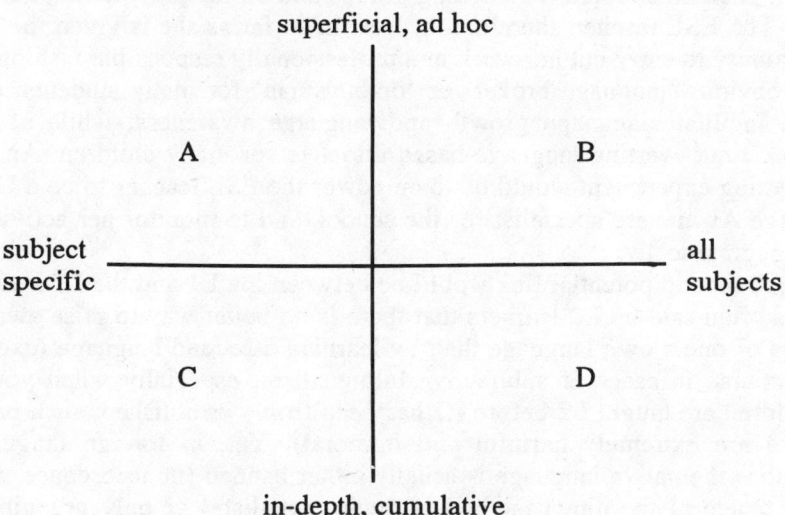

We can use this simple map of curricular options to help us decide what it is we want to do and what we want to avoid. We want to avoid limiting language education to haphazard and piecemeal activities in a single subject 'language lesson' (A). We must also avoid similar unfocussed language work across the curriculum, that is, talking about language in the different subject areas just when it occurs to us or to the textbook writer, thus running the danger of talking at cross purposes (B). We do not want to restrict language education to a designated 'language' or 'language arts' lesson, without systematic connections to other academic work (C). What we want to promote is a systematic in-depth approach to language education across the child's entire educational career, emphasizing the central instructional and social role of language all over the school (in the classroom, the corridor, the office, and the playground), and the role of language (and dialect, minority language, and so on) in society (D).

Eventually, the most satisfactory solution to language education will be a combination of C and D, with well-explicated links between the language lesson and other lessons, including of course the foreign language lesson. This is a long-term objective in need of much pioneering work, but a logical consequence of all I have said hitherto, if it has any validity. I would like to mention two aspects of such cross-subject links that lend themselves to immediate action research (I realize that a prerequisite for succes—or a result of success!—would be a breakdown of the compartmentalization which is so rampant in today's schools).

First, ESL teachers in schools are often ideally placed to assist LEP students in their various school activities, including subject lessons, encounters with counsellors, administrators, coaches, and other personnel, with peers in cooperative learning groups and on the playground, and so on. The ESL teacher, therefore, at least in so far as she is given the opportunity to carry out her work in a professionally responsible fashion, is an obvious 'language broker' or 'ombudsman' for many students, and can facilitate language growth and language awareness, while at the same time averting language-based disasters for many children. An interesting experiment would be to empower the ESL teacher to be a Language Awareness specialist for the school, and to monitor her activities ethnographically.

A second potential link would be between the L1 and the L2 lesson. It is often said by L2 learners that there is no better way to raise awareness of one's own language than by learning a second language (except of course in cases of subtractive bilingualism, especially when young children are taught L2 before L1 has been firmly established; such practices are extremely harmful and immoral). Yet, in foreign language lessons the native language is usually either banned (in accordance with the tenets of the direct method or audiolingualism) or only grudgingly tolerated as a last resort (in most communicative courses). Conversely, in the native-language lesson a discussion of foreign-language concepts and experiences is not considered relevant. This artificial separation is largely due to a very stubborn but unfounded popular belief that two languages necessarily compete with one another in the learner's mind. In actual fact there is an enormous potential for cross-fertilization between native language and foreign language(s) which is almost completely ignored in the schools (an exception is Duff 1989), and which could be an important vehicle in the development of higher cognitive skills and critical thinking.

I believe that this cross-fertilization is what Rudolf Flesch had in mind when he remarked that, for the sake of clear thinking, 'the important thing is not the learning of foreign languages, but the activity of translation' (1951:49). But we need an urgent note of caution here. Bearing in mind the ghost of grammar past that we encountered above, we must also guard against another ghost, the one of translation past. Let us not draw the conclusion that we should go back to the types of mindless translation exercises which used to be the mainstay of every solid foreign language program. The study of Language Awareness can suggest far more sophisticated ways of capitalizing on the cross-fertilization between languages (on using translating and interpreting as pedagogical activities for L1/L2 language development in the secondary school, see Walqui 1991).

2.6 The syllabus as road map: The Triple A of Awareness, Autonomy, and Authenticity. In the U.S.A., the AAA is the American Automobile Association. It has a wonderful service of providing the traveller with a free 'Triptik', a spiral-bound collection of maps tracing the route which the member has indicated when requesting the service. On these maps, which you flip over as you travel along, there is a lot of information: gas stations, interesting spots and sights, smaller-scale maps of larger areas of interest, town plans, side roads worthy of exploration, and so on. I like to use this Triptik as a picture of my ideal syllabus: a road map with information and options; a guide, but one which leaves you the freedom to stop wherever you want, for as long as you want to, to travel with other people or on your own, to go off on tangents when it occurs to you, coming back to the main highway whenever you are ready.

In language education, an ideal syllabus such as the Triptik pictured here is only possible if it is based on certain curricular ideals and principles. In addition to the principle of LANGUAGE AWARENESS (and Learning Awareness, as well as other kinds of Awareness) which is the subject of this paper, the principles of AUTONOMY and AUTHENTICITY are crucial. Autonomy in learning and teaching is essential if informed and responsible choices are to be possible, and choices are necessary to ensure the intrinsic motivation, and hence the depth of processing, which guarantees language learning (van Lier 1991). Authenticity is a complex notion encompassing much more than just the purposes for which the input (textbook exercise, story, dialogue, example, etc.) was created. Elsewhere (van Lier 1991) I have described five types of authenticity that are of relevance in the language classroom: authenticity of ORIGIN, of CONTEXT, of PURPOSE (context and purpose together constitute PRAGMATIC authenticity), and PEDAGOGICAL and EXISTENTIAL authenticity.

A syllabus based on the AAA principles is of course an ambitious and long-term project, requiring structural changes in educational practices and a fundamental rethinking of the role and aims of education, and its place in society. LAD makes a very small but essential contribution to such change. In the final section below I will look at some practical suggestions for LAD at the teacher education level, with some tentative projections towards Language Awareness work in actual classrooms.

2.7 Language Awareness Development: Some practical examples. In order to implement LAD courses for teachers in accordance with the requirements for relevance and authenticity mentioned above (section **2.4**), it is necessary to identify areas of perennial concern in education. It should be perfectly possible for teachers to generate their own list of such concerns. Here is one from my own courses and workshops:

1. Correctness in language. What is correct and what is not? When should we do something about incorrect language, and how should we do it? Who should do it?
2. Field work: the problem of collecting language samples in the world (including the classroom world). What to do with the samples once collected.
3. The language of control. Management, discipline, persuasion, manipulation, domination, submission, and so on, in the classroom, in the media, between sexes and ethnic groups, in government, and so on.
4. The language of advertising, propaganda, campaigning, political speeches.
5. Prejudice, stereotypes, cultural differences, assimilation, and multiculturalism.
6. Foreigner talk and teacherese: simplification, oversimplification, talking down.

And so on . . . the list can be extended indefinitely, depending on teachers' interests and needs and, most importantly, their growing awareness of language-related professional issues.

As an example I will use the theme of CORRECTNESS. The starting point is as follows: most teachers, and also most language students, tend to assume a rather clearcut distinction between what is 'right' and 'wrong' in language. There are a number of ways in which teachers can come to realize that in actual fact such a clear distinction is fictitious. I will briefly describe some activities that address the issue of correctness. Actual materials referred to are reproduced in the appendix.

(1) Activity 1 in Appendix 1 gives 30 actual sentences spoken/written by native speakers which might be regarded as odd or incorrect, or non-standard. By evaluating these and learning that these were all produced by native speakers, teachers can judge their degree of 'grammatical tolerance'. It can also lead to an investigation of dialect and idiolect.

(2) A series of activities addressing colloquial speech may begin with the 'Djeetchet' ad (Appendix 2). Many native speakers need some time and hints to figure out what is meant, but they can subsequently come up with other examples of absorption patterns in English (e.g., 'watcha', 'waintcha', 'wanna'). This can lead to an investigation of colloquial speech and how it differs from written language.

Adding the dimension of regional dialects, we can write the words *a norsy zedandle* on the blackboard. Nobody will know what these words mean. I actually took those words from a recording of *Albert and the Lion*, a Lancashire folk poem, read by a British friend of mine when he visited us. I play the recording, and eventually it turns out that the actual words are *a horse's head handle*.

Since all *h*s are dropped, and consonants are linked with subsequent vowels by the process of elision, the actual pronunciation can be transformed quite substantially (especially for foreign students, of course). Here is the verse in which the phrase first occurs:

A grand little lad was young Albert
All dressed in his best, quite a swell
With a stick with an horse's head handle
The finest that Woolworths would sell.

(3) In the past I have asked ESL students to bring an 'entry ticket' to every class. This is a 5x3 card on which they have noted some linguistic item they have heard outside class, together with contextual information. This 'field work' activity can easily be adapted for teacher development classes, since it will give practice in collecting field data, and trains the teacher to be attentive to actual language use in the environment (rather than assuming that the language norm is contained in the textbook).

(4) When we mishear or misinterpret a message, and this happens frequently among native speakers, this may be due to a variety of factors. Using the 'concentric circles' diagram in Appendix 3, teachers

can analyze actual instances of communication failures in terms of the linguistic/pragmatic systems that may have led to the breakdown.

(5) Finally, Appendix 4 presents 'The Grammar Stick', which I have used successfully in teacher inservice courses and ESL courses alike. Quite simply, it forces a modulated evaluation of some particular piece of language rather than a categorical 'right-wrong' one. The actual anatomy of the stick, and the particular labels chosen, are of course less important than the intended message. For example, when one teacher asked me why I used the word 'odd' in one place, and the word 'strange' in another, I could use the stick itself to say that they were each 'about five-and-a-half'. In its imperfection, the grammar stick therefore reflects the imperfection of our own continuous judgments of correctness and acceptability.

Conclusion. At times it seems as if we have been performing a slow LANGECTOMY on education. Although all of education is saturated with and driven by language, it seems that we fail to encourage students to take control of their language faculty and develop it fully to become clear thinkers and efficient communicators. In addition we routinely fail to forge links between school language and community language, with the result that we unwittingly contribute to family breakdown, community alienation, dropout, and youth gangs. These are very serious problems, and I am not suggesting that language problems are the prime cause of all of them. However, I am proposing that, for educators, especially language teachers, and linguists, language is the means whereby our profession can positively contribute to a solution. Beyond that, there is a plausible argument to be made that language can be a CATALYST for bringing about a series of educational and social changes.

As in all fields of human endeavour, AWARENESS is the first step towards improvement. Initially, many people may be as little aware of the importance of language in their lives as fish are aware of the importance of water. Through awareness, we can take control of language and use it to improve both cognitive and social processes.

In education, language has in the past been treated as an OBJECT to be analyzed, parsed, and studied. This treatment has often resulted in lack of motivation and in perceptions of language study as being irrelevant to real-life concerns. Whenever the subject of language study is brought up, this 'ghost of grammar past' comes back to haunt us. In addition, whenever we discuss the possibility of comparing languages in the classroom, the equally lugubrious 'ghost of translation past' rattles its rusty chains.

In both cases, I suggest, the crux of the problem is the treatment of language as an academic OBJECT for study, the CONTENTS of which are to be TRANSMITTED to the students. Instead, we must see language as a key ingredient in the PROCESSES of growing, living, and thinking.

I have reviewed a few proposals and attempts to implement Language Awareness courses in schools. The main problem that has been noted has been the area of teacher education. Unless teachers develop their own metalinguistic knowledge and skills, they are unlikely to be able to deal effectively with the developmental language needs of their students. For that reason I am proposing the development of pre-service and in-service Language Awareness courses, with subsequent implementation of carefully monitored (through action research) Language Awareness courses in schools.

Appendix 1. Grammatical Tolerance test by Leo van Lier.

Key: 1 - Grammatically correct; Standard American English.
         2 - OK, e.g. in dialect, jargon, but not Standard American English.
         3 - Sounds foreign, not proper grammar.
         4 - I can't make sense of this.

Sentences:
1. He dove into the icy water.
2. Let's take the microphone out at the street.
3. She will likelily be billed for these items.
4. Is your house rugged (/rʌgd).
5. These clothes need washed.
6. Benefits likely will be cut.
7. We're the busiest this fall than ever before.
8. The roads are safer and less people are getting killed anymore.
9. They all ran away except Ryan and me.
10. The government have broken all their promises.
11. Could you open the television, please? I want to watch 'Miami Vice.'
12. [Ringgg!] Can I speak to Margaret?—This is she.
13. Everybody got their money ready?
14. What time should I knock you up?
15. We're way ahead of them, rocketwise.
16. He carried her to the dance.
17. That's my brother, whom I think is waiting for us.
18. Who do you want to talk to?
19. This is strictly between you and I.
20. The sporting neneks sang and 'mengalaid' through the night.
21. I think it starts at half seven.
22. It's ten minutes in front of eight o'clock.
23. Tomorrow the Upper Mississippi Valley will get unseasonable amounts of precip.
24. I didn't use to wear seatbelts ever.
25. Hey, Valerie, you should've came!
26. Stones rule OK!
27. I ain't afraid of no ghosts.
28. OK, let's go in already.
29. Do you have a scissors?
30. Josh's brother can olly all kinds of high.

To find your score, add all your marks and divide by 30. For example, if you rated all sentences 1, your score would be 1+1+1... etc., 30 times = 30, divided by 30 = 1. You would have perfect tolerance!

Appendix 2.

Appendix 3. Interpreting a message (L. van Lier 1991).

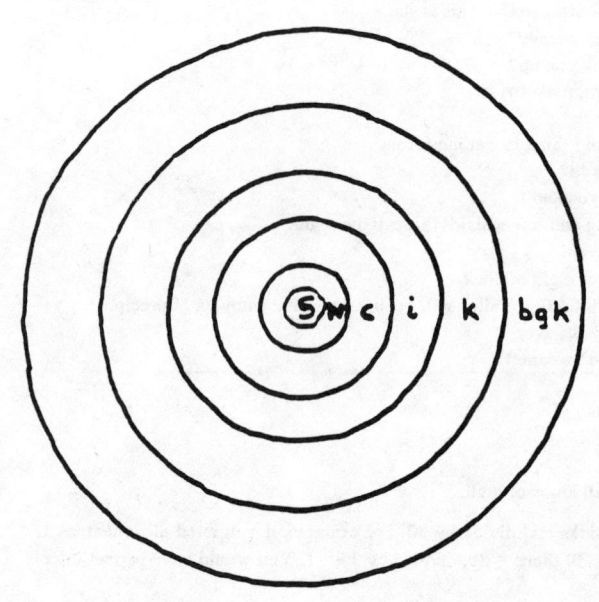

Key:

s   sound
patios vs. *pantyhose*
(nasal pronunciation)

w   word
estoy embarazada
'I'm pregnant'

c   clause
visiting aunts can be boring

i   intonation
she won't go out with anyone
(fall vs. rise-fall-rise)

k   kinesics
how interesting! (roll eyes)

bgk   background knowledge
A: *Let's buy a BMW.*
B: *Sure, we've got plenty of money.* [we don't, of course.]

Appendix 4. Grammar stick (L. van Lier 1990).

```
10 ──── obligatory
 9 ──── preferred
 8 ──── unmarked
 7 ──── OK: in this context
 6 ──── equivalent
 5 ────
 4 ──── strange: in this context
 3 ──── marked
 2 ──── odd
 1 ──── ?
 0 ──── *
```

References

Brumfit, C. ed. 1990. CLE Working Papers 1. Centre for Language in Education, University of Southampton.

Carter, R. ed. 1982. Linguistics and the teacher. London: Routledge and Kegan Paul.

Corson, D. 1988. Oral language across the curriculum. Clevedon, Avon: Multilingual Matters.

Corson, D. 1990. Language policy across the curriculum. Clevedon, Avon: Multilingual Matters.

Costa, A. ed. 1985. Developing minds. Alexandria, Va.: ASCD.

DES Department of Education and Science. 1975. A Language for Life (The Bullock Report). London: HMSO.

────── 1985. Education for All: Report of the Committee of Inquiry into the Education of Children from Ethnic Minority Groups (The Swan Report). London: HMSO.

────── 1988. Report of the Committee of Inquiry into the Teaching of the English Language (The Kingman Report). London: HMSO.

Donmall, B.G. ed. 1985. Language awareness. NCLE Reports and Papers 6. London: CILT.
Duff, A. 1989. Translation. Oxford: Oxford University Press.
Flesch, R. 1951. The art of clear thinking. New York: Barnes and Noble.
Halliday, M. 1982. Linguistics in teacher education. In Carter ed. 10-15.
Hawkins, E. 1987. Awareness of language. Cambridge: Cambridge University Press. Issues in Applied Linguistics 1,2
Larsen-Freeman, D. 1990. On the need for a theory of language teaching. In: James E. Alatis, ed. Georgetown University Round Table on Languages and Linguistics 1990: The interdependence of theory, practice and research. Washington, D.C.: Georgetown University Press.
Literacy and Language Task Force. 1990. The language of Australia: Discussion paper on an Australian Literacy and Language Policy for the 1990s. Canberra, Australia: Department of Employment, Education and Training.
Mitchell, R., and J. Hooper. 1990. Teachers' views of language knowledge. In Brumfit ed. 18-26.
OISE Ontario Institute for Studies in Education. 1990. Toronto.
Quinn, T.J., and M. Trounce. 1985. Some aspects of Australian experience with Language Awareness courses. In Donmall ed. 132-142.
Sinclair, J.M. 1985. Language awareness in six easy lessons. In Donmall ed. 33-6.
Sternberg, R.J., L. Okagaki, and A. S. Jackson. 1990. Practical intelligence for success in school. Educational Leadership 48,1.35-9.
Stubbs, M. 1982. What is English: Modern English language in the curriculum. In Carter ed. 137-155.
Tucker, G. R. 1986. Developing a language-competent American society. In: D. Tannen and James E. Alatis, eds. Georgetown University Round Table on Languages and Linguistics 1985. Washington, D. C.: Georgetown University Press.
van Lier, L. 1991. Inside the classroom: Learning processes and teaching procedures. Applied Language Learning. 2,1:29-68.
Walqui, A. 1991. Language awareness through translation and interpretation for bilingual high school students. Presentation at TESOL Convention, March 25, 1991, New York.
Wong Fillmore, L. 1991. Easy come, easy go: when learning a second language means losing the first. Plenary address, SLRF Conference, March 1991, Los Angeles.

The relevance of linguistic theory for language pedagogy: Debunking the myths

Suzanne Flynn*
Massachusetts Institute of Technology

Introduction. This paper is motivated in large part by observations I made during *GURT '90*. The theme of that conference was: *The inter-dependence of* theory, research and practice. Papers presented were supposed to clarify the relationship among these three domains in some way. While most attempted to do so, it became apparent during the course of the conference that there existed certain obstacles that blocked an effective integration of linguistic and pedagogic interests specifically. One 'theme' that emerged in several of the papers was a rejection of the usefulness of linguistic theory, in particular a generative theory, as a tool for effective language teaching. Such a repudiation is not new and one that can be readily understood in terms of early developments in the field of linguistics. Traditionally, linguistic theory and its related psycholinguistic research did not easily allow for meaningful extensions to language pedagogy. Consequently, little dialogue was encouraged or fostered between these two domains. When attempts were made to integrate the two in some way, they often proved unsatisfactory (see related discussion in Newmeyer 1983; Flynn 1990, 1991; Kim-Renaud 1991). Within the last decade, however, there have been significant advances made in linguistics and its related research. Yet the stalemate between linguistic theory and language pedagogy still continues. Why?

I argue that a major contributory factor to this problem are certain long-standing myths maintained by both linguistic theorists and language pedagogues about each other's endeavors and theories. In this paper I will attempt to address several of these fictions and demonstrate that they are based on faulty or fallacious assumptions. Once we have debunked these myths, we will be in a position to consider meaningful extensions and exchanges between linguistic theory and language pedagogy.

---

* The author wishes to thank and acknowledge Jack Carroll, Young-Key Kim-Renaud, and Gita Martohardjono for discussions concerning various aspects of the issues addressed in this paper.

Central to this paper is the belief that a dialogue between linguistic theorists and language pedagogues must be established. We can no longer afford the luxury of not 'speaking' to each other. Linguists need language teachers and language teachers need linguists. In order to develop explanatory theories of language, which by definition must account for how language learning is made possible, one must make reference to the second language learning process. At the same time, in order to teach effectively, one must have an adequate theory of the language to be taught, and the best developed theories have been those developed by linguists (see related discussion in Kim-Renaud 1991).

More simply stated, trying to develop effective teaching tools without reference to linguistic theory is analogous to trying to repair an engine without any theory of how an engine works. At the same time, developing theories of language without reference to the second language acquisition process is akin to designing an engine without any knowledge of how the engine is to be used. While not pretending to be able to address every relevant issue that emerged during *GURT '90*, I will limit myself to a discussion of three principal myths as well as several associated ones. The focus in this paper will be on issues germane to the role of linguistic theory for language teaching.

Before beginning, several definitions and clarifications are necessary. First, when I use the term second language acquisition, I am referring to both the learning of a second language and the learning of a foreign language. While it is important that we acknowledge the differences that exist in the circumstances surrounding each of these contexts, I will assume that the actual process of acquisition remains constant within each of these domains.

In addition, the term second language is meant to refer to the learning of any language after the learning of the first—be it the second, third, or fourth, etc. More appropriately, I am making claims about the acquisition of a 'next language.'

In this paper, I refer principally to a generative theory of language, specifically a theory of Universal Grammar as explicated in the work of Chomsky and many others (e.g. Chomsky 1986). I do this because at the present time it is the most well developed theory of both language and the language learning process existent.

In the way of clarifications, it is important to state the incontrovertible fact that language is a complex system consisting of several interrelated subcomponents or levels, each with its own associated set of properties and principles. The basic levels of language consist of the phonology, the morphology, the syntax, the semantics—including the word storage (the lexicon)—and the principles governing the use of language in communicative contexts (the pragmatics). To become a native speaker, or near native speaker of a language, one must acquire the competence for each of these highly abstract and interrelated systems.

Describing this process is the role of the linguist; developing this competence in a language learner is the role of the language teacher.

Having stated these preliminaries, we are now in a position to consider in more detail exactly those things that keep linguistics and language teachers at odds. We will begin with a consideration of the most commonly articulated and maintained myth.

Myth 1: Linguistic theory is irrelevant for language teaching. We hear this claim articulated in at least two different ways. The first version involves those who would argue that theory and teaching are simply unrelated: 'theories are theories' and 'teaching is teaching.' The second commonly heard version involves the claim that 'linguistics is a theory of competence and not a theory of performance.' A related version is that language is simply communication and linguistic theory is not an account of this. We will consider each of these versions separately as each is problematic from a number of different perspectives.

The first position, namely that linguistic theory and language teaching are totally unrelated, correctly acknowledges the theoretical nature of the linguistic enterprise but incorrectly identifies teaching as an atheoretical one.

As briefly noted above, linguistic theory aims to represent in a formal manner the structures and processes that underlie a human's ability to speak and understand language. The grammars that linguists develop to capture these facts refer to both the internal representation of a language within a person's head and the linguist's model or best guess of that representation.

Language pedagogy, on the other hand, aims to develop and foster those structures and processes that enable an individual to speak and understand a new target language.

In order to develop this competence, language teachers resort to methodologies that reflect some form of both a theory of language and the language learning process. Without such theories, it would be impossible to teach in any coherent manner as there would be no basis upon which to develop curriculum. While this state of affairs might exist in some classrooms, it clearly reflects the exceptional case. Thus, if we already operate with some theory about language and language learning, then why not make sure that they are ones that accurately characterize the language to be learned and the language learning process. This is not to say that the linguist's representations of these grammars are the final word; rather, if one wants to develop the most effective language teaching tools, then it only makes sense that one would want to make use of all that is available, especially that which is so centrally relevant. By analogy, one would never consider constructing an airplane without consulting the laws of physics and aerodynamics. Any attempt to do so, would simply be ostracized, not to mention result in a total disaster.

A related position that one could take is that linguistic theory is not important for language teaching because the really critical goal in language teaching is to expose your students to language and its use and give them the opportunity to develop their knowledge of language through those interactions. In response to such a claim, we know of no language teacher who provides their students with nothing but unstructured conversation. Whether we acknowledge it or not, we utilize our own implicit theories about language and language learning when we teach. Again, given that we already operate with such theories, why not make sure that they are the appropriate ones?

With respect to the second claim namely that linguistics is a theory of competence and not of performance, we need to begin by clarifying what it is that we mean by competence and performance. Linguistic competence refers to our tacit knowledge of the structure of our language. It is 'the system of rules and principles that we assume have, in some manner, been internally represented by the person who knows a language and that enable the speaker, in principle to understand an arbitrary sentence and to produce a sentence expressing his thought; . . .' (Chomsky 1980:201).

Linguistic performance, on the other hand, refers to 'actual use of language in concrete situations.' (Chomsky 1965:4). Essentially, linguistic performance is our language knowledge in use. Every aspect of language performance involves language competence in some way. To name a few, it is involved in our processing of language, our production of language, our recognition, recall. For example, we cannot identify sentences we hear as being ungrammatical, mispronounced, or anomalous without using our own implicit language knowledge to make such judgments. If a speaker accesses this impicit knowledge base to produce and comprehend language, then how can a teacher ignore this in a language classroom? Thus, development of any theory of performance must take into account a theory of competence as well as taking into 'account the structure of memory, our mode of organizing experience, and so on' (Chomsky 1980:225).

In this way, performance and competence are mutually dependent, almost inseparable. To thus claim that language teaching is only concerned with performance is simply ludicrous. In language teaching, the goal is to develop the linguistic competence of a speaker so that language learners can appropriately use the target language. We cannot teach our students to 'perform' correctly unless they have the linguistic competence needed to do so. Another way to look at this is to consider the fact that speakers do not produce utterances atheoretically. If they did not have an implicit theory of grammar in their heads, they would not be able to speak grammatically or recognize ungrammaticality.

In a related manner, one cannot simply dismiss linguistic theory by saying that there is more to language than merely linguistic competence.

No one would deny this fact. However, to attempt to deny the relevance of linguistic theory on the basis of this fact is simply preposterous.

In short, linguistic theory is not irrelevant for language pedagogy. It determines the core for what must be developed in the language learner.

Myth 2: Linguistic theory is too esoteric and too complicated. A second related myth arises among some of those who might in principle accept the relevance of linguistic theory for language teaching. Specifically, there are those who would argue that linguistic theory, though potentially relevant, is essentially incomprehensible or that it changes too quickly.

In response to this claim, one has to respond that 'yes, linguistic theory is complex and yes, it is a developing theory.' However, this does not distinguish it from any other theory or discipline that is dynamic and evolving—be it physics, biology or chemistry—nor can we use complexity as a convenient substitute for scholarship and rigor in the discipline. Language teaching itself is also very complex yet it does not mean that we stop attempting to teach language or stop attempting to try to articulate what it is that are trying to do.

At another level, admitting or acknowledging the complexity of linguistic theory does not mean that its basic principles are incomprehensible. The theory can be useful whether we understand the fundamental percepts or pursue the particulars in great detail. For example, Japanese and English differ in head-direction. What does this mean? In English, we have verb-object constructions, prepositions, noun-relative clause constructions, etc. In contrast, in Japanese we have object-verb constructions, postpositions, relative clause-noun constructions etc. (for a more detailed discussion see Stowell 1981; Flynn 1987). At a very general level, it is very useful for a language teacher to know as a consequence of these facts about language that her Japanese students, for example, expect to see their modifiers before the nouns, direct objects before their verbs, nouns before their postpositions, etc. But this will not be true for Spanish speakers as Spanish is a head-initial language like English. Thus, when learning a head-initial language like English, Japanese speakers will encounter difficulties not experienced by Spanish speakers (e.g. Flynn 1987).[1] If one knows about head-direction facts in languages

---

1 This is not to say that when learning English that the Japanese speakers will assume that English is Japanese and simply transfer their first language structures onto English. Flynn (1987) has shown that while these speakers at early stages of acquisition know that Japanese and English differ in head direction, they must reset the head direction parameter to cohere with English. Because Spanish and English match in this regard, Spanish speakers do not have to reset a parameter. Thus, when we examine and compare the patterns of development for both of these groups, we found certain differences (as well as similarities) that we can account for in terms of the match or mismatch in head direction among the languages.

like Japanese and Spanish, then one will have available a potentially very useful teaching tool to employ.

In short, by understanding the fundamentals, we can begin to understand what an individual is going through, i.e. what one has to achieve in the construction of an second language grammar. The more depth that one goes into with the theory, the more useful the theory will become. But the fact remains that in either case, if this linguistic knowledge is used in either a general sense or in a more detailed one, our teaching is likely to be more effective than if we did not use it all.

Another related myth is that the theory is only concerned with syntax. This is only partially true; phonology is also very well developed within linguistic theory. However, it is no accident that syntax is focal in much work. Syntactic patterns link the sounds and meaning together. Acknowledging this fact, however, does not mean that this is all that linguists believe constitute language or language knowledge. As stated above, language consists of a set of highly complex, interrelated subsystems. A central goal of linguistics is to represent the principles that govern each of these subsystems and to discover those that link each of these systems to each other as well as those principles that allow essential linkups with other cognitive domains. The claim that linguistics is only concerned with syntax is one that has been generated from outside the field, not within it. It is patently false.

Myth 3: We are a discipline in our own right and we should not rely upon linguistics and related research to tell us what to do. This is a claim that is becoming quite commonly heard within the field as it seeks to establish its own identity and agenda. However, while widely articulated, it is not clear what this claims means. It seems to reflect more of an insecurity within the field itself about its own identity rather than an articulation of position that is based on reason and logic. The field of language pedagogy does not exist in a vacuum; we are dealing with human beings and not robots. To effectively teach, one must make reference to other relevant fields. As stated above, the language learning task is extremely complex. It must often take into account a myriad range of theories that have sources outside of the field. This is simply a fact, given the nature of the endeavour.

Returning to our airplane building, if we want to construct a good airplane, we are not likely to be very successful if we ignore the laws of gravity or aerodynamics because we believe them to be too theoretical and irrelevant to the practical task of successful airplane building. The same relationship holds for the relationship between linguistic theory and language pedagogy. If your language students are to 'fly' right, we do not want to hand them a pair of inverted wings.

At this point one might ask, in what more specific ways can linguistic theory be used to inform our language teaching practices. As I have developed such ideas in work elsewhere (Flynn 1990, 1991), I will simply sketch out a few ways in which linguistic theory might prove important.

At the most general level, linguistic theory is important in terms of our understanding about what knowledge is available to the second language learner, how this knowledge is used, and how learning takes place. In turn, these insights have consequences for teacher training and classroom composition, as well as for the development of effective groupings and sequencing of curricular materials. I will briefly consider the relevance of linguistic theory for the development of curricular materials in one way.

To illustrate, current theory challenges many of our traditional ideas concerning the organization of materials to be presented in a class. Linguistic theory isolates ways in which the often seemingly unrelated, abstract properties of a language cluster together and can be accounted for in terms of a single grammatical principle. One simple illustration of this would be the head-direction phenomenon I referred to above for Japanese and English. This head-direction property, though easily tractable for some constructions within a language, is concerned with fairly abstract relationships in a language. Capitalizing upon all the ways that head-direction manifests itself in a particular language could serve as a basis of curricular development. For example, when teaching Japanese students English, one unit that could be developed would be one that focussed on the head-initial properties of English. In so doing, one would want to present the students with materials that dealt with noun phrase configurations, verb phrase configurations, and prepositional phrases as well as complex sentences. In this way, learners would be exposed to a range of linguistic phenomena associated with this particular property of the language.

While this is a very simple example (and I do not want to trivialize this endeavour in any way), it nonetheless specifies in a very concise manner how one might begin to implement insights garnered from linguistic theory in the language curriculum. Readers are referred to Flynn (1990, 1991) for a more detailed explication of these ideas.

Conclusions. To conclude, in this paper I have attempted to debunk several commonly articulated myths concerning the relevance of linguistic theory for language pedagogy. While historically we can understand how many of these myths were generated, at the present time there is no longer any basis for their continuance. In fact, to continue to hold onto such false beliefs will keep the field of language teaching forever outside the mainstream of any intellectual endeavour and will keep it enslaved by its own prejudices and illusions.

References

Chomsky, N. 1965. Aspects of a theory of syntax. Cambridge, Mass.: MIT Press.
Chomsky, N. 1980. Rules and representations. New York: Columbia University Press.
Chomsky, N. 1986. Knowledge of language. New York: Praeger Press.
Flynn, S. 1987. A parameter-setting model of L2 acquisition: Experimental studies in anaphora. Dordrecht: Reidel Press.
Flynn, S. 1990. Theory, practice, and research: Strange or blissful bedfellows? Georgetown University Round Table on Languages and Linguistics 1990: Linguistics, language teaching and language acquisition: The interdependence of theory, practice and research, ed. by James E. Alatis, 112-122. Washington, D.C.: Georgetown University Press.
Flynn, S. 1991. Linguistic theory and foreign language learning environments. Foreign language research in cross-cultural perspectives, ed. by K. de Bot, D. Koste, R. Ginsberg, and C. Kramsch. Amsterdam: John Benjamins Press.
Kim-Renaud, Y-K. 1991. The governance of foreign language teaching and learning: The issues for Korean. Paper presented at AAS, New Orleans.
Newmeyer, F. 1983. Grammatical theory: Its limits and its possibilities. Chicago: University of Chicago Press.
Stowell, T. 1981. Origins of phrase structure. Ph.D. dissertation, MIT.

What can real spoken data teach teachers of English?

Jan Svartvik
Lund University

December 10 is 'Nobel Day'. It is a big day in my country and, in fact, in the international scientific community at large, in being the day when the Nobel Prizes are 'received from the hands of his Majesty the King'. More often than not, those phrases are said in English by eminent senior Swedish scientists with such striking Scandinavian sing-song intonations that the younger generation exposed, both before and after their critical period to pop songs and CNN 24-hours-a-day satellite broadcasts, make fun of it. Yet these scientists read and write professional articles in English as a matter of course and master a vocabulary far larger than that of their younger critics.

This is one of the generation gaps that show up in the command of spoken and written English. The gap may be attributed to the different language teaching methods that the two generations have been subjected to, but also to the different types of English to which they have been exposed. The spoken English discourse that is part and parcel of our contemporary international lifestyle provides both input and motivation to the young and an advantage in gaining competence in spoken English.

Assuming that both teaching methods and exposure to authentic language are important for language learning—and I am here talking chiefly about the EFL context—the question I want to address is what we as teachers can learn from 'real spoken data', more specifically from 'computerized corpora of spoken English', i.e. samples of recorded, transcribed and analyzed spoken language which are intended to represent 'real language' as opposed to the 'concocted examples' often used in linguistic studies or the 'pedagogical language' as commonly encountered in language learning textbooks.

The attitude to the use of corpora in linguistic research has had its ups and downs. During the downperiod for corpus-based research it was widely claimed that there was no reason for linguists to gather data from outside their own competence in a language. For a number of reasons, this attitude has changed and we now find a growing demand, from various quarters, for the large bodies of computerized data we call 'corpora', in particular those that represent interactive spoken discourse.

Despite the quantitative dominance of speech over writing in most people's everyday use of English in the world and despite the growing realization—largely under the impact of the communicative approach—of the importance of actively teaching the spoken language, there is as yet little spoken material that is readily available, in machine-readable form, to an interested customer. As for the American variety, there are now advanced plans at the University of California, Santa Barbara, for producing a corpus of adult-spoken American English. There is also another project under way, the International Corpus of English, with the aim of compiling comparable samples of both spoken and written English as it is used in over 15 locations in the world (Greenbaum, forthcoming).

Producing a spoken corpus is an extremely time-consuming operation which goes a long way toward explaining the lack of such language data banks. The production involves several steps, some of which are not required for compiling a written English corpus: selecting a suitable range of situations to record, making the recordings, producing transcripts with prosodic notation, and computerizing the transcripts, preferably with the text 'tagged', i.e. supplied with linguistic analyses.

For well over a decade a major part of research in the English Department at Lund University has centered on the study of spoken English based on the London-Lund Corpus. This is a collection of about half a million words as spoken by native British English speakers in different types of discourse. As the name implies, the London-Lund Corpus of Spoken English derives from two cities, and it is the result of cooperation between our project at Lund and the Survey of English Usage, University College, London. Figure 1 (reproduced from Greenbaum & Svartvik 1990) shows the plan of the complete corpus of both spoken and written English. Within the branch labelled 'spoken' (which covers the texts of the London-Lund Corpus), a main distinction is made between dialogue, including conversation and public discussion, and monologue, including spontaneous and prepared speech. In its transcribed form this corpus is available on disk to scholars all over the world who are interested in working on the material with their PCs. (For further information about this and other generally available computerized corpora, see recent issues of *ICAME Journal*[1]). One third of our corpus, which includes conversation, is also available in print. Figure 2 gives an example of a transcript of a conversation between two female academics (A & B) talking about choosing art objects for their offices (from Text S.1.8 as printed in Svartvik & Quirk 1980).

---

1 *ICAME Journal*, published by the Norwegian Computing Centre for the Humanities, University of Bergen, P.O. Box 53, N-5027 Bergen, Norway.

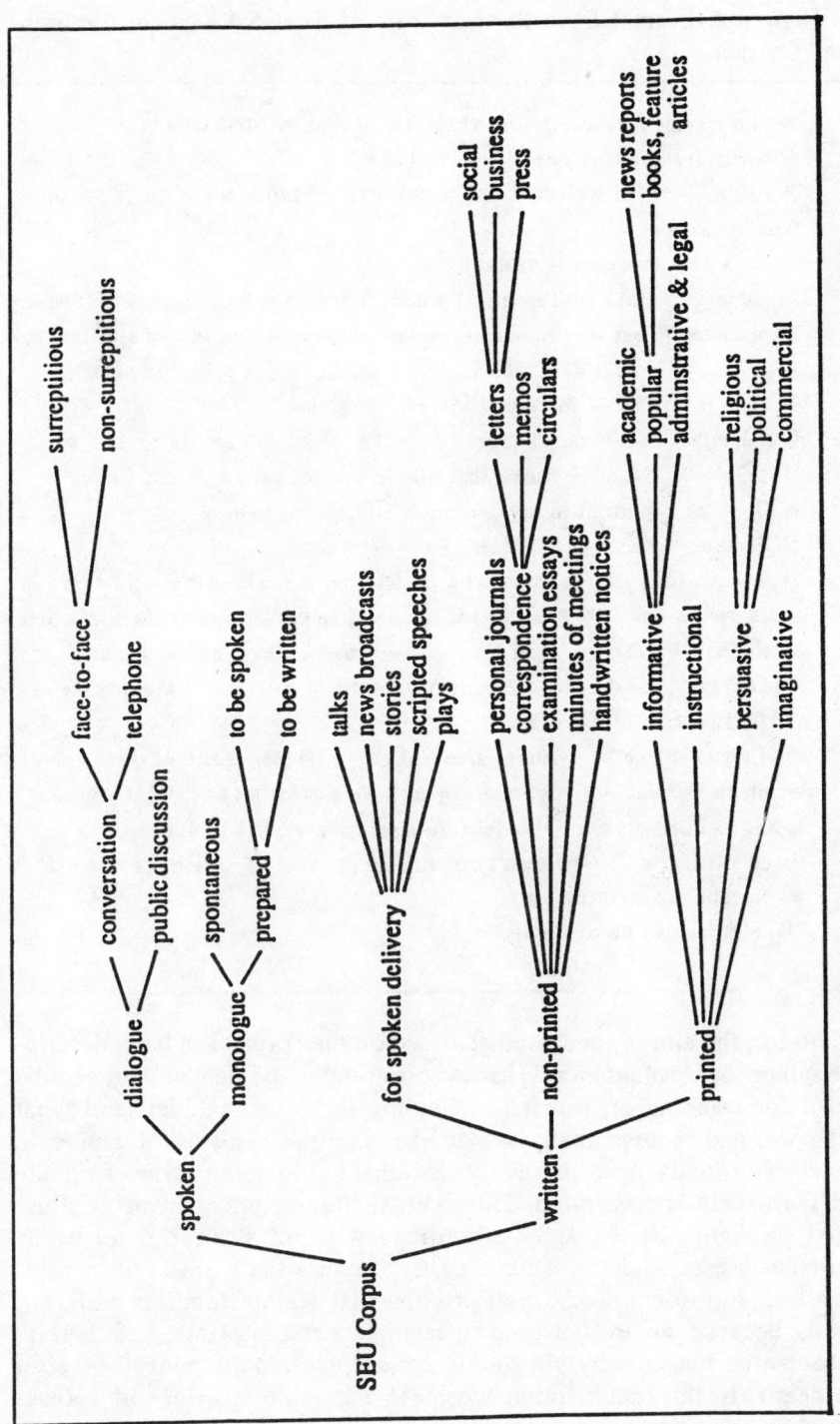

Figure 1. Corpus of the Survey of English Usage (Greenbaum and Svartvik 1990).

Figure 2. Extract from the transcript of Text S.1.8 in the London-Lund Corpus.

B	⁶⁵ that GRÈEN is is ▮not BÁD▪ ⁶⁶ ▮i̇s it▪ ⁶⁷ that ▮LÁND'SCAPE▪
A	⁶⁸ ▮what the ᴀBRÌGHT one▪ - ⁶⁹ ☆《it's》☆
B	⁷⁰ ▮YÈS▪ ⁷¹ ☆well it's☆ ▮not ᴀvery BRÍGHT▪ ⁷² ▮no I 'meant the +ᴀsecond 'one ALÒNG▪+
A	⁷³ +oh ▮that one 'over+ THÈRE▪
B	⁷⁴ ▮YÈS▪ - ⁷⁵ ▮NÒ▪ ⁷⁶ I'm ▮not I'm ▮not ÌNTERESTED▪ · ⁷⁷ the ▮STÀTUES are all RÍGHT▪ ⁷⁸ but they're · for a ▮small RÓOM▪ ⁷⁹ they're ▮not SÙITABLE▪ ·
A	⁸⁰ ▮[m̂]▪ - - ⁸¹ no I ▮think '《actually》 I ᴀthink they're a 'bit too BÌG▪ ⁸² 《you ▮KNÒW》▪ ⁸³ for my ▮RÒOM▪ · ⁸⁴ ▮[m̂]▪ -
B	⁸⁵ ▮[m̂hm]▪ - - - ⁸⁶ oh 《I ▮6 to 7 SỲLLS》▪ ⁸⁷ it's just ▮not one's LÎNE▪
A	⁸⁸ ▮[m̂]▪ - ⁸⁹ ▮YÈS▪ ⁹⁰ I ▮like that 'one in the ᴀCÒRNER▪ ⁹¹ but I ▮don't really 'want a 'portrait in my ▷room I ▷like · my ▷own ·
B	⁹² ☆▮YÈS▪ ⁹³ ▮YÈS▪ · ⁹⁴ ▮YÈS▪ · ☆ ⁹⁵ ▮[m̂]▪
>A	⁹¹ ☆ ▷individu▷ality to ᴀSPRÈAD▪ ⁹⁶ a▮round the ▷RÒOM▪☆ - · ⁹⁷ it's ▮NÍCE THÁT▪ - - - ⁹⁸ ▮yes [? ɔː] it ᴀÍS so 'Brenda▪ ⁹⁹ this ▮i̇s the 'nicest one▪ ·
B	¹⁰⁰ ▮[m̂]▪ ¹⁰¹ ▮YÈS▪ · ¹⁰² ▮if [əm] - - 'one were to 'have one at ÁLL▪ - - - ¹⁰³ [əm] ▮[m?] - ▷they're · ᴀreally 'UNDISᴀTÌNGUISHED▪ ¹⁰⁴ ▮ÀREN'T they▪
A	¹⁰⁵ I ▮THÍNK so▪ ¹⁰⁶ ▮YÈS▪
B	¹⁰⁷ I ▮think if 'one [ə] - ▮those aren't BÁD▪ · ¹⁰⁸ [əm] ▮SÒME of them are 'well 'painted▪ ¹⁰⁹ but · if you're ▮going to 'have a ᴀPÌCTURE▪ · ¹¹⁰ if you're ▮going to CONᴀFÈR▪ · ¹¹¹ a ▮picture ᴀinto your RÒOM▪ ¹¹² it's ▮got to be 'ᴀwell PÀINTED▪ · ¹¹³ I ▮can't 'do with an [i] ᴀaura of ᴀFÀILURE▪ ¹¹⁴ 《I》 ▮have enough FÀILURE▪ ☆ ·
A	¹¹⁵ ☆(- laughs) 《6 to 7 sylls》☆

So far, the aim of most studies based on the corpus has been descriptive rather than pedagogical. However, our authentic data should also be useful for teaching or, rather, for helping the teacher understand what real spoken discourse really looks like. For the analysis of authentic speech we usually need to have it documented in some form of visible and permanent transcription. However, in transcription (such as illustrated in Figure 2) the audio-recordings will not strike the reader as particularly user-friendly. This is partly because there exists no institutionalized form of prosodic transcription that we are familiar with, but mainly because we are not used to seeing speech in print—and there is of course no reason why we should be: speech is not meant to be seen but heard. In the transcription we meet a graphic structure of spoken language displaying bursts of brief chunks of vocalization (with arrows and capitalization denoting prosodic features) that are surrounded by stretches of non-vocalization (pauses being indicated by dashes and periods), hesitation phenomena realized as pauses, repetitions or word partials (appearing within square brackets), simultaneous speech (denoted by asterisks), etc. Such a transcript presents a radically different picture from that of written language with its closely-knit strings of sentences bounded by institutionalized punctuation marks.

Whereas the sentence of writing is well documented in linguistic theory, grammatical description, and teaching materials, there is far less information to be had about a corresponding unit of speech, and in fact no agreement about how such a unit should be named, let alone defined. The sentence is not an obvious candidate here. There is little in the phonetic signal that provides evidence of spoken sentences, and it is difficult, problematic, and perhaps irrelevant to analyze speech in terms of sentences (cf. Crystal 1980, Chafe & Danielewicz 1987). In our approach we use the term 'tone unit', and in the illustration its boundaries are indicated by a filled square. Here the tone unit is contour-defined, not pause-defined: it is only optionally bounded by a pause, and there is no one-to-one relationship between tone units and pause-defined segments. The tone unit may be viewed as different types of unit: prosodic, cognitive, textual, grammatical or physiological (cf. Altenberg 1987:47). In prosodic terms, it is a unit manifested as a coherent intonation contour optionally bounded by a pause and containing a salient pitch movement with a principal accent (variously called 'nucleus', 'tonic', 'main stress', etc) normally occurring at or near the end of the unit. In cognitive terms, it is a unit maximally consisting of one newly activated concept—which the speaker brings into his focus of consciousness—and, optionally, some already active (or semi-active) concepts. In textual terms, it is a unit consisting of a part typically carrying new information and optionally preceded or, less commonly, followed by a part carrying given information. In grammatical terms, it is a unit containing at least one phrase or clause element but often a larger grammatical structure. Depending on where the focus is laid, such units are variously called 'tone units', 'tone groups', 'intonation units', 'information units', 'idea units', 'chunks', 'phonemic clauses' or 'breath groups'.

Our assumption, then, is that the segmentation of speech into such units is not arbitrary but has linguistic significance. It appears to be a basic requirement of natural and intelligible speech. If so, there should be a lesson for the language teacher here. The importance of the prosodic information unit, rather than the grammatical sentence, as the unit appropriate to speech has to be seen in the light of the pressure under which spontaneous speech is produced, in particular the limit on time for planning and the lack of opportunity for unobtrusive revision—on top of which there is always the natural restriction of human memory capacity. One measurable difference between the two types of unit is length in terms of number of words: the written sentence is three or four times longer than the spoken tone unit. The average number of words per sentence is around 19 in written English (Johansson & Hofland 1989, vol 1:17) as compared with 4.5 words per tone unit, with a textual variation ranging from 3.9 words to 5 words. In the same study of the corpus the speech rate was found to be 1.9 seconds per tone unit, with a textual variation ranging from 1.1 seconds to 2.5 seconds (Altenberg 1987:22f). The written sentence is clearly too long a unit to handle in speech, particularly in interactive discourse, where planning and execution partly overlap. The real-time processing in speech appears to require a short prosodic segment, such as the tone unit, for comprehension as well as for production. The spoken unit represents a linguistic expression of 'focuses of consciousness' (Chafe 1980:15) and a meaningful segment of discourse, 'one quantum of the message, the way the speaker is organising it as he goes along' (Halliday 1985:53).

When it comes to teaching spoken English—and presumably any human language—the first lesson to learn from a large collection of real data is, I suggest, to become conscious of the difference in information structuring in speech as compared with writing. The emphasis on the tone unit rather than the sentence is not meant to imply that, in speech, all sentences have gone overboard but, rather, that the sentence is not the natural spoken processing unit. Nor is this to claim that there is one grammar of spoken and another of written English. The core of English grammar is the same for speech and writing but it is used differently in the two modes. For example, the dense packing of information by means of heavily premodified noun phrases, subordination, and nonfinite verb constructions is characteristic of writing but rare in speech (see further Brown & Yule 1983).

Probably the most comprehensive corpus-based study of linguistic variation in the two modes, including a unified analysis of the whole range of spoken and written registers in English, has been conducted by Douglas Biber (1988). His multi-dimensional, statistical comparison of linguistic characteristics of 23 genres does not lead him to make an absolute, two-way distinction between spoken and written discourse: '. . . the variation among texts within speech and writing is often as great as the variation across the two modes' (24). Yet, face-to-face conversation is described as the stereotypically oral genre and, with respect to three dimensions, the following poles are said to characterize academic exposition and conversation (162):

> Informational *vs.* Involved Production
> Explicit *vs.* Situation-Dependent Reference
> Abstract *vs.* Non-Abstract Information

Without questioning Biber's conclusions in this valuable study it seems relevant to emphasize, in the context of this Round Table, that the gap between the two modes of writing/reading, on the one hand, and speaking/listening, on the other, is actually wider than appears from his statement. The reason is that the linguist examines the end-product of a process, as evidenced in a corpus, while the learner is the actual performer/producer of the process and, as we have noted, the speech process is radically different from the writing process, in particular with its real-time constraint.

In foreign language teaching we have certain obligations to our students: one is to create awareness of the structure of the language, preferably also of its literature and other cultural manifestations, another is to promote proficiency in the actual use of the language. One type of awareness that should have high priority in our teaching is that speech is something special, and that we all have to help demolish the still widespread popular view that spoken language is some inferior form of written language. One way to do this is to expose students to transcripts of real spoken data, produced of course in a simpler form than in Figure 2 (which is intended for linguistic analysis rather than language pedagogy). One possible, reduced, and more user-friendly version of the text is given in Figure 3, which can no doubt be improved upon. However, the effect is lost if, as is often the case, the transcripts of speech are transformed into regular written text with the full punctuation of writing and without prosodic cues. Most important, of course, is to expose students also to the original aural data, i.e. recordings of English (preferably with visual support on video) as used in a range of situations. We have had tape-recorders readily available for over 50 years and they are getting smaller and cheaper every year, yet their full potential for language learning seems to be far from achieved.

In addition to drawing attention to how spoken discourse differs from written in terms of linguistic structure, we should highlight also other typical features of conversation: the informal context, the need to adjust to your partner, the interactive, real-time processing constraint which means that each participant has to take an active part in the circular process of planning a contribution, organizing it linguistically, producing it, listening to the other speaker's turn, interpreting it, reacting in a suitable way by planning another turn, and so on and on.

In view of the specific requirements of real-time processing, the teaching has to aim at promoting instantaneous understanding and use of 'discourse items', i.e. those linguistic features that are typical of speech. These can be divided into three groups (cf. Nattinger 1988:78-79 and Stenström 1990:144): social interactions, necessary topics, and discourse devices. Social interactions include greetings (*how are you doing*), closings (*be seeing you*), politeness routines (*if you don't mind*), refusing (*no way*); necessary topics cover language (*how do you say . . .*), time (*how

Figure 3. Extract from Text S.1.8 in simplified transcription.

```
B   that GR\EEN is is not B/AD▪  \IS it▪ that L\/ANDSCAPE▪
A   what the BR\IGHT one▪ - it's
B   Y\ES▪                 well it's not very BR/IGHT▪
    no I meant the second one AL\ONG▪
A                   oh that one over TH\ERE▪
B   Y\ES▪ - N\O▪ I'm not I'm not \INTERESTED▪ -
    the ST\ATUES are all R/IGHT▪ but they're - for a small R/OOM▪
    they're not S\UITABLE▪ -
A   \M▪ - - no I think actually I think they're a bit too B\IG▪
    you KN/OW▪ for my R\/OOM▪ - \M▪ -
B   \MHM▪ - - - oh I - - - it's just not one's L/\INE▪
A   /\M▪ - Y\ES▪ I like that one in the C\/ORNER▪
    but I don't really want a portrait in my room I like - my own -
    individu▪ality to SPR\EAD▪ around the R\OOM▪ - -
B   Y\ES▪ Y\ES▪ - Y\ES▪ - \M▪
A   it's N\ICE TH/AT▪ - - - yes @: it \/IS so Brenda▪
    this \/IS the nicest one▪ -
B   \M▪ Y\ES▪ - if @m - - one were to have one at /ALL▪ - - -
    @m m - they're - really UNDIST\INGUISHED▪ \AREN'T they▪
A   I TH/INK so▪ Y=ES▪
B   I think if one @ - those arent B/AD▪ -
    @m S\/OME of them are well painted▪
    but - if you're going to have a P\ICTURE▪ -
    if you're going to CONF\/ER▪ -
    a picture into your R\/OOM▪
    it's got to be well P\AINTED▪ -
    I can't do with an aura of F\AILURE▪
    I have enough F\/AILURE▪
```

long . . .), space (*how far . . .*); discourse devices include fluency devices (*you know*), sensory predicates (*it seems to me . . .*), reinforcers (*OK, and then what happened*), hedges (*sort of thing*), responses (*fine, quite, right, sure thing, fair enough, uhuh*). One slippery customer in spoken English whose function is peculiarly difficult to capture and describe adequately—let alone teach—is *well*, as in:

Do you feel like jogging?
Well, not this morning, I think.

This innocent-looking four-letter word has rank 14 in our corpus of conversations, i.e. it is more common than central grammatical items like *this, we, on, for, if, do, which*. While *well* as a discourse device (as opposed to a manner adverb) is to be found in the 'Top 20' list in speech, it is non-existent in writing and strikingly absent in pedagogical handbooks. Clearly, an item with this kind of frequency in the conversation of native speakers has got to be important also to foreign students who want to manage conversations adequately.

So far the most extensive dedicated pedagogical use of corpora has been producing statistics on frequency of vocabulary items and structural patterns. One form of information derived from word frequency counts is that, in most texts, a small number of different words (i.e. types) account for a very large proportion of all word tokens: in most written texts 5,000 words will account for up to 95% of the tokens, and 1,000 words will account for 85%; in speech, 50 function words account for up to 60% of the tokens (cf. Kennedy, forthcoming). Most native speakers with experience of talking with foreign students will probably agree with Gillian Brown and John Sinclair:

> ... it always seems a shame when one meets foreign speakers of English with a very impressive command of spoken English who speak in conversation as though they were addressing a public meeting. (Brown 1990:6)

> At present many learners avoid the common words as much as possible, and especially the idiomatic phrases. Instead they rely on larger, rarer and clumsier words which make their language sound stilted and awkward. (Sinclair 1987:159)

A 'lexical syllabus' has indeed been proposed by Sinclair and Renouf (1987), who have extensive experience from the COBUILD project at Birmingham University of how a large English corpus can be used in producing corpus-based dictionaries, grammars, and other handbooks.

What appears to be a most fruitful use of corpora is the analysis of specific semantic fields and pragmatic categories. In her study of epistemic modality as expressed in some ESL textbooks as compared with real corpus-data, Janet Holmes (1988) shows that many textbook writers 'devote an unjustifiably large amount of attention to modal verbs, neglecting alternative linguistic strategies for expressing doubt and certainty' (40). Such alternatives include lexical verbs (*appear, believe, doubt, seem, suggest, etc.*), adverbials (*apparently, certainly, doubtless, inevitably, necessarily, etc.*) and nouns (*belief, certainty, idea, opinion, possibility, tendency, etc.*). The reason for the traditional emphasis on modal verbs to the exclusion of lexical verbs, adverbials and nouns can be traced to structural grammars where the morphological peculiarities of modal auxiliaries (lack of third-person-*s*, infinitive, and participle forms, etc) naturally place these auxiliaries high on the list of teaching items. Other semantically equivalent expressions (*suggest, apparently, belief, etc.*) do not constitute any morphological problem and, consequently, have no place in a morphologically-biassed textbook.

Another promising, but as yet largely uncultivated, field is the use of real data for studying habitual co-occurrences of lexical items, whether they be called lexical phrases, collocations, prefabs, or preassembled chunks. Some such multi-word items belong to the speech-specific categories already mentioned (*if you don't mind, etc.*), but most types do not appear to be characteristic of either the spoken or written varieties. Yet I think there are two reasons why such prefabs may be considered particularly relevant for the student of spoken discourse. One is that interactive speech takes place in real time which—unlike written discourse—offers no opportunity of resorting for help to a dictionary, a friend or an embassy. Another reason is the typical information structure of speech: we speak in brief chunks which often consist of habitual co-occurrences.

In conclusion, what is the lesson that we, as language teachers, can learn from real spoken data? First and foremost to learn to understand (and make students understand) that, in a performance-perspective, impromptu speech (rather than prepared and scripted exposition) is radically different from—but not inferior to—writing. Consequently, our teaching of spoken English should focus on the interactive variety that we typically meet in informal conversations, which is the variety most different from writing. Hence we cannot expect to pick up this art satisfactorily simply as a spin-off from reading and writing. It is not that the grammar of spoken English is different from that of written English, only that it is used differently. Real-time performance in interactive spoken discourse makes heavy demands on both sender and receiver. The participants have to cope, on the spot and without recourse to handbooks, with any unpredictable topics, grammatical structures, lexical items, prosodic features, dialectal peculiarities, etc. that can crop up in a coffee chat.

Transcripts can be used to create and enhance linguistic awareness, but learning how to use and understand spoken English requires extensive exposure to original recordings: spoken language should primarily be heard, not seen (in print, that is, video is a bonus). While the typical textbook dialogue may do no harm it should be realized that it is a far cry from the real thing encountered outside the classroom. This should be brought home to students by making them conscious of what active speaking and listening participation really demands, and what a challenge it presents to the foreign learner. The teacher should provide exposure to a range of spoken discourse types, beginning with reasonably organized and slow speech but progressing towards natural speech, while pointing out the function of information units.

In the past the emphasis has been laid on the teaching of the pronunciation of English (Brown 1990). This may well be an unfair description of the situation also today—we can only guess what's going on in the English language classrooms of the world—but in my experience it is still the case that teachers tend to worry a lot about things like the choice of aiming at a British or American pronunciation, and the danger of mixing the two—yet it seems pretty trivial if we sing-song in the one or the other variety. Elements that are too often left alone to take care of themselves in teaching and practice are intonation, rhythm, and fluency in spoken production and, in listening, comprehension of fast, natural delivery as regularly used by native speakers when talking among themselves. Intonation is still often seen as decoration placed on top of sentences for emotional colouring—yet it is a speech-specific carrier of meaning and, more often than not, linked to grammatical structure and hence largely predictable (even if you're not a mind-reader). Rhythm is an outstanding feature of a stress-timed language like English with obvious importance to understanding and communication. Fluency is not just a sign of elegant language processing but a basic requirement for successful and comfortable interactive discourse. A conversation participant whose contributions are notably intermittent and consist of long terminal strings laboriously transformed from kernel sentences will soon discover that this manner of handling spoken discourse results not only in loss of fluency but also of a conversation partner.

References

Altenberg, B. 1987. Prosodic patterns in spoken English: Studies in the correlation between prosody and grammar for text-to-speech conversion. Lund Studies in English 76. Lund: Lund University Press.

Biber, D. 1988. Variation across speech and writing. Cambridge: Cambridge University Press.

Brown, G. 1990. Listening to spoken English. London: Longman.

Brown, G., and G. Yule. 1983. Teaching the spoken language. Cambridge: Cambridge University Press.

Chafe, W. ed. 1980. The pear stories. Norwood, N. J.: Ablex.

Chafe, W., and J. Danielewicz. 1987. Properties of spoken and written language. In: Comprehending oral and written language, ed. R. Horowitz and S.J. Samuels, 83-113. New York: Harcourt Brace Jovanovich.

Crystal, D. 1980. Neglected grammatical factors in conversational English. In: Studies in English linguistics for Randolph Quirk, ed. Greenbaum, S., G. Leech, and J. Svartvik 1980, 153-166. London: Longman.

Greenbaum, S. Forthcoming. A new corpus of English: ICE. In: Proceedings of Nobel Symposium on Corpus Linguistics. J. Svartvik, ed. Berlin: Mouton de Gruyter.

Greenbaum, S., and J. Svartvik. 1990. The London-Lund Corpus of Spoken English. In: Svartvik ed. 1990, 11-45.

Halliday, M.A.K. 1985. Spoken and written language. Deakin: Deakin University Press.
Holmes, J. 1988. Doubt and certainty in ESL textbooks. Applied Linguistics 9, 21-44.
Johansson, S., and K. Hofland. 1989. Frequency analysis of English vocabulary and grammar. Oxford: Oxford University Press.
Kennedy, G. Forthcoming. Preferred ways of putting things with implications for language teaching. In: Proceedings of Nobel Symposium on Corpus Linguistics. J. Svartvik, ed. Berlin: Mouton de Gruyter.
Nattinger, J. 1988. Some current trends in vocabulary teaching. In: Vocabulary and language teaching, ed. R. Carter & M. McCarthy, 1988, 62-82. London: Longman.
Sinclair, J. 1987. The nature of the evidence. Looking up: An account of the COBUILD project, 150-166. London: Collins.
Sinclair, J., and A. Renouf. 1987. A lexical syllabus for language learning. In: Vocabulary and Language Teaching, ed. by R. Carter & M. McCarthy, 140-160. London: Longman.
Stenström, A.-B. 1990. Lexical items peculiar to spoken discourse. In: Svartvik, ed. 1990. 137-175.
Svartvik, J., ed. 1990. The London-Lund Corpus of Spoken English: Description and research. Lund Studies in English 82. Lund: Lund University Press.
Svartvik, J., and R. Quirk. 1980. A corpus of English conversation. Lund Studies in English 56. Lund: Lund University Press.

Lexicography and syntax:
The state of the art in learner's dictionaries of English

Flor Aarts*
Katholieke Unversiteit, Nijmegen

1 Introduction. Among the questions we can ask when comparing and evaluating English learner's dictionaries are the following:

(1) Which headwords, phrases, collocations, idioms, etc. have been entered and which have not?
(2) What are the reasons for their inclusion or exclusion?
(3) What information does the dictionary provide on the headwords it contains?

In this paper I am only concerned with the last question. I shall be looking at three learner's dictionaries of English: the *Oxford Advanced Learner's Dictionary of Current English*, 4th edition, 1989 (henceforth OALD); the *Longman Dictionary of Contemporary English*, 2nd edition, 1987 (henceforth LDOCE); and the *Collins Cobuild English Language Dictionary*, 1987 (henceforth COBUILD), my purpose being to compare the information they provide on the syntax of verbs and the way this information is organized (cf. Heath 1982). 'Ordinary dictionaries', as Sinclair (1987b:106) points out, 'are designed primarily to offer support to the reader, and not to the writer. Given that restricted objective, it is not necessary to state the limits and constraints on structure and usage'. However, if they are also to cater to the needs of the writer, dictionaries should contain information not only on the meaning of words, but also on their use in contexts. (Cf. Béjoint 1981 and Cowie 1983). This is particularly true of verbs. Hornby (1975:v) claims that 'A knowledge of how to put words together in the right order is as important as a knowledge of their meanings. The most important patterns are those of the verbs'.

---

*For critical comments on an earlier version of this paper I would like to thank Bas Aarts.

All three dictionaries employ codes to indicate the syntactic patterns that verbs can occur in. OALD and LDOCE provide charts of the codes they employ inside the back and front cover, respectively. Codes are also explained at length in the Guides (OALD, pp. 1554-1570 and LDOCE, F39-F44). COBUILD prints a list of grammatical symbols (p. xiii), each of which is explained inside a box in the alphabetical entry list in the dictionary. Unfortunately COBUILD does not have a convenient one-page chart with examples, as do OALD and LDOCE.

Before dealing with verb codes in section 3, I shall first compare the way verb entries are organized in the three dictionaries (section 2). In section 4 I will present a proposal for a verb coding system which I believe to be more user-friendly than those in OALD, LDOCE, and COBUILD. This paper is summarized in section 5.

2 The organization of verb entries. In OALD and LDOCE every verb has the symbol *v* at the beginning of its entry, immediately after the pronunciation. If a verb has only one meaning, the symbol *v* is followed by the code(s) that show(s) in which pattern(s) the verb in question can be used. Compare, for example, the entry for *emancipate*:

OALD: *emancipate ...v* [Tn, Tpr] ...
LDOCE: *emancipate ...v* [T (from)] ...

If a verb has more than one meaning, the entry is subdivided into numbered sub-entries (which are sometimes further subdivided by means of letters). If all the meanings of a verb allow the same patterns, the codes in OALD are all given at the beginning of the entry, after the symbol *v*. If each meaning requires its own pattern(s), the codes appear at the beginning of each sub-entry. The verb *declare* has been taken as an example (see pages 533-35, *this volume*).

In OALD the first meaning (1a) of *declare* has as many as 8 codes:

declare ... *v* 1(a) [Tn, Tf, Tw, Cn.a, Cn.n, Cn.t, Dpr.f, Dpr.w].

These codes are followed by only 5 examples. This means that the reader will have quite a job matching the codes with the examples. He will discover that some of the codes have no corresponding examples and that some of the examples should be matched with more than one code. We also find cases in OALD where the number of examples exceeds the number of codes. Thus the first meaning of the verb *want* has 5 codes and 9 examples. This is fine as long as the reader is able to figure out which code(s) match which example(s). This is not always easy, however.

In OALD the verb codes are listed at the beginning of entries or sub-entries, not within the text. LDOCE differs from OALD in that entries

OALD *facsimile*

de‧clare /dɪˈkleə(r)/ v **1** (a) [Tn, Tf, Tw, Cn·a, Cn·n, Cn·t, Dpr·f, Dpr·w] formally announce (sth); make known clearly: *'I'm not coming with you — and that's final!' declared Mary.* ○ *declare that the war is over* ○ *They then declared (to us all) what had been decided.* ○ *They declared him (to be) the winner.* ○ *I declare the meeting closed.* (**b**) [Tf, Cn·a, Cn·t] say (sth) solemnly: *He declared that he was innocent.* ○ *She was declared (to be) guilty.* **2** [Ipr] ~ **for/against sth/sb** say that one is/is not in favour of sth/sb: *The commission declared against the proposed scheme.* **3** [Tn] tell the tax authorities about (one's income), or customs officers about (dutiable goods brought into a country): *You must declare all you have earned in the last year.* ○ *Have you anything to declare?* **4** [I, Cn·a] (in cricket) choose to end one's team's innings before all ten wickets have fallen: *The captain declared (the innings closed) at a score of 395 for 5 wickets.* **5** (idm) **declare an/one's ˈinterest** reveal to others any facts that might be thought to influence one's opinions or actions on a particular issue. **declare trumps** (in card-games) say which suit will be trumps. **declare ˈwar (on/against sb)** announce that one is at war (with sb): *War has been declared.*

and sub-entries often have only one symbol (e.g. T) at the beginning of the entry. Additional codes that go with (a) particular example(s) are printed within the text of the entry immediately in front of the example(s) they describe. The verb *declare*, for instance, has only one symbol (T) at the beginning of its first and second sub-entries (see *overleaf*). Within the text of these sub-entries we find the following codes and examples:

[+ *obj* + *n*/*adj*]: Jones was declared the winner of the fight.
I now declare this meeting open.
The medical examiner declared me fit.

[+ (*that*)]: She declared (that) she knew nothing about the robbery.

[+ *obj* + *n*/*adj*: She declared herself (to be) a supporter of the cause.
The police declared themselves (to be) completely puzzled by the lack of evidence.

This way of matching codes with examples makes things considerably easier for the reader, since it ensures that codes do not stand on

LDOCE *facsimile* **de·clare** /dɪˈkleəʳ/ v **1** [T] to make known publicly or officially, according to rules, custom, etc.: *Britain declared war on Germany in 1914.* [+obj+n/adj] *Jones was declared the winner of the fight.* | *I now declare this meeting open.* | *The medical examiner declared me fit.* **2** [T] to state or show with great force so that there is no doubt about the meaning: *He declared his loyalty to the government/his total opposition to the plan.* [+(that)] *She declared (that) she knew nothing about the robbery.* [+obj+n/adj] *She declared herself (to be) a supporter of the cause.* | *The police declared themselves (to be) completely puzzled by the lack of evidence.* **3** [T] to make a full statement of (property for which tax may be owed to the government): *The customs officer asked me if I had anything to declare.* **4** [I] (of the captain of a cricket team) to end the team's INNINGS before all its members have been put out **5** [I;T] (in a card game) to say which type of card will be played as TRUMPS **6 I declare!** *old-fash* (an expression of slight surprise or slight anger) —**-clarable** *adj:* *Have you any declarable goods?* —**-claratory** /dɪˈklærətəri‖-tɔːri/ *adj*

declare against sbdy./sthg. *phr v* [T] to state one's opposition to

declare for sbdy./sthg. *phr v* [T] to state one's support for

their own. Just as in OALD, we find cases in LDOCE where the number of codes exceeds the number of examples (see, e.g. *brake* and *inflate* (1)). There are also verb entries with codes, but without examples (e.g. *paddle* (1)). Moreover, the order of the codes in LDOCE does not always correspond to the order of the examples (see, e.g. *bump* (1), *fling* (2) and *meet* (2)).

The main difference between OALD and LDOCE, on the one hand, and COBUILD, on the other, is that the text of entries or sub-entries in COBUILD consists only of a definition, followed by one or more examples. All codes, both for word classes and for syntactic patterns, are given in what is called 'the extra column'. Verbs with more than one meaning have numbered sub-entries in COBUILD, which are sometimes further subdivided by means of numbers. Sub-entries are usually printed in separate paragraphs, each with its own code in the extra column.

The verb *declare* (see facsimile overleaf) shows how verb entries are organized in COBUILD. In COBUILD we find the same inconsistencies as in OALD and LDOCE: there are codes that are not illustrated by examples (see, e.g., *declare* (4) and *find* (1.1)), entries where the order of the examples deviates from the order of the codes (see, e.g., *mix* (2) and *remember* (2)), as well as entries where there is only one code for different patterns (see, e.g. *spend* (2)).

3 The verb codes in OALD, LDOCE, and COBUILD. In this section we will first look at the symbols for the verb and its various

COBUILD *facsimile*

declare /dɪˈklɛə/, **declares, declaring, declared.** 1 If you **declare**, you say something firmly and in a way that shows that you believe it is true. EG *Never before in her life, she declared, had she tasted such food as this... They were heard to declare that they would never steal again.*   V+REPORT-CL/ QUOTE = announce, assert

2 If you **declare** an attitude or intention, you make it known to other people by expressing it clearly. EG *He declared his intention to fight the election... The Labour Party declared its support for the Campaign for Nuclear Disarmament.*   V+O ⇑ say = proclaim, state

3 If you **declare** yourself as having a particular attitude or intention, you state clearly that you have this attitude or intention. EG *He declared himself strongly in favour of the action we were taking.*   V+O (REFL)+C = profess

4 If you **declare** something, you state officially that it exists or is the case. EG *War was declared on the enemy... The government declared a state of emergency... At his trial he was declared innocent... The clerk declared her duly elected to the committee.*   V+O, V+O+C, OR V+REPORT-CL ⇑ announce

5 If you **declare** goods that you have bought abroad or money that you have earned, you say how much you have bought or earned so that you can pay tax on it. EG *'Have you anything to declare?'-'No, nothing'.*   V+O

6 If you say **'Well, I declare'**, you are letting people know that you are surprised at something; an old-fashioned expression.   EXCLAM = goodness me

declare against. If you **declare against** something, you say that you are opposed to it. EG *They have declared against all war.*   PHRASAL VB : V+PREP ⇑ state = oppose

declare for. If you **declare for** something, you say that you are in favour of it. EG *A small group declared for the king.*   PHRASAL VB : V+PREP = support

---

subclasses (3.1). Next we will compare the codes for transitive verbs (3.2.).

3.1 Symbols for the verb and for verbal subclasses. In order to refer to the verb and its subclasses OALD employs six symbols, LDOCE four, and COBUILD two (see Table 1). In OALD and LDOCE *v* is used as a word-class symbol at the beginning of all verb entries. This symbol does not specify to what subclass a verb belongs. *I* and *L* stand for intransitive verbs and linking verbs, respectively.

In LDOCE there is only one symbol for the whole class of transitive verbs *(T)*. *T* can occur on its own, in which case it stands for a monotransitive verb. Ditransitive and complex transitive verbs in LDOCE are described by codes in which *T* is followed by two additional symbols.

OALD employs three symbols *(T, D,* and *C)* to describe transitive verbs. *D* stands for ditransitive (or double-transitive) verbs and *C* for complex-transitive verbs. In OALD *T* cannot occur on its own when it describes a monotransitive verb. It is always followed by additional symbols which specify what type of complementation the verb requires.

Table 1. Symbols for the verb and for verbal subclasses.

Verb classes:	OALD	LDOCE	COBUILD
Intransitive verb:	I	I	V
Linking verb:	L	L	V
Monotransitive verb:	T	T	V
Ditransitive verb:	D	T	V
Complex transitive verb:	C	T	V
Ergative verb:	—	—	V-ERG
Verb class not specified:	v	v	—

COBUILD employs only two verb symbols, *V* and *V-ERG*. *V* has two functions. It indicates that the word beside which it is printed in the extra column is a verb. Secondly, if *V* is not followed by another symbol, it stands for an intransitive verb. If followed by one or more additional symbols, *V* in COBUILD can refer to various verbal subclasses, depending on the number and type of the additional symbols. *V-ERG* describes verbs that can be both intransitive and transitive in the same meaning (the object of the transitive verb can function as the subject of the intransitive verb). The verb *open*, for instance, is an ergative verb, since we can have both: *She opened the door* and *The door opened*.

OALD and LDOCE do not have special symbols for ergative verbs. For the first of the above examples they employ the symbols *Tn* and *T*, respectively. For the second example both have the symbol *I*.

As far as the symbol for verbs is concerned, I believe that the COBUILD system is the best, because it is the simplest. All we need is the symbol *V*. The COBUILD symbol *V-ERG* is not necessary, provided ergative verbs are illustrated by examples that show how they can be used. The reason why I believe that symbols other than *V* are redundant is that students who want information about a verb are not interested in labels such as intransitive, monotransitive, ditransitive, etc. What they are interested in is the question 'By how many elements and by what type of elements can this verb be followed?' In order to answer that question the dictionary requires only one verb symbol.

3.2 Codes for transitive verbs. Having compared the symbols for verb classes in 3.1, I shall now examine the symbols that follow the verb symbol in the codes. In order to simplify the comparison I shall confine myself to the three classes of transitive verbs: monotransitive, ditransitive, and complex transitive. The most important codes are listed in Table 2. The OALD codes have been taken as starting-point.

Table 2. Codes for transitive verbs.

OALD	LDOCE	COBUILD	Examples:
MONOTRANSITIVE:			
1 Tn	T	V + O	adore sb/sth
2 Tn.pr	T(prep. specified)	V + O: IF PREP THEN...	accuse sb of
3 Tn.p	T(adv.specified)	PHRASAL VB:V +O +ADV	ring sb up
4 Tf	T + *that*	V + REPORT-CL	believe (that)
5 Tw	T + *wh-*	V + REPORT-CL	wonder (what to do)
6 Tt	T + *to-v*	V + to-INF	hate (to drive)
7 Tnt	T + *obj +to-v*	V + O + to-INF	cause (sth to happen)
8 Tg	T + *v-ing*	V + -ING	finish (reading)
9 Tsg	—	—	dread (Mary/'s taking over)
10 Tng	T + *obj + v-ing*	V + O + -ING	notice (sb doing sth)
11 Tni	T + *obj + to-v*	V + O + INF	feel (sb do sth)
12 —	T + *obj + v-ed*	V + O + PAST PART	have (one's hair cut)
DITRANSITIVE:			
13 Dn.n	T +*obj(i)* +*obj(d)*	V + O + O	send (sb sth)
14 Dn.pr	T (prep.specified)	V + O + A(prep.specified)	teach (sth to sb)
15 Dn.f	T + *obj + that*	V + O + REPORT-CL	tell (sb that)
16 Dpr.f	—	—	explain (to sb that)
17 Dn.w	T + *obj + wh-*	V + O + REPORT-CL	ask (sb what)
18 Dpr.w	—	—	indicate (to sb where)
19 Dn.t	T + *obj + to-v*	V + O +to-INF	advise (sb to do sth)
20 Dpr.t	—	—	signal (to sb to do sth)
COMPLEX TRANSITIVE:			
21 Cn.a	T +*obj +adj*	V + O + C (ADJ)	keep (sth cool)
22 Cn.n	T +*obj +n*	V + O + C (NG)	call (sb a fool)
23 Cn.n/a	T +*obj +adv/prep*	V + O + A	treat (sb as)
24 Cn.t	T +*obj +to-v*	V + O + to-INF	force (sb to do sth)
25 Cn.g	T +*obj +v-ing*	V + O +-ING	set (sb thinking)
26 Cn.i	T +*obj +to-v*	V + O + INF	make (sb do sth)

When we compare the codes in Table 2, we find the following major differences:

OALD:
- uses 25 codes in all for transitive verbs: 11 for monotransitive, 8 for ditransitive, and 6 for complex transitive verbs;
- does not have a separate code for pattern 12;
- has a rather puzzling code for pattern 23;
- employs 10 different symbols after the symbol for the verb (see Table 3);
- usually (but not always) has a dot to separate the second from the third symbol in the code;
- employs category symbols (such as *n*, *a*, and *f*) only;
- has a number of symbols that are not transparent, such as:
    f (= finite *that*-clause), *w* (= *wh*-clause), *t* (= *to*-infinitive),
    g (= *-ing* participle), *s* (= genitive/common case, as in *Mary's /Mary*), and *i* (= bare infinitive);
- employs codes that are very different from those in LDOCE and COBUILD.

LDOCE:
- has 11 codes for monotransitive verbs, 5 for ditransitive verbs, and 6 for complex transitive verbs. The total number of different codes for transitive verbs is 17;
- has a special code for pattern 12, but does not have separate codes for patterns 9, 16, 18, and 20;
- uses 13 different symbols after the symbol for the verb (see Table 3);
- uses the plus sign (+) to separate the symbols in the code;
- allows the symbol T to stand on its own (as in pattern 1). T can also be followed by a category label (as in patterns 6 and 8), by two function labels (as in pattern 13), or by a combination of a function label and a category label (as in pattern 10);
- employs transparent labels;
- bears a closer resemblance to COBUILD than to OALD, both as far as the number and as far as the form of the codes are concerned.

Table 3. Number of different symbols after the verb symbol.

OALD	LDOCE	COBUILD
a	adj	ADJ
f	*that*	REPORT-CL
g	*v-ing*	-ING
I	*∫ɸ-v*	INF
n	n	NG
p	adv	ADV
pr	prep	PREP
s	—	—
t	*to-v*	*to*-INF
w	*wh-*	REPORT-CL
—	*v-ed*	PAST PART
—	obj	O
—	obj(i)	O
—	obj(d)	O
—	—	A
—	—	C
10	13	12

COBUILD:
- has 10 codes for monotransitive verbs, 4 codes for ditransitive verbs and 6 for complex transitive verbs. The total number of different codes for transitive verbs is 13;
- has a special code for pattern 12, but does not have separate codes for patterns 9, 16, 18, and 20;
- uses 12 different symbols after the symbol for the verb (see Table 3);

- uses the plus sign (+) to separate the symbols in the code;
- allows the symbol *V* to be followed by function labels (as in pattern 1). *V* can also be followed by category labels (as in pattern 3), or by a combination of a function label and a category label (as in pattern 26);
- employs transparent labels;
- bears a closer resemblance to LDOCE than to OALD, both as far as the number and as far as the form of the codes are concerned.

For reasons of space it is impossible to comment on all the questions raised by the codes in Table 2. I shall therefore confine myself to two points.

The first point concerns the question whether verb codes should account for underlying syntactic differences. In other words, if verbs are followed by complementation patterns that are surface structurally the same, but underlyingly different, should we give those verbs different codes, or will one code do? In what follows I will look at three constructions involving an object, followed by a *to*-infinitive, a bare infinitive, or an *-ing* participle.

The first construction is illustrated by examples (1) to (3):

(1) I wanted her to answer that question.
(2) I told her to answer that question.
(3) I forced her to answer that question.

Although (1) to (3) look alike from a surface structure point of view, it is, of course, obvious that the verbs *want*, *tell* and *force* are followed by different complementation patterns. Syntactic tests bring out the differences. Compare:

(4)   She was told to answer that question.
(5)   She was forced to answer that question.
(6)   *She was wanted to answer that question.
(7)   I told her that.
(8)   *I forced her that.
(9)   *I wanted her that.
(10) I wanted that question to be answered by her.
(11) *I told that question to be answered by her.
(12) *I forced that question to be answered by her.

OALD employs three different codes for the constructions in (1) to (3) (*Tnt, Dn.t*, and *Cn.t*, respectively), but LDOCE and COBUILD have only one code.

The second construction is illustrated by (13) and (14):

(13)　　The children saw the cat steal the meat.
(14)　　His tutor made him work.

Underlyingly, (13) differs from (14), since we can have:

(13a)　　The children saw the cat.

but not

(14a)　　*His tutor made him.

Whereas LDOCE and COBUILD have only one code for both examples, OALD has two codes: *Tni* for (13) and *Cn.i* for (14) (the latter code, incidentally, is said to be used only for four verbs. (See *OALD, Detailed Guide*, p. 1567.

The construction involving an object and an *-ing* participle is illustrated by sentences (15) and (16):

(15)　　He noticed a child entering the courtyard.
(16)　　This remark set everyone thinking.

Again we do not have the same complementation patterns here. Compare:

(15a)　　He noticed a child.
(16a)　　*This remark set everyone.

Nevertheless, LDOCE and COBUILD employ one code for both cases, where OALD has Tng (for 15) and Cn.g (for 16). The latter code is said to be used for only 6 verbs (but presumably also for *catch*). (See *OALD, Detailed Guide*, p. 1566.)

For each of the above constructions LDOCE and COBUILD have only one code. This means that they have 3 codes in all where OALD has 7. From a learner's point of view one code for each construction is adequate. What learners want is information about surface structure possibilities. This information can be given by means of one code, even in cases where, on the basis of transformational constraints, it is possible to distinguish different constructions. In this sense the OALD coding system is unnecessarily complicated.

My second point concerns the treatment of phrasal (= multi-word) verbs. Phrasal verbs are fixed combinations (with a special meaning of their own), consisting of a verb, followed by an adverb (*look up*), a preposition (*look after*) or a combination of adverb + preposition (*look forward to*). OALD, LDOCE and COBUILD adopt the same approach to phrasal verbs in that they list them in alphabetical order at the end of the numbered sections of the entry for the main verb. In other respects, however, their approach is different.

First of all, OALD does not provide codes for phrasal verbs, LDOCE and COBUILD do. The question is whether codes for phrasal verbs are really necessary. Since phrasal verbs are verbal idioms consisting of a fixed number of elements that do not allow variation, the fact that they are listed by a dictionary is enough and would seem to make codes redundant. There is little point in giving phrasal verbs like *look forward to* and *put down to* the code *V + ADV + PREP* (as in CO-BUILD). What is important, however, (and this is where all three dictionaries are adequate) is that phrasal verbs should always be listed together with the complements they can take. In other words, instead of giving *put down to*, the dictionary should give *put sthg down to sthg*.

If phrasal verbs do not require codes, they do require information about two important syntactic properties. First of all, the dictionary should tell us (where this is relevant) where the object of a phrasal verb can go. If the object can go in more than one place, LDOCE uses a double arrow, as in *look sthg up*. This symbol also implies that a pronominal object comes immediately after the verb. In OALD and COBUILD the place of the object is not indicated by the codes, although it can often be inferred from the definitions and/or examples.

Secondly, the dictionary should tell us whether a phrasal verb can occur in the passive. LDOCE does not give information on this point. The COBUILD codes are not consistent: sometimes they contain the label HAS PASS and sometimes they do not (cf. *put at* and *put away*). In OALD the reader may assume that a passive construction is always possible, unless the entry in question contains the label *no passive*.

Considering the idiomatic nature of phrasal verbs I believe that dictionaries can do without codes. However, information about the place of the object and about the passive is essential.

4 Verb codes: A new proposal. In this section I wish to propose a new verb coding system. Although this system owes a great deal to those in OALD, LDOCE, and COBUILD, I believe it to be simpler and more accessible to the reader (cf. also Lemmens and Wekker 1986).

My system is based on the following considerations:

(1) the number of codes and the number of symbols should be kept to a minimum;
(2) symbols should be transparent;
(3) codes should contain category symbols only, not symbols denoting sentence functions;
(4) codes should represent surface syntactic structures; underlying differences between structures can be ignored;
(5) when V is followed by n we assume that a passive construction is possible, unless the code contains the label *no passive*;
(6) phrasal verbs should be listed in the dictionary with all their syntactic properties (where relevant), but do not require codes.

The system I propose contains only one symbol for the verb (*V*) and only 10 category symbols for elements that can follow *V* in the codes. The total number of codes is 22. They are listed below together with an explanation of their meaning and a few examples:

CODE	MEANING	Examples
1 V	The verb can stand on its own	Two of the victims have died.
		This meat stinks.
2 V + n	The verb can be followed by a noun phrase	He admired her paintings.
		All the students wrote an essay.
	No passive:	The film lasted 90 minutes.
		My watch cost £ 90.
		They remained friends.
		She became an expert.
3 V + adj	The verb can be followed by an adjective phrase	His son fell ill.
		We got ready.
		Water is running short.
4 V + prep	The verb can be followed by a prepositional phrase	Prices range from £ 25 to £ 40.
		The piano stood in the corner.
		This path leads to the river.
5 V + adv	The verb can be followed by an adverb phrase	My sister lives abroad.
		The party went well.
		His success won't last long.
6 V + (*that*)	The verb can be followed by a clause optionally introduced by *that*	I hope (that) you can come.
		She believes (that) I'm rich.
		John says (that) he's in love.
7 V + *wh-*	The verb can be followed by a finite clause introduced by a *wh*-word	Guess what happened.
		She asked who was responsible.
		He inquired whether this was OK.
8 V + *wh*-inf	The verb can be followed by an infinitive clause introduced by a *wh*-word	I wonder what to do next.
		She knew what to say.
		They've learnt how to do it.
9 V + *to*-inf	The verb can be followed by a *to*-infinitive	I hate to drive.
		She failed to see my point.
		We expect to arrive early.
10 V + *-ing*	The verb can be followed by an *-ing* participle	I have stopped smoking.
		She does remember posting the letter.
		We go shopping tomorrow.
		My shirt needs mending.
11 V + *-ed*	The verb can be followed by an *-ed* participle	She got booked for speeding.
		Her remarks went unnoticed.
		I stand corrected.

CODE	MEANING	Examples
12 V + n + n	The verb can be followed by two noun phrases	I can't lend you the money. She bought him a flat. They made her chairman. She has made him an excellent wife.
13 V + n + adj	The verb can be followed by a noun phrase and an adjective phrase	She prefers her coffee black. He declared the meeting open. That will make things difficult.
14 V + n + prep	The verb can be followed by a noun phrase and a prepositional phrase	She explained the problem to me. Let's put the table in the corner. He led me into the garden. The porter helped her out of the taxi.
15 V + n + adv	The verb can be followed by a noun phrase and an adverb phrase	Stand the ladder over here. Put the book there. They pulled the piano upstairs.
16 V + n + *that*	The verb can be followed by a noun phrase and a *that*-clause.	He told me that he would resign. She warned us that this was dangerous. Let me remind you that you are late.
17 V + n + *wh*-	The verb can be followed by a noun phrase and a finite clause introduced by a *wh*-word	She asked me where he was. Show me how you did it. He informed her when he was leaving.
18 V + n + *wh*-inf	The verb can be followed by a noun phrase and an infinitive clause introduced by a *wh*-word	He taught us what to say. She told me how to behave. Remind me where to meet you.
19 V + n + inf	The verb can be followed by a noun phrase and a bare infinitive	I heard the burglar come upstairs. She won't let me go. This will make them laugh.
20 V + n + *to*-inf	The verb can be followed by a noun phrase and a *to*-infinitive	He told us to leave. Do you want me to sell? I would hate her to stay. Did you get them to help you?
21 V + n + -*ing*	The verb can be followed by a noun phrase and an -*ing* participle	She kept the students waiting. This will set him thinking. We got the engine going again. He hates her coming home late. I heard them quarrelling upstairs.
22 V + n + -*ed*	The verb can be followed by a noun phrase and an -*ed* participle	You should have your hair cut. I want this done now. He could not make himself understood.

By way of conclusion let me give some comments on the above list:

(1) I believe that these 22 codes account for the vast majority of verb patterns in English. The list can be extended without using extra symbols. Among the codes that might be added (although the number of verbs that take these patterns is probably very small) are the following:

V + prep + prep:	*look upon sb/sthg. as ...*
V + prep + *that*:	*announce to sb. that ...*
V + prep + *wh*-:	*indicate to sb. where ...*
V + prep + *to*-inf:	*gesture to sb. to ...*

(2) A verb that can be followed by different categories can be given a code which indicates that the verb allows a choice, as in:

V + n/adj:	*seem a success/likely*
V + prep/adv:	*live in France/abroad*
V + *to*-inf/-*ing*:	*hate to go/going*

(3) Alternative patterns need not be indicated by means of an extra code. It is more economical to provide only one code and to illustrate variants by means of examples. This principle can be applied to so-called ergative verbs, which can be described as follows:

boil [V + n]: *You can boil eggs in a pan.*
  Eggs should boil for 3 minutes.

It also applies to cases like the following:

V + n + n:	*He sent his sister a present.*
	He sent the present to his sister.
V + n + n:	*She bought her husband a ring.*
	She bought the ring for her husband.
V + n + prep:	*They sprayed the wall with paint.*
	They sprayed paint on/over the wall.

(4) The use of category symbols in the codes has important consequences. It means that the same code can be given to verbs that are different from a syntactic point of view. Code 19 (V + n + inf), for example, can be given to perception verbs like *hear*, but also to the verb *make*. These verbs do not take the same complementation patterns. The question is whether codes should account for these differences. In my opinion they should not, since

this would require very complicated codes. We should bear in mind that dictionaries are often consulted by linguistically naive learners, who are not familiar with English syntax. The place to discuss syntactic issues is in the grammar, not in the dictionary.

5 Summary. This paper compares three learner's dictionaries of English (OALD, LDOCE, and COBUILD) on the information they provide on the syntax of verbs. The comparison involves the organization of verb entries (section 2) and the verb codes they employ (section 3). A proposal for a new verb coding system is presented in section 4.

A comparison of the way in which verb entries are organized in OALD, LDOCE, and COBUILD shows that all three dictionaries suffer from the same inconsistencies. If a verb entry which employs codes is to be accessible to the reader, it should meet at least three criteria:

(1) each code should be illustrated by at least one example;
(2) if a code is illustrated by more than one example, the examples illustrating one code should be clearly separated typographically from those illustrating another code;
(3) the order of the codes should match the order of the examples.

If these criteria are not met (and this is often the case in all three dictionaries), the reader has to work out for himself which codes go with which examples. In many cases he will find that difficult, if not impossble.

A comparison of the verb codes (and of the symbols used in the verb codes) shows that LDOCE and COBUILD are to be preferred to OALD for the following reasons:

(1) they employ fewer codes;
(2) their codes are less difficult to interpret;
(3) they employ fewer symbols for the verb;
(4) their symbols are transparent.

OALD is better than LDOCE and COBUILD on at least one score: it employs category symbols only, rather than a mixture of category symbols and function symbols. Moreover, OALD does not provide codes for phrasal verbs, which I believe to be redundant.

Section 4 presents a proposal for a verb coding system which I believe to be more accessible to students than those in OALD, LDOCE, and COBUILD. It consists of only 22 codes, has only one symbol for the verb and only ten (transparent) symbols for elements that can follow the verb. The system employs category symbols only.

References

Béjoint, H. 1981. The foreign student's use of monolingual English dictionaries: A study of language needs and reference skills. Applied Linguistics II.3: 207-22.
Cowie, A.P. 1983. On specifying grammatical form and function. In: Lexicography: principles and practice. Edited by R.R.K. Hartmann. London: Academic Press. 99-107.
Cowie, A.P., ed. 1989. Oxford advanced learner's dictionary of current English (OALD). 4th ed. Oxford: Oxford University Press.
Heath, D. 1982. The treatment of grammar and syntax in monolingual English dictionaries for advanced learners. Linguistik und Didaktik 49/50: 95-107.
Hornby, A.S. 1975. Guide to patterns and usage in English. 2nd ed. London: Oxford University Press.
Lemmens, M., and H. Wekker. 1986. Grammar in English learners' dictionaries. Tübingen: Niemeyer.
Sinclair, J., ed. 1987a. Collins COBUILD English language dictionary. London and Glasgow: Collins.
Sinclair, J. 1987b. Grammar in the dictionary. In: Looking Up: An account of the COBUILD project in lexical computing. Edited by J. Sinclair. London and Glasgow: Collins. 104-15.
Summers, D., ed. 1987. Longman dictionary of contemporary English (LDOCE). 2nd ed. Harlow, Essex: Longman.

Language teaching and learning:
Folk linguistic perspectives

Dennis R. Preston
Eastern Michigan University

Folk linguistics has never fared well. Linguists treat popular beliefs about language, at best, as innocent misunderstandings (perhaps minor impediments to introductory linguistic instruction) or, at worst, as the bases of social prejudice. Nonprofessional comment on language, what Bloomfield called 'secondary responses', may both amuse and annoy linguists, but the folk are not happy to have their beliefs contradicted and often retort with what Bloomfield called a 'tertiary response'. Bloomfield himself tells the following story (1944 [1970:418]):

> A physician, of good general background and education, who had been hunting in the north woods, told me that the Chippewa language contains only a few hundred words. Upon question, he said that he got this information from his guide, a Chippewa Indian. When I tried to state the diagnostic setting, the physician, our host, briefly and with signs of displeasure repeated his statement and then turned his back on me. A third person, observing this discourtesy, explained that I had some experience of the language in question. This information had no effect.

Bloomfield apparently believed that he understood not only the linguistic facts (Chippewa has more than a few hundred words!) but also the cultural ones which underlie the beliefs of Dr. X. Although Bloomfield insisted on rigorous scientific accounts in linguistics, he was apparently willing to guess about such tricky and complex ethnographic matters. We can only infer what Bloomfield believed to be 'the diagnostic setting', but it is not hard for a linguist to do so.

(1) Nonlinguists often believe that some languages are primitive, impoverished in various ways, perhaps especially in vocabulary size.
(2) Nonlinguists often believe in a genetics of language; therefore, a Chippewa guide can speak Chippewa fluently.

(3) Nonlinguists often do not believe in a science of language; therefore, native speakers (the guide) and intelligent laypersons (Dr. X) are authorities.[1]

Unfortunately, Bloomfield apparently imagined rather than discovered these beliefs. They may be based on the proper inferences to have drawn from Dr. X's behavior, but there is very little evidence to go on. From an ethnographic point of view, Bloomfield carried out a participant observation study of a few seconds and reached a judgmental conclusion. Such disregard for folk information makes it no surprise to discover that a dinner table game in the Bloomfield family was the recitation of *stankos*—ignorant observations about language heard from nonprofessionals. Little wonder that Bloomfield's and other structuralists' early forays into applied linguistics (second language teaching and reading instruction) met with such emotional rejection (Hall 1990:73-8 & 88-9, respectively); their contempt for nonspecialists' views was worn on their sleeves.[2]

In contrast, Hoenigswald (1970) claims that knowledge of the folk categories of language serves not only folkloristic, anthropological, and even general linguistic ends but also applied ones, and the ethnography of communication (e.g. Hymes 1972) has legitimized the study of the awareness of and regard for the shape and uses of language in standardized speech communities; anthropologists and folklorists had already been at work investigating folk linguistics in other societies for some time (e.g. Stross 1974). In spite of these efforts, what the folk say about rather than do with language is devalued in nearly every tradition of research, even the sociolinguistic, social psychological, and ethnographic.[3]

I will not review that situation here; examples are surveyed and evaluated in ongoing research by Niedzielski and Preston. Instead, although it may be an egocentric view, I will characterize my own concerns with folk linguistics, focusing on the increasing scope of those studies and describing more recent research which has direct bearing on language teaching and learning.

---

1 This last 'diagnostic' is elaborated in Preston 1984.

2 Even when contempt is not present, the failure to take folk linguistics into account can be disastrous in educational settings. Attempts in the Washington, D.C. area years ago to establish a bidialectal initial reading program for African-American children met with strong community opposition. UPI reports this year similar community rejection of a Montgomery County, Maryland after-school bidialectal program for older African-American children aimed at helping them '. . .move between "black English" and "standard English" and speak them both successfully.' One of the protesting African-American parents wondered why white children were not offered similar programs: 'If anything, they could have done something for the white kids geared toward their slang when they say "that's awesome" or "that's radical".'

1 Speech imitation. I suggested (in Preston (a), to appear) that linguistic 'caricatures' both added to and cut across Labov's division of linguistic variables into 'markers', 'indicators', and 'stereotypes' (e.g. Labov 1972:314).³ That claim resulted from data gathered in interviews in which respondents of the opposite ethnicity were asked to 'talk black' or 'talk white'.

Although the study revealed a considerable variety of linguistic and folkloristic detail, phonology was the overwhelmingly favorite level of exploitation in the whites-talking-black context. That task resulted in extensive modification of the segmentals and suprasegmentals and even modification of vocal quality (falsetto, lowered overall pitch, breathy and/or raspy voice). Of course, the data reveal varying degrees of accuracy and consistency, but they show considerable folk ability to radically alter phonetic realizations even in allegro speech delivery. Post-task interviews in such studies show that even the most successful imitators cannot characterize (except in the most global terms) the articulatory facts behind the imitation. Although there are sensitive social issues involved, I believe clever language teachers have long exploited such folk linguistic imitative abilities of learners.

Minor and Preston (1980) tried to exploit this resource in an introductory French text:

> Speak English with French rules: This is an especially helpful practice since it allows you to concentrate on the timing of French without worrying about what you want to say. First try some English words:
>
> (1) Mississippi
>
> Remember, the syllable division in French almost always ends syllables in a vowel; therefore, this word should be divided *mi-si-si-pi*, not *mis-i-sip-i* as in English.
>
> (2) abracadabra   (5) irregularity
> (3) pessimistic   (6) monotonous
> (4) possibility

---

3 The strongest position in this regard is perhaps Labov's 'observer's paradox' (e.g. Labov 1972:209) in which even the performance (let alone the opinions) of speakers who know that their language is being observed is of lesser value for linguistic purposes. Apparently only two linguistic traditions—the structural and the generative-transformational—value overt language observation. In the first, linguistically naive speakers of (generally) non-Indo-European languages were taken to be expert reporters on their own languages (at least, when samples were cleverly presented to them by field linguists); in the second, linguists, apparently as a by-product of their training, achieve an ideal native speaker-hearer intuitive state and are capable of unerringly identifying strings which do and do not belong to their languages.

Now try whole sentences; say anything you like (in English) to your instructor or another student. Use French rules of timing, stress, and intonation. (5-6)

Although this lesson combines analytic skills with folk ones, it differs from analysis and imitation of an authentic model by exploiting the folk skill of phonological caricature.

2 Perceptual dialectology. In 1980 I began the study of American English folk dialectology, the first results of which are reviewed in Preston 1989; a summary of later work is also provided (in Preston (b), to appear).[4] The perception of language varieties differs not only between folk and professional accounts but among folk accounts, and these differences result not only from the various areas where the respondents live but also from such demographic facts as age, status, ethnicity, and gender.

Figure 1 shows the generalized perceptions in United States dialect areas of 147 respondents from southeastern Michigan and 123 from southern Indiana who were asked to draw maps of regional speech. Although there are differences in the number, shape, and relative salience of areas, there are interesting similarities as well. For neither group did this task suggest the relativistic position supported by linguists—for the folk, dialect areas are prescriptive as well as descriptive units. The South is the most salient region for respondents from both areas, and, as another study which ranks the states for 'correctness' from the same respondents shows (Figure 2), it is the South which ranks lowest for both. Regional salience, therefore, is tied to prescriptivist notions.

Evidence of differences between the two respondent areas, however, may be seen as well in Figure 2, in which the linguistically secure Michigan raters place themselves at the top of the correctness scale while the comparatively insecure southern Indiana raters place themselves lower. The source of the Indiana raters insecurity may be seen in a folk linguistic assessment of degree of difference (Figure 3). While the Michigan raters find themselves most different from the southernmost areas (the only ones they rate unintelligibly different), the Indiana raters find themselves most different from the northeast and rate Massachusetts as the only area unintelligibly different. Undoubtedly, the Indiana raters see themselves as not completely unlike those speakers to the south whom they did not rate highly for correctness, and, tellingly enough, those they rated the highest (the northeast) are unintelligibly different.

---

[4] The more recent work in perceptual dialectology was supported by a grant from the National Science Foundation (BNS-8417462).

Figure 1. Computer-generalized hand-drawn maps of U.S. speech areas by respondents from (A) Southeastern Michigan (MI) and from (B) Southern Indiana (IN) speech regions.

A. Southeastern Michigan Speech Regions

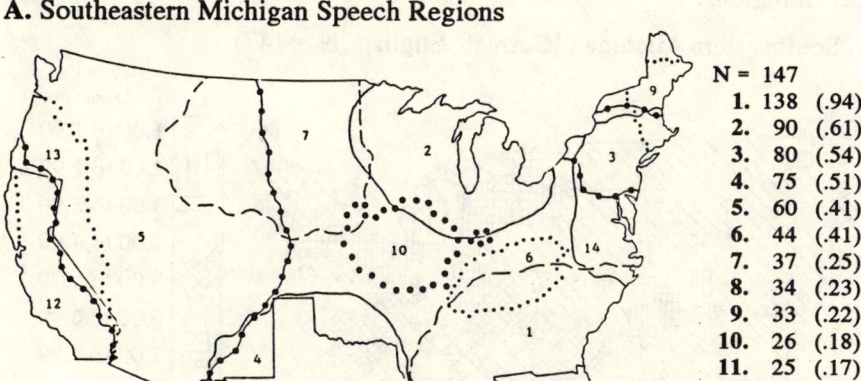

N = 147
1. 138 (.94)
2. 90 (.61)
3. 80 (.54)
4. 75 (.51)
5. 60 (.41)
6. 44 (.41)
7. 37 (.25)
8. 34 (.23)
9. 33 (.22)
10. 26 (.18)
11. 25 (.17)
12. 25 (.17)
13. 25 (.16)
14. 25 (.16)

1. South
2. North
3. Northeast
4. Southwest
5. West
6. Inner South
7. Plains and Mountains
8. Texas
9. New England
10. Midwest
11. Florida
12. California
13. West Coast
14. East Coast

B. Southern Indiana Speech Regions

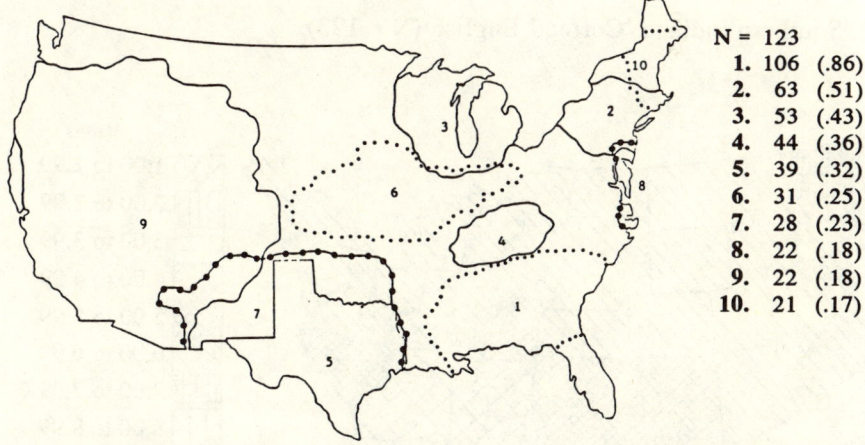

N = 123
1. 106 (.86)
2. 63 (.51)
3. 53 (.43)
4. 44 (.36)
5. 39 (.32)
6. 31 (.25)
7. 28 (.23)
8. 22 (.18)
9. 22 (.18)
10. 21 (.17)

1. South
2. Northeast
3. North
4. Inner South
5. Texas
6. Midwest
7. Southwest
8. Mid-Atlantic
9. West
10. New England

Figure 2. Mean scores for 'Correct' English (where 1 = 'least correct' and 10 = 'most correct') for respondents from (a) Southeastern Michigan (MI) speech regions and (b) from Southern Indiana (IN) speech regions.

A. Southeastern Michigan 'Correct' English (N = 147).

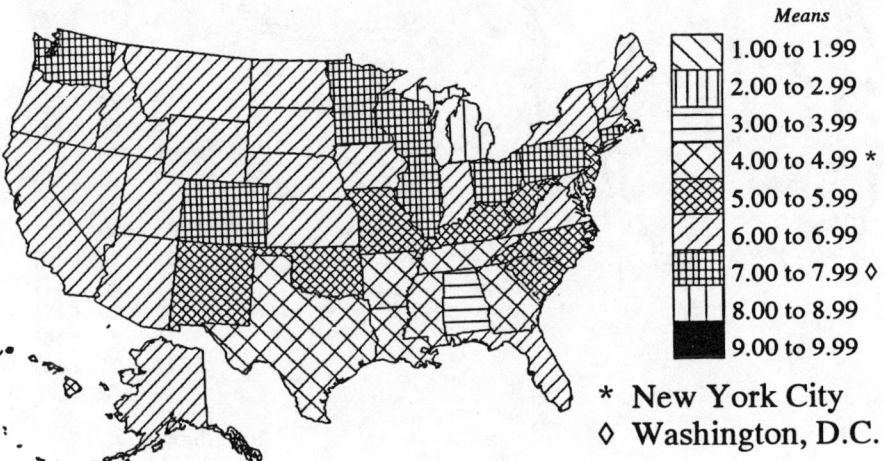

B. Southern Indiana 'Correct' English (N = 123).

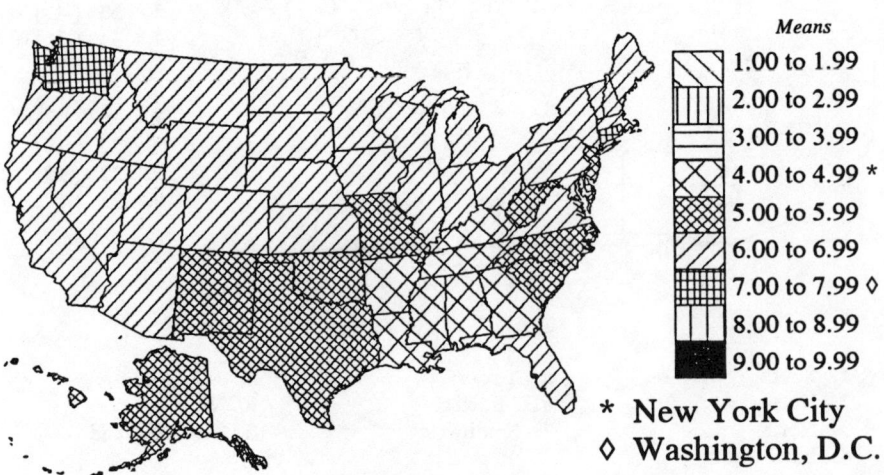

Figure 3. Mean scores for degree of difference in spoken English from that used in the home site of respondents from (a) Southeastern Michigan and (b) Southern Indiana, where 1 = 'same', 2 = 'slightly different', 3 = 'very different', and 4 = 'unintelligibly different'.

A. Southeastern Michigan 'different' English (N= 147).

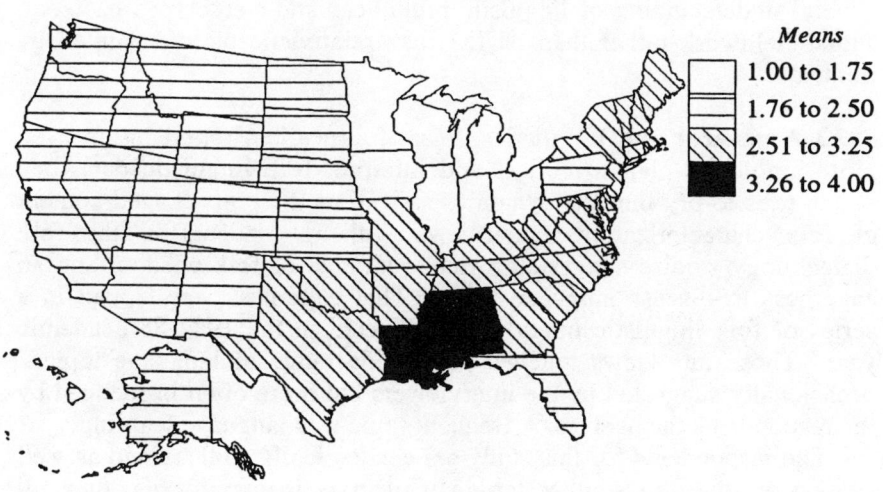

B. Southern Indiana 'different' English (N = 123).

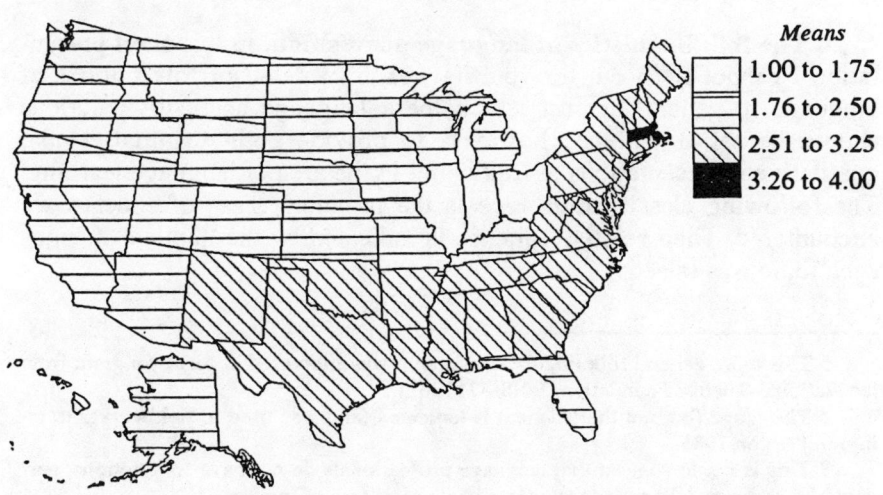

Folk dialectology offers new perspectives for areal linguistic investigation and supplementary information for language attitude study. One applied result is a reassessment of the linguists' claim that a standard American English exists in every region; for folk linguists, the ones who count in such matters, that claim is obviously false. Teachers of English as a second language will be better informed if they have a general understanding of linguistic prejudices and stereotypes based on actual fieldwork rather than on the rosy relativistic picture painted by linguists.

3 A general folk linguistics. What follows is a report on an even more ambitious plan to collect and interpret folk linguistic data, one which tries to pry into the dynamics as well as the prepackaged content of folk characterizations. Interviews with respondents in the folk dialectology studies suggested a rich catalogue of folk wisdom and an eagerness to discuss language topics. That eagerness was tapped in a series of folk linguistic interviews conducted in the 1987-88 academic year.[5] Those interviews touched on a wide range of language topics,[6] occasionally suggested by the interviewers but more often introduced by the respondents themselves. A frequent topic was language learning.

The respondents for this study are academically well-trained as well as poorly educated southeastern Michigan residents; for us, they all count as folk. To catalogue the folk belief of a modern, United States speech community on the basis of a caricaturistic, old-fashioned notion of folk, one which focuses on poor, minority, rural, or particularly conservative members of the community, serves no useful purpose. Only linguists were excluded.[7]

4 The folk linguistics of language acquisition. In this short presentation I cannot flesh out for you the wealth of detail of folk notions of language in general against which these language acquisition notions should be set. I will try, however, to provide both quantitative and qualitative representations of folk belief in the area of language learning. The following classification reveals the principal areas of concern we encountered. Their relative salience is indicated by the number of times each topic was raised:

---

[5] This more general folk linguistics research was supported in part by a grant from the National Science Foundation (BNS-8711267).

[6] The range (but not the balance) is indicated (and was used in fieldworker training) in Preston 1986.

[7] This is not to suggest that language professionals do not have folk notions, particularly, perhaps, folk notions connected with their area of inquiry.

A. Conditions for learning and retention: 37
    1. Linguistic structure   15
    2. Frequent use   8
    3. Natural settings   7
    4. Exclusivity of the target language   6
    5. Teaching techniques   1

B. Results of learning: 26
    1. Linguistic   8
    2. Social: 18
        a. Responsibility   7
        b. Tradition   6
        c. Benefit   5

C. Learner characteristics: 24
    1. Motivation   9
    2. Talent   9
    3. Age   5
    4. Intelligence   1

In our work on folk linguistics so far, we have found no better illustration of the need for empirical data than what must surely be for many the surprising level of concern the folk have for linguistic structure in language learning (A.1). Linguists and language teachers who intuit folk linguistic concerns would surely rate this item very low,[8] but it covers a variety of linguistic levels. I begin by citing the phonological:

```
M: I thought German was supposed to be one of the harder languages to
learn. I don't know if it's because they gurgle when they talk or (    )
you know. Yeah that's got to be hard it's like you're trying to clear your
throat - while you're=
       [
E:                                          (Laughs)
M: =speaking. I mean that would really be hard for me.
F: Yeah well if you
              [
E:                    ((Laughs)) ( )
              [
M:                          Huh?
E: I said you do it all the time.
```

---

8 I admit to caricaturing rather than investigating the folk beliefs that language professionals have about the linguistic folk belief of nonprofessionals, but I hope to be granted this one lapse into intuition. Besides, 'Language Teacher Beliefs about the Linguistic Folk Belief of Language Learners' sounds like a great thesis topic.

M: ((Talks while clearing throat)). Let me clear all this phlegm out of my throat.[9]

French nasals and French 'flat' intonation are also singled out as particularly difficult phonological phenomena. The folk confusion of sounds and spelling is as much a part of second as it is of first language education.

```
G: The verb forms are standard throughout, and - English is not standard,
   the verb forms aren't standard, like 'would,' where=
                                       [
F:                                     Yeah, uh huh.
G: =does THAT come from,
```

According to this same respondent, Spanish verbal morphology is simpler than English as well:

```
G: The verb forms are standard throughout, and - English is not standard,
   the verb forms aren't standard, like 'would,' where=
                                       [
F:                                     Yeah, uh huh.
G: =does THAT come from,
```

One possible interpretation of this surprising folk notion is that G's study of Spanish has given her an analytic knowledge of the language which she equates with regularity.

Higher levels of structure are also dealt with, and the respondents clearly have well-developed notions of contrastive analysis:

```
D: I've studied uh French, and I know (.hhh) and I know that the STRUCture
   sentence structure changes (.hhh) uh between languages, and that's one of
   the, that's one of the things that translators have (.hhh) have to do is
   you know - (to make-) uh: to underst- to take the structure and underst-
   and understand exactly what's being said and then put it in the (.hhh) uh
   in the in the context of the language. And this- people that (.hhh) uh
   that that take uh - uh - uh take a- another language, they realize that
   this - this is typically what happens. Whi- uh 's'il vous plait', 'if=
                                                                        [
F:                                                                      Uh huh.
D: =you please'. We don't go around saying, (.hhh) oh uh 'pa- pass the
   potatoes, if you please.' (We don't do that, ). We=
```

---

9 Space does not permit me to detail the conventions used in data transcription. Anyone experienced in discourse transcription will note our debt to the classical ethnomethodological tradition (e.g. Sacks, Scheghloff, and Jefferson 1974), although we avoid allegro-form respellings for reasons outlined in detail elsewhere (Preston 1982, 1985). Space also prevents me from providing sketches of the respondents. The fieldworkers are always identified as 'F' (even though their identities may change from one sample to another). Initials identifying respondents always refer to the same individual throughout the examples.

```
                                        [
    F:                                  Uh huh.
    D: =say 'pass the potatoes, please'. (.hhh) So - this, you know=
                                                                  [
    F:                                                            ((laughs))
    D: =bu- w- when we go from from English to Chinese, I'd probably try and
    bring my English structure to your Chinese language and then it will not
    work. ((laughs)) And that's what you do when you come to English, you try
    and bring your good Chinese to our=
         [
    F:   ((laughs))
    D: =good English language and - you'd have a lot of - bumping heads.
```

Another respondent makes the specific claim that related languages are easier to learn.

Finally, the folk see contrastive structure at the level of communicative competence and comment on indirection in conventionalized speech acts. The following folk account characterizes the 'come and see me sometime' leave-taking of American English which caused a Chinese student to get a cool reception when she actually followed up on it:

```
    A: It's the way you say good-bye.
    F: It's a way (of) say good-bye?
    A: Yeah, sometimes what is necessarily SAID, is not - what is actually
    meant.
```

Other linguistic elements mentioned include the degree of difficulty of a language (e.g. one respondent ranks Spanish, French, and Latin as increasingly difficult but claims that related languages are not necessarily easier to learn; another claims that English is by far the most difficult since it is a result of a 'mish-mash' of languages and seems to have only exceptions rather than rules. In fact, that respondent notes that English is so illogically spelled that engineers, who have logical minds in her opinion, are among the worst spellers of it. Also mentioned is the difficulty of understanding language varieties and allegro speech.

The second most-frequently mentioned condition influencing second languages is frequency of use (A.2):

```
    T: It's just like anything else. You use it or lose it. Um at the time
    there was not anybody that I could talk to on a regular basis. Okay.
```

This second concern is probably related to the third: that natural (or natural-like) situations promote language learning and retention and that classroom learning does not result in communicative ability:

```
    T: So therefore - I knew the book way=the textbook way how to speak it,
    but actual conversation okay was in high school okay, but once I got to
    college it was null and void. Impossible.
```

Finally, both naturalness and frequency may be related to the last-mentioned concern—exclusivity. Several respondents felt that one needs to hear the language being learned exclusively if it is to be learned well:

> L: I never did well in German. The centers were kind of like- they had three centers I think in Germany. They were based a lot on speaking level ability and mine was the lowest. And because I had an English roommate - an English speaking roommate, she would never really ( ) much German. So I could understand general conversation and get around okay but I never was fluent at all. Which was too bad.

Exclusivity is an especially sensitive factor for children who face schooling in another language:

> K: My parents are Norwegian. And they didn't speak Norwegian at home. My mother had been here less than two years when I was born. And they had really kooky idea- ( ). They just believed that we would have a lot of problems learning- at school, if we had spoken only Norwegian at home.

It may be surprising to teachers that techniques and methods of language teaching engage the interest of folk so little. One respondent speculates on the preference for native speaker teachers at beginning or advanced levels, and another wonders if sleep teaching will work.

In general, the folk believe that languages are tricky, at every level of structure, but that frequent use, natural settings, and exclusive use of one language may overcome the difficulty. Not much time is given to teaching methods, although it is interesting to note that one particularly successful adult multilingual noted that classroom study of the structure of a language was an optimum prerequisite to gaining fluency in a natural setting.[10]

In addition to their concern for the conditions for language learning, the folk are concerned with the results; and one concern is with the linguistic form of the product itself (B.1).

An interesting belief, which appears several times, is that non-native speakers are actually better users of the language than native speakers along several dimensions. The following comment is made to a Chinese fieldworker:

> A: (.hhh) Well - yeah. The difference really is, is if you speak English, actually speak proper English, (.hhh) you are probably speaking it better than we. - I know that sounds strange.

This is perhaps related to the commonplace that non-natives speak more formally. One respondent comments on a mutual acquaintance from Switzerland:

---

10 That, of course, is not unlike comments made in earlier studies of 'good' language learners (e.g. Rubin 1975, Schmidt 1986).

```
V: Yeah he's very - v- ver- more formal I think in his- in his=
   [
F: Yeah.
V: =English, more formal in his speech.
```

A number of respondents noted that accent was the principal difficulty in understanding non-native speech, and several mentioned groups which they found especially difficult to understand (e.g. Koreans). Some respondents related bad overall results to poor opportunities for learning (already discussed) or to detrimental learner characteristics (to be discussed).

In their discussion of language learning results, however, the respondents were concerned with a number of social as well as linguistic matters. The responsibility of individuals to speak the languages of their environment was particularly strongly expressed and reveals a deep folk disparity between the regret for the loss of language abilities in succeeding generations and the emphasis on accommodation (B.2.a).

```
J: If you're going to be in the United States you got to teach- you got to
   speak English. You know and there's a lot of flack about teaching Spanish
   in the uh in the schools in in uh California and in Texas and they had to-
   they had to go to the Supreme Court? And the Supreme Court said they have
   to be taught in their own language.
F: Uh huh
   [
J: Well you know but then if that person wants to - uh really go places
   in the United States you've got to have a good hand- handle on English.
   You've got to be able to be able to speak=
                                                                     [
F:                                                            Uh huh
J: =English because uh - if you just want to speak Spanish in your own
   little uh area, i- in your community, fine. Teach them=
                                    [
F:                              Uh huh
J: =in Spanish then- but then (.hhh) they c- it's very difficult for them
   to move out of that into the main stream. (.hhh) So they should be taught
   English and- but not take their Spanish away from their culture and every-
   thing by (.hhh) uh switching them over completely to English.
```

Although some folk are a good deal less ambivalent:

```
O: I mean I- I think that language is the one- the one that unifies the
   country.
F: Uh huh.
O: I mean we have different religions, we have different - ethnic back-
   grounds, we have - teRIFfic different socio-economic standards and differ-
   ent lifestyles from one part of the country=
                    [
F:                Uh huh.O: =to the other. I mean - what's a lifestyle and
   way of living to somebody that lives in - Birmingham Alabama is certainly
   almost foreign to someone in Boston, Massachusetts or Seattle, but - the
   one unifying thing in the country is the language, and and - and to sug-
   gest that we want to start a bilingual language- country is-
                    [
```

F: I don't know, oh I think-
            [
O: I mean I think it is - people are just
crazy. - I mean if you look at history countries that have bilingual
things are countries that have problems because=
F: =Well yeah I guess that's all true.
O: You jus- I just can't believe that anybody - when they start on this
business. - I mean when foreign people come to this country, I think that
when the foreign kid from - Japan arrives I think we should have a time
and someone to help him adjust, but I think the ultimate goal should be
for that kid to learn English if he's going to stay here.
F: Huh.
O: It's just - the same thing like all these people coming from Mexico and
this kind of stuff? I- I just think that the ultimate goal should be for
them - for these children to have to learn to speak English. I- I can't
see setting it up so that they can - because I mean - You're talking to a
person that couldn't learn a foreign language for her life depended on it,
but I really think that if you're going to go to another country to live
that that's just something you should accept and they should have to do.
....
O: Well or anything else, I mean I can't see that we should have to - have
bilingual things on driving? I mean what is the point in giving someone -
a- a- a driving test in Spanish and saying Oh swell they can read, they
can have this driver's license because they can read in Spanish, and they
get on the road and all the signs are in English?
F: ((laughs))
O: I mean that's kind of=
F: =It doesn't - mesh.
O: It- it just doesn't uh - I don't know, to me that's really that's really something. I can't worry about their rights. Their rights are that
they should learn.
....
O: ... when you listen to the stuff about all the stuff that we should
have for - bilingual students and should we be making the poor Mexicans
out in wherever it is learn English and - YES if they're going to be part
of this country.
F: Uh-huh.
O: I think you're just creating another subculture that is=
                                                           [
F: Yeah.
O: =always going to be a down-trodden subculture. To me if you take this
little Mexican kid who's come over with his family and you structure it so
that he really doesn't have to learn English you forever condemn that
child to a second-class living. I think you take something away from him.
You OWE that kid something, and part of what you owe him is forcing him to
learn and become assimilated into the English world.
F: He's not going to get a job at IBM-
                                      [
O: No he isn't. You forever condemn that
kid to a second-class life if you structure his education so that so that
he can get by without speaking good English.[11]

---

11 It is easy to pooh-pooh these apparently uninformed folk opinions, but one
need not look exclusively to such organizations as English Only to find echoes:

The political and social situation created by linguistic diversity ranges from the harmony of Switzerland ... to India, where the entire political fabric is torn with linguistic conflict. Although both represent extremes, *there is usually at least some conflict
and dissent within multilingual nations* (Lieberson 1970 [1981:1], emphasis mine).

It is as nearly universally held, however, that Americans fail in their responsibilities -to learn other languages:

> J: I would love to be able to speak another language. I- I think that that's one of the bad things about Americans, that we (.hhh) go into other countries and we expect everybody else to be able to talk to us - but we don't - think it's necessary for - it's=
>   [
> F: To ((laughing)) speak English.
> J: really very arrogant I think.

In addition to these strong feelings of linguistic responsibility, many respondents feel that language learning is often simply a part of the tradition of a country or people.

> J: But uh- other countries are way ahead of us in that. You know=
>   [
> F: So-
> J: =like uh Jose from Chile he could speak five languages.
> F: Who?
> J: Oh that- that - yeah. He could speak Spanish, he spe- spoke=
>   [
> F: Chile person - Aw
> J: =uh Portuguese, he spoke - French, he spoke English, and uh a little German.
> F: But where did she- did he learn all these - in Chile
>   [
> J: In Chile - He didn't learn it here. Sure. Of course Chile has a big Ger- uh German=
>   [
> ?:   (   )
> J: =population there (.hhh) and uh if they want to - study overseas they've got to be able to speak the language. And=
>   [
>   F: Uh huh
> J: =that's what they do. They go to France s- to study or go to (.hhh) (hhh) uh Germany or to Great Britain - you know or to the=
>   [
> F: Uh huh
> J: =United States,

Finally, though less important, the instrumental consequences of language learning are mentioned.

> J: Well you know the Japanese come over here and they- they've got wonderful engi- engineers. They- they come and they learn they study they come here and they can speak English as well as any one of us. They don't come over here speaking=
>   [
> F: Um:
> J: =Japanese to us.
> F: ((laughs)) that's right.
> J: Yeah. I mean uh that's because they want to get ahead, (.hhh) and if they're meeting with people (.hhh) that they're going to sell their com-

modities to or whatever they want to be able to speak good English. Because uh - because we don't understand Japan- Japanese.

In some cases the instrumental gains are even more baldly stated:

R: You know if s- a person was smart, we'd s- academically and thinking of their future, - any kind of person that could - grasp a language, to- boy could they ever make the money, couldn't they:?

In general, the folk seem more concerned with social outcomes than with linguistic ones. Linguistically, they are especially tolerant, even admiring of non-native speech, but they note pronunciation as a particularly difficult area. Socially, although individual bilingualism is usually seen as a plus, the folk are suspicious of societal bilingualism or of plans which might result in it.

Finally, there are folk opinions of learner characteristics (C); and motivation and talent vie for first place in this area. Without proper motivation, learning is doomed:

```
R: ...but I think the trouble is that the kids get turned off because they
   - they need to learn conversational language more than they do. Unless
   they're going to be some- I mean if they=
   [       [
F: Uh huh    (       )
             [
J:           Yeah.
R: =could - knew what they were going to go into I suppose maybe=
   [
J: I agree.
M: they know- need to know the grammar and all this declaring=¹²
                                  [
S:                                Uh huh.
R: =and all this (.hhh)- because mostly if they could learn to speak it-=
J: =There'd just be a kind of a s- just a second - second=
                                                         [
R:                                                       Uh huh.
J: =language tha- that you- they picked up.
```

And social demands are seen as powerful motivators:

K: ... Because there are children around here who've been here for a year or two, and they sound like they were - they were born in America. An:d it's something to do, I think with fitting in, too. They really want to fit in.

But some feel the American situation itself may be responsible for poor motivation:

---

12 'Declaring' is probably an idiosyncratic folk term for 'declension', which, as an earlier part of this conversation shows, actually refers to 'conjugation'.

F: Do you think that people don't have interest? or desire?
K: We don't need to. It's such a large country and we don't- Most people don't need to. They don't come into contact with other languages.

Motivated or not, however, many respondents feel that some have a talent for language learning:

H: It is just something that comes more easily to me.
F: Why - why [
H: I never worked at it. I do not know. People just have different gifts and that is something that was easy for me.

And there are apparently different gifts for different linguistic levels. R was apparently a successful Spanish student, but she never learned to roll (presumably her 'r') and remembers to this day a nun who modeled the sound for her:

R: It never rolled off my tongue. I never really even though I=
                                 [[
J: Yeah.   Yeah.
R: =Spanish, (.hhh) it came easily to me. I mean I could never=
                                                    [
J: Yeah.
R: =get my tongue to roll:. To sound right. Yeah. You know, and=
           [
F: Uh huh
                 [
J: To sound right. Yeah. Uh huh. (I=
R: =you had to roll:, I can remember the nun, [imitates nun?].=
J: =remember that.)
                                                [
F: ((laughs))
R: =Never forget it.
[
J: Heh yeah. Yeah.

One respondent seems to relate musical with language learning talent since she notes her 'tone deafness' along with her poor language learning skills. Our most delightful explanation of why some have it and some don't, however, came from a respondent who believes in reincarnation. Those who have spoken a language in an earlier life will obviously have an easier time picking it up the second time around.

All the respondents who mention age (C.3) believe that younger learners are more adept, particularly in achieving good pronunciation, and one respondent felt that adapting to even different rules of communicative competence was easier for younger people. Once when a linguistically sophisticated fieldworker let slip the information that language learning after puberty is difficult, a respondent was quick to exclaim: 'I'm not lazy, guys, I'm past eleven'.

Only one respondent felt that intelligence is important in language learning, although we have already noted that another believes that logical engineers are bad spellers of illogical English.

In conclusion, the folk hold strongly to talent and motivation as the principal learner characteristics for success, and they give younger learners the edge.

Figure 4. *A*. General linguistics, *B*. language attitudes, *C*. folk linguistics.

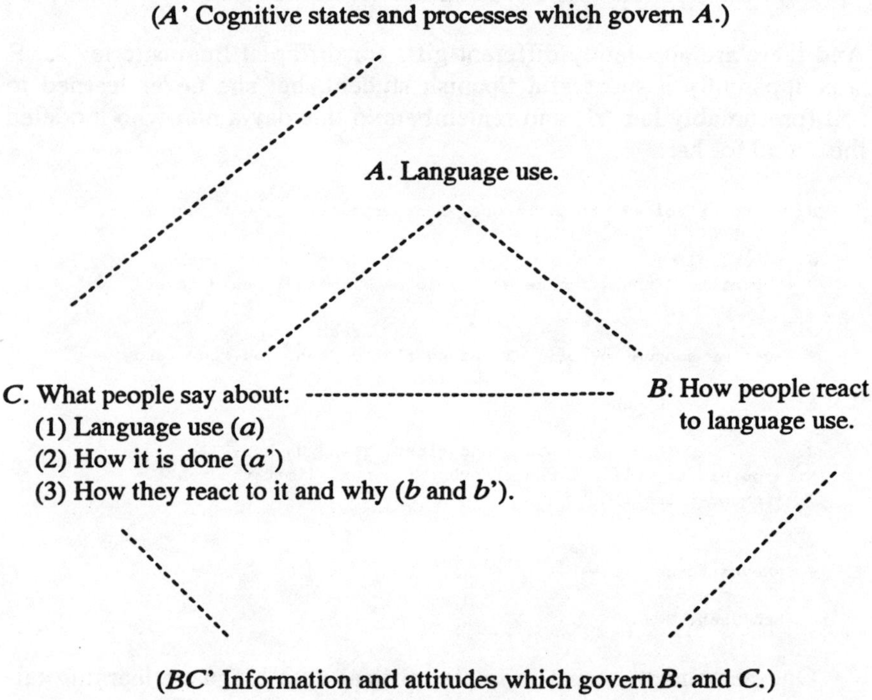

(A' Cognitive states and processes which govern A.)

A. Language use.

C. What people say about:
  (1) Language use (a)
  (2) How it is done (a')
  (3) How they react to it and why (b and b').

B. How people react to language use.

(BC' Information and attitudes which govern *B*. and *C*.)

Conclusions. So what! First, it might be easy to yuk it up at imagined stankos about language learning, but these actual data collected from real folk are not all that strange, not all that distant from professional opinion, and not so outrageously or obviously false. Second, even if they were only quaint folk imaginings, they are the beliefs and the products of reasoning about such questions based on folk knowledge and folk ways of bringing resources to bear. Only those who hold to the radical opinion that overt knowledge never has anything to do with ways of acquiring and employing language would regard this information as trivial. In fact, we see folk linguistics in general as an important third corner of a triangle of concerns (Figure 4). Mainstream theoretical linguists are concerned with a' (and avoid the messiness of a by using intuitions).

Other theoreticians (e.g. sociolinguists, so-called 'functionalists', ethno-methodologists, ethnographers of communication) see an interesting interplay between A and A'. Social psychologists till the fields of B (and B' in their interpretations). They try to devise techniques (e.g. 'matched guise') which allow us to peer into attitudes towards languages, varieties, and users without the overt knowledge of the respondent.

We believe, however, that C (and C') and its subcategories adds the important dimension of overt language concern to every other area of investigation. What people believe about how they learn, how difficult the target of their learning is, what special talents they have (or lack) for learning, what social outcomes await them, and the host of other matters that only an empirically designed folk-linguistic investigation can lay bare is surely an important matter for applied linguistics. Teacher trainers, national and local curriculum developers, materials developers, and classroom practitioners will surely fare better with knowledge of the speech community's understanding of the language learning process. And as it is with most scientific matters, it is better to find out what those understandings are than to imagine them.

References

Bloomfield, L. 1944. Secondary and tertiary responses to language. Lg. 20.45-55 (reprinted in A Leonard Bloomfield anthology, 1970, ed. by C. F. Hockett, 413-25. Bloomington and London: Indiana University Press.
Hall, R. A., Jr. 1990. A life for language. Amsterdam and Philadelphia: Benjamins.
Hoenigswald, H. 1970. A proposal for the study of folk-linguistics. In: Sociolinguistics, ed. by W. Bright, 16-26. The Hague: Mouton.
Hymes, D. 1972. Foundations in sociolinguistics. Philadelphia: University of Pennsylvania Press.
Labov, W. 1972. Sociolinguistic patterns. Philadelphia: University of Pennsylvania Press.
Lieberson, S. 1970 [1981]. Language and ethnic relations. Chapter 1 of Language and ethnic relations in Canada. New York, N.Y.: Wiley (quoted from Language diversity and language contact, 1-18. Stanford: Stanford University Press).
Minor, L. and D. Preston. 1980. Do it in French. Fredonia, NY: State University College (mimeographed).
Niedzielski, N. and D. Preston. In progress. Folk linguistics.
Preston, D. R. 1982. Writin' fowklower daun 'rong. Journal of American Folklore 95.304-26.
Preston, D. R. 1984. Linguistics: Science's best-kept secret. Indiana English 7,3.16-22.
Preston, D. R. 1985. The Li'l Abner syndrome. American Speech 60.328-36.
Preston, D. R. 1986. Fifty some-odd categories of language variation. International Journal of the Sociology of Language 57.9-47.

Preston, D. R. 1989: Perceptual dialectology. Dordrecht: Foris.
Preston, D. R. To appear (a): Talking black and talking white: Two studies in the ethnic ethnography of speaking. Surprise Festschrift.
Preston, D. R. To appear (b): Folk dialectology. American dialect research, ed. by D. Preston. Amsterdam and Philadelphia: Benjamins.
Rubin. J. 1975. What the 'good language learner' can teach us. TESOL Quarterly 9.41-51.
Sacks, H., E. Schegloff, and G. Jefferson. 1974. A simplest systematics for the organization of turn-taking for conversation. Lg. 50.696-735.
Schmidt, R. 1986. Developing basic conversational ability in a second language. Talking to learn, ed. by R. Day, 237-326. Rowley, Mass.: Newbury House, 237-326.
Stross, B. 1974. Speaking of speaking: Tenejapa Tzeltal metalinguistics. Explorations in the ethnography of speaking, ed. by R. Bauman and J. Sherzer, 213-39. Cambridge: Cambridge University Press.

Metaphors we are healed by:
On the use of metaphors in medical language

Maria Ibba
Università Cattolica del Sacro Cuore, Rome

Background. The considerations I set out to share in this paper stem from my current research and practical pedagogical concerns in the field of teaching/learning a language for specific purposes.

The advances made in foreign language pedagogy that we have witnessed in the past two decades include the fundamental shift of the point of departure for such endeavor (as learning/teaching) **from** the object of the teaching/learning process, i.e. the language, **to** the subject/agent of the learning activity, i.e. the learner.

Hence, we hear, now with increasing frequency, phrases such as the following: 'learner-centered approach to language teaching', 'assessment and definition of learner communication needs', 'situations of language use as subjectively perceived by the prospective learner', compared to the situations objectively taken into consideration by the curriculum designer-language teacher, and so on; all clearly reflecting the aforementioned mentioned shift.

Thus, responding to the identified needs of the learner, the study of a second language is no longer one of the many branches of a general education curriculum, but it has become a study area for the rapid mastery of verbal communication skills, to be used in a specific work situation, within the shortest time possible.

'Communicative competence' (see Hymes 1971) and, more pertinently for the scope of my talk, 'communicative cooperativeness' (see Grice 1957) are central to the definition of the aims of foreign language pedagogy to take place in the context in which I operate.

The use of metaphors in the various contexts of verbal communication constitutes a challenge for the adult learner of a foreign language.*

After mention of some insights gained from relatively recent, theoretical language studies, and a brief survey of work on metaphor by

---

* See Lakoff, George, and Mark Johnson. 1980. Metaphors we live by. Chicago: University of Chicago Press, p. 5.

scholars in fields other than linguistics, a sample of metaphor occurrences will be provided—with some discussion thereof—taken both from everyday language use and from the specific language of the medical profession. The conclusions will include some implications for the foreign language learning monitoring task.

Some theoretical considerations. A reasonably sound approach to second-language pedagogy cannot possibly dispense with at least some of the main insights gained from the major trends in the formal study of language. I proposed elsewhere (Ibba 1980) the pursuit of some sort of 'selective eclecticism' towards laying the theoretical foundations and formulating realistic working hypotheses because no one theory of language could alone provide the needed basis, and a sufficient set of 'clues', for the complex endeavor of meeting the learner group-specific needs of a foreign language. A complete survey of the major contributions that the formal study of language has provided to contemporary approaches to language learning/teaching is not deemed appropriate here, due to the time constraints of this talk and, especially to the very scope of the presentation. The considerations in this section shall be limited to what seems to be the bare minimum for the indispensable theoretical framework.

The above mentioned learner-centered approach to language teaching prompts the question of what amount of language knowledge a learner ought to master in order for him to be truly communicatively competent, in view of the specific context of language use in which the communication tasks are going to be carried out (learner-specific needs assessment). For Dell Hymes (1971:5), to whom we owe the term 'communicative competence', the speaker in good standing in a given sociocultural community is one who not only knows the language system proper (in its phonological, syntactic, and semantic aspects) but one who can communicate 'appropriately something (adequate, happy, successful) in relation to a context in which it is used'.

With Lyons (1977:6) one raises the question as to 'what kinds of knowledge the participants in a language event must possess, over and above their knowledge of the phonological and grammatical rules of the language-system and the sense and denotation of lexemes, in order to produce and understand contextually appropriate utterances?' He continues with his successful attempt of an answer: 'Much of this additional knowledge, we may assume, is of very general nature, which is not restricted to the use of language, but is relevant to all kinds of semiotic behavior.' In Lyon's view a theory of language should thus be comprehensive of a theory of contextual appropriateness, linguistics semantics being 'taken to be that branch of semiotics which deals with the way in which meaning (of all kinds) is conveyed by language.' But such theory it is not yet possible to formulate acceptably, Lyons regrets, although he himself has got very close to one.

I gradually and rather cautiously, I admit, am now approaching the heart of the subject matter of my paper, i.e. the metaphor.

While I am still within this theoretical reflections section, one question must be asked: whether and where, in the formal language system, metaphors find their collocation.

Except for those simple lexemes which, used metaphorically, have acquired institutionalized senses, and have therefore become part of the lexicon, metaphors are usually considered a matter of 'style', and not possible of inclusion in the lexicon of a traditional generative theory.

Metaphorical extension of the meaning of a given lexeme is viewed by Lyons as a product of the speaker's 'creativity, the language-user's ability to extend the system by means of motivated, but unpredictable, principles of abstraction and comparison.' Creativity, a part of linguistic competence, does not appear to be rule-governed, but it is rather to be considered as a result of 'strategies'.

A rigid theory of semantics would find it difficult to accommodate unpredictable operations such as metaphorical extensions of lexemes.

Avoiding, by necessity, several intermediate steps I now come to Grice's (1957) maxim of 'cooperative interaction' by means of language in the interpretation of metaphors. Grice views a metaphor as 'one contextually acceptable way of using language *to convey something other than what is actually said*' [emphasis mine]. The interlocutor then needs to recognize the 'contextual appropriateness' of the metaphor. It must be kept in mind that sociocultural factors are implied in this recognition of contextual appropriateness of metaphors.

There is yet no such theory of text interpretation, which can predict the results of such operations.

Grice's notion of language-behavior as cooperative interaction seems to fit quite well in Austin's (1962) theory of a speech act which does recognize the social basis of language, a theory; as Lyons (1981:9) calls it, of social pragmatics, in which context is relevant to the interpretation of utterances.

Thorough knowledge of the context makes native-speakers participants in a conversation able to use and interpret most lexemes in syntagms that have not been previously encountered.

On the contrary, the nonnative speaker-participant in a conversation may not always be capable of Grice's cooperative interaction, for language and sociocultural differences can interfere. The nonnative speaker may not be aware of some of the relationships that hold between a given lexeme and the reality it is referred to, which is external to the language system.

Metaphorical extension of lexemes further complicates nonnative speaker's task of interpretation of a metaphor (which, we remember, using Lakoff and Johnson's expression (1980), is 'understanding and experiencing one kind of thing in terms of another').

Lakoff and Johnson (1980) claim that 'metaphor is not just a matter of language, that is, of mere words, . . . on the contrary, human thought processes are largely metaphorical.' For these authors, metaphor means 'metaphorical concept'. They go further to talk of a coherent system of metaphorical concepts, as characterized, by metaphorical entailments such as, for example, those possible in the metaphorical concept 'time is money', or in orientational metaphors.

Not in all cultures would the conceptual metaphor 'time is money' be understood the way it is in the Western countries nor, as a consequence, would its entailments be possible.

Since 'a metaphor can serve as a vehicle for understanding a concept only by virtue of its experiential basis', . . . no metaphor can be interpreted or produced without such experiential basis.

If one wanted to do justice to the undeniably stimulating and challenging subject of metaphor much more ought to be said about it. I intend to do that in a more comprehensive study on the subject, which is in progress.

Scholars from different fields look at metaphor. The concept 'metaphor' has been the object of interest and of inquiry also for scholars outside the linguistic, philosophic, and pragmatic fields. These include writers in the literary field, sociologists, medical ethicists, medical doctors, and writers with professional experience both in the literary field as researchers and teachers as well as in the medical profession.

Viewed from different standpoints metaphor provides opportunities for a variety of considerations.

An author from the literary field proper, having been a cancer patient herself, (Sontag 1978) experienced 'the subtle sequestration, the social isolation often experienced by people with cancer (Sontag 1978) comparable to that of patients affected by AIDS, and she lashes out at the insensitivity and foreclosure of hope that (in both cases) the metaphor of 'plague' seems to impose! Sontag (1978) attacks what she calls the 'crippling effect' of metaphor, with the following words: 'The metaphoric trappings that deform the experience of having cancer have very real consequences: they inhibit people from seeking treatment early enough, or from making greater efforts to get competent treatment. The metaphors and myths, I was convinced, kill.' Metaphor in the case of the AIDS patient kills, i.e. the metaphor is itself a plague as it stigmatizes and thereby compounds the agony of the HIV-positive individual.'

D. S. Diekema (1989) approaches metaphor starting from Lakoff and Johnson's work. He applies their insights to the use of metaphor that is made by medical professionals, of whom he is one, and goes on to pursue moral implications.

Some of the medical metaphors which Diekema discusses are going to be briefly mentioned here. The first one is 'removing fetal tissue' which is the terminology of choice for abortion advocates. Such a phrase would appear at least ambiguous in its linguistic form; but it happens to mean for the non-abortionists only 'murder of the unborn', . . . Another metaphorical concept the author attacks is the 'body-as-machine' metaphor. Within such a frame of metaphorical thinking the human organism is seen as the 'sum of the body's parts' (Diekema 1989).

My experience of work in hospital wards still leaves me with a vivid memory of a physician once addressing a nurse with the request to 'keep an eye on the pump of room 47'—a metonomy within the body-as-machine metaphor. Only the addition of information on the part of the nurse in her reply—'oh, yeah, the little Italian guy, I'll take good care of him, we're buddies'—helped me understand at least that 'the pump' was not the mechanical object known to us all, but a human being, a heart patient. As to why the patient was labeled a 'pump' took me, a foreign bilingual observer, a while to figure out—in spite of my considerable familiarity I had at that time with . . . 'medspeak'. From my standpoint I feel no need to share any more except what was implied in what I just said: that more than the language can be a hindrance to understanding—there is the matter of cultural attitude and metaphor. Within the realm of metaphorical thinking, the care of the ill person could be understood as some sort of assembly-line work.

One would hope that at the end of that 'line' someone would be capable of assembling the fragmentary information gathered by the different specialists and, eventually provide for him-/herself and for the whole medical team the assembled picture of a whole body, and hopefully—of the person.

The medicine-as-war metaphor also is mentioned by Diekema as well as by Sontag and Ross. In the case of this metaphorical concept, just as in most such cases, the associated entailments can lead farther than one would expect. In this case the patient would be the battlefield where the war between the medical team and the disease would be fought. Continuing with the metaphorical thinking process Diekema goes farther to talk about 'burnt-out shell' and 'fragmentary ruins, if the war is won'.

One could at least wonder, in the case of so far 'incurable' diseases, such as cancer and AIDS, whether it is at all legitimate to talk about winning a war rather than more realistically talking about winning, at the most, some battles.

The medicine-as-war metaphor does not constitute any particular communication problem between medical people of the two different languages/cultures, English and Italian.

The 'burnout' metaphor is discussed by the sociologist E. Maher (1989). Its identification as 'the high cost of high achievement' is taken from Freud's (1961) view of human activity—'human energy is a scarce and limited resource' of which 'an individual has only a fixed quantity'; 'the malaise of modern civilization'.

The interlocutor of Italian language and culture background would understand the burnout metaphor by referring to the image of a candle which burns out, and therefore is consumed; but it is not a readily understood metaphor.

Albert H. Carter, III (1989) holds an almost opposite view of metaphor as compared to Sontag's. Carter (1989) talks about the 'healing potential' of metaphor and even of the 'necessarily metaphoric nature of medicine'. He claims that the use of metaphor in medicine contributes: '(1) to enhanced communication between patients and physicians and (2) to the use of healing resources, however poorly understood, within the patient'. Carter recognizes that metaphors are 'linguistic structures that bear epistemological weight, both personal and cultural'. He sees them as 'a synthetic way of perceiving the world, evaluating and interpreting it, and preparing for decisions and actions...'

More considerations on metaphor-language-culture. The metaphor 'in everyday life' is very frequently encountered both in informal situations such as in the home, among friends, and in formal ones, such as in newspapers, in news broadcasts and the like. A few examples are here provided in order to illustrate this statement:

1. Young adults find their wings clipped by skyrocketing housing costs, so many of them are returning to their nests.
2. For nest-building commuters the place to go is X.
3. Envy can be the price of success.
4. He managed it in the teeth of the most terrifying odds.
5. The three main arteries of downtown traffic have been in trouble lately.
6. Joe is a fox.
7. Schools seem to be turning out less educated mainstream youngsters nowadays.
8. My old man has had a pain in his side for the past three days.
9. This side of the mountain is particularly dear to climbers.
10. Don't worry, my lips are sealed.

We observe that a native speaker of Italian would have no difficulty understanding the metaphorical concepts 'wings clipped' and 'nest' in sentence 1, 'price' in sentence 3, 'arteries' in sentence 5, 'fox' in sentence 6 and 'side' in sentences 8 and 9. This is because the 'metaphorical thinking' is taking place within the same conceptual framework in the two languages/cultures involved. Whereas 'nest-building' of sentence 2 and 'mainstream' of sentence 7 are not readily understood yet by the native Italian speaker. The Italian's difficulty in interpreting example 7 might be explained by the fact that mass immigration into Italy is a phenomenon of only the past few years, consequently the implied comparison of immigrant school children vs. mainstream children has not yet been a pressing reality. As to 'side' in sentences 8 and 9, the use in 9 is a metaphorical extension of the use in 8, the comparable form is used in the same way in Italian as it is in English. 'Sealed' of sentence 10 would be *cucite* 'sewn' in Italian: the lips are kept 'closed' by means of thread rather than by glue or a wax seal.

Returning to metaphors used in medical language I shall attempt some sort of organization of what appears to be a considerably extensive use of metaphors.

A. One very old area of use of metaphors in medical language is in anatomy where the names of parts of the body are clearly taken from other realities in the surrounding world. A few examples, taken from hundreds of them, are in order:

trunk	arch	apex	sinus
branch	atrium	axis	fornix
stem	wall	labyrinth	valve
root	chamber	aquaduct	invagination
tree	threshold	aditus	tunnel, etc.

These examples need no illustration as the referents in the known world are shared by the two language/culture groups Italian-English.

B. Pathological conditions are also referred to by means of metaphorical extensions of known lexical items or of phrases. For instance:

English:
1. funnel chest
2. duck gate
3. wheezing heart
4. clubbed finger
5. green stick fracture
6. frostbite
7. helicopod
8. thrust breast heart
9. cake kidney
10. cells that have gone crazy

Italian:
1. torace da calzolaio, a imbuto
2. andatura anserino
3. cuore a timbro pigolante
4. dito a bacchetta di tampuro
5. frattura a legno verde
6. assideramento
7. andatura falciante
8. cuore a petto do tordo
9. regne a focaccia
10. celle impazzite

and so on . . . .

Of the examples in group B, exactly half of them (1,2,3,5, and 10) are readily understood by the Italian speaking medical student/doctor, not so for the remaining five. This is again the case of choice of different realities from which the word/phrase was borrowed in the two different cultures.

C. Other expressions such as the following:

Italian:
1. danza delle arterie
2. sutura a borsa di tabacco
3. addome batraciano
4. respiro paradosso
5. urine marsala
6. vomito caffeano

and many more of this type are not immediately intelligible to the English speaker and undeniably constitute a problems for the English speaker working in an Italian environment.

I must omit the discussion of details, which could be of some use towards a better understanding of the idea I have been trying to convey. While I apologize for not being more specific I hereby commit myself to make a more thorough treatment of the subject available to the interested colleagues within the current solar year.

Let's now draw some conclusions:

1. We have observed that, as Wittgenstein (1988) would put it, there are meanings that can be easily said in language and those which must be shown more indirectly by some sort of indirect use of language.

2. Metaphorical concepts vary according to the culture within which the speakers verbally interact, for as Aristotle in his *Poetics* states 'metaphor consists in giving the thing a name that belongs to something else; the transfer being either from genus to species or from species to genus, or from species to species, or on the grounds of analogy'.

3. Foreign professionals working across language and culture barriers can find mutual understanding to be particularly difficult. 'Such understanding is possible through the negotiation of meaning. To negotiate meaning with someone, you have to become aware of and respect both the differences in your backgrounds . . .' (Lakoff and Johnson.)

One pedagogical implication that demands to be shared in this context concerns: (a) directly, by the medical professional learning English for a better performance on his work across language/culture barriers, and (b) indirectly, bythe principal beneficiary of the medical professional's work, the patient.

As to point (a) these particular students of English need to be specifically guided towards an awareness and mastery of the unsuspected number of metaphors (not shared by their culture). Such awareness is not easily gained by some unmonitored learning effort. In those cultures where Latin and Greek are not so well known as they are in the Western world a special effort must be made to help understand those metaphors which are based on these classical languages.

As to the patient, in relation to the physician's use of metaphors, it ought to be kept in mind that the negotiation of meaning is of paramount importance in the verbal exchange between patient and physician (if the patient is to be considered a partner in the healing process). Unless the physicians are themselves perfectly aware of, and have become truly proficient in, the metaphorical conceptualization processes of the culture in which they operate, they will not be able to provide the right kind of care the patient needs; for, the (claimed) inevitable use of 'med-speak' would be compounded by the use of undecodable metaphor-like expressions.

The specialist in foreign language pedagogy called to work in the medical setting must feel the obligation to face the challenge that metaphors represent for the target learners, and consequently devise adequate teaching materials and create classroom situations to facilitate acquaintance with and mastery of at least those metaphorical items which the learner is more likely to be exposed to both receptively and productively.

It is my hope that the audacity it took to address the subject of metaphor within very severe time and space constraints has resulted in at least 'lighting a candle', even a small one, in the much feared (if not cursed) darkness of 'metaphor and language pedagogy'.

References

Aristotle. Nichomachean Ethics. I.1.
Austin, J. L. 1962. How to do things with words. Oxford: Clarendon Press.
Bruner, J. 1986. Actual minds, possible worlds. Cambridge, Mass.: Harvard University Press.
Carter, Albert H. 1989. Metaphors in the physician-patient relationship. Soundings 72(1).
Cassell, Eric J. 1985. Talking with patients. Boston: MIT Press.
Diekema, Douglas S. 1989. Metaphors, medicine and morals. Soundings: 72(1).
Durkheim, Emile. 1951. Suicide. Translated by J.A. Spaulding and G. Simpson. New York: Free Press.
Engel, G.L. 1971. The deficiencies of the case presentation as a method of clinical teaching. New England Journal of Medicine 184: 20.
Freud, Sigmund. 1961. Civilization and its discontents. New York: W.W. Norton.
Grice, H.P., Meaning. Philosophical Review 66:337-88. 1957.
Hodgkin, P. 1985. Medicine is war. British Medical Journal 291.
Hymes, Dell. 1971. On communicative competence. Philadelphia: University of Pennsylvania Press.

Ibba, Maria. 1980. L'Inglese della Medicina. Milano: Vita e Pensiero.
Katz, Jay. 1984. The silent world of doctor and patient. New York: Free Press.
Lakoff, George, and Mark Johnson. 1980. Metaphors we live by. Chicago: University of Chicago Press.
Lakoff, G. 1972, Hedges: A study in meaning, criteria and the logic of fuzzy concepts. In: Papers from the 8th Regional Meeting, edited by P.M. Peranteau, et al. Chicago.
Lee Whorf, Benjamin. 1956. Language, thought and reality. New York: Wiley.
Lyons, John. 1977. Semantics. Volumes 1 and 2. London: Cambridge University Press, 1977.
Lyons, John. 1981. Language, meaning and context. London: Fontana Linguistics.
Maher, Ellen L. 1989. Burnout: Metaphors of destruction and purgation. Soundings 72(1).
McCullough, Laurence B. 1989. The abstract character and transforming power of medical language. Soundings 72(1).
Moser, Robert H. AIDS and the plague metaphor. Review and Opinion. Ob.Gyn. News, Vol. 24, No 13, 15.
Pellegrino, Edmund D., et al. 1981. A philosophical basis of medical practice. New York: Oxford University Press.
Ross, Judith Wilson. 1989. The militarization of disease: Do we really want a war on AIDS? Soundings 72(1).
Searle, John R. 1975. Indirect speech acts. In: Cole and Morgan, eds., Syntax and Semantics, Vol. 3. New York: Academic Press.
Searle, John R., et al., eds. 1980. Speech act theory and pragmatics. Dordrecht, Holland: D. Reidel, p. 317.
Sontag, Susan. 1978. Illness as metaphor. New York: Farrar, Strauss and Giroux.
Tolstoy, Leo. 1981. The death of Ivan Ilych. Translated by L. Solotaroff. New York: Bantam Books.
Tracy, D. 1987. Plurality and ambiguity: Hermeneutics, religion, hope. New York: Harper and Row.
Wittgenstein, Ludwig. 1988. Wittgenstein's lectures on philosophical psychology, 1946-47. Notes by P.T. Geach, K.J. Shah, A.C. Jackson; edited by P.T. Geach. London: Harvester Wheatsheaf.

NC